ANCIENT CEYLON

THE DANCE OF THE GALÉ DEVIY
(After a native painting.)

[*Frontispiece.*

ANCIENT CEYLON

H. PARKER

WITH ILLUSTRATIONS BY THE AUTHOR

GYAN

Published by

Gyan Publishing House
5, Ansari Road
Daryaganj, New Delhi-110002
Phone: 011-47034999, 9811692060
E-mail: books@gyanbooks.com

Distribution Network
gyanbooks.com
India, USA, Canada, UK, Australia, France

ISBN : 978-81-212-3119-0 (PB)
First Published, 1909

2nd Impression 2020

Printed at: Gyan Press, Delhi.

Ancient Ceylon
Author: H. Parker

ANCIENT CEYLON

An Account of the Aborigines and of Part of the Early Civilisation

By

H. PARKER

Late of the Irrigation Department, Ceylon

WITH ILLUSTRATIONS BY THE AUTHOR

LONDON
LUZAC & CO.
PUBLISHERS TO THE INDIA OFFICE
1909

PREFACE

IN the last thirty years our acquaintance with the interior of Ceylon, a country four-fifths of the size of Ireland, has made great advances. The researches of members of various Government Departments have extended throughout the whole island, until it may now be said that there is no part of it which has not been investigated.

During this period, however, little new information regarding it has been published in England otherwise than in the Journals of various Societies, with the exception of some excellent studies of its natural history; a work by Professor Rhys Davids on the Ancient Coins and Measures; and two books prepared for the Government, one by Mr. Smither, the former Government Architect, containing an architectural description of the dāgabas at Anurādhapura, and the other, by Dr. Edward Müller, giving a first account of the ancient inscriptions.

Evidently the time has arrived when part of the other recently obtained knowledge of the country should be presented to the world. My employment in the Irrigation Department from the middle of 1873 to the end of 1904 having given me opportunities of acquiring some information of the interior of the island, I have therefore prepared the present work, which describes some phases of the early civilisation, beginning with the history, life, and religion of the aborigines, and ending, as regards local matters, with the village games. Although the subjects included in it are dealt with in a disconnected manner, it will be seen that they advance from the primitive stages to more recent times.

The character of such a work must naturally render it more useful to students of the subjects treated of than attractive to the general public. For this reason it has been my endeavour as far as possible to furnish accurate and detailed information rather than generalities among which the student might search in vain for the particulars he requires. I may be permitted to express a hope that my critics will deal leniently with the errors which must be inseparable from such a publication.

In transliterations I have followed Dr. E. Müller in indicating by *æ* the vowel which appears as *e* in publications of the Ceylon Government. The form accepted by me, when pronounced as a diphthong as in the Oxford Dictionary, both gives the sound of the letter and is historically accurate, the letter having been in most cases derived from an ancient *a*.

The consonant which is often expressed by *v* has been represented by either *v* or *w*, so as to be in general agreement with its local sound. In Ceylon it is a *w*, and any one who pronounced it otherwise in nearly all words would make himself ridiculous. In the case of Pāli words, especially the names of places and books, I have used only the letter *v*, in order to avoid confusion through being in disagreement with other works. I adhere in general to the Pāli forms of names.

I have to express my obligations to the Secretary of State for the Colonies for his readily granted authorisation to reproduce some of Mr. Smither's drawings of the dāgabas; and to my friends Mr. H. T. S. Ward, the recent Director of Irrigation, and Mr. H. C. P. Bell, the Archæological Commissioner, the former for permission to copy and utilise the drawings of irrigation works in his office, and the latter for allowing me to include in this work a description of some early coins in the possession of the Ceylon Government, without which the account of the first local coinage would have been incomplete.

In the various chapters in which it has been utilised I have acknowledged the information furnished by several kind friends in Ceylon, and by Mr. C. H. Read of the British Museum and Dr. C. G. Seligmann, to all of whom it is a small return to tender my grateful thanks.

Messrs. H. B. Andris and Co. of Kandy were so good as to bring about the publication of a Sinhalese work on the Kohomba Yakā in order that it might be available for me, and to the kindness of Mr. H. W. Codrington, of the Civil Service, I am indebted for native accounts of this deity compiled in various provinces. To my friend the late Dr. Paul Goldschmidt I owe my interest in the early inscriptions.

With regard to the scales of the drawings, which are usually expressed in fractions, the denominator divided by twelve gives the number of feet equal to one inch.

Through an inadvertence the word *Vyādha* appears in some places as *Vyāda*.

CONTENTS

LIST OF ILLUSTRATIONS AND PLATES

CEYLON
Scale of Miles
Point Pedro
Jaffna
Mullaittivu
NORTHERN PROVINCE
Mannar
Trincomalee
NORTH CENTRAL PROVINCE
Puttalam
NORTH WESTERN PROVINCE
Dambulla
Chilaw
Kurunegala
CENTRAL PROVINCE
Batticaloa
EASTERN PROVINCE
Negombo
Kandy
UVA
Colombo
WESTERN PROVINCE
Nuwara Eliya
Badulla
PROVINCE
Adam's Peak
SABARAGAMUWA PROVINCE
Ratnapura
Kalutara
Bentota
SOUTHERN PROVINCE
Hambantota
Galle
Matara
Tangalla

[To face p. 1.

Part I

THE ABORIGINES

I

THE FIRST INHABITANTS

WHEN the first Āryan invaders entered India they brought with them an exaggerated belief in the existence of various classes of evil beings, among whom those termed Rākshasas occupied the most prominent place. These demons were thought to be especially active and powerful during the darkness of the night, when, though invisible in their true shapes, they acted in many objectionable ways in opposition to the new settlers; and most of the ills which beset the Āryans were attributed to their malevolence. Every mysterious sound heard during the night, and especially the weird calls of the forest owls, showed them to be then in the immediate neighbourhood of the villages or encampments, but with the first gleams of sunrise they vanished; the spear-like rays of the mighty Sun-god had annihilated them, or at the least had driven them away into the obscurity of the trackless forests. Being thus powerful during the nocturnal hours, it was naturally believed to be they who inspired the night attacks of the aboriginal tribes, the constant enemies of the Āryan settlers; and many and fervent were the prayers addressed to Agni, the Fire-god, and Indra, the God of the Firmament, the Lord of the Thunder and the Controller of the Heavenly Fires, to arise and disperse and overwhelm them. In the fourth hymn of Book iv of the Rig-Veda (Griffiths' translation) the prayer runs :—

> Rise, Agni, drive off those who fight against us: make manifest thine own celestial vigour.
> Slacken the strong bows of the demon-driven. . . .
> Destroy the cursing Rākshasas.

As the Āryans advanced further into the country their belief in the existence of these demons of the night remained firmly impressed on their minds. They afflicted both man and beast, and were devourers of raw flesh. Sometimes they appeared bodily—not in their true forms, but in the shape of dogs, owls, and other birds—and obstructed the sacrifices of the Āryans in various ways, and especially by the pollution of their presence. In the hymn 104 of Book vii, the Maruts—the Gods of the Storm-winds—and Indra are appealed to :—

She, too, who wanders like an owl at night-time, hiding her body in her guilt and malice,
May she fall downward into endless caverns. May press-stones with loud ring destroy the demons.
Spread out, ye Maruts, search among the people: seize ye and grind the Rākshasas to pieces,
Who fly abroad, transformed to birds at night-time, or sully and pollute our holy worship.
Indra hath ever been the fiends' destroyer who spoil oblations of the Gods' invokers:
Yea, Sakra, like an axe that splits the timber, attacks and smashes them like earthen vessels.
Destroy the fiend shaped like an owl or owlet, destroy him in the form of dog or cuckoo.
Destroy him shaped as eagle or as vulture: as with a stone, O Indra, crush the demon.

They were considered to be especially-malignant sorcerers. The same hymn continues: 'Slay the male demon, Indra! Slay the female, joying and triumphing in arts and magic.' It concludes with the prayer, 'Indra and Soma, watch ye well. Cast forth your weapon at the fiends: against the sorcerers hurl your bolt.'

The hymn 87 of Book x is entirely devoted to denunciations of these demons, and appeals to Agni to destroy them :—

Where now thou seest, Agni Jātavedas, one of these demons standing still or roaming,
Or flying on those paths in air's mid-region, sharpen the shaft and as an archer pierce him.
The fiend who smears himself with flesh of cattle, with flesh of horses and of human bodies,
Who steals the milch-cow's milk away, O Agni—tear off the heads of such with fiery fury.
Agni, from days of old thou slayest demons: never shall Rākshasas in fight o'ercome thee.
Burn up the foolish ones, the flesh devourers; let none of them escape thine heavenly arrow.

FIG. 4. Rākshasa as Guardian, Tanjore Temple.

To face p. 5.

In the Sāma-Veda (Stevenson's translation) the Rākshasas are said to be indomitable (Adhyāya xii, 2), and to be all around (Prapāthaka vi, 6).

In the hymns of the Atharva-Veda (Bloomfield) we learn that the Rākshasas robbed people of their senses (vi, 3), and 'possessed' them (ii, 9), and that errors made in the prescribed ritual of the sacrifice were also sometimes due to their malicious interference (vii, 70). They were unable to face Indra; 'Indra forced the demons into the nethermost darkness' (ix, 2).

Such were some of the earliest ideas of the Āryans concerning the Rākshasas, in the second or third millenium before Christ. In the first half of the pre-Christian millenium, the Ordinances of Manu confirm the statement that the Rākshasas were flesh-eating demons, and that night was the special time of demons' activity they also place them in a position of high respectability after the Gods and Manes, along with other classes of supernatural beings. In the Sutta-Nipāta (Fausböll's translation, S.B.E., p. 51) we find the Rākshasas uniting with the Gods in reprobating the slaughter of cows.

When the Indian epic poem, the Rāmāyana, was composed, the Rākshasas had developed into beings who constantly made their appearance before men, in their own or other forms which they took at will. They were first described as wandering malignant demons of the great Vindhya forest, which extended far to the south in India; and afterwards, in the later portions of that work, they were represented as occupying all Ceylon, then (and still) denominated Lankā, under the rule of their own king, Rāvana. The Mahā-Bhārata has the same tradition.

The latest account of them in these works is as follows[1]: When Brahmā created the Waters he formed Rākshasas to guard them.[2] Visvākarman, the general architect and builder of the Gods, erected a city termed Lankāpura for them in Ceylon, on the top of the mountain Trikūṭa, 'Three Peaks,' on the shore of the southern ocean. Three of their princes

[1] Muir. *Original Sanskrit Texts*, Vol. iv, pp. 414 ff.

[2] Two Rākshasas are carved in relief as guards in Fig. 159. I know of no other representation of them in the Sinhalese carvings.

performed intense austerities for which they were rewarded by the grant of long life and a certain amount of invincibility. They made use of these gifts to oppress the Gods and sages, and at last prepared to attack heaven itself. The Sāma-Veda mentions another Rākshasa called Kravi, who had previously got heaven and earth into his power and desolated them (Adhyāya xiii, 8). They were defeated by Vishnu, and driven back to Ceylon, and afterwards to the underworld, Pātāla, as stated also in the Atharva-Veda, where the deed is attributed to Indra (see above).

Ḳuvēra, the God of Wealth, with his attendants the Yakshas, who were demons of another type, in some respects not much better than the Rākshasas, but of a higher rank, then took up his residence in Ceylon, at Lankāpura. Eventually, his half-brother Rāvana, the Rākshasa king, by means of thousands of years of austerity obtained from Brahmā the boon of indestructibility by all beings of a higher class than man. This enabled him to re-occupy Ceylon, which once more became the headquarters of the Rākshasas. He also conquered Kuvēra, whose magic car he took, Yama, the God of Death, and Indra, and generally made the lives of the Gods extremely unpleasant. 'The Gods then addressed a word to Brahmā, the Creator of the world: "A Rākshasa named Rāvana having obtained a boon from thee, O Brahmā, in his pride harasses us all. Obedient to thy words, we endure everything at his hands. . . . We are therefore in great fear of this Rākshasa of horrible aspect"' (Muir, *O.S.T.* iv, p. 140).

The Rāmāyana recounts at great length how these truculent demons interfered with or polluted the sacrifices of the anchorites in the Vindhya forest, and even devoured those holy men. The situation was evidently insupportable. In the meantime, the Gods had a rod in pickle for the demons. Vishnu, the younger brother of Indra, had acceded to the unanimous request of the deities, and become incarnate as Rāma, the son of Dasaratha, the king of Ayōdhya or Oudh. Rāma, who was suitably provided with magic weapons, first destroyed the Rākshasas in India on account of their crimes

FIG. 5. Vibhīsana as King of Ceylon, his Wife Amman, and Lakshmana. (Three Rākshasas below.)

To face p. 7.

there; and then, assisted by an immense army of monkeys and bears, proceeded to attack and kill Rāvana in Ceylon, after the demon king had carried off his wife Sītā to Lankāpura. He then returned to Oudh with Sītā. According to the Rājāvaliya, one of the Sinhalese historical works, the date of this event was 1844 years before Gōtama Buddha entered on his mission, that is, about 2370 B.C.

Although he had promised to do it, Rāma did not exterminate the Rākshasas. Vibhīsana, the younger brother of Rāvana, a good and devout worshipper of Vishnu, who had joined Rāma's forces in the war against the Rākshasas, was appointed the sovereign of the survivors in Ceylon, in the place of Rāvana; and there the story ends so far as it concerns Ceylon. The Rākshaṣas also vanish from history, with the exception of an occasional appearance of a fever- or ophthalmia-causing demon who is termed a Rākshasa in the Sinhalese chronicles. They are found, however, in early times and down to the present day in the folk-stories of the villagers, both in India and Ceylon. In Ceylon they have degenerated into mere man-eating ogres of the European Jack-and-the-Beanstalk type,[1] who are much more powerful than the Yakshas—according to one story four Yakshas took to

FIG. 6. A Modern Rākshasa.
(After a Native Painting.)

[1] The reader may remember the striking description of one in the Third Voyage of Sindbad the Seaman:—'A huge creature in the likeness of a man, black of colour, tall and big of bulk, as he were a great date-tree, with eyes like coals of fire and eye-teeth like boar's tusks and a vast big gape like the mouth of a well. Moreover, he had long loose lips like camels', hanging down upon his breast, and ears like two Jarms [a kind of barge] falling over his shoulder-blades and the nails of his hands were like the claws of a lion.'—*Arabian Nights*, Lady Burton's Ed., iii, p. 485.

flight when opposed by one Rākshasa—but are outwitted by clever girls and men. The Rig-Veda had already termed them foolish.

Although there is nothing in this legend of the Rāmāyana to indicate that the composer of even the last section possessed more than the slightest knowledge of Ceylon, most of the geographical outlines referring to the island are accurately pourtrayed. He knew that Ceylon was an island near the southern coast of India, and tied to it, as it were, by a chain of islands or sandbanks. He was aware that the country was

FIG. 7. Riṭigala, from the South.

about 100 leagues in length—the actual distance is about 266 miles [1]—and that there are mountains in the southern part of it. He had also learnt that on the side of the ancient highway leading from the end of Mannār to the southern districts, the traveller passed a hill termed Arishṭha, the Ariṭṭha of the Pāli histories of Ceylon, now called Riṭigala, near the foot of which the high road certainly ran in historic times. The name Suvēla, which is also mentioned as that of a hill, cannot be identified as such, but may be a reference to the land round the town called Uruvela. In the northern

[1] The earliest Sinhalese history, the Dīpavansa, p. 196, says that it is 32 yōjanas ; at 8½ miles per yōjana this is 272 miles.

part of the Kandian hill-country there are also three very conspicuous peaks on one of the higher mountains, when viewed from the northern low country, from which the idea of the mountain Trikūṭa may have been derived.

It is evident that before this knowledge of the interior of Ceylon could be available in India, the island must have been thoroughly explored by intelligent travellers. This could only be done in a settled and peaceable country such as we find under the Sinhalese kings, and there is no probability that it was ever feasible at an earlier period. As European scholars now agree, the whole account of the invasion of Ceylon by Rāma must therefore have been invented during historic times, and it thus becomes simply and purely a poetic fiction, an improvement of the original story without any basis whatever in fact. Even such a slight foundation for it as the spread of the Hindu religion, or Āryan civilisation, among the tribes of the south must be swept away so far as Ceylon is concerned, since the descendants of the original inhabitants of the island, the Vaeddas of the interior, have never adopted the worship of the Hindu gods, nor, until historic times, the civilisation of the Āryans.

We now come to the Sinhalese annals, and here we soon begin to feel our feet on firmer ground.[1] Of these histories, the two most important ones are written in the Pāli language —the Dīpavansa and the Mahāvansa The former, which ends with the death of King Mahā-Sēna (277–304 A.D.), and appears to have been completed not later than the beginning of the fifth century A.D., and possibly nearly a century earlier, is believed by its translator, Dr. H. Oldenberg, to consist chiefly of extracts from histories or chronicles of much earlier date.

The Mahāvansa was written at various times, and has been continued to the end of the eighteenth century. My references will be to the English translation made for the Ceylon Government by the late Mr. L. C. Wijesinhe. There is no doubt that the author of the first part of it was a Buddhist

[1] The Rt. Rev. Dr. Caldwell termed the writers 'on the whole, the most truthful and accurate of oriental annalists.' (*Dravidian Grammar*, Introduction, p. 121.)

monk who bore the title Mahānāma, and was the uncle of King Dhātu-Sēna (463–479 A.D.); and that most probably soon after the death of that king he completed the book up to his own day. It is recorded in the Ṭīkā, or 'Commentary' on the Mahāvansa, a work of somewhat later date, that he derived his materials from Chronicles written long before in Sinhalese, one of which owed its authorship to the monks of the Uttara Piriwena (the Northern Monastic residence) at the Mahā Wihāra, the great Buddhist temple founded at Anurādhapura in the middle of the third century B.C.

It is expressly mentioned that several histories were extant in his time, and were consulted by him. Some of them were also termed Mahāvansas. In the Commentary it is stated: 'Thus the title "Mahāvansa" is adopted in imitation of the history composed by the fraternity of the Mahā Wihāra. . . . In case it should be asked in this particular place, "Why, while there are Mahāvansas composed by ancient authors in the Sinhalese language, this author has written," ' etc.[1] Mahānāma himself insists on the accuracy with which he adheres to the accounts of the early chroniclers. At the beginning, he states: 'Having bowed down to the supreme Buddha, immaculate in purity, illustrious in descent; without suppression or exaggeration I celebrate the Mahāvansa.' It can hardly be doubted, from the amount and accuracy of the details which Mahānāma gives in his work, that at least one of these prior Chronicles was begun in the third century B.C., and certainly not later than the second century B.C.

It is important to understand clearly that as regards the pre-Christian and early post-Christian details which are found in the Mahāvansa we have got, not the opinions or fancies of a monk who lived 500 years after Christ, but a work carefully compiled from annals that were committed to writing in the second or third century before Christ, and continued without a break up to the time of the reverend author. With respect to the information to be collected from the work regarding the earliest rulers, we have at least the opinions of

[1] Turnour. *The Mahawanso*, Introduction, pp. xxxi, xxxii.

annalists, or traditions recorded by them, dating from a time that was perhaps only a century and a half later than the earliest local events of which they preserved the story. Some of these early chroniclers may have seen, or have known persons who had seen, the great king Paṇḍukābhaya, the record of whose reign is of the utmost value for the light it throws on the position occupied by the aborigines in the third and fourth centuries before Christ.

There are other historical works of subsequent date, nearly all written in the Sinhalese language. Occasionally they contain supplementary details of the early period which are not found in these two first books, thus showing that their composers had also access to some manuscripts that are now lost. Among such works may be noted the Rājāvaliya, the Rājaratnākara, the Pūjāvaliya, the Thūpāvansa, and the Dhātuvansaya.

It has been already mentioned that the later parts of the Rāmāyana and the Mahā-Bhārata contain the statement that Ceylon was once occupied by a class of beings termed Yakshas, under their sovereign Kuvēra or Vaisravana, the God of Wealth, the Wessawanā of the Sinhalese. The Rāmāyana also incidentally adds that some Yakshas dwelt on the Arishṭha hill at the period of the mythical invasion by Rama, and on the mountain Mahēndra—at the southern end of the Vindhya chain, the Western Ghāts—on the opposite coast of India. It is possible that the person who composed that part of the epic had heard of the stories related by Indian traders regarding the first settlement of the Sinhalese in Ceylon.

Apparently, at the time when the first Magadhese traders [1] came to Ceylon from the lower part of the Ganges valley, they described the inhabitants whom they found occupying the central and southern forests as beings who were scarcely

[1] The way of the tradesman [is the occupation] * of Māgadhas. *Ordinances of Manu,* Translation by Burnell and Hopkins, x, 47. The translators state that the Commentator Medhātithi specifies 'the way' as referring to both land and water.

* Throughout this work, the words in square brackets are inserted by me.

human, a custom of many later travellers when delineating aborigines. They may have exaggerated and embellished their accounts of them with a view to deterring others from venturing into Ceylon, so as to enable them to retain a lucrative trade in their own hands. However this may be, the chronicles of their descendants, the Sinhalese, applied the Pāli term *Yakkha*, 'demon,' to the beings whom they found in the island, but described them as devoid of most of the supernatural attributes of the Yakshas of the early Indian works. They were no longer beings of a semi-divine nature, but were looked down upon as approaching much more nearly to the class of evil demons, just as the references to the aboriginal Dasyu of Vedic times are often couched in terms that might equally describe the characteristics of demons. They no longer possessed the power of aerial flight and of passing through the water.

The historical works of Ceylon contain a mythical story of three visits that were supposed to have been paid to the island by the last Buddha, Gōtama, as well as by the three previous Buddhas. It is not found in the canonical works, and is therefore not accepted by the more intelligent Buddhists in the island, whether monks or laymen; but it is credited as an article of faith by the less-instructed classes, and it has had the effect of greatly enhancing the prestige of the Buddhist remains at Anurādhapura and Kaelaṇiya, the sites of two of the supposed visits.

In them an account is related of the miraculous expulsion of the Yakkhas from the island at the last Buddha's first visit, in the ninth month after he attained Buddhahood, in order to render it habitable by the Gangetic settlers who were about to occupy it after his death. The Dīpavansa gives the story as follows (i, pp. 46 ff., Oldenberg's translation): 'At that time the ground of Lanka was covered with great forests, and full of horrors: frightful, cruel, blood-thirsty Yakkhas of various kinds, and savage, furious, and pernicious Pisāchas [a lower form of demon] of various shapes and full of various (wicked) thoughts, had all assembled together. [The Teacher thought] "I shall go there, in their midst; I shall dispel the

Rākkhasas and put away the Pisāchas ; men shall be masters (of the island).'' '

He came through the air from the Anōtatta Lake in the Himālayas, and alighted at Mahiyangana, on the eastern side of the Central mountains. There he first sent down 'rain, cold winds, and darkness,' and afterwards intense heat, to escape from which the unfortunate Yakkhas could merely stand on the shore.

In the end he permitted the Yakkhas and Rākshasas (who are suddenly introduced into the story) to escape to an island called Giridīpa, 'the Island of Hills,' a name which may possibly indicate Malayālam, 'the Mountain Region.' The Rājāvaliya terms the place Yak-giri-dūwa, 'the Island of Demon Hills.' This place is described as 'beautifully adorned by rivers, mountains, and lakes . . . full of excellent food and rich grain, with a well-tempered climate, a green, grassy land . . . adorned by gardens and forests ; there were trees full of blossoms and fruits.' It was situated 'in the great sea, in the midst of the ocean and the deep waters, where the waves incessantly break ; around it there was a chain of mountains, towering, difficult to pass.'

The second visit of the Buddha is stated to have been paid in the fifth year of his mission. In this case he visited the Nāgas, a class of beings entirely different from the Yakkhas, who were engaged in a civil war in Northern Ceylon.[1] He first cowed them in the manner which had proved so effective with the Yakkhas, by means of a 'deep terrifying darkness.' and then reconciled them and converted great numbers to Buddhism. On this occasion he was accompanied by Indra as his attendant, who brought with him a large Kiripalu tree (*Buchanania angustifolia*) in which he commonly resided, and held it as a sunshade over his illustrious master, finally planting it in northern Ceylon as an object for the Nāgas to worship.

The third visit was made in his eighth year. On the full-moon day of Wesak (April–May), accompanied by 500

[1] The Rājāvaliya fixes the incident at Kaelaṇiya, and states that he then remained three days in Ceylon. It omits his visit to that place on the occasion of his third journey.

monks, he is represented as going to Kaelaṇiya, on the western side of Ceylon, near Colombo, at the invitation of Maṇi-Akkhika the Nāga king of Kaelaṇiya, who had undertaken a journey to India in order to invite him to come. Maṇi-Akkhika, who is stated in the Dhātuvansa to have been the maternal uncle or father-in-law of Mahōdara, one of the kings who was at war on his former visit, is described as a devout Buddhist, having been converted at the Buddha's first visit to the Yakkhas. The Nāga king erected a highly-decorated pavilion for the reception of the distinguished visitors, and distributed a great donation to the monks. After this, the Buddha is believed to have first left the impression of his foot on the Sumana Kūṭa mountain (Adam's Peak), and to have afterwards proceeded to the site of the future Dīghavāpi, on the eastern side of Ceylon, and finally to Anurādhapura, where he visited the sites subsequently occupied by the celebrated Bō-tree and three dāgabas.

According to these accounts, the Nāgas were apparently considered to be a comparatively civilised race. The incident of the planting of the Rajayatana (*Kiripalu* in Sinhalese) tree of Indra in their country Nāgadīpa, 'the Island of the Nāgas,' plainly shows that they belonged to the older faith of India, and were worshippers of Indra, and not of Śiva. They were ruled by their own kings, and had a settled and regular form of government. They seem to have been confined to the western and especially the northern part of Ceylon, this latter tract being invariably referred to in the histories for many centuries as Nāgadīpa. In these works the expression 'island' is often applied to a tract of land only partly surrounded or bordered by water. Similarly, in the Sinhalese histories India is always known as Jambudwīpa or Dambadiva, 'the Island of Jambu (trees).'

Nāgas are generally understood to be a form of nondescript beings with the bodies of serpents attached to the upper parts of human beings; but they are never represented in this manner in Sinhalese carvings, nor at Bharhut and Amarāvati in India. In the Bharhut carvings they resemble human beings in all respects, and can be recognised as Nāgas only

FIG. 8. Nāgas as Guardians, Jētavana Dāgaba.

To face p. 15.

by the addition of this descriptive title to their names. In the reliefs at Anurādhapura and Amarāvati, Nāga princes and princesses are only distinguishable from human beings by means of the cobras' heads with outspread hoods which appear behind or at the side of their heads. The Pūjāvaliya mentions dancers among North Indian Nāgas, and refers to the arms of the Nāga raja, Aravala. The old notion regarding them appears to have been that they had two forms which they could assume at will—either a human shape or that of a cobra.

Just as the Rākshasas disappear from history after the events described in the Rāmāyana, so the Nāgas of Ceylon are never mentioned again as inhabiting the island after their supposed partial conversion by the last Buddha. Yet the fact that the only name for the northern portion of Ceylon was 'the Island of Nāgas,' must be held to prove that some beings designated Nāgas once inhabited it.

The word Nāga may be applied either to human beings—there are still people of this name in north-eastern India—or cobras, or elephants, or to the class of supernatural beings referred to above, whose home was in the water, or below Mount Mēru, the centre of the universe. The latter were especially beings of the water, as the Yakshas were beings of the land. We may venture in these days to leave such creatures out of consideration, and to assume that the early occupiers of Northern Ceylon were human beings, as the account of them in the histories indicates.

The original home of such a race must evidently be looked for in the most southern part of India. In such a case, I think we must naturally turn first to the people of an identical name in Southern India, the Nāyars, who still occupy practically the extreme south-west part of the country. Their situation itself renders it in every way likely that Northern and Western Ceylon might be colonised by a branch of this race. There is no direct proof of the occurrence of such an immigration, but some evidence of it may be found in the fact that it would provide an explanation of the existence among the Kandian Sinhalese, who are a more or less mixed race, of some social features resembling those of the Indian Nāyars. Among these may be especially noted (1) the practice of polyandry; (2) the elasticity, or rather the slenderness, of the marriage tie, which permits the discarding, without any disgrace being attached to it, of undesirable husbands or wives; (3) the re-marriage of such wives, and of widows, with others, as a universal national custom; and (4) the absence of 'Sati,' or widow immolation. These are all customs that with perhaps the exception of the last, apparently cannot have been brought to Ceylon by the settlers who came from the valley of the Ganges; but they are still maintained by the Nāyars and the Kandian Sinhalese. Neither Sati nor the first three practices are found among the Vaeddas, the wild inhabitants of the inland forest tracts, and the three social customs must therefore have been introduced by others. It would be difficult to account for their presence in Ceylon by any other probable hypothesis than a Nāyar connexion of early date, since in historical times there has been no special intercourse between the island and Malayālam, beyond the enlistment of a few mercenary soldiers who were natives of the latter country. I suggest, therefore, that the Nāgas who occupied Northern Ceylon long before the arrival of the Gangetic settlers were actual Indian immigrants, and were an offshoot of the Nāyars of Southern India.

During the reign of the first king of Ceylon we find a town to the north of Anurādhapura, on the Kadamba river, which may have been then, as it is now, the boundary of the Drāvidian territory, that is, of Nāgadīpa, specially referred to by the annalists as the seat of 'the Brahmanical Upatissa.' Thus it may possibly have been a town or settlement of early Drāvidian colonists.

Returning to the Yakshas, the Yakkhas of the Pāli works, who evidently occupied the portion of Ceylon which was not included in Nāgadīpa, we find that in addition to Mahiyangana, which is stated to have been the scene of one of their battles (Mah. i, p. 4), they are more than once mentioned as being present in north-central Ceylon. They are expressly said to have been numerous 'in the south,' where the Indian prince Wijaya, the future ruler of the island, and his party from the

Ganges valley are reported to have landed; one of their capitals, Sirivattha, or the headquarters of one of their chiefs, was near this landing-place.

FIG. 9. A Yaksha (Wihāra Painting).

Notwithstanding their supposed previous removal from the island about forty-five years before his arrival (according to the statement that he came in the year of Buddha's death) we are told that Wijaya found the country still occupied by the Yakkhas. This is explained by the Rājāvaliya, which states that some Yakkhas had concealed themselves in the midst of the forest, and thus escaped banishment. According to the Mahāvansa, Wijaya married a Yakkha princess, called Kuwēnī, and with her advice and assistance succeeded in overcoming her countrymen and making himself master of at any rate a considerable part of Ceylon. A great part of the story of Wijaya's exile from his father's realm, and his journey to the island appears to be fictitious; but the whole account is valuable as indicating the early beliefs current in pre-Christian times regarding the aborigines.

In the Jātaka tales, or instructive incidents in the former

lives of the last Buddha, Gōtama—the most recent stories of which are at any rate of earlier date than the period of the compilation of the Dīpavansa, while others date from the fourth or fifth century B.C.—some interesting evidence is forthcoming regarding the tract inhabited by the Yakkhas.

After the usual introductory remarks, the Valāhassa Jātaka (No. 196) begins as follows: 'Once upon a time, there was in the island of Ceylon a goblin town called Sirīsavatthu, peopled by she-goblins. When a ship is wrecked these adorn and deck themselves, and taking rice and gruel, with trains of slaves, and their children on their hip, they come up to the merchants.' The story relates how they entice the traders to accompany them to the goblin city; 'then, if they have any others already caught, they bind these [other men] with magic chains, and cast them into the house of torment. And if they find no shipwrecked men in the place where they dwell, they scour the coast as far as the river Kalyāni [Kaelaṇiya, which enters the sea at Colombo] on the one side and the island of Nāgadīpa on the other. This is their way.'[1] Then follows an account of the ensnaring of five hundred shipwrecked merchants in this manner, and the escape of two hundred and fifty of them by the aid of the Bodhisattva [Gōtama Buddha, in this former life], who assumed the shape of a wonderful flying horse which carried them back to India. When some new men were entrapped the Yakkhas are described as killing and eating the two hundred and fifty who were left behind.

This anecdote implies that the Yakkhas occupied all the coast districts outside the limits of Nāgadīpa and Kaelaṇiya.

[1] The 'goblins' were Yakkhas. It is to be regretted that the translators of these stories, as well as other translators, decided to transform the appellations of the various inferior supernatural beings who are mentioned in them, into words that are assumed to be their English equivalents, but in reality belong, in some cases, to beings of different characteristics. The word 'goblin,' for instance, would never mean to the ordinary reader both a being, Yaksha, who was sometimes ranked in India close to the Gods—in the Atharva-Veda Yakshas precede the Rishis and the Father —and also a ghūl, *Vētāla*, an eater of dead bodies. 'Demon' and 'fiend' are used to designate such different beings as Dānavas, Daityas, Rākshasas, Yātudhānas and Pisāchas.

Taken with the information gleaned from the histories, this Jātaka story renders it clear that the old authors believed them to have held the southern two-thirds of the island, including one-third of the western coast. The fact that the Nāgas are described as being in possession of two-thirds of the western coast districts tells very strongly in favour of their coming from some part of the Malayālam tracts.

There is good reason to suppose that the accounts which the early writers have given respecting the Yakkhas have some foundation in fact. If so, they must necessarily refer, not to any supernatural beings who had made Ceylon their home, but to the aborigines, who in any case must have been driven out of the northern districts of the island by the intrusion of the Nāgas. It is the general consensus of opinion that they are now represented by the Vaeddas, the hunting and fishing tribe who at one time occupied all the central forests as well as the southern coasts.

The late Mr. H. Nevill, of the Ceylon Civil Service, and others, have traced the identification of the Vaeddas with the Yakkhas, by the old authors, to a similarity of the names of the two classes of beings. According to this view, the Pāli expression *Yakkha* was wrongly applied to the aborigines because of its resemblance to a title which is supposed to have been given to them as descriptive of their calling as hunters. It is believed by these writers that they were known as 'Arrow-persons'; this would be expressed by the word *iya*, 'arrow,' plus the personal suffix *ka*, forming the word *Iyaka*, which in sound is sufficiently close to *Yakkha* for such a confusion to arise. Although the arrow is certainly given a very prominent place in the ceremonies and worship of the Vaeddas, there appears to be no other evidence in favour of this derivation of the name applied to them by the ancient authors.

On the other hand, we have unmistakable evidence that they were known in pre-Christian times by the name which they still bear. The statement of the Mahāvansa that in the fourth century B.C. King Paṇḍukābhaya provided a site at Anurādhapura for the Vyāda-Dēva, 'the Vaedda deity,' and erected special dwellings for the Vyādas there, appears to prove conclusively that at that early date the aborigines were known as Vyādas or 'hunters,' that is, Vaeddas, and not Iyakas. In the Mahāvansa they are also once termed Pulindas, that is, savages or barbarians, a name applied by Indian writers to the Bhīls; and in place-names they are Sabaras, a word with the same meaning. It was probably due to exaggerated tales about these hunters, which the primitive Indian traders told their credulous countrymen on their return from their long and arduous expeditions to Ceylon, that the aborigines came to be denominated Yakkhas, that is, demons or goblins.

For the original home of these first comers we must search in the nearest aboriginal tracts of the adjoining continent, the hills of Southern India, or their neighbourhood. It has been already noted that the Rāmāyana mentions the existence of Yakshas on them. Professor R. Virchow has shown that the character of the skulls of the present Vaeddas indicates a race with an affinity to some of the South Indian hill tribes. In several respects their customs incline to those of other South Indian hill-men, and their supreme deity is the Hill-God, whose cult prevails throughout the Western and Southern Ghāts. Perhaps the strongest evidence of the country of their origin is their own tradition that this deity came to Ceylon from Malawara-desa, 'the Country of the Hill-region,' that is the Malayālam hills. It remains to be seen whether any affinities can be recognised between their dialect—which is practically a compound of modern Sinhalese, old Sinhalese, and a few Tamil words—and those of the South-Indian hill tribes.

There is nothing to indicate that the Vaeddas were ever the cannibals that the Jātaka story represents them to be; the tale of their eating shipwrecked persons is an embellishment regarding the truth of which the later legends of the supposed habits of the true Yakshas would leave no doubt in an Indian mind. It may be taken to have no better basis than the fact that like many other aboriginal tribes they may have robbed and perhaps killed some of the traders wrecked on their shores, and seized the cargoes of their ships. On the other hand, the statement that the Pulayars of Travancore, who are believed to be the aborigines of the plains in South-west India, habitually file their teeth [1] must be admitted to afford some evidence that cannibalism was formerly a practice of that race, the habit of sharpening the teeth being almost always associated with anthropophagy. Had man-eating been also a custom of the aborigines of Ceylon, however, some distinct reference to it, in addition to the very doubtful story of the habits of the Sirīsavatthu residents, would almost certainly be found in the Sinhalese historical works, and the teeth of the Vaeddas would probably be filed to the present day, like those of the Pulayars.

On the whole, it may be concluded that the advance of the Drāviḍians to the south of India, which may have occurred before the entry of the Āryans into the north-western regions, may have eventually led to an exodus of an aboriginal and probably pre-Drāvidian hunting and fishing tribe across the shallow strait that separates Ceylon from India.[2]

That this tribe in early times obtained food by fishing as well as hunting, may be gathered from the facts (1) that some Vaeddas live entirely by fishing at the present day; (2) that they are stated in the Valāhassa Jātaka to have wandered along the shores round the southern and eastern part of the island; and (3) especially that in the eastern part of Ceylon, where the people who retain the name of Vaeddas are still found, the shark is a forbidden food to the Kapuwas (or demon-priests) of the jungles of the interior who conduct the worship in honour of their supreme deity. This prohibition must have arisen from an acquaintance with the man-eating proclivities of the shark, regarding which the natives of the interior could have no direct knowledge. Such a prohibition would never be thought of by any but residents on the sea coast who were accustomed to catch and eat the shark, and it would be quite useless among others who lived far from the sea. The shark is not a forbidden food to the Kapuwas in other parts of the

[1] Rev. S. Mateer, *Native Life in Travancore*, p. 41.

[2] Dr. R. Virchow has already stated that 'we cannot avoid the conviction that they stand in a close affinity to the Aborigines of India.' (*The Veddās of Ceylon*, Translation, p. 131.)

island. The custom is an evident survival from a time when a considerable part of the race gained a living by sea-fishing, and were aware of its necessity in order to preserve from defilement the officiators at the services in honour of their deity. I may add that it appears to completely negative the Indian story of the cannibalism of the aborigines. If they were eaters of human flesh they could have no reason for declaring the shark an impure fish because it ate the same food as themselves.

Many centuries must have elapsed before these wanderers could penetrate and spread through all the dense forests of the interior, and in considerable numbers occupy all the southern coast districts, as they are represented to have done by the fifth century B.C. It may thus be accepted as certain that their advent dated, at the latest, from the second millennium before Christ, if the primitive state of the wilder members among their descendants, and the advanced state of the more civilised portion of the race in early historical times, do not indicate an even more distant arrival in the island.

II

THE ANCIENT VAEDDAS

THE Sinhalese histories contain several references to the aborigines of Ceylon, whom they usually denominate, in the Pāli language, Yakkhas. The narrative of the Buddha's supposed visit to them has been given already. They are next mentioned in the tale of the arrival of Wijaya, the first Sinhalese king; and the story, even if partly or chiefly fictitious, is valuable as an illustration of some of the notions which the invaders or new settlers held regarding them. On this occasion only two Yakkhinīs (female Yakkhas) showed themselves and endeavoured to entrap the travellers, who were only saved because Vishnu had taken the precaution to tie charmed threads on their arms.

One of the Yakkhinīs proved to be a princess named Kuwēnī, whom Wijaya married. She provided the adventurers with a good meal of rice and other articles taken from ships that had been wrecked on the coast of Ceylon. She is then represented as proceeding to recommend Wijaya to attack the Yakkhas of the neighbouring town, in the following terms (Mah. i, p. 33):—"In the city Sirivattha [the Sirīsavatthu of the Jātaka story], in this island, there is a Yakkha sovereign Kālasēna, and in the Yakkha city Lankāpura there is another sovereign. Having conducted his daughter Pusamittā thither, her mother Kondanāmikā is now bestowing that daughter at a marriage festival on the sovereign there at Sirivattha. From that circumstance there is a grand festival in an assembly of Yakkhas. That great assemblage will keep up that revel without intermission for seven days." The prince acted as advised by her, and 'having put Kālasēna, the chief of the Yakkhas, to death, assumed his court dress. The rest of his retinue dressed themselves in the vestments [or ornaments] of the other Yakkhas. After the lapse of some days, departing from the capital of the Yakkhas, and founding the city called Tambapaṇṇi Wijaya settled there.'

According to the narrative, Wijaya subsequently married a daughter of the Pāṇḍiyan king of Madura, and discarded the Yakkha princess, who went to Lankāpura, where she left her two children outside the town (Mah. i, p. 35). 'The Yakkhas on seeing her enter the city, quickly surrounded her, crying out "It is for the purpose of spying on us that she has come back." When the Yakkhas were thus excited one of them whose anger was greatly kindled put an end to the life of the Yakkhinī by a blow of his hand. Her uncle, a Yakkha named Kumāra, happening to proceed out of the Yakkha city, seeing these children outside the town, "Whose children are ye," said he. Being informed "Kuwēnī's," he said, "Your mother is murdered; if ye should be seen here they would murder you also; fly quickly." Instantly departing thence, they repaired to the neighbourhood of Sumanakūta (Adam's Peak). The elder having grown up married his sister and settled there. Becoming numerous by their sons and daughters, under the protection of the king they resided in that Malaya [mountain] district. This is the origin of the Pulindas.' Thus it is plain that at the early date when the first annals consulted by the compiler of the Mahāvansa were written it was known that the so-called Yakkhas were in reality the aborigines, the Pulindas.

In the time of the fourth king of Ceylon, Tissa, the chronicler returns to the old idea of the Yakkhas as a form of demon, and narrates (Mah. i, p. 41) that 'A certain Yakkhinī named Cētiyā [1] (the widow of Jūtindhara, a Yakkha who was killed in a battle at Sirivatthapura [2]) who dwelt at the Dhūmarakkha mountain [which the context shows was close to the Kasā ford on the Mahawaeli-ganga, near Polannaruwa], was wont to walk about the marsh of Tumbariyangana in the shape of a mare,' which was of a white colour, with red legs. Prince

[1] In this and all other transliterations the letter *c* represents the sound *ch*, as in *church*.

[2] The words in brackets are only given in Turnour's *Mahawanso*.

Paṇḍukābhaya, the nephew of the king, who had taken the field in an attempt to seize the throne, and now held all the eastern and southern districts, to the south of the river Mahawaeli-ganga, succeeded in catching this mare, and by her supernatural advice and help, that is, with the assistance of the Yakkhas or Vaeddas, defeated and killed the king his uncle, and the latter's brothers, with the exception of two, and thus secured the sovereignty.

He reigned at Anurādhapura, which he enlarged and rearranged, so that during his reign it became an important city. The chronicler relates that 'He established the Yakkha Kālavēla in the eastern quarter of the city; and the chief of the Yakkhas, Citta, he established on the lower side of the Abhaya tank [that is, on the south-western side of the town]. He who knew how to accord his protection with discrimination established the slave [Kumbōkatā], born of the Yakkha tribe, who had previously rendered him great service,[1] at the southern gate of the city.' Thus he arranged that his Vaedda allies should be established on three sides of the city, doubtless as its defenders.

The cemetery was fixed on the western side of the town; and to the northward of it, and apparently near the main road which led to Mahātiṭṭha, the port from which travellers sailed for Southern India, 'a range of buildings' was also constructed for the 'Vyādas,' the Vaedda populace in general.

The Mahāvansa also informs us that 'he established within the garden of the royal palace the mare-faced Yakkhinī.' It will be noted that this Vaedda chieftainess is no longer called a mare, but only mare-faced, just as nicknames such as 'moon-faced,' 'crooked-nosed,' 'large-toothed,' etc., were applied to the Sinhalese kings.

Thus it is clear that a large proportion of the population of Anurādhapura or its outskirts at that time consisted of the

[1] She had saved his life when an infant. According to the history, the so-called Yakkhas protected him from the time when he was born, his uncles having endeavoured to kill him on account of a prediction that he would destroy them. If there is any truth in this, his father's mother may have been a native princess.

Vaedda supporters of the king. It has been already mentioned that he provided a site for the Vyāda Dēva, 'the Vaedda God,' also. The chronicler proceeds to indicate in unmistakable language the commanding position of the Vaedda rulers of this period: 'In the days of public festivity, this monarch, seated on a throne of equal eminence with the Yakkha chief, Citta, caused joyous spectacles, representing the actions of devas [gods] as well as mortals, to be exhibited.'

This important sentence proves that the supreme Vaedda chief of that day occupied a position little, if at all, inferior to that of the Sinhalese king.

The chronicler continues, 'This monarch befriending the interests of the Yakkhas, with the co-operation of Kālavēla and Citta, who had the power of rendering themselves visible,[1] conjointly with them enjoyed his prosperity.'

It is easy to see that it was by means of a close alliance with the Vaeddas that this astute king, the greatest organiser the country has ever had—who is recorded to have made the first land settlement by defining the boundaries of the villages throughout the country—succeeded in deposing his uncle and gaining the throne. The natives were evidently far too numerous and powerful and well-organised to be put aside afterwards like the unfortunate Kuwēnī; and the politic king found it advisable to recognise the authority and influence of their leaders as nearly equal to his own. His political sagacity in this respect doubtless saved the country from many years of bloodshed and insecurity, and converted the Vaeddas into peaceable inhabitants devoted to his interests. In religious matters he was equally liberal and impartial; he made special provision for all religious bodies at his capital. It was he, also, who gave the first stimulus to reservoir construction in the northern districts, and probably also irrigation. The historian rightly referred to him as 'this wise ruler,' and stated that at his death the country was 'in a state of perfect peace' (Mah. i, p. 44). This great monarch was born in about 345

[1] We may recognise the hand of the reverend historian of the fifth century in this little parenthesis.

B.C., and reigned from 308 to about 275 B.C., or possibly a little later.

In the middle of the third century B.C. the account of the arrival of Mahinda, the son of the Indian emperor Aśōka, on a mission to convert the Sinhalese and their king Dēvānam-piya Tissa to Buddhism, possibly indicates a certain retention of power by the Vaeddas, and the brusque manner in which they ventured to address the king. When Mahinda first met the king in the jungle, 'the thera [superior monk] said to him, "Come hither, Tissa." From his calling him simply "Tissa" the monarch thought he must be a Yakkha' (Mah. i, p. 50). Whether the story is true or false, it proves that the writer believed that the Yakkhas, who must have been either supernatural beings or the Vaeddas of that time, did not exhibit much deference towards the Sinhalese sovereign.

In the time of Duṭṭha-Gāmiṇi (161–137 B.C.) there is a reference to a temple of a deity termed 'Pura-Dēva,' which is stated to have been on the northern side of the cemetery, where we have seen that the Vaeddas were settled. This god seems to be the Vyāda Dēva of the time of Paṇḍukābhaya, the word apparently meaning 'the Ancient God' of the country.

When the great Ruwanwaeli dāgaba[1] was constructed by this king at Anurādhapura, among the paintings depicted on the wall of the relic-room inside it the list runs: 'The four great kings of the Cātumahārājika heavens stood there with drawn swords; and thirty-three supernaturally-gifted dēvas [inferior gods] bearing baskets of flowers and making offerings of pāricchatta flowers [*Erythrina indica*, now used only for demon-offerings]. There stood thirty-two princesses bearing lighted torches, and twenty-eight Yakkha chiefs ranged themselves as a guard of protection [for the relics in the chamber], driving away the fierce Yakkhas' (Mah. i, p. 121).

In the Hatthi-pāla Jātaka (No. 509) a tree-deity is repre-

[1] A dāgaba is a solid mound built to contain relics of Buddha, or important personages, especially monks, or sometimes only to commemorate an event which occurred at the site. It is usually a semiglobe or a bell in shape, with a terminal spire; but there are other forms, of which an account is given in a subsequent chapter. Dāgaba =dhātu-garbha, 'relic-chamber.'

sented as applying to the 'eight and twenty war-lords of the goblins' to grant a son to a king. The beings mentioned in the Mahāvansa are thus probably the same Yakkhas of the Indian authors. At the dāgaba at Bharhut, in India, these beings were carved in relief at the gateways of the 'Buddhist railing' in the third century B.C., as guards, together with Nāga chiefs.

On the other hand, in Southern India it is the Rākshasas who always act as guards at the Hindu temples, in accordance with the derivation of the word from the root *rāksh*, to guard. When deities are represented on the gōpuras or ornamental gateways at the entrances of the great temples, figures of the Rākshasas are invariably present as their guards, and the Yakshas are never found in such positions of trust.

In the later wall-paintings of the Buddhist wihāras in Ceylon, the Yakshas always form the army of Māra, the god of Death, which attacked the Buddha; but this has been shown to be a conception of later date than the canonical works, and it may not have found acceptance in the country in the time of Duṭṭha-Gāmiṇi. It is, however, somewhat strange to find Mahānāma inserting the description of these figures in such a position in the dāgaba without some explanatory remark. He may have understood them to be representations of aboriginal chiefs.

I believe the Vaeddas only make their appearance twice more in the early Sinhalese histories. The Rājāvaliya relates that King Mahā-Sēna (277–304 A.D.) employed Yakkhas as well as [Sinhalese] men in the construction of a large number of reservoirs that were formed in order to store water for the irrigation of rice fields. Some confirmation of this story may be seen in his deification at some subsequent period, with the title of Sat-Rajjuruwō, that is, 'King of (all) living creatures,' —both the men and the supposed demons whom he forced to work for him. Worship is still paid extensively to him in this capacity in the northern Kandian districts.

The Vaeddas still formed a great part of the population in the twelfth century. The Mahāvansa (ii, p. 151) recounts how King Parākrama-Bāhu I (1164–1197 A.D.), while his cousin

Gaja-Bāhu ruled at Polannaruwa, made preparations for a campaign for the conquest of the latter's dominions, and enlisted for it large numbers of his subjects. Among these we are told that 'He trained many thousands' of Vyādas, that is, Vaeddas, 'and made them skilled in the use of their weapons, and gave them suitable swords, black clothes, and the like things.' Thus in the twelfth century we see the Vaeddas in a state of comparative civilisation, taking their place in the army with the other levies.

It is extremely probable that contingents of Vaeddas formed part of the Sinhalese army not only then but in every war. We find them still serving with the other troops under Raja Sinha in the early part of the seventeenth century. Captain Robert Knox, in his *Historical Relation of the Island Ceylon*, p. 62, states of those living near Hurulla, in the North-central Province, 'The King once having occasion of an hasty Expedition against the *Dutch*, the Governour summoned them all in to go with him, which they did. And with their Bows and Arrows did as good service as any of the rest; but afterwards when they returned home again, they removed farther in the Woods, and would be seen no more, for fear of being afterwards prest again to serve the King.'

As the immigration, such as it was, from the Ganges Valley appears to have practically ceased from the time of Paṇḍukābhaya's birth, his policy of admitting the natives to an equality with the Indian settlers must have caused a rapid fusion of the two races. This was the birth of the Sinhalese nation.[1] We must believe that such a broad-minded ruler would not

[1] The tradition of the origin of the name is given as follows in the Mahāvansa i, pp. 33, 34. 'By reason of the King Sīhabāhu [the father of Wijaya] having slain the lion (*Sīha*), his sons and descendants are called "Sīhalā" (the lion-slayers). This Lankā [Ceylon] having been conquered by a Sīhala, from the circumstance of its having been colonized by a Sīhala, it obtained the name of Sīhala.' At a much later date it became the fashion to adopt Sanskrit forms of words in writing, and instead of the Pāli word *Sīha* the Sanskrit expression *Sinha* was used. The word meaning the country and people thus became 'Sinhala' (pronounced with a nasal *n*, but no *g* sound). The Vaeddas have retained the old name of the country.

refuse equal rights to the northern Drāvidians of Nāgadīpa, and thus the whole population must have gradually coalesced, with a great preponderance of the Vaedda blood. In the same manner as in England in Norman times or after the Roman domination, the natives in the lapse of years totally absorbed the newcomers, and a later very slight admixture of Tamil blood at last produced the race which we now find in the Kandian provinces. It differs from that of the western and southern coast tracts in all respects but colour, religion, and language.

In a note on the subject of Polyandry, the late Mr. E. Goonetilleke, the learned Sinhalese editor of the *Orientalist*, said in Vol. iv, p. 93 of that publication, regarding the two races of Sinhalese, 'They are as distinct from each other in their dress, habits, manners, and customs, and in their very ideas and manner of thinking, as if they formed two different races, rather than two sections of one nation.' The Kandian villagers certainly look upon the people of the western coast tracts as a separate race, and do not term them Sinhalese, but always speak of them as *Pāta ratē minissu*, 'Men of the Low-country.'

The difference is not altogether due to a preponderance of Vaedda blood in the interior. The dwellers near the western coast have always been exposed to foreign influences. The various races who have either settled among them in considerable numbers or held the western coasts as conquerors include Drāvidian and Arab traders and settlers; and as conquerors, Malays, Chinese, Portuguese, Dutch, and lastly English. It would be strange if the resultant people did not vary greatly from those of the interior.

That the Kandian Sinhalese are thus the modern representatives of the great bulk of the ancient Vaeddas is, I venture to think, beyond doubt. The people who were so numerous throughout the country in the twelfth century, that in half the island 'many thousands' could be enlisted as soldiers, have certainly not been exterminated. They, like the Vaeddas of preceding centuries, have simply settled down as Kandian villagers. An insignificant number still retain their ancient designation, but even these, with the exception of a few families, have become ordinary villagers, and in outward appearance are indistinguishable from many other Kandians.

This abandonment of the wild forest life of their ancestors apparently began at a very early date. After the time of Paṇḍukābhaya the next proof of the fact is found immediately after the introduction of Buddhism into the country. The evidence derivable from the caves or rock-shelters, thousands in number, under the sides of the boulders lying on the slopes of all the hills of the Low-country, whether in the eastern and southern part of the Northern Province, or the North-western, the North-central, the Eastern, or the Southern Provinces, all points to the settling down of the Vaedda populace in early times as peaceable villagers.

The researches of the Drs. Sarasin and Dr. C. G. Seligmann have shown that the first inhabitants of the caves were aborigines who made use of stone implements. Then, at a later date, which we know from the dedicatory inscriptions to be in nearly all cases pre-Christian, the caves throughout the whole of the above-mentioned Provinces (I have no knowledge of those of other districts) were turned into shelters for ascetic Buddhist monks. There is hardly a hill possessing such cave shelters, some of which, at least, were not so converted. Even where no inscription records the fact, the cutting of the *katāra* or drip-ledge to prevent rain-water from trickling down the face of the rock into the cave is indubitable proof that this was the case.

Had the aborigines been forcibly ousted from these caves in order to permit the monks to occupy them, we cannot suppose that they would not have felt resentment, which would have led to reprisals of a violent character. It is clear that in many instances little establishments of only two or three monks must have occupied the caves on some of the most secluded of these hills, buried in the depths of the dense forests of the wildest parts of the island. In such sites the aborigines could have regained possession of their caves with ease and impunity, and with practically no fear of punishment by the Sinhalese authorities. In the histories, also, there is no hint of any quarrels with the natives after the time when Paṇḍukābhaya became king.

If the monks who occupied the caves had been in danger of attacks by the aborigines, it is extremely improbable that they would have utilised the caves on practically all the hills during the short period between the middle of the third century and the early part of the first century B.C., as the form of the letters of the inscriptions cut on so many of them—'hundreds and hundreds,' according to Dr. E. Müller—proves was the case. A few caves, but only an insignificant number, have inscriptions cut in letters of a later date than this. Thus there seems good reason to believe that when the monks came to occupy the caves their original residents had already voluntarily abandoned them, and, like the Vaeddas of Anurādhapura, had established themselves in villages.

Even the people who still call themselves Vaeddas are to some extent of mixed blood. This applies almost equally to the wildest members of the race, and is proved conclusively by the wide variation in the colour of the skin, and in the amount of hair on the face, even if the general outline of the features does not indicate it.

It was probably due to the union of the races on nearly equal terms that the Vaeddas accepted the language of the Gangetic settlers in preference to their own, which they have totally lost. Had they kept more aloof from the newcomers, they might have maintained their own tongue nearly intact down to the present time. The new language spread through Nāgadīpa also; there is not a single very early Drāvidian inscription in the whole of Northern Ceylon. The adoption of the Buddhist religion throughout the entire country—including Nāgadīpa, as the numerous remains of ancient wihāras prove—must have accelerated this change of language; at every monastery the monks would teach the dialect of Pāli which had become the Sinhalese speech, in the same manner as at present.

Notwithstanding the alteration of language and ideas and the spread of the new religion, the population of whole districts must have remained more or less pure Vaeddas for many centuries, with some gradual slight intermixture of foreign blood as the intercourse with Nāgadīpa and Southern India led to an intermittent influx of Drāvidians, culminating in occasional invasions of the island by South Indian armies. In some cases, in what are now thought to be pure Sinhalese districts, many of the people were still distinguished from the other inhabitants by the name of Vaeddas down to the seventeenth century, after which they appear to have abandoned this title to the wilder residents of the eastern districts.

Although declaring themselves Buddhists and attending the services at the temples, many of these Sinhalese-Vaeddas still adhered to the worship of the ancient Hill-God of their ancestors, the Vyāda Dēva of the old annalists. The philosophical reasoning of the new faith might appeal to their minds, but it did not afford the practical protection which they received from their old religion. They still felt the need of the kindly supreme deity to whom they could appeal in time of trouble, for which the new faith provided no remedy, but only taught resignation to the inevitable. The ancient god could still, it was thought, assist them out of their physical difficulties, without interfering with their general belief in the truth of the Buddhist doctrines. In some parts of the Kandian districts the two religions have therefore settled down side by side to the present day.

Dr. R. Virchow, as the result of an examination of a series of Vaedda and Sinhalese skulls, expressed the following opinion regarding the affinity of the Vaeddas and Sinhalese: 'The Vaeddas would appear rather as representatives of the aboriginal race; the Sinhalese, on the other hand, as hybrids produced by a union of immigrant Indians with Vaeddas, and therefore varying according to the measure of their participation of either of these elements. This indeed strikes me as being the solution of the anthropological problem before us, so far, at least, as the material at present reaches. The linguistic difficulty, that also the unmixed [1] natives adopted the Āryan language of the conqueror, without, so far as we can

[1] It is extremely doubtful if there are any groups of Vaeddas of unmixed blood in these days.

judge, having been forced to do so, appears to me no longer insurmountable, since from personal experience I have established the fact that in the Baltic provinces of Russia one part of the Finnish population after the other, through imperceptible but steady progress, has become letticized to such an extent that the Courland language has wholly, the Livonian almost wholly, disappeared, and only the Esthonian still offers any resistance.' [1]

His final conclusions on the subject are : '(1) That manifold resemblances exist between the Vaeddas and the Sinhalese, and that the origin of the Sinhalese race from a mixture of Vaeddas and immigrants from India possesses great probability, as well upon historical as also upon anthropological grounds.

'(2) That the Vaeddas as well as the Sinhalese in the main features are distinguished from the Ceylon Tamils, and equally from those of Tanjore (Sōla).

'(3) That, on the other hand, among the remnants of the old Drāvidian or perhaps pre-Drāvidian tribes of Hindustān we find even to-day evidence of analogies with the Vaeddas' (p. 136).

[1] Monograph on the Vaeddas, published in the *Memoirs of the Royal Academy of Science of Berlin*, in 1881, and translated for the Ceylon Branch of the Royal Asiatic Society in 1888, p. 110.

III

THE MODERN VAEDDAS AND WANNIYAS

THE following account of these races depends on original observations of them made by myself during official visits to their districts, largely supplemented by quotations from articles on the Vaeddas by the late Mr. Hugh Nevill of the Ceylon Civil Service, which he published in 1886, in his magazine, *The Taprobanian.*[1] I have endeavoured to credit him with all information taken from his papers. He had the advantage of being stationed in the Eastern Province for a considerable time, first as Assistant Government Agent of the Trincomalee district, and afterwards as District Judge of Batticaloa; and being an indefatigable student and an accurate observer, and well acquainted with the native languages, he was able, owing to his official position, to collect a large amount of valuable information regarding the Vaeddas, as well as other subjects, which would not be readily available to others. It is greatly to be regretted that the part of it relating to the ceremonies used in their demon worship was never made public by him. I have also quoted some remarks on the Vaeddas by Professor R. Virchow, together with the sizes of their skulls as noted in the valuable monograph on them already referred to. Throughout this account of them I have instituted comparisons between them and the present Kandian Sinhalese. I am well aware of the defective nature of this account; but as it contains some information which is not elsewhere available. I have thought it advisable to publish it.

[1] I am indebted to the courtesy of his brother, Mr. Ralph Nevill, for permission to utilise them.

The Vaeddas of the present day, or those known as such, are found only in the eastern half of the island. They are usually divided into three classes, which I shall distinguish as follows :—

(1) The wild Forest Vaeddas, few in number, who live entirely by hunting, and dwell in the depths of the forests near the eastern base of the Kandian mountains. At Nilgala, where I expected to find them well known, I was surprised to learn that they are rarely seen ; all of whom I could hear in that neighbourhood consisted of one small party who sometimes visited or resided on a hill about five miles away in the forest. There are more of them on the western side of the valley of the Madura-oya.

(2) The Village Vaeddas of the eastern interior and the south-eastern coast districts, who in many cases, but probably not in all, have some intermixture, recent or ancient, of Sinhalese blood, though practically forming the same race as the Forest Vaeddas. There are two villages of these Vaeddas in the North-central Province, near Hurulla tank, and several others on the eastern side of the lower part of the Mahawaeli-ganga, but the great majority live in the Eastern Province.

(3) The Tamil-speaking Vaeddas, who live in scattered villages on or near the central coast tract, from the north of Trincomalee to about ten miles north of Batticaloa. These have intermarried with the Tamil residents of that part of the country, and have adopted their language, and some of their customs, while still retaining some of their own.

Distributed among some eighteen small hamlets along the northern border of the North-central Province, which is the boundary between the Tamil districts of the north, the ancient Nāgadīpa, and the Kandian Sinhalese, there is also a race of hunters, probably less than 500 in number, who, like the others, are termed by the Tamils Vēḍan (in English pronunciation *Verdan*), plural Vēḍar. They themselves repudiate this appellation, except in its ordinary meaning of 'hunter,' and they deny that they are in any way connected with the Vaeddas, of whom they speak in very contemptuous terms. Their own name for themselves is Waṇṇiyā, 'person of the Waṇṇi,' as the forest and jungle of northern Ceylon to the south of Elephant Pass is called. They all speak Sinhalese, with the exception of the inhabitants of one or two hamlets lying to the west, but all the men also know a certain amount of Tamil. As their habits when engaged in hunting do not differ from those of the Vaeddas, it will be useful to include them in dealing with the latter, especially as some consider them to be true Vaeddas, with whom, in fact, it is not unlikely that they are connected, although they have lost all tradition of it, and neither know the Vaedi [1] dialect nor, so far as I am aware, worship quite the same deities.

Like the Vaeddas, they all claim to be of good caste (in their case the Goyiwansa, or cultivating caste), although, like them also, many have names such as elsewhere now belong only to persons of the low castes like the Tom-tom beaters; among these may be mentioned Kandā, Vēlan, Kaṭā, Kōnā, etc. Others have what are considered to be good caste names.

On examining the inscriptions and histories, however, we learn that two thousand years ago, or more, the short names that are now confined to the lower castes were borne by the chiefs, and even by the members of the royal family. In Ceylon, in early times there seem to have been no names that were specially distinctive of the high and low castes; where a distinction was made it was provided by the addition of a separate ending, of which instances occur in the names found both in the cave inscriptions and the histories, such as the

[1] Vaedi is the adjectival form. In Sinhalese, the masculine noun is Vaeddā, plural Vaeddō, and the feminine noun is Vaeddī. I believe these nouns are only employed by Sinhalese. I have not heard the Vaeddas term themselves otherwise than as 'Vaddī men' (*Vaedi minissu*). In their own dialect this would be *Vaedi minu*, but a Vaedda has been represented as calling one of his race *Wannikuḍē minā*, and the word *Mal* occurs for Vaeddas in the invocations collected by Dr. Seligmann. The Tamil-speaking Vaeddas call themselves *Vēḍan*. Reasons have been given for doubting if the word *Vaedda* could be derived from the Pāli word *Vyādha*. In any case, that Vyādha, however, signified Vaedda is, I think, clear from the use of this term in the Mahāvansa to describe the 'many thousands' enlisted by Parākrama Bāhu I. In a footnote at the end of the chapter on the Primitive Deity of Ceylon I have given an intermediate form found in one old work.

terminations Gutta (Gupta), Sēna, Dēva, Mitta (Mitra), and Nāga. As regards their characteristic names, therefore, the Wanniyas and also the Vaeddas have simply retained the custom of pre-Christian times.

At the Census of 1901 the total number of all classes of Vaeddas, including, I presume, the Wanniyas, was found to be 3,971. The numbers obtained at the two preceding decennial enumerations were so defective that no conclusions can be based upon them regarding the increase or decrease of the race.

Little is known of the Vaeddas of the first of the three classes, who are almost inaccessible in their wild forests.[1] Formerly they were accustomed to lead a more or less wandering life, which in the case of each little family party was confined to a definite tract of forest, sleeping in caves at the foot of the hills, or under trees. They still make use of the caves, but their village neighbours informed me a few years ago that all now build huts in the forests and inhabit them at times when they are distant from their cave shelters. Those whom I have seen were indistinguishable from the Village Vaeddas; they appeared to be healthy and well nourished. According to Mr. Nevill, they change their quarters from time to time when the game and 'Iguanas' (large terrestrial lizards) of their neighbourhood are killed or driven away. So far as my own limited observation extends, I quite agree with Mr. Nevill that the Forest Vaeddas and the wilder Village Vaeddas are the same people. It is a mistake to suppose that all Village Vaeddas are of more mixed descent than the Forest Vaeddas; many are simply Forest Vaeddas who have settled down in recent times in more or less permanent hamlets.[2]

Clothing.—They are a wild-looking race, wearing a minimum of clothing, which consists, in the case of the men, of a small rag or strip of calico suspended in front from a bark string tied round the waist, and when hunting a larger strip of discoloured

[1] Dr. C. G. Seligmann, accompanied by Mrs. Seligmann, has succeeded in finding some families of these Forest Vaeddas, and is about to publish an exhaustive account of them and their customs and beliefs.

[2] See the footnote at the end of this chapter.

cloth which is passed round the abdomen in three or four folds, forming a narrow flat band about four inches wide. It is recorded that in the early part of last century some Vaeddas wore a short skirt made of the liber or fibrous inner bark of the Riṭi tree (*Antiaris innoxia*), like the material of the bark bags which they still prepare for household purposes. It may be considered certain that where these trees were found this must have formed the general costume of the wilder individuals at a time when cotton cloth was unobtainable; and I was told that a very few of the poorer people still employ it for the same purpose.

Some have also been reported to wear green leafy twigs suspended from a bark string tied round the waist; but this may have been merely a hunting device to avoid notice of their cloth by wild animals. I have seen the Wanniyas using this primitive costume on such occasions, but only as a temporary expedient. Mr. Nevill mentioned that he was informed that in ancient times leaves were so worn as clothing in districts where there were no Riṭi trees. Only the poorest among them wore this dress, and that not from choice but necessity. He considered that there is no reason to suppose that they ever went about in a state of nudity. I never heard that any of them have worn skins.[1] The account of the natives at the time of Wijaya's arrival would lead one to suppose that some at least wore clothing which the newcomers did not consider primitive.

When in the forests, the Village Vaeddas of the interior, as well as the Wanniyas, dress in the same manner as the ordinary Forest Vaeddas, and roll up their cloth and fasten it round the abdomen like them. The females of both classes have similar clothing, a short skirt of cotton fastened round the waist and reaching to the knees or below them. When visiting other villages the men wear a similar cloth from the waist to the knees or below them.

[1] Ribeyro, whose work was written in 1685, stated that those who lived in the forests north of Trincomalee (? Wanniyas) wore the skins of animals, but he does not say that he ever saw them. Knox would not be likely to omit mentioning the custom if it had been practised in his time.

The Tamil-speaking or Coast Vaeddas dress like Tamil villagers, with a cloth reaching from the waist nearly to the ankles; the women wear a long calico robe which is passed round the body under the arm-pits and hangs straight down nearly to the feet. It is the ordinary costume of the village Tamil women of northern Ceylon, and is singularly ungraceful.

General Description.—I may premise that as regards Anthropology, so far as it relates to the scientific description of the human body, I possess neither qualifications nor knowledge, and I have therefore collected no information beyond that of a casual observer who is well acquainted with the other races of Ceylon.

The skin of the first two classes of Vaeddas is commonly of a dull dirty-looking dark reddish-brown colour, which may be termed a dark walnut hue. There is nearly always a distinct reddish tint in it. The difference between it and the colour of some low-caste Kandian Sinhalese is so slight that I am unable to define it; I should say that it consists chiefly in the duller appearance of the Vaedda skin. Many of the Coast Vaeddas and a few of the Village Vaeddas and Forest Vaeddas are much darker than this, and of a brownish-black colour, this shade evidently indicating a mixture with Drāvidian blood.

Mr. Nevill considered that the Vaeddas belong to a light brown race, and the Sinhalese to a light yellow race, and he even thought that both the Sinhalese and Vaeddas 'are of one original colour, yellow, with an olive tint.' This does not account for the reddish hue of the Vaeddas, which can almost always be seen in a full light, and sometimes very conspicuously. It has reddish-brown or reddish-purple shadows. It is often present in the skins of Kandian Sinhalese, some few of whom are even of a clear dull copper-red colour. This tinge is never seen in the skins of Tamils, and is hardly observable among Telugus, at any rate those of low castes; but I have noticed it very plainly in several Kanarese from Maisūr, some of whom are of a clear copper-red colour. The pale brownish-yellow tint of Sinhalese is only found in the members of families of what is now thought to be the purest descent, such as those of many of the leading chiefs; it is the colour of those who most closely represent the original settlers from the valley of the Ganges, and is far from being the average colour of the race who comprise the Kandian or Low-country Sinhalese of the present day, which is much nearer a dark walnut tint. In the ordinary Kandian villager all shades are found from clear copper-red through varieties of reddish-browns to the deepest blacklead black, but the tints at the extremes of the scale are uncommon.

The height of the Village Vaeddas is less than that of the ordinary northern Kandian villagers, and in the case of the men averages probably five feet, or an inch more, the Sinhalese being two inches or three inches taller. Recorded measurements of Forest Vaeddas show that they, or many of them, are much shorter than this, and vary between four and five feet, but always above the lower figure.

Although their figure is always very slight, with narrow hips and weak-looking calves and thighs, the Vaeddas are active and lithe in the forests, and can thread their way for many hours among the trees and jungle without apparent fatigue. When alone one morning in thick forest remote from any villages, I met a party of Vaeddas who were in search of honey. In reply to my inquiry regarding their hamlet, they informed me that it was 'quite near' a tank (reservoir) which was four miles away, but I afterwards learnt that the place was several miles beyond it. They had made the journey that morning, and probably would return also, through a forest full of undergrowth.

Nearly three hours later, as I was returning along the path after visiting the reservoir, I sat down at the side of a tiny streamlet of clear water, fresh from a neighbouring spring, in order to get a drink, and enjoy a quiet pipe under the cool shade of the tall forest trees, when suddenly one of the party, an intelligent young fellow with a pleasant countenance, stepped out of the thick bushes and joined me. He had left the others some distance away, and had come on for a drink. I gave him the contents of my tobacco pouch, and found him quite communicative and acquainted with Sinhalese, which he spoke intelligently, although he addressed me as *Umba*, you, an expression which is usually applied only to inferiors. He stated that they only knew and visited the people of one small settlement several miles away. No others lived within some hours' journey from their huts. He laughed at the fears which some Tamils had expressed to me regarding the demons who were supposed to infest that part of the forest, though he admitted that it was full of them. These people were apparently true Vaeddas, but not now the Forest Vaeddas, who are, I believe, unacquainted, or only slightly acquainted, with ordinary Sinhalese. In physical appearance and colour they resembled Kandian Sinhalese of some low castes. Their ancestors were Forest Vaeddas in the first half of last century.

Vaeddas have not the slightest negroid appearance. Their jaws are not prognathous, the facial angle is good, like that of the Kandian Sinhalese, and according to my observation their noses are usually straight and rather well-formed, though somewhat wide at the nostrils. They have not very large orifices. Mr. Nevill said that they are 'squat, with no bridge to them'; evidently they are of two types. Mr. F. Lewis, of the Forest Department, has informed me that the Village Vaeddas whom he has seen had commonly straight noses and somewhat thick lips. In the case of those whom I have observed the lips were perhaps thinner than those of the Sinhalese. The cheek bones are always somewhat prominent, but this may be partly due to the absence of superfluous flesh on the face. The eyes are rather deep set, but otherwise resemble those of Kandians. Some faces are practically hairless below the eyes, and there is rarely more than a very sparing growth of hair on the face, a very thin short moustache and a little short hair on the chin being all that is usually present. In this respect, also, they resemble many Kandian Sinhalese, but not Low-country Sinhalese, who are a distinctly hairy race, and often have thick beards, hairy chests, and a central line of hair down to the navel, which is said to be thought a mark of beauty. This is quite uncommon among Kandian Sinhalese, and apparently totally absent among the Vaeddas. A few Vaeddas have more beard than others, but it is always thin; such a feature may indicate some mixture in their blood; I have seen it with a very dark skin. The forehead is narrow and not high; it does not recede much from the line of the face.

Dr. Virchow gave the following proportions of their skulls, together with those of Sinhalese [1] and Tamils :—

	Number of Skulls	Capacity in Cubic Centimetres	Height / Length	Breadth / Length
Vaeddas	20	1261	74·9	71·6
Sinhalese	10	1438·8	75·4	72·4 *
Tamils	4	1247	77·5	75·3

* In sixteen skulls this was 72·2.

He remarked that the average index of the ratio between the length and breadth proves that the skull is 'decidedly dolichocephalous,' only four out of the twenty being mesocephalous, with an index of seventy-five, while the index of seven was under seventy. He also stated that 'no elaborate proof is needed that neither Sinhalese nor Vaeddas, at least in the form of their skulls, present the slightest indication of any relationship to the Mongols. Such a remarkably dolichocephalous tribe has never yet been found among the Mongols.' I may add that neither do they resemble the Australians in any respect, to judge by the illustrations of them in the elaborate works of Dr. Howitt and Messrs. Spencer and Gillen. On this subject Dr. Virchow said: 'One glance at the skull, and still more at the skeleton, of the Australian convinces us that here a great and unmistakable contrast exists.' [2] Some have endeavoured to connect the Vaeddas with the Andamanese. This is at once disposed of by Dr. Virchow, who remarked: 'The Andamanese, as well as the Negritos generally, are in reality brachycephalic, and this one circumstance distinguishes them definitely from all the Ceylon races. If we add to this that their hair grows in spiral coils, and is to be classed with the woolly hair of the genuine negro, then every possibility disappears of a union with the Vaeddas unless we assume that climatic influences have specially affected the hair.' [2]

The hair of the Vaeddas is black with a slight brownish

[1] It is uncertain how many of these were the skulls of Kandians.
[2] *Op. cit.* p. 131.

tinge, and, if attended to, is not more frizzly than that of ordinary Kandian Sinhalese. It is never cut, and is tied in a knot at the back of the head (as stated by Knox, p. 62), exactly like that of all Sinhalese. Photographs of some Village Vaeddas who have been brought to Kandy and elsewhere to be exhibited represent men with wild unkempt frizzly locks; but I have never seen anything of the kind in their own districts, and it is probable that the heads of those who have been so pourtrayed have been 'made up' specially, in order to increase their wild appearance—as, in fact, I was informed by their Sinhalese neighbours has been done on similar occasions. The wildest Vaeddas whom I ever met, in the middle of dense forest, had their hair tied up in a knot at the back of their heads in the usual way of the villagers; these were the true Forest Vaeddas who could speak only the Vaedi dialect.

It may occasionally be a practice of the Vaeddas when hunting, as it is of other hunters in Ceylon, to wander in the forest with unfastened hair; but from my own experience of them, and from that of Sinhalese who live in their district and are well acquainted with them, I am able to state that it is not otherwise done habitually by any but an extremely limited number. In answer to special inquiries, I was informed that some few individuals do neglect to attend to their hair, and allow it to stand out in this wild-looking manner. Instead of their hair being naturally frizzly, I have never seen a Vaedda with hair more wavy than that of the Low-country Sinhalese of the western coast districts. I may repeat that so far as superficial appearances go, there is nothing in the figure (except the smaller height), the features, or the ordinary coiffure, and very little in the average colour of the skin, to distinguish the Vaedda from many low-caste Kandians found in the northern and north-western Sinhalese districts.

There is only one race in Ceylon with curly hair; they are the Kinnaras or Karmāntayō, the mat-weavers, the lowest caste in the island. In the case of some of the men the whole hair of the crown consists of a mass of very short thick curls, while the lips of those I have seen were invariably rather thick, although the jaws were not prognathous. Their faces resemble in other respects those of Kandians, and are not of the Mongolian type. The hair of the women is tied up in a knot like that of the ordinary Sinhalese. The men never allow their hair to hang down beyond the upper part of the neck, even in the case of those whose locks are not so curly as others; it is always cut off when it reaches this length. The colour of these people is the same dark brown as that of the average Kandian villager; I have seen none who were much darker than this.

Their mode of life does not indicate any connexion with the Vaeddas, none of them being either hunters or fishers; all gain their living by weaving mats in frames, and by cultivating millet and rice. They have village tanks and rice fields, and keep cattle; their villages and houses are clean and neat, being exactly like those of the Kandian Sinhalese. They have no tradition regarding their origin, and no dialect of their own, knowing not one word except Sinhalese; and nearly all their folk-stories are the same as those of the Kandians. Those which vary from the latter are chiefly Buddhistic, the race being all Buddhists, though not permitted by the Kandians to enter the wihāras, or the houses of other villagers. Their rank is so low that, as some of them admitted to me, they address even the Roḍiyas, whom many wrongly believe to be the lowest race in the island, as Hāmaduruwō, 'my Lord,' and do not pass them on a path without first asking permission to do so. I was informed that the Roḍiyas at once interfere if any of the men attempt to allow their hair to grow beyond the upper part of the neck, and order them to cut it shorter.

I believe that they are now found only in the district immediately to the north and north-west of Kandy and near Kurunāegala; but a Sinhalese folk tale places some on the western coast. This may indicate that we have in them the remnant of another tribe who came from the Malayālam country. It is interesting to note that, like the Vaeddas, they have completely abandoned their original language.

On the other hand, there is another race, of which only a few villages exist in the North-western and perhaps in the North-central Provinces, called 'Waga' or 'Waga men,' who are traditionally supposed to be the descendants of some of the Tamil captives brought from Southern India by Gaja-Bāhu I, in the second century A.D. These people, though nearly as much isolated among the Sinhalese as the Vaeddas, but not so much as the Kinnaras, still retain and speak their original Tamil tongue, in addition to Sinhalese. They closely resemble Sinhalese of some low castes, and are rather darker in colour than the average Sinhalese villagers. Why some races should have abandoned their mother tongue and others have retained it is a fact for which I am unable to offer any satisfactory explanation.

The Waga people, although they are supposed to have been originally only charcoal burners, are now cultivators exactly like their neighbours. They term themselves of good caste, and the men have the usual names which denote that position, such as Maeṇikrāla, Kapurāla, etc. ; but the women have names that belong to persons of low caste, such as Bokkī, Baṇḍī, Baḍī, Kombī, Gaembī, Ṭikirī, Lattī. One might expect the name of the race to mean Vanga, that is, Bengal, but that the people both speak Tamil and claim to be Tamils.

The figure of most of the Tamil-speaking Vaeddas naturally approximates to that of the Tamils with whom they are intermarried—so much so that there is little in it to distinguish them, and especially the women, from many village Tamils of a rather low caste. In the greater width of the hips and the amount of posterior tissue, the difference between the females and the Village Vaedda women is marked. Their colour is also commonly darker than that of the Vaeddas of the interior, and is sometimes black, with brownish shadows.[1] The character of the features of the men approaches that of the Village

[1] The only races I have seen with jet-black skins, which always have distinctly blue or purple shadows, are many of the Tamils of Southern India (not Ceylon), and all the Wolofs of the Senegal and Gambia coast districts, who have no resemblance to the true negroes. Some of the Andamanese are also described as having skins of this black-lead colour. The same peculiar colour is to be seen in some few northern Kandians, but such cases are quite exceptional, and are doubtless due to a strain of Drāvidian blood. It does not occur among the Vaeddas.

Vaeddas; there are the same scanty hair or absence of hair on the upper lip and chin, and the somewhat prominent cheek bones, and, according to my observation, straight noses. The hair is always tied in a knot at the back of the head.

The description of the Village Vaeddas is generally applicable to the Wanniyas, who, however, are perhaps an inch or two taller, on an average, and I think have slightly less prominent cheek bones. Their eyebrows are low and fairly straight, their eyes deep set, their noses generally straight, and their lips not thicker than those of the average Kandian villager. There may also be a slight difference in the shade of the skin, which is perhaps not quite of the same dull dirty tint as that of the Vaeddas; but otherwise, like theirs, is nearly always a dark brown with a reddish tinge, though darker shades are also seen. There are variations in the colour, some having distinctly reddish skins, and others skins of a deep walnut hue. The hair is nearly straight, and excepting sometimes when they are hunting is always tied in a knot at the back of the head. The face is commonly nearly hairless below the eyes. The women differ in appearance from Tamils; they have oval faces, pleasant comely features, and not ungraceful figures. Among all Vaeddas and Wanniyas the superciliary ridge is rather prominent; it is never absent in Kandian Sinhalese, but is often unnoticeable in Tamils and the so-called 'Moormen.'

Ornaments.—The Tamil-speaking male Vaeddas and those of the south-eastern coast tract, who are brought into communication with the Tamils, or Sinhalese who have adopted some of the habits of Tamils, carry a ring or stud in the lobe of each ear after marriage, and some of the former also wear silver bangles. The Vaeddas of the interior and the Wanniyas often have silver rings in their ears, and I have observed the Forest Vaeddas with similar ornaments, which some of the most northern Kandian villagers, as well as the Roḍiyas, also commonly wear, but not other Sinhalese men, nor the Kinnaras.

Mr. Nevill remarked that the females put on necklaces of coloured glass beads when they can get them, and shell, ivory, glass, or brass bangles. The Village Vaedda women are said by him to have worn in former times a considerable amount of costly jewellery made of gold and gems, in the form of necklaces and bangles, but not anklets or nose ornaments (which Sinhalese also never wear) ; there cannot be much of this left among them now. They also had ear-jewels, set like those of the Kandian Sinhalese, in a large hole which is bored through the lobe of the ear and expanded to receive them, to a diameter of about three-quarters of an inch ; some of them were made of ivory, horn, or bone, and were carved and etched. Brass ones are now worn. Sinhalese women have a cylindrical tube of silver, closed at the outer end and having a projecting rim at it ; in this end are inserted pieces of red glass or garnets, round a central stone or boss.

Mr. Nevill also observed that when properly dressed in their villages both men and women adorn their hair with bright or fragrant flowers and leaves, and occasionally add garlands of flowers for their necks, red and orange being their favourite colours. I have noticed that Kandian girls do the same. He added that the Vaeddas also crush fragrant leaves and rub them on their hair, neck, arms, and breast. He learnt that the marrow of the Sambar deer (*Rusa aristotelis*) is applied about once a week to the hair, if procurable ; or the fat of the Talagoyā or Monitor Lizard (*Varanus dracaena*), commonly called in Ceylon the 'Iguana,' is used for this purpose. He was of opinion that the number of split bones left by prehistoric people may be due to a similar custom.[1]

Dwellings.—Mr. Nevill states regarding the Forest Vaeddas : 'If possible, a cave is chosen for the home, and improved by a slight roof in front, if too exposed, and around this the food-winner ranges' during the rainy season, when the Sambar deer frequent the neighbourhood of the hills. 'A good cave becomes an hereditary possession. . . . Where an overhanging rock can be found, it is of course sufficient. Otherwise any rock is chosen, and some sticks being laid sloping from in front of it, it is roughly thatched with twigs, rushes, and large pieces of bark. A few elk [Sambar] hides, if not bought up

[1] *The Taprobanian*, Vol. i, p. 189.

by pedlars, will form a screen at one end. If it is only to exclude dew, a very few branches or bits of bark suffice.[1]

'In the dry hot months when brooks and ponds dry up, the game collects in the low forests around the half-dried river beds. He then takes wife and children, aged parents, or crippled relatives, and settles them in a hut close to where water can be got. From this he makes his hunting forays, and returns to it with his game.

'Besides his high-ground [cave] residence, and his low-ground residence, if a tract of forest burst suddenly into flower that attracts vast swarms of bees, or into useful fruit, the family will make a little picnic party, and go there for a week or a month, if it be too far from the home for daily visits. He cannot, however, be called nomadic.'[2]

The houses of the Forest Vaeddas are flimsy, easily erected, low rectangular huts or shelters under shady trees, built of thin sticks, and usually in a reversed wide **V** shape, without walls, though some have them. They have a covering of grass on the roof, or in default of it the skins of Sambar deer, or broad pieces of bark. The temporary huts of the Village Vaeddas are quite similar; and their more permanent houses are also rectangular,[3] with a low roof raised on walls which are covered with broad strips of bark, or have the spaces between the sticks filled with leafy twigs. A few fill up the walls with mud. Nearer the eastern coast, where suitable trees for barking are scarce or absent, they have only grass roofs, and leafy twigs are almost always employed for closing the spaces in the walls. Mr. Nevill remarked that there is little difference between the homes of the Village and Forest Vaeddas except that the former makes his house sufficiently substantial to keep out rain as well as dew; and that he leaves his family at it, and does not usually take them to his temporary hunting quarters. The Wanniyas erect similar huts roofed with grass;

[1] Dr. Seligmann is giving a full account of the cave dwellings of the Forest Vaeddas.

[2] *The Taprobanian*, Vol. i, p. 186.

[3] With the exception of a few Tamil villages in the Northern Province there are no circular dwelling-houses in Ceylon.

nearly all those I have seen had only walls of sticks, filled up with leafy twigs, but a few possessed mud walls—or rather, mud was used in them instead of the twigs.

Any bushes growing at the front of the huts are cleared away, so as to leave an open space under the trees, in which the occupants can sit, or lie, or cook, and peg out deer-skins for drying, or dry their surplus meat on a rectangular stick frame over a slow fire, this being a common custom of all hunters in Ceylon. They all abandon the site for very slight reasons, and establish themselves a mile or more away, often, in the case of those who cultivate millet, in order to be near the piece of ground which they are clearing for millet-growing, and at which, in any case, the men generally reside for some months in huts like those of the Forest Vaeddas, to protect the crop from Elephants, Deer, and Buffaloes.

Sometimes they form a new hamlet because they find themselves too near a road used by the public, or on account of an outbreak of sickness. In the latter instance it is thought that the old site was haunted by local devils who caused the disease. I have known the northern and north-western Kandian Sinhalese abandon villages for the two latter reasons, even when their huts had mud walls and raised earthen floors, which require much more labour to reconstruct.

Food.—The food of the Forest Vaeddas consists of fruits, roots of wild yams, and especially honey and the flesh of any animals they can kill, which are chiefly 'Iguānas,' Pigs, and Deer. All the Village Vaeddas, and the Tamil-speaking Vaeddas (with the exception of a very few who are solely fishermen), and the Wanniyas eat the same food, and have in addition the small millet above-mentioned, called *Kurahan* by the Sinhalese, the Indian *Rāgi* (*Eleusine coracana*). This is grown in temporary clearings (termed *hēna* in Sinhalese), made in the forest, all bushes and grass being cut and burnt off, but not the larger trees. After one crop, or sometimes two, have been taken off the ground, the clearing is abandoned, and allowed to be overgrown once more with jungle, and is not recultivated until from five to seven years have elapsed. In these clearings, which are exactly like those of the Sinhalese, are also grown a few red Chillies and Gourds, and sometimes a little Indian Corn, and a small Pulse called *Muṇ* (*Phaseolus mungo*). A very few Village Vaeddas and Wanniyas who live in suitable places for it grow and irrigate a little rice, which the Forest Vaeddas are now learning to cook and eat when they can procure it.

Mr. Nevill was informed that 'of all food the greatest delicacy is considered to be little bits of lean flesh, chopped up, and wrapped in fat of the Iguana, taken from the entrails apparently. This is broiled.'[1] The flesh of this lizard is white, and rather wanting in flavour, but not in any way unpalatable; I have often eaten it when stationed in the jungle, and it is a favourite dish of the Kandian Sinhalese villagers.

Following the example of their Tamil neighbours, the Wanniyas and the Tamil-speaking Vaeddas do not eat Monkeys, which, however, form a regular item in the diet of all Vaeddas of the interior, and with the exception of the small brown Monkey (*Thersites*) are eaten by the majority of the northern Kandian villagers. The flesh is dark-coloured, and somewhat strongly flavoured; I have tried it more than once, feeling at the time that I was, as it were, the next-door neighbour of palaeolithic man, and practising something allied to cannibalism.

The Tamil-speaking Vaeddas informed me that they have no forbidden meats excepting the Monkey and some of the 'Vāhanas' of their Hindu Gods, that is, the animals on which the Gods ride, such as the Peafowl and the Rat, the Vāhanas of Skanda and Gaṇēsa.

The Coast Vaeddas subsist on fish, in addition; they alone catch them by netting or spearing them. Like the Sinhalese and Tamils of jungle villages, all are accustomed to capture fish in the dry seasons either by baling the water out of shallow pools, or by stupefying the fish by means of poisonous leaves or fruits thrown into the water. The crushed leaves of the Timbiri tree (*Diospyros embryopteris*), or the crushed fruit of the Kukuru-mahan bush (*Randia dumetorum*), and also, accord-

[1] *The Taprobanian*, Vol. i, p. 191.

ing to Mr. Nevill, the roots of a species of creeper called Kalavael (*Derris scandens*) are especially used for this purpose.

Unlike the Low-country Sinhalese, they never fish with the hook, a peculiarity that they share with the Wanniyas and nearly all Kandian Sinhalese, who for some reason, unknown even to themselves, hold that it is quite improper to do so.[1] Whether the Sinhalese name for fish-hook, *bili-katuwa*, the word *bili* meaning also offerings made to devils, has had any influence, I cannot say; but the feeling may be connected with the fact that the north-western Kandians also think it a disgraceful act for a female, even though a child, to capture a fish in any way whatever. I have never been able to discover an explanation of this prohibition. Whatever the objection may be to the fish-hook, it is not applicable to the Tamils; I have seen Tamil women of jungle villages fishing with a line and hook, and proud to show the number of fish they had taken.

The millet is ground into flour on a flat stone, or in a quern by those who possess one, and is cooked by baking it inside a wood fire. The flour is first mixed with water on a deer-skin or some broad leaves, into a stiff paste, which is made into a circular cake more than an inch thick and some nine inches in diameter. This is then covered on both sides with the large green leaves of the Halmilla tree (*Berrya ammonilla*). After the fire has burnt for some time, so as to contain a supply of redhot charcoal, it is raked away, and the cake is laid on the hot ashes, and covered up by more ashes and the burning charcoal, the heat of which in a few minutes is considered to have baked it sufficiently. The Wanniyas term this cake *Alupota*, 'Ashes-slab'; it is the *Ginipūwa*, or 'Fire-cake,' of the Sinhalese hunters, who also make it. Mr. Nevill states that cakes are also made of the dried and ground-up seeds of the Tree-fern (*Cycas circinalis*); the 'cabbage,' or bud of unopened leaves at the crown of the wild Date (*Phoenix zeylanica*), is doubtless also eaten, as by Sinhalese villagers.

As in the case of all hunters, meat is cooked by broiling.

[1] Plutarch mentions that the natives of Oxyrhynchus in Egypt did not eat fish that had been caught with a hook.

The few who have rice boil it; being in the neighbourhood of Sinhalese or Tamil villages, where common pottery is obtainable, such persons are able to procure earthenware pots for the purpose.

Including even the wildest Forest Vaeddas, all are accustomed to chew sliced Areka-nuts with Betel-vine leaves, when they can get them from other villagers. In default of them they (like the inhabitants of remote Kandian villages who are without them) use the leaves of aromatic herbs, especially a Basil, Talā (*Anisochilus suffruticosus*), and the bark of the Kaeppiṭiya (*Croton lacciferum*)—one of the bushes on which stick-lac is found—and other trees, among which Mr. Nevill includes the Demata (*Gmelina asiatica*) and Dawata (*Carallia integerrima*), and the seeds of a Lac-bush (*Gardenia carinata*). He states that lime is sometimes burnt from shells of *Cyclophorus involvulus*, and taken with the barks as a luxury. Some Forest Vaeddas looked with suspicion on some cut tobacco which I offered them for chewing, and refused it, as they had not previously seen any like it; but they readily took the uncut leaf.

According to Mr. Nevill, 'they will drink the clear water in a natural [rock] cistern, but will not drink the clear water of pools in the bed of a river or in forest hollows. If water is wanted at a stream, they scoop a little hollow in the sand, where it looks clean and sharp, and wait until the water filters through into it. They particularly like water lightly tinged yellow with mud, called *Bora-diya*, and it is considered better flavoured and more wholesome than plain water. They will drink river water, unless it be clear and stagnant; and the clear water of streams, running, they also drink if there be no sand in their bed in which to scoop a hollow. Stagnant clear water is considered very bad, in fact, poisonous.'[1] Kandian villagers also prefer 'bora-diya,' and the water of pools which are covered with a green vegetable growth. I have found this water always good and sweet.

Utensils.—At their dwellings the simple wants of these people are easily supplied. In some parts of the interior the

[1] *The Taprobanian*, Vol. i, p. 187.

wilder Vaeddas have a few large hollow black shells of the hard fruit of a high tree which grows in the eastern forests, the name of which I omitted to note, slung by some bark strings for carrying. More commonly they use the shells of small Pumpkins, with a section cut off at the stem, similarly strung, and termed *Panliya*. These are about seven and a half inches in diameter, and are used for carrying water or honey (Fig. 18).

The only other household article that they really require is a bag, or perhaps two, made of the inner bark of a short slightly tapering length of the Riṭi tree, which is stripped off or drawn off in one piece, after being well beaten, and is sewn together at the larger end. This makes a strong and very durable bag, called a *Riṭi-malla*, which lasts for some years, and has almost the appearance of having been woven. One in my possession, blackened with age, is thirty inches long, ten and a half inches wide near the mouth when laid flat, and fourteen inches wide at the other end (Fig. 19). The bag is used for carrying or storing millet, or any other food. Some also make small baskets of the same inner bark. The Wanniyas and those who live near the sea have, like the Kandians, whole gourds (*labba*) for holding water, and also use common earthenware pots, obtained from Sinhalese potters, for cooking and for containing water. Mr. Nevill learnt that in ancient times the [Village] Vaeddas had household vessels made of copper and even gold, for holding water and for cooking, and he saw copper ones still in use. There is no probability that the wilder Vaeddas ever possessed such articles. Neither Vaeddas nor Wanniyas are acquainted with the art of making pottery, and certainly the former, and I believe also the latter, do not understand any form of mat or other weaving. Deer-skins supply the place of mats for sleeping on, or when preparing food.

The blades of axes and especially those ot arrows answer all the purposes for which knives are usually thought to be indispensable. Those who cultivate millet or rice purchase for the purpose, by exchange of honey, meat, deer-skins, or horns, or beeswax made into thick circular cakes, the digging

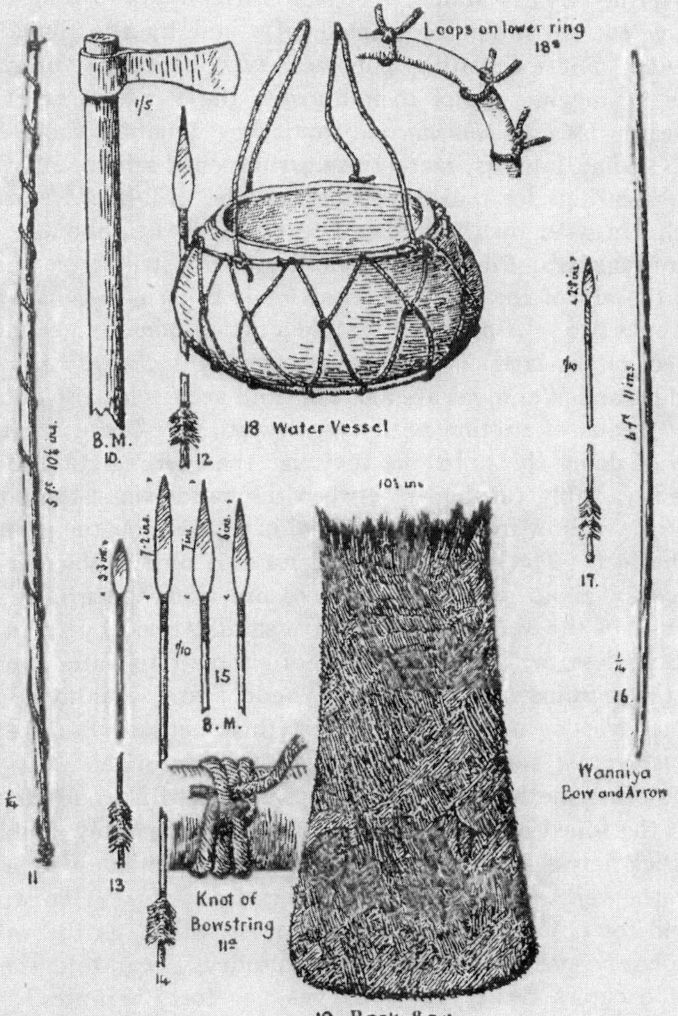

FIGS. 10–19. Weapons and Utensils of Vaeddas.

hoes termed by us 'Mamoty'—(more correctly, the Tamil word *man-veṭṭei*, earth-digging implement)—and by the Sinhalese *Udaella*. For excavating purposes, such as taking up wild yams, or digging out of their burrows the Pangolin or Scaly Ant-eater (*Manis pentadactyla*) and the 'Iguana,' they, like the Kandian hunters, merely use a sharpened stick. All who make clearings for millet-growing buy the Bill-hooks (*kaetta*) which are used by their Sinhalese or Tamil neighbours.

Fire-making.—Fire is commonly got by striking a spark with the aid of the axe, the word for it being *gini-gahanawā*, 'to strike fire.' A piece of flint and a little tinder are generally carried, or the latter is soon made from a bit of rag. But all Vaeddas and Wanniyas are also able and accustomed to obtain it by means of friction with two dry sticks. There are two ways of doing this. In one they use the twirling-stick, both races invariably turning it between the hands while the point rests in a hollow in a lower stick which is held on the ground by the feet. The expression used for this by the Vaeddas is *gini-gahen ginna gannawā*, 'to take fire from the fire-tree'; it is one of the very few alliterative sayings used by them or the Sinhalese, with the exception of simple duplicated words and the refrains of songs. The Vaeddas and Wanniyas use various woods for getting fire by this method, but Velan (*Pterospermum suberifolium*) is a general favourite.

The other method, which when practised with wood picked up in the forest is much more laborious, is by simply rubbing one stick across another; the Wanniyas and Sinhalese express it by the verb *mandinawā*. Only extremely dry Velan wood is used for obtaining fire by this process, which, as the wood is probably even then not thoroughly dry, I was told sometimes occupies nearly two 'paeyas,' or forty minutes.[1]

This is the mode of fire-making employed by some tribes of Central Australia, but not other Australians, the edge of a

[1] Dr. Schweinfurth, in *The Heart of Africa*, 3rd Ed., Vol. i, p. 254, describes this method of obtaining fire in the Higher Nile districts, 'the whole proceeding being a marvel which might well nigh eclipse the magic of my lucifer matches.' It is also practised in Senegal. (Caillié, *Travels through Central Africa*, Vol. i, p. 123.)

piece of wood used as a spear-thrower being rubbed 'backwards and forwards upon the shield; in a short time the light wood is charred, then it glows, and with judicious blowing the glow is fanned into a flame.'[1]

This method of getting fire is found in Malayālam and Travancore, the very district from which it is probable that the earliest settlers came to Ceylon. In Mr. Thurston's *Ethnographic Notes of Southern India*, pp. 468, 469, it is stated that fire is made by cross-friction by the Pulayans of Travancore and the Paniyans who live at the base of the Western Ghāts of Malabar. He gives an illustration of two members of the latter race engaged on this work, which he describes as follows: 'A portion of a bamboo stem, about one foot in length, in which two nodes are included, is split longitudinally into two equal parts. On one half a sharp edge is cut with a knife. In the other a longitudinal slit is made through about two-thirds of its length, which is stuffed with a piece of cotton cloth. The latter is held firmly on the ground with its convex surface upwards, and the cutting edge drawn, with a gradually quickening sawing motion, rapidly to and fro across it by two men[2] until the cloth is ignited by the incandescent particles of wood in the groove cut by the sharp edge. The cloth is then blown by the lips into a blaze.'

When no flint or chert is available, the Kandian Sinhalese also employ both processes, but naturally they prefer the twirling stick, which they always turn by means of a bow and slack string, using in the north either Velan wood for both sticks, or often the wood of the Lōlu tree (*Cordia myxa*) for the lower stick, and Mayila wood (*Bauhinia racemosa*), which is very hard, for the upper one, or twirling-stick. The use of

[1] Messrs. Spencer and Gillen's *The Native Tribes of Central Australia*, p. 586; *The Northern Tribes of Central Australia*, p. 619.

[2] In the illustration only one man is doing the sawing work, while the other holds the lower stick. Captain Lewin described a nearly similar method employeu by the Chittagong Hill Tribes. A semi-circular groove was cut round a split bamboo, and a flexible strip of bamboo worked in it until the dust became incandescent.—*Wild Races of S. E. India*, p. 207.

the bow for this purpose is one of the very few practices which differentiate the Sinhalese from the Vaeddas.

There is a third method of making fire by means of two sticks; in it the pointed end of one stick is rubbed in a long groove made in the other. I believe it is unknown in Ceylon. Dr. Guppy, who calls it 'the Polynesian method,' saw it used in the Solomon Islands, and stated that 'the friction in some three or four minutes produces smoke; and finally a fine powder, which has been collecting in a small heap at the end of the groove, begins to smoulder. After being carefully nursed by the breath of the operator, the tiny flame is transferred to a piece of touch-wood, and the object is attained.'[1]

Darwin also observed this mode of fire-making in Tahiti, and wrote of it, 'The fire was produced in a few seconds'; he himself tried it, and found that it required 'the greatest exertion.'[2]

In the Eastern Archipelago A. R. Wallace noticed that cross-friction was employed.[3]

Thus we find that fire may be obtained from two pieces of dry wood by three different methods: (1) by drill-friction of a point in a hollow, the mode most generally used, which is again subdivided into hand-drill friction, bow-drill friction, and cord-drill friction (as used for the sacred fire of Hinduism); (2) by transverse friction of a knife-edge in a groove; and (3) by longitudinal friction of a point in a groove.

The fact that even those Vaeddas who have seen fire obtained by turning the twirling-stick with a bow never copy this method, although they understand the action of the bow and the ease with which fire can be obtained by using it, shows how extremely conservative in their ideas such people are. When they had said of it to me, "The Sinhalese do it, but it is not our custom," there was an end of the matter, so far as they were concerned. This is exactly the way of the northern and north-western Kandian Sinhalese. When I asked one of the latter whom I knew well why he did not try the effect of

[1] *The Solomon Islands*, p. 65.
[2] *A Naturalist's Voyage*, ed. 1882, p. 409.
[3] *The Malay Archipelago*, 5th ed. p. 325.

manure on his rice field, which he complained was not very productive, he made the usual reply, "We are not accustomed to do it." After I had explained the matter further, and suggested an experiment on one small patch, he ended the discussion by remarking, "My father did not do it. Am I a better man than my father?"[1] When this is the mental position of primitive races, it is clear that immense periods of time must be allowed for the development of the slightest and simplest advances towards civilisation.

Weapons and Tools.—The weapons of all the Vaeddas and Wanniyas consist only of a diminutive axe (Fig. 10) and a bow and arrows, generally two in number according to Mr. Nevill, and rarely three among the former race; but usually three among the latter people. Mr. Nevill had an axe that was two and a half inches wide and five and a half inches long in the blade; but some are much smaller than this. These axes have handles from eighteen inches to two feet in length, which are passed through a socket-hole in the head. Nearly similar tools are in general use by the Kandians, and are illustrated in a later chapter. Neither Vaeddas nor most Wanniyas carry knives, which Kandian Sinhalese find indispensable. The steel heads of these tools are obtained from Sinhalese or Tamil smiths in exchange for skins, honey, or meat.

The correct length for a Vaedda or Wanniya bow is considered to be a little more than the owner's own height, but there is no fixed standard, the length partly depending on the strength of the person who is to use the bow. Some considerably exceed their owner's height; but short ones are often preferred for use in thick forest, as being more convenient to carry than long ones. One Wanniya bow that I got (Fig. 16) is only four feet ten inches long,[2] and the old man from whom I obtained it stated that he always used similar short ones;

[1] It is laid down in the Ordinances of Manu (iv, 178) that a good man should always follow the path of his father and grandparents, so the attitude of the villager was quite correct.

[2] Some bows of British archers in mediaeval times were only five feet long.

other men informed me that they preferred longer ones. The longest are perhaps six feet in length.

The Vaeddas of the interior make them of Kolon (*Adina cordifolia*) and Kaekala wood (*Cyathocalyx zeylanicus*), split and thinned down to the required size, and also of Kobbā or Kobbae-wael (*Allophylus cobbe*). The Tamil-speaking Vaeddas to the south of Trincomalee employ the wood of the Ulkenda tree for them. All are rough, round in section, and not always straight, and are without notches. They are not decorated in any way. The Wanniyas informed me that they only cut their bows during the south-west monsoon, as they have an idea, possibly well founded, that the constant bending and relaxing of the fibres caused by the strong winds of that season render the wood more elastic and tougher than at other times. The roughest sort of Sinhalese bow does not differ from that of the Vaeddas; but others vary in the material used, the length and thickness, and in having elaborate decoration in coloured lac. The length is usually greater than that of the Vaedda weapon.

Mr. Nevill states that pellet-bows like those of the Sinhalese, with two strings at the middle of which a piece of skin is fixed, are used by Vaedda boys for killing small birds.

When shooting, the bow is commonly held by the left hand, but occasionally by the right. Some Vaeddas and Wanniyas are also accustomed to shoot while sitting on the ground, holding the bow by the foot, between the big toe and the next one. This is chiefly, if not entirely, done in shooting animals at night when they come to drink at a water-hole.

The twisted inner bark of two or three different trees is used for bowstrings, or where they are available the exceedingly tough fibres found in the long narrow leaves of a rock plant called Niyanda (*Sansievera zeylanica*). Many Vaeddas of the interior employ for this purpose the fibres of the thin aerial roots of the Banyan tree (*Ficus indica*). The Tamil-speaking Vaeddas make use of the inner bark of a creeper called Gaera-vaela in Sinhalese or Tevalan-koḍi in Tamil. The Wanniyas employ the inner bark of Velan trees. The string is sometimes rubbed with the split fruit of the Timbiri tree, which is said to strengthen it. It is permanently fastened to one end of the bow, and tied round the other when about to be used (Fig. 11[a]).

The shafts of the arrows (Figs. 12–15)[1] of all alike are made of small Velan saplings, thinned down to about half an inch in thickness, and the whole length is often three feet, but varies from two to three. A wide notch is cut at the butt end. Whether used by Vaeddas, Wanniyas, or Sinhalese, they invariably have flat, narrow, and elongated steel heads rounded at the points, without barbs. The Vaedda arrow-heads are wider near the butt than those of the modern Sinhalese, and very slightly concave on the sides, but some ancient Sinhalese arrows nearly resembled those of the Vaeddas in shape. They vary from two and a half inches to nearly eighteen inches in length, the latter size being of course rarely used, and only for large game such as Elephants ; the smallest are required for Hares and birds. The usual length of the blade is four or five inches. A set of three which a Wanniya used varied from four to eight inches in length. The arrows have nearly always either three or four feathers, which in every case, even among the Sinhalese, are the primaries (or long feathers) from the wing of the Peahen.[2] These are rarely fixed in slight grooves cut in the stem. Occasionally five feathers are employed, and Mr. Nevill stated that in some instances they are placed in a slightly spiral direction. The fine strings of bark which tie the feathers to the shaft or bind the shaft at the head are sometimes protected from wear by being covered with a hard gum. A Wanniya arrow in my possession (Fig. 17) is wrapped at the head with a thin strip of deer-skin in a spiral. In former days, according to Mr. Nevill, pieces of the shells of River Mussels (*Unio lamellatus*

[1] The arrows numbered 13 and 14 are in the possession of Mr. H. B. Christie, recently Provincial Engineer in the Public Works Department, and were obtained by him from Village Vaeddas. They differ from the usual Vaedda type shown in the other arrow heads, and Fig. 14 resembles those now employed by Sinhalese.

[2] Used in India also. Kālidāsa describes an arrow which Raghu used against Indra, as being 'fledged with peacock's plume.' (*Raghuvança*, Johnstone's translation, p. 26.)

and *U. marginatus*) were used by some Vaeddas of the interior as arrow-blades ; and he observed that the Sinhalese who live in their district in the Eastern Province still term these bivalves 'arrow-head mussels.'[1]

Until recent times no ancient stone weapons or implements had been discovered in Ceylon, and it was therefore assumed that the aborigines were unacquainted with the art of their fabrication. It was thus with great interest that I learnt from my friend Mr. F. Lewis, of the Forest Department, that for a considerable number of years several types of primitive stone implements have been found in the Kandian hill-tract in Maskeliya, by Mr. John Pole and Mr. G. B. Gardner. Through the courtesy of these gentlemen I am able to append the following particulars of their discoveries.

Mr. Pole, who has recently published a short account of his collection in the *Journal of the Ceylon Branch of the Royal Asiatic Society*, writes that the first examples of these weapons and tools were discovered twenty-five years ago by himself and Mr. E. E. Green, who is now the Government Entomologist in Ceylon, on some hillocks at Imbulpitiya, near Nāwalapitiya. He states (*in epist.*) : 'I have collected within the last twenty-four years over a thousand of these stones, in all their fantastic shapes and material, and my conclusion is this : The men of this age arrived at no type of implement. They split the stone and made the implements they immediately required, from the shards as they split them off, according to their adaptability. A serviceable shard or flake was helped to an "edge," and when they found a "point" amongst their shards they chipped the sides to make the point more serviceable. There was no attempt at copying any known design ; the material was too obstinate to allow this.' He states that he considers that the agreement of a few specimens with some primitive types is merely an accidental coincidence. Of course in these remarks Mr. Pole is referring only to the stone implements in his own collection.

In his paper on them he mentioned that similar flakes have been found in the districts of Puttalam (that is, in the early

[1] *The Taprobanian*, Vol. i, p. 33.

Nāgadīpa), and Hambantota in the Low-Country ; and Mātale, Nāwalapitiya, Dimbula, Dikoya, and Maskeliya in the mountain region. He added that the Drs. Sarasin of Basle also discovered some in Uva, and in caves at Nilgala ; and from Mr. Pole and Mr. Gardner I learnt that Mr. J. Still, formerly Assistant to the Archaeological Commissioner, Mr. H. C. P. Bell, met with some made of quartz and chert in the North-central Province.[1]

In a letter to the *Ceylon Observer*, dated August 8, 1907, Mr. Pole remarked of the makers of those found by him on the mountain ridges in Maskeliya, 'These people must have lived in cordons of single families, for they must have entirely occupied the vantage points of every spur of our mountains. Not many flakes are found in the flats.'

He expressed the opinion that 'There was never more than a single family in one spot ; there was no village artizan, around whose domicile a larger number of shards and débris might be found. . . . Each man was his own armourer, found his own quartz stones, smashed off his own pieces from the native rock, just as he was able ; made use of the most serviceable by coaxing off from them some extra thick edges. . . . There was no getting rid of an obstinate angle in the stone fractured. There was no subsequent rounding off of the edges and corners.

'As to shape and size, they took the chance chippings of the stones, satisfied with the natural fracture, and worked the blunter edges. The material was quartz of various formations and compactness ; some as clear as glass, some clouded and milky, and others of a granulated structure.' It appeared to him that the stones 'had been brought from great distances —for although there is scarcely a ridge up-country on which no "flakes" occur, it will be found that the material of which they are formed exists nowhere in the vicinity.' He added that there could hardly be any distinct classification of the stones excepting into those with points and those with edges.

[1] Dr. C. G. Seligmann informs me that he also found worked quartz chips under the earth in some caves now or formerly occupied by Vaeddas, and he has since published an account of them in 'Man.'

Mr. G. B. Gardner, of Belihuloya, had, however, a different experience, and all the worked stones which he discovered seem to have been arrow-heads. They were lying on the ground on the summit of a hill. He states (*in epist.*): 'They generally consist of a natural stone of the right size with one natural edge, and the other edge seems to have been chipped to make it double-edged.' These stones were not of the type of any of those found by Mr. Pole.[1] They were roughly triangular, and were notched on both sides near the butt end for tying to the shaft. He noticed the resemblance between them and others in his collection, from Arizona and New Mexico, made by the Red Indians within the last forty years.

Specimens of all the types were sent from Ceylon to Mr. Bruce Foote of the Indian Geological Survey, and were reported by him to be identical with those which he has found throughout Southern India; he considered them to be of Neolithic age. According to Mr. Pole, the Drs. Sarasin (who, I believe, had not inspected those found by Mr. Gardner) thought them to be palæolithic, and of the 'Madeleine' or Magdalénien period—the time when the Mammoth and Aurochs and Reindeer were hunted in France and England.

Any doubt as to their date which these conflicting opinions might leave has now been definitely removed by the high authority of Mr. C. H. Read, of the British Museum—to whom I submitted Mr. Pole's tracings of typical examples of the stones and Mr. Gardner's drawing of the type found by him—and who has been courteous enough to furnish me with the following expression of his opinion of their age: 'I should think there can be no question that the age of the stone implements is either neolithic or relatively modern. These stones seem to me to have much the same relation to the Vaeddas as the stone implements of North America have to the existing Red Indians.'

[1] I am indebted to Dr. Seligmann for a cutting from the *Ceylon Observer* (weekly edition) for March 5, 1909, in which Mr. Pole gave an account of the discovery of numerous flint implements and cores in a cave on Scarborough Estate, in Maskeliya. Among them was one 'beautiful example' of an arrow-head, but of what type is not stated.

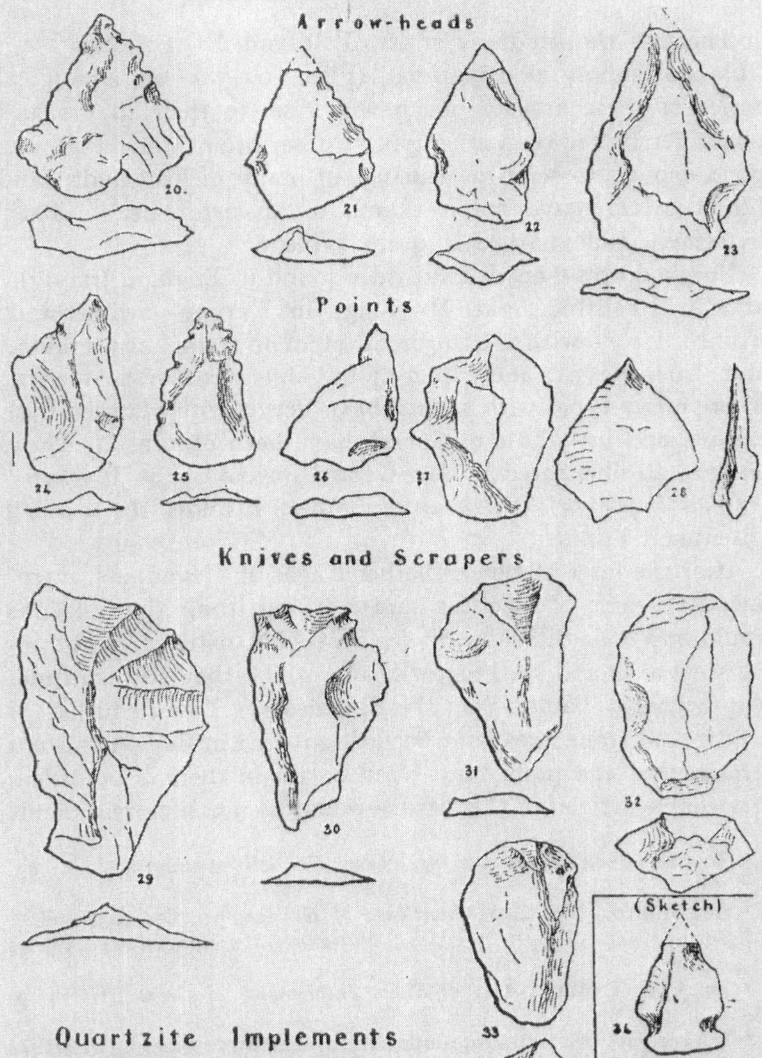

FIGS. 20–34. Stone Implements. (Half Scale.)

F

Through the kindness of Mr. Pole and Mr. Gardner I am able to supply illustrations (Figs. 20–34) of a typical series of these articles which will indicate their shapes and character better than attempts at description. Mr. Pole was good enough to send me tracings of many of his 'finds,' and Mr. Gardner gave me a sketch of an arrow-head. Their extremely rude nature is quite evident.

Notched arrow-heads have been found in England (rarely),[1] and in Neolithic Lake Dwellings in Europe—Switzerland, France, Italy—with a slight broad stem or 'tang' at the butt,[2] and also in Egypt [3] and Japan [4]; but chiefly in North America, where many types with a straight or very slightly curved base or butt end like those of Ceylon have been obtained. These last are all illustrated by Mr. Gerard Fowke in the *Thirteenth Annual Report of the Bureau of Ethnology*, under the heading 'Stemmed Flints.'

After the later settlers, whether Nāgas or Magadhese, introduced the arts of smelting and working iron,[5] the Vaeddas would find little difficulty, in the accessible districts, in obtaining steel axes and steel arrow-heads, which they still continue to procure by barter from the Sinhalese or Tamil smiths.

Since no stone axes have been discovered in Ceylon, it is not certain that the prehistoric Vaeddas made them. Doubtless serviceable articles of this nature would be much more difficult

[1] Jowitt. *Half-Hours among some English Antiquities*, p. 45, Fig. 61.

[2] Dr. Munro. *The Lake Dwellings of Europe*, pp. 65, 103, 268.

[3] Seton-Karr. *Report of U.S. National Museum*, 1904, Plates 2, 4, 9.

[4] Sir John Evans. *Ancient Stone Implements of Great Britain*, p. 362.

[5] I have met with low mounds and scattered fragments of refuse from very ancient smelting furnaces in three or four places in the Northern Province, but I think not elsewhere. All trace of the furnaces had disappeared. To the best of my recollection all the heaps were in uninhabited forest in places where kidney iron abounded on the surface of the ground. There were some small fragments of a very rough type of pottery mingled with the refuse in at least one of the heaps, but nothing else to assist in determining the age. The pieces of refuse resembled black slag from English smelting furnaces, and not the scoriae rejected from forges.

to fabricate than the simple tools shown in the illustration. The axe seems to be more indispensable in Ceylon than the arrow; both Vaeddas and Wanniyas (and I may add Sinhalese hunters also) are accustomed to procure a supply of food by its aid, without employing the bow and arrow. It is difficult to comprehend how the aborigines could exist in the wild forests of Ceylon without it.

If they did not make stone axes, it is just possible that in some way or other the primitive inhabitants may have been able to procure metal ones. If so, they must have got them from India, as it cannot be assumed that the Nāgas, who may have made them at a later date, arrived in the country until several centuries had elapsed after the coming of the Vaeddas, otherwise they would have occupied a greater portion of the island. There may have been a trade in such articles at an extremely early date. Iron or steel weapons and tools of various kinds were in common use by the Āryans in the early Vedic times, and it is possible that their manufacture may have been understood in some part of Southern India also, in the second or third millennium B.C. The Vaedda word for an axe, *gal-raekki*, in which the first half of the compound means 'stone,' appears to refer to the sharpening of the weapon on a stone, according to Mr. Nevill's information,[1] and until some examples have been discovered in Ceylon it cannot be accepted as affording any proof of the employment of stone axes by the first comers, no tradition of their use having survived.

The earliest Sinhalese iron or steel axes that have been found in Ceylon, apparently belonging to the second or third century B.C., are mere socketless 'celts.' They are described and illustrated in a subsequent chapter. They are of a shape which was found elsewhere in the later Neolithic period, the polished-stone age. Although such tools must have been in general use by the Sinhalese from the time of the arrival of the first Gangetic settlers, the fact that only two examples of this form of axe have been discovered, and that by the mere accident of the excavation of a deep channel at Tissa through

[1] *The Taprobanian*, Vol. i, p. 189.

a hollow in which the refuse of an artificers' settlement was deposited, shows how unsafe it would be to assume that tools which have not been found yet have never existed. All later types of axes found in Ceylon are removed by centuries from this primitive form. If, therefore, of the immense number of iron or steel axes that were used in clearing away the forests throughout all the civilised districts of Ceylon for probably more than five hundred years, only two examples have been met with, it may easily have occurred that the dwellers in the forests had axes, either of stone or iron or some other metal, of which no specimen has yet been seen by us.

A few Wanniyas and Village Vaeddas who can afford to buy guns now use them in the dry season, when the rustling of the crisp leaves that cover the ground at this time renders it difficult to approach game without being observed.

Some of the Coast Vaeddas, but no others, have an iron-headed spear or harpoon for catching fish, but I have not examined one, though I have seen them using it while wading in the brackish or salt water of the lagoons near the sea. As no other form of spear is employed by Vaeddas, they may have learnt its use from their Tamil neighbours in comparatively recent times.

Bathing.—Many of the Forest and Village Vaeddas do not bathe. One man stated that he caught cold after the only bath he ever took, and therefore he had abandoned the practice as too dangerous. It will easily be understood that many of them are not very cleanly in their persons. A gentleman in the Survey Department who had occasion to make use of some of them as guides in the forest informed me that they appeared to spend most of their spare time in pursuit of their insect comrades; these appear to have been unfavourable specimens of their race. It is also a common recreation of Sinhalese villagers, especially females, and is looked upon as an exhibition of disinterested friendship, to institute a searching examination of the heads of their friends for this purpose.

Hunting.—It is especially as hunters in thick forest that the Forest and Village Vaeddas and Wanniyas are distinguished, and in this respect they are exceedingly skilful, if not altogether unrivalled. Lazy and inexpert as they seem when idling about their houses, the rapidity with which they can pass like shadows through thick jungle, without making the least sound, is astonishing. They have assured me that when the leaves lying on the ground are not too dry they can steal up to any animal in the forests without rousing it, and kill it while asleep, or at the least give it a mortal wound, with the sole exception of the Peafowl, which is too wakeful to be caught in this manner. Living in woods frequented by Elephants, Bears, Buffaloes, and Leopards, they state that they have no fear of any beast that the forest contains; and judging by my own experiences when in the forest with some of them, I should suppose that in any ordinary circumstances they could escape from any of the three first-mentioned animals with ease; the Leopard does not attack them. Occasionally, however, a savage Sloth-bear (*Ursus labiatus*) mauls them when met face to face at a sudden turn in a narrow jungle track.[1]

A Vaedda once related to me a story of an incident of this kind, which cost him the loss of half a finger. On rounding a corner in such a path he found himself close to a Bear which immediately attacked him, knocking him down and endeavouring to seize his face. He described vividly how he felt its hot breath on his face as he caught its open jaw with both hands while he lay on his back, with the Bear standing over him. He succeeded in holding it thus for some minutes, in the meantime getting half his finger bitten off; and at last by a great effort he threw it backward and sprang to his feet. Luckily for him, the Bear thought the adventure not worth pursuing, and did not renew the attack, but disappeared in the jungle.

On another occasion a Village Vaedda was assaulted in the same manner by a Bear, and came out of the encounter much more seriously injured, being badly bitten on the arms and head. He told those who found him lying on the path and carried him home, how he heard a loud report while the Bear

[1] I have seen Kandian villagers who have been frightfully injured by these Bears. In one case the whole side of the face was bitten away.

was worrying his head; this was caused by the fracture of his own skull by the animal's teeth. He was seriously ill when the account was given to me, and I did not learn whether he succumbed to his injuries or not. The way in which these jungle-dwellers recuperate after extremely severe injuries is sometimes surprising. I have known a Kandian recover under home treatment by a village practitioner or 'Vedarāla' when his thigh was half cut through in the middle and the bone exposed, by his falling backwards across a razor-edged piece of newly-blasted granite.

While engaged on a hunting expedition, these hunters—and Kandians likewise—glide along in single file, avoiding every leafy twig the rustling of which might betray their presence, or if game be near holding it until the next man can take charge of it, and hand it over in the same manner to the man behind him. At such times all tread in the footprints of the first man, who when putting his foot on the ground first glides his toes along it in order to push aside any twigs or leaves that might emit a noise if crushed. Their eyes and ears are fully alert to catch the slightest sound or movement among the thick jungle around them. With a lifetime's experience and hereditary perceptive faculties to assist them, the secrets of the deepest forest appear to them as an open book which they read as they pass. They hear sounds and see objects that to a person whose perception is dulled by civilisation might as well be altogether absent, so far as his power of observation is concerned. Their trained ears detect the footfall of the wild forest animals walking through the jungle at considerable distances away, and can distinguish even the species by means of the sound, which is quite inaudible to less experienced observers. If any uncertainty exists regarding it they crouch down, or kneel down with one ear on the ground, and soon clear up their doubts. When they are in search of Deer or other animals with keen sight, they hide their cloth by hanging leafy twigs round their waist-string. This certainly gives them a very wild appearance, but there is no trustworthy evidence to show that it was the primitive dress of the aborigines of Ceylon.

Wild honey being one of their favourite foods, their vision and hearing are trained to an astonishing quickness in detecting every Bee that flies across their path, and noting its species, and whether it is flying laden or is only in quest of food. When it is carrying a load of honey and flying straight through the trees, they at once move off in the same direction, if it be the season in which the hives contain honey, that is, August and September, knowing of course that the laden insect makes a direct flight to its hive—the proverbial bee-line. As the nest is approached other Bees are seen converging towards it, and in a few minutes it is certain to be discovered.

Four species of Bees are found in the forests of Ceylon. The greatest one, a giant among Honey-bees and as large as a Hornet, is called the Bambarā, its hive being a Bambaraya. It hangs an immense white comb longitudinally under a substantial branch of a tall tree, or high up in the face of a cliff, sheltered by overhanging rock. The Wanniyas have a belief that the next species of Bee does not permit the Bambarā to make any part of its comb on the upper side of the branch. If it did so, the Danḍuwaellā would carry off the honey in that portion, the right to place any above the branch belonging to it alone.

The largest of these combs is about five feet deep, but somewhat less in length. The comb is without any cover excepting that provided by the bodies of the Bees, which usually cluster thickly over it, and completely hide it, thus protecting it from both sun and rain. The honey is chiefly used medicinally by the Sinhalese, but for the Vaeddas it is an important addition to the dietary. An old Wanniya once told me, as a good joke, that when moral pressure was put upon him by a Raṭēmahatmayā, or principal district chief, in order to make him supply some honey, he took care that it should be of this kind, and after receiving the thanks of the chief, who anticipated some pleasant eating, decamped before it was tasted. " I was never ordered to bring honey again," he said, with a chuckle.

Mr. Nevill noted that to get this honey when the hives are attached to rocks, the Vaeddas sometimes descend from above by long frail ladders made of cane. These swing about in an alarming manner, rendering the task a very dangerous one, especially at night. In order to appease the Spirit of the rock, called Kandē Yakā, 'the Demon of the Rock,' and induce him not to cause or permit the climber to fall, they sing songs loudly [I presume in his honour] while engaged in the work. Before undertaking the task a song is also sung, and a little honey sprinkled, to propitiate the Spirit.

The next Bee in size, called Daṇḍuwaellā, its hive being the Daṇḍuwaellaya, also hangs a single uncovered small white comb vertically under a branch, but never under a very high one; it is commonly found in a low bush. A very small portion of the comb is always constructed on and round the upper side of the branch also. No larvae are placed in this part, which is reserved for storing honey. This Bee protects the comb in the same manner as the large species. The honey is clear, rather pale-coloured, and sweet; and is eaten by all who find it. As in the Bambarā's comb, the cells are on both sides of the comb, the more advanced larvae being in the outermost cells; these are often separated from the rest by one or two rows of short empty cells. In the middle portion of the comb the largest larvae are found round the centre. The largest combs I have seen were from twelve to fourteen inches wide and deep.

The third kind of Bee makes its hive in hollows in trees. It is termed the Mī-maessā, the 'Bee-fly,' the hive being the Mīya, and it bears a close resemblance to the common Honey-bee of Europe. The honey is darker coloured but perhaps sweeter than that of the last species. This is the kind that is specially searched for by the hunters; as there are many combs in the hive, of course much more honey is obtained from it than from the single comb of the Daṇḍuwaellā, and eight or even ten quarts of honey are taken from a very good hive. The Forest Vaeddas are said to still occasionally preserve surplus meat in this honey, placing it in the hollows of trees, which they fill up with honey, and afterwards closing the orifice with clay or wax.

The last Bee is an interesting one called the Kuḍā-Mī-maessā, the 'Small Bee-fly,' no bigger than a small House-fly, which at a first glance it somewhat resembles. It is a fat-bodied little insect, less than a quarter of an inch long, and is extremely tame; when one perspires with the heat in the jungle several of them often alight on one's hand to drink the moisture.[1] It is black in colour, as are also its comb and honey. There is very little of the latter in a hive, but it is the sweetest of all. The nest is often found in a small dead branch or stump; and the entrance is built up with wax so as to leave an orifice sometimes not wider than the lead of a common pencil, barely permitting the insect to enter. The Wanniyas consider this Bee to hold higher rank than the others, notwithstanding its diminutive size; it is the Himi, 'Lord,' of the Bees, because, they say, its hive is sometimes established at a higher level than those of the other kinds.

The honey of the two last-mentioned Bees is procured by enlarging the entrance to the hive, or cutting a new one, with the little axe which these hunters always carry by passing the handle downward through their cloth belt. The work is easily done, as the stings of the Bees are ineffective and rarely cause injury; in fact, they are not often inflicted upon the hive-robbers; but the Bambarā is a dangerous insect when the community is aroused—there being often several combs in proximity on the same rock—and its hive can be cut down only at night, after stupefying the Bees with a smoking torch on which resin has been sprinkled.

Unless the wax be required for household use or barter, the finders divide and eat it, and everything taken out of the hive, excepting only the full-grown young which crawl out of their cells in time to escape this fate; all the rest of the larvae, however much developed, being thought to be little, if at all, inferior to the honey, and having, as a Kandian assured me, "a pleasant flavour like milk."

In districts where there is suitable forest, the Kandian Sinhalese make exactly similar, but temporary, excursions in search of honey, and are fairly expert in observing the Bees, without which they could not expect to meet with any success.

[1] I met with a similar Bee, which was equally tame, in the Gambia district in West Africa.

Among some Sinhalese it is a custom for the man who discovers a hive which he intends to take afterwards, to make a cut with his axe on the stem of the tree; the honey will not then be removed by others. It is believed that if more than five cuts were made the Bees would abandon the nest. While on such expeditions in one northern district, it is a significant fact that they still address each other as "Vaeddā."

All the forests and jungle where the hunting races live are apportioned among them for the purposes of hunting, getting honey, taking fish, and collecting shed deer-horns; and they informed me that they respect each other's rights over them. When I was out in the forest with some Wanniyas on one occasion, one of them observed a half-broken twig hanging at the end of a small branch—a common hunter's mark in the jungle—and remarked at once that somebody had been passing through their forest, which was a wild tract far from villages. It was evidently a matter which caused them considerable misgiving, and they discussed it long and eagerly, and eventually agreed that it was done by a certain person of another hamlet, who was known to them as an unscrupulous character. "It must have been Tikkā," they said, "he is a bad man; no one else would do such a thing. He has been collecting some of our horns."

It is well known that Deer shed their horns annually. At the season when they are dropped the hunters wander about in the forest in all directions in search of them, knowing that they are useful for barter at the little roadside 'boutiques,' or shops, which they visit in order to procure cloth, salt, etc. It is somewhat strange that many horns are found badly gnawed, sometimes more than half through; this is said to be done by Porcupines. The work of collecting the horns is laborious, and to our minds would not appear to be worth the little that their finders obtain for them. A Wanniya who was with me carried for three days, at considerable inconvenience, a small gnawed horn for which he only expected to receive a penny. After reaching his home he would still have a journey of eight miles in order to dispose of it, but probably he would carry some honey or other horns with him. At any rate this work would appear to be performed without much danger ; but I have known a man when so engaged to be attacked by a Sambar deer, which knocked him down and broke his collar-bone.

The Vaeddas, and also Kandian hunters, usually go on hunting or honey-collecting trips for a few days at a time; but the Wanniyas are absent in the forests for about two months together, returning home at intervals in order to fetch a little millet-flour, or to leave horns, skins, or honey. They take with them as food merely a small bag of millet-flour. When other food fails they cook the large cakes that have been described above, one of them sufficing for a day's eating. Of course the wilder Vaeddas who do not cultivate millet are without this resource, and live entirely on the forest products and animals at these times.

The Vaeddas are sometimes reduced to starvation if continuous rain fall while they are distant from their home on these trips. At such times, they informed me that they seek a large Riṭi tree (the bark of which is easily detached in large pieces), and immediately make a long cut across it with an axe, near the foot, and from each end of this a vertical cut of about their own height, or a little more. The piece of bark within the cuts is then lifted off the tree at the lower end, and supported at the loose corners on two sticks set in the ground for the purpose. This makes a tiny watertight shed under which a man can sit and sleep while the rain lasts. I was assured that sometimes they have been obliged by bad weather, when the forest streams were impassable, to remain in such a shelter for three, and in extreme cases even four days, without food. They are so well inured to privation of this kind that they seem little the worse for it, in the opinion of the Sinhalese who know them best. They remarked that they had never heard of a Vaedda's dying of starvation.

When I was in the forests for several days with a party of Wanniyas, a heavy rain-storm came on in the evening, and lasted all night. Using my breakfast-cup as a gauge, I found that the fall amounted to more than three inches. It was an awkward predicament, as we were quite without shelter, and were merely camping under trees. There were no Riṭi trees in that part of the country, but the hunters were equal to the emergency, the threatening appearance of the sky having given us warning of the approaching storm, which many earnest supplications addressed to one of their special Forest-Deities, the Sat-Rajjuruwō, the deified King Mahā-Sēna, had failed to avert, though accompanied by abundant offerings of leafy twigs hung over the horizontal stems of suitable creepers.

They scoured the forest all around until they found a tree with a large hollow up the trunk, at its foot. Dried wood was collected, and hastily crammed inside this shelter. Then a fire was made round another large dead tree, which soon became ablaze, and the whole night's rain failed to extinguish it. It will be observed that the fire was taken to the wood, and not the wood to the fire; this is a hunter's custom; a hunter always makes his fire close to a supply of dry wood. Round this tree we all camped, the men lying on improvised beds of small leafy twigs which kept their bodies off the wet ground, while I was in a hammock, between two blankets, out of which the water was wrung in the morning. When the rain at last ceased at 7 a.m., the dry wood was brought out of its hiding-place, and a roaring fire was made at the burning tree. This soon warmed us, and thoroughly evaporated all the moisture in my clothes—no one else was much overburdened with such articles—and the drenching had no injurious effect on any one.

When animals have been wounded by their arrows, the hunters track them through the jungle until they find them exhausted or dead. Elephants are killed by means of heavy arrows with the eighteen-inch blades. These are driven into them behind the shoulder at very close range—a distance of two or three yards—and as both edges of the blade are sharpened, every branch touched by the shaft of the arrow as the animal rushes through the jungle causes it to enlarge the wound, until the loss of blood is so great that the Elephant is exhausted. An old Wanniya, Kōnā by name, told me that he had killed nine Tusk-elephants in this way. Sambar deer are taken in a similar manner. Deer and Pigs are often killed on moonlight nights, while drinking at small pools in the forest, the hunter sitting behind a low bush or a small shelter of leafy branches made on the leeward side of it. It is on such occasions that the bow, if a very strong one, is sometimes held by the foot.

By the Wanniyas, at least, if not also the Vaeddas, the flesh of the Pig is never removed until the epidermis has been scorched off by fire. On one occasion when one was shot they refused to cut it up until this necessary preliminary work had been done. "Whoever heard of cutting up a Pig before the skin was burnt off," they said; and I was obliged to wait and watch the proceeding. As the Pig is considered to be an 'unclean' animal by the Kapuwas, or demon-priests, in the Vaedda districts, there may be some idea of first purifying the meat by the application of the great purifier, fire, before taking it away. A fire is made against one side of the animal until it is charred, after which the body is turned over and the other side, and, in fact, all parts are equally burnt, firebrands being applied to the legs. The skin is then easily removed by scraping it with sticks.

Kōnā was quite an original character. I never saw him sleep in the ordinary way; he merely sat with his back in a comfortable position against a large tree, and he seemed to obtain a good night's rest in this manner. He hobbled about with a bent back, and supported by a long stick, and appeared to be quite incapable of any useful work; but as soon as we began to make our way through the bushes he took the lead and kept it, at a pace that was almost too rapid for me. He knew, he said, every rock and game track in the forests in which he and his friends were accustomed to hunt, and his opinion was always listened to with respect, and his advice followed.

The idea of locality of these hunters is perfectly developed. On one trip I was taken by some Wanniyas through a piece of wild pathless forest ten or eleven miles across, near Padawiya tank, at the north-eastern boundary of the North-central Province. The jungle was dense, and the journey therefore occupied all day. Of course we were unable to proceed in a straight line, and more than once we deviated into a right-angle from our proper direction in order to avoid thorny jungle that was said to be in front of us. At about one o'clock we came to a high rock, as they had promised, on the top of which good rain-water is always retained in a hollow. There we cooked and ate some food, after which we resumed our tramp. In the middle of the forest, as we were proceeding along a deer-track, one of the men drew my attention to a half-broken twig hanging at the side of the path. "I broke that two years ago," he said; he was then proceeding at a right-angle from the line we were taking.

When I asked him if he never lost his way in such thick forest, full of undergrowth, he at first could not understand my meaning. After I had explained it—feeling while doing so that I was making an interesting exhibition of my ignorance—he laughed consumedly, and thought it a capital joke. "How *can* one lose it?" he said. He had never heard of such a thing before; to him it appeared to be quite impossible,[1] apparently as much so as getting lost in an open field would be to us. "When we look at the sun we always know which way to go," he remarked. The men justified my confidence in their powers by emerging, just before dusk, at the very spot where I wished to arrive, many miles from the homes of any of the party. Those who had acted as guides lived some twelve miles or more away, by the nearest footpath; and the house of the man who lived nearest was five miles from the point where we left the forest. I have always thought it a very clever feat.

There can be no doubt that something more than the mere sight of the sun is necessary when one is in the midst of such thick leafy jungle as that of Ceylon. Accompanied by two Kandian trackers, I once followed the tracks of a 'Rogue-elephant' that I had alarmed, for more than half a day, in thick forest, ending, nearly at dusk, seven miles from my quarters by the shortest path; and nothing would convince

[1] A hunter near Benin, in West Africa, stated that 'it was quite impossible for him to be really lost in the forest.' (Roth, *Great Benin*, p. 144.)

me that we were not returning in a diametrically wrong direction out of the jungle, until we got into a path which I recognised. I was then no longer inexperienced; I had lived for several years in jungle stations, and had been accustomed to jungle shooting and elephant tracking. The men who were with me could not possibly be acquainted with the part of the forest where we ended, as it was eight or ten miles from their village, and was totally uninhabited; yet they understood their position perfectly, and rightly decided that if we adhered to a game-track it must lead us to a village tank which they knew.

Progression in the right direction in open forest is a simple matter; it is different when one is in the midst of thick leafy jungle. Some in Ceylon is so dense and full of leaves that it is no exaggeration to say that an Elephant would be invisible at a distance of six feet; and in one case I was charged by a Rogue-elephant which I could hear approaching but of which I could not get a glimpse until his head was ten feet from me. I can recommend such an experience as a good test for the nerves. In this instance, a Kandian young man of about twenty years of age, who at his earnest request had been allowed to accompany my two trackers, was so overcome by fright that he stood perfectly still, paralysed and speechless, with wide-open mouth and staring eyes, and shaking all over more violently than the proverbial aspen. I have also seen a 'Moorman,' perhaps thirty years old, in exactly the same state under similar circumstances. Some minutes elapsed before they recovered the power of speech. Of course all the forests frequented by these hunters are not so dense as this; some of the high forest is comparatively open in parts, and they avoid the thicker jungle.

As illustrating the observant nature of the Vaedda, I may mention that I once showed some Village Vaeddas who lived far from others in the forest the illustrations, the first they had ever seen, in a copy of the *Graphic*, among which was one representing the landing of some troops from boats. They understood the scene immediately, one of them having once seen some boats at the coast, he said; and to my surprise a

Vaedda remarked that the persons in the background who appeared to be smaller than the rest must be at a greater distance than the others. He explained that they had noticed that the more distant objects always seemed smaller than those near at hand.

On the other hand, when I exhibited a drawing in the same paper to a learned Buddhist Abbot or Anunāyaka, who lived at a remote temple, and was deservedly respected by all, and well acquainted with the Pāli and Elu (old Sinhalese) languages, he said, regarding the more distant persons, " I suppose those men are a smaller race." The Buddhist scholar, deeply versed in the classical languages of his country and intimately acquainted with the abstruse philosophy of his religious works, who, in fact, was then about to found a small college for training Buddhist monks, was surpassed in intelligence by the Vaedda, who had never looked inside a book in his life, perhaps had never seen even the outside of one before.

A road was opened near the hamlet of these Vaeddas, and when I passed that way again and wished to renew my acquaintance with them, I found that they had withdrawn some miles further into the forest to avoid the publicity thrust upon them.

The Wanniyas believe that when the Grey Mungus [1] (*Herpestes griseus*), which they term the Nay Mugaṭiyā, or ' Cobra Mungus,' meets with a Cobra that it is afraid to attack or which has attacked it, it goes off in search of a White Mungus or Eli Mugaṭiyā, which is said to be a very small and rare species, and fetches it to the scene of combat, where it pays homage to it, bowing down before it. Fortified by the presence and authority of this superior animal, the Cobra Mungus at once attacks the Cobra and kills it, after which it and any others proceed to eat the snake, the White Mungus, however, taking no part in the feast.

Character.—The Wanniyas closely resemble the Kandian Villagers as regards their intelligence. The instances I have given are evidence of the amount of mental quickness shown

[1] It is incorrect to spell the name ' Mongoose ' or ' Mungoose ' ; the original Pāli word is *Mungusa*.

by the Village Vaeddas with reference to subjects with which they are acquainted.

The Vaeddas and Wanniyas bear the character of being thoroughly honest, and they are said to be faithful in their marriage relations. Unlike the Kandian Sinhalese, they are strict monogamists, and do not practise polyandry, according to my information ; and the former, at any rate, are reported to be good to their wives according to their ideas. I have no reason to doubt that the same can be said of the Wanniyas.

They are quite as lively and ready to enjoy a small joke as the Kandian villagers, but there is not much to amuse them in their forest life. While the Vaeddas often dance and sing on suitable occasions this does not appear to be a trait of the Wanniyas, who thus resemble the Sinhalese villagers as regards the former amusement. Fortunately for them, they are not exposed to the temptation of drinking alcoholic liquor, and probably not one of them knows the taste of it. Crime is practically non-existent among them all.

With respect to their truthfulness, of which Mr. Nevill had a very high opinion, my own experience is that although they are generally truthful, many individuals are prepared to deny a knowledge of facts of which they are fully aware, when to do so suits their convenience for the moment. In this respect they are like the Sinhalese villagers, so far as concerns their dealings with strangers. They will not work for hire except under the compulsion of hunger, and they might thus be thought lazy by those who see them idling about their huts at times when they are not engaged in hunting. But their active life at other times, when they are out in the forests, entirely disproves it.

I found them all converse readily with me, without any appearance of the fear, or hesitation, or shyness that one often notices in Kandian villagers. Many Forest Vaeddas have loud harsh grating voices. I was told by those who knew them well, and I observed the same peculiarity in those I met, that under ordinary circumstances, as well as inside their dwellings, the conversation of some of them is carried on in an extremely loud tone, the people almost shouting at each other, so that they appear to strangers to be in a towering passion with each other when in reality they are having a friendly chat.

Vaedda children are said to be fairly healthy; but owing to want of good drinking water, in very dry years outbreaks of dysentery sometimes occur which carry off many of them as well as the adults, who also suffer considerably from malarial fever and the peculiar disease called 'Parangi Leḍa,' allied to the West Indian 'Yaws.'

Every race has its own etiquette. When visiting an ancient abandoned reservoir in the forest with some headmen who knew the Vaeddas well and could speak their dialect, I once offered the usual 'chew' of Betel-leaf and Areka-nut to two wild-looking Forest Vaeddas whom we met there. The elder man said immediately, "What is there here for me to take to my wife?" and refused it; but he accepted the offer of a whole roll of the leaves and an adequate accompaniment of the nut. It was explained to me that everything they receive is invariably shared with their wives. They expect, therefore, never to be given less than a handful of anything, and to present a smaller quantity to them is considered to be a breach of ordinary courtesy. As an example of this feeling, I was told a story of a gentleman who offered a Vaedda a rupee in turn for information supplied by him. It was scornfully declined, but was readily taken when changed into copper cents, one hundred to the rupee.

The wildest Vaeddas now understand the use of money; one of the men above mentioned suggested to me that I should give him some.

I cannot do better than quote some of Mr. Nevill's remarks respecting their character: 'The true Vaedda varies between a taciturn and almost morose state when hungry, and a laughing reckless mood when not hungry. Their temper changes rapidly, and hence, if offended, in former times they were often guilty of sudden murder. They would carry on a feud until they considered justice done,[1] and then their minds would

[1] This must always be necessary among people who have no chiefs or court to which they can carry their grievances for redress. The

cherish no future malicious rancour. The Vaedda is proud in the extreme, and considers himself no man's inferior. Hence he is keenly sensitive to ridicule, contempt, and even patronage.

'He is thoroughly truthful and straightforward; a little kindly sympathy makes him an attached friend, and for his friend, as the Sinhalese nobles over and over again proved, he will readily give his life. The women are chaste and industrious, and have seldom a wish to attract the envy of other women, or the admiration of men.

'They are a merry people, delighting in riddles, songs, and jests. Those I have seen, of all clans, laugh often and merrily. They burst into a verse of song now and again, apparently from sheer exuberance of spirits, and any ludicrous incident amuses them as much as it would a Malay.

'A Vaedda is exceedingly jealous, and this jealousy, coupled with a quick temper and a reckless craving for revenge, probably developed the chastity and monogamy of the race. In any case, its honesty, truthfulness, and obedience to family or clan discipline, stand out in bright pre-eminence.

'As a rule, among the purer Vaeddas the younger women are rigorously excluded, or rather protected, from contact with strangers. They occupy, however, an honourable and free position in the society of their relations.'

A 'Mission' established a few years ago to 'rescue' and civilise these people was, like previous attempts, a failure. Nearly all the persons who joined it had Sinhalese names, and probably most of them were not true Vaeddas, though leading nearly the same life as the Village Vaeddas. I learnt that they only remained at it for the sake of the free food which they received. The true Vaedda is not a person who could be induced to settle permanently at such a station. When the hunting season came round it would be impossible to prevent these hunters from feeling an irresistible desire to return to their forest life, which some of them informed me they greatly prefer to any other. A small grant of funds to enable a supply of millet to be given to them in years when unfavourable seasons

same custom is, or was, in vogue among the Jōlas of West Africa, among whom the conditions which affect this practice were similar.

damage their crops, and, if possible, the provision of some kind of inexpensive wells at their hamlets, such as those made by the ancient Sinhalese and lined with rings of common earthenware, would be of more practical and immediate benefit to them.

The late Mr. Frank Fisher, who was formerly in charge of the Eastern Province as Government Agent, and who understood the natives of Ceylon better than most Europeans, was of opinion that the best method of dealing with the Vaeddas would be to restore one of the larger ancient reservoirs in the middle of their district, and to induce them, by a little pressure if necessary, to settle on the irrigable land below it. As such a scheme would be of benefit to the other inhabitants of the district it might eventually prove successful, but not for some years, and possibly never as a commercial undertaking. In any case it would be a costly experiment. Probably it was through the introduction of irrigation and rice cultivation that the ancient Vaeddas were converted into the Sinhalese of the present day. It was certainly not by means of well-meant but ineffective 'Missions.'

As one village tank after another was constructed—until every valley, however shallow, had a chain of them, one below the other, each supplying a separate rice-field with water—and the benefits due to these works became appreciated, the Vaeddas who lived near them would be gradually led to adopt rice cultivation as a chief means of gaining a livelihood, while still, like the Wanniyas and many Kandians of jungle villages, devoting a large part of their time to hunting. The example of agricultural settlers from Southern India, and occasional intermarriages with them, would doubtless give a further impetus to this transformation of the race into a nation of cultivators. We can see the very same advance in civilisation taking place among the Vaeddas of the present day. Some who live near the recently constructed irrigation works have already voluntarily adopted rice cultivation, and of their own accord have planted Coconuts and other fruit trees about their houses.

Time Reckoning.—Neither the Forest nor Village Vaeddas

keep any account of time. They have no words for the days of the week, and do not recognise such periods as the hours and their subdivisions, nor even weeks, months, or years.

Counting.—I now come to the question of the Vaedda's ability to count, which has been denied by some. I did not specially investigate the extent of the knowledge of the Wanniyas in this direction. All those whom I met appeared to resemble the ordinary Sinhalese villagers in this respect, and their common reference to numbers up to a thousand showed that they are well acquainted with them.

Regarding the Vaeddas, I may state that my inquiries were made without interpreters, in Sinhalese or Tamil. I was definitely assured by the Village Vaeddas, and this was confirmed by Sinhalese headmen who speak their dialect, that in the dialect which they call their own they have no words to express either numbers or periods of time. A Village Vaedda who came from the wild tract in the Madura-oya valley in which the Forest Vaeddas are chiefly found, informed me, in Sinhalese, that Vaeddas never make use of any numbers when conversing, and are unable to count. He remarked that he himself could not count; but on making further inquiry I learnt that this only referred to the Vaedi dialect. He could count quite correctly in Sinhalese, and seemed rather proud to do it for me until I stopped him. As apparently all Village Vaeddas are more or less acquainted with Sinhalese, it is safe to assume that they are all able to count in that language.

Regarding the knowledge and use of numbers possessed by the Forest Vaeddas, I have no positive information. If their dialect does not, as I was told, contain words for them, it is just possible that they are unacquainted with them; but before believing this I should require convincing evidence which at present is not forthcoming. That they have a considerable acquaintance with Sinhalese is certain, and if so why should they omit to remember the words for numbers? The parents of many persons who are now ordinary Village Vaeddas were true Forest Vaeddas sixty years ago,[1] yet all the former class understand and speak Sinhalese.

[1] See the footnote at the end of the chapter.

There is a Vaedi measure of length, the *Pilluma,* which represents the Sinhalese *Saetaepma* or *Hatakma,* the distance marched by a man carrying a load while on a journey, between two resting-places, called *Rūppē* in the Vaedi dialect. Its use appears to postulate the employment of some method of stating a distance of several Pillum ; and the Village Vaeddas readily mention (using Sinhalese words) the number of Pillum on a well-known path, for instance one which leads to their own village.

It is also quite likely that the Forest Vaeddas, even if they are unacquainted with any words for expressing numbers, may indicate them by means of marks made on the ground, or pieces of stick, or stones, or by their fingers, a common method used by Sinhalese villagers. In the course of conversation the wild Village Vaedda above mentioned indicated a number to me by his fingers of both hands, and a half by crossing his right forefinger over his left one ; and they may do the same.

Some have remarked that the Vaeddas can count only up to five ; and the same reply has been made to me by Tamil-speaking Vaeddas. On inquiry, however, I ascertained that it merely meant that they, who spoke Tamil and could count easily in that language, were only acquainted with the Sinhalese words for numbers up to five ; they thought them Vaedi words.

The Village Vaedda above referred to, who was much nearer the state of a Forest Vaedda than the ordinary villager, declared that he and his acquaintances never employed numbers when conversing among themselves. In reply to my special questions he assured me that they would never use such expressions as 'three trees' or 'three buffaloes'; he insisted that they would only say the words 'trees' or 'buffaloes,' without specifying the number. He seemed to think that the actual number would be of little importance ; it would be enough to know that there were more than one. I have no doubt that this is correct, as others confirmed it ; but it is far from proving their inability to count when they desire to do it.

Mr. Nevill remarked on this subject : 'The earlier observers are right in saying that they do not count. Practically one, two, several, many, very many, make up their use of numbers.' I am not satisfied that this can be accepted as final, even in the case of the Forest Vaeddas, if it was meant to indicate not only their use but also their knowledge of numbers, since it is quite certain that the Village Vaeddas, at any rate, both can and do count without difficulty by employing Sinhalese words or their fingers, although they, too, have been supposed to be unable to do it.

Whatever the final result of the investigation of the knowledge of numbers possessed by the Forest Vaeddas may be, the absence of special Vaedi words for them is of little value as evidence of the state of Vaedda civilisation, either now or in past times. If the vocabulary which I append be examined it will be found that there is in it only a single pronoun, and that is practically a Sinhalese, that is, an Āryan word. If they adopted the Sinhalese pronouns in the place of those which they possessed originally, they could equally employ the Sinhalese words for numbers instead of their own. Their long and intimate connexion with the Sinhalese is evident in their vocabulary.

The only indication of their use of numbers in early times is the statement in the Mahāvansa that the wedding festivities at the marriage of one of the local chiefs were to last seven days. Even if this was an invention of the early Sinhalese annalist, it proves that he, who must have had some acquaintance with the ways of the aborigines, believed not only that they were able to count, but that they kept a time record.

I am strongly of opinion that if any Vaeddas do not habitually make use of numbers, it is merely because they do not find it necessary to employ them, and not from any incapacity to understand them.

As an illustration of this, I give a practically literal translation of a few lines from a folk-story told in Sinhalese by a Village Vaedda of the interior, called Yāpā, a typical Vaedda name, and written down *verbatim* in that language.

It is evidently a story originally learnt from the Kandian Sinhalese, and there is nothing in it to indicate any connexion with Vaeddas; but the mere recollection and repetition of it prove that the Vaedda and his hearers had a good acquaintance with numbers, including simple addition and subtraction, otherwise they could not understand the point in it. It is too long to be given in full here. It relates the adventures of a Gamarāla, or minor village headman (who is often the butt of folk-story jokes), who being anxious to eat some cakes, after a quarrel with his wife over them, took some rice and asked the women at another house to prepare them for him.

It then continues as follows: 'Having given them a little rice, he said, "Make and give me five cakes (*Kaewun*) out of this, please." The people of the house replied, "Very well," and taking a little of the rice fried some cakes. The woman who fried them then looked into the account. "For the trouble of pounding the rice and grinding it into flour, I want ten cakes," she said. "Also for the oil and Coconuts [1] I want ten cakes; and for going for firewood, and for the trouble of frying the cakes, I want ten cakes." So that on the whole account for cooking the cakes it was made out that the Gamarāla must give five cakes.

'Next day the Gamarāla, having eaten nothing at home, came to eat the cakes. Having sat down, "Where are the cakes?" he asked. Then the woman who fried the cakes said, "Gamarāla, from the whole of the rice I fried twenty-five cakes. For pounding the rice and grinding it into flour I took ten cakes. For the oil and Coconuts I took ten cakes. For going for firewood, and for the trouble of frying the cakes ten more having gone, still the Gamarāla must bring and give me five cakes."

'Then the Gamarāla thought, "Adā! What sort of a cake-eating has happened to me!"'

It is evident that the persons who can enjoy such a story as this have as good an acquaintance with numbers as the ordinary Kandian villager.

There is also among the Sinhalese and Tamils of the villages in the jungle a laconic mode of expression which closely ap-

[1] Scraped Coconut was put inside them, and they were fried in Coconut oil.

proximates to the Vaeddas' talk without using numbers. For instance, if a drove of wild pigs or a herd of deer cross the path, these villagers would rarely draw attention to them by uttering more than the single word " Pigs," or " Deer " (pl.). If a man fire at some birds and miss them, his comrade does not say, " You missed them ; all three have flown away " ; but merely *Giyā*, " gone." It is nearly the same in some parts of India. In the folk-tales, the European man-eating giant exclaims when he scents the youth hidden in his house, " Fee, fi, fo, fum ! I smell the blood of an Englishman " ; but the laconic Eastern ogre only says, *Mānush-gandah*, " Man-smell " !

In the same way the Vaedda finds the simple plural a sufficient numerical expression. He is not conversational, but very laconic ; he says no more than is necessary. The intelligence of his hearers easily supplies the blanks in his speech, which consists of concise statements of simple facts, or opinions upon matters with which all who are present are conversant. Thus he needs few nouns, and still fewer verbal forms, and practically no abstract expressions, except such adjectives as good, bad, and the like. The ordinary conversation of the Wanniyas and of the Kandians of the more secluded jungle villages is nearly similar.

Gestures.—When a gesture will convey his meaning, the wilder Vaedda uses it in preference to spoken language. If the thumbs be placed side by side, and the forefingers be raised and curled forward until their tips approach each other, he thinks that any one will understand that this must mean a buffalo's horns, and therefore a buffalo.

The head is often utilised for this purpose. Instead of saying *Otta*, ' there,' or *Oba*, ' on that side,' a slight inclination of the head sideways fully expresses his meaning. A similar movement implies ' yes,' or ' very well,' when an affirmative answer is expected, just as the least shake of the head suffices for a negative, as with us. Anything in front is indicated by the chin, the head being tilted slightly backward.

A double nasal grunt conveys various ideas according to its tone ; it means ' yes,' ' is it so,' ' no ' or ' do not,' in which senses it is used by the Sinhalese. A near approach to it is the affirmative aspirate *Hă*, which is also in constant use by the Kandian Sinhalese, but not those of the Low-country ; it is noteworthy that I found it (as well as the Sinhalese affirmative *ehe*) nearly equally employed by the inhabitants of the Gambia valley, in West Africa.

When out in the forests, the Wanniyas and Vaeddas call to each other by an exact imitation of the bleating cry of the small Hornbill (*Tockus gingalensis*). This does not disturb any animals, of course. The former race, and probably the Vaeddas, are also on such occasions accustomed sometimes to utter the grunt of the Buffalo. I think this is done if a slight rustle be made when game is near, so as to allay any suspicion which it might arouse. It may have other meanings, and it is also a call to each other when near at hand. I do not remember hearing them imitate any other animal.

Domestic Animals.—The Vaeddas are said by Mr. Nevill to keep only Dogs as their domestic animals, but I was informed by the Sinhalese headmen of their districts that many of the Village Vaeddas also possess Buffaloes. A few Wanniyas have some fowls, as well as Buffaloes, Black-cattle, and Dogs.

The dogs are trained for hunting, and will track any wounded animals, or follow up unwounded ones, through the thickest jungle ; they are specially taught to catch the small Mouse-deer, or ' Mīminnā ' (*Meminna indica*), and the ' Iguana,' and Mr. Nevill says also Porcupines and Hares. He found that from three to five are generally maintained by each Village Vaedda household.

Well-trained dogs of this kind, of no particular breed, sharp-snouted, pointed-eared, little bigger than an Airedale terrier, in colour commonly yellow-brown or black, the ordinary nondescript dogs that are seen in every village, are wonderfully intelligent in the forest. I have myself seen a small pack, the general set of curs that are found about cooly huts in the jungle, perform a feat that astonished me.

I was then engaged in the restoration of an ancient tank or reservoir, which had an embankment a mile in length, and covered 170 acres. A party of earthwork labourers were excavating soil in the jungle at the low side of the embankment, at about half-way from each end. On going to work one morning the men startled three Axis deer that were grazing close to their working-place, and the dogs belonging to these coolies at once set off by themselves in pursuit of them. They followed them for some hours, gradually bringing them close round the upper side of the reservoir, as we could hear by an occasional faint yelping which reached our ears across the water; and after a chase of several miles through the thickest thorny jungle, they finally drove the exhausted animals completely round the reservoir, and into the very spot from which they had commenced the hunt; and their masters killed all three there.

The same or similar dogs were greatly interested in a tame Leopard which I had at that time, and parties of three or four of them, or on rare occasions single individuals, made periodical visits to my quarters, a mile from their homes, to inspect it. On their arrival they sat on their hams at a very safe distance, and watched the Leopard for some considerable time, finally trotting back after, as a rule, behaving in the manner customary when dogs meet with odorous corners or objects.

A trained dog of this description will lie flat on the ground, with his ears, if they be not cropped close to avoid injury by thorns, laid close to his head; and in this attitude and on his own initiative draw himself forward by his forelegs until he has passed completely under heaps of thorny bushes that have been piled up for burning, and seemed to have no passage through which such an animal could crawl. These are favourite hiding-places for the Mouse-deer and Forest Hares. One hunter with a gun assured me that with a single trained dog in a leash, to prevent its too rapid progress, he was certain to kill any wounded Sambar deer that he followed up.

Such dogs as these are invaluable assistants to the hunters in the dense forests of Ceylon, and an old Wanniya informed me that four which he kept had run down and captured many Sambar deer for him. As Mr. Nevill remarked, the dogs act as guards of the huts as well as the camp, and when they are present their masters know that they will have ample notification of the approach of strangers, whether bipeds or quadrupeds.

We are told by Mr. Nevill that in former times the [Village] Vaeddas kept Buffaloes which were trained for use in hunting; they are still employed for the purpose by some few Sinhalese and Tamils. The animal obeys orders communicated to it by means of a string which passes through the septum of the nose, 'and the archer stalked his game behind it, shooting either over or under it, as occasion required. They are now trained to allow use of firearms.'[1] A gentleman who had been out shooting with one informed me that he experienced no difficulty in approaching various kinds of game in this manner, round the sides of open grass plains. The time selected for the purpose is a bright moonlight night, when the animals can be seen at a considerable distance.

Mr. Nevill also learnt that when they had them the Vaeddas used milk taken from the Buffalo cows; and he remarked that 'well informed old Sinhalese have told me that the Unāpāna Vaeddas, and allied clans, used to ride Buffaloes, the wife sitting beside her husband. This is mentioned in one widely known song also.'

A very few Vaeddas who grow rice must make use of either their own or borrowed Buffaloes in its cultivation, for converting the surface of their rice fields into mud prior to sowing, by trampling it continuously while wet. Some Wanniyas also use them for the same purpose; at a hut in one of their hamlets the mud hole in which the animals wallowed was so close to the door that the occupants could hardly avoid passing through part of it on entering or leaving the house. When I asked one of the occupants if they did not get malarial fever in such a site his reply was characteristic. "Why not?" he said; "we do get it." He added that they were considering the advisability of moving their quarters, and abandoning the site to the Buffaloes.

Games.—I made no inquiry regarding the games played by either the Wanniyas or Vaeddas. Mr. F. Lewis has informed

[1] *The Taprobanian*, Vol. i, p. 191.

me that the only one of which he heard was played with the small red seeds of the Olinda Creeper (*Abrus precatorius*), which one person tossed to another. I feel no doubt that other amusements are known to them.

Folk-Stories.—The most secluded Village Vaeddas [1] of the interior told me that they are acquainted with many folk-stories. The names of several that they mentioned, as well as others that I have collected from people of different villages, show that they are the same as the tales related by the Kandian Sinhalese of the North-western and North-central Provinces. They appear to have been learnt, like the one already given, from Kandian Sinhalese visitors or settlers, or perhaps have been passed down from the earlier Vaeddas of the North-central Province, who must have acquired them from their neighbours in that case. There is not one among them, so far as my information extends, which describes the primitive life, or ideas, or customs of the Forest Vaeddas. This almost makes one doubt if the Forest Vaedda is an altogether primitive being.

I reserve the stories for publication with a collection of other Sinhalese tales ; but I append a translation of one, evidently of early date, about a Vaedda, that was written in Sinhalese for me in the North-central Province. Its conclusion is interesting. It will be observed that notwithstanding his poverty, the Vaedda is represented as being appointed the local king of the district in which he lived. I have adhered to the words of the story as they were written, and have inserted in brackets a few others that are required to explain the meaning in some places.

'A Story of a Vaeddā'

Once upon a time in a city a dāna [or feast for Buddhist monks] was given at the royal palace. On the next day the surplus rice was deposited for animals to eat, and dogs, cats,

[1] Excepting one small Vaedi hamlet, there is not a village within ten or twelve miles of theirs.

pigs,[1] fowls, and crows came and began to devour it. Then a Vaedi youth, who had gone to kill some game and was hungry, came and saw the fowls and pigs eating some cold cooked rice, whereupon he went to the heap of rice, and pushing aside the upper part of it took a little from the bottom and ate it.

At that time the royal Princess was at the open upper story of the palace. She saw this action of the Vaeddā, and remarked to her mother, " Anē ! Ammē ! However poor a man may be he does not do that disgusting work." The Queen admonished the Princess, and said to her, " Appā ! My daughter, do not say so of any man whatever ; you do not know what may happen to you. [It might be your fate to be married to such a person.] " Then the Princess, speaking in ridicule of the Vaeddā's want of good looks, replied, " If so, why should I wear this costume ? [I may as well begin to dress like my future husband's people.] " The Vaeddā, after stopping and overhearing this conversation, went away.

As a lion used to come to that city [and carry off the inhabitants] the King subsequently caused the following proclamation to be made by beat of tom-toms : " I will give my daughter to any person whatever who kills the lion which comes to this city [and devours the people.]" On hearing this, the Vaedi youth dug a hole in the path by which the lion came, and having got hid in it, when the animal approached shot it with his bow and arrow and killed it.

When the King learnt that somebody had killed the lion, he gave public notice that its destroyer should be sought for. The Vaedi youth then came forward, and after he had [proved that he was the person who killed it] the King gave that royal Princess to him in marriage [and he went away with her].

While she was living with him another good-looking Vaedi youth accompanied him one day. On seeing him, the Princess trickishly drove away the Vaeddā who was her husband, and married that handsome Vaedi youth.

It was not long before this Vaeddā one night killed a Buffalo, and [taking some of the flesh] said to the Princess, " Cook this

[1] No pigs are now kept by Kandian Sinhalese of the North-central or North-western Provinces.

and give it to me." The Princess replied, "It would be disgusting work for me to do; it is no business of mine"; [and she added] "What does it matter if my first husband is not good looking? he was good to me." Saying this, she drove this Vaeddā away, and seeking the place where the first Vaeddā whom she had married was stopping, went up to him, and said, "Let us go [home together]." But the Vaeddā refused.

After that she put on her Princess's robes as before, and came away.

In a little while afterwards that very Vaeddā was appointed to the kingship, and everybody subsequently lived prosperously and in health.[1]

When they can repeat, as they have done for me, page after page of these stories, varying in almost no detail from those of the Kandians, it does seem rather absurd that some who have described these people should have remarked that their memories are defective. What better test of their retentive powers could be desired?

Are the Forest Vaeddas Primitive?—I have ventured to utter a doubt as to the position of the Forest Vaedda of these days. Is he, at least in part, the degenerate descendant of more civilised ancestors, and not altogether primitive? There are one or two facts which to a certain extent tell in favour of such an hypothesis.

It is made clear by Captain Robert Knox [2] that in the middle of the seventeenth century the majority of those who retained the name of Vaeddas were such as we should now term Forest Vaeddas. They were then found throughout a large tract of country in addition to the present Vaedi-raṭa or 'Vaedda Country,' on the east of the Kandian mountains.[3] He mentioned that about Hurulla, in the North-central Province, 'there are many of them that are pretty tame and

[1] A proof, according to Eastern notions, of the excellence of the ruler.

[2] *An Historical Relation of the Island Ceylon*, 1681, p. 61.

[3] At the beginning of last century Percival mentions Vaeddas as being found in considerable numbers in the Northern Province. Probably these were Wanniyas. (*An Account of the Island of Ceylon*, p. 273.)

come and buy and sell among the people,' and that he saw many of their camping-grounds in the forests between Anurādhapura and Arippu. Even if 'the tamer sort' could be found 'it must be with a great search in the woods,' as 'they have no Towns nor Houses.' All lived solely by hunting; 'they never Till any ground for Corn, their Food being only Flesh.'

I shall assume, therefore, that a few centuries ago the ancestors of all the present Village Vaeddas were in reality Forest Vaeddas—as we know was actually the case with many of them during the last century—and that at that period they acknowledged the same deities as their descendants.

The evidence, chiefly found in succeeding pages, which tends to indicate either the lapse of the Forest Vaeddas from a more civilised state, or their close connexion in former times with civilised people, is as follows:—

1. They claim to belong to the highest castes of Vaeddas. Some of the wildest of them are members of the Baṇḍāra Warigē, 'the Chiefs Clan,' from which alone the Vaedda chiefs and kings were taken in ancient times. If these chiefs were civilised, many of the other members of the same leading clan were probably equally civilised.

2. Their knowledge of the Sinhalese language, which they spoke even in the time of Knox. Had they always been isolated from civilisation, as at present, it is difficult to comprehend how they could acquire this language. The fact that they understand and use in invocations such classical expressions as *Nirindu,*[1] 'Chief of men,' a poetical title meaning a king, proves a more or less intimate acquaintance with the tongue in ancient times. Such a word is never employed in modern colloquial Sinhalese.

3. Their adoption of the worship of the Goddess Mōhinī, which must have been acquired through Sinhalese who had taken it over from Tamils, if not directly from Tamils. In either case it postulates an intimate and lengthened acquaintance with civilised people.

[1] This word, the Sinhalese form of *Nara + indra,* occurs in an invocation of the Vaeddas which Dr. Seligmann was good enough to show me.

4. Their cult of Panikki [the] Vaeddā, a distinguished Vaedi chief who lived in the North-western Province, and was created a Baṇḍāra Mudiyansē or Mudaliyār (the title of a superior chieftain), in the latter half of the fifteenth century.

5. Their adoption of a whole series of the demons of the Sinhalese, which were acquired by the latter from the Drāvidians of Southern India. Nothing but a very close connexion with the Sinhalese or Tamils can account for their taking over these evil deities and learning their attributes.

6. The mixed blood of the Forest Vaeddas, as well as that of the Village Vaeddas. While the majority are brown, some have black skins, which cannot have descended from Sinhalese, among whom a really black colour is quite exceptional; it must be derived from a strain of Drāvidian blood. To acquire it they must have been on terms of intimacy with Sōla or Pāndiyan Tamils.[1]

In the face of these facts it is difficult to resist the conclusion either that nearly all were once partly, if only slightly, civilised, or that at the least they must have been joined in their forest life by considerable numbers of Sinhalese and a few Tamils, that is, by civilised people. Knox even stated that this was the case. He remarked, 'They are reported to be courteous. Some of the *Chingulays* [Sinhalese] in discontent will leave their houses and friends and go and live among them, where they are civilly entertained' (p. 63). This adoption of the hunting life by occasional civilised villagers most probably continued for many centuries, and the cumulative effect of its influence on the Vaeddas is evident in their language and beliefs.[2]

I have already drawn attention to the incontrovertible fact that there was a considerable Vaedda population at Anurādhapura in the time of Paṇḍukābhaya; and I may remark that the evidence of the caves is conclusive as to the abandonment of the cave life by nearly all the Vaeddas in pre-

[1] Dr. Seligmann has met with some Tamil expressions in the invocations of the Vaeddas.

[2] [illegible] Bell says of the Vaedda villages in the North-central Province, [illegible] ountry Sinhalese squatters have settled in [illegible] hamlet.' (A[illegible]haeological Survey. *Annual Report* for 1897 [illegible] 10, footnote.)

Christian times. There is good reason to believe that the caves were not re-occupied by them until several centuries had elapsed after the time of Christ. The people who had lived in them must have become villagers. It is possible that heavy taxation, or misgovernment, or Tamil invasions induced a certain number of these villagers, who had always lived partly by hunting, to revert to the forest life of their ancestors. Parties of Kandian hunters often occupy some of the caves for a considerable time at the present day.

High Rank of Vaeddas.—The Vaeddas claim to be of high caste, and their leading clans hold that they are not inferior in this respect to any Sinhalese, whom they consider to be interlopers. One of them remarked to me, "The whole country was ours before the Sinhalese came." It is significant that their rank does not depend on their present state of civilisation; some of the wildest Forest Vaeddas belong to the highest clan, from which their chiefs were selected.

The ending of the story which has just been given was considered by Sinhalese villagers of the North-western Province to be quite appropriate, and they stated that it was in accordance with their traditions. They saw nothing incongruous in the appointment of a Vaedda over people of their own race.

There are other examples which confirm the Sinhalese and Vaedi traditions of the high rank held by their chiefs. One of them occurs in an inscription.

At the side of a flight of steps cut in the rock at Dambulla to facilitate the descent from the celebrated cave-temple, the largest in Ceylon, to the quarters occupied by the Buddhist monks, near which many other monastic buildings stood in former times, several short inscriptions in colloquial Sinhalese of about the third or fourth century A.D. were left as records of the commencement of the chiselling work for cutting out the steps. They record the names of pious personages who perhaps bore part of the expense of the work. Such records as *Amataya Wahabaha taṇi patagaṭi*, 'The place begun by the Minister Wasabha'; *Naka lakhi kahi patagaṭi*, 'Nāga having made a mark began (the work here)'; *Humanayaha patagaṭi*, 'Begun by Sumana'; *Mitaha buja patagaṭi*, 'Begun by the landed proprietor Mitta,'—leave no doubt as to their general import.

Another [1] of these notices runs, *Sidha. Raja Pulida Abaya nakare Sidahata kapa gala,* ' Hail ! the stone cut by Siddhattha, King Abhaya, the Pulinda, having caused it to be done.'

The appellation Pulinda shows that this king was a Vaedda. When the expression occurs in the Mahāvansa it certainly refers to the Vaeddas, and there is nothing to indicate that in the present instance the word has a different meaning.

So far as it is of value, the Sinhalese story also supports this interpretation, which at once sets aside all doubts as to the high caste-rank of the ancient Vaeddas, and the commanding position of the superior Vaedda chiefs even seven or eight centuries after the accession of the first Sinhalese king.

Coming down to much later times, there is conclusive evidence of their power in a manuscript (the Wanni Kaḍa-in Pota, ' the Book of the Wanni Boundaries ') of the time of King Bhuvanēka Bāhu VI of Kōtta (1464–1471 A.D.), which contains an account of the appointment of a chieftain called Panikki Vaeddā, of Eriyāwa, a village near Galgamuwa in the Kurunāēgala district, to define the boundaries of the Four Wanni Pattus or divisions of what is now the North-western Province. He was granted the title of ' Baṇḍāra Mudiyansē,' an expression which could only be applied to a chief of very high caste. After stating the limits of the district, the account concludes as follows in one manuscript : [2] ' Having received the orders from the Lord, the Sinhalese [3] King, Bhuvanaika Bāhu, Panikki Vaeddā fixed and gave the boundaries.'

Panikki Vaeddā was evidently one of the most important chiefs in Ceylon at that time. He was not merely the supreme chief of the Four Wanni Pattus (Puttalam Pattuwa, Munissaram Pattuwa, Demala Pattuwa, and the Wanni Hat Pattu) ; these districts were granted to him and his heirs for

[1] A facsimile will be found in Fig. No. 153.

[2] There are variations in the wording, but not many in the matter, of different manuscripts.

[3] As this expression also shows, there is some reason to believe that the book was written by a Vaedda, reference being made in it to ' our servitude ' (*apē daskama*), which Bhuvanēka Bāhu abolished.

ever. This record is so important that I give the words in full, with a translation.

Sītāwaka waeda un Bhuvanēka Bāhu ḍēvi mahā rajjuruwannen yedī Eriyāwē Panikki Vaeddāṭa me hatara pattuwa kaḍa-in koṭa irahanda pawatina tek laebunāya.

'Having fixed the boundaries, these four Pattus were granted to Panikki Vaeddā of Eriyāwa as long as the sun and moon last, by the Great King His Majesty Bhuvanēka Bāhu who dwelt at Sītāwaka.'

He is elsewhere termed *Wanni hatara pattu Eriyāwē Panikkirāla*, 'the Elephant-catcher Chief of Eriyāwa over the Four Wanni Pattus'; and the leaders under him, called Panikkirālas or merely Panikkiyās, are mentioned as *me hatara pattuwē Vaeddan*, 'these Vaeddas of the four Pattus' or districts.

He was an Elephant catcher (*Panikkiya*); and as stated in Upham's *Buddhist Tracts*, p. 236, he and another chief named Dippitigama Liyana Vaeddā, or in another manuscript, Lēkan Polpiṭiyē Liyana Vaeddā, a Secretary or Registrar, were ordered by the king to capture a Tusk-elephant and take it direct to Sītāwaka, where they showed the king the manner of tying up a wild elephant, the newly captured animal having been freed for the purpose inside a circle of tame female elephants. The men who tied up the elephant received presents and high-sounding titles; one of them became Eriyāwa Wanninayaka Siṇhappu Mudiyansē, and another was called Rājapaksa Kumāra Siṇha Wanniyā.

The villages of these men, or the chiefs who assisted in the capture of the animal, are mentioned as Eriyāwa, Gāla-waewa, Dunupota-gama, Kaekuna-waewa, Wilawa, Warā-gammana, Hulugalla, Hātā-gammana, Wenda-kaḍuwa, Mahagalla, Uḍuwēriya, and Polpiṭi-gama; they are nearly all still occupied by Kandian Sinhalese who must be the descendants of these Vaeddas of the fifteenth century. Large tracts of rice fields were cultivated at these villages, the sowing-extents being stated in the manuscript.

These are not the only records of the deeds of Panikki Vaeddā. When some princes with armed followers arrived from India at Ponparappu, his 'Archer Vaeddas' (*Malalu Vaeddan*) at once notified the matter to this chief, and Panikki, who is also termed Panikki Maetiyō, 'the Minister Panikki,' proceeded to the spot with a large force of Vaeddas to inquire into the cause of their coming. He translated into Tamil the words of the Vaeddas, for the benefit of the visitors, made them show him the presents which they had brought for the king, and sent his royal master a full report, stating that they carried swords slung from their right shoulders and shields in their left hands, but that they stated that they came as friends, and were in want of food; he awaited instructions. Eventually he was ordered to feed them, and to allow them to proceed to Sītāwaka for an audience with the king. A large guard of Vaeddas under Panikki accompanied them, apparently to see that they caused no damage on the way. The visitors stopped at Munessaram to pay their devotions at a temple of Vishnu, who granted them permission to proceed to the king.

In the first half of the seventeenth century we find Vaeddas still holding important positions in the country. A short manuscript in my possession which apparently dates from about 1640, contains some particulars of the efforts made by Prince Wijapāla to retain the control of the Mātale district. As we learn from the Mahāvansa (ii, p. 330), the Prince's father was King Wimala Dharma Suriya I (1592–1620); and his uncle Seneratna (1620–1627) having succeeded this king placed him in charge of the Mātale district.

The account commences by stating that 'Wijapāla Maha Rājayāno, of the Goḍapola Maha Wāsala,' or palace, having failed to conquer his enemies—that is, his cousin, Rajasinha, who had followed Seneratna on the throne, and with whom he had quarrelled—called out his adherents in the Mātale district, and with their assistance dispossessed several chiefs of their territories. The representatives of 'the three Mātale Houses' responded to his summons; they were Kulatunga Mudiyansē of Uḍupihilla, Candrasēkara Mudiyansē of Dubukala, and Waniśeka Mudiyansē of Alu Wihāra.

The following Vaedda chiefs are also mentioned: The Vaeddā chief of Hulangomuwa, Yahamipat Vaeddā, Kannila Vaeddā of Pallakanan-gomuwa, Hērat Vaeddā of Nikakoṭuwa,

Maha Tampala Vaeddā of Palapatwala, Maha Dombā Vaeddā of Dombawala, Wallī Vaeddī of Wallivela (a female Chief), Maha Kawuḍellā Vaeddā of Kawuḍupalla, Nairaṇ Vaeddā of Nāran-gomuwa, Hērat Banḍāra Vaeddā of Madawala, Imiyā Vaeddā of Kampalla, Makarayā Vaeddā, Koduru Vaeddā, Raekā Vaeddā (evidently a title, as he was the Guardian of the district boundary), Maha Kanda Vaeddā of Kandapalla, Hēmpiṭi of Galēvela, Bāju of Uḍugoḍa, Minimunu of Pallēsiya Pattuwa, Dēvakriti of Melpiṭiya, and Kaḍukāra of Bibile. All these are stated to be Vaeddas; they were 'of the Vaedi wāsagama.'

As no other leaders are mentioned, it is certain that these Vaedda chiefs were included among the most important personages next to the three superior Kandian chiefs. The Mātale district was evidently full of Vaeddas at that period.

The manuscript also contains a bare reference to the reason of the invasion of Ceylon by the Sōlians of Madura in the reign of Wankanāsika Tissa (110–113 A.D.). This is termed 'the War of the short-horned Buffalo (*ankoṭa miwuwāgē haṭana*) of the widowed Vaeddī, Simī of Dodandeniya.' Unfortunately, no explanation of the phrase is furnished. Doubtless it commemorates some incident that was popularly supposed to have led to the war between Ceylon and Madura, regarding the cause of which the histories contain no information. We may conjecture that some traders from Madura killed or carried off the widow's buffalo, and that the reprisals made by the Vaeddas eventually induced the Sōlian king to avenge his subjects by invading the country. Whether the dispute originated in this manner or not, the traditional phrase may be taken to prove that the Vaeddas possessed buffaloes in the second century A.D.

Their high caste-rank is still admitted by most Sinhalese who are acquainted with them. I was informed thirty years ago by the brother of one of the Raṭēmahatmayās, the superior Kandian chiefs, that his family was intimately allied to the Vaeddas by marriage, and that such a connexion was considered to be by no means a *mésalliance*.

No one who knows the intense family pride of the Kandian

chiefs could suppose that they would allow their sons to marry wives selected from the Vaedda clans if these were thought to be of much lower social status than themselves; and still more rigorously would they be debarred from marriage with them if they had been, as Professor R. Virchow said, mere primitive savages of a lower type than the Australians and Andamanese. It would be an insult to them to even suggest that they would ever, in a single instance under any circumstances, consent to such unions.

It is also impossible that a race of savages would be selected as the special guardians of the important Hindu temple of Skanda, the War God, at Kataragama, in South-eastern Ceylon.

Evidence of Former Civilisation.—Professor R. Virchow has written of the Vaedda race that 'One may call it among the smallest [in stature] of the living human tribes'; and after stating that he thought it just conceivable that some remains indicating their former higher culture might yet be discovered, he proceeded to remark, 'But what will be gained even by this? At best the possibility of placing the Vaeddas on a level with the Andamanese and the Australians, whilst, according to present facts, they must be placed decidedly lower. A people who do not even possess clay vessels, who have no knowledge of domestic animals beyond the dog, who are unacquainted with the simplest forms of gardening and agriculture, who lack almost every kind of social institution, who are not even counted among the outcasts by their civilized neighbours, cannot possibly ever have had the means which make a higher culture of any kind possible. The hypothesis of a return to barbarism must hence be definitely given up.' [1]

Had the learned Professor been in possession of the information which I have given in the last few pages, he might perhaps have modified this sweeping condemnation of the race to the lowest place among the lowest savages. But even the early Sinhalese annalists furnished particulars which, if they are to be credited, disprove the Professor's conclusions.

The references to the Vaeddas in the Sinhalese histories and

[1] Monograph on the Vaeddas (Translation), p. 108.

the Valāhassa Jātaka story show clearly that in pre-Christian times, when it must necessarily be admitted that they were numerous and well known in the country, part of them at least were believed to have held a far higher position in the scale of civilisation than their direct representatives of the present day. It must not be forgotten that the accounts which we possess were compiled from annals that were almost certainly—as the accuracy of the details in other respects shows—committed to writing by the second if not the third century B.C. The more our knowledge of the early history of the country progresses the more evident does the general truthfulness of the early accounts become. The careful Sinhalese chroniclers of that time would be most unlikely to attribute to the aborigines more advanced customs than those which they saw for themselves among them, or to place them in a higher social position than they occupied in their day or in the traditions of their forefathers.

In describing the uncivilised natives of a conquered or newly acquired territory, the general tendency among writers down to comparatively recent times, and not among the early authors only, has been in the opposite direction. They have represented people with a certain amount of culture as mere savages, and savages have been even described as no better than the wild beasts, and as using no human form of speech. On this account, any evidence of the civilisation of the ancestors of the Vaeddas which occurs in the early histories may be accepted with much confidence.

What is this evidence? [1] Assuming it to be trustworthy, let us see what deductions may be legitimately drawn from it.

We are told that the country was politically organised, that is, that in the fifth century B.C. it was ruled over by chiefs who lived at settled towns or villages which had a considerable population. Eighty years after the first Sinhalese king began his reign, we find a supreme sovereign of the Vaeddas, whose name is given as Citta, residing at Anurādhapura almost on an equality with the Sinhalese king, and sitting on a similar throne to his when the royal party were present at public

[1] It will be found in detail in the preceding pages.

festivals and sports. It is specially added, in order to mark the position held by the Vaedda chief, that both the thrones were of the same height. According to eastern custom, and even western also, this proves that the Vaedda ruler took precedence of all persons in the country except the Sinhalese king himself, who thus publicly acknowledged their equality of rank. Had the annalist been a Vaedda, we might suspect that he had invented such a description of his sovereign's status at the court ; we may feel sure that no Sinhalese chronicler would have deliberately perpetuated a story which placed the ruler of the aborigines in such a prominent position unless he and his compatriots believed that the Vaedda chief had actually occupied it.

In addition to the sovereign of the Vaeddas, another Vaedda chieftain, Kālavēla, who held a post of almost equal importance in the country, is mentioned as residing at the Sinhalese capital. It is explicitly stated that it was with the assistance of these two chiefs that the Sinhalese king ruled over the country. It may be said, therefore, that this account completely supports the more doubtful one which is given of the social position of the local chiefs in the time of Wijaya. They were persons with whom the Sinhalese rulers could associate on terms of practical equality. I suggest also that it is difficult to account for the devotion of the Vaeddas to Paṇḍukābhaya, before he became king, unless he was connected with their race through his grandmother.

The reference to the wedding festivities of even the local rulers of the Vaeddas indicates that they were elaborate festivals which lasted some days, and that the etiquette of the country rendered it necessary for the princess who was to be married to be escorted by her mother to the town or settlement at which the ruler dwelt to whom she was to be united.

The Vaeddas are described as being well dressed. The kings had a special ceremonial costume which even a prince from the court of one of the sovereigns of the Ganges valley was not ashamed to wear when he assumed the sovereignty over them. The costumes or ornaments of the royal retinue were also found suitable for the followers of the Indian prince. It is clear that the dresses of such people were no mere waist-cloths of Riṭi bark, or girdles of leafy twigs. They must have consisted of imported cotton cloth of an ornamental pattern, brought into the country either by Magadhese or South-Indian traders.

These statements are supported by modern Sinhalese traditions, and the accounts of the Vaeddas which were collected by Mr. Nevill. These name even the clan, the Baṇḍāra warigē—the 'Chief's Clan,' which still exists, and to which some of the wildest Forest Vaeddas belong[1]—from which the kings and chiefs were chosen in former times; and they mention the coloured dresses and jewels, and the golden household utensils which their more settled representatives still possessed in the last century. Among the names of modern Village Vaeddas given below it will be seen that one is called Randunu Wanniyā, 'the Wanniyā of the Golden Bows.'[2]

If the Vaeddas were in the state of civilisation which these facts indicate, it would be unjustifiable to suppose that they could be ignorant of all knowledge of numbers.

The Sinhalese annalists and the writer of the Valāhassa Jātaka agree that trading vessels were often wrecked on the shores of Ceylon before the advent of Wijaya, that is, in or before the fifth century B.C. The tradition of the Vaeddas is also quite definite as to the arrival of their supreme deity in a ship from Southern India, 'in the olden time,' which we know by the reference to him in the reign of Paṇḍukābhaya must have been prior to the fourth century B.C.

These were not local ships; it is practically certain that they were vessels which came from ports on the Indian coasts. In the Sankha Jātaka (No. 442) there is a reference to a ship built of planks, with three masts; and voyages were certainly made at an early date from the Ganges valley to Suvanna-bhūmi, 'the Land of Gold,' that is, Burma. In the *Indian Antiquary* for 1876, vol. v, p. 340, Dr. J. Muir published translations of some maxims from the Mahā-Bhārata, one of which

[1] I have stated that I met some who belonged to it.

[2] This is strong evidence that the Wanniyas are really Vaeddas; another Vaedda is also called 'Wanniyā.'

runs, 'On seas, in forests wild, the bold will risk their precious lives for gold'; and even in Vedic times sea-voyages, some of which occupied several days, are often mentioned. It must have been such vessels as these which brought the first Gangetic travellers, and at a much later date Wijaya and his relatives, and their followers.

With what object did the first Magadhese traders venture upon the dangerous voyage to Ceylon from their distant country on the Ganges, a journey of more than 1,600 miles? This long voyage cannot have been undertaken for any other purpose than to obtain the articles produced in the country, ivory, wax, incense, and probably also pearls and gems,[1] being part of them. We know also that these were not paid for with money, which would have been useless to the natives; the traders must have brought with them cargoes of other goods, like those taken to Burma according to the Jātaka stories (in which whole shiploads of merchandise are mentioned)—to be disposed of in exchange for the local commodities. We shall probably be correct in assuming that these cargoes consisted largely of cotton materials, beads and other ornaments, axes and arrow-heads of steel, and cooking and other vessels of earthenware, copper, or brass, all of which would be readily taken by the natives in exchange for the produce of the country.

This at once presupposes an internal trade in these articles, like that of prehistoric people in Europe. All would not be retained in the hands of the dwellers on the coast; a part of them would be distributed throughout the whole country by some form of barter,[2] or possibly by local traders established at settlements far inland, in the 'forests wild' of the Mahā-Bhārata, where the produce of the district would be collected in exchange for them, exactly as at present.

[1] The Mahāvansa states that Wijaya sent to his father-in-law the King of Madura, gems, pearls, and chanks (i, pp. 34, 35).

[2] So also it is stated of the natives of Central Australia, 'The trading propensities of the Australian natives have led long ago to the disposal far and wide over the continent of the iron tomahawk of the white man. . . . One group barters what it makes for the products of another living, it may be, a hundred miles away.' (Dr. Howitt, *The Native Tribes of Central Australia*, p. 575.) There was a similar prehistoric trade among the American Indians, and in Europe in Neolithic times.

The mere tact that Indian traders came so frequently to Ceylon that vessels were known to be often wrecked on the coasts, proves, without any other evidence, that many natives were in a far more advanced state that the present wild dwellers in the eastern forests, with whom no regular trade could be possible. Permanent trading centres must have been established at fixed and well-known points on the coast, near native settlements, at which the vessels called, and to which the articles produced in the country would be conveyed for barter with the adventurous merchants who came for them with the monsoon winds. All this must necessarily follow if such traders came to Ceylon ; and that they did visit the island is confirmed by the presence of the natives of the Ganges valley as settlers in the fifth century B.C. It is impossible that these settlers were the first persons to visit Ceylon from Magadha. The Magadhese were a nation of traders (as the Ordinances of Manu tell us), and probably knew all the coasts of the Bay of Bengal. If they were acquainted with the voyage to Burma they would experience no greater difficulty in finding their way down the Indian coast to Ceylon. In the Sussondī Jātaka (No. 360) merchants are stated to have proceeded by water from Benares to Nāgadīpa, that is, northern Ceylon, in former times.

If some of the inhabitants were carrying on a trade with Indian merchants, and their rulers were considered by the Sinhalese sovereigns to be sufficiently civilised to associate with them, we may still surmise that a great number of the natives continued to gain a living wholly or partly as hunters, leading while in the forests the same wild life as their descendants of the present day.

The annalists evidently believed that no rice was grown in the country before Wijaya's time, since they specially explain that the rice which was cooked for travellers when they landed was procured from stores brought by ships that were wrecked on the coast. According to the custom or law regarding such matters in other countries, of which many examples might be quoted, these wrecked vessels would be looked upon as lawful prizes, either sent by their Gods for their special benefit, or rejected by the God who ruled over the waters.

I assume that as the newcomers from the Ganges valley, introducing various arts of their own country, settled down permanently, and exhibited a more stable form of civilisation than that of the aborigines, they must necessarily have intermarried with the more advanced natives. While they were being gradually absorbed by them—which would not occupy a long period after immigration, which was probably never extensive, from the Ganges valley ceased—they imparted to them their own culture, and to a great extent their language.

But the physique, and colour, and hunting proclivities remained unchanged. Many of the villagers of the North-central and North-western Provinces merely require to be sent to live in the forests in order to become once more practically the same Forest Vaeddas who lived by hunting before the time of Wijaya. If these people were isolated in the forests for a very short period, I am sure that in most respects they would be indistinguishable from the Vaeddas, just as the Wanniyas resemble them. It would be an unavoidable result of the environment. They could make neither pottery, nor iron or stone implements [1]; and dogs would be the only domestic animals that they could retain in the forests. All Sinhalese and Wanniya hunters lead the life of the Forest Vaeddas after they leave their villages on their hunting expeditions, carrying only a small bag of millet-flour, gourds for water, an axe, a knife, and usually, but not always, either a gun or bows and arrows. They all anticipate such a life with pleasure; they are still Vaeddas at heart. They dress almost like the Vaeddas, and get the same food in the very same manner.

This shows that the appliances of the Vaeddas are such as are best suited to their forest life, and that the absence of others is not a proof that they are the lowest savages. It only proves that they have practically all the implements that are necessary in these dense forests. I cannot imagine that any others but the knife would be of the least use to such hunters.

The omission to keep any record of time, whether days of the week, or months, or years, cannot be considered to be

[1] If the potters and smiths were excluded.

conclusive evidence of a primitive state. I found it equally absent among the Adjammāteyi or Jōlas (the Diolas of French authors) of West Africa, who are admitted by other natives to be the best agriculturists in the Gambia valley. They stated to me that they only recognised the season for preparing the ground for crops by observing the flowering of certain forest trees. Yet they have fully inflected verbs, with eight tenses and eight persons, and no less than eight regularly formed conjugations derived from each verbal root.

So, also, to the early Greeks Hesiod said :—

> 'When Atlas-born, the Pleiad stars arise
> Before the sun above the dawning skies
> 'Tis time to reap ; and when at sunrise now
> They sink beneath the West, 'tis time to plough.'

The small cranial capacity of the Vaeddas is not a proof of their low intellectual status. Dr. Virchow has shown that the size of the brain in four Tamil skulls is practically identical with theirs, and he states that other South-Indian skulls are similar. No one, I presume, will venture to maintain that the Tamils, or rather the Drāvidians, are not a highly intellectual race, to whom India possibly owes a part of its present culture. The Rt. Rev. Dr. Caldwell, the greatest authority on the subject, said in the Preface to his *Grammar of the Drāvidian Languages*, 'It is impossible for any European who has acquired a competent knowledge of any of the Dravidian languages—say Tamil—to regard otherwise than with respect the intellectual capacity of a people amongst whom so wonderful an organ of thought has been developed' (2nd ed., p. ix).

M. de Quatrefages also remarked that 'the development of the intellectual faculties of man is to a great extent independent of the capacity of the cranium, and the volume of the brain.'[1]

As to the opinion which is sometimes expressed regarding the intellectual effect of variously proportioned brains, there is nothing to show that the Vaedda cranium is inferior in mental power to that of other dolichocephalic people. As a matter of fact, it is open to doubt if the mere proportions of the cranium are more than insignificant factors in the case. Bra-

[1] *The Human Species*, p. 384.

chycephalic races are not necessarily of greater mental power than dolichocephalic races. Thus the Lapps are at the limit of brachycephaly, with a cranial index of 85; and Mongols, Turks, Javanese, North Americans and even Andaman Islanders have a higher index than Parisians.[1]

In dealing with the position of the Vaeddas, we are faced with this difficulty—that a portion of the race was relatively civilised in ancient times, while certain members of it are found at the present day almost in the state occupied by some of the most primitive peoples. We must adopt a theory which will include all the facts of the case; and not one which ignores some of the most important and significant and incontrovertible historical details and traditions. We cannot select the smallest and wildest group of Vaeddas, and because of their simple life as hunters place the whole race in the position which they continue to occupy, not because, like the aborigines of Australia and the Andamans, they are intellectually incapable of rising above it, which the example of the others has completely disproved, but partly by accident and partly of their own free choice.

My conclusion therefore is that whether there has been any retrogression of the present Forest Vaeddas from a certain low state of civilisation or not, in very early times a great part of the race had reached a much more advanced state of culture than the wilder members of it, whose more or less isolated life either as hunters, or as hunters-and-villagers, did not in many cases induce them to feel any desire to participate in it. This more civilised portion has absorbed the Gangetic settlers, and acquired their status and language, and with some intermixture of Drāvidian blood, or in many instances without it, has become the existing Kandian Sinhalese race.

The ancestors of the present few hunting Vaeddas—who now most probably number much less than one hundred—either abandoned, some centuries after Christ, a form of village life in which they were partly or chiefly hunters, and reverted to the forest life of their forefathers; or, like some of the wild hunting tribes of the South Indian hills, remained, at least until very

[1] Topinard, quoting Broca and Hamy, in *Anthropology*, pp. 241, 242.

recent years, in nearly the original condition of the first comers to Ceylon, apparently simply because they preferred the free untrammelled life in the woods, and found their accustomed habits and household articles suited to all the requirements of a hunter's existence in the forests of Ceylon. The evidence afforded by the caves appears to me to be in favour of the former theory, which is also supported by the loss of their original language and their adoption of the Sinhalese tongue.

The majority, however, of those who did not coalesce with the Gangetic settlers and their descendants, or accept their mode of life and culture, have, in comparatively modern times,[1] and in certain instances partly through compulsion—since portions of the forests in which they were accustomed to hunt have been cut down in order to permit rice and millet cultivation—to some extent adopted the more civilised existence of their neighbours. Many keep buffaloes, and all but those few who live only by hunting and fishing, grow millet and other plants suited to their jungle clearings. An exceptional few in favourable sites for it even cultivate rice, and, as some of them informed me, in recent years have settled down permanently and have planted such fruit trees as Coconuts, Areka-nuts, and Plantains about their houses.

No arguments of the supporters of the hypothesis that the Vaeddas are, 'at the best, on a level with the Andamanese and Australians' (which must imply an incapacity for intellectual development), can lay aside the examples which have been given of their high status in former times. Historical facts such as these must necessarily supersede any theories that are not in accordance with them; if the theories do not agree with the facts, so much the worse for the theories.

[1] As an example, I may note that according to Sir Emerson Tennent a number of Forest (or, as he terms them, Rock) Vaeddas settled down in hamlets between 1840 and 1850, at one of which there were twenty-five families. He adds, 'it may thus be said that the distinction of the Rock Vaeddas has ceased to exist in that part of the country; all having more or less adopted the customs and habits of villagers.' (*Ceylon*, 2nd ed., Vol. ii, p. 447.)

SOCIAL DIVISIONS AND CUSTOMS

THE Vaeddas are socially divided into a series of tribes or clans, called by them Warigē (or Warugē, according to Mr. Nevill), of which three hold much higher rank than the rest, with whom their members do not intermarry. These are (1) the Baṇḍāra warigē, 'the Chief's clan'; (2) the Morāni warigē; and (3) the Unāpāna warigē.

The members of at least these three clans, and I believe those of the other clans also, are admitted by the Kandian Sinhalese to belong to the Goyiwansa or Cultivating caste, the highest among the Sinhalese, though there are several different grades in it. Mr. Nevill was informed that in ancient times the Vaedda kings and chiefs were selected only from the Baṇḍāra warigē, as the name indicates. He stated that this clan is supposed by some to derive its origin from the children of the Vaedda princess Kuwēnī, whom Wijaya married, their names being thought to be Sabarā and Sabarī. Of course no dependence can be placed on any claim to such a descent, though the fact remains that the clan is acknowledged by all Vaeddas, as well as the Sinhalese who are acquainted with it, to be of higher rank than the others.

How it came about that part of the Forest Vaeddas are members of this clan is a matter deserving special investigation. It may possibly be an indication of their relapse from a more cultured state for the reasons suggested by me, or owing to some cause which cannot now be traced.

Below these come the following clans: (4) Ūrana warigē, which Mr. Nevill called Ūruwa, and put in the sixth place; (5) Nabudena or Namada warigē; (6) Ūrāwāḍiya warigē; (7) Aembalāna, or Aembala warigē; and Mr. Nevill added also (8) Kōvila wanamē; (9) Talā warigē; and three territorial groups, those of (10) Tambalagama, (11) Kaṭṭakulam, and (12) Anurādhapura (? Tamankaḍuwa); as well as (13) the Coast Vaeddas. The warigē names of the last four have been lost. Possibly the Wanniyas should also be included as an additional clan.

He found that the Kōvil wanamē has four territorial sections, those of Dambāna, Miyangoḍa, Mākanda, and Galkaeṭa; but their representatives are now very few in number, and apparently they could give no account of their ancestry, beyond a tradition that it was some members of the Dambāna section who discovered the Goddess Valliyammā as a child in the forest near Kataragama, and adopted and reared her until the War-God Skanda married her. He learnt that it was formerly the duty of this clan to act as guards of the Kataragama temple in south-eastern Ceylon, and that they resided in the district adjoining it.

This temple, dedicated to Skanda, is considered to be one of special sanctity, and is visited by pilgrims from all parts of India, including even the North-west Provinces. How it came to be established in such a site, and to acquire such importance is, I believe, unknown; it must have been partly due to encouragement and support given by the kings of Southern Ceylon in the times when they resided at Tissa or Māgama, which is not far distant.

Possibly Kataragama may have been an important site of the worship of one of the deities of the aborigines. Dr. C. G. Seligmann has informed me that the Forest Vaeddas highly reverence a deity said by them to be the spirit of a Vaedda known during life as Kandē Wanniyā, by which title he is frequently addressed in their invocations. If he was an ancient deity the new settlers may have identified him with Skanda, who is also a hill-god, and to whom worship is paid on the hills by some of the wild tribes of Southern India, according to information derived from a respectable Tamil eyewitness of it. Skanda's usual name in Ceylon, Kanda Kumāra, may have assisted in this identification, which would account for the Vaeddas' becoming the guardians of his temple, with which, however, Kandē Wanniyā is not now connected.

FIG. 35. Skanda and Valliyammā (Tanjore Temple).

To face p. 115.

The princes (who may have been Vaedda chiefs) of Kājaragāma, as the place was then called, were included among the distinguished persons who were present when the celebrated Bō-tree was planted at Anurādhapura in 244 B.C.; and that an important Buddhist monastery was established at the spot at that time is proved by its being selected by King Dēvānampiya Tissa as one of the first places at which a shoot of the Bō-tree was planted. The only inscription that Dr. E. Müller saw there was a defaced one of the fourth century A.D.[1]

Mr. Nevill referred to a local legend that it was at Kataragama that Skanda and his forces defeated the Asuras; and that he also met Valliyammā and married her there, after she had been adopted in a Vaedda family[2]; but I never heard of her being treated as a special goddess by either Sinhalese or Vaeddas. I give an illustration of these two deities (Fig. 35). It represents a panel at the great Saivite temple at Tanjore, and may date from the thirteenth century A.D.

When Dr. Davy visited Kataragama in 1819 he found two enclosures there, and said of them, 'In the largest square are the Kataragama Dēwāla [temple], and the Dēwāla of his brother Gaṇa [Gaṇēsa]; a wihāra dedicated to Buddha in a state of great neglect, and a fine Bo-gaha [Bō-tree]; and six very small kōvils [temples], mere empty cells, which are dedicated to the Goddess Pattinī[3] and to five demons. In the smaller square are contained a little karaṇḍuwa sacred to Īsvara [Śiva], the Kalyāna Madama [shed], a kōvil dedicated to the demon [God] Bhairava, a rest-house for pilgrims, and some offices.'[4]

The tenth, eleventh, and twelfth clans are said by Mr. Nevill to be practically extinct, their members having died out or been absorbed by the surrounding people. The others, who with the exception of the Ūrana warigē, the Ūrāwāḍiya warigē, and the Coast Vaeddas, are very few in number, appear to

[1] *Ancient Inscriptions in Ceylon*, p. 46.

[2] *The Taprobanian*, Vol. i, p. 180.

[3] An account of her will be found in a later chapter, on the Ancient Games.

[4] *An Account of the Interior of Ceylon*, 1821, p. 420. I have corrected the spelling of the names and native words.

have lost all tradition of their origin; but it is possible that patient inquiry by a competent person might elicit some interesting facts, or legends at least, regarding their ancestors.

Pending the publication of Dr. Seligmann's researches, there is not much definite information concerning their social customs. The Village Vaeddas have a simple but formal ceremony similar to that of the Sinhalese, on the day when the child first tastes the food of adults. When the infant is about seven months old the parents fry some Indian corn, or cook some millet porridge, and give a little of this to it, together with a taste of any other food that they possess. It is probably at this ceremony that a name is bestowed on it.

As regards their marriages, Mr. Nevill has condemned the inaccuracy of those who stated that the Vaeddas are accustomed to marry their sisters. This was an Indian custom of early times, however, and the Mahāvansa mentions two traditional cases at least—the parents of Wijaya, and the children of Kuwēnī—in both of which the contracting parties were the children of the same parents. According to the Dasaratha Jātaka (No. 461) Rāma married his sister, Sītā. It seems also probable that Mahā-Nāga, the brother of Dēvānam-piya Tissa, married his sister Anulā; while in the Kunāla Jātaka (No. 536) we find the people of Koliya reviling the Sākyas of Kapilavastu (from whom Mahā-Nāga was descended) as persons who 'cohabited with their own sisters.' Regarding the practice of the Vaeddas I have no direct information; I should accept Mr. Nevill's statement on the subject in preference to those of others who had not the same opportunities of obtaining correct accounts of their ways. Such marriages with sisters are unknown among the Sinhalese of the present day.

Mr. Nevill learnt that among the first eight clans marriage into another territorial section was usual. His remarks are so interesting that I quote them rather fully: 'Thus if A and B are adjacent territories, the bachelor in A goes to B, and marries a wife, if possible his mother's brother's daughter, or the nearest collateral relative similarly connected [that is, through the mother]. The difficulty of finding out who this might be was remedied by adopting the territorial title as a quasi-gotram division ; and our bachelor in A, whose mother came from A and bore that name, would go to B, and marry the first eligible maiden of the B name, with perfect confidence that she belonged to the correct division of the family.

'This caused an apparent division into family clans [subdivisions] which, however, are better termed territorial clans [sections], to avoid confusion with the true hereditary clan. The necessity of taking a wife from a territorial clan [section] C, D, or E, if no available maiden could be found in B, often led to breaks in the propinquity of the descent, and even intermarriage with a new warugē, as distinguished from a territorial section of the same warugē. The warugē divisions [clans], once political or ethnic in origin (at times of mixed ethnic origin by intermarriage out of the Vaedda race), have now become quasi-gōtra or family clans, and are thus to be distinguished from what I term the territorial clans [sections, which are] all branches of the one true gōtra or family clan.

'The rule for marriage was stringent. The daughter represents her mother's family, the son also represents his mother's family [? father's family, as among the Kandian Sinhalese]. In no case did a person marry one of the same family, even though the relationship was lost in remote antiquity. Such a marriage was incest. The penalty for incest was death. Thus the daughter must marry either her father's sister's son or her mother's brother's son, neither of whom would be of the same clan name. [This is the common Kandian custom also.] Failing these she may marry any of their name, and should no such bridegroom be available, marriage into a third family becomes necessary.

'The Vaeddas marry young, and are strict monogamists. Consequently the husband and wife are watchfully jealous, each of the other, and love intrigues are few and far between. Nothing short of murder would content the injured party. This strict morality extends to unmarried girls, who are protected by their natural guardians with the keenest sense of honour. It does not extend, however, to widows, however young and pretty, and a widow who avoids exciting the jealousies of the wives may have love affairs with half the men around, without exciting any wish for revenge among her relations, who would have given their lives at once to avenge any impropriety of conduct while she was single. The women also are said not to show any excessive jealousy of a widow, if her allurements be not too openly talked of.

'As might be expected, when a wild race marries young and the husband and wife remain constant, any unusual festival is often the occasion for riotous sensuality between husband and wife, who then discard all decency in their private intercourse, and break out into licentious love-songs and gestures.

'There are no special marriage ceremonies.'[1]

I was informed by the Village Vaeddas that when a young man thinks of marrying, he selects a suitable girl himself, and speaks on the subject to either her father or mother. Having obtained the necessary consent, he takes up his residence at their house without further ceremony, and the girl becomes his virtual wife. After three or four months have elapsed, and he has cut, and sown, and reaped a temporary clearing in which millet is grown, or has otherwise assisted in providing a supply of food for the family, he is considered to be formally united to the girl. Prior to this, I presume that the union is looked upon as a probationary one, according to the similar practice which is still occasionally followed in the more backward Kandian villages of the interior. It is also a common custom of Kandian villagers not to register their marriage until after the birth of the first child; this leaves the parties free to separate, if they desire to do so, without the trouble of applying for a formal divorce. In such cases the marriage prior to registration is practically a probationary one, like that of the Vaeddas.

The formal consent of a parent, or of the natural guardian if the parents be dead, is the only absolutely necessary part of the Kandian marriage ceremony, which is thus in agreement with the practice of the Vaeddas, and is doubtless derived from them. This consent having been obtained, the living together of the young couple, with or without any other ceremony, constitutes a valid marriage, by ancient Kandian custom. I have known several cases of this kind, in which the permanent union

[1] *The Taprobanian*, Vol. i, p. 177.

was unaccompanied by any ceremony. A recent law of the last decade renders registration compulsory in order to secure the legality of all marriages.

To show that this practice of the Vaeddas is not a mere primitive trait, it is only requisite to refer to the custom in China, where we are told that 'the only *essential* feature of a Chinese wedding is the delivery of the bride at her husband's home.'[1] Among the West African Mandinkō and Jōlas, too, who are certainly not primitive, the consent of the parents renders any marriage valid, and among the latter people there is no formal ceremony.

I am obliged again to borrow the following information regarding funerals from Mr. Nevill's account of them:[2] 'Bodies were never buried until the English Government endeavoured to enforce burial. The Vaeddas have not the least objection to the corpse being buried, but object greatly to being forced to dig the grave, a waste of labour, over mere perishable matter, from which the spirit has gone free, they say.

'The Vaedda religion seems to have been such that the spirit alone was recognised as human, and the flesh, when the spirit has left it, receives neither veneration nor superstitious reverence. Where the life left the body, there the body was left, if safe from wild beasts, or if the family were in a hurry. It was usual to put it in a crevice between rocks, or to cover it with boughs; if no rocks were near, boughs were laid over it. This was merely done in a sense of decency, to prevent wild beasts from feeding upon it. Spirits were not thought to haunt the spot, as among Sinhalese and Tamils, nor did superstition require any funeral rites. Two to five days after the death, however, the relatives were invited to the scene of funeral, and a feast was held. The original object of this seems not to have been religious, but civil. It was in fact a coroner's inquest, and was held to satisfy relations that there had been no foul play. I have hitherto had great difficulty in getting real Vaeddas to discuss the funeral, as they seem to think that I am secretly

[1] Rev. Dr. Smith. *Village Life in China*, p. 269. The italics are his.

[2] *The Taprobanian*, Vol. i, p. 179.

laughing at their want of etiquette on such occasions, and there is nothing a Vaedda dislikes and dreads so much as being despised as a savage.

'The Vaeddas of Bintenna, however, having assembled relations and neighbours, procure rice or other grain, and decorate the pot in which it is cooked with sprays of the Līniya tree (*Helicteres isora*), a shrub with leaves like our hazel, but with bright scarlet flowers. If no flowers can be got, bits of red cotton or other cloth should be used. The celebrant then dances round the pot of food with an arrow in his hand, singing any chant he knows, and making obeisance to the food by a wave of the arrow. The food is then distributed, and it is etiquette not to revisit the spot until the flesh has decayed away. There does not seem to be a dread of pollution ; but rather that feeling which makes us think it bad taste to be seen in a night-dress, etc., by our friends makes the Vaedda think it bad taste to go and stare at the decayed and abandoned body of his friend and neighbour.

'It is evident that this custom cannot apply to those who formerly did not eat grain. These, however, were few. Roasted game would probably with such take the place of grain, and the latter seems only used as the best and most unusual food procurable, much as our poor try to provide cake, and not bread and cheese, etc., at weddings.'

My own information regarding this ceremony is scanty. I was told by them that a few days after the burial they prepare food, in the same manner as the Sinhalese make ready a 'dāna' or feast for the Buddhist monks who attend at their houses on such occasions, and proceed with it to the grave, upon which they place it. They then call the deceased loudly by his name, to come and eat it. After waiting a little time, during which the spirit is supposed to partake of the essence of the food, all the persons present at the grave themselves eat up the whole of the food. After this feast they return to their houses.

The summoning of the dead to share in the repast makes it clear that this ceremony is a farewell feast with the spirit of the deceased person, who, as the honoured guest, is first fed before the rest of the party take their shares of the food.

The Telugu-speaking Gypsies of Ceylon have a similar custom, but in their case the cooking of the food is also done on the grave itself immediately after the burial. Those present at the grave then eat it at the spot. The 'dāna' of the Sinhalese appears to be in its origin the same, or a closely allied, ceremony.

Among the Tamil-speaking Vaeddas the ceremony becomes a religious one, approaching in character that of their Tamil neighbours in honour of the Manes, rather than a farewell feast with the dead, and I therefore include it with other religious ceremonies.

I have no information regarding the social customs of the Wanniyas.

I append a list of some names of Vaeddas, in addition to the few chiefs previously mentioned:—

Vaeddas of the Interior.

MALES.

Patabaendā	Siripālā	Kōnaruwā	Siribaddanayā
Dematānan	Rani	Kirā	Hēratā
Milalānan	Radduwā	Sellā	Haedayā
Kuppeyā	Wanniyā	Vīrā	Milalānā
Bōndā	Roḍḍā	Tissahāmi	Panamayā
Kandā	Yāpā	Puncā	Baḍapissā
Kundā	Randunu Wanniyā	Mutuwā	Kiritandā
Kummā		Rangā	Vannaku Baṇḍa
Kayirā	Nilā	Punyā	Hudu Maeniki
Vaedibekki-rāla	Maenikā		

FEMALES.

Wallī	Rongī	Hudī	Wēratti
Madalēna	Ukku	Wayirī	Rāmī
Rangī	Kandī	Maenikī	Rangaru
Attī	Kirī	Garu	Lattī

Names given by Mr. Nevill, in 'The Taprobanian.'

MALES.		FEMALES.[1]	
Janaya Kattandi	Ahugada	Handi	Maedini
Kalingurāla	Waeliyā	Kawenihami	Rukkuli
Dahagonayā	Siyātū	Kumi	
Binākaya	Rākā		

[1] Probably the final vowel is long in all these names; but it is not so marked by Mr. Nevill.

Southern Vaeddas, chiefly Sinhalese names.

Males.		Females.	
Nanhāmi	Kandā	Kanāttī	Puncihāmī
Maeddam-Appu	Siññō	Umayāttī	Silinduhāmī
Manawālayā	Hudu Baṇḍāra	Kalu	Garu
Sudu-Appu	Raṭērāla	Ranhāmī	Salangu
Isanhāmi	Ganaeti	Maenikī	Kiribaṇḍu
Undiyarāla	Potāna [1]	Wāsanī	Kirō

Tamil-speaking Vaeddas.

Males.		Females.	
Kanakkan	Pālan	Kālī	Nākī
Siddenā	Periya Tūtan	Vallī	Karatī
Pattar	Sinna Tūtan	Tēvī	Vayirī
Sinna	Kayilan	Kandī	Sinnī
Karaval	Yāpan	Sempālā	Pattī
Kanavadi	Vēlan		
Sinnaya	Karatan		
Kandan			

[1] So-called because he was born at a village of that name. There are several place-names in the list of chiefs previously given.

THE VAEDI AND KAELĒ-BĀSA VOCABULARIES

THE Vaedi dialect is to a great extent the colloquial Sinhalese tongue, but is slightly changed in form and accent. Yet closely as it resembles the latter, these differences and the manner in which it is pronounced render it quite an unknown language when it is spoken to one who has not a special acquaintance with it. Besides this, the Vaeddas use their own terms for the wild animals and some other things about which they often find it necessary to converse. Such words are usually a form of Sinhalese, or admit of Sinhalese or Tamil derivations; but a very few may possibly belong to, or be modifications of words in, their original language, forming, with perhaps a few forms of grammatical expression, the only remains of it that have been preserved, with the exception of some doubtful terms found in Sinhalese.

Strange to say, the Kandian Sinhalese and the Wanniyas apparently imitate the Vaeddas while they are hunting in the forests, and also when engaged on ceremonies at their threshing-floors, and use another series of expressions or nicknames for many of the same animals, to the exclusion of the usual names for them. They have acquired a belief that unless a special dialect be employed while they are in the forest, they cannot expect to meet with any success or good luck in seeking honey, or hunting, or in avoiding dangerous animals.

This dialect of the forest is termed Kaelē-bāsa, 'Jungle language.' It consists of the employment of new words not only for animals but also for a few other nouns, and for verbs used to denote acts most commonly performed on such trips. In addition, all negative (that is, unlucky) modes of expression are totally debarred from use on such occasions, as well as the words meaning 'insufficient' and 'too much,' which are inauspicious as indicating dissatisfaction with the number or quantity to which they are applied.

As it appears to have some bearing on the connexion between the Kandian Sinhalese and the Vaeddas, I give a list of the words of this dialect (but not the words used at threshing-floors), together with the Vaedi words, the colloquial Kandian expressions, and their English equivalents.

Where the letter N is suffixed the word is taken from Mr. Nevill's writings. In the cases where no word is given in the Vaedi dialect or Kaelē-bāsa, both the Vaeddas and other hunters employ colloquial Sinhalese words, often slightly altered in pronunciation by the Vaeddas, as by using *c* for *s*, etc. It should be noted that in these lists the letter *c* is pronounced like the English *ch* in *church.* The Vaedi vocabulary which I append is extremely deficient, but that of the Kaelē-bāsa is nearly complete.

The whole of the Kaelē-bāsa vocabulary is not employed in one district. Many words are common to all Sinhalese districts, including even the extreme south of the island; others are found only in special localities.

It is interesting to note that in the north, when a Kandian hunter is addressed in the forest the title 'Vaeddā' should be suffixed to his name; for instance, a person called Baṇḍā would be addressed by his hunting comrades as Baṇḍā-Vaeddā. Among the Wanniyas it is often the forest custom, when telling others to perform actions, to prefix the interjection *Hō*, as *Hō! Yamallā,* 'let us go'; *Hō! Warillā,* 'Come ye.' When inviting persons to eat food they similarly prefix *Hā*, as *Hā! Balāgallā,* 'eat ye.' These interjections are not so used by Sinhalese.

English.	Sinhalese	Kaelē-bāsa.	Vaedi.
		Animals.	
Ant-eater	Kaballayā Kabaellāewā	Pottā, *f.* Potti Āēyā Talkola-pettiyā	Malinyāwā Gal-mundā, N. Gal-gawarā, N.
Axe-man	Poro-kārayā	Waḍuwā	—
Bear	Walahā *f.* Waelihīnī	Uyangowwā Tadiyā, *f.* Tadī Kaluwā, *f.* Kalu-Waelihīnī Gamayā, *f.* Gamī	Keriyā Balā Haeccā, N. Walā, N. Araci, N. Baraci, N. Keri-boṭā, N.
Beast	Sīpāwā	—	Boṭā Sipā, N. Hipā, N. Haturā, N.
Bee, honey	Mī maessā	—	Kuḍā Maehikeli Kuḍā Maeyikeli
,, humble	Bumbaeli-maessā	—	Penda-uli, N.
,, large	Bambarā	—	Mā Maehikeli Mā Maeyikeli
,, small	Kuḍā Mī-maessā	—	Hīn Maehikeli Hīn Maeyikeli
Bird	Kurullā	—	Cappiyā, *f.* Cappī Sappī, N.
Buffalo	Mīwā	Ambaruwā Gawayā Pimbinnā, N.	Manyā, *f.* Manyī Wal Mannya, N.
Cattle	Harak	Bolla, N.	Mannya, N.
Child	Lamayā	—	Kaekulā, *pl.* Kaekul-petō Ammī, N. Bilindā, N.
Civet Cat	Urulāēwā	Appala-baeṭaeyā Hoṭaembiliyā Hōtambayā	—
Cobra	Nayā	Bōyi-satteyā	—
Cow	Eladena	—	Gonadena, N. Gonī, N.
Crocodile	Kimbulā	Gamayā	—
Deer, Axis	Pit-muwā	Ambaruwā Pit-paelaellā	Kewulā Kabara-boṭā., N. Muwa-kewarā, N.
,, Mouse	Mīminnā	Kekkā, *f.* Kekkī Yakaḍayā Dangarayā, N.	Lembu, N. Kewurā, N.
,, Red	Waeli-muwā	Rat-baḍayā, N.	—

English.	Sinhalese.	Kaelē-bāsa.	Vaedi.
Deer, Sambar	Gōnā	Ambaruwā Karakolayā Pollā, *f.* Pollī	Gawara Mahagallā Hela-kaṭā, Keri-gonā Gawarā, N. Gal-gawara, N. Kaṭa-kaebaelā, N. Māgāl, N.
Deity	Deviyā	—	Hurā
Dog	Ballā	Aedurā Bandinnā, *f.* Bandinnī Hatara-bāgayā Hatara-bāga-aettā	Kukka, f. Kikkī Balo, N. Koṭawā, N.
Elephant	Aliyā Aetā (tusker)	Uhallā Usallā, *f.* Usallī Usangallā Gajjarā, N.	Boṭā, *f.* Boṭī Boṭa-kandā Gōmbara-Uhallā Aet-boṭā, N. Boṭa-Kabalā, N. Kadā, N. Kota baebēlā, N. Mōlā, N.
Father	Piyā Appā	—	Appā-latto, N.
Fish	Mālu	Mas	—
„ small	Kuḍā-massaṇ Uriyan Tittayō	Gembō	—
Hare	Hāwā	Yakdessā Yaddessā	Yak-kadayā, N.
Hornbill (*Tockus*)	Kāēndettā	Aeṭa-raetiyā Aettiriyā Raetiyā	—
Hornet	Debarā	Patarambayā	Dembara-maeccā, N.
'Iguana' (*Varanus*)	Goyā, *f.* goyī	Kaeraellā Kapurāla (aged) Mandā, *f.* Mandī	Mundā, *f.* Mundī Go-kandā, N. Go-mundā, N. Goy-boṭā, N. Mūndā, N.
„ tied in a circle for carrying	—	Mandu-walalla	—
Kingfisher	Piḷihuḍuwā	—	Tākan, N. (Tamil)
Kite, Brahminy	Ukussā	Māralu	—
Lapwing (*Lobivanellus*)	Kiralā	—	Aeṭi
Leopard	Koṭiyā	Diviyā Siwupāwā Baedi-mutā, N. Raenaya, N.	Kapuru-ballā Polleccā Mitā, N. Mita-boṭā, N.
Little one	Pettiyā	—	Peccā, *f.* Peccī

English.	Sinhalese.	Kaelē-bāsa.	Vaedi.
Lizard (*Calotes*)	Kaṭussā	—	Kaṭ-tombā, N.
Lord	Swāmi	Himi	Hurā
Man	Minihā	Hobarayā	Minā, *pl.* Minu Minna, N.
Monkey (*Semnopithecus*)	Wandurā	Gas-gonā Gas-gōnā	Uḍa-kelinnā Keri-bandurā, N. Mā-bandurā, N.
Monkey (*Thersites*)	Rilawā	Kandaṇ-paninnā Paṭagahāpu-ekā	Hil-bandurā, N. Hossā, N. (?) Nilawā, N. Rila-patayā, N.
Mungus	Mugaṭiyā	Appalą-baeṭaeyā Hō-tambayā	—
Pig	Ūrā	Hoṭa-barayā, *f.* Hoṭa-barī Tadiyā, *f.* Tadī Tel-kaliyā	Dolā, *f.* Dolī Hocca-dikkā Gal-boṭā, N. Hossa-ullā, N.
Porcupine	Ittāēwā	Ittaeyā Kaṭuwā	Iddāēyā, N. Hiccā, N. Nittāēwā, N.
Snail (land)	Gombaellā	—	Tombā, N.
Snake	Sarpayā	Isa-gora-satteyā	Tola-gaeccā Sara-boṭā, N. Urasā, N.
Turtle	Ibbā	Diya-kukulā, N.	—
Wife	Hirē	—	Nāenā, N.
Woman	Gāēnī	—	Minī, *pl.* Minilā Maeli, N.
Youth	Ilandārayā	—	Kaekulā, *f.* Kaekulī

GENERAL NOUNS.

English.	Sinhalese.	Kaelē-bāsa.	Vaedi.
Areka-nut	Puwak-geḍi	Golaeya (unripe) Kahata-geḍi Kaeppiṭi-geḍi	—
Arrow	Īgaha	—	Ītala, N. Moriyan-kecca, N.
Axe	Porawa	Koṭanna Poro-waḍuwa Waḍuwa	At-barawa Gal-raekki Porawa-pecca
Bark bag	Malla	—	Riṭi-malla Patta-malla
„ basket	Peṭṭiya	—	Patta-peṭṭiya
„ of branch	Atu-potta	Rana-potta	—
Betel-leaf	Bulat kola	Bōl Bōl-kola Bōl-pana Daehaet Paengiri	—
Billhook	Kaetta	Āwudae Kaeti-waḍuwa	Adināta Malā-koti

English.	Sinhalese.	Kaelē-bāsa.	Vaedi.
Billhook, golden	Ran-kaetta	—	Manna-kaetta
Blade	Talē	—	Kaecca, N.
Blood	Lē	Tuwāla	—
,, track	Lē-pāra	Kiri-pāra	—
Body	Sarīra	—	Bo-pata, N.
Bow	Dunna	—	Dun-gā, N.
,, string	Dunu-lanuwa	—	Dunu-ḍiya
Cave	Gal-gē	—	Galigē
	Lena		Rukkula, N.
Chillies	Raṭa-miris	Serapalu	—
Clan	Gōtra	—	Warigē
			Warugē, N.
Clouds	Walāhula	—	Gal-pēriya, N.
Cold	Śīta	—	Ehna, N. (?)
Cross-roads	Maṇ-handiya	—	Rūppē.
Earth (ground)	Bima	Būmi	Polawē-waeli
			Bimi, N.
Eye	Aeha	—	Eccel, N.
Fat	Tel	Kapparu, N.	—
Fire	Gindara	Ratta	Ginna
	Gini		Ginname
	Ginna (body-heat)		Pimbināta
Fire-wood	Dara	Pīrumbu	—
Flesh	Mālu	Higaman, N.	—
	Mas		
Flock	Raela	Kāya, N.	—
Food (cooked)	Kāēma	Pas	—
Forest	Mūkalāna	Himāla	Baedde, N.
		Uyana	Gāla, N.
Found things	—	Tāēgi (with *v.* lebenawā)	—
Friend	Yāluwa	—	Kimbune, N.
Gourd	Labu-geḍi	Kalu-gaeṭaeya	—
		Suraya	
		Titta-gaeṭi	
Gourd, for water	Labba	Dabarāēwa	Panlīya
		Pāndāwa	
Hair (of head)	Isa-kes	—	Īca-Kola, N.
Halting-place	Wāḍiya	—	Rūppē
Head	Isa	—	Īca, N.
	Oluwa		Isi, N.
			Iya, N.
Heat	Ushna	—	Gina, N.
Hive (of Mī-maessā)	Mīya	Gabaḍāēwa	Maehikeli-gama
		Gabaḍāwa	
Honey	Mī-paeni	Bora	Meccan, N.
			Micca, N.
			Mijja, N.
			Mijjaka-pēni, N.
			Minji-paeni, N.

English.	Sinhalese.	Kaelē-bāsa.	Vaedi.
Honey-comb	Mī-wada	Padaya, N.	—
Horns	Aṇ	Araṭu Tōḍu Wakaṭa-padaya, N.	—
House	Gē	—	Gal-gama Tūn-gē (hut) Rukkula, N.
Jungle	Kaelē Wal	Himāla Uyana	—
Ladder (cane)	Wē-wael ini-maga	—	Ran-kendiya, N.
Leg	Kakula	—	Danis patul, N.
Lightning	Widuliya	—	Gini-waeṭunu, N.
Loin-cloth	Kōnama	—	Kōnam-poḍge
Millet	Kurahan	Alu	—
,, cake	Roṭi	Alu-lēlli Alu-pota Alu-pūwa Gini-pūwa	—
,, flour	Kurahan-piṭi	Alu-kuḍu	—
Moon	Handa	—	Pāna-pojja, N.
Noise	Sabda	—	Anda, N.
Nose	Nāhē	—	Naya N.
Piece	Kāēlla	—	Kate, N.
Porridge	Talapa	Kūla	—
Rain	Waessa Warusāwa	—	Diya-pompa, N. Waecca, N. Waecca-wata, N.
Rice, cooked	Bat	Arambu Bubbara	—
,, uncooked	Hāl	Lawal-aeṭa	Pubbura, N. Waṭa-kuru, N.
,, unhusked	Vī	Kiri lawal-aeṭa	Depaṭulaṇ, N. Depurul, N.
River	Oya	—	Diya-gama, N.
Sea	Muhuda	—	Sawu, N.
Sky	Ahasa	—	Dewu-ula, N.
Stage (of journey)	Hatakma	—	Pilluma
Stream	Aela	—	Diyagama, N.
Snout	Hossa	—	Hocca
Sun	Ira	Sūriya	Ira-pojja, N.
Thorn	Kaṭuwa	Panaraela, N.	—
Thunder	Ahasa gaera-wīma	—	Dewu-ula ande, N.
Tobacco	Duṇ-kola	Paepol-roḍu Sera-kola	—
Touchwood	—	Pīrumbu	—
Tree	Gaha	Hoṇḍa Hoṇḍe Hoṇḍeya	Gā, *pl.* Gāyi Guye (?), N.

English.	Sinhalese.	Kaelē-bāsa.	Vaedi.
Troop	Raela	Kāya, N.	—
Village	Gama	—	No word
Water	Diya Watura	Dīra Gangula, N. Hoṇḍa Pāēdi Paeheyiya Paeṇ	Diya
Wind	Hulanga	Wātaya	—

VERBS, AND OTHER WORDS.

English.	Sinhalese.	Kaelē-bāsa.	Vaedi.
Arise, to (from sleep)	Naegiṭinawā	Suṇ elāgannawā	—
Before	Issarahaṭa	—	Iccaṭa, N.
Behind	Passaṭa	—	Paccaṭa, N.
Call, to	Andagahanawā	—	Kilāpā, N. Anda-talāpā, N
Cannot	Bāē	Issaraṭa (with dative) Passē puluwani	—
Catch, to (with hand)	Allanawā	(Ata) gahanawā	—
Chew, to	Koṭanawā	Koṭabānawā	—
Chop, to (with axe)	Koṭanawā	Waḍulanawā Waḍuranawā	—
Cohabit, to	Saṇwāsaya karanawā	—	Penna-ganna, N.
Cold, to be	Sītā-wenawā	—	Hītā-gana, N. Hītā-pura, N.
Come, to	Enawā	Bandinawa, N. Pahāsu-wenawā	Enna (Fut. 1st pers. sing. Ennammā)
Cook, to (broil, etc.)	Uyanawā	Tambanawā	—
Cut, to	Kapanawā	Mān-karanawā, N.	
Die, to	Maerenawā	--	Miya, N. Miyala inda, N. Miyala yā, N. Sala yā, N.
Dig the ground, to	Polawa hāranawā	Bin-dinawā	—
Distant	Āēta	—	Naekat, N.
Do not	—	Issaraṭa Passē puluwani	—
Drink to	Bonawā	Balanawā	Diya ka, N. Ukā, N.
Eat, to	Kanawā	Balanawā	Baḍa-banda, N. Kāpā, N. Kāpāt-ena, N.

English.	Sinhalese.	Kaelē-bāsa.	Vaedi.
Go, to	Yanawā	Baendenawā Haerenawā Issarahāēṭa bahinawā Karana karanawā Issara balanawā, N.	Mangaccana (Fut. 1st pers. sing. Maŋgaccan. Imp. 2nd pers. sing. Mangaccapa). Palacca, N.
„ to jungle	Kaelēṭa yanawā	Himāla wadinawā	—
Here	Mehi	—	Meṭṭa
Hold, to	Allanawā	Bandinawā	—
Hot, to become	Unu-wenawa	—	Radaga, N.
Hungry, to be	Baḍagini allanawā	—	Dālaga, N.
Insufficient	Madi	Bōyi	—
Journey, to	Gaman-karanawā	—	Gamana Miṭa-gana, N.
Jump, to	Paninawā	—	Boṭa-dama, N. Duwa, N. Paena, N. Paran-dena, N.
Kindle (fire), to	Pattu-karanawā	Mahi-karanawā Pawatanawā, N.	Awuccana, N.
„ (by cross-friction)	Mandinawā	Mandinawā	—
„ (by twirling-stick)	Gini-gānawā	Gini-gānawā	Gini-gāna Gini-gahen ginna ganna
Large, great	Maha	Gaja	Mā
Little	Kuḍā Puñci	—	Taenak, N.
Long	Diga	—	Dikka
Mend (fire), to	Bō-karanawā	Mahat-karanawā Pawattanawā	—
Meet with, obtain	Samba-wenawā	Haeppenawā	—
No	Nāē	Bōyi	Koḍāwā[1]
Not	Naeti	—	Koḍāwā
Pudendum (*f.*)	—	—	Hantāna patiliya, N. Mala kabala, N.
„ (*m.*)	—	—	Hantāna pole, N.
Quickly	Lahi Wigahaṭa	—	Numā, N. Perumāt, N.
Rain, to	Wahinawā	Gangula-bānawā, N.	Diya pompa, N.
Run, to	Duwanawā	—	Paena uccā, N.
See, to	Dakinawā	—	Reviga, N.
Shoot (with arrow), to	Widinawā	—	Penna-ga, N. Wida-bacca, N. Wida-ga, N.

[1] Compare Sin. *nokaḍawa*, always, ever (*lit.* unbroken); without the negative particle *kaḍawa* would thus mean 'never.'

English.	Sinhalese.	Kaelē-bāsa.	Vaed
Skin, to	Hama-gahan-awā	Honda-karanawā	—
Sleep, to	Budi-wenawā Ninda-gan-nawā	Bōyi-karanawā	Nida, N.
So much	Occara	—	Witara, N.
Speak, to	Kiyanawā	Galu-karanawā, N.	Bana, N. Guwā-kara, N. Guwā, N. Katan-kiya, N. Kewili-la, N.
There	Ohe	—	Oṭṭa
,, (distant)	Aha	—	Aramba
That side	Oya petta	—	Oba Obba, N. Otaka, N.
This side	Mē-petta	—	Meba Mebaga Mobba, N.
Tie (an Iguana), to	—	Manduranawā	—
Walk, to	Ewidinawā	Tamananawā	Gaman ila gana, N. Gaman ina, N. Miṭa gana, N.
Where	Kohē	—	Kōde, N. Kōyde, N.
Whet, to	Madinawā	Honda-karanawā	—
Why	Eyi	—	Ayi
Yes	Hā Ēhē Owu	—	Hā Īta, N.
You	Tō (thou), *pl.* Tōpi Umba	—	Toba, N. Toban, N. Topa, N. Topan, N.
Young	Lapati Taruna	—	Elama, N.

IV

THE RELIGION OF THE VAEDDAS AND WANNIYAS

THE DEITIES

THE Vaeddas are not Buddhists, but a few who live in the villages of the interior sometimes visit a Buddhist temple and offer flowers there, if there is such a place in their neighbourhood. Neither the Forest nor Village Vaeddas pay any regular worship to the superior Indian Gods under their present names, although some of the latter make occasional offerings to Skanda, as the god of Kataragama.

The northern Tamil-speaking Vaeddas to the south of Trincomalee periodically visit and present offerings at the Hindu temples of their vicinity ; these are devoted to Skanda, who is known as Kumāra Tēvan, and Gaṇēsa, called by them Pulikāra Tēvan, 'the God Pilleiyār.' They also make offerings in the jungle to seven Goddesses, termed 'the Seven Kannimār,' or Maidens, whose names they do not know.

The Wanniyas of the north-eastern part of the North-central Province describe themselves as Buddhists, and sometimes pay visits to the Buddhist temples near them ; and the older men at times take the eight vows, or 'Aṭasil,' of the Upāsakas or lay-devotees. These are the vows of adherence to the prohibitions against murder, theft, falsehood, drinking intoxicating liquor, and unlawful sexual intercourse, forming the 'Pansil,' or five vows that all devout Buddhists should keep ; and three additional ones against nocturnal eating, the personal use of garlands and perfumes, and sleeping on anything but a mat laid on the ground. Persons who adhere to the Aṭasil are expected to be regular in their attendance at the temples on the Poya days, at the quarters of the moon, and also must particularly avoid taking life of any kind.

With possibly the sole exception of the Wanniyas, all Village Vaeddas alike, according to my information, when cautiously interrogated, acknowledge that their chief deity is the God whom they know as the Galē Yakā, although some who afterwards showed me a temple erected to him in their village at first denied all knowledge of him when I questioned them regarding him. The Vaeddas of the interior, including those of the Madura-oya valley, stated to me that all worship him. One man remarked to me, "He is the greatest of all Gods." As the ancestors of many who are now classed as Village Vaeddas were certainly true Forest Vaeddas three-quarters of a century ago it would appear that the Forest Vaeddas cannot be ignorant of this deity, but most probably have the same belief in him. I mention this as Dr. Seligmann, who has recently investigated the religion of the Forest Vaeddas, has informed me that he obtained no information regarding him from the Madura-oya villages.[1] After my own experience of a refusal of Village Vaeddas to divulge their worship of him to me I am inclined to believe that their knowledge of him was intentionally concealed.

Literally the name means 'the Demon of the Rock'; but as their male deities are all termed 'Yakā,' whether beneficent or malevolent, the true signification of the expression, as it was explained to me in Sinhalese by them, is 'the God of the Rock,' a name identical with that by which he is known and worshipped by the Kandian Sinhalese, who call him the Galē Deviyā.

The Tamil-speaking Vaeddas term him Malei Pei, 'the Hill Demon'; Kallu Pei, 'the Rock Demon'; Maleiyan, 'He of the Hill'; and Maleiya-swāmi, 'Hill Lord.' I give an account of his worship in a separate chapter ;-it appears to be the primitive cult of the island. It was apparently this deity

[1] He is mentioned by name as the 'Indigollāē Yakā' in one invocation of the Forest Vaeddas which Dr. Seligmann was good enough to send me, and another was apparently addressed to him as the 'King of the Hills.'

who was known as the Vyādha Dēva, 'the Vaedda God,' in the time of Paṇḍukābhaya, that is, in the fourth century B.C.; and possibly he was the God mentioned under the name of Puradēva, 'the Ancient God,' in the time of Duṭṭha-Gāmiṇi (Mah. i, p. 100), as having a temple at Anurādhapura.

The Village Vaeddas also greatly reverence a Goddess known as the Kiri-Ammā, which means in Sinhalese 'Grandmother,' but in reality in its use by the Vaeddas is equivalent to the Indian and Sinhalese word Dēvī, 'Goddess,' which is not employed by them.

Mr. Nevill considered her to be a form of Parvatī, the wife of the God Śiva, who, as the mountain-born goddess, the daughter of the Himālaya personified, is called in Tamil Kiri-Amman, 'the Hill Mother,' *kiri* being the Tamil form of the Sanskrit word *giri*, hill or mountain. So far as the name and position of the goddess are concerned, this identification appears to be quite satisfactory. On the other hand, it is to be observed that the expression 'Kiri-Ammā' is applied by both Vaeddas and Sinhalese to other goddesses who are not connected in any way with hills. For this reason the name itself cannot be accepted as proof that the goddess in question is really Parvatī, unless there is some confirmation of her personality from other directions. It is also noteworthy that the Tamil-speaking Vaeddas do not recognise her, although they worship other Hindu gods.

In the villages of the interior, where the ancient traditions and practices are better preserved than near the coast, where Tamil influences have affected some of the religious notions of the Vaeddas, this goddess is held to be the most important deity next to the God of the Rock or Hill, whose wife she is supposed to be. This would tell strongly in favour of her being Parvatī if the God of the Rock were Śiva. Yet we do not find her worshipped on the hills like the Galē Yakā; she is chiefly, if not entirely, a Forest-Goddess, and it is to her that the Village Vaeddas of the interior especially appeal for protection and good-luck in hunting, their chief occupation. She is known as the Indigollāēwa Kiri-Ammā—her husband the Galē Yakā being also called the Indigollāēwa Yakā—or the Kukulāpola Kiri-Ammā. The last place is a village of the Vaedi-raṭa (as the district inhabited by the Vaeddas is termed), on the west bank of the Madura-oya; while Indigollāēwa is in the North-central Province, near Kalāwaewa, and there is a temple at it devoted to her and her husband.

According to the tradition of that district she is not Parvatī, but Mōhinī, the beautiful incarnation of Vishnu, who was also a Hill-God,[1] and who, according to Indian authorities, took her form temporarily so as to enable the Gods to cheat[2] the Demons at the celebrated Churning of the Ocean by the Gods and Asuras (or demons) in order to produce Amrita, the Liquor of Immortality. The admiring and unsuspecting demons agreed that the lovely Mōhinī should divide the Amrita between them and the Gods. She separated them into two rows, and then distributed the whole to those in the Gods' row, to whom she gave it first.

One Asura sat among them, and thus obtained a share of the precious drink. The Sun and Moon observed this and pointed him out to Mōhinī, who promptly cut off his head; but the magic liquor had already conferred immortality on him, and therefore Brahmā, who always found a way of dealing with apparently insuperable difficulties, transformed the two parts into heavenly bodies. The tail or body became a comet, and the head a planetary sign called Rāhu, which as a heavenly dragon endeavours by way of revenge to swallow the Sun and Moon, and thus causes eclipses. On account of the unfair treatment of the demons by the Gods on this occasion, there has been undying feud between the two classes of supernatural beings from that day.

Some confirmation of the identification of the Kiri-Ammā as Mōhinī is to be seen in the fact that throughout the interior of Ceylon, Ayiyanār, the son of Mōhinī, is everywhere considered to be also a Forest-God, who specially guards travellers in the forests and jungles when they appeal to him for pro-

[1] In the Rig Veda, i, 154, 3 (Griffiths' translation), he is called 'The Bull far-striding, dwelling on the mountains.'

[2] Her name is derived from the word *Mōhani*, delusion, fascination, and in South India she is always colloquially termed Mōhanī.

FIG. 36. Mōhinī (Rāmaswāmi Temple, Kumbakōnam).

To face p. 136.

tection—and is certainly not a Hill-God. On the whole evidence, therefore, and especially since the Vaeddas do not treat her as a Hill-Goddess, I am inclined to accept the only native explanation of the identity of the Kiri-Ammā which I have been able to find, and to look upon her as a form of Mōhinī rather than Parvatī.

Seven other Goddesses, who are also termed Kiri-Ammās, are revered collectively in the south. They are stated to have been originally influential chieftainesses who have been deified, possibly in comparatively recent times. Their names are given as : (1) Mīriyabaedda Kiri-Ammā, the most important of them ; (2) Pusmarāga Kiri-Ammā ; (3) Unāpāna Kiri-Ammā ; (4) Kosgama Kiri-Ammā ; (5) Bōwelagedara Kiri-Ammā ; (6) Bālagiri Kiri-Ammā ; and (7) Ginigal Dēvatāgē Kiri-Ammā. The last one evidently belongs to a different class from the others, and is clearly the Śaktī or female manifestation of the minor deity called Ginigal Dēvatā. There is some doubt regarding the class to which Bālagiri Kiri-Ammā belongs. These are all beneficent deities, that is, Goddesses.

Of the same class, according to Mr. Nevill, is Bōwala Dēyā, who may be connected with the fifth one in the list just given. He is believed by Mr. Nevill to be a late instance of the propitiation of a local chief who became an evil spirit after his death. He resembles the numerous Baṇḍāras of the Kandian Sinhalese, by whom more than one hundred are enumerated, some having protective powers though all are ranked as demons. Panikki Vaeddā, already mentioned, is included among them ; Dr. Seligmann informs me that a person of this name is a spirit deity of one group of the Forest Vaeddas. He traced the belief in him to a Vedarāla, or village doctor, of mixed descent. The older men do not recognise him.

According to the description of them supplied to Mr. Nevill, a group of deities called the Uḍa Yakō, 'the Upper Yakās,' or 'the Yakās who live Above,' are the most important gods of the Vaeddas. Their individuality is stated by him to be ill-defined ; they occupy the position of superior nebulous spirits who are 'like little children,' and who apparently neither do much good nor much harm to mankind. The expression evidently merely corresponds to the collective term, Ātāla Deviyō, of the Sinhalese, 'the Gods of the Upper World,' in contradistinction to the Pātāla Deviyō, 'the Gods of the Lower World.'

After the Uḍa Yakō, Mr. Nevill places the Bilindu Yakō, literally 'the Children Demons,' said to be a father and son, the mother of the latter being thought to be the Kukulāpola Kiri-Ammā, while the child is supposed 'to have died shortly after birth, and to be now separately gifted with divine powers.' Some state that the Bilindu Yakō are two brothers; others say that they are seven in number. It is apparent that their identity is uncertain. I have no knowledge of them, but perhaps it may be assumed that the first account of them, being the most definite, is the most likely to be correct.

The younger one is said by Mr. Nevill to be the Ilandāri Dēvatā of the Coast Tamils, who is also one of the deities of the Wanniyas, and is known to the Kandian Sinhalese as a son of the Kiri-Ammā, thus confirming the relationship.

The elder one is identified by Mr. Nevill as a Mūdē Dēyiyā, or 'God of the Sea,' of the Coast Vaeddas, but I am not aware for what reason, as the Sea God is not described by him as being the husband of the Kiri-Ammā. As her consort, the elder Bilindā Yakā would appear to be the Hill God. The functions of these deities are said to be warding off disease, granting food, and generally protecting their worshippers from unseen dangers; they are thus similar to those of the Hill-God.

Mr. Nevill also mentions a Mā Yakinī,[1] 'the Great Goddess,' who appears to be the Indigollāēwa Kiri-Ammā; (2) Unāpāna Yakinī, who is evidently the Unāpāna Kiri-Ammā; (3) Kino-mal Nāccī,[2] 'the Blue-lotus (coloured) Lady,' whose symbols are an arrow and a bowl of water, and who is the protectress of hunters, and therefore apparently another form of the Indigollāēwa Kiri-Ammā; and (4) a Baedi-Maelī, 'the Woman of the Jungle,' who has similar functions and

[1] Yakinī, or Yaksanī, the usual colloquial expression, is the feminine form of Yakā.

[2] The letter *C* is pronounced as *Ch* in all transliterations.

may be the same person. These deities are beneficent, and therefore are Goddesses.

I also heard of one called Gōmbara Nāccī Yaksanī, 'the Freckled Lady'; she is said to be the wife of the Galē Yakā. She must therefore be a form of the Kiri-Ammā, all these deities being, like the Vaeddas, strictly monogamous.

So far as I learnt, there is only one other kindly deity, the Gangē Baṇḍāra, 'the Chief of the River,' whose aid and countenance are sometimes invoked in the interior when the Vaeddas are about to proceed on a hunting trip. He is known also in the north-western Kandian districts. The Vaeddas locate him at Yāngala, near the Mahawaeli-ganga, but he has no temple there.

King Mahā-Sēna, who is worshipped by the Kandians and the Wanniyas under the title of Sat Rajjuruwō, is not known to the Vaeddas, either in the form of a deity or otherwise.

Next come the malevolent deities also called Yakās, a title which in their case means 'demons.' They cause the various evils that afflict the Vaeddas, and their position is exactly the same as that of the evil spirits whom the Sinhalese denominate Yakās. Sickness or misfortune of every kind is especially attributed to them; but some of them also exhibit their spite by throwing down rocks from the cliffs when people are passing by, and by frightening them in the night by strange cries and noises, the latter including the clapping of hands.

These other Yakās, who are thus generally harmful, belong to two categories, those known by names found only in the interior tract of the Vaedi-raṭa, and those recognised in other parts.

Of the former, Paeraet Yakā is one of the most powerful, he may represent the Daeḍimuṇḍā Yakā of the Sinhalese districts, if, as is probable, his name contains a reference to his being defeated (*paeraeddunā*) by Buddha in his conflict with the forces of Māra. According to the Sinhalese accounts, this demon alone did not run away when Māra's army was defeated, but crept under Buddha's throne; he was therefore called by Buddha "Daeḍiyā," 'the Resolute One,' a title that does not strike one as being particularly applicable under the circumstances. Daeḍimuṇḍā is connected by a legend with the construction of Alut-Nuwara or Mahiyangana, apparently an early Vaedda settlement, which has been already mentioned as the site of one of their early battles. He is also known by the Sinhalese as Dēvatā Baṇḍāra, 'the Godling Chief,' and Alut-Nuwara Baṇḍāra, 'the Chief of Alut-nuwara.' As Daeḍimuṇḍā, I was informed by them that he is considered to be an 'Aemaptya,' or minister, of Vishnu, and the son of a demon termed Mānawakā or Mānōkā, who was the spirit of a Mānā or Black Stork (*Dissura episcopa*), which was caught by a pandita named Widurā,[1] yoked to a plough, and forced to plough a field for him. Daeḍimuṇḍā is considered by the Sinhalese to be the most powerful of all demons, and to rank next to Wessawana, or Kuvēra, the Overlord of all Yakshas. It seems possible that the Vaedi name 'Paeraet' has suggested his identification with a Yaksha of the Sinhalese. His connection with Mahiyangana, which he is said to have built, may indicate that he was an original deity of the Vaeddas.

Among the Yakās of this class mentioned by Mr. Nevill, the Kumbē Yakā is noted by him as being the most dreaded by the Vaeddas, and as being a very powerful and vindictive demon. I have no other information regarding him, and not having a full account of his attributes and special powers I cannot state if he is a demon of the Sinhalese. Their Saeda or Haeda Yakā is said by some to hold the next rank to Daeḍimuṇḍā. His name, which means 'strong' or 'cruel,' shows that his character is like that of the Kumbē Yakā; but it is uncertain if the two are identical.

There is also a possibility that the name of the powerful Kohombē Yakā of the Sinhalese, and of Southern India, 'the Demon of the Margosa (tree)' may have been contracted; or perhaps it may be derived from the Vaedi name Kumbē Yakā. There are reasons for believing that the Kohombē

[1] The hero of the Vidhura Pandita Jātaka (No. 545). It was as a punishment for his cruelty to the unfortunate Stork that the demon Puṇṇaka subsequently ill-treated the saint.

Yakā is an original demon of the Vaeddas; he has as subordinates three 'Vaedi Yakās,' and also twelve others who are termed 'Vaedi Kaḍawarayō,' and who are of inferior rank under him. The Kumbē Yakā is not likely to be the zodiacal sign Kumbha (Aquarius), which is represented by the Sinhalese as a demon with a human body and the head of a dog.

The Gini Rāhu Yakā, 'whose worship seems a little mixed up with a Goddess known as Alut Yakinī, the New Demoness,' who is represented as his wife, is thought by Mr. Nevill to be a form of Agni, on account of his name, and his symbol, a burning torch. This identification seems to me to be doubtful, partly on account of the character of the Śaktī, who is said to be connected with water, and apparently to have been produced in the sea; and also because no worship is paid to Agni in any form by the Sinhalese, so far as I am aware.

He is more likely to be a form of the demon Rāhu already mentioned in connection with Mōhinī, than of Agni. The Sinhalese consider that Rāhu the dragon has the form of a snake, and that he rides on a horse, holding a fish as his symbol.[1] This indicates some connection with water. Offerings are made to Rāhu by the Sinhalese, as well as to other planetary signs, which are all considered to be evil demons who afflict mankind.

There are only three deities to whom fire-worship, termed Gini Mangalya, is paid by the Sinhalese; in order of importance these are Pattinī Dēvī, an incarnation of Durgā, Vīramuṇḍā Deviyā, and Devol or Devel Deviyā. All are importations from Southern India. The Tamils of India and Ceylon have fire ceremonies in honour of Vīrabhadra, Ḍraupadī and Dēvī-Amman, who is either Paṭtinī or a form of Śaktī, the daughter of Daksha and wife of Śiva. The Gini Rāhu Yakā does not appear to be one of the two male Sinhalese

[1] The description of Rāhu in *Hindoo Castes* is taken from Ward as follows:—'This god is painted black; wears black garments; rides on a lion; has four arms, in which he holds a scimitar, a spear, and a shield, and with the other hand he gives a blessing.' The Vaedi name may mean 'the Fiery Rāhu Demon.'

deities, who are termed Gods and not demons. Torches are used freely in many dances in honour of demons, and in themselves are no proof of any connection with fire-worship.

If the Wana-gatta Yakā is, as Mr. Nevill said, the deity whose power extended over the forests, and who 'is propitiated only when great want of success follows the huntsman's toils,' his character among the Vaeddas is very different from that of the Forest-Deities of the Sinhalese and Wanniyas. Mr. Nevill described this demon as 'a dreaded spirit, and the sacrifices and incantations are regarded with intense terror and faith, and only resorted to in extremities.'[1] He stated that the offerings made to him are 'clothes and blood,' and he therefore considered him to be 'clearly a form of Bhairava.' Blood, however, is offered by the Sinhalese to many demons, if not to all. Clothes are not presented to any demons by them, I believe, and in any case would appear to be an unnecessary and inappropriate gift to beings of this type. Have the irresistible forces of civilisation begun to affect their ideas of propriety?

Bhairava is not a Forest God; in Ceylon he is known as Bahirawā Deviyā, and as a form of the God Śiva he is a deity of the Underworld, or Pātāla. In Ceylon his special function is acting as guardian of sacred edifices such as dāgabas or wihāras, and treasures, and everything underground (see Fig. 160). He has eight forms, termed the Ashṭa Kāli Bahirawayō, to whom, collectively, worship is paid by the Sinhalese. In another aspect he is a truculent demon called Bahirawā Yakā, whose duty it is to punish those who break into temples, or dāgabas, or who open the ground (as for wells or mining work), or excavate treasure, without first obtaining the permission of the Bahirawā Deviyā.

The characteristics of the Wana-gatta Yakā, as abovenoted, do not, if he is a Forest Deity, point either to Bahirawā, or to the usual Forest-Gods, whose functions are decidedly

[1] *The Taprobanian*, Vol. i, p. 196; at p. 183, however, he is identified by Mr. Nevill with the 'Wanni Dēva,' that is, the Wanni Deviyā (Wanni Baṇḍāra of the northern part of the North-central Province), who is said by some to be Ayiyanār, but who possibly may be Bilindā Yakā, and he is not a demon, but a Guardian Forest God.

protective, and who are appealed to on the slightest pretext by all travellers in the jungle, whether under the name of the Wanniyā Baṇḍāra of the Wanniyas, or the Wanni Deviyā, or Ayiyanār, or Skanda as the 'Kataragama God,' of the northern and north-western Kandians.

Regarding Kalu Vaedda Yakā I have no knowledge. Mr. Nevill identifies him as the Kalu Yakā, 'the Black Demon' of the western Sinhalese, apparently only because both are termed 'black'; but there are several who are similarly described, and it is very unsafe to trust merely to similarity of names for an identification of these obscure deities.

All Sinhalese recognise 'Vaedi' Yakās to whom offerings are constantly made on account of the illnesses of men and women, but chiefly the latter, and especially after childbirth. If his functions are similar, the Kalu Vaedda Yakā may be one of these demons, the Kalu Yakā not being known to the Sinhalese as a 'Vaedi' Yakā, but as an Indian prince of Madura, who became a demon after his death. The latter's usual designation is Kalu Kumāra Yakā or Baṇḍāra, the 'Black Prince Demon' or 'Chief'; and King Gaja-Bāhu I (113–135 A.D.) is believed to be an incarnation of him because of the cruelties traditionally attributed to him during his invasion of Southern India, in revenge for the deeds of the Sōliyans in the 'War of the Short-horned Buffalo,' during his father's reign.[1]

Kandē Yakā, 'the Yakā of the Hill,' may be, as Mr. Nevill says, the Galē Baṇḍāra, 'the Chief (or minor deity) of the Rock,' of the Sinhalese; but this assertion is not conclusive in the absence of some further basis than the resemblance of the names. He is said to haunt precipices, and only to be invoked locally, whereas the Galē Baṇḍāra is appealed to throughout a large tract of country in north-western Ceylon. A Kandē Baṇḍāra is found in a list of deified chiefs and other deities contained in a very old manuscript of the Kurunāegala district, and he may be the Vaedda deity. There is a possibility that the name may be another term for the Galē Yakā,

[1] This demon is illustrated in Callaway's *Yakkun Nattanawā*, 1829, p. 4, and is there dressed as a Kandian Chief.

whom I have mentioned as the highest god of the Vaeddas, of whose status Mr. Nevill appears to have been unaware.

These rock and hill deities are difficult to identify without acquaintance with their attributes and functions. The Sinhalese recognise three if not four special forms of them: (1) the Galē Deviyā, 'the God of the Rock,' who is undoubtedly the Galē Yakā of the Vaeddas; (2) the Galē Baṇḍāra, 'the Chief of the Rock,' an Indian demon who arrived on the southern or western coast with others, in a boat made of stone, and is by some confounded with No. 1; (3) the Kandē Baṇḍāra, 'the Chief of the Hill,' about whom I have no information; and (4) Kurunāēgalē Postimā Baṇḍara, 'the Chief Postimā of Kurunāēgala,' a local demon of the Kurunāēgala district, who is the spirit of the Prince Postimā who was thrown down the precipice at the Kurunāēgala rock.[1]

Mr. Nevill states that Māra, the personification of Death, is largely invoked by the Coast Vaeddas 'as a later conception of Kumbē Yakā as the God of Death, the opponent of youthful vigour.'

Among the southern Vaeddas, I found that offerings are made to a second series of ..ckness-causing demons, several of whom are identical with those of the Sinhalese, from whom they appear to have been borrowed. These latter are as follows, each having a Śaktī, or female manifestation of the same name, who is considered to be his wife, this being a local development, and I believe unknown to the Sinhalese.

Name of Demon.	Name of Śaktī.	Functions.
1. Sanni Yakā	Sanni Yaksanī	Causes Sanni-rōga (sickness accompanied by convulsions, such as cholera), and other illnesses, and is the worst of the group.
2. Hūniyan Yakā[2]	Hūniyan Yaksanī	Causes the ills that follow curses, magical spells, and the glance of the Evil Eye.

[1] See the account of it in *Eleven Years in Ceylon*, by Major Forbes. Vol. i, p. 194.

[2] Illustrated in *Yakkun Natta...ā*, p. 10. In the plate he rides on a horse, holding a sword in the left hand and fire in a vessel in the right. He is surrounded by snakes, which coil about his limbs and head.

Name of Demon.	Name of Sakti.	Functions.
3. Maha Sōna Yakā or Samaya Yakā[1]	Maha Sōnī Yaksanī	Causes fever, head-ache, and pains in the body.
4. Waṭa Yakā	Waṭa Yaksanī	Afflicts the stomach, limbs, and eyes.
5. Sīri or Rīri Yakā	Sīri Yaksanī	Causes fever, loss of appetite, and pains in the limbs.
6. Maralu Yakā	Maralu Yaksanī	Causes ulcers and tumours.
7. Abimāna Yakā	Abimāna Yaksanī	Spits at men, and takes away their appetite.
8. Billē Yakā	Billē Yaksanī	Causes head-ache, tears, etc.

In addition to these there is the Kumāra Yakā, 'the Prince Demon,' who is most likely the Kumāra Baṇḍāra of the Kandians and the Sinhalese of the western coast, a son of a King of Madura and brother of the Kalu Kumāra Yakā. He cannot be Skanda, the War God, who is also called Kumāra, as he has distinctly demoniacal traits, and among other things causes fever and swelling of the body—probably dropsy.

There are other evil female deities : Sīri Kaḍawara Yaksanī, and Madana Sīri Yaksanī, whose names indicate a belief in the respective male forms Sīri Kaḍawara and Madana Kaḍawara ; and at least three termed Girī, the feminine form of Garā, are known in the south, where they afflict women and children.

There are no less than twelve demons who are especially called 'Vaedi' Yakās. Unfortunately I could not obtain their names, as my informants, although Vaeddas, were unacquainted with these details. They are said to be extremely malignant, so much so that if they strike one recovery is impossible. Mr. Nevill refers to apparently the most important one under the name 'Maha Vaedde Yakā' ; another is clearly the Kalu Vaedda Yakā already mentioned, and possibly some of the others whose names have been given belong to this class.

The Kandian Sinhalese also recognise twelve Vaedi Yakās ; two of them may be the demons termed Pudana Vaedi Yakā

[1] Illustrated in *Yakkun Nattanawā*, p. 7, as a black demon with a bear's head, who carries a spear in his left hand, and an elephant (which he is about to devour) in his right. He rides on a pig.

and Hella Vaedi Yakā, who, however, are not so deadly as the Vaedi Yakās of the Vaeddas. I have already stated that there are three Vaedi Yakās who are subordinate to the Kohombē Yakā, and twelve others under him in an inferior position who are termed Vaedi Kaḍawarayō. Very little appears to be known about them. Lists of these attendants and other particulars for which I am indebted to the kindness of Mr. Codrington of the Ceylon Civil Service, do not throw much light on the subject, as they do not seem to contain the names of Vaedi deities.

Lastly, there is Kurumbuḍa Yakā, ranked by the Sinhalese as a very malignant (*wasa napuru*) demon. He is the minister and attendant of the Galē Yakā, whom he accompanied from India.

Doubtless there are others of whom nothing is yet known, and especially an immense array of nameless minor local demons, who are found throughout the whole country, inhabiting rocks, and pools, and trees, and waste grounds. Dr. Seligmann has stated at a meeting of the Ceylon Branch of the Royal Asiatic Society that he found the Forest Vaeddas largely worshipping a number of spirit deities, who are the spirits of deceased persons, their relatives. He will doubtless give a full account of them in his work on the Vaeddas. He terms them the Nāē Yakās, 'the Kinsfolk Demons' or deities.

On a review of this formidable list of the deities, beneficent and malevolent, of the Vaeddas, it will be seen that the close connection between their religious ideas and those of the Sinhalese, and especially the Kandian Sinhalese, exclusive of Buddhism, is very prominent. In fact, the chief line of divergence lies in the deification of the Kiri-Ammās and the recent Nāē Yakās. Sacrifice of some kind is paid by the Kandians or the Sinhalese of the western coast districts to practically all the other deities of the Vaeddas, with the exception of Bōwala Yakā, and possibly of Kumbē Yakā, and Wana-gatta Yakā. I have no acquaintance with the Mūdē Yakā, the God or Demon of the Sea, of the Fishing or Coast Vaeddas; he may be a deity borrowed from the Sinhalese or Tamil fishermen with whom they come in contact, or possibly is aboriginal.

The point of particular interest is the supreme position assigned to the God of the Rock, or Hills, as a beneficent deity. Nominally, at least, he does not hold this rank among the north-western Kandians, who term him merely one of the most powerful of the demons, and one who does not often trouble himself with the affairs of men, although as a matter of fact they often appeal to him for assistance in case of the outbreak of epidemics or great want of rain. He is quite unknown to the Sinhalese of the western coast. I think there can be no doubt that he is the Hill God of the wild tribes of the South Indian hills. The legend regarding his arrival in Ceylon, and the particulars of his worship as it still survives among the Village Vaeddas and Kandians are given in the next chapter.

The statement of the Vaeddas that the Goddess known as the Indigollāēwa Kiri-Ammā is his wife finds confirmation in the North-central Province, where the same temple at Indigollāēwa is the local centre of the cult of both deities. If the Kiri-Ammā is really Mōhinī, as I was informed, we have here a cult that has been to some extent developed independently of India, and that perhaps may be connected with the legends respecting the conquests of the Asuras by Skanda and his half-brother Ayiyanār. People who found themselves surrounded by such a numerous band of evil spirits as those of Ceylon naturally would be inclined to pay honour to deities like Mōhinī, who had proved themselves their outwitters.

After the demons had been cheated by the gods at the great Churning of the Ocean, Mōhinī regained the form of Vishnu, and left the scene. The God Śiva subsequently heard of the incident, and proceeded to Vishnu, who to satisfy his curiosity resumed the shape of the fascinating beauty. The susceptible Śiva was overcome by her charms, and the result was the birth of a son after Vishnu had returned once more to his own form. We learn this from the Bhāgavata Purāna.

The infant made his appearance in the world from the back of the God's right hand, and received the name Eiyanār (in Tamil), or Ayiyanār (in Sinhalese), or, according to the Tanjore temple authorities, who may be taken to represent South Indian opinion, more correctly Keiyanār, 'He (who was born) from the Hand.' He is also known as Nāyanār, and as Hari-Hara-putra, the son of both Hari, or Vishṇu, and Hara, or Śiva. His colour is dark blue or black, and in Ceylon his Vāhana, or the 'Vehicle' on which he rides, is a white elephant. In India he rides both the elephant and the horse.

The vāhanaṣ, an elephant, a bridled horse, and apparently another smaller animal, part of the head of which appears behind the horse, at the side of a guardian deity carved in high false relief on a pillar at one of the wāhalkaḍas, or ornamental altar-backgrounds, at the Jētavana dāgaba at Anurādhapura, show that the figure may represent Ayiyanār. He wears a cloth from the waist downwards, and has the usual heavy ear-rings, two jewelled necklaces, and large armlets and bangles. He holds an upright cross hanging from the fingers of his uplifted right hand. On the other side of his head flames emanate from a chalice-like object carved in relief on an upright slab or stele. In the panel below him is represented one of his wives, who carries a large flower or bouquet in her left hand, and has a long twist of hair hanging down on her right breast (Fig. 37). This carving probably dates from the early part of the fourth century A.D.

In the reliefs on the gōpura of the eleventh century A.D. at the Tanjore temple he is represented as a child on a diminutive elephant, and has one face, but twelve arms (Fig. 39). Pushkalā and Pūrnā or Pūranā were his two wives.

A different account of him is given by Dr. Burgess, in describing the rock-cut temples at Bādāmi in the Dekhan.[1] It is taken by him from Foulkes's *Legends of the Shrine of Harihara*, and agrees with the Bādāmi carvings, which may be four or five centuries earlier than those at Tanjore. In this story Harihara had a different origin and mission. It was

[1] *The Indian Antiquary*, Vol. vi, p. 358.

FIG. 37. Ayiyanār as Guardian (Jētavana Dāgaba).

To face p. 148

FIG. 38. Ganesa, Vibhīsana, and Pattinī.

FIG. 39. Ayiyanār on Elephant (Tanjore)

To face p. 148.

Śiva who assumed the form of Vishnu in order to destroy an Asura called Guha, who by his austerities had obtained powers from Brahmā which enabled him to conquer the Gods, and turn them out of their paradise. Śiva killed the demon with his magical arrow.

In accordance with this legend the statue at Bādāmi represents a figure who is half Śiva and half Vishnu. He has one face and four arms, and carries as a battle-axe the crescent-shaped 'Ketēriya' of the Sinhalese, round the handle of which a cobra is curled. He wears a high crown, the frustrum of a tall cone, decorated with symbols of the God Śiva on the right half.

According to a Sinhalese tradition Ayiyanār came to Ceylon from Madura. His name seems to show that his place of origin was in a Drāvidian country. The honorific title Nāyanār, 'the Nāyar' appears to indicate that he was originally a deity of the Nāyars. If so, he was an early South Indian god, and his high position as the special Forest Deity of Ceylon may be due to his introduction by the early Nāgas. If he were not aboriginal it is unlikely that he would be thought so important in the forests of Ceylon.[1] The story of his wonderful birth must be a later invention in order to bring him into the Hindu pantheon.

After the account of his birth had been generally accepted it would be logically concluded that if the father, Śiva, and the son, Ayiyanār, deserve worship, so must also the mother of such a son, especially as she was an incarnation of Vishnu, and had acted so successfully against the demons.

The Vaeddas, who were in close contact with the Sinhalese of the interior, probably acquired from the latter their knowledge of this goddess, and adopted her either as suitably filling an unoccupied place in their pantheon, or as being identical with some pre-existing goddess of theirs. This Mōhinī worship must therefore be a later addition to their cult. Neither the Vaedda nor Sinhalese traditions which are given in the next

[1] In South India his special function consists in his acting as night-watchman of the villages. In performing this duty he rides on a horse.

chapter mention the Kiri-Ammā as having accompanied the Hill God when he came to Ceylon from India, but on the contrary state definitely that he had with him only one attendant minister. This is strong evidence against Mōhinī's being an aboriginal goddess of the Vaeddas. In the Sinhalese districts her star has paled before the brilliance of a later goddess, Pattinī, who was introduced from the Pāndiyan Madura; and offerings, in addition to those of the Vaeddas, are now made to her only in the north-central districts, and in Uva and the south-east part of the island.

Ayiyanār, the son of Mōhinī, divides with his half-brother Skanda, the God of Kataragama, the attentions of all Sinhalese travellers in the forests and jungles of the interior of Ceylon. So far as the Kandians are concerned, they are the deities, above all others, whose powers are specially protective in such places. In the south-western part of the North-central Province it is stated that the first-mentioned deity and the Forest-God termed Wanni Deviyā[1] are identical, and this latter deity is manifestly the Wanniyā Baṇḍāra of the northern parts. A Kandian invocation shows that he may be Bilindā and not Ayiyanār.

In view of the close connection between the religions of the Vaeddas and the Sinhalese, it is probable that the worship of Ayiyanār exists in some form among the Village Vaeddas, at least, if not the wilder Vaeddas of the forests. There is nothing to show that one of the Bilindu Yakō is Ayiyanār, excepting his relationship to the Kiri-Ammā; the identification of the younger one as the Ilandāri Dēvatā precludes his recognition as Ayiyanār, unless these two are the same deity under different titles, which the names do not support.

With regard to the other Kiri-Ammās, the local titles attached to them confirm, at any rate as regards five of them, the statement of the Vaeddas that these are their deified female chiefs. In the list of chiefs of the seventeenth century

[1] An incantation of the Forest Vaeddas which Dr. Seligmann has allowed me to see throws some doubt on this identification. According to it this Forest-deity may possibly be the Galē Deviyā. But the Vaeddas may have confounded the two gods (see p. 159).

the name of one important female leader is found; and there is a distinct and unmistakable reference to one in the story of Paṇḍukābhaya—the 'horse-faced' Yakkhinī. The worship of these Kiri-Ammās proves the exalted position held by the women in former times—a sure mark of at least a certain amount of civilisation—and such deification is rendered the less unlikely by the existence among the Sinhalese of a custom permitting queens to rule over the country at various times from the first century B.C. down to the sixteenth century A.D.

It is strange that an entirely different group of seven Kiri-Ammās are worshipped by both Kandians and Low-country Sinhalese. They are described as seven manifestations of the Goddess Pattinī. Pattinī is never treated as a Hill Goddess, but is venerated only in her aspects as the Goddess of Chastity and the Controller of Epidemics. The worship of these seven Sinhalese goddesses seems to be an independent cult which has borrowed the nomenclature of the older one, and has ousted it in some districts.

The commanding position of Pattinī among the Sinhalese is doubtless chiefly owing to her being an incarnation of the Goddess Durgā, the wife of Śiva, a great foe of the demons collectively called Asuras. She has so entirely supplanted the terrible Indian Goddess Kālī that it is now considered that the 'Ashṭa Kāliyō,' the eight forms of Kālī, have sunk into the position of mere attendants on her, a clear proof that she is a form of Durgā.

I know of no trace of Pattinī's special cult among the Village Vaeddas, and she is not ascertained to be included among the seven Kannimār, or 'Maidens,' to whom offerings are made by the Tamil-speaking Vaeddas, who, however, were unable to furnish me with their names. A list of seven Kannimār published by Mr. Nevill[1]—possibly a different set of deities—shows them to be chiefly evil aspects of Kālī, whom these half-Tamil Vaeddas may have merely taken over from their Tamil neighbours. By the Tamils of the southern part of the Eastern Province, and perhaps elsewhere in Ceylon,

[1] *The Taprobanian*, Vol. ii, p. 146.

as in India, Pattinī is worshipped as a Goddess, under the name Kannakei Amman.[1]

To what extent the Vaeddas borrowed their religious notions from the Sinhalese, and the latter from the Vaeddas, must be partly a matter for conjecture. The legends regarding the Hill God, or God of the Rock, prove that he at least was an original deity of the aborigines; and his cult must have descended from them to the Kandian Sinhalese.

That the twelve or fifteen demons called Vaedi Yakās or Vaedi Kaḍawaras were originally primitive evil deities is at least extremely likely. It is regrettable that practically nothing is known about them. The two or three uncertain demons are perhaps included among them.

The origin of the custom of deifying important spirits such as those of chiefs, male and female, or of special ancestors, is doubtless very ancient; it appears to be widespread in India as well as in Ceylon, the worship of the Manes being well known. The Buddhist monks of Ceylon are of opinion that the spirits of some deceased persons become Yakās. In the Jātaka story No. 545, it is stated of the Kuru King Dhananjaya, 'his mother in his last existence but one before this was his guardian deity.' In the story No. 544, Angati, King of Mithilā, inquires of Nārada, "I ask thee this matter, O Nārada; give me not a false answer to my question; are there really gods or ancestors—is there another world as people say?" Nārada answered: "There are indeed gods and ancestors,[2] there is another world as people say." In the Jātaka story No. 512, it is related that the spirit of the chaplain of the King of Benares supplied the latter with fruit daily after he had become an ascetic.

In Southern Indian Tamil districts and in Ceylon it is believed that a person who has been inordinately fond of his house and its surroundings becomes a spirit termed in Ceylon the Gewalē Yakā, 'the Yakā at Houses,' and in India, Muni. Although considered to be an evil spirit, his love of his old home induces him to act as its protector to a certain extent;

[1] *The Taprobanian*, Vol. iii, p. 16.
[2] That is, ancestral spirits.

and he is supposed to remain in its immediate neighbourhood. It is considered to be a lucky thing to have such a Yakā about the premises, since his care of them and the inmates brings good fortune and prosperity; but, on the other hand, if the residents neglect him and do not make offerings to him he afflicts them in various ways. This is not done through vindictiveness but because, as it was explained to me by a Kapurāla, "One must live, and this is the only way in which he could make people give him food." As I understand the position, this nearly coincides with the ideas of the Vaeddas concerning the spirits of their deceased relatives and chiefs.

Such Yakās as this one and the Baṇḍāras mentioned below are generally believed to notify their position in the spirit world by appearing to persons in dreams and saying, "I am now a Yakā"—or a Baṇḍāra, as the case may be; but some do this by performing supernatural feats, and then informing the people through an authorised person—a soothsayer, when 'possessed'—that they have caused them, and that they require offerings. One Yakā who resided at Jaffna is stated to have left that place in disgust, and come to the North-Western Province, because he was half starved there, he said. This was the Kambili Unnáehae, mentioned below as a Forest Deity.

The earliest instance of such deification in Ceylon is that of the Sōlian king who invaded Ceylon in the second century A.D.

The next person is King Gaja-Bāhu I, who lived in the second century, and who is believed to have been in reality an incarnation of a demon of Madura. Nīlā, a chief of his time, about whose prowess in the invasion of India some stories have been preserved, is also now a deity called Kalu Kumāra or Dēvatā, apparently one of the 'Five Gods' of the Wanniyas.

After him comes King Mahā Sēna, of the third century A.D., who is still worshipped as a Forest Deity by both Sinhalese and Wanniyas.

In the ranks of the deities termed Baṇḍāras, who are the spirits of important chiefs, or heroes, or ancestors, are found six chiefs of a King Wijaya-Bāhu ; but whether he was the first who bore that name, and who reigned from 1065 to 1120 A.D., or a later one, I am unable to say. It is not probable, however, that the king was one of the later rulers of that name, who were all unimportant personages, although he may have been the second one, who was at war with the Tamils in Ceylon for a short time in the thirteenth century.

Among these Baṇḍāras there are also included Postimā Baṇḍāra, who has been already mentioned as a prince who was thrown over the precipice at the Kurunāēgala rock, about 600 feet high, in the thirteenth or fourteenth century ; and Panikki Vaeddā, a Vaedda Chief of the fifteenth century. Another of these deities who can be dated is a chief who lived under a son of Wimala Dhamma Suriya I or II, in the seventeenth century.

An addition was made to the list in the time of Kīrti Śri (1747–1780), this being a chief called Kīrti Baṇḍāra: and during the early part of last century the cruelties practised by the last king of the Kandian territory, Śri Vikrama Rāja Siṃha (1798–1815), caused him also to be enrolled in the ranks of the evil spirits.

Lastly comes a folk-story of a man of the Western Province, who, being thought to be dead, was taken for an evil spirit or Yakā when he returned home late one night. Every one in his village refused to open a door and admit him when he knocked at each house in turn, and informed the inmates who he was. It ended in his accepting the situation, and demanding abundant food, which was deposited for him nightly. I understand that he is now enrolled among the regular Yakās, and that offerings are still made to him.

Nearly all the other deities of the Village Vaeddas are undoubtedly of South Indian origin. Whether the belief in any of them was introduced into Ceylon by the Nāgas, or the knowledge of all was acquired at a later date, possibly through the intermarriages of the royal families of Ceylon and Madura, or through their introduction during some of the various Tamil invasions, there is no evidence to prove, excepting a doubtful

Sinhalese tradition of the Kapurālas that their cult originated in the time of King Paṇḍuwāsa Dēva, that is, in the fourth century B.C.; and other stories which state that many of the demons landed on the western or southern coast at some unknown time.

So far as these researches have extended, the result, as regards the primitive cult of the aborigines, may be summarised in a few words. The original religion of the Vaeddas appears to have been this: They worshipped one beneficent deity, the Hill God of Southern India, who provided them with food, sent them rain, and checked their illnesses and epidemics. They also believed in the existence of at least twelve evil deities or demons, who caused the ills that afflicted them. They may have had a Sea God also; but respecting this the evidence is insufficient. Probably, also, they shared with the other inhabitants of India a belief in the existence of ancestral spirits, to whom offerings were made, and whose functions were partly hurtful and partly protective.

One thing at least may be remarked with confidence respecting the Vaeddas—that their religious conceptions contain no beliefs that tend to show any connexion with other aborigines than those of Southern India. I am not aware that there is any adoration of the sun, or planets, or astral bodies, or the powers of Nature, nor apparently is there any snake worship by them. How far their magical ideas extend is unknown; that some of the more settled of them must be acquainted with many of the practices of the Sinhalese is proved by their faith in the existence of the Hūniyan Yakā, the demon whose special function is to give effect to curses, and magic, and evil spells.

The full story of Ayiyanār's miraculous birth may be contained in the Skanda Purāna, which has not appeared in English. I translate the legend as it was related to me in a Sinhalese village near Indigollāēwa; it is in close agreement with that which I heard at the great Saivite temple at Tanjore. Some explanatory additions are inserted in brackets.

The Origin of the Sons of Śiva.

Great Vishnu [Mā Vis Unnānsē] having taken the appearance of a woman whose name was Surānganā ['Celestial Nymph,' that is, Mōhinī] was rocking in a swing. At that time Basmasurā [1] was a servant of the God Īswara [Śiva]. The Goddess Umayanganā [Parvatī] was married to Īswara. While Basmasurā was employed under Umayanganā she went alone to the river to bathe, and taking off her Ābarana [insignia] placed them near the river. Leaving them alone there she pulled up a small quantity of *Singarael* [a plant] and created from it a prince, and instructed him to remain beside the Ābarana [to guard them]. She then entered the water. A tale-bearer went and falsely told Īswara that Basmasurā had gone to watch the Goddess bathe. Then Īswara being angry mounted his elephant, and taking his sword proceeded to the spot. [Seeing a person sitting on the river bank] he cut off the prince's head, which fell into the water.

The Goddess thereupon came out of the water, and said to Īswara, "Why did you behead the prince whom I have created?" Īswara replied, [" I thought he was Basmasurā]. If you can create another prince, do so." Then the Goddess said, "If you will cause the prince whom I created to come to life again, I will create [not one, but] seven more." Īswara agreed to this. But he was unable to find the head [*oluwa*], and he therefore entered the water, and created a white lotus plant [*olu-gaha*]. He then cut off the head of his elephant, and fixed it on the neck of the beheaded prince, and named him Gaṇa [2] Deviyā [Gaṇēsa].

Then the Goddess created a prince from a kind of grass; she made another from Singarael; a third from a piece of cloth; a fourth from leaves; a fifth from sand; a sixth from creepers; and a seventh from a kind of fruit that had fallen from a tree. Those seven remained in one place. The God

[1] A Rākshasa in Indian legend. The name is a compound of *Bhasma*, ashes, + *Asura*, demon. Śiva is called *Bhasma-priya* 'Fond of Ashes.'

[2] Evidently deriving the word from the Skt. *ghana*, slaying.

Īswara, saying, "I am going to eat [1] my sons," clasped his arms round them, and all seven were caught, but one escaped beneath his hand and fled. The other six were crushed together, and became the God Kanda-Swāmi [Skanda], with six faces and twelve hands, who rides on a peacock. The prince who had escaped became the Kaḍawara [2] Dēvatā ['the Celestial who escaped,' generally considered to be a demon in Ceylon].

After this, Īswara entered the river to bathe [to purify himself], and handed to Basmasurā the arrow [3] which he held in his hand. Basmasurā thinking "I will kill Īswara with this arrow, and marry the Goddess Umayanganā," made off with the arrow. The God Īswara, being afraid, ran away, and got hid under the swing in which the Goddess Surānganā was swinging. When Basmasurā came up with the arrow Surānganā asked him, "What are you doing?" "I am running to kill the God Īswara," he said. "Why?" she asked. "In order to marry Umayanganā," he replied. "What is [the use of] that; should I be a bad match for you [*mama narakada* ?]," she asked. Basmasurā answered, "It is good" [expressing his approval of the match]. Surānganā then said, "We will swear an oath never to give each other up." "Yes," rejoined Basmasurā [forgetting that her name Mōhinī means 'Deluder'], "what oath shall we swear?" "Take your right hand and put it on your head," answered Surānganā, "and I will take my right hand and put it on my head." At that time Basmasurā having become foolish through the sentiment of Kāma [love], without giving up the arrow placed it on his head in his hand. Thereupon he was burnt up by [the magical properties inherent in] the arrow. Then [Īswara came out from under the swing and embraced Surānganā,

[1] This is the correct translation of the Sinhalese words, *magē puttō kanṭa;* but the last word, like the whole story, is taken over from the Tamil, in which it must mean 'embrace.' Compare Skt. *kaṇṭha-graha*, an embrace. In Tamil, *kantam* or *kaṇḍam* is a neck.

[2] From Tamil *kaḍa*, to step aside, or escape from, + *varar*, celestials.

[3] I have a very short Sinhalese spear or assegai, which the owner termed an 'arrow'; the arrow mentioned in the story appears to have been a stabbing weapon, as no bow is referred to.

and] Basmasurā, through his love for her was conceived in her womb. Afterwards Surānganā resumed her male form [as Vishnu]. Ten months being fully accomplished, he split his right hand, and took out the prince, who received the name of Ayiyanār Baṇḍāra. Surānganā's name became Kiri-Ammā.

This story was told to me in order to explain exactly who Ayiyanār was, and his relationship to the Kiri-Ammā. Thus it is plain that by the Sinhalese, at any rate, the latter is believed to be Mōhinī, and not Parvatī.

A different version of this story is current in Maisūr, and is given in the *Indian Antiquary*, Vol. ii, p. 50. In it Śiva handed to Basmasurā his middle fiery eye, the glance of which consumes everything on which it gazes. Vishnu in the form of a bewitching female came to Śiva's assistance, and the wicked Rākshasa was burnt up himself. The interview with Mōhinī resulted in the production of three Lingas.

Among the Wanniyas the chief deities [1] are (1) The Wanniyā Baṇḍāra, (2) the Five Dēvatās, and (3) the Hat (or Sat) Rajjuruwō.

The Wanniyā Baṇḍāra is the Wanni Deviyā, the Forest God who is said by the Sinhalese of the North-central Province to be Ayiyanār. Invocations collected by Dr. Seligmann indicate a possibility that he may be the Galē Yakā, the special reason against this identification being the facts that the Wanniyā Baṇḍāra or Deviyā of the Sinhalese is not a Hill God, and the Galē Yakā is not a special Forest God. The name of the Wanniya god means the 'Forester Chief'; he is not worshipped on hills like the God of the Rock.

The five Dēvatās are said to be Ilandāra Dēyiyā, Ayiyanār Dēyiyā, Kalu Dēvatāwunār, Kaḍawara Dēvatāwunār, and Mangalya Dēyiyā. The Hat Rajjuruwō is, as already stated, merely a title of King Mahāsēna. All these act as guardian deities.

If the names of the Dēvatās are given correctly, Ayiyanār

[1] I made no inquiry as to their knowledge of the God of the Rock or the Kiri-Ammā, having myself no information regarding them at that time (1885).

reappears among them in a minor position, where one would not expect to find him. This considerably strengthens the probability that the Wanniyā Baṇḍāra is the Galē Yakā. On the other hand deities often reappear with varying names under different aspects, and various persons hold divergent views regarding them.

Ilandāra Dēyiyā is known to the Coast Vaeddas and the North-western Kandians; he is said by the latter to have been a chieftain under King Mahā-Sēna, and to have resided at Minnēriya tank. The Kandians of the North-central Province state that he is a son of the Kiri-Ammā. The Kalu Dēvatā is also reported to be a special deity of the North-central Province. Kaḍawara Dēvatā has been already mentioned as the prince who avoided the squeeze of Śiva which compressed the six others into one.

Although it seems clear that Ilandāra and the younger Bilindā are the same deity, the identity of the Wanni Deviyā is less certain, notwithstanding the information given to me that he is Ayiyanār. Such statements always require sifting carefully. The name of the latter deity in both Tamil and Sinhalese is an honorific form meaning 'Elder Brother,' an expression that would not be used unless there was a younger brother, that is Ilandāra, 'the youth,' or Bilindā, 'the child.' Thus the latter deity and Ayiyanār appear to be the two Bilindu brothers of whom Mr. Nevill heard.

In a poetical Sinhalese invocation addressed to 'the Twelve Gods,' references made to the Wanni Deviyā (also called in it Wanni Baṇḍāra) indicate that he is Bilindā, and not Ayiyanār. It states that he, the 'God of the Wanni Country,' went to Kataragama in order to receive offerings, and that ***napuru ayayi me puraṭa aewidin yak mennē waran laeba***, 'the wicked elder brother having come to this city obtained power like a Yakā.' Dr. Seligmann heard that Kandē Yakā killed Bilindā; perhaps reference is made to this in the poem. From it we also learn that the Wanni Deviyā was born at a place called Kiwiyaluwa, and was king of the Vaedi country, and king of Bintaenna, who promenaded round Sorabora tank. He protects the people of jungle villages, rides wild elephants, and always carries a goad; and it 'comforts his heart' to see Sambar and other deer, and to visit the *Uḍa raṭa*, the Upper-country. It is not unlikely that some sovereign or chief of the Vaeddas has been canonised (or possibly two legends have been united), and identified as a son of Mōhinī.

Mangalya Dēyiyā evidently is the God Mangala, whom Mr. Nevill mentioned[1] as being anciently worshipped in the Trincomalee and Batticaloa districts. He stated that when offerings were presented to him invocations were addressed to a number of deities called by Tamils 'The 160 Vatanamār,' who were subject to his orders. He remarked that 'Mangala was specially invoked by elephant-hunters and by wild buffalo hunters.' He learnt from the hymns to him that 'both they [the chiefs] and their subjects, these votaries of Mangala, evidently came from the Malabar coast, and followed the Nāyik custom of inheritance of ancestral property in the male [female] line.' Here is another practice which points to the early Nāyar connection with the people of Ceylon. Mr. Nevill considered this god to be 'a personification of the influence of the seven or nine planets conjointly'; but on reading over the two hymns which are given by him it seems to me clear that the God Mankala in whose honour they are composed is shown by his name Nāyinār in them, and his vāhana, an elephant, to be Ayiyanār, as an avatāra or incarnation of a part of Vishnu. One of the names of Ayiyanār is Nāyanār, according to Winslow's Tamil dictionary. Vishnu, as the husband of Lakshmī, who is termed Mankalei in Tamil, is called Mankalanār, a title given to his son also in these hymns.

The second hymn begins :—"I sing the sacred story of the glorious Mankalārs [Vishnu and Ayiyanār]. O Sankāra [Śiva] of vast Kayilāsa! graciously aid me to sing the praise of Narāyana [Vishnu] on the ever-writhing snake-couch."

The first hymn relates the capture of the elephant which became Ayiyanār's vāhana, and part of it is so interesting as giving a description of the god that I quote it :—

'Mankalanār came and rose forth from a beauteous lotus flower, at the white-lotus flowering, bliss-giving, great city

[1] *The Taprobanian*, Vol. i, p. 54.

called Kāsi, called Mūlam. At that very time was the Avatāram of Mankalanār. When Nāyinār was born at the auspicious hour, all came and worshipped the Mankalār.

'When twelve years fulfilled had passed by, wearing thrice three jewels [the nine gems], and assuming the triple-twisted cord [the sacred thread] Nāyinār was seated, with bow, arrow, javelin, strong cord, axe, nāga-like-cane like a goodly circlet, with girdle, indescribably-flowered clothing, girt with a curved club, and wearing a gem-set ring and ear-rings, with goodly coat and hat ; wearing all these Mankalanār was seated !'

The capture of the elephant by noosing it is then described, and the hymn ends, 'they bathed it for beauty in the white-lotus-flowered pond. Placing on its feet bangles, on its neck bells, on its body spreading white cloth and so forth, they brought it. Wearing a coat, wearing a cloth, wearing a hat, putting on a crown, like the Katpakam grove surrounded by the Ganges, surrounded on all sides, he was pleased to become seated.'

In this story Kāsi, that is, Benāres, is mentioned as the birthplace of Nāyanār, and the account of his origin is quite different from those previously given.

I made no inquiry into the demonology of the Wanniyas ; but it may be accepted as certain that, like the Sinhalese and Vaeddas, they are acquainted with a long array of evil spirits.

RELIGIOUS CEREMONIES

THE commonest religious ceremony of the Village Vaeddas is performed on the occasion of their setting out on one of their hunting excursions, of which it, or an allied ceremony, is the invariable preliminary. This is a prayer for protection and success in hunting, offered to a deity, usually the Indigollaēwa Kiri-Ammā, whose powers are supposed to be specially manifested in the forests. It is always accompanied by offerings of food made according to a simple fixed ritual. For this purpose a trained intermediary or priest is not needed; any member of the hunting party who knows the form of prayer which is necessary temporarily undertakes the office.

The Vaeddas of the interior villages prepare a covered shrine resting on four sticks, under a large shady tree. The bottom of the shrine is made at a height of about four feet from the ground; it is nearly two feet square, with a roof arched over from side to side and the front open, but not the back. It is covered with grass on the top and has the walls enclosed by leafy twigs. The inside is lined with white calico, if available. Similar frames or temporary shrines are erected by the Sinhalese for holding offerings to evil or beneficent deities.

Inside this are laid on separate green leaves the best foods they possess—fresh meat of some kind, Rice boiled with Coconut-milk if obtainable, small cakes of Rice-flour or Millet, some bits of Coconut if they have them, and a little water in a piece of Coconut shell. A few red flowers of the Ratmal tree (*Ixora coccinea*), or Eramudu tree (*Erythrina indica*) are also placed inside the shrine before the offering; and in front of all a wick made of a bit of rag saturated with fat is fixed in anything available—often a piece of Coconut husk. Lustration of water is made in front of the shrine, and obeisance is performed to the offerings with the hands raised in front of the face and the palms touching each other. This is the dedication of the offerings.

The wick is now lighted, and the officiator turns aside until it expires. He then steps in front of the shrine, and dances there slowly, holding an arrow in his hand, after which he says loudly "Aybō! Aybō! Aybō! Indigollāe Kiri-Ammē! Hail! Hail! Hail! (literally, 'may life be long'), O Indigollāewa Kiri-Ammā! Eat. Drink. Give us livelihood. Give us meat got by hunting. Do not cause us to meet with the Elephant. Do not cause us to meet with the Bear. Do not cause us to meet with the Leopard. You must make us a livelihood by (means of) the Pangolin. You must make us a livelihood by (means of) the 'Iguāna.' You must make us a livelihood by (means of) the Monkey. We must meet with the Sambar deer. We must meet with the Pig. To the end while going, to the end while coming back, you must promote and give livelihood and protection, O our esteemed Goddess."

When the offerings are made to the Gangē Baṇḍāra, the River Deity, the hunters first fix a day for them, and give notice to a professional devil-priest, termed a Kapuwā, who purifies himself by bathing on the three days preceding the ceremony. The offerings consist only of Betel-leaves, Areka-nut cut in pieces, and a little water. In fact, the deity is merely offered the usual 'chew' of Betel—the eastern form of the Stirrup-cup—before the hunters set out. The shrine is erected as in the preceding case, but lined with a torn cloth. This ceremony may take place anywhere; there is no fixed site for it. After presenting the offering, and lighting one wick, and dancing, the Kapuwā repeats the same prayer as before, simply changing the address to the Gangē Baṇḍāra instead of the Goddess.

When going only to collect honey they usually say aloud for the information of the deities, "We are going to cut a hive for the Yakās." In their own interests the deities are then expected to see that the men are successful. On their return, some present part of the honey they have obtained, and cooked rice if they can provide it, to the Kataragama God. Many offer the honey to the Kiri-Ammā; but if they have found very little they punish her by withholding this offering, apparently without fearing any act of reprisal on her part.

Village Vaeddas who know more Sinhalese, as well as the neighbouring Sinhalese villagers, place the offerings in a similar shrine, lined with a white cloth, and use a longer prayer to the Kiri-Ammā. It is made—so I was informed, but this may be a mistake—before the lights expire, two being set in the shrine, one for the Goddess and the other for her husband, the Galē Yakā. The prayer was repeated for me as follows, the utterer holding an arrow in his hand while saying it:—" Aybō! Aybō! Aybō! O Indigollāēwa Kiri-Ammā, who became famous through splitting the Sapphire Gem at the Sapphire Mountain[1] in the country of the Seven Seas, and even the country beyond it! While you are looking at this beautiful cooked food this is our supplication, telling you to give a good Sambar deer, having caught it with this Vaedi arrow. O my Kiri-Ammā! This is our supplication asking you for a good Horn-bearer[2] [Sambar deer], for a Speckled One [Axis deer], for a Fat-maker [Pig], for a Meat-bearer [Buffalo] to be daily placed for us."

When the same people pray for honey an identical formula is used up to the word 'food,' after which it runs:—" This is our supplication, telling you, O Indigollāēwa Kiri-Ammā to grant your loving favour, giving us a bee-hive until our eye is blind." The concluding part is a common saying among village Sinhalese; its meaning here is 'even more than we can want.'

In order to avoid dangerous animals, and the difficulties of the path, they say after 'food,' " This is our supplication telling you, O Indigollāēwa Kiri-Ammā! to grant your loving favour, beating and driving afar Leopards, Elephants, enclosing and filling up hollows, blunting pointed stones,

[1] Alaka, on Mt. Kailāsa, the home of the Yaksha sovereign Kuvēra. In the *Mēghadūta* (Ouvry), v. 76, the exiled Yaksha says, "On the banks of this (lake) is a beautiful mountain for sport, whose summit, composed of sapphires, is worthy to be seen on account of its being enclosed by golden plantains."

[2] These names of animals belong to the Kaelē-bāsa, and not the Vaedi dialect.

beating and driving afar Serpents, giving livelihood and protection in the forest, and [making up] all deficiency."

Among the southern Village Vaeddas, and in the adjoining Sinhalese districts, offerings of the first-fruits obtained by hunting are made in a similar way, with one light, to the Kukulāpola Kiri-Ammā. They consist of fresh meat and honey.

To the seven Kiri-Ammās of the south, a single offering is made in the same kind of shrine when the men are about to leave on a hunting expedition, and also when children are sick or fretful. If they are procurable, it consists of milk-rice (rice boiled in Coconut milk), Jak-fruit, the flower-bud of the Plantain tree (which is used in curries), Betel-leaf and sliced Areka-nut, Sugar-cane, and a little Sandal-wood.

In this case, the shrine is subdivided into seven compartments in which seven leaves are placed on a white cloth, one for each Goddess; and on each of them a small portion of each kind of offering is laid. Water is sprinkled over these articles, and in front of the shrine, and the offering is also purified by incense (a resinous gum which exudes from the bark of the Dum tree), which is burnt on a fire-stick, and waved round it. A wick is then placed near each end of the offering and lit. After the lights have expired, the offerer takes a Betel-leaf in his right hand, between the first two fingers, and waves it from side to side in front of the shrine, and then, still holding it, makes a long prayer to the seven Goddesses, which I had no opportunity of writing down.

When children are ill, and the parents do not possess things suitable for giving to these seven deities, or the time is inauspicious, or there is not an opportunity of doing it (as in the case of a sudden violent attack), they make a vow to present an offering to them; and hang up a *bārē*, a visible token of the forthcoming sacrifice. There is no magic, as some have supposed, in this act; a bārē, which has various forms according to the personage to whom the offering is to be made, is like an engagement ring in Europe, and is invariably necessary among all Sinhalese when a vow to present an offering has been made. It must not be removed on any account until the vow has been accomplished. In the present instance it consists of a Mango-leaf and a strip of Palmira-palm leaf, strung on a thread, which is then tied across the doorway of the hut. On one side of the Palmira leaf are written the words 'Paṭṭa-Girī, Bāla-Girī, Mōlan-Girī,' probably to indicate that the child is to be specially guarded against the evil actions of the female demons who bear those names.

Among the Kandian Sinhalese, Girī is the feminine form or Śaktī of a class of demons, twelve or more in number, called Garā (plural Gaerae or Garayō), who afflict only women and children. The word *gara* means sickness or disease, and is derived from the Sanskrit root *grah,* to seize ; these demons are thus personifications of certain diseases.

In this case, the offering, as described above, is usually made after the child has recovered, or as soon as the requisite articles for it can be procured ; but sometimes, as when an infant has been fretful in the night, it is presented on the following day, if possible.

Respecting the ceremonies used in presenting offerings to the Bilindu Yakō, Mr. Nevill merely remarked, 'The offerings are those, omitting rice, still used in India and Ceylon at the festival of Pongal, in honour of the January sun. The symbol used is the arrow.' [1]

Mr. Nevill observed concerning the religious ceremonies of the Vaeddas: 'In almost all their religious rites the arrow is used ; it receives worship as an emblem, or is waved in the hands of the celebrant, around the sacrifice.

'They leave tiny babes upon the sand for hours together, with no other guard than an arrow, stuck in the ground by their side. Their belief in the efficiency of this has received no shock. They never knew such a child to be attacked by wild beasts, pigs, leopards, jackals, etc., or harmed. They say, "Are we not the children of our Gods, and if we leave our child under their care will they not watch over it ?" The arrow being the God's symbol, they themselves are practically, as his children, the iya-vans, or "sons of the arrow," and this fully accounts for the name Yaka or Yakkho,' [that is, as

[1] *The Taprobanian,* Vol. i, p. 195.

I have already stated, iya-kō, arrow-persons. I have previously expressed my opinion of this derivation ; I may add that the Vaeddas never claim to be called either Yakās or Iyakās].

Offerings of food are made by the Tamil-speaking Vaeddas to their deceased relatives, excluding infants. As the manner in which they make the gifts was certainly not derived from their Tamil neighbours, this ceremony may have been developed by their ancestors in ancient times, although its absence elsewhere shows that it is not a primitive one. The offering is first made seven days after the death, and subsequently once a year, after the Hindu custom.

A shrine like that already described is erected under a shady tree in the jungle. It is from three to five feet high and is usually, but not always, arched over ; it is lined with a white cloth. The foods placed in it are cooked meat if available, cooked rice, Betel-leaves, Areka-nuts, and Plantains. Of course they are purified by lustration. In front of the offering one wick is lighted inside the shrine. Tom-toms are beaten loudly to attract the notice of the deceased person, and a dance is performed in front of the offering in his honour, after which the officiating relative merely says, "Lord, eat and go." The party then return home.

The ceremony of the offering to the Seven Kannimār is said to be quite similar, the shrine having, as in the case of the seven Kiri-Ammās of the South, seven compartments, one for each Goddess, whose share of the food is thus given separately. I do not know the prayers addressed to them. An arrow is certain to be held by the dancer.

Regarding the manner in which offerings and invocations are made for propitiating the various evil demons of the Vaeddas, I regret that I have no information, my visits to their district having been too short to permit me to collect the particulars. Those who live in the forests informed me that they are accustomed to place offerings of food for them in shallow hollows in the surface of rocks. This matter has now been investigated by Dr. Seligmann.

When the Wanniyas are about to set out on a hunting trip they first purify themselves on the preceding day by bathing in their little village tank, and then perform the following ceremony to ensure success in their expedition, no women being allowed to see it.

Under a large tree at the foot of the embankment of their tank, one of the party, who becomes the temporary officiator or priest, cleans, by pounding, four quarts of paddy (rice in its husk), and boils the rice so obtained. Others fix in the ground three sticks in a triangle, with a platform in it well above the ground level. The boiled rice is placed in a new earthenware pot, or 'chatty,' which is deposited by the celebrant (who alone performs the whole ceremony), on the frame, resting on the tops of the sticks; and a little saffron is sprinkled on the rice.

On the little platform below the pot seven Betel leaves are next arranged in a circle, with their points together, and an Areka-nut is put on each; a pinch of Camphor is also placed near the outer end of each leaf, a light is applied to it, and it is burnt.

Water is then taken in a washed gourd, or new 'chatty' (or pot) and with the hand a little is sprinkled three times on the ground in front of the offerings. Dummala incense is next laid on a fire-stick, and while it is burning the stick is waved round the platform and the pot of rice. The officiator now steps back, and with his palms joined in front of his face pays obeisance to the offering by bowing to it three times. This completes the dedication.

He next takes three wicks soaked in fat, one of which he fixes on the end of an upright stick set in the ground in front of the frame, so as to be higher than the pot of rice, and the other two he arranges on the ground on each side of the taller one. The three are then lighted. Before they expire he walks aside, and turns his face away until they have completely ceased burning. After this he returns, and again sprinkles water three times in front of the frame.

He now raises his joined hands, and standing in front of the offering three times repeats the following invocation:—
"You, O Wanniyā Baṇḍāra [? Ayiyanār] are required to take the offering of a feast of cooked food. Wanniyā Baṇḍāra, we

must meet with the Royal Great Hive ; we must meet with Horns ; we must not meet with an Elephant, a Bear ; we must not meet with a Snake ; we must meet with livelihood."

The celebrant then removes the offering, of which all the hunting party partake.

On the return from their expedition the same offering is repeated in the same manner ; but the officiator merely says, " Wanniyā Baṇḍāra, we met with a livelihood."

Hunting parties of the Kandian Sinhalese of the North-central Province perform a ceremony which is very similar to that of the Wanniyas and Vaeddas, when about to leave their village on one of their expeditions in the forest. Under a large shady tree they prepare a *maessa*, or small covered shrine, which is raised about three feet off the ground, and is open only in front ; it is supported on four sticks set in the ground.

In this they offer the following articles if available, or as many as possible of them :—One hundred Betel leaves, one hundred Areka-nuts, Limes, Oranges, Pine-apples, Sugar-cane, a head of Plantains, a Coconut, two quarts of rice boiled specially at the site of the offering, and silver and gold. Also the flowers of the Areka-nut tree, the Coconut, and Ratmal tree. All are purified by lustration and incense, as usual, and dedicated.

They then light a small lamp at the front of the offering, and remain there watching it until it expires, differing in this respect from the practice of the Wanniyas, who must never see the light go out.

Before the light expires they perform obeisance towards the offering, and utter aloud the following prayer for the favour and protection of the Forest Deities, which must also be repeated every morning during the expedition, after their millet cake, gini-pūwa, has been eaten, before starting for the day's hunting :—

" This is for the favour of the God Ayiyanār ; for the favour of the Kiri-Ammā, for the favour of the Kataragama God [Skanda]; for the favour of the Kalu Dēvatā ; for the favour of Kambili

Unnaehae [1]; for the favour of Ilandāri Dēvatā Unnaehae; for the favour of Kaḍawara Dēvatā Unnaehae; for the favour of Galē Baṇḍāra; for the favour of the Hat Rajjuruwō.

"We are going to your jungle (*uyana*); we do not want to meet with even a single kind of [dangerous] wild animals. We do not want to meet with the Tall One [Elephant], the Jungle Watcher [Bear], the Animal with the Head causing Fear [the Snake], the Leopard. You must blunt the thorns. We must meet with the Horn-bearer [Sambar deer], the Deer [Axis], the One full of Oil [Pig], the Noosed One [Iguāna], the Store-house [Beehive]. We must meet with about three pingo [carrying-stick] loads of honey. By the favour of the Gods. We ask only for the sake of our bodily livelihood."

The first, fourth, sixth, seventh and ninth personages are included among the deities of the Wanniyas previously enumerated. The Kiri-Ammā is the Goddess of the Vaeddas. I have already stated that the Galē Baṇḍāra is not the God of the Rock, but a deity who landed on the south coast of Ceylon, with others from Madura. Kambili Unnaehae is an evil deity who is well known in the North-western Province. Thus these deities of the Forest are a miscellaneous gathering of Gods and evil deities.

In the hunting-prayer of the Wanniyas the first thing asked for is the Royal Beehive, the wish to find which occupies a foremost place in the hearts of all these northern hunters, though the Vaeddas have no knowledge of it. From the Wanniya Kōnā, whose grandfather was said to have taken one, I obtained the following account of it.

The entrance to the nest of the Bee-King is always at the foot of a large hollow tree, up the inside of which it extends. It is surrounded by seven other nests, which are those of his seven Adikārams, or Ministers; and they also have their entrances at the foot of their respective trees. The Royal Hive is the largest; it extends up the hollow tree higher than a man's height; but all honey above the level of the chin must be left for the Bee-King. From each Adikāram-miya or Minister's hive there will be got two gourd-fuls of honey, and

[1] Unnaehae is equivalent to our 'Mr.'

from the Raja-miya or Royal hive fourteen gourd-fuls and seven large chatties or pot-fuls.

Whoever may first discover the nest, no one but a Wanniya can cut out the honey, and that only after a solemn ceremony, otherwise the bees of all the hives would attack and kill him. This result is said to have nearly occurred on one occasion when some Sinhalese villagers were rash enough to attempt to take one themselves ; the boy who found it was badly stung, and would have died had not the Wanniyas been summoned in time to save his life by their prayers and magic spells, which appeased the bees, and enabled the hunters to get the honey.

The taking of the Raja-miya being an event of such extreme importance, a special offering is necessary as a preliminary. For this there are required one hundred ripe Plantains, one hundred Limes, one hundred Oranges, one thousand Areka-nuts, one thousand Betel leaves, seven quarts of unhusked rice (paddy), and seven Coconuts.

The first Wanniya who sees the Raja-miya must make the offering, and conduct all the proceedings on the occasion ; and for the time being he is called the Wanniyā Kapurāla, or demon-priest. For the seven days prior to cutting out the honey he must bathe, after anointing his head with lime-juice. He must continue to wear the same cloth all the time, and on each day he must wash it, whether it be an old or a new one. These must appear to be very unusual purifications to persons who rarely perform such acts in ordinary life, and they evidently indicate the extraordinary character of the occasion.

On the day when the honey is to be taken, the party proceed to the site of the Royal Hive ; and there, within the circle of the Ministers, the offering is presented to the Forest-Gods, to ensure the success of the undertaking.

The Kapurāla first pounds the paddy, and having arranged seven new cooking-pots in a row in front of the Raja-miya, he boils the rice in Coconut milk separately in each. He next spreads a new white cloth on the ground in front of the Raja-miya, and places on it in a row opposite the pots seven large leaf-plates, which must consist of either pieces of Plantain leaf or leaves of the Halmilla tree. After these have been lustrated the rice is deposited on them, that from each pot being put on the leaf adjoining it. The Betel leaves, Areka-nuts and fruit are then laid beside the rice, and sprinkled with water; and Camphor is burnt on one spot in front of all. Incense burning on a stick taken out of the fire is now waved round the cloth, and a triple obeisance completes the dedication.

A wick soaked in fat is next fixed opposite each offering, and lit; and, as in the ordinary ceremony, the Kapurāla turns aside until these lights have expired. He then returns, and makes a lustration three times round the cloth.

He now stands facing the offering, with palms joined in front of his face, bows thrice to it, and says, "Wanniyā Baṇḍāra, Five Dēvatās, Hat Rajjuruwō! This is for the favour of the Gods. To cut the Raja-miya came we." The others then respond in the Kaelē-bāsa, or jungle dialect, "Kapurāla, Gabaḍāēwa waḍulāpan," (cut the hive,) whereupon he proceeds to cut out the honey, and place it in the gourds and pots which have been brought for the purpose. Lastly, he removes the rice, and shares it with the party, who all eat it up at the spot; after this they carry home the honey.

When northern Kandian Sinhalese meet with a hive on their honey-collecting expeditions, the person who cuts it out is addressed as "Waḍuwā," Axe-man, in Kaelē-bāsa. Under no circumstances, however, must he take out and divide the honey among the party. This can only be done by a second person, who is addressed as "Purawannā," 'He who fills' the receptacles brought for it.

In the North-central Province and the adjoining part of the North-western Province, Ayiyanār is not merely a forest deity; he also exercises a general supervision over the village tanks.

In the former district Mr. R. W. Ievers stated [1] that when a village tank has filled, the elders of the village perform a ceremony called Muṭṭi Mangalya or 'Cooking-pot Festival.' They proceed to a special tree at the tank, and a salute of

[1] *Manual of the North-central Province*, p. 109. Note A.

two guns is offered there to the deity. The chief elder, a 'Gamarāla,' then steps forward, and announces to the God that the tank is becoming full, that cultivation will now be commenced, and that after the harvest the festival will be celebrated. A *bārē* is then deposited in the shape of a few copper coins wrapped up in a piece of rag coloured yellow with saffron, which is tied to a branch of the tree. The ceremony is ended by the Gamarāla's commending the tank, the village, its residents and their cattle to the protection of the deity.

After the harvest is finished the villagers at a public meeting appoint a day for the fulfilment of the promised ceremony, called the Muṭṭi Mangalya. The nearest Anumaetirāla (the title of a dancer in honour of a god and not of a demon), is invited to conduct it, and notices are issued to the washermen whose duty it is to supply the necessary white cloth, and to the tom-tom beaters who must take part in the ceremony. The Gamarāla directs that every shareholder in the rice-field should contribute to the feast.

On the appointed day these contributions are collected; they consist of rice and other materials for curries, Coconut oil, cakes, sweet Plantains, and Betel and Areka-nuts. The food is then cooked, and at the evening the assembled people eat it.

The meal being over, the Anumaetirāla, accompanied by all the people and the tom-tom beaters, proceeds in procession with two new earthen pots to the tree on which the bārē was hung. Under it on a raised altar of sticks (*yahana*) overhung with cloth and erected earlier in the evening are placed the two pots (muṭṭi) after being purified with water and incense as usual, and marked with saffron; Betel and Areka-nuts are also deposited on it [and no doubt a light also]. The deity is then addressed by the Anumaetirāla [presumably thanking him for his favours and requesting him to accept the offering], and ceremonial dancing by him to the strains of the tom-toms continues till dawn. The two pots are then removed from the altar and laid on the stumps of two branches on or under the tree.

By the mouth of the Anumaetirāla the god now makes it known that he has accepted the offering, and that the tank, the village, its inhabitants and their cattle are taken under his protection for a period of one, two, or three years, as the case may be.

The people then return to the village, where the Anumaetirāla again dances, and the tom-toms are beaten until the mid-day meal is cooked. This is eaten up at noon, after which all disperse. Mr. Ievers stated that a somewhat similar ceremony is performed in case of an epidemic among either men or beasts. Thus in that part of the country it is clear that the place of the God of the Rock, the Galē Deviyā, whose worship and functions are described in the next chapter, is at least partly occupied by Ayiyanār. He is said to have fifty names, each one indicating a different function or power possessed by him.

The villagers catch the fish when their tanks are nearly emptied, by wading out in the water and suddenly dropping in it a conical wicker basket or creel (karak-geḍiya) without bottom, and with a small opening at the top through which the arm can be inserted for removing any fish that have been imprisoned. In the case of tanks infested by crocodiles in the eastern part of the North-western Province these fishers appeal to Ayiyanār to protect them while so engaged. They break some leafy twigs, and hang them on a horizontal branch or creeper, and say, "It is for the favour of the God Ayiyanār. Do not permit any living creature whatever in the tank to bite us." After this, the crocodiles are said never to molest them even when close to them (I have seen them only a few feet distant from the men), provided they do not defile the tank in any way— including expectoration in the water.

When they are travelling through wild forest which is believed to be infested by wild animals, or possibly robbers, or by evil demons, both Kandian Sinhalese and Wanniyas are accustomed to make a very simple offering to one of the Forest Deities, who is usually Ayiyanār, accompanied by the prayer, "It is for the favour of the Gods," or "the God Ayiyanār." The offering merely consists in hanging a leafy twig across a horizontal creeper or branch at the side of the path, and usually under a large shady tree. In some places where no suitable creeper or branch is available two sticks with forked tops are set firmly on the ground, and a horizontal one laid across them, on which the offerings are hung. These sometimes accumulate through the action of successive travellers until they form a large heap of such twigs. In the last chapter I mentioned that the Wanniyas made this offering to the Hat Rajjuruwō when supplicating him to stop the approaching rain-storm. I do not remember noticing these twig offerings in the districts of the Vaeddas.

V

THE PRIMITIVE DEITY OF CEYLON

IN the account of the religion of the Vaeddas it has been mentioned that their chief deity, the Galē Yakā, is probably identical with the Hill God of the aborigines of Southern India. It may be assumed that the knowledge of him was either brought to Ceylon by the first comers, or was acquired by them at an extremely early date, as nothing is known of him by the Sinhalese of the coasts, or the northern Kandian Sinhalese, or by the Tamils of Northern Ceylon. If his worship had been introduced at a later date, after these races had arrived in the country and had occupied all the coast-line, some, at least, of them would be acquainted with it. This god is regularly propitiated in the interior, however, by the Kandian Sinhalese in part of Uva, and the southern half of the Eastern Provinee, and especially in the tract to the north-east of Kurunāēgala. The residents in these districts may have acquired a knowledge of him from their ancestors the Vaeddas

Although he is known by the name of Galē Deviyā, 'the God of the Rock,' in these latter districts the Sinhalese consider him to be a powerful demon, and state that they apply the expression 'God' to him merely as an honorific title calculated to please him. It will be seen, however, that it has a much more honourable meaning. It is an excellent illustration of the degradation of an ancient deity into the position of a demon. I have already given the names by which he is known to the Vaeddas, and pointed out that there was a deity at Anurādhapura—'the Vaedda God'—in the fourth century B.C., who appears to have been this one.

A similar legend regarding his arrival in Ceylon from India is current among the Vaeddas and the Kandians; and all who are acquainted with him agree that he came from a country called Malwara-dēsa or Malawara-dēsa, 'The Country of the Hill Region,' which can be no other than some part of the Malayālam tract, our Malabār, for which. however, a separate expression, Malayāla-dēsa, is now commonly used in Ceylon.

The tradition of the Tamil-speaking Vaeddas, which is very definite, is that accompanied by his minister Kurumbuḍa, 'in the olden time' he landed from a vessel on the east coast, at a place called Periya-kaḍuvei-karei, close to Vāleichēna, which is twenty miles north of Batticaloa. A temple was established there for his worship, and it was in existence down to comparatively recent times, when the residents of the place having died out or left, it was abandoned, and the

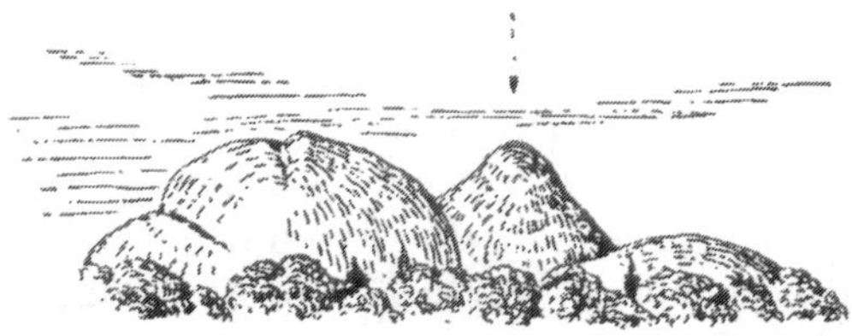

FIG. 40. Kokkā-gala.

site became overgrown with jungle. They state that he did not remain at this spot, but went to some place in the interior with which they are unacquainted. "When he came," they said to me, "he told us the names of things, trees, and animals, and how we should make offerings and dance to him when going into the jungle to hunt, and at other times. He told us everything we know." Such teaching is distinctly a characteristic of only a primitive deity.

The Vaeddas of the interior state that the Galē Yakā came over the sea, and alighted on two hills of their district in succession, on which dances are still performed in his honour one of them is called Kokkā-gala, and I believe the other is Ōmun-gala. Ōmun may be the Sanskrit word *ōman*, 'favour'; the name would then appear to mean the rock on which the God granted favours—probably a translation of an ancient Vaedi name for it. Some thought that this deity afterwards proceeded to Kataragama; I have already referred to the probability that this place was a site where a Vaedda deity was worshipped in early times.

The Sinhalese who inhabit villages in the same district carry his movements a step onward, and repeat a tradition that he and Kurumbuḍa went to some place further inland, where they killed a number of Buddhist priests, and took possession of a cave in which they resided. Neither the name of the district to which he proceeded, nor the site of the cave is known by them.

To follow up the God's travels it is now necessary to move to the Kurunāēgala district of the North-western Province, where the latter part of the story is much more definite, and is related as follows. The Galē Deviyā, attended by Kurumbuḍa Dēvatā, alighted from Malwara-dēsa on Riṭigala, the hill called Arishṭha in the Rāmāyana, and thence came to Maeṇikpāya-kanda, the upper part of Raṇa-giriya, called also Dēva-giriya, 'the Hill of the God,' a steep forest-clad rocky hill near Nīrammulla, about fifteen miles north-east of Kurunāēgala. Some say that they landed first at Wilbāwa, two miles from Kurunāēgala, before going to Raṇagiriya; others believe that they came direct to Raṇagiriya from India.

They were pleased with the general convenience of a large Buddhist cave-wihāra or temple which they found established under a rock on the slope of the hill, and wished to take possession of it; but the sixty monks who occupied it refused to hand it over to them, and began to chant 'Pirit,' or sacred stanzas, for protection against evil in general and demons in particular, as a spell to keep them out. If they could persevere in this course, and continue the chanting without intermission for seven days and seven nights, demons would have no power over them. In the meantime the Galē Deviyā could not harm them while the magical verses were being repeated. So he said to his minister Kurumbuḍa, "Kill these monks for me." But the monks went steadily on with the Pirit, and Kurumbuḍa could not touch them unless he could make them stop. It must have been an interesting spectacle. Six days passed, and the demons had made no progress whatever. At last, on the seventh day, the resourceful Kurumbuḍa threw down into the midst of the holy men the quarter of a bull, at which all the monks started, and raised their hands higher than their shoulders in astonishment, and said with disgust, " Ish " ! It was a little word, or hardly a word, but it was fatal to them. The Pirit was stopped for an instant, and in that instant Kurumbuḍa plucked off their heads, and drank their blood.

The Galē Deviyā then took possession of the cave and the hill, which has ever since been his headquarters in Ceylon, his ' Mula-gala.' He wanted to live at this place because it was in the great Pallēkaelē Forest, nine gawus long and nine gawus broad,[1] without a village in it. Here he could live undisturbed by the busy world around. Over this forest he placed his minister Kurumbuḍa Dēvatā, in charge as Mura-kārayā, or Guardian, with his residence at Kurumban Kanda, a hill in the northern part of it.

By some, the Galē Deviyā is spoken of as the Demala Yakā, the Tamil demon, all South-Indians being collectively called ' Tamils ' by the Sinhalese villagers.

As at most of the detached metamorphic hills of Ceylon, there are several large natural caves, due to weathering and flaking of the rock, on the sides of Raṇagiriya, which retain evidence of their former occupation as residences of Buddhist monks, or temples ; but all are now abandoned to the forest, and to the bears and leopards which sometimes take shelter in them. It is not definitely known which of them was the scene of the legendary contest, but it is supposed to be one of the higher caves. There is a small ruined dāgaba, or solid dome-shaped relic-mound, built of brick, near some lower caves, and over a cave close by it the following inscription has been cut in the earliest form of letters, with the bent *r*, which shows that it is probably of not later date than the second century B.C. :—

Gamikā sita sala Parumaka Tisasa ca.
The cool hall (of) Gāmikā and of the Chief Tissa.

[1] Thirty-six miles square.

Gāmikā being a feminine form may be presumed to be the name of the pious headman's wife, who evidently joined her husband in causing the place to be prepared for the reception of the monks. The inscription proves that the legend of the expulsion of the monks cannot have originated before the second century B.C.

The bricks used in the enclosing wall of a room formed at another cave, termed the Uḍa wihāra, the upper temple, are 12·75 inches long, 8·12 inches wide, and 2·75 inches thick, the contents being 285 cubic inches, and the product of the breadth multiplied by the thickness, 22·3 square inches. According to the table given in the next article, these dimensions point to about the third or fourth century A.D., as the approximate time when they were moulded. Thus the monks were still on the hill at that period. The good state of preservation of the plastering on the wall may be taken to indicate a tenancy of the cave extending to perhaps the thirteenth or fourteenth century, or even later. Therefore it would appear that the monks were never driven away from the hill up to comparatively recent times.

In view of this, it is strange to find that the villagers living on the eastern side of the Central mountains, who are totally unacquainted with this district, have preserved the same tradition of the contest for one of the caves. It is strong evidence of the antiquity of the story; and the presence, from early times, of a temple to this God is also indicated by the names of the hill itself. A possible meaning of Raṇagiriya is 'the hill of the battle.'

By way of explaining the legend, it may be surmised that while in early times an upper cave was utilised as a dēwāla, or demon temple (literally, a god's-residence) for the Galē Deviyā, the Buddhist monks occupied the lower ones, and wished to get the dēwāla removed. If the death of some of the monks occurred through an epidemic disease, or in any mysterious manner, it would certainly be attributed to the malicious action of this so-called demon; and in this manner the outlines of the story may be accounted for, so far as this hill is concerned. The dēwāla of the Hill God has long ago been transferred to a more convenient site at the village of Nīrammulla, nearly two miles from the hill.

The legend evidently contains a reminiscence of a conflict between the two religions, Buddhism and the worship of the Hill God, in which the latter was victorious. As a matter of fact, in spite of the overwhelming position of Buddhism, the belief in the power of the Galē Deviyā has survived down to the present day in considerable vigour throughout a large tract of country surrounding his headquarters at Nīrammulla, even while all the inhabitants also adhere to Buddhism. It is doubtless due to this faith in Buddhism that the God has been relegated by the Kandians to the ranks of the demons of the island, although he must originally have been a deity friendly to them.

FIG. 41. Vaedda Temple of the Galē Yakā.

Evidence of this is to be seen in the fact that notwithstanding their present opinion of his character as a demon, the Kandian Sinhalese of the district where his cult prevails still attribute beneficent actions to him. When unfavourable seasons ruin or seriously damage their crops, it is to him that a group of villages will unite to make offerings, and appeal for suitable rains or better times. In wide-spread outbreaks of malarial fever, or in serious epidemics affecting man or beast, the people of the whole country-side equally turn to him collectively for alleviation of their misfortunes. His commanding position is shown by their very rarely or never asking him to exert his powers in the case of minor evils, or those affecting single families.

In spite of the Buddhist story of his killing the monks, it is undeniable that the functions generally credited to him by the Kandians are those of a superior beneficent God, and not those of a maleficent evil spirit. This is nearly the position that he occupies among the Vaeddas, who, however, are on more intimate terms with him, and in some parts even expect him to attend to their little hunting requirements, and undertake the provision of game for them, like the Kiri-Ammā. In sickness, too, he is the benevolent deity to whom each Vaedda family turns for assistance and medical aid, and who protects their districts from epidemics and misfortune.

FIG. 42. Rock Temple of the Galē Deviyā.

The general character of the edifices constructed in honour of such a powerful and kindly deity certainly leaves much to be desired. Among the Tamil-speaking and other village Vaeddas, the building erected as a temple for him is an extremely simple and economical oblong structure, a mere hut, consisting of only one room, with an entrance at the middle of one end. It is roofed with grass, and has the spaces between the sticks of the walls closed by leafy twigs, like their own houses, which, in fact, it closely resembles. The service to the God is sometimes conducted in front of the entrance.

In the north-western Sinhalese districts the Hill God's temples, termed dēwālas, like those devoted to all minor deities or demons, differ in no respect from the latter structures. As a general rule, they are dedicated to several of these godlings or demons, as well as to the service of the God, who thus finds himself in a somewhat mixed company.

They all consist of two rooms, one being a small rectangular chamber with 'wattle-and-daub' walls, plastered over with mud, in which the *Ābarana*, or symbols of the deities, are stored, as well as any lamps required for the services, a copper or bell-metal vessel for containing sandal-wood, and at least one earthenware cup used for holding lustration water (Figs. 51–53). Attached to this is the *Dig-gē*, 'the long-house,' an oblong shed extending longitudinally in front of the sanctum, in which part of the services are held, and tom-toms and pipes are played. At one side, a small structure called the *Mulutaen-gē*, the 'kitchen-house,' is built for use as a kitchen when food is cooked for the gods and demons. In some places the dēwāla is a small cave-shelter under an overhanging rock, with the front enclosed by a wall of brick or dried clay. The reader is referred to the illustrations of both kinds of dēwālas devoted to this deity, including a celebrated one at Nīrammulla, which is held to be the leading one in Ceylon provided for him.

FIG. 43. The Nirammulla Dēwālaya.

CEREMONIES

WHEN the Tamil-speaking Vaeddas are about to leave their village on a hunting-trip they erect under a Velan tree, the tree whose wood is always used for arrows, a little shrine termed *kuḍāram,* like those of the Kiri-Ammā, a rectangular structure supported by four upright sticks set in the earth, with the floor of the shrine about three feet off the ground. The top is usually arched over, and the inside is lined with white calico. In it are laid the bright yellow flowers of the Raṇawarā bush (*Cassia auriculata*) and those of the Red Lotus (*Nelumbium speciosum*), with two wicks soaked in oil or fat in front of them.

On the ground immediately in front of the shrine, resting on a white cloth, are placed a small ' chatty ' or earthen pot, holding rice boiled in Coconut milk, and in two circles round it seven small earthen vessels (*kuncaṭṭi*) and seven larger ones (*mancaṭṭi*) containing the other usual cooked food as offerings—meat, cakes, etc. Round these are thirty nuts of the Areka palm, laid on thirty leaves of the Betel vine. Water is sprinkled over these articles and in front of the shrine, obeisance is paid to the offering, and the dedication is complete.

The wicks are now lighted, and the officiator, an ordinary villager acquainted with the service, dances in front of the offering, holding a flower-staff, called *mugura*, in his right hand. He is dressed in a good white cloth, and has a head-dress of the same yellow and red flowers as those in the shrine, which covers the whole top of his head. The mugura is a stick, eighteen inches long, covered over with the same kinds of flowers, and having a looped handle in the middle, so that it may be held horizontally without touching the flowers.

He then chants in a Sinhalese doggerel some words the meaning of which he, being acquainted only with Tamil, does not comprehend, although he knows that he is asking for deer. The purport, as nearly verbatim as I could follow them, is :—

"Pāta tantāna thanum! Ōm! Tāna tantāna! I have placed for you a gift, cooked food, Deity of the Country [*Dēcamu Hurā*]. Tāna tantāna tana! Stopping a Sambar deer at the place where it is to be killed, O Protector and Friend of Dharma, at the corner where the Sambar is shot with an arrow make it over to us. When the Sambar has fallen make over three more to us."

These men ask for no other animals but Sambar deer. After the celebrant has again danced before the offerings, he sits down cross-legged in front of them, holding the mugura vertically, and makes 'dabs' at, or points it at, the seven smaller vessels one by one. He then sets it upright in the middle of the milk rice.

The God now says in Tamil by the mouth of the celebrant :— "Go ye! To whatever place you go, you will overcome the thing encountered." The food is then eaten by the hunting party at the site of the ceremony. On their return no further offering is presented.

In case of sickness, the Lord of the Hills is again appealed to. The officiator, the interested relative of the patient, proceeds to the front of the temple, and stands erect there, facing the doorway; in his outstretched right hand he holds horizontally an arrow, near the butt-end, just beyond the feathers, with its point towards the doorway. He then says, "Lord God (*Āndavana Swāmi*)! Hill-Lord! By this, as it is brought and held in the hand, health must go (to the sick person)." He at once leaves without awaiting any intimation of the result of this order—or perhaps request, as the word which expresses an imperative 'must' is also used, as in Sinhalese, with the meaning 'hoping that (something) will occur.'

The Village Vaeddas of the interior appeal in a similar manner to the same deity for the cure of sickness, carrying with them their bow at the time. They admitted to me, with a laugh, that holding the arrow with its point towards the shrine had the appearance of a threat; but the God is thought to be so powerful that probably this is not their intention.

Those in the south prepare a little shrine, like that already described, under a shady tree, and offer inside it cooked rice, pieces of Coconut if available, a small cake made of rice-flour, and a little meat, these foods being purified by lustration of water; one lighted wick is fixed in front of the offering.

The officiator holds an arrow upright in his right hand, and while repeating his prayer to the God for the removal of the sickness makes little cuts with it at the rice, believing that as he cuts it the sickness passes into the rice. At the conclusion of the offering, a ceremonial dance is performed by the celebrant, in front of the shrine, holding the arrow in his hand.

Now comes the peculiar part of the ceremony. Although the sickness is supposed to have been communicated to the rice, it is thought that a ceremonial sprinkling of water over the latter will drive it out again. This is now done, and the food having been thus purified is divided among the persons who are presenting the offering and the patient, and is eaten together with the other things offered.

This ceremony is called the *Gaḷē-Yak-maḍuwē bat pūjāwa*, 'the Offering of the Rice of the Galē Yakā's Shed,' the shed being the shrine. Similar dances and offerings are customary in the neighbouring parts of Uva.

The Vaeddas of the interior and their Sinhalese neighbours also dance to the Galē Yakā and his wife the Kiri-Ammā, in order to avert apprehended epidemic disease, or misfortune. This is before the occurrence of the sickness or bad-luck; after the sickness has set in the village becomes ceremonially impure, and it is held by them to be imperative that no dance to the God should take place within its boundary, which includes all the neighbouring jungle. The dance, which is usually performed once or twice a year, and preferably, by those who keep an account of the days of the week, on a Saturday or Sunday, is commonly executed under an Ironwood tree (*Nā, Messua ferrea*) when it is in flower, or a Banyan tree (*Nuga, Ficus indica*).

The dancer, a professional devil-priest, or a Vaedda, significantly termed Deyiyannē Kapuwā, 'the Devil-priest of the

God,' is dressed in a white cloth, and has a red handkerchief wrapped over his head. He also wears several bead necklaces, and any kind of bangles that his small store can furnish. If a Sinhalese man, he holds in his right hand a small *āwudē*, literally 'weapon,' a stick roughly shaped like an arrow; if a Vaedda an arrow is held by him.

He now becomes 'possessed' by the God (*mayanwelā*, in Sinhalese), after which everything he does or says is supposed to be the action or speech of the deity himself. While dancing in front of the shrine containing the offerings, he chants verses in honour of the two deities who are being worshipped. The usual food offerings made at such ceremonies are presented, the dance being begun after the two lights which are placed in front of the offerings have expired. Tom-toms are also beaten as an accompaniment by those who have them.

But the special place for such dances to the God of the Rock, for the Vaeddas particularly, and also for the Sinhalese who live near them, is on the summit of precipitous crags on or near the top of certain hills of the district, on which this form of worship has been performed from ancient times. On these they dance once a year to ensure the general prosperity of the district. The Officiator, the Deyiyannē Kapuwā, is accompanied in the Vaedda ceremony by any two men as assistants, who alone climb up onto the rock with him. Among the neighbouring Sinhalese the assistants are the washerman who washes the Kapuwā's clothes, and the smith who made the God's emblem; the former stays at the foot of the crag, and the latter alone goes with the dancer to the summit. The three persons wear no special head-covering, but each one has a handkerchief on it, and is dressed in the Sinhalese ceremony in a clean white cloth. In the Vaedda ceremony, I was assured that each one is dressed in an old torn cloth, and not a new one. It appears to represent the traditional dress of their ancestors.

The dancer carries up the symbol of the God, which is not an arrow, as one would expect, but a short-handled bill-hook, called a Raṇ-kaetta, 'Golden Bill-hook,' in Sinhalese, or Mannà-kaetta, in the Vaedi dialect. The latter word probably means 'Bill-hook of Honour'; or it may be connected with the word *mantra*, prayer, spell. He holds this in his right hand while performing the dance.

No particular day of the week is selected by the Vaeddas for the ceremony, all days being alike to them. It usually takes place during the daytime, but occasionally at night, torches being then carried by the assistants. This appears to point to planetary influences over the hour selected for it, which in such cases will be determined by a Sinhalese Kapuwā.

The dance performed by the Vaeddas is an extremely simple one. The body is slightly bent forward, with the elbows near the sides, and the fore-arms extended horizontally. In this attitude the performer lifts up and lowers his feet alternately, turning round gradually to the right while chanting verses in honour of the God, to the air, which begins each stanza :—*Tānan tańdĕni tā'nā nē'ē*, the last part being sometimes varied to *tadi nā nē*, when repeated at the end of a verse. As my informant, himself an officiator at these services, was unfortunately obliged to leave immediately owing to his child's sickness, in order to arrive at his home, far away in the forest, before complete darkness set in, I had not an opportunity of writing down the invocation which accompanied his dance; it consisted of eight or ten four-line stanzas of a very simple character.

For three days before the dance the Kapuwā must make himself ceremonially pure by bathing daily, and by not entering a house. For three days after it there is the same restriction against entering houses. Apparently time is required, as in ordinary devil-ceremonies, for the divine afflatus to become dissipated, and while it lasts the 'possessed' person lives in a state of tabu. During his whole life the professional Kapuwā must specially avoid eating, under penalty of death inflicted by supernatural power, any part of certain animals which are 'unclean' to him. These are the Pig, *Ūrā*; the large Monkey, *Wandurā* (*Semnopithecus priamus*); the Peafowl, *Monarā*; the Shark, *Mōrā*; and a large river-fish called *Magurā*.

This prohibition appears to have no connection with Hinduism, or the common Brown Monkey, *Rilawā* (*Macacus pileatus*), would be included, and also the Rat, as the vāhana of Gaṇēsa, and the Turtle as representative of Vishnu ; or some of these. I have already referred to the significance of the inclusion of the Shark. The Pig must appear in the list for the same reason, that is, as an eater of dead bodies, which might be those of human beings. The Magurā is probably added for a similar cause. The plumage of the Peafowl is generally thought to be auspicious, but I am not aware if this is the opinion of the Vaeddas. The primary feathers of the wing are always employed for feathering arrows, which it will be seen, by their use in the religious services, have something of a sacred character attached to them. I can offer no suggestion regarding the inclusion of the Wandurā, unless it be on account of its human appearance. I think it is clear that there is nothing totemistic in these prohibitions.

In the district of the Vaeddas, the following are all the hills on which are found the so-called ' Dancing Rocks ' (*natana gal*), one on each hill, of which I could obtain information :—Ōmungala near Rūgama tank, Henannē-gala, Kokkā-gala, Dambarā-gala, Unakiri-gala, Māwarā-gala, and one near Diwulāna tank.

It is among the north-western Kandian Sinhalese, however, that the ceremonies in honour of the God of the Rock, as he is there called, have survived, or have been developed, in the most complete manner. Yet it is evident that even there the cult has seen its best days. The dance is no longer an annual event at several of the rocks devoted to it ; occasionally intervals of some years elapse between two celebrations, and in a few cases it has altogether fallen into disuse. This is said to have been caused by the death of the officiating priests, and the want of successors, and not through lack of support by those who provide the expenses.

In these districts, in all cases the dance, which is a very important part of the proceedings, and indispensable in the complete ceremony, takes place on a high precipitous projecting crag near the top of a prominent hill, or on the summit of the hill if it is a single bare rock. These rocks commonly face towards the south, but not invariably; and I have stood on one that was on the northern end of a long hill (Dolukanda) which has a high vertical precipice on its top, facing due east, that might have been selected for the purpose, if desired. This fact is of some value as almost necessarily indicating the absence, from an early date, of any connection with sun or moon worship, at any rate with adoration of the rising sun, which is further emphasised by the performance of the ceremony on all the rocks at or after noon, and never in the early mornings. The occasional dances at night by the Vaeddas also prove that the cult is quite unconnected with sun worship.

The following is a nearly complete list of all the hills in the Kandian districts on which the Dancing Rocks are situated, together with the names of the dēwālas at which the subsequent proceedings are carried on, and from which a procession accompanies the performer to the hill where the dance is to take place. An asterisk is prefixed to the names of those hills at which dancing has now ceased.

Hill.	Dēwāla.
Gōpallawē-gala	Ganēmulla.
,,	Gōpallawa.
,,	Maedagampola.
Deviyannē-kanda.	Gōkaraella.
*Ganēmullē-gala	Ganēmulla.
Dēvagiriya (Kabara-hīnna and Kaeṭa-gala-hīnna)	Nīrammulla.
Hummuttiyāwa Galpaya, or Aematiyā Galpaya, in Pallēkaelē Forest.	?
*Nelliya-gala.	Nelliya.
*Mānapaya-kanda.	Yāpāgama.
Kandalawa-kanda (two rocks)	Kandalawa.
Kōmbuwē-gala.	Kōmbuwa.
,, ,,	Malla-waewa (abandoned).
*Bōgamuwa-kanda	Bōgamuwa.
Aragama-kanda.	Ganēgoḍa.
*Dolukanda (Rāsamūna-gala).	Bārubē.
Madahapola-kanda.	Madahapola.
Dekanduwala-gala.	Kanduboḍa-gama.
Nikawāē-gala.	Nika-waewa.
*Rock on Moratta-oya.	Kahalla.
Āṇḍiya-gala (N. C. Province)	Āṇḍiya-gala (Indigollāēwā).
Bambā-kanda (Mātale District)	Galēwela.

Dancing Rocks of the Galē Deviyā.

All but the last two are in the eastern part of the Kurunāēgala district.

The ceremony takes place in the months Aehala (July–August), or Nikini (August–September), sometimes on a Monday, but generally and preferably on a Wednesday or Saturday, and never on a *pōya* day (the Buddhist Sabbath, which is kept at each quarter of the moon), but sometimes on the day following it. Wednesday and Saturday are specially devoted to demon ceremonies, and are the two most inauspicious days of the week, and as such are invariably avoided for beginning any journey or work.

The months in which the dance is performed are two in which the full force of the winds of the south-west monsoon is felt in this district, and the work of the dancing-priest is thus on some occasions excessively dangerous on such exposed sites, a few of which can be reached only by means of ladders. In one instance, at Aragama-kanda, it is stated that the dancer was blown clean away and never seen again ; and that any dancer escapes unhurt is attributed to the protection afforded by the God.

For two days prior to the ceremony the dancer must not enter a dwelling-house, and he usually lodges at the dēwāla ; for three days after it he is subject to a similar ban. He then bathes, anointing himself with lime-juice, and the restriction ends. He must never enter a house in which a birth has taken place, until a month has elapsed after the event—some say seven days only—nor a house in which a death has occurred until three months have passed, and then only after it has been cleaned and purified by having new cowdung plastered on the floors.

As long as he lives he must not drink any spirituous liquor, and he cannot, on pain of death, eat the flesh or eggs of Fowls, *Kukulā*—including any bird which bears this Sinhalese name. Thus, the prohibition applies to the Jacana, *Diya-Kukulā* (*Hydrophasianus chirurgus*) ; the Spur-fowl, *Haban-Kukulā* (*Galloperdix bicalcaratus*) ; and the Ground Cuckoo, *Æṭi-Kukulā* (*Centrococcyx rufipennis*). Included in the prohibition are also Pigs. *Ūrā*, among which is reckoned the Dugong, called in Sinhalese the Sea-Pig, *Mūdu-Ūrā* (*Halicore dugong*); Sea-Turtles, *Kaesbā*; and Eels, *Āndā*. The 'Iguāna,' *Goyā*, is added by some, but not the Peafowl.

No devil-priest may eat these animals, whether he dances or not; they are termed 'unclean' (*kilutu*). If he has once officiated as a priest they are forbidden foods for the rest of his life, whether he takes any part or not in the services of either the God of the Rock or demons.[1] From infancy, it is customary for the male children of the priests not to be permitted to taste them, as possibly they may become devil-priests, and it is advisable to guard them from unnecessary defilement. The girls are allowed to eat them. Only men of good caste, *raṭē-minissu*, can officiate at the ceremonies in honour of the Galē Deviyā; but the caste has no influence affecting these food-prohibitions, which are equally applicable to low-caste dancers who take part in the services in honour of certain demons.

We have here a different set of animals from those considered unclean in the Vaedda districts, with the exception of the Pig. The Fowl may be forbidden partly as a bird whose blood is offered to demons, and perhaps also as a household bird, the cock being often kept at Buddhist temples to awake the monks early in the morning. Many Buddhists think it wrong even to eat the eggs. The Eel may be included on account of its feeding on garbage, and because it resembles a snake, which has protective powers.

I know no reason why Sea-Turtles, and no other kind of Turtles or Tortoises, are forbidden food, unless it be the Turtle-incarnation of Vishnu, who was at least very highly respected in Ceylon in pre-Christian times, and even now is permitted to have his statue in the Buddhist wihāras. It was he who took the precaution to tie charmed threads on the arms of Wijaya and his comrades, in order to preserve them from the Yakshas.

The story of the incarnation goes back to the time of the

[1] In Southern India, the Pūsāris, the officiators at demon offerings, are also forbidden to eat Fowls, Pigs, Peafowls, and Turtles, as well as certain grains and pulse.

great Churning of the Ocean in order to make Amrita.. The Gods and Asuras or Demons agreed to work together for this laudable purpose, which was effected like the production of the sacred fire. They took a mountain, Mandara, for a twirling-stick; and the King of the Serpents, Vāsuki, allowed his body to be utilised as the cord to be passed round it once, and pulled at the ends alternately, the Gods holding it at the tail, and the Asuras at the head. At first the effort failed; the mountain sank in the water or mud by its own weight, until at last Vishnu transformed himself into an immense Turtle, and permitted it to rest and turn on his back. It is called a Tortoise in the translations of the legend; but being in the sea it must have been a Sea-Turtle.[1]

It is almost needless to remark that such a restriction must have been originated among a race who knew and ate the Sea-Turtle. It cannot have come from an inland district where the Sea-Turtle would be unknown. This excludes all inland tracts, as none but fishers or those living near the sea would be affected by it. It appears to date from ancient times; at the present day and for more than two thousand years the people in Ceylon who are chiefly, or almost entirely, influenced by it in the case of the ceremonies in honour of the God of the Rock have never seen such an animal.

On the other hand, not one of the Vāhanas of the Indian gods is prohibited as food; even the Bull may be eaten by Sinhalese Kapuwās, as well as the Peacock and the Rat. It will be observed that these are Saivite 'vehicles,' and do not belong to the worship of Vishnu.

The dance on the rock takes place about noon, or in the afternoon, and it sometimes lasts for nearly an hour. The day is fixed some weeks in advance, in order to allow time

[1] In the *Ordinances of Manu*, v, 18, the Tortoise is included among the animals which 'the wise have pronounced eatable'; tame Cocks and tame Swine are excluded (v, 19). Monkeys come under the category of animals with five toes, which are forbidden. Peafowl are not expressly excluded, but it is ordained (xi, 136) that the slayer of a Peacock or an Ape must present a cow to a Brahman—the same fine as for killing wild carnivorous animals (xi, 138).

for the necessary provisions to be collected for the offering and feast which follow the dancing.

On the appointed day, the dancing priest, who is termed Anumaetirāla,[1] and not Kapurāla (the ordinary title of a good-caste devil-priest), dons at the dēwāla the traditional dress of the God,[2] consisting of a many-flounced coloured skirt or skirts, an ornamental jacket with puffed out sleeves reaching to the elbows, and especially a tall tiara-like conical white hat (*toppiyama*), made in three tiers or sections, as well as a jingling anklet, *salamba* (in Tamil, *silampu*), and any other usual ornaments, bangles, etc., of his profession.

He also takes in his right hand the Ābarana, or symbol of the deity, a Bill-hook, nearly sickle-shaped, with an ornamental handle about two feet long, to which is tied a much smaller one, having its blade immediately below that of the large one. This latter is the symbol of the God's minister, the redoubtable Kurumbuḍa Dēvatā. In his other hand he sometimes holds some flowers of the Areka-palm, merely for the dance, and not as offerings.

The Anumaetirāla now becomes 'possessed' (*mayanwelā*) by the God, and henceforward his actions are no longer under his own control but are those of the deity. Holding the symbols of the deities, he marches to the Dancing Rock, generally about a mile from the dēwāla, accompanied by his two assistants, the smith who made the weapons, and the washerman who washes the Anumaetirāla's clothes; he is preceded by tom-tom beaters, and followed by an indiscriminate crowd of villagers. Meanwhile, others have collected near the hill which is his goal, selecting vantage grounds whence a good view of the proceedings is obtainable. The crowd often numbers several hundred people.

The Anumaetirāla and his two assistants alone ascend the hill, the former being assisted by the other two to mount the crag, if necessary. At some places all three climb onto the

[1] From *Anumatiya*, sanction or command. Thus he is the person who acts under the God's command, that is, because he is compelled by the God to do it. It is supposed to be involuntary on his part.

[2] See the Frontispiece.

Dancing Rock, but generally only the smith goes onto it, in order to be ready to render him any assistance which may be needed on account of the wind; in such a case the washerman waits for them at the foot of the crag.[1]

On this wild and often extremely dangerous platform, on some hills a mere pinnacle, usually hundreds of feet above the plain below, and in one case—(Dolukanda)—more than a thousand feet above it, and in full view of the spectators gathered there, the Anumaetirāla now performs his strange dance, like that of all so-called devil-dancers. He chants no song in honour of the ancient deity (according to my information), but postures in silence with bent knees and waving arms, holding up the Bill-hooks—the God himself for the time being. In a rough outline drawing, representing this dance, on the wall of the ancient temple of the God at Mallawaewa (Fig. No. 42)—from which I obtained the cup and lamp illustrated below—the deity is drawn with a triangular beard, and he holds a Sword instead of a Billhook. When he begins to feel exhausted the performer brings the dance to an end, but sometimes his excitement makes it necessary for his assistant to seize him, and forcibly compel him to stop. He then descends from his dizzy post, assisted by his henchmen, and returns to the dēwāla with the tom-toms and the crowd.

While the party are absent at the Dancing Rock, the women of the village at which the dēwāla is established cook at the house of another priest, called the Muḷutaen (kitchen) Kapurāla, a feast consisting of cakes, milk-rice (rice boiled in coconut milk, that is, not the liquid found in the coconut when it is opened, which is never used, but some made by squeezing grated coconut in water until the latter acquires the colour of milk), rice, and also curries made of three kinds of vegetables termed *tun-mālu*.

The whole party from the rock come to this place, and the Anumaetirāla examines and expresses his approval of the food, which has been laid ready for his inspection in earthen

[1] At some sites it is said that only the Anumaetirāla goes on to the rock on which the dance takes place.

vessels deposited on a clean white cloth on the floor, each covered by a small round grass mat. He then proceeds to the dēwāla, in which he replaces the Ābarana, and removes the hat and the other habiliments of the God, being then no longer possessed by him. After this, he comes back to the house of the Mulutaen Kapurāla, and he and all the rest of the people eat the food that had been prepared. I was informed that on one occasion seven and a half bushels of

FIG 51. Black Earthenware Cup.

FIG. 52. Beaten Copper Cup.

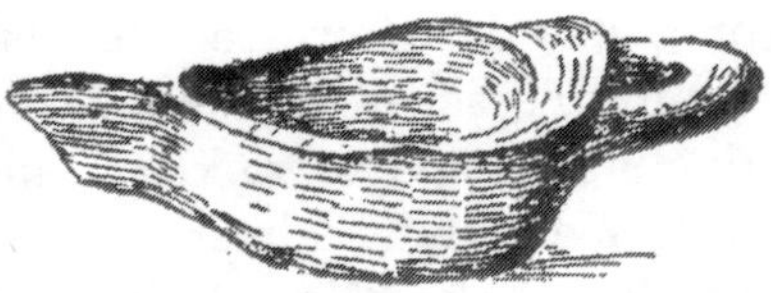

FIG. 53. Black Earthenware Lamp.

Ancient Utensils of the Galē-Deviyā.

rice were thus disposed of, making a good meal for five or six hundred people.

During all this time the deities have been left without food. After the conclusion of this feast and the indispensable chew of betel which follows it, the Anumaetirāla, the Mulutaen Kapurāla, and some of the people return to the dēwāla, and there the Mulutaen Kapurāla himself cooks, in the Mulutaen-gē or kitchen, some of the same foods for the Gods. The Anumaetirāla never takes any part in these duties, but when the cooking is finished it is he who makes the offering of the food. At other times, in the case of other Gods and demons, this is done by a third priest, called the Tēwāwa Kapurāla, all having strictly defined duties.

On a *yahana*, an oblong stand or altar, with a flat top, prepared previously in the dēwāla, the Ābarana, or insignia, of all the deities to whom the dēwāla is dedicated, are separately placed on a white cloth by the Anumaetirāla, after sprinkling in front of it saffron-water, that is, water in which a piece of saffron or turmeric had been placed. Incense laid on burning charcoal deposited in a censer is also waved in front of it. This always follows the lustration with the saffron-water, and is invariably a part of all such purifications.

He now once more assumes the dress of the God, and other ornaments of devil-dancers, but not the tall hat, which is reserved for the dance on the rock, of which it thus indicates the special character. Its place is taken by a white cloth which covers his head and shoulders. The Muḷutaen Kapurāla now brings into the dēwāla the food which he has cooked, and the Anumaetirāla offers it to the deities.

As a good illustration of this service, I shall take the case of a dēwāla at which the insignia of five other deities are kept. These are Pattinī Dēvī, whose symbol is her hollow jingling bangle or anklet, called *salamba* ; Dēvatā Baṇḍāra or Daeḍimuṇḍa, already mentioned in connection with the Vaeddas, whose symbol is a *yakaḍa-āwudē*, 'iron weapon,' a thin rod of iron, thicker at the butt end than the other, which is bent over to one side ; Kumāra Baṇḍāra, an Indian evil spirit or demon, the son of a king of Madura, whose symbol is a straight sword, *kaḍuwa* ; Dahanaka Baṇḍāra, whose symbol is a bill-hook, and Yāpawu Baṇḍāra, whose symbol is also a bill-hook, these two last being deified chiefs. There is also the sword of Kurumbuḍa Dēvatā.

The Anumaetirāla lays on the altar, on a white cloth extended in front of the Ābarana of the seven deities, seven sets of pieces of fresh green Plantain leaf, to act as dishes, each consisting of two pieces, laid one over the other. These, like everything else used, are purified by sprinkling them with saffron-water and fumigating them with the incense.

He then takes four strips of Areka-palm flowers, and lays them on each plantain dish, so as to form a hollow square on each; and in the centre of each square he places a little of the newly-cooked rice and the other food, after first purifying it, and reverently offering it with both hands towards the Ābarana. Great care is necessary to apportion the rice equally among the seven deities, so that none may be offended at receiving less than his neighbours; this is a detail regarding which they are unduly sensitive. A little sandal-wood, *handun*, is now rubbed on each leaf, and one or two little earthenware oil-lamps are lit in front of the offering. In some places a narrow-mouthed, round-bodied flower pot, called *kalasa*, filled with Areka-palm flowers, is placed there, with an earthenware lamp resting across its mouth, on the flowers.

A yaṭa yahana, or 'Lower Altar,' is now formed by a mat laid on the floor in front of the God's altar. On this six sets of Plantain-leaf dishes are first prepared for the reception of the meats, after the same purification as before; and on them is divided the rest of the cooked food, after being first purified, and offered in the hands towards the Ābarana. No light is placed on this altar. This food is said to be presented to six minor deities, called Dēvatāwas, whose names are unknown. They are considered to be a form of demon; and judging by the practice elsewhere part of the food is doubtless an offering to all absent minor deities or demons collectively, who always expect to receive a small share when others are fed.

Invocation is now addressed by the Anumaetirāla to the Gods of the upper altar, calling on them to come and partake of the feast prepared for them. After a short interval the foods are removed, and sliced Areka-nut laid on Betel leaves is deposited in its place, purified as usual, on the seven leaves of the upper altar, but none is presented on the lower one for the inferior personages.

Both before and after offering the food, tom-toms and other instruments are sounded as loudly as possible, so as to arouse the attention of the Gods, who are also held to feel satisfaction when this music is executed zealously and in an artistic manner. The instruments used for the purpose at the dēwāla in question are as follows:—one drum, *dawula*; one common tom-tom, *bera-geḍi* (not the long tom-tom used for demons, which is called *yak-bera*); one double kettle-drum, *temmattan* (used at wihāras); one horn trumpet, ***horanāēwa***; one reed-pipe, ***nalāwa***; and one perforated conch-shell, ***hak-geḍi***. When all these instruments are emitting their loudest sounds it will be understood that the result is a fine medley of noise.

After offering the Betel, and while the instruments are being played, the Muḷutaen Kapurāla may dance, holding a sword and not the Billhook in his hand, and chanting at the same time verses in honour of the various deities; but this is not an indispensable part of the ceremony. In the end, the Anumaetirāla puts back the Ābarana in their places in the sanctum, removes his habiliments, and thus brings the affair to a conclusion. He and the Kapurāla, but no one else, may now eat the offerings, the deities being supposed to have taken as much of the essence of the food as they required.

The rock-dancing ceremony takes place not more than once a year in connection with each dēwāla of the God of the Rock; but this offering at the dēwāla itself is, in the case of this one temple, made every three months, and is devoted to all the deities of the dēwāla collectively, and not alone to the God of the Rock. The ceremony is the same at places where he and his minister are the sole recipients of the offering; in such case a separate altar is constructed for Kurumbuḍa at a lower level than that of his master, but well above the ground.

The whole service is considered to be in honour of Gods, and not to be a demon ceremony. In all ordinary services for demons, meat in some form, or blood, is a necessary part of the food. It is clear that the Galē Deviyā's aspect as a beneficent deity is alone kept in view in these proceedings.

To my mind, the detailed account which I have been able

to present respecting this god leaves no room to doubt that we have here the worship of the original deity of Ceylon, dating from pre-Buddhistic times. The oldest gods of the East were mountain deities. In Babylonia they were born on the mountains, and Enlil, the greatest of the early gods, was especially the God of the Mountain. Such also were the great Indian Gods, Indra, Vishnu, Rudra, and the Maruts.

What is the explanation of the curious fact that in most respects the God of the Rock resembles the Rudra of the early Āryans of India? It is unlikely that an aboriginal deity of the hated Dasyus would be elevated by the first Āryan invaders of India to the high rank indicated by his being addressed as 'the best among the Gods,' a term applied to Rudra. In any case, the earliest Āryans of north-western India could have no knowledge of the religious notions of the South-Indian hill tribes. Did the aborigines, then, take over Rudra from the Āryans at a later date? This also seems improbable, as apparently the mountaineers, at all events, kept aloof from the invaders, and were little affected by their civilisation.

If they did not so borrow him, perhaps we may conclude that there was a wide-spread primitive belief in such a deity, extending not only throughout the hills of Central and Southern India, but also through the country from which the Āryans came. As some of the chief Āryan gods were hill-deities this must have been to some extent a mountainous tract It could only be in such surroundings that a belief in mountain-gods could be developed.

Rudra was the parent and Lord of the forty-nine Maruts who were the deities of the storm, and who dwelt 'on the lofty mountains.' So far as my information extends, he differs from the God of the Rock chiefly in being a Destroyer; the later story of the destruction of the sixty monks cannot be held to be sufficient proof that the original Vaedda God had this character.[1] But Rudra's aspect as such is not strongly emphasised in the Rig-Veda. He was pre-eminently

[1] Dr. C. G. Seligmann has, however, met with an invocation in which the Indigollāē Yakā is referred to as drinking human blood.

the beneficent kindly deity of the Āryans, the Health-Giver, the 'Best of all Physicians.' In this respect, Rudra and the Vaedda deity have identical functions and attributes, as the following extracts from the Rig-Veda, (Griffiths' translation,) show plainly.

Book i, 43.

1. What shall we sing to Rudra, strong, most bounteous, excellently wise?
4. To Rudra, Lord of Sacrifice, of hymns, of balmy medicines, we pray for joy and health and strength.
5. He shines in splendour like the Sun, refulgent as bright gold is he,[1] the good, the best among the Gods.
6. May he grant health unto our steeds, well-being to our rams and ewes, to man, to woman, and to kine.

Book i, 114.

1. To the strong Rudra bring we these our songs of praise, to him the Lord of Heroes with the braided hair,
   That it be well with all our cattle and our men, that in this village all be healthy and well fed.

Book ii, 33.

2. With the most saving medicines which thou givest, Rudra, may I obtain a hundred winters.
   Far from us banish enmity and hatred, and to all quarters maladies and troubles.
4. Let us not anger thee with worship, Rudra, ill praise, strong God! or mingled invocation:
   Do thou with strengthening balms incite our heroes; I hear thee famed as best of all physicians.
10. Worthy, thou carryest thy bow and arrows; worthy, thy many-hued and honoured necklace;
   Worthy, thou cuttest here each fiend in pieces; a mightier than thou there is not, Rudra.
11. Praise him the chariot-borne, the young, the famous, fierce, slaying like a dread beast of the forest.
   O Rudra, praised, be gracious to the singer; let thy hosts[2] spare us and smite down another.

---

[1] In modern paintings the God of the Rock is represented with a skin of a golden yellow colour.

[2] The Maruts, the Storm Gods.

Book v, 42.

11. Praise him whose bow is strong and sure his arrow, him who is Lord of every balm that healeth.
Worship thou Rudra for his great good favour.

Thus, although their symbols differ at present, though perhaps not originally, one carrying a billhook, and the other the bow and arrow, both are great sickness-removers from man or beast, the givers of health to their worshippers; and as such, both being gods of the mountains, they may have been in their origins the same deity. If so, the belief in such a god must extend back to a very remote age.

No reason has been discovered why certain hills only, sometimes in close proximity, were selected as the sole spots on which the dances to the God of the Rock should be performed. I could not observe that a specially sacred character is attributed to them by the Sinhalese, although I obtained some verbal evidence, possibly of little value, in favour of it;[1] but I believe the Vaeddas have some idea of the kind regarding those in their district, and Mr. F. Lewis heard this said of Kokkā-gala.

Riṭigala and many other prominent Kandian mountains are not known, according to tradition, ever to have been the sites of Dancing Rocks. Even a commanding rocky peak a few miles from Kurunäēgala, known as Yak-dessā-gala, 'the Devil-dancer's Rock,' is stated never to have been one of them, notwithstanding its suggestive name.[2] This is

[1] Mr. Bell states regarding the Dancing Rocks at Indigollāewa and Nikawāe-kanda, 'The rocks are so sacred that no one dares venture near them, except on the *perahaera* [procession] day; even hunters worship as they pass! (*Arch. Survey. Annual Report* for 1895, p. 5.)

In the Kurunāēgala districts I have never known any one show any reluctance to go with me onto the hills, or even onto the Dancing Rocks. I have also seen men go readily to cut grass on such a hill, and a party of villagers once spent a night with me at a cave close to one of the rocks.

[2] In the work on the Kohomba (or Kosamba) Yakā to which allusion is made in the Preface, Vaeddas are mentioned as living at this hill and at Alagala, on the side of the railway to Kandy. In it the word 'Vaeddas' is written *Vaeddan* and *Vaeddhan*; the latter shows the transition from *Vyādha*

probably correct, as no Yak-dessā, a title applied only to dancers of two very low castes, could ever take any part in the services in honour of this supreme deity of the country. With the decline of the cult, the use of many rocks for the dancing ceremony may have been abandoned and forgotten. In early times its practice must have extended over the whole country.

From the foregoing statements it may be concluded that the God of the Rock is a form of the original Rudra, who was developed at a later date into the great deity Śiva.

In his South Indian form he appears to have had two sons, Eiyanār or Ayiyanār, 'the elder brother,' and a younger one termed Ilandāri, 'the youth,' in Tamil, or Bilindā, 'the child,' in Sinhalese. To the sectarian feelings of the worshippers of these younger deities may be due the story of their enmity. Both are Guardian Gods of the forest districts of Ceylon, and as such both may have the title Wanni Deviyā, God of the Wanni.

Having these sons, the father must have had a wife, who would be the Hill Mother, Giri-Ammā, a word which became Kiri-Amman in Tamil, and thence Kiri-Ammā in Sinhalese. As the mother of Ayiyanār, she must be identified with the Indian goddess termed Mōhinī.

When Rudra had developed into Śiva the northern form of the Hill Mother, Parvatī, supplanted this southern deity as the wife of the Hill God in Hinduism.

According to the Mahā-Bhārata the birth of Skanda was 'full of all mysteries,' and in one legend he was the son of Rudra. Thus, if the God of the Rock be Rudra it would seem that, as his son, Ayiyanār may be a form of Skanda; and in that case Ilandāri or Bilindā may be a southern form of Ganēsa. The latter's name in Tamil is Pilleiyār, 'the child,' and both deities alike were killed while young, and revivified.

Part II

STRUCTURAL WORKS

VI

THE ARCHAEOLOGICAL VALUE OF BRICKS IN CEYLON

THE references in the early histories of Ceylon to the construction of any very ancient structures that can be identified at the present day, with the exception of some reservoirs and a few special dāgabas, are so rare and meagre that it is almost impossible to learn from the existing writings anything of value regarding the ages of nearly all the remains of buildings of various kinds that are scattered over the whole island. Even in the case of such well-known edifices as the earliest and most celebrated dāgabas there are many points of great interest to the antiquarian respecting which the histories are silent. As an instance of the neglect of the chroniclers to transmit to us a satisfactory record of buildings of even great importance, I may cite the absence of any reference to the addition of an outer shell enclosing the celebrated Ruwanwaeli dāgaba which was built at Anurādhapura in the second century B.C.

By a long series of measurements and sketches taken whenever opportunities occurred for a period of more than twenty years, I endeavoured to ascertain whether the mouldings and decorations of the various edifices disclose any types of detail that afford a clue to the period when the buildings at which they are found were constructed or repaired. In Europe, each arch or moulding and almost any kind of decoration is stamped, as it were, with the approximate date of its construction ; and it seemed possible that some similar gradation might be discovered in Ceylon. It proved, however, to be nearly hopeless to expect to meet with much success in this research, since it was ascertained that nearly identical mouldings were reproduced in buildings the erection of which is certainly separated by many centuries.

Probably the only conclusion to be arrived at, from an examination of these details, is that the simpler forms of outlines or decorations in buildings of a similar class may often indicate an earlier date of erection than the more elaborate ones. But this would be a very untrustworthy guide, as such details might be affected by the amount of the funds available for the work. There are also some peculiarities in the various modes of building with stone, and in the style of decorative design, that may point to earlier or later work. Thus, there are three entirely different types of holes cut for wedging stone, which indicate early, middle-age, and twelfth century work. But as general guides to the ages of structures it is evident that conclusions derived from such data are too vague to be of much use for practical purposes.

As a last resource, we are reduced to the bricks and brickwork. It has been already learnt that in some countries, as in Rome and Persia, the sizes of the bricks employed in buildings afford a valuable guide to the date of their manufacture. In India, although no definite scale of the dimensions may be possible, it is at least known that bricks of large sizes are a trustworthy indication of early work. I shall endeavour to show that in Ceylon, also, they may be utilised, in some instances, to a much greater extent than in India, but within somewhat wide limitations.

In order to obtain a satisfactory basis for such a conclusion the first requisite is a list of the dimensions of the bricks used in certain structures of varying ages, the dates of the construction or restoration of which are already known from the records found in the histories or preserved in the inscriptions that have been cut on them. It is in this respect that the chief difficulty lies. Even when a building is stated to have been erected during the reign of a special king, it may have been subsequently enlarged or repaired at some unknown time; and we might thus be led to accept as bricks of a certain age some that were burnt centuries afterwards. It was also a common custom, in the case of slight repairs that were executed at a later date, to utilise ancient bricks and cut stones brought from some pre-existing ruin of the neighbourhood.

But as knowledge of the different types of bricks and building work accumulates, the greater part of these difficulties tends to be overcome. For instance, when any extensive repairs have been carried out we always find a large proportion of broken bricks laid in the re-built work, and nearly invariably bricks of two or even three or four sizes, which have been moulded at the time when each repair was done, or additional work built.

The data on which the value of any tables of the sizes of the bricks must chiefly depend are as follows. The list of structures of various periods will probably be accepted as belonging to the dates here assigned. For the basis on which the first dates rest, reference may be made to the genealogical table of early kings at the end of the chapter on inscriptions, and to the remarks appended to it.

1. The large dāgaba, called the Maha Sāēya, at Mihintale, was constructed by King Dēvānam-piya Tissa in about 240 B.C.

2 and 3. The older dāgabas at Tissa (or Māgama) in the Southern Province, the Mahā-nāga dāgaba and the Yaṭṭhāla dāgaba, date from the reign of King Mahā-Nāga, that is, the second half of the third century B.C.

4. The Sanda-giri dāgaba, at the same place, belongs to the time of Kākavaṇṇa-Tissa, who reigned in the first half of the second century B.C. (Pūjāvaliya, p. 16.)

5. The Miriswaeṭi dāgaba at Anurādhapura, was built by king Duṭṭha-Gāmiṇi in 158 B.C.

6. The inner work of the Ruwanwaeli dāgaba at Anurādhapura was built by the same king in 137 B.C.

7. The Lankārāma dāgaba at Anurādhapura was erected by King Waṭṭa-Gāmiṇi, 76–88 B.C.

8. At Millāēwa-gala wihāra in the North-central Province, near Tantirimalei, an inscription in letters of the first or second century A.D,[1] refers to the construction of

[1] This inscription, a facsimile of which is given in Fig. No. 153, is as follows :—

(1) Sidha. Wihāra mawita puriha cata gowaka Sivaha leṇe (2)

the wihāra in the reign of King Nāga, that is Iḷa-Nāga, 38–44 A.D. or one of the earlier Nāgas of the second century.

9. Hurulla Tank, in the North-central Province, was made by King Mahā-Sēna, 277–304 A.D. (Pūjāvaliya, p. 27.)
10. Padawiya tank, in the North-central Province, appears to have been built by King Mahā-Sena. According to my information, it is called in a rare manuscript (the Maha Jalanandana) Maha Ratmala tank, which is included in the list of those made by him (Mah. i, p. 151).
11. The Vaṇṇāṭṭi Pālama, the dam on the river below Padawiya, for utilising the water of that reservoir, is of about the same age.
12. Nīrammulla Tank, in the North-western Province, on the Kimbulwāna-oya, is included in the same list, as Kumbhīla-vāpi, and is of the same age.
13. The inner room of the building called the Daḷadā Māligāwa, 'the Palace of the Tooth-Relic,' at Anurādhapura was probably built early in the fourth century A.D.
14. Tōpāwaewa, the tank at Polannaruwa, was made by King Upa-Tissa I, 370–412 A.D. (Rājāvaliya, p. 54).
15. The Gallery at Sīgiriya was built by Kassapa I, 479–497 A.D.
16. The Rankot, 'Golden-Spire,' dāgaba at Polannaruwa was built in the latter part of the twelfth century A.D.
17. The Thūpārāma Hall at Polannaruwa was built in the twelfth century.
18. The wall of the Fortifications at Polannaruwa also belongs to that period.

ca(tu disa sa)gaya niyate. Naka rajaha rajahi mawita. Hail! Having built the wihāra, the cave of Sīva, Guardian of the City Dāgabas, is assigned for the community of the four quarters. Constructed in the reign of King Nāga.

The meaning of *Cata* is doubtful when qualified by *puriha*; as the word often stands for *caitya* in inscriptions I have given it this interpretation. Sīva or Siva may have been an official whose duty it was to undertake the repairs, whitewashing, etc., at the Anurādhapura dāgabas.

The following table exhibits the contents and mean dimensions in inches of the bricks used in this series of ancient works. I add also, for comparison, the sizes of the bricks used in the large dāgaba at Sāñchi in India, which dates from the time of Aśōka[1] (263–222 B.C.), although the measurements are only given roughly by Sir A. Cunningham in his work on *The Bhilsa Topes*, p. 270.

Because of a reference to the name Cētiya-giri in Turnour's edition of the Mahāvansa i, 49, as the place where Dēvī, the mother of Mahinda and wife of Aśōka lived, and as there was a Buddhist heresy in the fourth century B.C. called 'the Cētiya schism,' Sir A. Cunningham stated his belief that this dāgaba may be as old as 500 B.C.,[2] but his argument is not satisfactory. In the first place, the corrected reading of the word in the Mahāvansa is Vēdisa-giri, Vēdisa being mentioned in several of the inscriptions found there ; and in the second place, the name Cētiya-giri is not a proof that a dāgaba existed there, the early meaning of Cētiya being merely 'a religious building,' and only secondarily a dāgaba. The Mahāvansa says plainly that the wihāra at Vēdisa was established by Dēvī, the wife of Aśōka, who himself left an inscription at it.

I look upon the Sānchi bricks as of the greatest interest. They are perhaps the earliest Indian bricks to which a date can be attached,[3] yet their dimensions demonstrate, without any doubt, that others of the same shape had been burnt in India long prior to this date. The measurements bear no definite ratio to each other. The length of the original

[1] *The Bhilsa Topes*, p. 124. [2] *The Bhilsa Topes*, p. 271, note.

[3] They are far from being the earliest Indian bricks, of course. In addition to the Greek references to the use of bricks in the structures of the fourth century B.C., the employment of burnt bricks one foot square, for building the altar of Nirriti, the Goddess of Destruction, the mother of Fear, Terror, and Death, is enjoined in the Satapatha Brahmana (vii, 2. 1) :—'They measure a foot square . . . they are unmarked—[an expression which shows that it was the custom to mark some other bricks] . . . they get baked by rice husks . . . they are black.' They were to be laid loosely, evidently not like other bricks—'he does not settle them—settlement being a firm footing—lest he give a firm footing to evil.' The date of this may be any time in the early part of the pre-Christian millennium.

bricks of this type would almost certainly be fixed at the cubit, like those of Ceylon, and the breadth and thickness would be simple fractions of the length. Yet nearly two inches had already been struck off the length, and probably an equal amount off the breadth when the Sānchi bricks were burnt. I refer here to this Indian question as it is of some value in connection with possible early brick-making in Ceylon, where this art may have been practised by 300 B.C., if not in the first half of the fourth century B.C., as I have explained in dealing with the first irrigation works.

No	Name of Structure.		Date.	Length.	Breadth.	Thickness.	Breadth × Thickness.	Contents.
	Large dāgaba, Sānchi .		B.C. 3rd Cent.	16·00	10·00	3·00	30	480
1	Mahā Sāēya, Mihintale	N.C.P.	3rd Cent.	17·92	8·87	2·91	25·8	461
2	Mahānāga dāgaba, Tissa	S.P.	3rd Cent.	17·35	8·84	2·83	25	434
3	Yaṭṭhāla dāgaba ,,	,,	3rd Cent.	17·85	8·64	2·90	25	447
4	Sanda-giri dāgaba, ,,	,,	Early 2nd Cent.	17·14	8·67	2·81	24·4	418
5	Ruwanwaeli dāgaba, inner work . . .	N.C.P.	2nd Cent.	—	9·67	2·79	27	—
6	Miriswaeṭi dāgaba, Anurādhapura . .	,,	2nd Cent.	—	10·41	3·0	31·2	—
7	Lankārāma dāgaba, Anurādhapura . .	,,	Early 1st Cent.	17·37	8·94	2·62	23·4	407
8	Millāēwa-gala dāgaba .	,,	A.D. 1st or 2nd Cent.	15·57	8·00	2·72	21·7	339
9	Hurulla tank, central sluice	,,	Late 3rd Cent.	—	8·40	2·70	22·7	—
	Hurulla tank, high-level sluice	,,	,,	—	8·35	2·51	21	—
10	Padawiya sluice . . .	,,	,,	14·02	8·50	2·46	20·9	293
11	Vaṇṇāṭṭi Pālama . .	,,	,,	13·61	8·48	2·70	22·9	311
12	Nīrammulla sluice . .	N.W.P.	,,	—	8·45	2·70	21·5	—
13	Daḷadā Māligāwa, inner room	N.C.P.	Early 4th Cent.	14·10	8·45	2·52	21·3	300
14	Tōpāwaewa sluice . .	,,	Late 4th Cent.	—	7·40	2·43	18·00	—
15	Sīgiriya gallery . .	,,	Late 5th Cent.	13·09	7·32	2·31	16·90	220
16	Rankot dāgaba, Polannaruwa	,,	12th Cent.	12·52	8·40	2·00	16·80	210
17	Thūpārāma hall, inside, Polannaruwa . . .	,,	,,	12·00	8·36	2·00	16·70	201
18	Fortification wall, Polannaruwa	,,	,,	12·63	8·20	2·00	16·40	207

Although when the bricks used in other buildings are examined the actual irregularities in the sizes become much more evident than this table shows, if the contents and area of the side be alone considered, it is quite clear that there is a generally-diminishing scale in the dimensions of the bricks from the earliest period down to the thirteenth century. But although the gradation is found to be often characterised by irregularity, this is not present in such an excessive degree as to prohibit the use of the dimensions—with a certain amount of discrimination—for determining the probable dates of the structures in which the bricks are found. For instance, the short table already given would at least enable any one to distinguish, by the bricks alone, a work of the tenth or twelfth century from one of the second or third century A.D., and the latter from one of pre-Christian date. Even if some exceptions occur in which the age of the construction is doubtful, or even with regard to which a dependence on such measurements might lead to an actual mistake in the time, they should not be allowed to outweigh or to throw much doubt upon the general advantage to be attained by the use of such an accessible method of ascertaining or corroborating the probable dates of structures.

In taking the dimensions of the bricks it is of less importance to measure a great number of lengths than to take a good series of thicknesses, so as to obtain a trustworthy mean thickness; the breadths occupy an intermediate position in value. The reason is plain. The average thickness is about 2½ inches, one twenty-fifth of which is only one-tenth of an inch, a dimension that can hardly be correctly noted on ordinary bricks, which often vary to this extent, or more, in different parts of the same brick; and thus it can only be accurately measured by taking the mean thickness of several bricks. In the case of the lengths of the bricks, however, one twenty-fifth of even the shorter bricks is half an inch, beyond which the error due to utilising the average size of only two or three bricks as the mean length is not likely to extend. Thus an error of half an inch in the length is of equal importance to an error of one-tenth of an inch in the thickness.

A clear understanding of this fact is of practical service, firstly, because it saves time on the ground, especially in searching for more whole bricks than are necessary; and secondly, because the accidents of time or the repairs of edifices have resulted in the fracture of nearly all the longer bricks, with the exception of those laid in buildings that were specially protected from damage by their mass or situation.

It is still more important in another way. In cases where no whole lengths can be found it permits the use, within certain limits, of a length calculated from the thickness or breadth, or derived from a comparison with other similar bricks, the error in such instances being probably often little more, *in proportion*, than that made when only two or three measurements of the thickness are possible. This is especially the case if the bricks have been moulded on the ground, and not on planks or tables.

On comparing a large series of measurements of bricks employed in various parts of Ceylon it is clear that the proportions varied in different periods. In the earliest times the length was commonly about six times the thickness, and the breadth was about half the length. Afterwards, the length was reduced to about five or even four times the thickness, though it never reached the English ratio of three times the thickness. The breadth also latterly varied between one-half and two-thirds of the length, but was commonly near the latter ratio.

The contents fell from a possible maximum of about 673 cubic inches [1] to 77 cubic inches; and the area of the side was reduced from 34 square inches to 7·7 inches. In actual dimensions, the length varied from a possible 19·8 inches to 8·2 inches, the breadth from 10·4 inches to 5·0 inches, and the thickness from 3·4 inches to 1·55 inches.

I have consigned to an Appendix a Table containing the sizes of the bricks measured at a large number of ruins in Ceylon,

[1] The contents of the largest bricks of which the three dimensions were actually measured was 583 cubic inches; but at three other sites larger ones appear to have been burnt, although unfortunately their lengths could not be measured, no unbroken bricks having been found (see Appendix).

which it is desirable to preserve for the use of local archaeologists, and in some instances for general reference. In preparing it I was confronted by the difficulty caused by the absence of the lengths in places where no whole bricks could be found, or were not in a position where their lengths could be measured, as in some dāgabas where the outer bricks are all 'headers'. In these examples I have inserted in brackets in some cases an approximate length and contents, obtained by making the length a definite proportion of the breadth or thickness. Of course it will be understood that the figures so included in brackets merely indicate the *probable* length and contents, and nothing more.

As regards the periods into which the table has been divided, it is evident that their limits cannot be accurately defined. It may at least be asserted with some confidence that the first one, ending at about the Christian era, is nearly correct; and the same remark may possibly be applicable to the second period.

Owing to the slight change in the sizes from the sixth to the twelfth centuries there will always be considerable uncertainty as to the dates of that period. It is probable that by a reference to the table, however, the date of any bricks may be fixed at that time without an error of much more than one hundred and fifty years; and prior to that time usually within the limits of about one hundred years.

I give a few examples of the application of the information obtained from the table in determining the ages of some structures. Many others will be found in the following chapters, where I have made full use of it.

The Thūpārāma wihāra and dāgaba at Anurādhapura were built by Dēvānam-piya Tissa (245 — B.C.); but the latter was at least partly pulled down and rebuilt subsequently, and in any case the bricks used in it, which would doubtless consist chiefly of those originally employed, are covered up by a coat of plaster. In a small building which still remains on the same platform, and close to the south side of the dāgaba, there are bricks measuring 19 inches by 9·15 inches by 3 inches, with a contents of 521 inches, and a side area (which in future will be termed Bt, that is, the average breadth multipled by the average thickness) amounting to 27·4 square inches.

From an inspection of the table it is safe to conclude that these bricks must belong to some period B.C., and possibly to a late date in the second century, or early in the first century. The building in question must have been a house for statues or relics, or both, no buildings intended for the occupation or personal use of the monks being ever permitted within the inner enclosure round a dāgaba in Ceylon, according to information given to me by Buddhist monks. References to such a building occur in the histories, and are given in a later chapter on the dāgabas. It is only the measurements of the bricks which prove that the building is of pre-Christian age.

The size of the bricks found in the Maeṇik dāgaba at Tissa shows that it was built at about the same time as the Sandagiri dāgaba at the same city; or in other words that it was erected in the first half of the second century B.C.

The table also proves that there are many other works that in all probability date from the last three centuries B.C., and it may be also stated as a general rule that where any early bricks are found in rock-caves at which inscriptions in the earliest characters occur, some of them are of a size which indicates that they belong to the same period.

The great value of the bricks in assisting in the determination of the ages of some of the dāgabas at Anurādhapura is apparent in a later chapter.

The bricks of the structures built at Anurādhapura in the second half of the second century B.C., and early in the first century B.C., exhibit great irregularity compared with those at both earlier and later works. It is not known why such variations were made in the sizes at this period. Perhaps it was a time of experiments, and trial was being made of some bricks of a larger size than had been used previously. The difficulty that must have been experienced in burning and handling such clumsy and heavy ones apparently soon led to the adoption of smaller and more convenient dimensions.

At Polannarudwa, the larger bricks used in the little Pabulu,

'Coral,' dāgaba are demonstrated by the table to be of pre-Christian age; while those at the Gal-wihāra at that city belong probably to the first century after Christ, and agree closely with the largest ones at the sedent Buddha at Tantirimalei. Mr. Bell, the Government Archaeologist, has already drawn attention to the similarity of the carving at these two places, the works at which he attributed to the same period.[1]

Although the whole construction at the Gal-wihāra is credited to King Parākrama-Bāhu I in the Mahāvansa, it is now shown by the bricks that his work there consisted only of some repairs at the old structure, and perhaps some additional rock excavation and carving. It is impossible to believe that the larger bricks found at these two sites were brought in each case from pre-existing ruins of their vicinity, at which, by some wonderful coincidence, bricks of practically identical sizes had been burnt more than twelve hundred years before. If the Tantirimalei bricks were burnt for use at the work at which we find them, so also were those of the Gal-wihāra; and it is certain from the table that they do not belong to the twelfth century.

In the case of the irrigation works, the table, as might be expected, yields some interesting information, part of which is utilised in later chapters. It will suffice here to draw attention to the evidence of the bricks at Pāvat-kuḷam, Sangili-Kanadara tank, Batalogoḍa, the Allē-kaṭṭu dam, and Nuwara-waewa, the largest reservoir at Anurādhapura, as well as the channel for filling it. The construction of not one of these important works is mentioned in the histories. Other works not now described, such as the Māmaḍu tank in the Northern Province, and Kaṭiyāwa tank, and Kītikaḍawala tank, and some others, in the North-central Province, appear to have been formed in pre-Christian times, although these also are not mentioned by the historians.

At the head-works of the channel for conveying water to the Giant's Tank, it is the bricks alone which prove the antiquity of this great irrigation scheme, as explained in the chapter

[1] Annual Report, 1896, p. 8.

on the 'Lost Cities.' Even without the inscription that was discovered at the reservoir, the dimensions of the bricks would enable any one acquainted with this table to affirm that the enlargement or improvement of this irrigation work was undertaken in about the twelfth century.

VII

ANCIENT ROCK CUP-MARKS

AS the Vaeddas were unacquainted with the art of smelting iron, or making any metal tools, and appear never to have had any stone tools of their own manufacture excepting very rudely made arrows and 'scrapers,' etc., no early stone-cutting in any form can have been done by them. What knowledge of the art was possessed by the primitive Nāgas is quite unknown, as no work that can be attributed to them has been discovered, nor, I believe, have any stone tools or weapons been found in the northern part of the island. Any early rock-cutting must thus have been done by the later immigrants or those who learnt the art from them, or by persons employed by them.

Some of the most ancient and undoubted work in stone which can be recognised at the present day in Ceylon consists of the cutting of the *kaṭāra*, or drip-ledge, over the earliest caves, and the carving of the earliest cave inscriptions under it—(both, however, works that indicate a good prior acquaintance with the ordinary use of the stone-cutter's chisel)—in the second half of the third century B.C. For reasons which are given in a later chapter, there is a possibility that some excellent stone-cutting in some sluices may be of about the same date.

It is certain that the men who employed the tools for such purposes were not mere learners of the art of trimming stone. The cutting at the earliest cave inscription exhibits a freedom and accuracy of touch which are a clear proof of previously-acquired skill. It may be concluded with certainty that these stone-cutters had either been brought over for the special purpose from India—where the Bharhut and Gayā sculptures prove that stone-cutting had been practised for a long period prior to the reign of Aśōka—or had possessed in Ceylon a long acquaintance with the art, even although any very early work done by them cannot be recognised now.

The Mahāvansa (i, p. 149) refers to a 'colossal and beautiful stone statue' of Buddha which was carved during the reign of Dēvānam-piya Tissa, probably in about 235 B.C. (and which *may* be the large statue now at the Abhayagiri monastery); but a special work of this kind might be done by one or two men imported from India, and does not prove, like the other works, a general knowledge of stone-dressing in Ceylon at that period.

Neither dolmens nor circles of stone posts, on which cup-markings are sometimes cut in other countries, being known in Ceylon, the only cup-shaped holes that have been met with occur on the natural faces of rock masses or boulders. Some later outline carvings were also left on a few stone slabs or steps, evidently the work of the stone-cutters who were engaged in trimming them; or were cut on rocks as boundary marks of the various districts into which the island was subdivided.

The shallow cup or saucer-shaped holes such as are found on rocks elsewhere are uncommon in Ceylon, and I know of only a few places where they occur. One of these is the hill Riṭigala, where Mr. H. C. P. Bell, the Government Archaeologist, informed me that he met with some, accompanied, I understood, by circles. He has not yet published a description of them, I believe.

Another site is a rock lying in the bed of the Kallāṛu, a stream in the Northern Province. As an ancient stone dam of unknown date, but probably pre-Christian, now called the Allekaṭṭu (Fig. 147), was built across this stream at the place, the work of cutting the holes appears to have been done by the men engaged in its construction. The holes are six in number, and in shape are excellently cut deep saucers, with well-smoothed sides and bottoms. The illustration, (Fig. No. 54), shows that after making seven wedge-holes in order to split off this stone for use in the dam, the masons left it untouched,

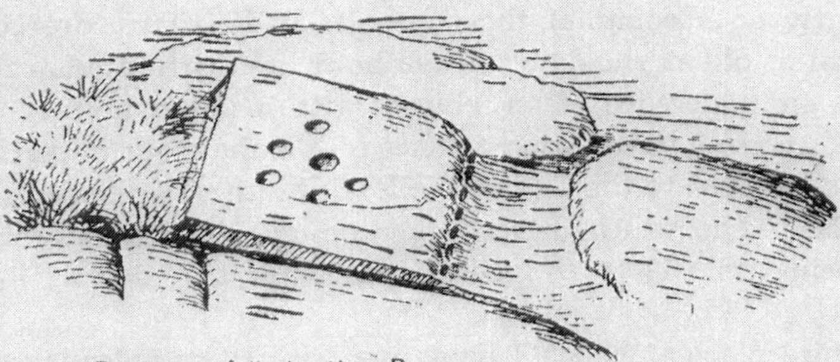

FIG. 54. Rock at Allekaṭṭu Dam

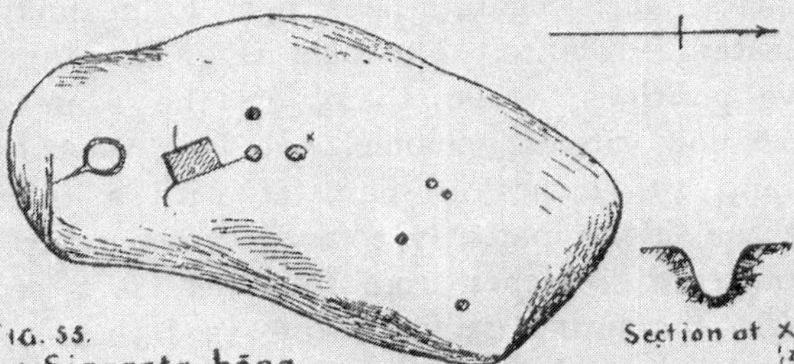

FIG. 55.
Boulder at Sigarata-hēna

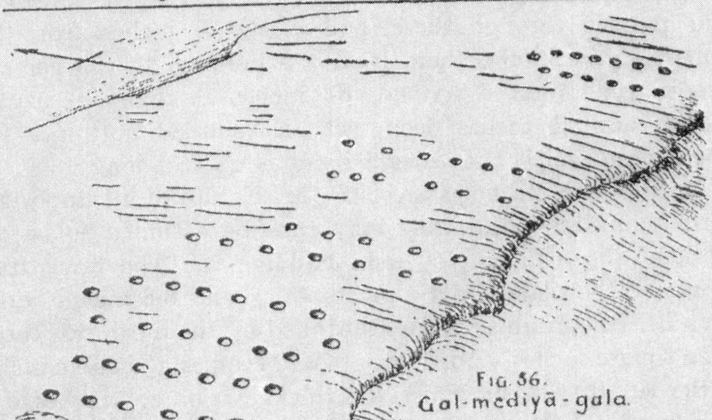

FIG. 56.
Gal-mediyā-gala.

Shallow Cup-holes.

evidently on account of the cup-holes in it. They are thus at least as old as the dam. Five holes are distributed nearly in the circumference of an ellipse, with a larger hole at its centre, an arrangement that at once recalls the mode of placing the food offered to the God of the Rock by the Tamil-speaking Vaeddas. The width of the whole design is 11 inches, each hole being from 1½ to 2½ inches in diameter, and about 1 inch deep.

A third place at which I have met with these holes is on a nearly flat-topped boulder at the side of a path in the forest, at a place called Sigaraṭa-hēna, near Pulugannāwa tank, in the Eastern Province. The plan (Fig. No. 55) shows their relative positions. Near them, on the same rock, there is a shallow circular channel one inch wide, half an inch deep, and 16¼ inches in diameter, with a tapering radial cut at one side, apparently to drain away water or oil. At a distance of 18 inches from this there is a peculiar sunk rectangle, measuring 23 inches by 15 inches, with a short curved channel cut from one corner. In a north-and-south line passing through these, and 7 feet 6 inches from the centre of the circle, there is also a hole of the larger and deeper type next described, 8½ inches in diameter at the mouth and 5¼ inches deep, with a rounded bottom. The boulder on which the holes are cut is 24 feet long.

In this case the holes are close to the site of an important early monastery, and they may thus be assumed to be the work of the men employed in building it. The brick fragments at the place are 2·5 inches thick and 8·8 inches wide; thus Bt. (the mean breadth multiplied by the mean thickness) is 22 square inches, and the contents becomes 330 cubic inches if the length was six times the thickness, or 275 inches if it was five times the thickness. These dimensions point to the second, third or fourth century A.D. as the period when the bricks were burnt, and the holes may be of the same age.

A fourth site is on the sloping surface of an immense rock termed Gal-maediyā gala, 'the Stone-Frog Rock,' which rises high above the surrounding forest, two and a half miles above the point where the river Siyambalan-gamuwa-oya crosses the minor road from Kurunāēgala to Anurādhapura. There are traces of a small building on the crest of the rock, and the remnants of a monastery on another rock termed Nelun-gala, 'Lotus-Rock,' a short distance away; while on the other side of the Frog Rock is the embankment of the Siyambalan-gamuwa tank, where a considerable amount of stone-work was used. The cutting of the holes may in this case also be attributed to some of the men employed at these works. The bricks used at the sluice of the tank and at the monastery at Nelun-gala, are of similar sizes, and indicate the second, third, or fourth century A.D. as the time when they were made. They average 2·56 inches thick, and 8·45 inches wide; Bt. is 21·6 and the probable contents does not exceed 332 cubic inches.

The holes (Fig. No. 56), which are in roughly parallel rows that run north and south, are 67 in number. The lines of holes are in five pairs, each line consisting of either six or seven holes, with in three cases an additional hole at the end, and in one case a hole at each end. The holes are shallow saucers in shape, about an inch and a half in diameter on the average, and a quarter of an inch deep; many of them are perfect circles in plan and beautifully hollowed out. They appear to have been intended for playing the game called in Arabic 'Mankala,' and termed Olinda Keliya 'the Olinda game' in Ceylon.[1]

It is strange that a site should have been selected in which the lower holes are on a part of the rock which slopes downward considerably, close to the edge of a precipice. The place is also quite exposed to the sun, and, as I myself experienced, the surface of the rock becomes greatly heated during the day-time, when one would expect the game to be played on such a site. It would seem to be unnecessary to cut this large number of holes in such close proximity, and in lines almost parallel, if they were merely intended for a game at which two persons require only one set of two rows. There are other parts of the rock that appear to be much more suitable for playing this game, where it would be needless to crowd

[1] For a full account of it, see *The Ancient Games.*

the holes together. The Sinhalese villagers who accompanied me to the rock, and who were well acquainted with the game, could offer no elucidation of the use for which the holes were intended ; they were unable to understand why any one should desire to play the game on such a site. Yet notwithstanding these reasons for doubt, and partly because of the holes next described I assume that these cup-holes were intended for the Olinda game. I may observe that for some reason which is unexplained it is possible that there may have been something of a sacred character in this game in Ceylon ; it appears to be specially connected in some way with the celebration of the festival of the New Year.

Another site was discovered by Mr. F. Lewis, at that time a member of the Forest Department in Ceylon, at Pallebaedda, in the Sabara-gamuwa Province, and I am indebted to his kindness for my information regarding it. The holes are cut in a rock immediately in front of three caves that were prepared in ancient times for the occupation of Buddhist monks. Mr. Lewis states, 'In front of the wihāra cave is a rock of a 'hog's back' outline, on the ridge of which are two well-cut [square] holes evidently to receive the wood-work of a shrine. A little to the right of them is what appears to be a sort of cribbage-board, in which there are 18 holes cut in the rock, ending with a crescent-shaped hole. The smaller holes are each about 1½ inches in diameter, spaced 1½ to 1¾ inches apart.' His sketch shows this to be an unmistakable Olinda board of nine circular cup-holes in each row.

The antiquity of the holes is indicated by the number of them, fourteen being invariably employed at the present day in Ceylon and Southern India. If the holes do not actually date from the period when the caves were being prepared for the monks it is probable that they belong to some time during the next few centuries.

As to the date of the work at the caves, there is definite evidence in the forms of the letters in the dedicatory inscriptions cut over them, below the kaṭāras. One inscription copied by Mr. Lewis is, *Tapasa D(e)vasa leṇe sagasa,* and in a second

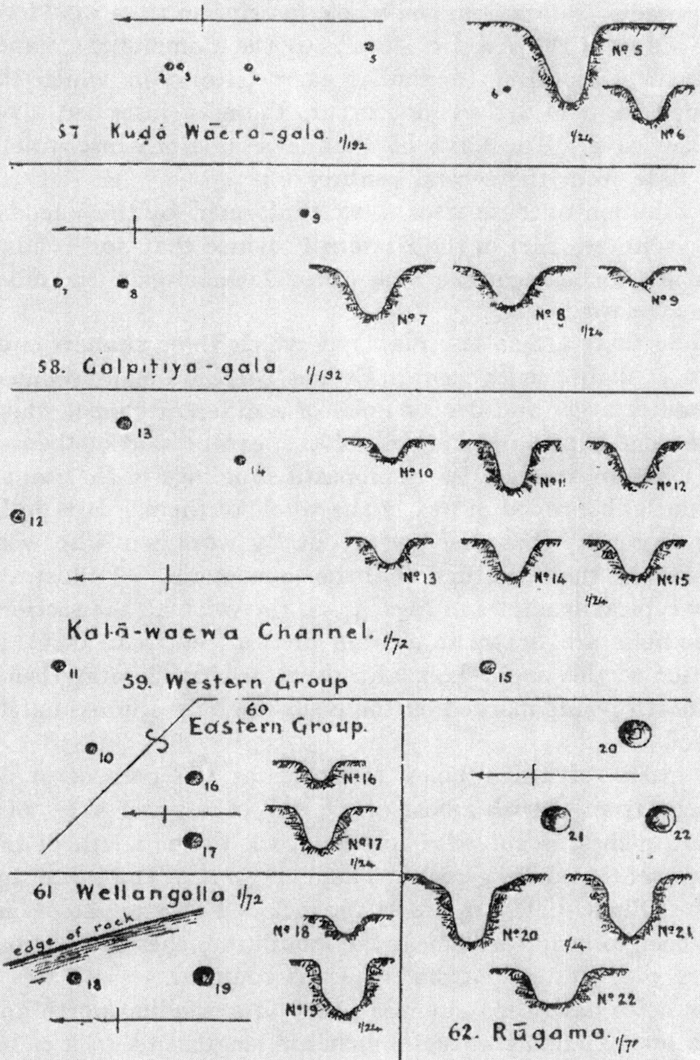

Plans and Sections of large Cup-holes.

line a word which in his hand-copy is *Tūsasa*. This may be in reality *Gutasa*, and the whole inscription then would be,—'The Cave of the Ascetic Dēva; to the Community; (and) of Gutta (Gupta).' In similar early letters, in which the rounded form of *s* does not occur, there is inscribed over another cave, 'The Cave of Pusadēva.'[1] Both inscriptions may date from the second century B.C.

In addition to these sites, I was informed by the Vaeddas of the southern part of the Eastern Province that some small holes are to be seen on a rock called Lenama-gala, six miles from Haelawa.

While there are so few places at which these shallow cups or saucer-shaped holes occur in Ceylon, there are many peculiar and much larger and deeper holes of a different shape, which await some explanation. This at least can be said of them—that there are traces of early monastic buildings in the immediate neighbourhood of nearly the whole of them. It is probable, therefore, that they were cut by workmen who were engaged on the construction of the monasteries. I illustrate a few typical examples in Figs. 57–62 (in which all the sections of the holes are drawn to a scale of two feet to an inch), in addition to the single hole already noted at Sigaraṭa-hēna. The north points marked on the plans are only approximately correct.

A group of three holes arranged at the corners of an isosceles triangle with a base of 3 feet 6 inches and sides of 4 feet 10 inches, is cut on a low flat rock to the south of the above-mentioned Frog-rock. They may be of the same age as the Olinda holes in the latter rock. They are all of one size, being 6 inches wide near the mouth, 6 inches deep, and 2 inches wide at the bottom, which is rounded.

Six holes have been cut in a group in a winding north and south line extending 40 feet 8 inches in length, in a rock called

[1] There is nothing to connect this person with the Phussadēva of the Mahāvansa, the great Archer-Chief of Duṭṭha-Gāmiṇi. On the other hand, it may be noted that the name is a most uncommon one; I have not met with it elsewhere. There remains a possibility, but nothing more, that the inscription was cut by orders of this Chief, but in that case one would expect to find him termed *Parumaka*, 'Chief.'

Kuḍā Wāēra-gala, 'the Small Dāgaba-rock,' at Wambaṭuwā-gama, in the North-central Province (Fig. No. 57). Close by, to the south, there is a large rock on which are the remains of a monastery, including a small dāgaba at which the bricks have a mean thickness of 2·75 inches, and a breadth of 8·8 inches, Bt. being thus 24·2 inches. The size exactly agrees with that of others found at an old ruined monastery of the immediate neighbourhood, where the length is 15·70 inches and the contents 382 cubic inches. This size indicates the latter part of the first century B.C. or the first century A.D. as the time when the bricks were burnt. As the holes in the rock are of such a character that they must have been made by skilled stone-cutters, it may be taken as certain that they were cut by the men who were engaged in preparing stone for the adjoining monastery.

The holes numbered 3 and 6 may be considered typical of the smaller kind of these holes. Of all the holes which I have examined I believe that No. 5 is the only one with an axis considerably out of the perpendicular. The dimensions in inches are as follows :—

Number.	Top Width.	Bottom Width above the Curve.	Depth.	Number.	Top Width.	Bottom Width above the Curve.	Depth.
1.	9	2¼	9¾	4.	9½	2½	10¾
2.	9¼	2½	12½	5.	9	2½	10¾
3.	6¾	2	6	6.	6¼	2	4¾

On another rock not far away, called Galpiṭiya-gala, three holes have been cut (Fig. No. 58). The hole No. 7 is 11 inches wide at the top, 1½ inches at the bottom, and 7½ inches deep; No. 8 is 10½ inches wide at the top, 2 at the bottom and 6 inches deep; No. 9 is 6 inches wide at the top, 1½ at the bottom, and only 2½ inches deep.

At a rock in the jungle, on the side of the ancient channel from Kalāwaewa (tank) to Anurādhapura, which may date from the end of the third century A.D., there are two groups of holes, which may have been cut by men who were employed on the channel works. No ruins are known near them, it is said. The larger group (Fig. No. 59) consists of six holes, of which the dimensions in inches are as follows :—

Number.	Top Width.	Bottom Width above the Curve.	Depth.	Number.	Top Width.	Bottom Width above the Curve.	Depth.
10.	6	2⅝	2⅞	13.	6½	(weathered)	3¾
11.	8	3	6⅞	14.	8	(„)	5½
12.	8	2⅝	6	15.	8½	(„)	4¾

The smaller group (Fig. No. 60) consists of only two holes in an east and west line, of which one is 9 inches wide at the top, 3 near the bottom, and 6 inches deep; and the other is 6¼ inches wide at the top, 2½ at the bottom, and 3 inches deep.

At Wellangolla, in the North-western Province, two holes are cut in a sloping rock over which passes a track leading to some caves that were made over to Buddhist monks, apparently in the second century B.C. An inscription cut over one of them in two lines, in the earliest characters, with the bent *r*, runs :—(1) *Supaḍu... leṇe sagasa*, (2) *Asiya Nagasa gapati Anurudi kulasa ca dine.* 'The 'Very Pale' cave of the Community; given by Asiya Nāga, and by the family of the (female) householder Anuruddhī.' Three brick fragments at it average 2·8 inches in thickness, and one is 9 inches in breadth, Bt. being thus 25·2 square inches. If the length was six times the thickness, this being the usual proportion in pre-Christian bricks, it would be 16·8 inches, making the contents 423 cubic inches. The dimensions thus point to pre-Christian times, and possibly the second century B.C., as the period when the bricks were made. There is also a small stone flower altar 2 feet 6½ inches square, but its age is uncertain.

The holes (Fig. No. 61) lie in a north and south line, which is not parallel either to the adjoining edge of the rock or to the path; their centres are 4 feet 4 inches apart. Hole No. 18 is 6 inches wide at the top, 1 inch at the bottom, and 2¾ inches deep; and hole No. 19 measures 6½ inches in width at the top, and ends in a point at the bottom; it is 8½ inches deep. Holes ending in an actual point are very rare, and I have examined only one other hole which was of this type.

Near the Wellangolla holes a long inscription has been cut on the rock by 'the great king Jeṭṭha-Tisa, son of the great king Mahā-Sēna,'[1] recording grants made to the monks. Jeṭṭha-Tissa reigned from 332 to 341 A.D., and the holes may have been cut by the person who chiselled his inscription, if they were not made when the caves were being prepared for the monks.

At Rūgama tank, in the Eastern Province, there are three holes in a triangle, cut in the rock at the flood-escape (Fig. No. 62). At hole No. 20 the rock is broken away at the mouth; below this it is 5½ inches wide, and it has a total depth of 10 inches. Hole No. 21 is the pointed hole referred to above. It is also worn at the mouth, and is 6 inches wide below this part, and 9 inches deep. Hole No. 22 is 12 inches wide to the outer part of the curve at its mouth, and is 5 inches deep, with a flat bottom, a very unusual feature.

On a rock close to the cave called 'Great Beautiful,' in the Eastern Province, at which an inscription was left by the great chieftain of the second century B.C., Nandimitta,[2] there is one hole 6 inches wide at the top, and 6¼ inches deep, with a well-rounded bottom. It may have been cut at the same time as the inscription, or, as there was a monastery near it, at a somewhat later date.

Two holes are cut in a north and south line below 153 steps chiselled out of the steep sloping face of an immense rock called Tumbullē Waehaera-gala, in the North-central Province. They are cup-shaped, one being 2¼ inches deep, 4½ inches wide at the top, and 2 inches at the bottom, while the other is 3¾ inches deep and 6 inches wide at the top.

There are monastic ruins on the rock and part of a dedicatory inscription over a cave near its base, in letters probably of the second century B.C., by *Sumana Tisagota*, 'Sumana of the Tissa clan' (?). Bricks at this cave measure 15·70 inches by 8·80 inches by 2·75 inches, Bt. being 24·2 and the contents 380 cubic inches. They apparently are of a late pre-Christian date, or an early date in the first century after Christ. An inscription by a 'Tisa Maharaja,' near the cave, belongs to the second or

[1] No. 102 of Dr. E. Müller's *Ancient Inscriptions in Ceylon.*

[2] See *The Earliest Inscriptions*, No. 47.

third century A.D. The steps and the holes may have been cut at the same time as this inscription, if they were not made by the person who prepared the cave for the monks.

At Nagadarana-gama, in the North-central Province, Mr. Bell met with one of these holes surrounded by two concentric circles cut in the rock. His account of it is as follows :—'Here, too, is one of the unexplained incisions in concentric circles not infrequently met with ; the outer ring 3 feet in diameter by 1 inch in depth, the middle 2 feet 3 inches and 3 inches deep, whilst the central hole is cylindrical, 1 foot in diameter and depth.'[1] This is evidently of a different type from the holes above described.

In his Annual Report for 1891, p. 7, he mentioned a similar hole, a foot deep, at Tamara-gala. A circle 2 feet in diameter was cut round it, and outside that another 13 feet 6 inches in diameter, 'shallowly cut.'

There are many other rocks in the North-central and North-western Provinces where holes similar to those I have described are cut, and in some instances single holes are found. The Vaeddas informed me that they have seen groups consisting of seven and even ten holes of this kind on rocks in the southern part of the Eastern Province. I have observed a group of, I think, seven such holes arranged in an extended line on a long low rock in the North-central Province, at the side of a path leading to a wihāra. At that time I recorded no particulars of these holes, though I often met with them on rocks in the jungle. In the case of the row of seven holes, I was informed that these were utilised at festivals as lamps for illuminating the path, oil being poured into them on water, and a floating wick fixed on it, resting on four cross-sticks, in the manner often employed for hanging coconut-oil lamps.

However much the holes of this description vary in size they are always exactly circular in cross section, with the upper edges carefully rounded. The sides and bottom are always beautifully smoothed and in some instances almost polished. No chisel mark can be seen on any of them, and it is evident that the smoothness is due to much friction,

[1] Arch. Survey. Annual Report for 1892, p. 8.

which must have been caused in the case of the deeper holes, if not in all, by turning round inside them a stone or iron implement of a special shape, or by constant rubbing. There is nothing to indicate if the smoothness was originally given to them by the men who cut them, or is due to long use of them for some purpose or other. The latter is the probable cause of it. At each group of holes there is usually at least one small one; but in some groups there are no deep holes.

With the exception of the single group now occasionally employed as lamps I have never met with any villagers who could even suggest any use for the larger holes just described. Their Sinhalese name is *kōwa*, which commonly means 'crucible'; and a word like it, but with a slightly different spelling (*kowuwa*), is used in inscriptions as the name of the stone flooring slabs laid round the dāgabas at Anurādhapura. If the modern name indicates the employment of some of them as mortars for preparing medicines, this apparently can only apply to the shallower ones, and the mode of utilising the others is left unexplained, as well as their excellent finish and perfect shapes.

Although the holes are usually close to the sites of temples, I know of no purpose for which they could be required in connection with the services at them. I have been told by Vaeddas that they sometimes present offerings of food to demons in hollows on rocks, and such a use might account for some saucer-shaped holes, especially those in other countries; but it will not explain the reason for cutting the deeper holes.

Holes are sometimes cut in boulders or rocks near temples for use in pounding paddy (rice in the skin); but they are wider and of a different shape from these, being always cylindrical. Others in which money or valuables have been concealed are also cylinders, with an offset round the top into which the covering slab was inserted and cemented, earth being then sprinkled over the spot. Sockets for holding wooden or other posts are also cylindrical, or square in section.

It seems possible that some of the deeper holes may have been cut for expressing oil by hand labour for temple illumination, as an act of merit for the piously disposed, in the manner now practised for extracting coconut oil by a 'chekku,' that is, by means of a pair of bulls which turn a loaded wooden pestle in a large wooden mortar. The pieces of coconut are compressed between the pestle and the side of the hole or mortar, and the oil is gradually squeezed out of them. It is a practice of great antiquity, and notwithstanding its primitive appearance is said on the best authority to be as effective at the latest European machinery. Even this explanation does not satisfactorily account for some of the groups of holes, and especially for the rounding of their edges, although, on the whole, it is the best one that I can offer.

VIII

THE LOST CITIES OF CEYLON

Tambapaṇṇi and Wijita

IN the account which has been given of the aborigines of Ceylon, I have endeavoured to show that at the time when the written history of the country begins they held only the southern two-thirds of the island. The first capital of the Gangetic ancestors of the Sinhalese was established in some part of this district, and was believed by the early annalists to be in the neighbourhood of one of the coast settlements of the aborigines, as the extracts which record the fate of their princess Kuwēnī render quite clear. It was near this settlement or town, Sirivatthapura, that Wijaya and his followers were understood to have landed. It follows that the early writers were aware that the Sinhalese capital was close to the place of their debarkation, at a spot where the natives had an opportunity of collecting treasure-trove in the form of the cargoes of vessels that were wrecked on the adjoining coast. This fact, about which there can be no doubt, throws aside all the inland sites that are connected with the story by modern tradition. Such tales are not of the slightest value when compared with the written beliefs of the pre-Christian chroniclers from which the historians gathered their information.

Many different places have been selected by European and later Sinhalese writers as the site of the first capital, but the early annalists appear to have had no doubt regarding its position. It was then known as the city of Tambapaṇṇi, an early name of the island itself, apparently borrowed from Southern India, where there is a river of this name. The Dīpavansa says (p. 162) of this place, 'Tambapaṇṇi was the first [Sinhalese] town in the most excellent Lankādīpā [Island of

Ceylon]; there Vijaya resided and governed his kingdom. . . . The town of Tambapaṇṇi surrounded by suburbs was built by Vijaya in the south, on the most lovely bank of the river.' [1] The history being written at Anurādhapura, all sites to the north, east, and west of that city are at once excluded by this sentence.

In this story the tale about Kuwēnī is altogether omitted, but unless the new-comers had formed an alliance with some of the natives it is difficult to comprehend how they could acquire the supremacy over more than a small part of the country. What probably occurred was that for a long period antecedent to the appointment of a Gangetic prince as ruler, the Magadhese merchants had been accustomed to visit the island in ships that sailed direct from the mouth of the Ganges, or perhaps called at other trading stations on the way. At last an adventurous member of one of the northern royal families accompanied a party of these merchants to Ceylon, and by allying himself with some of the natives succeeded in acquiring the general sovereignty of the island in the districts where the influence and power of the traders were sufficiently extensive. Other parts of Ceylon probably retained their own rulers in a state of complete independence until at least the time of Paṇḍukābhaya, the fifth sovereign, who by his wise policy of conciliating the native chiefs succeeded in inducing all to accept his control.

The annalists state that the first Gangetic prince (who is mentioned only as Wijaya, 'The Conqueror') married a Pāṇḍiyan princess of the southern Madura, by whom he had no children. Shortly before his death he despatched messengers to his father's capital, Sīhapura, 'the Lion City,' in the Ganges valley, to request another prince of his own family to come to Ceylon in order to succeed him. His nephew, called merely Paṇḍuwāsa Dēva, 'The Deity or King of the Pale Race,' son of his elder brother, Sumitta, who had succeeded to the throne on the death of his father, accompanied the ambassadors to Ceylon, and became its second sovereign. One of the late king's ministers, called Upatissa, faithfully managed

[1] Translation by Dr. H. Oldenberg, p. 162.

the government during the year's interregnum that followed the death of Wijaya, early in the fourth century B.C.

It is the descriptions of the journey of this prince to Ceylon, and that of the princess who followed him afterwards in order to become his queen, which afford definite information regarding the place in the south of Ceylon at which the first capital was founded.

According to the Mahāvansa, Wijaya died soon after despatching the ambassadors to Sīhapura, and the Regent had settled down at another early town, called Upatissa, to the north of Anurādhapura, and on the bank of the Malwatta-oya, then known as the Kadamba river (Mah. i, p. 34). The returning members of the mission could not be aware of these facts, and evidently landed at the usual port near the old capital. The Mahāvansa states (p. 36) that they arrived at the mouth of the Mahā Kandara river, and Mr. Turnour has added, apparently from the Ṭīka or Commentary, 'at Gōnagāmaka tiṭṭha,' the ford or landing-place of Gōnagāma.

Following this prince, there arrived the princess who became his queen, who also landed at the same port of Gōnagāma. whence she also proceeded to Upatissa, the new capital. The Mah. says (i, p. 36), 'The ministers having already consulted the fortune-teller Kālavēla, and having waited on the females who had arrived at Wijita [on their way to Upatissa] in fulfilment of that prediction, having also made enquiries there regarding them and identified them, presented them to the king at Upatissa.'

Where was the town Wijita, to which these ministers proceeded from Upatissa, a city north of Anurādhapura, in order to meet the distinguished traveller from Gōnagāma? It has been long believed that it was at Kalā-waewa, in the North-central Province, where a small Buddhist temple, called Wijitapura wihāra, exists to the present day. I have examined this place, and failed to find signs of any early works of importance. The best evidence, the dimensions of the bricks, is uncertain. Those accessible in the dāgaba at the wihāra are all more or less in pieces, and are of two sizes, averaging 2·71 inches in thickness, which it is possible may be pre-Christian, and 2·10 inches. There are also some worn fragments of inscriptions of the fifth or sixth century A.D., cut on the steps leading to the temple enclosure. Nothing but this monastery is locally known to have been constructed at this spot.

In the story of the re-conquest of northern Ceylon from South-Indian invaders by King Duṭṭha-Gāmiṇi before 161 B.C., there is a long and fanciful account of his capture of a very strong fort at Wijitapura, with triple fortifications, the strongest fortress in the country next to Anurādhapura, which was at that time the capital; but no such place is known anywhere near Kalāwaewa. The account of this campaign is fully related in the Mahāvansa (i, p. 96 ff.). Duṭṭha-Gāmiṇi, marching from Māgama or Tissa in the extreme south-east of Ceylon, began it by capturing the town of Mahiyangana, an early settlement on the eastern side of the Kandian mountains; after which he gradually made himself master of a chain of forts established by the invaders along the banks of the Mahawaeli-ganga. The history then states (p. 97) 'All those Damilas [Tamils] who had escaped the slaughter along the bank of the river threw themselves for protection into the fortified town called Wijita.' It is clear, therefore, that this town was not far from the lower section of the Mahawaeli-ganga; and, as we know from the journey of Paṇḍuwāsa Dēva's bride, was on a public road leading direct from the port of Gōnagāma to the northern capital. By holding it the Indian troops evidently hoped to check Duṭṭha-Gāmiṇi in his victorious march on Anurādhapura.

A later historian who described the extensive works of King Parākrama-Bāhu I (1164–1197 A.D.) at Polannaruwa, his capital, relates (Mah. ii, p. 201) how he formed three suburbs of the city:—'Afterwards the king caused three smaller cities to be erected, namely, the Rājavēsi Bhujanga, the Rāja Kulantaka [also called Sīhapura on p. 259] and Wijita.' It then states that in the space between the palace and these three towns he built three wihāras, thus indicating that they were not far from the capital. At p. 260 reference is again made to 'the branch city, Wijita.' It is a constant habit of the later historians to use the word meaning to construct when the actual work done is a repair or re-construction; and whether it was the case in this instance or not, it is at least proved by these records that close to Polannaruwa there was a Wijitapura in the twelfth century. Can it be the celebrated fortified city captured by Duṭṭha-Gāmiṇi?

When that king had taken it he next marched on a post termed Girilaka, the station of a chief called after it[1] Giriya, 'the Giri person.' This may have been the place eight miles north of Polannaruwa now known as Giri-talāwa, on the present road to Anurādhapura. The meaning of the name, 'Giri plain,' shows that it may be derived from the Giri village, where the chief Giriya lived.

From there the king proceeded to Mahēla, which may be the village now termed Maha Aela-gamuwa, on the road from Dambulla to Anurādhapura. With these very probable identifications to confirm the line of Duṭṭha-Gāmiṇi's march, I feel justified in assuming that the fort of Wijita which he captured was close to Polannaruwa, and possibly either an early name of that city itself, or a place at the site of Parākrama-Bāhu's 'branch city.' It cannot have been a town on the north-western side of Kalā-waewa, at the site of the Wijita-pura wihāra, which is completely out of the line of march to Anurādhapura from any point on the lower course of the Mahawaeli-ganga, and is also too far from that river to be a rallying-ground for troops who were blocking the king's advance on the capital.

We now return to the journey of Paṇḍuwāsa Dēva's bride from the coast to Upatissa. If Wijitapura where the king's ministers met her was near Polannaruwa we see at once that the meeting-place was nearly half-way on the great highway which passed from Māgama to Anurādhapura and Upatissa, through Guttahala (now Buttala), and across the Mahawaeli-ganga at Dāstoṭa. This old highway, part of which is now called Kalu-gal baemma, 'Black-Stone Embankment,' is still in existence, but overgrown with forest; and it is said that it can be traced from Buttala to the river. Where I examined it

[1] 'Each village gave its name to the Damila chief in charge of it.' Mah. i, p. 97.

near Nilgala, and at the present high road to Batticaloa it is well defined. Near Nilgala it runs on an earthen embankment which is about twenty feet high near some stream-crossings; it is five feet high at the path from Nilgala, and one hundred feet wide at the base. The top of this bank appears to have been thirty or forty feet broad, or even more.

It is clear that if the true site of Wijita-pura is even approximately fixed by me, the landing-place from which it was necessary to pass through it in order to arrive at the capital cannot have been at any point on the western coast, or even on the central part of the eastern coast. We are therefore reduced to southern and south-eastern Ceylon in which to find the port where the princess disembarked, the same Gōnagāma at which Paṇḍuwāsa Dēva landed.

The name of the river, Mahā Kandara, is of little use in the quest without further corroboration of its position, there being several Kandura streams in Ceylon. But the name of the port itself may now be utilised. Where is there a Gōnagāma landing-place in southern or south-eastern Ceylon? This query is easily answered. Four miles inland from the mouth of the Kirindi river which runs past Māgama or Tissa there is a natural pool still termed Gōnagama-wila, 'the Gōnagama pool.' I suggest that, taken with the other evidence, it proves that the mouth of this river was the landing-place in question. If so, the Mahā Kandara river is the present Kirindi river, the old name of which in the Mahāvansa was Karinda. The 'Sambar village' which gave its name to the pool, but may have been near or the mouth of the river, has long since disappeared.

This, then, is the place, unlikely as it may seem at the extreme south-east of Ceylon, at which the two Indian travellers, one from the same country as Wijaya, and the other from its immediate neighbourhood, landed in Ceylon. It is a fair inference that this was the usual route of the early Gangetic traders, and that the journey of Wijaya was believed to have followed the same course.

That such is the case is confirmed by the Rājāvaliya which says (p. 20), in unmistakable terms, that Paṇḍuwāsa Dēva landed 'at the haven of Tammaṇṇa,' the Sinhalese name of Tambapaṇṇi city. Thus Gōnagāma was the port or haven of Tambapaṇṇi.

It was at the same spot that Wijaya and his men landed :— 'When the ship made for land in the direction of Ruhuṇa [southern Ceylon], they saw the rock Samanta Kūṭa [Adam's Peak] while at the sea, and concluded among themselves that it was a good country to live in. Having seen the sea-coast they landed at Tammaṇṇā-toṭa, and rested beneath a Banyan tree' (Rāj., p. 16). From the sea or the coast near Kirindi, Adam's Peak is clearly visible in fine weather, as the writer from whom this account was taken by the historian evidently was aware, or he would not have specially mentioned the fact, which itself excludes every site on the eastern coast.

Having once found this landing-place of Wijaya, Paṇḍuwāsa Dēva, and the latter's queen, the fact that the first capital was so close to it that it was termed 'the port for Tammaṇṇa' leaves no room to doubt that the later Māgama, now called Tissa, at the side of the Kirindi river, and only six miles from its mouth, was the spot selected by the settlers as the first seat of government. All the early settlements of the leading chiefs are termed *gāma*, 'village,' in the Mahāvansa, and the capital became the Mahā-gāma, 'the Great Village' of the country. The appellation still survives as the name of a small village, Māgama, on the bank of the river, between Tissa and its mouth.

The city was established along the higher ground on the left bank of the Kirindi-oya. In a slight hollow to the left of this again the Tissa reservoir or 'tank' was made for supplying the place with water. Tissa appears to have been the name of a suburb on the eastern shore of the reservoir, where an inscription of about the second century A.D., cut on a pillar to record the suppression of a heresy, refers to it as *Asatisa rajakaya gāma*. 'Āsatissa, the royal village.'

It is not my intention to give a description of the present state of the early cities. I shall be satisfied if I can succeed in identifying the sites of some of them, and thus clearing up certain difficulties in the early topography of the island.

Wijitapura is described as follows in the second century B.C., at the time of Duṭṭha-Gāmiṇi's war: 'The fortress of Wijitapura was in this wise. It was girt about with three moats filled with water. Around it was a rampart of bronze closed by a gate of eighteen cubits. Amongst the fortresses reduced there was none like unto this. Except the city of Anurādhapura none of the other fortresses equalled it.' (Rāj., p. 38).

According to the Mahāvansa it was founded by a chief called Wijita, who accompanied Prince Wijaya to Ceylon, and it was then an 'extensive settlement' (Mah., i, p. 34). Paṇḍuwāsa Dēva subsequently removed there from Upatissa-nuwara, and made it his residence in the early part of his reign (p. 37), and the brother of his queen also lived at it, probably as 'Governor,' like other princes mentioned in the histories. Thus it was evidently one of the most important towns in the country at this time. It was then abandoned by the sovereign in favour of Upatissa, and it does not re-appear in history until the war of Duṭṭha-Gāmiṇi; nor after he captured it is it again mentioned until the twelfth century A.D.

The measurements of some of the bricks still to be found at Polannaruwa prove that buildings of pre-Christian date existed there or in its immediate neighbourhood; but beyond this meagre evidence which they have preserved nothing further is known of the early settlement at this town on the greatest highway in the kingdom. Its position on this route was too commanding, however, for it to be totally given up; and in all probability the new city, Polannaruwa, merely supplanted the old one.

Upatissa

In the Mahāvansa (i, p. 34) it is stated that the chiefs under Wijaya settled down at important stations throughout the country. 'Thereafter the followers of the prince formed an establishment, each for himself, all over Sihala[1] [Ceylon].

[1] The Vaeddas still use this expression to designate the districts occupied by Sinhalese. The Sinhalese expression for the island is Lankā or Lankāwa.

On the bank of the Kadamba river [the Malwatta-oya], the celebrated village called after one of his followers Anurādha. To the north thereof, near that deep river, was the village of the brahmanical Upatissa, called Upatissa. Then the extensive settlements of Uruwēla and Wijita, each subsequently a city. Thus these followers, having formed many settlements, giving to them their own names, thereafter having held a consultation, solicited their ruler to assume the office of sovereign.'

Of these towns, neither Upatissa nor Uruwēla has been identified. Upatissa is described in the Dīpavansa (p. 162) in eulogistic terms :—'Upatissa founded Upatissa nagara, which had well-arranged markets, which was prosperous, opulent, large, charming, and lovely.' It ought to be discovered when the ruins along the course of the Malwatta-oya have been completely explored.

A highway formerly ran northward from Anurādhapura through what is now the Northern Province, the ancient Nāgadīpa. It crossed the Malwatta-oya by a bridge formed at the ends by stone posts fixed in rocks in the bed of the river, a few of them being still visible at the banks, according to information given to me by villagers. It passed immediately below the embankment of a large and very early reservoir, now called Pāvat-kuḷam, the original name of which is unknown. Across the water which escaped over the waste weir or flood escape, the road was carried by means of another bridge consisting of stone beams, laid on stone posts, part of it still remaining at the spot (Fig. No. 125). It is extremely probable that this great highway, a continuation of that from Tissa, was carried through or close past Upatissa-nuwara, the only large town which is described as being north of Anurādhapura. I believe, however, that no ruins likely to be the remains of such a city have been found as yet.

After a lapse of more than two thousand years the ground occupied by the early houses will doubtless be covered by an accumulation of soil. At Anurādhapura, the floors of many buildings the majority of which must have belonged to post-Christian times have been buried under two or three feet of soil. Only slight mounds, or the ends of a few broken stone posts may be visible at the surface as an indication of the site of what may once have been an extensive town. Even at Tissa, which was an important town down to the twelfth century A.D., nothing but the excavation of an irrigation channel revealed the portion of the city which once must have been thickly covered by the ordinary houses of the populace, now traceable merely by a layer of ashes, and bits of charcoal, and fragments of pottery some three feet in depth, which was entirely hidden under a coating of soil over which a dense growth of thorny jungle had spread. There was no mound of any kind to show that houses had formerly existed at the spot.

When it is considered that all the dwellings, with the exception of those devoted to the Buddhist monks, and perhaps also to royalty, would be made of mere sticks and mud, or, at the best, of wood alone, it is easy to comprehend that all trace of a great city may totally disappear from view in a few centuries, unless some prominent Buddhist ruins attract attention to the site. Still, it is always somewhat surprising to discover how completely these early cities disappear from view, while many insignificant hamlets, with their little mud-walled huts under the shelter of their ancestral trees, are found still occupying the spot on which they were established, in some cases more than two thousand years ago, with the inhabitants doubtless leading nearly the same simple life as their distant forefathers.

At a few miles to the north-west of the great north road, and three miles south of the Malwatta-oya, there was an extensive and very early monastery at a place now known as Tantiri-malei, a wilderness of rocks about a quarter of a mile across.[1] The bricks in the dāgaba are 3·23 inches thick and 9·04 inches wide, Bt. being 29·2, and the length either 18 inches, making the contents 525 cubic inches; or, if it was six times the thickness, 19·38 inches, which would make the

[1] Reference is made to it in Mr. Bell's Annual Report for 1896, pp. 7 and 8. He met with an inscription which is cut in the rock there, for which I made unsuccessful search on my visit ten years previously; but he does not state its contents.

contents 565 cubic inches. In either case the size points to a time late in the second century or early in the first century B.C., as the date when the bricks were burnt, that being probably the only period when these excessively large ones were made.

Colossal sitting and reposing statues of Buddha cut out of the solid rock, at which the bricks are of pre-Christian date or the first century A.D., and other works, prove its importance; while fragments of rough pottery which cover the beds of small water-courses near it show that many people lived there for a long period. Yet it seems to be too far from a dry-season water-supply sufficient for the inhabitants of a town, to be the site of a city that was the capital of the country for half a century or more. I incline to the opinion that the city called Upatissa was more likely to be close to the place where the northern road crossed the Malwatta-oya, at a point probably some miles to the north-west of Anurādhapura, a neighbourhood that I had no opportunity of exploring, though I heard of a low hill near it on which some carvings (statues or reliefs) are to be seen.

The references to the town in the Mahāvansa are very meagre. I have already mentioned that it became the station of one of Wijaya's chiefs, probably in about 400 B.C. When that king died, the ministers who carried on the government are said to have made it their headquarters, notwithstanding its great distance from the former capital at Tissa. Paṇḍuwāsa Dēva seems first to have made Wijitapura his capital (Mah., i, p. 37), but in the latter part of his reign he is described as living at Upatissa, where he is represented as having an extensive establishment.

The next king, Abhaya, his eldest son, is stated to have reigned at Upatissa for twenty years (Mah., i, p. 41). He was deposed, and was succeeded by his brother Tissa, who also resided at Upatissa for seventeen years (Mah., i, pp. 42, 44). The following king, Paṇḍukābhaya, transferred the seat of government to Anurādhapura, and little more is known of the old capital; but during the reign of Dēvānampiya Tissa in the third century B.C. it is mentioned that five hundred youths of Upatissa became monks. Thus it is seen that Upatissa continued to be the capital for fifty or sixty years in the fourth century B.C., during which period it may have been the largest city in the country.

Uruwēla

The other early city, Uruwēla, never became the capital of Ceylon. After the reference to the settlement of Wijaya's chieftain at it, it is next mentioned in connection with Duṭṭha-Gāmiṇi, in the second century B.C., as follows :—'To the westward of the capital [Anurādhapura], at the distance of five yōjanas, at the Uruwēla town, pearls of the size of the Āmalaka fruit [Myrobalan], interspersed with coral rose to the shores of the ocean. Some fishermen seeing these, gathering them into one heap [lucky fishermen !], and taking some of the pearls and coral in a dish, and repairing to the king, reported the event to him' (Mah., i, p. 107). Thus the writer of the original annals was aware that Uruwēla was on the western coast, close to some pearl-banks, where coral also was found.

The town is mentioned again as a place where King Subha (60–66 A.D.) built a wihāra (Mah., i, p. 140). There is no further information respecting Uruwēla until the reign of King Parākrama-Bāhu I (1164–1197 A.D.), who is stated to have (re)-built two hundred and sixteen tanks that belonged to the Buddhist monks, among which is specially included 'the great tank Uruwēla' (Mah., ii, p. 265).

Thus there is not much information in the histories to enable even the approximate position of this town and its 'great tank' to be ascertained, yet when utilised with a knowledge of the country these indications are not quite so vague as they appear at the first glance.

It should be noted that the early writers are rather indefinite in their accounts of the direction in which places lay from Anurādhapura. They generally refer to them as being to the east, west, north or south, and often omit the intermediate points of the compass. When, therefore, they describe Uruwēla as being 'to the westward' this may have a rather wide application, and does not necessarily mean due west of the capital. If this assumption be permissible, we may at once proceed to search for Uruwēla near the site of the pearl-banks of the Gulf of Mannār.

In that part of the country there were only two tanks of importance. One is now called Periya-kaṭṭu-kuḷam; its embankment, two miles from Marisi-kaṭṭu, a village not far from the ancient Kutirei-malei, or 'Horse-hill,' promontory, is extremely low; and it cannot have held more than a depth of three or four feet of water. A low masonry dam, forty feet thick, was built across the Mōdaragama-oya, a stream which is usually dry throughout the summer months, in order to divert water into this tank. This appears to be a construction of much later date than the embankment of the reservoir, which would perhaps have been raised had these improvements been completed. No stonework has been found at the embankment, which, however, may have retained enough water to ensure a crop of rice off suitable lands lying near it. Although the tank had a long bank it could hardly be described as a 'great' reservoir.

The other reservoir is the work now known as the Giant's Tank;[1] its original name has been lost. This also was an unfinished work until its recent restoration, but a lower embankment may have existed from ancient times, sufficiently high to impound a shallow sheet of water which would cover a great extent of ground, the bed being extremely flat. Even a depth of five feet of water would have spread over 1930 acres. Thus, although the bank was low, the expression 'great' was a suitable one to apply to this work.

A stone dam, 90 feet thick, called in Tamil the 'Tēkkam,' was built at a later date across the Malwatta-oya, at a point twelve miles away, in order to turn water into this Giant's Tank. At a much earlier period a line of square socket-holes was cut in the rock on which the dam is founded, in the bed of the river, evidently in order to permit strong wooden posts to be inserted into them. These would then form the main supports of a temporary dam which must have crossed the

[1] A translation of its Tamil name, *Sōḍayan kaṭṭu karei*, Giant-built embankment.

river at the site of the present stone dam. At the distance of a few feet on the down-stream side of each post-socket, a sloping socket-hole was also cut in the rock, to hold the lower end of a sloping strut that would support the post near it.

FIG. 63. The Giant's Tank (before restoration).

All the sockets, excepting a few at the northern end of the structure, have been covered up by the later stone dam, but sufficient remain visible to prove clearly and unmistakably for what purpose they were made.

It is manifest that the sockets were cut long prior to the building of the stone dam, in order to enable a dam of sticks and earth that could be repaired easily, to be made across the river for the purpose of diverting water down the only channel cut from it, which runs directly into the Giant's Tank. We see, therefore, that these first works are of early date, for increasing the water-supply of the reservoir. They may be considered proofs that a shallow tank existed there long before the stone dam was built, and that the later work both at the dam and the reservoir consisted only of an improvement and enlargement of the original scheme.

Some kind of regulator was built of brickwork, at the inlet

of the channel, in order to check too great a flow of water down it ; and the bricks which still remain at the spot, being of two sizes, may indicate the age of the first wooden dam and of the later stone one. The average size of a good series of the larger bricks is a thickness of 2·51 inches and a breadth of 8·57 inches ; Bt. is thus 21·5 inches. If the length was six times the thickness it would be 15·06 inches ; if five times, 12·55 inches, the proportion being almost invariably between these figures in the case of such bricks. The contents would be 324 cubic inches, or 270 cubic inches ; and the dimensions point to some time from the second to the fourth century A.D. as the date when the bricks were burnt. It may be assumed that the Giant's Tank was already in existence before this period ; such a long channel would not be opened until it had been found that a better supply of water was necessary. The later and smaller bricks resemble those found at Polannaruwa in buildings of the twelfth and thirteenth centuries, and this would appear to be the time when the stone dam was built.

We have seen that the Mahāvansa records the repair or re-construction of 'the great Uruwēla tank' by Parākrama-Bāhu I. This monarch, or Niśśanka-Malla, who reigned a few years later, had a most laudable habit of leaving a record cut on a stone pillar at the larger reservoirs restored by him. There is one at Padawiya tank, another at Paṇḍā-waewa in the North-western Province, and there are several at the chain of tanks adjoining Tōpā-waewa, the reservoir at Polannaruwa. If the so-called Giant's Tank is the ancient Uruwēla tank enlarged, we might accordingly hope to find at it a similar record of its repair.

In clearing out the bed of one of the breaches at the tank, the late Mr. N. M. Walker, the engineer who completed the recent restoration of the work, discovered a considerable number of cut stones, evidently brought to the spot for the purpose of building a sluice for passing water out of the reservoir. These had been previously covered up by soil washed over them by floods, and their presence was unsuspected. They were all stones such as might be found at abandoned temples, and some of them had parts of inscriptions on them, two of which recorded grants to wihāras. Another was an octagonal pillar; and on its lower part, which was square and had been fixed in the ground at its former site, was cut the following inscription (see Fig. No. 153), ready to be set up on the embankment when the work was completed, the pillar being then reversed :—

> Śrīmat Sihapure jata Śrī Parākrama Bāhu nakāritan wiswa lokāttha kāryyavya pāritat manā.
>
> Made for the benefit of the whole world by the prosperous Śrī Parākrama-Bāhu, born at Sinhapura, minded of what was fit to be done.[1]

The record is almost a copy of that which was left at Padawiya, in which the king gives himself the epithet *Śrīmat*, prosperous, which therefore is to be applied to him and not to the town. It is merely placed first in order that, according to an old custom, the record may begin with an auspicious word.[2]

It is surprising to find that the king records his birth at Sinhapura. It appears to be clear from the statements in the Mahāvansa (ii, p. 118) that Parākrama-Bāhu I was born at Punkha-gama in southern Ceylon, whereas we find Niśśanka-Malla stating in more than one inscription that he himself was born at Sinhapura, in India. As he also in his long Dambulla inscription gives himself only the name 'Parākrama-Bāhu,' it would appear either that all these records at the great tanks in reality belong to him, or otherwise, as is more probable, that he carried on and completed some of the works begun by his great predecessor, and copied his records when writing this and perhaps other inscriptions. Parākrama-Bāhu and not Niśśanka-Malla receives all the credit of the works in the histories.[3]

[1] I have followed the words of Mr. Bell's translation of the Padawiya inscription so far as the two inscriptions are identical.

[2] Cicero says in his work on Divination 'Our ancestors were persuaded that much virtue resides in certain words, and therefore prefaced their various enterprises with certain auspicious phrases.'

[3] Dr. E. Müller thought 'that some of Niśśanka-Malla's deeds may have been put on Parākrama-Bāhu's account in the Mahāvansa.' (*Ancient Inscriptions in Ceylon*, p. 19.)

It may be concluded that the Giant's Tank was one of the more important irrigation works the improvement of which was at least begun by Parākrama-Bāhu I, and that it was in existence for centuries before his time. This alone does not amount to proof that it is 'the great tank Uruwēla'; but as there is no other reservoir in the neighbourhood of the pearl banks which can be accepted as such, it would seem that in the present state of our information the identity must be granted.

If so, the Uruwēla city must have been somewhere near the coast in that part of the country, where remains of ancient Buddhist edifices have been found in many places, as well as statues of Buddha. There are some ancient remains also at Mantota (called in Tamil Maka-toṭṭal, and Maka-tōtam) opposite the southern end of the island of Maṇṇār, including those of a celebrated Tamil temple dedicated to Tirukēsvaram, that is, Vishnu; but this place is generally believed to be the Mahātiṭṭha of the historians, 'the great landing-place' of travellers from southern India, although I am not aware that there is anything but the Tamil name to confirm the identification.

I should be inclined, however, to look for Uruwēla nearer the mouth of the Malwatta-oya, or Aruvi-āṛu as it is called in that district, where a permanent supply of fresh water would be obtainable easily by means of shallow wells, and where the attraction of the pearl fishery would induce a considerable population to reside. In all probability this was the original reason of the establishment of a town or trading settlement at the place, long before Wijaya's time. Beyond this general idea of the position of Uruwēla city we cannot go until the discovery of some suitable remains produces evidence of its actual site.

Parana Nuwara.

I next come to another city, regarding the early history of which the annals are silent. Unfortunately its original name has been lost; for many centuries it has been called merely Parana Nuwara, 'the Old City.' Its site is well known in the district around it, but elsewhere even its modern name is not recognised. It is on the bank of the Daeduru-oya, and about a mile from an ancient reservoir at Batalagoḍa, near Kurunāēgala, which was restored by me in the last decade (see Fig. 134).

At one time it was a very important post for the protection of the frontier districts of the kingdom of Kaelaṇi, or south-western Ceylon, and perhaps of Ruhuṇa, or southern Ceylon. The fort established at it agrees more closely with the account of that at Wijita-pura than any other I have seen, being surrounded on three sides by three high earthen banks separated by wide ditches; on the fourth side the steep bank of the river acted as a protection, and only one earthen embankment was raised there.

The extent of the town itself is unknown; it stretched along the side of the river and over some adjoining ground on the opposite side of a narrow rice-field. It had also several subordinate villages near it in which the various classes of artizans and workpeople whose services were necessary in the city were quartered. In one the smiths and tom-tom beaters lived, in another the washermen, and the same castes still occupy them. At a third a caste of hunters kept the king's hounds. A small wihāra and dāgaba were on the bank of the river to the south of the fort.

For the water-supply of this town the Batalagoḍa tank was made in pre-Christian times, according to the evidence of the bricks found at it. It now covers 635 acres, and is about twenty feet deep. Bricks at one of the sluices were 2·83 inches thick and 9·9 inches wide; Bt. is 28, and the contents 476 cubic inches if the length was six times the thickness. The width and thickness closely resemble those of the inner part of the Ruwanwaeli dāgaba at Anurādhapura, and therefore the bricks may belong to the second half of the second century B.C.

From a high-level sluice at the reservoir water was carried by a channel into the city.

Of the great antiquity of the town there can be no doubt. The bricks found at what is traditionally reported to be the remains of a wihāra are of a size which indicates that they were burnt in the second century B.C. or early part of the first century B.C. Their width is 9·5 inches and thickness 3 inches; Bt. is 28·5, and the contents may be 513 cubic inches; they resemble those in the dāgaba at Oṭṭappuwa in the North-central Province, which an inscription [1] proves to have been in existence before 30 A.D., and which tradition attributes to Dēvānam-piya Tissa.

Even in the third century A.D. it had lost its first name, and was already 'the Ancient City.' An inscription of this period (see Fig. 153 for facsimile) cut over the entrance to a cave-shelter under a rock at Pēddawa, a village six miles away, is as follows: *Siddham, Pubaga nakaraka wasike bhojike Cuḷutaha leṇe.* 'Hail! The cave of Cuḷuttha, a headman dwelling at the Ancient City.' Incidentally, we may infer from this inscription that there was already in existence another town termed 'the New City,' that is Alut-Nuwara, at Mahiyangana.

The town is believed locally to have been the seat or capital of the 'Great Scholar' king, Kumāra Dhātu-Sēna (515–524 A.D.), and it is said to have been here that the incident occurred which led to his self-immolation on the funeral pyre of his friend the Sinhalese poet Kālidāsa. Another and better-known, but perhaps not better-founded, tradition places the tragic event at Mātara, in the extreme south of Ceylon, an unlikely spot to have been selected in those days for the residence of the king.

The place is first mentioned in the historical works in about 1081 A.D., when the Mahāvansa (ii, p. 100), includes it with others of the district, in a list of towns captured from the Sōlians by a general of King Wijaya-Bāhu (1065–1120 A.D.). It was then called Badalat-tala. It was here that the ceremony of the investiture of Parākrama-Bāhu with the sacred thread was held with great pomp and rejoicing (Mah., ii, p. 125).

At a little later date the importance of the fort is shown by the story regarding it in the Mahāvansa (ii. p. 128 ff.) which relates how Prince Parākrama-Bāhu, who afterwards became

[1] See Fig. No. 152.

the first king of that name, and the most energetic ruler whom the country ever had, first proceeded to this place on his way to attack his cousin King Gaja-Bāhu, who reigned at Polannaruwa, from whom he hoped to acquire the sovereignty.

At that time a general, Sankha Sēnāpati, 'a man of great weight and valour, the most powerful general in the kingdom,' was stationed at it by the king of south-western Ceylon, with a body of troops, in order to guard the frontier districts, which then extended up to the Kalā-oya. The general received the prince well, but on various pretexts continued to detain him pending the receipt of instructions from his master as to the course to be pursued regarding him. In the end, Parākrama and his men, losing patience, killed him at this fort. We find it mentioned several times afterwards during the desultory fighting of that period.

The last reference to the place is contained in an inscription which was left on a large slab on the embankment of the reservoir, by Queen Kalyānawatī (1202–1208 A.D.), the widow of King Niśśanka-Malla, in the third year of her reign, that is, 1204 or 1205. In it she recorded her restoration of the tank at 'Badalagoḍa at Mahalā-pura,' the old town, and her (re-)construction of a wihāra—now termed Koṭā-wēriya, from its 'short' dagaba, the Koṭa Waehaera—at an adjoining village, Pannala, as related in the Mahāvansa (ii, p. 268).

After this, the history of the old town relapsed into the fatal silence of all the other forgotten sites in the island, the fort was abandoned, and the inhabitants disappeared.

Siriwaḍḍhana-Nuwara

Another city of some interest on account of the prominence given to it by the Right Rev. Dr. Copleston in his work *Buddhism* (Appendix, p. 487 ff.), is Siriwaḍḍhana-nuwara, as to the position of which considerable doubt has existed owing to the vague statements regarding it in the histories. Dr. Copleston has given a summary of the history of its identification with a village called Nanbambaraya, said to be eight miles from Dambadeniya, in the North-western Province, which was the capital of the kingdom in the thirteenth century

A.D. He has expressed his approval of this identification, and has held it up as an example of the critical acumen of the modern Sinhalese students of their country's history. I may add that if their judgment is correct in this case it is almost the solitary instance in which they have cleared up a single doubtful point in the history of Ceylon.

Dr. Copleston has explained how, by a mistaken reading of the manuscript of the Mahāvansa, or through defective copies, the learned editors of the Sinhalese edition—not, I think, an independent translation from the Pāli language, but an amended edition of an early manuscript—made the distance of Siriwaḍḍhana-nuwara from Dambadeniya *aṭṭha*, 'eight,' yōjanas, instead of *aḍḍha*, 'half,' a yōjana. The translator of the English edition followed the same reading, and made the distance eight yōjanas. The author of the Pūjāvaliya also adhered to this distance.

The statements in the Bishop's summary tend to show that Siriwaḍḍhana-nuwara had been wrongly supposed to be much further from Dambadeniya than was really the case, and that the highway the lavish decorations of which are fully described in the history of the Festival of the Tooth-relic of Buddha (Mah., ii, p. 286), instead of being many miles in length was in reality a very short one.

In connection with this identification he remarked that the length of the yōjana is twelve miles (p. 488), but this is not in accordance with the latest researches. Several estimates have been made of this distance. At first it was supposed to be sixteen miles; this was afterwards reduced to twelve miles, as given by Mr. Childers in his Pāli Dictionary; and an estimate by Professor Rhys Davids in his work *On the Ancient Coins and Measures of Ceylon*, p. 17, made it between seven and eight miles. This, however, depends chiefly on Indian distances. The Mahāvansa contains several references to it, some of which may assist in showing what this measure of length was in Ceylon.

When King Duṭṭha-Gāmiṇi was about to build the Ruwanwaeli dāgaba at Anurādhapura, we are told (p. 106) that some silver was discovered at Ambaṭṭha-kōla—now called on account of it, Ridi-gama, 'the Silver Village,' in the North-western Province—which is stated to be eight yōjanas from Anurādhapura. The actual distance in a straight line is 55·3 miles. If we add one-tenth on account of the windings of the road we get 60·8 miles, or a length of 7½ miles for a yōjana.

Uruwēla city is also said (p. 107) to be five yōjanas from Anurādhapura. The distance in a direct line to the mouth of the Malwatta-oya, near which it may have been built, is 45·6 miles. Adding one-tenth again the distance becomes 50·1 miles, which makes the yōjana 10 miles. The sea due west of Anurādhapura, at Ponparippu, is 39·2 miles away; this, with the same addition, would make the yōjana about 8½ miles if Uruwēla were there, and on the shore, at the point on the coast which lies nearest to the capital. Thus, in this instance we have a maximum of 10 miles and a minimum of 8½ miles, as the possible length.

Pēlivāpi is stated (p. 107) to be seven yōjanas north of Anurādhapura. This tank is the reservoir now called Vavuṇik-kuḷam, formed by raising an embankment across the valley of the Pāli-āṛu, on which no other tank is known. The river at the breach in the embankment is 51·2 miles from the capital, and the addition of one-tenth makes the yōjana 8 miles.

We also learn (p. 106) that going seven yōjanas eastward from Anurādhapura takes us into the district across the lower part of the Mahawaeli-ganga. Measuring up to any part of the river there the general distance is about the same, that is, 56 miles; so that when one-tenth is added the yōjana becomes in this case a little over 8½ miles. Professor Davids adds a little more to allow for the winding of the path; it would of course increase the length of the yōjana slightly if this were done.

Although these are only approximate estimates in the Mahāvansa, they agree so closely that the mean length of the yōjana found by them may be accepted as being nearly correct when applied to similar records of distances in Ceylon. If, as I believe, Uruwēla was near the mouth of the Malwatta-oya, the mean length of the yōjana becomes 8½ miles. This is not necessarily the actual length of a measured yōjana; it is probably the length ascertained by the time occupied in walking from one place to another.

The identification of Nanbambaraya village as the site of Siriwaḍḍhana-nuwara depends on three statements in the history :—firstly, the distance of the place from Dambadeniya, variously given as half a yōjana and eight yōjanas, neither of which agrees with the actual distance of the village from the capital ; secondly, the statement that before his accession to the throne Parākrama-Bāhu II lived at Nanbambaraya ; and thirdly, another statement that his wife, who of course lived there with him, was termed the Siriwaḍḍhana Bisawa (queen).

According to the Mahāvansa, he himself was born at Siriwaḍḍhana ; thus the third piece of evidence merely shows that he married a lady whose native place was the same as his own. The second statement would be of value only if the traces of some early city, and of the temple to which the Tooth-relic was taken, had been discovered at Nanbambaraya ; but regarding this point the Sinhalese scholars furnish no information, although it is one that they could easily investigate. Without this support the whole argument hangs in the air, awaiting the construction of some solid foundation on which it may rest. All is paper evidence of an unconvincing type. Although much has been written to show that in the opinion of the writers Siriwaḍḍhana-nuwara ought to be at Nanbambaraya, there is not a line to prove that it really was there.

The evidence seemed to me so unsatisfactory that I made careful enquiry into the matter from the Kōrāla, or chief of that district, who knew the country well, and lived in the neighbourhood. He informed me that there is no local tradition that Siriwaḍḍhana-nuwara was in that part of the country, or that the Tooth-relic was ever deposited at any place in the district excepting Dambadeniya. He knew of no traces of any ancient city anywhere round that town. As a matter of fact, he and all others whom I interrogated on the subject stated that the people of the district had always understood that Siriwaḍḍhana-nuwara was not there, but in the Wanni Hat Pattu, which extends between the Daeduru-oya and the Kalā-oya. This might merely point to the ancient town at Yāpahu, which was also sometimes termed Siriwaḍḍhana-nuwara, and was the capiṭal for a short period in the thirteenth century A.D.

As a result of other enquiries, I learnt that there is a place at Kaṭuwannāwa, a village two miles north of the junction of the Kimbulwāna-oya with the Daeduru-oya, which still bears the name of Siriwaḍḍhana-nuwara ; and I took advantage of the first opportunity to visit it.

There is an early wihāra at the spot, with a small brick dāgaba, called the Sīgiriya Waehaera, a raised platform round a Bō-tree, and two small rock-caves prepared for the monks. The only inscription known consists of four letters, of the second or third century A.D., on a flat rock near the dāgaba, reading *mi simiṭa*, with a probable meaning, 'this (is) for the boundary.' The bricks of the dāgaba are of two sizes, of which those of the earliest type average 2·93 inches in thickness, 9·07 inches in breadth, and are nearly 18 inches in length, a fragment being broken off the most perfect one I could find. Bt. is 26·5, and as the length is evidently, as usual, six times the thickness, or 17·58 inches, the contents becomes 466 cubic inches. These dimensions indicate the third century B.C. as the probable time when the bricks were burnt.

Water was supplied to the place by a cut channel with a bed from 15 to 18 feet wide, which branched off from a main channel that was opened from a stone dam, now breached, built across the Kimbulwāna-oya. This main channel was carried on to Talagalla tank, a large reservoir about four miles away, The restoration of these works by Parākrama-Bāhu I is mentioned in the Mahāvansa (ii,. pp. 148 and 265), the site of the dam being there termed Sūkara Nijjhara. In the ground all around, the villagers informed me that when digging for cultivation purposes they met with large-sized ancient bricks, the presence of which proves the existence of numerous monastic buildings there at an early date.

There is, however, a general absence of ruins above the surface of the ground, with one notable exception. This is a ruin known as the Daḷadā Māligāwa, the Palace of the Tooth-relic. It was a circular building of a special type, perhaps unique in Ceylon, 40 feet in diameter to the outer sides of the 20 octagonal pillars that supported the roof, each being about 14¾ inches thick, and standing now 7½ feet out of the ground. Four larger square pillars, with sides of 18 inches, are arranged in a square 10 feet 6 inches across, in the centre of the circle. Inside this central chamber there is a stone flower-altar formed of a single well-cut slab 8 feet 7 inches long and 3 feet 7½ inches wide, close to which, on the west side, in the middle of the room, is the spot now pointed out as the site occupied by the case or 'karaṇḍuwa' of the Tooth-relic. A second stone flower-altar 4 feet 10½ inches wide, is fixed to the eastward of the inner room, in the outer circular chamber which surrounds it.

According to the local tradition, the building had three stories; all the upper part must have been built of wood, as in practically all other instances in Ceylon, and it has of course disappeared. The whole place was overgrown with jungle, which was partly cleared away to enable me to examine it.

At the time when the great Festival of the Tooth-relic took place the king is said to have restored the present wihāra and the dāgaba. The villagers expressed surprise that doubts had been cast upon the identity of the town.

According to the Waṇṇi Kadayin Pota, 'the book of the Wanni (district) Boundaries,' the limits of that part of the Visideka Kōrale of the Wanni Hat Pattu, in which the town lay, was defined as follows in the fifteenth century:—'Having first taken the Daeduru-oya up to Śrī-warḍḍhana-nuwara, the boundary was made as follows: On this side of the rocky ridge at Ratmala; the Degaḍaturā mountain; Potuwē-piṭiya; Moragoḍa hill; Gurugoḍa wihāra; the wihāra of Niyandawana were made the boundaries. This additional country is the end of the boundaries for the Visideka.'[1]

This extract proves that the city was close to the Daeduru-oya, and at the edge of the district; that is, at the site just described at Kaṭuwannāwa. It is evident that it does not

[1] See also Upham's *Buddhist Tracts*, p. 215, where the translation is defective.

apply to Yāpahu-nuwara, which is neither near the river nor is the boundary of the district.

The road running from the city in the direction of Dambadeniya is said to have crossed the Daeduru-oya by means of a bridge on wooden posts set in sockets cut in the rock in the bed of the river. That capital was 24½ miles away in a direct line; and if, as before, one-tenth be added, we get about 27 miles as the probable length of the path to it—or a little over three yōjanas.

In any case, it is difficult to see how the distance given in the history is to be reconciled with the facts; but some of the other measurements supplied by later writers are also widely wrong. For instance, in the Mahāvansa (ii, p. 309) it is stated that Polannaruwa is five yōjanas from Dambadeniya, while the distance in a straight line is about 71 miles, or by the present road, which is very devious, 86 miles. The relics were taken there in a procession like that to Siriwaḍḍhana-nuwara, during the reign of the same king.

Possibly the word *yōjana* was written instead of *gawuwa*, which commonly means about four miles. If the road was more devious than usual its length would be a little less than eight gawuwas. It is to be noted that in the translation of the Mahāvansa published by Upham in 1833, the distance of Siriwaḍḍhana-nuwara from Dambadeniya is not mentioned; apparently it was not in his manuscript.

The Mahāvansa relates (ii, p. 288) how, after causing the road to be levelled 'like the face of a drum' and covered with sand, 'the king, followed by the sound of the five instruments of music, and forming a procession of great magnificence, carried the relics [the Tooth-relic and the Alms' Bowl of Buddha] by stages along the decorated highway into the city of Siriwaḍḍhana, and placed them on the seat that was prepared for Buddha in the spacious ornamented hall that was built in the middle of the wihāra.' The chief quality of the music was its loudness; it is described as being 'like a blast proceeding from the sea of his merits, which sufficed to drown the roar of the ocean and put to shame the thunder of the clouds.'

IX

THE EARLIEST DĀGABAS

WHEN the ancient Egyptian desired to give the earthen mound or tumulus that was raised over the dead a form that would permanently guard his remains he designed a four-sided pyramid of stone or brick. In the East the structure took the form of a solid dome of stone or brick, called in Ceylon a *Waehaera, Sāēya, Dāgaba* (relic-chamber), *Thūpa,* or *Cētiya,* and in India *Caitya* or *Sthūpa* (tope). In Ceylon two of the intermediate stages between the plain earthen mound and the solid stone or brick structure have survived, one being in the form of an earthen mound enclosed in a hemispherical shell of brickwork, and the other being a wide cone of brick. Both these forms are comparatively rare.

Whether the people of the East borrowed the idea of the dome-shaped building from the Phoenicians it is impossible to say; there is at least a great probability that they did so, since before such dāgabas or sthūpas were constructed in India and Ceylon Phoenician tombs were already in existence of a nearly similar design, consisting of a segment of a hemisphere resting on vertical-sided cylinders of larger diameter. As they borrowed the alphabet from the Semites they might equally adopt this form of durable tomb, seeing that many other 'motives' in the art of the East are derived from those of the Euphrates valley and Phoenicia. In Ceylon, at all events, the majority of the details used in early decorative art can be traced to those countries. That such copying of the shape of the tomb took place is rendered the more probable by the fact that in Ceylon the dome, in all the types of the dāgaba, was almost invariably raised from the ground on one or more basal cylinders, as in Phoenicia. It was from India, in the third century B.C., that the idea of the dāgaba was first directly borrowed in Ceylon, and the earliest ones of which we have any record were constructed during the reign of the famous Indian Emperor Aśōka.

Having once adopted this type of relic-tomb the constructive and artistic genius of the Sinhalese race proceeded in the following century to develop the design to an extent not found elsewhere. The most important examples erected in Ceylon are comparable with the greatest pyramids of Egypt. By some persons this comparison is looked upon as inappropriate, but as a matter of fact the two largest dāgabas at Anurādhapura surpass in contents, and three dāgabas exceeded in height, all but the two enormous pyramids of Khufu and Khafrā, at Gizēh.

The minor structures of this class are found throughout the whole country, and must have eventually amounted to thousands. The present account deals only with the earliest works which can be identified, regarding some of which no measurements are yet available.

THE ANURĀDHAPURA DĀGABAS.

Putting aside the mythical story of the building of a small dāgaba at Mahiyangana, in Eastern Ceylon, during the life-time of the last Buddha, in order to enshrine a handful of his hair, the first historical notice of the erection of this kind of relic-tomb in Ceylon belongs to the reign of Dēvānampiya Tissa (245 — B.C.), who is recorded to have built two, the Thūpārāma Dāgaba and the Paṭhama Cētiya, at his capital, Anurādhapura, and apparently one at Mihintale, a rocky hill eight miles away, besides other unnamed small ones elsewhere. The first and last of these three are still in existence, but the Paṭhama Cētiya has not been found, and therefore it cannot have been a large building. Of the two which are known, the first to be erected was the Thūpārāma dāgaba, in about 244 B.C. The others must have been built within the next ten or fifteen years.

FIG. 64. The Thūpārāma Dāgaba, 1873.

THE THŪPĀRĀMA DĀGABA

The Thūpārāma dāgaba was formed in order to enshrine two relics of Buddha, his right collar-bone (*dakkhiṇakkhaka*) and the plate off which he was accustomed to eat his food. Its original shape is not recorded; but at the early date at which it was constructed it is unlikely to have differed from that of the dāgaba built in the same reign at Mihintale, which is a hemisphere resting upon three very short wider cylinders that form basal ledges round it. Like it, the Thūpārāma dāgaba would have a square block of brickwork, now termed a 'tee,' an expression borrowed from the Burmese, on the top of the dome, and a spire rising out of a short cylinder set on this. Unlike other works of the same character, it is not stated to have been provided with a terminal member in the shape of a 'chatta,' or solid umbrella, on the summit of the spire.

Around its base was formed a circular paved court-yard 164 feet 6 inches in diameter,[1] raised 11 feet 4 inches above the adjoining ground, the ascent to this being made by two sets of stone steps on the east and west sides, each consisting of two flights. This enclosure is supported by a brick retaining wall, which has evidently been reconstructed since its erection, and in which bricks of the earliest type are not found.[2] Extremely graceful slender stone pillars with ornamental capitals, but no bases, were fixed in the court-yard in four concentric circles round the dāgaba.

It is recorded that various later kings, by way of showing their piety, caused costly decorated network coverings to be placed on the dome. It is uncertain if a roof was ever built over the dāgaba, nor is there any actual record of such a construction, although artists of the eighteenth century, if not earlier ones, have represented one in their wall-paintings in various wihāras. This must remain a doubtful point, as it is mentioned in the histories that two other dāgabas at Anurādhapura, of nearly the same size, were sheltered by roofs erected over them, as well as a few dāgabas in other parts of the island. A work containing relics of such importance as those deposited in the Thūpārāma dāgaba would be likely to receive the same protection.

The chamber in which the relics of Buddha were placed was formed in the upper part of the dome, and according to the account of it appears to have been a small one. No description of its original internal arrangement or decorations has been preserved.

[1] For almost all the dimensions of the Anurādhapura dāgabas I am indebted to Mr. J. G. Smither's valuable work on them entitled *Architectural Remains, Anuradhapura*. It was prepared by order of the Ceylon Government, Mr. Smither being then the Government Architect.

[2] The size of the larger bricks appears to belong to a late date in the first century B.C. The wall must have been completely rebuilt by one of the first two Parākrama-Bāhus, as there are 2-inch bricks in the mouldings at its base. It has half octagonal pilasters, 7½ inches wide and 8 feet 9 inches apart.

A small room for containing other relics was also built on the southern side of the dāgaba in the paved court-yard. It was looked upon as a building of extreme importance, and in the reign of Dappula III (827–843 A.D.) we are told that his 'General named Vajira who was a man large at heart . . . covered the Thūpa house at the Thūpārāma with tiles of gold as became it, and fixed doors also of gold in the house' (Mah., ii, p. 61). Mahinda IV (975–991 A.D.) made a door of gold for it 'like the Mount Sineru shining with the rays of the sun' (Mah., ii, p. 87).

King Lajji-Tissa (119–109 B.C.) is stated to have 'enclosed the cētiya in a superb case of stone' (Mah., i, p. 128). If this was a course of cut stone which covered the whole dome no trace of it remains. A golden pinnacle was fixed on the spire by King Upatissa II (370–412 A.D.), the dāgaba being despoiled of it by Dāṭhōpa-Tissa I (640–652 A.D.).

In the time of Aggabōdhi II (598–608 A.D.) a large section of the structure slipped down, exposing the relic-chamber, in which the relics were found lying undisturbed. They were replaced when the repairs were made by this king. Of the relic-chamber it is said (Mah., ii, p. 21), 'he arranged four images throughout the relic-room, also a throne made of solid stone, and a golden canopy, and other works of art inlaid with stone and ivory.' The room as rebuilt appears to have been one of considerable size.

During the reign of Aggabōdhi III (624–640 A.D.) it is related (Mah., ii., p. 31) that this dāgaba was rifled by the sub-king Kassapa of the invaluable relics and gems placed in it in the time of Dēvānampiya Tissa, and was completely demolished; but doubtless this refers only to the upper part of the dome, where the relic-room was made. It was restored probably to its original form during the same king's reign, at a cost of only 1,000 pieces of money, an amount which shows that the damage was partial only (Mah., ii, p. 31); and a pinnacle studded with gems was fixed on the top of the spire by Kassapa after he succeeded to the throne, and found it advisable to conciliate the influential Community of Monks.

Mahinda III (787–807 A.D.) made for this dāgaba a cover of gold and ornamented it with bands of silver. These were carried off by Pāndiyan invaders from Madura, in the reign of Sēna I (846–866 A.D.). His nephew Sēna II (866–901 A.D.) invaded Southern India, and sacked Madura in revenge for this and other spoliations (Mah., ii, p. 69).

Udaya I (901–912 A.D.) 'covered the Thūpa at the Thūpārāma with a band of gold,' and Mahinda IV (975–991 A.D.) also fixed bands of gold and silver on the dome.

It was broken into during the domination of the Tamil invaders in the eleventh century, and was surrounded with jungle when Parākrama-Bāhu I (1164–1197 A.D.) undertook its repair.

During the reign of the Kālinga conqueror Māgha (1215–1236 A.D.), the dāgabas throughout the whole country were ransacked for treasure, and that at the Thūpārāma was certainly one of the first to suffer, but it was restored again in the reign of King Parākrama-Bāhu II (1240–1275 A.D.).

In the first half of last century the illustration given by Major Forbes[1] shows it as nearly flat on the top, which was covered with brushwood; it was considerably narrower below. An earlier drawing belonging to the time of Kirtti-Śri (1747–1780) on the wall of the Dambulla cave wihāra represents it as being of the ordinary bell-shape, and without a 'chatta,' or umbrella, on the top of the spire, the general idea being perhaps copied, as the monks at the temple state, from an earlier illustration of it there, done in the reign of Niśśanka-Malla (1198–1207 A.D.).

It was finally restored in the form of a bell-shaped structure of very graceful proportions. The diameter at the springing of the dome of the bell is 31 feet, and at the base 40 feet 6 inches, the latter being probably nearly its original measurement. The height to the top of the spire is 55 feet 6 inches.[2]

[1] *Eleven Years in Ceylon*, Vol. i, p. 226. It was in the same state when Sir Emerson Tennent visited the town in 1848; it must have been restored soon afterwards.

[2] Smither. *Architectural Remains*, p. 3.

The arrangement of the pillars, all being of gneiss, which surround the dāgaba is stated by Mr. Smither to have been as follows. In the inner circle there were 52 pillars, each, like those in the next two circles, being 12 inches square in the lower part and octagonal in the upper part; they are 22 feet 10 inches high to the tops of the capitals, which have long tenons projecting. In the second circle there were 36 pillars, 21 feet 3 inches high, also with tenons on the capitals; in the third circle 40 pillars, 19 feet 9 inches high, with a round boss

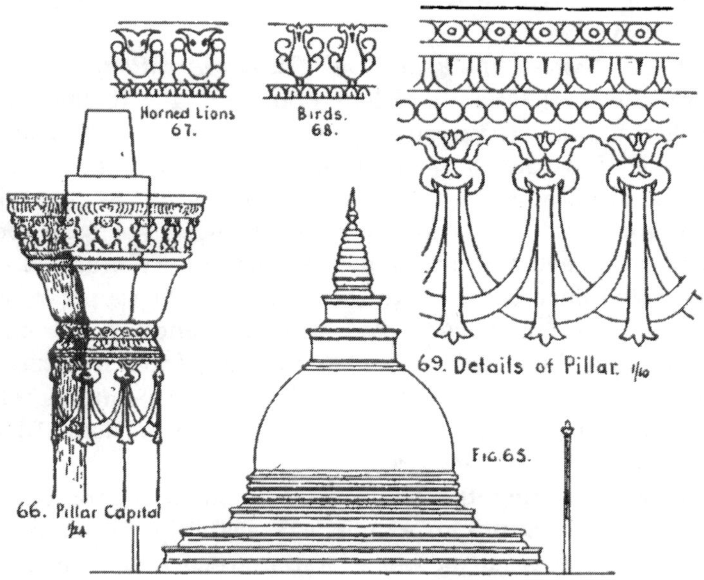

FIGS. 65–69. The Thūpārāma Dāgaba. $\frac{1}{380}$

in place of a tenon; and in the outer circle 48 octagonal pillars, 14 feet high, with a similar boss. The shafts are all monoliths, and they and the capitals are admirably cut. The histories do not record their erection; doubtless they are of considerably later date than the body of the dāgaba, and their general resemblance to those fixed round the Ambatthala dāgaba, described below, although some of the details are of an older type, may indicate that they belong more nearly to the period when the latter were cut (which was possibly early in the first century A.D.), or to some time approaching that date, say, the first century B.C.

The illustrations (Figs. 65–69) show the outline of the dāgaba as now restored,[1] as well as the form of the capitals and the decorations of these beautiful pillars. The dwarfs carved on them are repeated on the outermost pillars ; on the others their place is taken by horned lions, sitting upright on their haunches and facing front, with their fore-paws raised to the level of their faces, as though about to spring forward, and by standing crested birds with elevated wings, also facing outwards.

In his *History of Indian and Eastern Architecture*, p. 194, Fergusson stated his confident opinion that 'it can hardly be doubted that these [pillars] represent, and take the place of, the rail of the northern [that is, Indian] topes, and subserve the same purpose, but in what manner is not at first sight very apparent. Referring, however, to what was said above, about the Ceylonese preferring painting to sculpture, it does not seem difficult to explain the anomaly. These pillars were originally, I fancy, connected with one another by beams of wood on their capitals, and from these, frames or curtains may have been suspended covered with the paintings which are so indispensable a part of Buddhist decoration.' In this view Mr. Smither concurred.[2]

Notwithstanding the high authority in favour of this explanation, I venture to express my inability to accept this theory. It does not account for the absence of tenons from the tops of the pillars of the two outer circles. Mr. Smither believed that the frames were hung only at the two inner circles of pillars ; this still leaves the outer circles without any apparent function, and the tenons of the inner pillars, some of which are 8½ inches long, are much larger than such a purpose would require.

It is evident, also, that the meaning of the 'Buddhist

[1] Reduced from Mr. Smither's drawing, by the kind permission of the Secretary of State for the Colonies.

[2] *Architectural Remains*, p. 5.

railing' has been completely misapprehended. The railing forms a magical protection against evil spirits—the magic circle or square—for the relics enclosed within it; and the three rails usually found in it most probably typify the three protecting 'Refuges' of Buddhism—the Buddha, the Law, and the Community of Monks. That this is the chief if not the only function of the railing is proved by the stationing Nāgas and Yakshas as guards at the entrances in it at Bharhut, in India; they were not there to keep away the human beings for whose use the openings were made, but to forbid the approach of evil spirits, whom they alone could detect and stop,[1] just as Nāgas (Fig. 8) guard the great dāgabas of Anurādhapura, and Rākshasas act as protectors at the Gōpuras of Southern India (see Fig. 4).

Thus the principal member is the railing itself; the uprights, however much they may be decorated, are merely secondary, as its supporters. It is therefore impossible that a series of slender pillars can fulfil its function and take its place.

At Maederigiriya, five miles south-east of Kawdulu tank, the late Mr. Ievers, when Government Agent of the North-central Province, found a dāgaba, 'a copy in miniature of the Thūpārāma [dāgaba],' at which, between the outer pillars there was 'a wall about three feet high, generally formed of a single slab of stone deeply carved in the post-and-rail pattern.'[2] There is nothing to indicate that any detached fence of this kind existed at the Thūpārāma or any other dāgaba at Anurādhapura.

No example of the hanging of paintings round dāgabas, either in Ceylon or elsewhere, has been quoted by Fergusson—nor is it necessary. The purpose for which the circles of pillars were erected round them is explained quite clearly in the histories, and will be found stated in my account of the Ruwanwaeli dāgaba. They were employed for supporting festoons of lamps, and two instances are mentioned in which such pillars

[1] On the principle of setting a thief to catch a thief.
[2] *Manual of the North-Central Province*, p. 240.

were so utilised. This was not merely a subsidiary function ; it was their chief purpose. It is recorded that wooden pillars were fixed round two of the dāgabas, at one of which this is explicitly stated to have been the special reason for their erection. Such festoons of lamps were not hung simply as decorations ; they were well-known demon-scarers. Even at the present day large numbers of small lamps are lighted round some of the dāgabas at festivals, and I know that one procession of pilgrims from the North-western Province presented one thousand lamps, as well as oil for them, on one of these occasions.

With respect to the tenons on the capitals of the two inner circles, the facts that the pillars of the innermost circle are only two feet distant from the base of the dāgaba, and that their centres are only about four feet apart, afford strong indications in favour of their being originally intended, as one of their duties, to support a light roof over the dāgaba ; and in my opinion the chief evidence which tells against the existence of such a covering is the record of the fixing of a golden pinnacle on the spire in the fourth century A.D. It is possible, however, that such a roof may have been erected, and may have been removed by that date. It would not be a very difficult matter to construct a conical roof resting on the two inner rows of pillars, that would exert no outward thrust. The weight being well distributed over a large area its stability would depend on the character of the foundations. If these pillars did not uphold such a roof, the tenons show that the two inner rows must have sustained a covering over a circular procession-path round the dāgaba, in addition to the special duty of all the pillars as supporters of festoons of lamps.

The Topography of Anurādhapura

It is necessary to gain a clear idea of the general outline of Anurādhapura in early times in order to understand any arguments regarding the positions of the chief dāgabas in it, and the reader is referred to the annexed plan in connection with the following remarks.

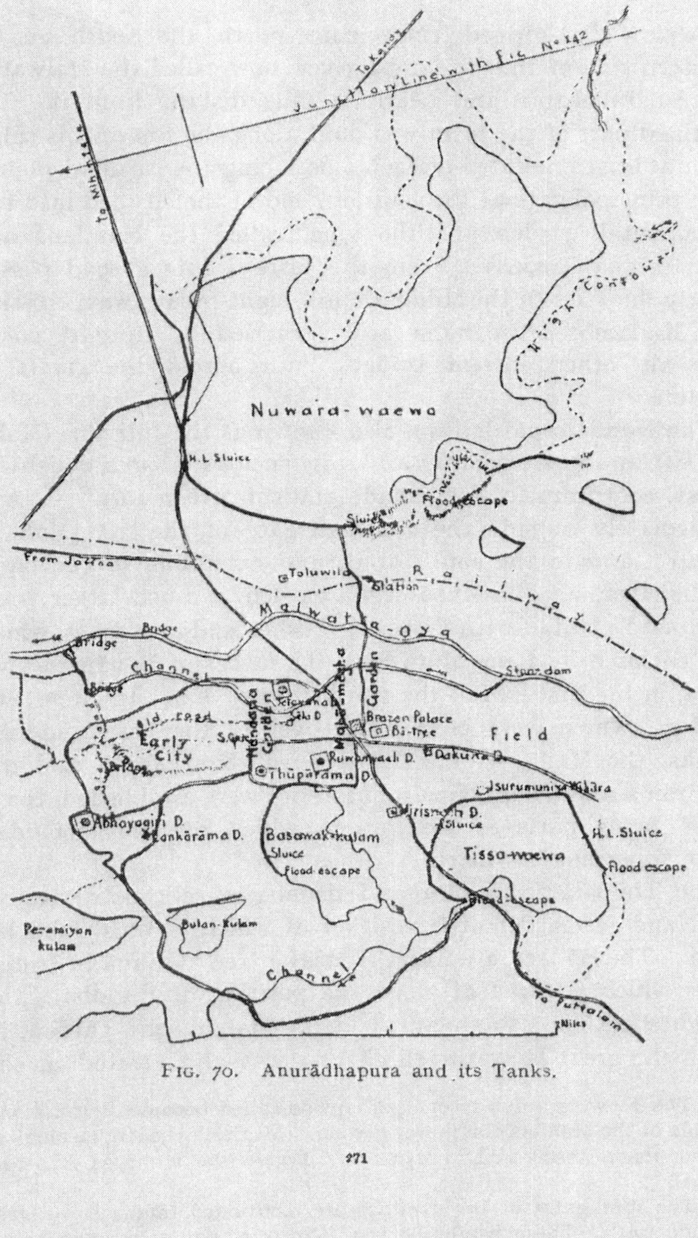

FIG. 70. Anurādhapura and its Tanks.

A low flat-topped ridge runs north and south on the western side of the Kadamba river, now called the Malwatta-oya,[1] parallel to it and nearly a mile distant from it. The fortified part of the town was built along the top of this ridge, with at least one gate[2] on each side facing the cardinal points. The principal gate at the southern end of the city led into two ornamental gardens of the king, called the Nandana and Mahāmēgha Gardens. From the eastern gate a road passed nearly due east to the Mihintale hill, eight miles away, crossing the Kadamba river by a bridge carried by upright posts, like all other ancient bridges built across the rivers of Ceylon.

The Nandana garden was also known as the Jōtivana (Mah., i, p. 64), and was evidently a narrow enclosure, 'in a delightful forest, cool from its deep shade and soft green turf.' It was immediately outside the southern gate of the city (Mah., i, p. 54); and to the south of it, and extending to the bank of the river, lay the Mahāmēgha garden, a much larger tract of ground planted with flowering bushes and fruit trees, which was enclosed by King Muta-Sīva, the father of Dēvānam-piya Tissa, in the first half of the third century B.C. In these two gardens, which were both made over to the first Buddhist monks, the Mahā Wihāra, 'The Great Monastery,' and the Tissārāma and Thūpārāma monasteries were established, these latter being parts of the former, which probably included other subordinate wihāras.

The Thūpārāma wihāra and dāgaba were constructed in the Nandana garden, the position of which is thus fixed by them. The Bō-tree, a cutting from the tree at Gayā in India, under which Gōtama attained the position of Buddha, 'the Enlightened One,' was planted in the Mahāmēgha garden, in which the great Ruwanwaeli dāgaba was also erected in the

[1] 'The Flower-garden river,' perhaps so called because it ran along one side of the Mahāmēgha flower garden. Mr. Bell, the Archaeological Commissioner, terms it Malwatu-oya; I give the name as I heard it in 1873.

[2] 'The four gates of the capital' are mentioned (Mah., i, pp. 119, 136 and 141). These would be the four principal gates, one being near the middle of each side.

second century B.C. As the Abhaya tank, now called Basa-wak-kuḷam, was in existence before this garden was enclosed, it is clear, from the references to it in the Mahāvansa, that the latter included all the land from the embankment of the tank, which is to the west of the garden, up to the river. The Mahā-mēgha garden was bounded on the north by the Nandana garden, and on the south by the low ground which forms a rice field.

The limits of the Nandana garden, or Jōtivana, on the east and west are not stated by the old writers. We may safely assume that on the west it included the narrow strip of ground extending up to the Abhaya tank; but on the eastern side it is uncertain if it reached quite up to the river. On the northern side there can be no doubt that it was separated from the city by the ditch of the fortifications, the position of the southern gate of the town being definitely indicated by the story given in the Pāli Thūpāvansa regarding the transport of the cutting of the Bō-tree from the port at which it was landed to Anurādhapura, by King Dēvānam-piya Tissa, in 244 B.C.

After describing its arrival at the port called Jambukōla, and the proceedings there, the account is as follows:—'Then, on the fourth day he took the Great Bōdhi (tree), and making superb offerings in due course reached Anurādhapura. Having given it a great reception at Anurādhapura, too, on the fourteenth day of the month, with the growing shadows, he brought in the Great Bōdhi by the northern gate, and having conveyed it through the middle of the city, and taken it out by the southern gate to the site, five hundred bow-lengths from the southern gate, where our Supreme Buddha seated himself and entered into the Nirōdha meditation, and the three former Supreme Buddhas indulged in meditation and sat, and where the Sirīsa Bōdhi of Kakusandha the Blessed One, the Udumbara Bōdhi of Kōnāgamana the Blessed One, the Nigrōdha Bōdhi of Kassapa the Blessed One were established—in that place, cleared for the occasion, which was like the forehead mark (*tilaka*) of the Mahā-mēgha garden, at the portico of the palace he caused the Great Bōdhi to be fixed.'

My friend Mr. J. A. Balfour, of the Irrigation Department, was good enough to get the distance carefully chained from the Bō-tree along the road which passes the Ruwanwaeli dāgaba, to the middle of a trench which runs east and west at a short distance to the north-east of the Thūpārāma dāgaba, and which appears to be the ancient ditch outside the southern wall of the city. The actual length is 3986 feet, and it is 33 feet further to a raised bank on the northern side of the trench; so that if the southern gate was on that road, and at the line of this bank, it would be 4020 feet from the Bō-tree. This would give a measure of eight feet for a bow-length, a size in excess of the length of most modern bows, which are usually six or seven feet long, but not greater than one in the British Museum. In some manuscripts there is mentioned a measure which is termed a 'Great Bow'-length (*Maha Dunna*); this may be the measurement referred to by the author of the Thūpāvansa. Dr. Davy, writing in 1816-1820, stated that the length of a bow was then usually nine feet.[1]

The distance from the Bō-tree to the city gate cannot be reduced, or it would fail to meet with any trench or bank such as would mark the boundary of the city; and in fact were the city wall more than a trifling distance nearer the Bō-tree it would run into the buildings that were erected round the Thūpārāma dāgaba, which are known to be outside the wall of the city. Although the number of bow-lengths mentioned in the Thūpāvansa must be merely an approximate round number it thus sufficiently confirms the position of the southern gate of the city. As the line along which the measurement was taken is that of an ancient road leading directly from the Bō-tree into the old city it is thus practically certain that the southern gate was at the point where it crosses the bank at the side of the trench, which is now marked by an irrigation channel from Basawak-kuḷam, laid out by me along the old ditch in 1873. The two royal gardens included all the ground from this channel up to the ricefield to the south of the Bō-tree.

The position of the northern boundary of the fortified part

[1] *An Account of the Interior of Ceylon*, p. 244, footnote.

of the city is more doubtful. In all probability it was fixed at the point where the ridge ends at that side, at a distance of about three-quarters of a mile from the southern gate. If so, the shape of the fortified part would be a narrow oblong, extending only along the top of the ridge, and not into the low ground on the east and west sides. The sites of the various suburbs of the city are not now distinguishable, but one or two of them will be considered in dealing with the identifications of the edifices mentioned below.

The Paṭhama Cētiya.

The second dāgaba erected at Anurādhapura was the Paṭhama Cētiya, which was raised to commemorate the spot where the Buddhist apostle Mahinda and his companions were supposed to have alighted when they proceeded from Mihintale on the occasion of their first visit to the city. From the account of their coming which is given in the Mahāvansa (i, p. 53), it is clear that this place was on the side of the public highway leading out of the town to Mihintale, and we are expressly told that it was 'in the eastern quarter of the city.'

In the description of the consecrated boundaries fixed by Dēvānam-piya Tissa, which included the city, this dāgaba is mentioned as lying north-west from two special trees that were on the bank of the Malwatta-oya. Thus it appears to have been at some moderate distance from the river, but not very far away. It was also distinguished by being selected as one of the places where the eight first shoots of the great Bō-tree were planted.

The dāgaba is mentioned only once more in the Mahāvansa, in the description of a royal procession through the city, on which occasion King Mitta-Sēna (435-436 A.D.) rode on the white elephant that was kept for the temple services. The words are, 'And he mounted him, and rode through the city in procession, and commanded that he should be stationed at the Paṭhama Cētiya, outside the eastern gate.'

The Mihintale Maha Sāēya

The third dāgaba, built on the hill at Mihintale, is stated, but not in the historical works, to contain a single hair of Buddha. It seems to have been a structure in which the old annalists took little interest, and as a result there are almost no records respecting it. I have already mentioned that it was one of the works of Dēvānam-piya Tissa, who built it probably about 243 B.C.

Its shape is a hemisphere resting on three low circular basal platforms, and it had the usual square tee, faced with post-and-rail work in false relief, and doubtless also a spire, probably surmounted by a chatta or umbrella, like all the other large dāgabas.

FIG. 71. The Maha Sāēya, Mihintale.

It is much larger than the Thūpārāma dāgaba. The dome is about 84 feet in diameter and some 44 feet high. The tee was about 20 feet wide and 10 feet high. The total height of the present ruin is 65 feet. The basal platforms form steps each about 4 feet wide and rather less in height; there is a quadrantal moulding round them. The 'wāhalkaḍas' found at the other great dāgabas of Anurādhapura are absent, and there are no encircling stone pillars, but wooden pillars were erected in their place between 9 B.C and 21 A.D.[1] The above noted dimensions are taken from a photograph by Messrs. Skeen and Co., of Colombo.

From the Mahāvansa (i, p. 128) we learn that King Lajji-Tissa 'encased with stone' this dāgaba (as well as the Thūpārāma dāgaba) at a cost of one hundred thousand pieces of money; but like the similar covering at the Thūpārāma all traces of such work have disappeared, impossible as it would seem at such a site. Considering the size of the dāgaba, I should think it not improbable that there has been some misunderstanding regarding some expression of the pre-Christian annalist; and that it is most likely that the laying of the flooring of the platform round the dāgaba was the work done at both structures.

It must have suffered like the Anurādhapura dāgabas during the periods when South-Indian invaders ruled the country in the eleventh and thirteenth centuries, and we may assume that it was included among the sixty-four dāgabas which Parākrama-Bāhu I repaired at Mihintale in the twelfth century.

In the latter part of last century it was in little better state than some of the other early works, and the spire had fallen, as well as large sections of the face work of the dome, and the structure was nearly surrounded by a talus of fallen brick-work covered with bushes. Its repair made considerable progress under the direction of the late Mr. R. W. Ievers, when he was the Government Agent of the Province, and its further destruction was thus arrested.

The dimensions of the bricks used in this structure have been given in a former chapter. It is of archaeological interest to note that when vainly searching for letters or marks that might have been left on them by their makers, I found on the side of one of them, which I handed over to the Archaeological Commissioner, a representation of a plain 'Buddhist railing,' consisting, I think, of three uprights and three cross bars, a post and rail fence like those built in stone in India. As the brick was one that had fallen out of the body of the

[1] Pūjāvaliya, p. 20.

dāgaba with others, and is also of the size of the earliest ones used in the dāgaba, which must belong to the original work, the discovery of this design on it proves that the knowledge of this form of construction dates in Ceylon from the middle of the third century B.C.

SMALL DĀGABAS

During the reign of Uttiya, brother and successor of Dēvānampiya Tissa, it is recorded that two dāgabas were built over the ashes of the introducer of Buddhism, the great apostle Mahinda, and his sister Sanghamittā, the first Superior of the Nuns. Evidently they were comparatively small structures.

The remains of a dāgaba 21 feet in diameter, which now bears the name 'Sanghamittā Thūpa' and lies north-east of the Thūpārāma dāgaba, were excavated by Mr. Bell; although he found nothing to prove that the modern name is correct he thought it possible that 'some of the ashes of the princess may have been deposited at this site.' [1] The dāgaba in which the ashes of Mahinda were laid was in the eastern part of the grounds of the Mahā Wihāra; it has not been traced.

The same king is also stated to have built a dāgaba, also doubtless a small one, to mark a spot where two previous Buddhas, Kōnāgamana and Kassapa, were supposed to have preached at the Sudassana or Sōmana Mālaka, 'the Beautiful Enclosure.' This place also has not been identified; the context seems to show that it was not far from the site of the Ruwanwaeli dāgaba, and probably to the southward of it.

To the south of the Thūpārāma dāgaba another small structure of this kind was also erected by a younger brother of King Uttiya, called Aśōka (Mah., i, p. 61), who is perhaps the same as the Asēla who subsequently succeeded to the throne

[1] Annual Report, 1895, p. 2. He found a small broken *cella* or relic chamber, in the form of 'an even cross,' in it, at about the level of the top of the basal platform or step. The dāgaba was built on a circular platform, 31 feet in diameter, paved with brick.

FIG. 72. King Duṭṭha-Gāmiṇi.

To face p. 279.

near the end of the third century B.C. Its object was to commemorate a site at which the preceding Buddha, Kassapa, was said to have preached when he visited the fabulous Visālā Nagara, which was supposed to have been at that time the capital of Ceylon.

Another similar dāgaba to mark a place called the Nāga Mālaka, 'the Cobra Enclosure,' where the Buddha Kōnāgamana was believed to have preached, was erected in his father's life-time by Thūlathanaka, who was king in 119 B.C. This structure was to the southward of the last-mentioned one. Thus there were three that were roughly in a north and south line, that erected by Aśōka being in the middle, and the Thūpārāma dāgaba at the northern end of the line. Both these small works seem to have completely disappeared, unless a mound that is now surmounted by some well-cut pillars of a later ruin is one of them.

The Ruwanwaeli Dāgaba

We next come to the period of King Duṭṭha-Gāmiṇi (161–137 B.C.), who built two large dāgabas at Anurādhapura. As one of these was north of the Bō-tree, and south-east from the Thūpārāma dāgaba, there can be no doubt as to the identification of the building now known as the Ruwanwaeli or 'Gem-Sand' dāgaba, and formerly called also Hēmamāli, Sonnamāli, Ratanavali, and the Mahā-Thūpa, 'Great Dāgaba,' even after larger ones had been erected. Owing to the interest with which the work was invested on account of its originator, and through its being the earliest of the greater dāgabas at Anurādhapura, we possess a much more complete history of it and its construction than of any other early building, either in Ceylon or India.

Duṭṭha-Gāmiṇi is described as dying in 137 B.C., before this work was finished, and his brother and successor, Saddhā-Tissa (137–119 B.C.), is said to have completed it after his death. According to the narrative the dome itself was built during the life-time of Duṭṭha-Gāmiṇi to hold some undescribed relics of Buddha; and his brother constructed the spire, its base, and an enclosing wall 'decorated with the figures of elephants.' We learn from the Mahāvansa (i, p. 114) that the original dāgaba had the usual three basal ledges.

King Lajji-Tissa (119–109 B.C.), the son of Saddhā-Tissa, then erected three stone 'altars' at the dāgaba, each costing one hundred thousand coins of some kind. The amount expended on them shows that the 'frontispieces' or *wāhalkaḍas* must be referred to or included, and not merely the ordinary flower-altars. Up to this time the square round the dāgaba had not been paved with stone slabs, since it is stated of the next king Khallāta-Nāga that 'enclosing the beautiful Great Thūpa Hēmamāli, he formed a square strewed with sand with a wall built round it' (Mah., i, p. 129).

In the reign of Bhātikābhaya (20 B.C.–9 A.D.) 'two basement cornice ledges' were built at the dāgaba. What these were is not quite clear; the remark does not seem to be applicable to the stone-work on the basal platforms which surround the dome, as these have no cornices. Some additional stone cornices on the wāhalkaḍas perhaps may be referred to.

The next king, Mahā-Nāga (9–21 A.D.), laid the flooring on the square round the dāgaba, and appears also to have made the lower outer square, which was 'strewed with sand, (Mah., i, p. 136). His son Āmanda-Gāmiṇi 'fixed a chatta [or umbrella-shaped top] over the chatta of the Mahā Thūpa, as well as cornices on the base and crown [tee] of that edifice' (Mah., i, p. 137). The first chatta may have been part of the original work of Saddhā-Tissa. Evidently the spire had now two chattas, one superimposed over the other.

In the reign of Siri-Nāga I (196–215 A.D.) we read (Mah., i, p. 144) of the construction of a gilt chatta at this dāgaba; this apparently was a third one fixed above the other two. The Dīpavansa attributes to his son Vōhāraka-Tissa (215–237 A.D). the construction of another also. Sangha-Tissa I (248–252 A.D.) caused the chatta to be re-gilt, and we learn that on each of the four faces of the base of the spire [in reality the tee] there was a representation of the sun, in the centre of each of which the king placed a gem which cost one hundred thousand coins. A glass pinnacle was also placed on the summit of the spire (which thus appears to have passed through the upper chatta), from a mistaken idea that it would prove a protection against lightning. Evidently the spires of some dāgabas had been damaged by thunderstorms before this date, as might naturally be anticipated; they could not fail to be struck sometimes. A golden chatta was again constructed at this dāgaba by Dhātu-Sēna (463–497 A.D.); this may have been merely a restoration of the former upper one.

King Moggallāna (608–614 A.D.) presented a new cloth covering to the dāgaba; and Kassapa II (652–661 A.D.) fixed

FIG. 73. The Ruwanwaeli Dāgaba.

a jewelled pinnacle on the spire, which again indicates that it passed through the uppermost chatta.

In the time of Kassapa V (929–937 A.D.) the second queen, Rājini, 'made an offering of a silken covering for the Hēmamālā cētiya' (Mah., ii, p. 80). This offering was repeated in the reign of Mahinda IV (975–991 A.D.).

The dāgaba appears to have been damaged by invaders from southern India in the eleventh century, and with the other chief structures at Anurādhapura was repaired by Tamil prisoners of war during the reign of Parākrama-Bāhu I (1164–1197 A.D.). A relic of this work is to be seen in an inscription on one of the stones of the flooring of the enclosure:—*Gaja-*

Bāhu sabhā pahaṇayak, 'a stone (presented by) the Gaja-Bāhu Assembly.'

It was again broken into by the invaders from Kālinga in the time of Māgha (1215–1236 A.D.), and was restored for the last time in the reign of Parākrama-Bāhu II (1240–1275 A.D.). This work had been commenced by his father, who was unable to finish it (Mah., ii, p. 306).

The dāgaba was then left to fall into ruin once more, by the neglect of centuries, and the spire, the greater part of the tee, and the upper part of the side of the dome slipped down in a high talus that covered all the base of the structure, which then became once more overrun with bushes and trees. At the beginning of 1873, its restoration was again undertaken by the energetic young Buddhist monk who was in charge of it, and it is still making slow progress, dependent on the subscriptions furnished by the large numbers of pilgrims who visit the old city at the annual and other festivals. The re-facing of the dome is not yet completed.

After the fallen *débris* had been dug away, and the support which it had given to the lower part of the cupola had been thus removed, a slip occurred of a section of the brickwork on the southern side of the dome; and on the occasion of a visit that I paid to the town at Christmas, 1886, I was surprised to find that this slip, which had taken place in 1885, had exposed the finished but unplastered surface of an inner dāgaba, round which a shell of brickwork, twenty feet thick, had been built.[1] The mass of brickwork that had fallen consisted merely of this outer shell; the inner work was intact, and disclosed throughout all the exposed surface the original face-work of unbroken and evidently undisturbed bricks, all laid as 'headers,' with very fine joints. I was informed that there is a tradition that this also is only a shell, and that inside it there is a still smaller dāgaba; but no reliance can be placed on such tales when they are unsupported by the authority of any of the historical works.

In any attempt to explain this method of building the dāgaba

[1] The actual thickness as measured by me was 19 feet 11½ inches.

it is obvious that the evidence afforded by the sizes of the bricks employed in the two portions of the work must be all-important. Those in the outer shell average 8·99 inches in width, 2·90 inches in thickness, and only 14·06 inches in length; Bt. is 26·1, and the contents 366 cubic inches. Those in the inner work average 9·67 inches wide and 2·79 inches thick; Bt. is 27. The length could not be measured as all are 'headers.' The difference in the average widths proves that entirely different moulds were used for the outer bricks; the manner in which the outer shell is built is also much rougher than in the inner work. It is therefore certain that the outer work was not carried on without a break or stoppage in the brick-moulding, and probably also in the building work; and thus there is every probability that the outer shell was built by another king than Duṭṭha-Gāmiṇi.

On making a careful examination of large numbers of bricks that had fallen out of this outer shell, I discovered on several of them a small series of letters that must have been inscribed on them before they were burnt, by the persons who made them. They are of the early angular types which date from prior to the time of the Gal-lena inscriptions,[1] or say 85 B.C.; and thus we must ascribe the building of the outer shell to some period between that date and the death of Duṭṭha-Gāmiṇi in 137 B.C.

We are therefore reduced to five kings who reigned during this period, to one of whom the work, which would occupy several years, must be attributed. Of these, Waṭṭa-Gāmiṇi was fully engaged with the construction of two other dāgabas, one of them being much larger than the Ruwanwaeli. His brother Thullathana reigned only forty days. Of the other three kings, Saddhā-Tissa and his sons Lajji-Tissa and Khallāta-Nāga, by far the most likely person to undertake the work was Saddhā-Tissa, who reigned for the longest period (137–115 B.C.), and was the brother and successor of Duṭṭha-Gāmiṇi. The completion of the dāgaba is attributed to him by the Mahāvansa, which says:—'This monarch, whose name implies

[1] See below, *The Earliest Inscriptions*, Nos. 68–72 (Fig. 153).

the sincerity of his faith, completed the pinnacle and plastering of the dome, and the enclosing parapet wall decorated with figures of elephants, of the Mahā Thūpa' (i, p. 128).

There is still a brick wall round the upper enclosure at the dāgaba, which has the fore-parts (heads and fore-legs) of elephants built in relief, four feet seven inches apart, in the outer face. The bricks used in these figures are of varying sizes, some of the lower ones being only two inches thick; these belong to some time in the ninth to twelfth centuries, and they clearly prove a complete reconstruction of the wall at about that period, perhaps by Parākrama-Bāhu I. The larger bricks are 17 inches long and about 2·85 inches thick, dimensions which are certainly pre-Christian. The difference between their length and that of the bricks in the outer shell of the dāgaba proves that they were not moulded at the same time as the latter; they may belong to the time of Khallāta-Nāga, who is recorded to have enclosed the square round the dāgaba.

In that case, the figures of elephants attributed to Saddhā-Tissa may perhaps be those in the uppermost platform or basal ledge, which is ornamented with the heads of elephants carved in limestone and set in the face of the top course. If so, he must have been the king who enlarged the dāgaba. The similarity of the dimensions of the bricks in the inner and outer work points to the lapse of a very short interval between the building of the inner dāgaba and the resumption of brick-making for its enlargement.

On the available evidence, it may be decided as a practical certainty that Saddhā-Tissa added the outer shell of the dāgaba. Evidently the early annalists or later historians, in their desire to exalt the fame of their favourite hero, Duṭṭha-Gāmiṇi, omitted to give his brother the credit due to him for the greater part of the work done by him.

In other respects, the fact that there is no trace of plaster on the surface of the inner dāgaba is another proof of the extreme accuracy of the account in the Mahāvansa, which states (i, p. 123), 'When the construction of the spire and the plastering of the cētiya alone remained to be completed, the king was afflicted with the disease which terminated his existence.' We now see that his brother decided to enlarge the whole structure, and then, only, to add the necessary protection of the plaster. It was no slight work to undertake ; if the outer shell is of the same thickness throughout, the amount of building done by him forms considerably more than one-third of the whole volume of the dāgaba.

The description of the relic-chamber leaves no doubt that it was in the upper part of the dome, like that of the Thūpārāma dāgaba, and was a comparatively large room. It is described as having the walls covered with paintings, and containing in the centre a Bō-tree with a silver stem and golden leaves, above which was suspended a priceless canopy hung with pearls, while at each of the four sides of the chamber there was a small golden statue of Buddha sitting on a golden throne. On another throne, relics believed to be those of Buddha, enclosed in a golden casket, were placed by king Duṭṭha-Gāmiṇi in person. Above this relic-apartment another room was formed in which the chiefs and people deposited large quantities of jewellery. (Mah., i, p. 123.)

A very much smaller dāgaba at Heṭṭipola in the North-western Province, broken into by treasure-seekers in 1877, has similarly two large (but undecorated) relic-chambers one over the other, the intervening floor being formed by slabs of stone that passed across from wall to wall, partly supported by two stone beams fixed under them transversely, an arrangement evidently like that of the Ruwanwaeli dāgaba. In the Heṭṭipola dāgaba eight small sedent figures of Buddha, made of some kind of cement and covered with gold, were placed on thrones similarly made and covered with silver, which were set in four rectangular niches formed in the four walls of the lower compartment. In front of each throne there was a small relic-casket or *karaṇḍuwa* of clear quartz, enclosed in a golden dāgaba-shaped case, with a spire and tee. Unfortunately I have no measurements of the bricks of which this structure is built, and therefore I can express no opinion regarding the age of the work. It may be an early one.

Inside the relic-chamber of a smaller dāgaba near it there is part of a pillar on which a royal grant in letters of the tenth century had been cut. This dāgaba can hardly be of earlier date than the twelfth century. As far as I remember, the chambers in the larger one were six or eight feet across.'

With this example before us it is easy to believe that with the exception of the enormous dimensions attributed to it (80 cubits square, which may be safely divided by ten),—the detailed account of the room in the Ruwanwaeli dāgaba, as preserved in the Mahāvansa, is a true description of the apartment and its decorations, written by a contemporary annalist who either actually saw it, or heard it described by others who had seen it.

The shape of the Ruwanwaeli dāgaba is thus explained in the Mahāvansa (i, p. 112). Duṭṭha-Gāmiṇi enquired of the architect in what form he proposed to build it. It is therefore clear that various shapes of dāgabas were even then known. 'The bricklayer, filling a golden dish with water, and taking some water in the palm of his hand dashed it against the water in the dish; a great globule like a ball of crystal rose to the surface; and he said, "I will construct it in this form." The monarch, delighted, bestowed on him a suit of clothes worth a thousand, a pair of slippers, and twelve thousand kahāpanas.' It is refreshing to read of a king who gave such desirable marks of his appreciation of an architect's intelligence; he resembled in this respect some of the worthy Egyptian monarchs. At the present day even the slippers are not given to successful architects in Ceylon.

When drawings of the chief dāgabas at Anurādhapura were made in 1877 by Mr. Smither, the Government Architect, he was of opinion that the dome of this dāgaba was a hemisphere, as described by the old writer. It is 254 feet in diameter. It rests on three short cylinders, the upper one having a diameter 12 feet greater than that of the dome and being 5 feet 6 inches high; the middle one is 14 feet wider still and 4 feet 9 inches high; and the bottom one is 14 feet wider than the middle one and 5 feet 9 inches high. Thus the height of the three cylinders is 16 feet, and they form three basal ledges or nar-

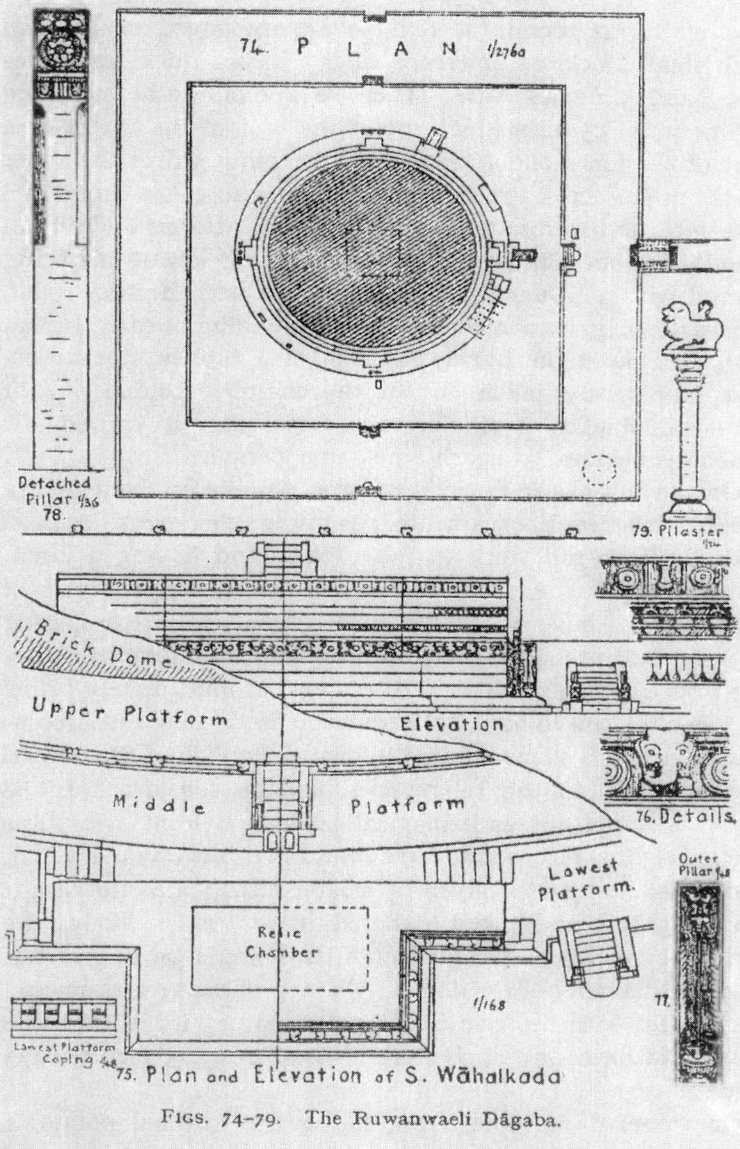

FIGS. 74–79. The Ruwanwaeli Dāgaba.

row platforms round the dome. All are paved on the top with small blocks of limestone each 3 inches thick, 10 inches long, and 5 inches wide. There is a quadrantal moulding of limestone 15 inches high round the base of the lowest one. Out of the limestone coping of the retaining wall of the upper platform projected 133 elephants' heads, also cut in limestone. The face of the retaining walls of the platforms is built of small limestone blocks, the top course of the lowest one being carved with a 'Buddhist railing' of two bars in false relief, evidently in imitation of the detached railing of early Indian works. Round the upper platform of a broken stone relic-case, apparently taken out of the chamber behind one of the 'wāhalkaḍas,' a similar rail of two bars is carved; it probably belongs to nearly the same period.

On the top of the dome there would doubtless be a square 'tee' of brickwork, ornamented, as in the other great dāgabas, with post-and-rail work in false relief, and having a circular disk of the sun, the great demon-scarer, in the centre of each face. Above this must have risen the spire, tapering slightly, and probably, like those of similar buildings, springing from a cylindrical base. At its top, or immediately below it, there appears to have been from the first a solid mushroom-shaped or lens-shaped 'chatta,' as a symbol of the royal honours paid to the relics, and perhaps considered to be quite as important as a magical protection from evil. The whole height is recorded to have been 120 cubits (Mah., i, p. 62), and the same figure is given by a later historian as the height when Parākrama-Bāhu I restored it. If, as is likely, the early cubit was two feet in length, this would be 14 feet less than the diameter of the dome. The top of the present mound is 178 feet 8 inches above the pavement at its base. The paved platform on which it rests measures 475 feet by 473 feet.[1]

On three, if not four sides, facing the cardinal points, a

[1] By the kind permission of the Secretary of State for the Colonies, I have reduced from Mr. Smither's drawings a plan of this dāgaba, and a plan and elevation of the Southern Wāhalkaḍa. (See Figs. Nos. 74 and 75.)

rectangular 'frontispiece,' as Mr. Smither termed it, in Sinhalese commonly called a *Wāhalkaḍa*, was built, projecting outwards from the dāgaba. This consisted, in the face, of a series of tiers of horizontal stone cornices or projecting moulded bands, separated by plain smooth-dressed stone-work. It was flanked at each end by two pillars, a high inner one on which sat a lion, looking outwards, with open mouth, and a short outer one, on each exposed side of which were conventional decorations in sunk relief. In 1886, I observed fragments of gilding on one pillar, and of painting on another. Slabs with roughly carved five-headed cobras, and in other respects like those at the Jētavana dāgaba described below, were fixed outside these pillars. Twenty-six elephants' heads [1] carved in stone project from the plain course above the lowest cornice of the wāhalkaḍa.[2]

The object of these highly decorated offsets, each 34 feet 2 inches long, appears merely to have been to form ornamental and also protective backgrounds for disengaged stone flower-altars placed on the pavement before them. Steps were also built behind these wāhalkaḍas, leading to the two upper basal platforms, and a room for relics, measuring about 13 feet by 6½ feet, was constructed behind each of them.

The Dīpavansa states that King Bhātikābhaya (20 B.C.–9 A.D.) 'made strong pillars for placing lamps round the foot of the Thūpa' (p. 213); and the Pūjāvaliya (p. 20) also records the erection of wooden posts round it and the large dāgaba at Mihintale, by King Mahā-dāṭhiya Mahā-Nāga (9–21 A.D.),

[1] The elephants' heads at this and the dāgabas next described were probably inserted for protective purposes. Those in the wall round the court-yard would have a similar function; others were also built in the surrounding walls of two other dāgabas (Mah., i, p. 163). See my remarks on the protective power of all auspicious objects, in the final chapter. The elephant, as the Vāhana or riding-animal of Indra, was a demon-scarer.

[2] Although it is not a suitable name for these structures, since it commonly means the gate-way of a palace, I employ their usual colloquial Sinhalese title, in preference to Reredos. 'Frontispiece,' the term applied to them by Mr. Smither, is inapplicable, as they are in reality projecting backgrounds, and 'Altar-background' is cumbersome. 'Offset' and 'Screen' fail to indicate their chief function.

apparently in order that festoons of lamps might be hung on them. Similar strings of lamps were hung round the Ambatthala dāgaba at Mihintale, which is surrounded by two rows of stone pillars (Mah., i, p. 136). This certainly indicates the chief purpose of such pillars round the dāgabas.

After the original structure was erected, a small attached relic-house, of a rectangular shape, was built on the eastern side, standing out onto the pavement like that at the Thūpārāma dāgaba. The bricks behind it are 16·78 inches long, 8·26 inches wide, and 2·36 inches thick ; Bt. is 19·5 and their contents 327 cubic inches. These dimensions point to about the second century A.D. as the time when they were made. It is possible that a room of this kind existed on that site at a much earlier date, and was replaced by a new building in the second century.

On each side at the bases of the steps at this dāgaba, as well as at all the more important buildings of Anurādhapura, a thin upright slab with an arched top is erected across the end of the balustrade. It resembles the stelae of Assyria on which the statues of the kings were carved. Many have plain tops like those of Assyria ; others end in a blunt point at the centre of the arch. In the more elaborate examples the figure of a protecting deity is carved in high false relief on the face of the stone (Figs. 157 and 160) ; on others a vase is represented out of which spring lotus flowers, buds, and leaves ; some are without any decoration of this kind.

An interesting feature at many of these stelae at Anurādhapura and a few other early sites, is a pilaster in relief on the outer side of each stele. (Figs. 79 and 157), often surmounted by an animal facing outwards, which is always a lion, a humped bull, an elephant, or a horse. On the face of a guardian slab at Mihintale there is a bird—probably a hansa—standing on a pillar at the side of a figure of the Indian goddess Kālī or Durgā.

The function of these animals in these sites has not been explained ; it appears to be similar to those of the processions of the same animals that are sometimes carved on the semicircular slabs termed 'Moon-stones' (in Sinhalese, *Irahanda-*

gala, 'Sun[1]-and-Moon Stone'), which are often placed on the ground at the foot of the lowest steps at the entrances to religious edifices. Processions of this kind are carved in relief on the uppermost band of the wāhalkaḍas at the Miriswaeṭi dāgaba, which is next described. With these may be also compared the elephants' heads that project from the face of these dāgabas, and the fore-parts of elephants that were built of brick and plastered over, on the outer face of the wall of the inner enclosure at the Ruwanwaeli and two other dāgabas. Processions of the sacred geese termed *Hansa* (which is identified with the Sun in the Rig Veda) are also carved on moon-stones; and hansas, lions, horned lions, and elephants are carved round the capitals of pillars at dāgabas and monastic buildings. The Mahāvansa states (i, p. 114) that 'rows of animals and hansas' were painted in the Ruwanwaeli relic-chamber, along with representations of 'the eight auspicious objects.' This appears to show that all these animals were carved because they were believed to have protective powers against evil spirits. This was certainly a function of the hansa, the elephant, the horse, the humped bull, and also of the lion.[2] The whole subject

[1] On one of these stones at Anurādhapura a half sun is carved, the central part having lotus petal decoration, outside which are the rays.

[2] At Saessēruwa, in the North-western Province, Mr. Bell found a dog and a ram-like animal carved with the others on a moon-stone. (Arch. Survey. Annual Report for 1895, p. 12.) The dog was a powerful demon-scarer; see my remarks on it in *The Earliest Coins*.

The lotus which appears so often on moon-stones and elsewhere seems also to have had protective functions. In Egypt it was closely connected with Rā, the Sun-god, of one of whose forms it was considered to be a type. Nu is represented in *The Book of the Dead* (Translation by Dr. Budge, p. 141) as saying, "I am the pure lotus which springeth up from the divine splendour that belongeth to the nostrils of Rā." In a variant of the same Chapter 80 it is addressed, "Hail, thou lotus, thou type of the god Nefer-Temu! I am the man that knoweth you, and I know your names among (those of) the gods, the lords of the underworld" (*op. cit.*, p. 141).

In Fig. No. 78 and on the moon-stone above-mentioned it is represented as the central part of the Sun-emblem. I believe that wherever the lotus appears at the entrances of buildings and at the dāgabas, although its purpose was partly decorative it had also a highly-protective

is rather obscure; further information regarding it will be found in the chapters on the early coins and the Swāstika.

In Fig. No. 79 I have illustrated on the right side one of these little pilasters, surmounted by a crouching lion, which is at the eastern entrance to the Ruwanwaeli dāgaba. The shaft is only 2⅓ inches wide. On the opposite side of the page is an elevation of a detached square pillar (Fig. 78) 8 feet 2 inches high, of an early type, which stands near the dāgaba. At the top it has a procession of three hansas, each

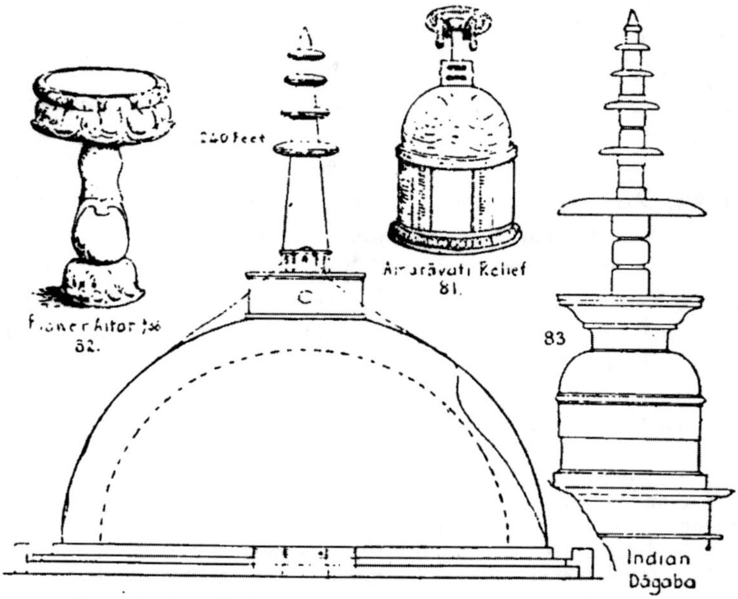

FIGS. 80–83. The Ruwanwaeli Dāgaba (restored). $\frac{1}{1200}$.

carrying a lotus bud by its stem. The design below it is a Sun-disk, the rays being incised between the outer circles; the next space in the figure contains lotus petals, and there is a flower in the centre. A row of pearls (which were very auspicious objects) follows, and below them and separated from them by a row of short bars are two plain loops separated by three bars. The pillar is highly symbolical and protective.

In Figure No. 80 I have ventured to give a drawing which attempts to reproduce the outline of this interesting dāgaba when in its complete state, according to the description supplied by the chroniclers. The winding line indicates the outline of the dāgaba before its restoration, and follows the contour in a photograph taken more than thirty years ago by Messrs. Skeen and Co., of Colombo. The inner dotted semicircle shows the size of the dome built by Duṭṭha-Gāmiṇi.

The restored dome is shown as a half sphere, agreeing in this respect both with the other great dāgabas of Anurādhapura and the account of it in the Mahāvansa. The tee and base of the spire follow the proportions of those of the two other great dāgabas which are described below. The height to the top of the lowest chatta is 240 feet, that is, 120 cubits at two feet per cubit, according to the scale adopted in a later part of this chapter.

The chattas follow the type of one carved in a crystal relic-case found at Tissa, and illustrated in Fig. No. 95. I have followed this unique example of an actual chatta in assuming that there was no pinnacle above the original one. There is also the authority of a later example in the Amarāvati carvings at the British Museum (slab No. 34), of which I give a sketch (Fig. No. 81), as well as a beautiful stone flower-altar in the Ruwanwaeli enclosure which, as Mr. Bell has already pointed out, is of this form (Fig. No. 82). At the Mahānāga dāgaba at Tissa, in the Southern Province, there is a much plainer flower-altar of this type.

I have represented, from a photograph for the loan of which I am indebted to Mrs. Waterfield of Malvern, the outline of the upper part of a highly decorated miniature stone dāgaba with five chattas, which was dug up at a village thirty-six miles from Peshāwar in India, by Mr. Stuart Waterfield of the Indian Civil Service, and which is now in the Calcutta Museum (Fig. No. 83). Although it is of much later date than the Ruwanwaeli dāgaba, I have accepted the arrangement of the chattas on the upper part of the spire as a guide in drawing those of the latter work.

The total height to the top of the pinnacle thus becomes 305 feet ; it may have been 25 feet lower if the spire passed through the first chatta.

The appearance of the great white dome covered with plaster and periodically white-washed, and of this high spire towering aloft in the blue sky, with its gilded upper chattas reflecting the bright rays of the tropical sun, must have been extremely effective and picturesque. It was a striking memorial of its great founder, and of the artistic genius of the Sinhalese race. But it was doubtless a far too prominent target for thunderstorms; and when Parākrama-Bāhu undertook the restoration of the structure he found it advisable to leave the summit of the spire at its original altitude of 120 cubits.

The Miriswaeṭi Dāgaba

Duṭṭha-Gāmiṇi also constructed the Maricavaṭi dāgaba, now called the Miriswaeṭi or Mirisawaeṭiya dāgaba, at Anurādhapura, immediately after he gained the throne, completing it and the surrounding buildings in three years, that is, in 158 B.C. It was erected in order to enshrine the relic which had been his palladium through all his fighting with the South Indian invaders. It is related in the Mahāvansa (i, p. 96) that when about to undertake the re-conquest of northern Ceylon, and while still at Māgama, he fixed a relic of Buddha in the head of his sceptre; and doubtless he would attribute to its magical power his constant series of victories over his enemies. The sceptre containing this relic is stated to be placed in the base of the dāgaba.

The Miriswaeṭi dāgaba shared in the vicissitudes that befel the others at Anurādhapura.

King Vōhāraka-Tissa (215–237 A.D.) restored the chatta on the spire, which is not previously mentioned and thus appears to have been an original work of Duṭṭha-Gāmiṇi. Kassapa IV (912–929 A.D.) handed over the charge of the dāgaba to the nuns of the Mahā Wihāra.

It was included in the dāgabas which the Tamils ransacked in the eleventh century; and it was restored, with the other large works, by Parākrama-Bāhu I. In the time of King Māgha of Kālinga, though allusion is not specially made to it by the historians, it was evidently broken into again;

FIG. 84. S. Wāhalkaḍa, Miriswaeṭi Dāgaba.

To face p. 295.

and like the other dāgabas it was repaired for the last time during the reign of Parākrama-Bāhu II.

Although Anurādhapura was visited by one or two later kings, there is no record of any further restorations of the dāgabas there; and all alike were allowed to fall into ruin and become overgrown with jungle. When I first saw the Miriswaeṭi dāgaba in 1873 it was little more than a conical mound covered with large trees and bushes, all the upper part having slipped down in a talus round its base.

Bricks of three sizes were used in the outer work. The largest, and certainly the original ones, were 10·41 inches wide and 3 inches thick. The intermediate bricks measured 14·2 inches in length, 8·2 inches in width, and 2·34 inches in thickness, Bt. being 19·19, and the contents 272 cubic inches. These dimensions indicate a restoration in about the fourth century A.D., which the historians have not recorded. The smallest bricks were those of the restoration effected by Parākrama-Bāhu I.

The shape of this dāgaba seems to have been a hemisphere, resting on three short cylinders which formed three basal platforms or ledges round it, like those at the Ruwanwaeli dāgaba. On the top of the dome there would be the rectangular tee, ornamented as usual with posts and rails on each face in sunk relief, above which rose the spire. Apparently only one solid chatta surmounted the spire.

It had three high rectangular stone wāhalkaḍas (Fig. No. 84), 25 feet long, facing the north, south, and west cardinal points, each formed of a series of cornices or deep mouldings separated by bands of plain stone-work. Twenty-one elephants' heads project from the band above the lowest cornice; and on the uppermost band are carved in relief four processions of animals in one line, all marching to the left, and consisting of horses, humped bulls, lions, horned lions, and elephants. At the left of the six animals in each wing of the wāhalkaḍa, a man or deity stands facing them, and holding up his left hand; and a similar figure stands facing each group of five animals in the central part.

The wāhalkaḍas are flanked at each end by two rectangular

monolithic pillars, 13 inches wide in the face, the inner one being as high as the uppermost cornice, and being surmounted by a stone lion sitting on his haunches on a square capital with a Buddhist railing of two bars on its face; he is looking outwards, with half-open mouth. The outer one, which is very short, has vertical flutings on the face, and the lower half of a rayed sun emblem above them. The taller pillars have as ornaments on their face, a dwarf at the base, supporting on his head a vase out of which springs a tree decorated with a series of pairs of men and animals alternately, climbing upwards on each side of it. At the top, above the tree, there is a disk or 'dharma-chakra,' a Wheel of the Law, on a pedestal, over which is a conical chatta in relief, with a snake lying head uppermost on each side of the pedestal. Above each snake is a Yak-tail fly-whisk, the emblem of a guardian deity. Behind the wāhalkaḍas steps led to the two upper basal ledges.

According to Mr. Smither's drawings, the diameter of the dome was 135 feet 6 inches. The upper basal cylinder had a diameter 9 feet 9 inches greater than that of the dome and was 3 feet 11¼ inches high; the middle one was 11 feet 6 inches wider still and 4 feet 2½ inches high; and the lowest one was 12 feet wider still, and 5 feet 2¾ inches high. Thus their total height was 13 feet 4½ inches. The height to the top of the ruin was 52 feet 7 inches; and the paved basement platform on which it stands is raised 4 feet 11½ inches above the ground level, and supported by a retaining wall of stone. The total height when Parākrama-Bāhu I restored it is stated in the Mahāvansa to have been 80 cubits.

This work and the Ruwanwaeli dāgaba prove that Duṭṭha-Gāmiṇi and his brother Saddhā-Tissa may claim the credit of being the first rulers to appreciate the grandeur of the effect of an enormous white dome, far greater than anything of the kind previously erected in Ceylon or India, and admirably adapted to be an expression of stability, and permanence, and inaccessibility, such as the purpose of its construction demanded. The bold rounded outline gives one the feeling of a finish and completeness which, to my mind, the pyramid, with its salient angles, does not possess. The simplicity of a very large dome is one of its charms ; its appearance of strength and nobility would be lessened by any decorative additions on its surface. The effect of the three platforms round the bottom of the dome is decidedly good ; they increase the idea of stability and add a finish to the base of the structure that is missing in early Indian works.

Sēla Caitya

Lajji-Tissa (119–109 B.C.), the second son of Saddhā-Tissa, built a dāgaba of stone, called in the Mahāvansa the Silā Thūpa, the Stone Dāgaba, 'in front of the Thūpārāma' (i, p. 138). In the Dīpavansa (p. 211) its site is better defined as being to the east of the Thūpārāma, and the structure is termed in that work the Dīgha Thūpa, the Long Dāgaba, the name doubtless indicating a different shape from that of the other dāgabas in Anurādhapura.

There is only one small dāgaba, now known as the Sēla Caitya, in the position described, and although it is built of brickwork like all the others it appears to be the building erected by this king. If so, it must have been destroyed, and afterwards rebuilt in brick. Mr. Bell discovered that the material in the interior consisted of 'earth and brick fragments, cased in by burnt brick,' an indubitable proof of its reconstruction.

The largest bricks found at it are apparently those of an early post-Christian date, being 9 inches wide and 2·53 inches thick, with Bt. 22·8. If the length was 6 times the thickness it would be 15·18 inches, and the contents would be 345 cubic inches. The size points to the 1st century A.D. or late B.C. as the period when they were burnt. There are bricks of three other sizes at this dāgaba, which belong to later restorations, probably of the second, twelfth, and thirteenth centuries.

The dome of this dāgaba is 37 feet 8 inches in diameter at present, according to Mr. Bell, this being possibly nearly its original width ; it is a mere ruin 10 feet high on a platform raised 5 feet 3 inches above the ground level, and 46 feet 8 inches square. The original form can only be surmised ; its name, 'the Long Dāgaba,' shows that it must have been either of a high bell-shape, or more likely almost a cone, these being the only two forms that appear very high in proportion to their width.

On sinking a shaft down the axis of the dāgaba, Mr. Bell found that the relic-chamber was 'a brick-cased *cella*, 3 ft. 6 in. in breadth by 2 ft. 6 in. high. Its bottom was on a level with the *maluwa* [enclosure] platform, and formed by a monolith slab, a foot thick, which covered a square *yantragala* [a slab with rectangular holes, often 25 in number, sunk in it to receive valuables] of nine partitions all empty.'[1]

We next come to the reign of King Waṭṭa-Gāmiṇi Abhaya, who after being dethroned in 103 or 104 B.C., in the first year of his reign, by South Indian invaders, afterwards re-occupied the throne from 88 to 76 B.C. There can be no doubt that he built a great dāgaba called Abhaya-giri, at the extensive monastery of that name which he established. There is no account of the relics which it enshrines.

For some unknown reason it has always, in modern times, been pointed out as one which is to the eastward of the Sēla Caitya and the Ruwanwaeli dāgaba, a mis-identification that perhaps dates from the restoration by Parākrama-Bāhu I, in the twelfth century. The state of the great dāgabas at Anurādhapura at that time is graphically pourtrayed by the old historian :—'These three Thūpas that the Tamils had destroyed were covered with great trees in which lurked tigers [*sic*, literally, leopards] and bears. And because of the great heaps of bricks and clay and the thickets of the forest no man was able to have access thereto' (Mah., ii, p. 260). This tends to prove that the place had been totally abandoned for so long a period that the ruins were practically unknown, and this might give rise to their wrong identification by the officials sent by the king to restore them. In giving an account of this restoration the Mahāvansa mentions that the Abhayagiri dāgaba was 140 cubits high and another large one, the Jētavana dāgaba, 160 cubits high; whereas we have the statement of the Rājāvaliya (p. 52) that the latter work was built 140 cubits high by Mahā-Sēna. Thus it is clear that

[1] Annual Report, 1895, p. 2.

there is an error regarding the nomenclature in one of these works. If, as I shall endeavour to show, the present names of these two dāgabas are wrong and should be transposed, this would seem to transfer the mistake to the twelfth century, since in more modern times the place was never so much overgrown that these sites could not be visited by pilgrims, and it is on record that several later kings went on pilgrimage to Anurādhapura. As the error involves both structures it will be convenient to deal with them together.

Identification of the Jētavana and Abhaya-giri Dāgabas

The account of the establishment by King Mahā-Sēna (277-304 A.D.) of the Jētavana wihāra at which the Jētavana dāgaba was built is given in the Mahāvansa as follows :—When Mahā-Sēna was a youth his tutor, who belonged to the (Vaitulya) Abhaya-giri Community of Monks, then engaged in a violent religious feud with the (Thēravāda) Community of the Mahā Wihāra, had induced him to adopt the doctrines of his own sect ; and as the result of this partizanship, when he succeeded to the throne he prohibited the giving of alms to any priests of the Mahā Wihāra. Afterwards, having a high opinion of a (Vaitulya) monk called Tissa, he decided to build a special monastery over which this person might preside, and he 'constructed the Jētavana Wihāra for him, within the sacred limits of the garden called Jōti, belonging to the Mahā Wihāra. He then applied to the priests [monks] of the Mahā Wihāra to abandon their consecrated boundaries in order that the ground might be consecrated for the new temple' (i, p. 151).

It has been noted previously that the Mahāvansa clearly explains (i, p. 64) that the Jōtivana is only another name for the Nandana garden, which I have shown to be a narrow enclosure wedged in between the city and the Mahāmēgha garden. It is in this strip of land that we must look for the Jēṭavana dāgaba ; and it seems inexplicable that any doubt should be felt that the only great structure of the kind in that part, although it is now commonly called the Abhaya-giri dāgaba,[1] is the building in question. As the Nandana or Jōtivana garden had been granted to the Mahā Wihāra by Dēvānam-piya Tissa, along with the Mahāmēgha garden, the application to the monks to make over part of their consecrated land for the new monastery can be easily understood.

This identification leaves only one other dāgaba of the largest size to be named at Anurādhapura, and this must be the Abhaya-giri, which is now mis-called the Jētavana dāgaba.

The description of its site given in the Mahāvansa (i, p. 131), although doubtless sufficiently definite at a time when the different details of the surroundings were well known, is not very clear in these days when all is buried in jungle. A large body of Tamil invaders had marched straight on the capital from Mahātiṭṭha, close to Mannār, and they were encamped at a village near the city, called Koḷambālaka, just as in the wars of the king's uncle, Duṭṭha-Gāmiṇi, a similar force under Bhalluka, the nephew of the Tamil king Elāra, had camped at the same place when advancing on the city from the same port (Mah., i, p. 100). The march of the two invading armies along the same route shows that this village was on the direct highway leading from Mahātiṭṭha to Anurādhapura, and therefore on the north-western side of the town.

Waṭṭa-Gāmiṇi led his forces out to meet the invading army, and fought a battle at Koḷambālaka, in which he was defeated; and 'mounting his chariot, fled through the Titthārāma gate. This Titthārāma had been built by Paṇḍukābhaya, and had always been assigned as a residence to people of foreign religions. . . . A certain Nigaṇṭha [a Jain anchorite] named Giri, seeing him in his flight, shouted in a loud voice, "The great black Sīhala [Sinhalese] is flying." The Maharaja hearing this resolved within himself "when my wishes are realised I will build a wihāra here"' (Mah., i, p. 129). Subsequently he regained the throne, and the account states that 'Thereafter this monarch demolished the aforesaid Nigaṇṭhārāma, at which he was reviled in his flight, and on the site thereof built a wihāra of twelve parivenas [monastic residences]. . . . By

[1] A local tradition which could point out the Dakuṇu dāgaba as the tomb of Elāra cannot be accepted as possessing much authority.

reason of the Ārāma having belonged to Giri, and by reason of the wihāra having been made by the king Abhaya, therefore it was called Abhaya-giri Wihāra' (Mah., i, p. 131). Thus the account shows that the monastery was between the fortified city of that period and the village to the north-west where the battle was fought.

In the account of Paṇḍukābhaya's arrangement of the suburbs (Mah., i, p. 43) it is stated that a range of buildings for Vaeddas was established on the northern side of the cemetery, and to the eastward of these dwellings, that is, on the north-east of the cemetery, ' he provided a residence [the Titthārāma] for five hundred persons of various foreign religious faiths.' Unfortunately the site of the cemetery is unknown. It was crossed by the consecrated boundary fixed by Dēvānam-piya Tissa (Mah., i, p. 62), and the route followed by the king shows that it was on the western side of the city. A site to the north-east of it could not therefore be very far from the position occupied by the dāgaba now wrongly termed Jētavana.

The clearest independent evidence in favour of this identification is contained in the account of Anurādhapura supplied by the Chinese monk, Fa Hien, in his narrative of his travels. He came from China to India for the purpose of obtaining copies of Buddhist manuscripts, and after spending six years there, he devoted two years to the same research in Ceylon, returning to China in the following year, 413 A.D. His words are (Dr. Legge's translation, p. 102) :—' When Buddha came to this country, wishing to transform the wicked Nāgas, by his supernatural power he planted one foot at the north of the royal city, and the other on the top of a mountain [Adam's Peak], the two being fifteen yōjanas apart. Over the footprint at the north of the city the king built a large tope [dāgaba], 400 cubits high, grandly adorned with gold and silver and finished with a combination of all the precious substances. By the side of the tope he further built a monastery, called the Abhaya-giri, where there are five thousand monks.' At this time, he states that the Mahā Wihāra had only three thousand monks, and it was thus inferior in size to the Abhaya-giri monastery.

The Chinese traveller's reiterated statement that the monastery was at the north of the city must be conclusive as to the identity of the only great dāgaba in that neighbourhood. I shall therefore refer to the two dāgabas by the names that appear to me to belong to them, terming the northern one the Abhaya-giri, and the one to the east of the Sēla Caitya the Jētavana dāgaba.

There is, however, further evidence regarding the identity of the northern dāgaba. When part of the *débris* collected round its base was removed by Mr. S. M. Burrows, late of the Ceylon Civil Service, he discovered a series of large stone relic-cases placed behind one or more of the wāhalkaḍas which are annexed to the dome at the cardinal points. Several of these were uninscribed, but round two of them the following sentence was deeply cut in one line (see Fig. No. 153 for facsimile).

> *Siddham. Maṭu Tisa Maharajaha raji nimi tabi hada tani jani.* Hail! Fashioned, established (for sacred purposes), put in the prepared place (in) the reign of the Great King Maḷu-Tissa.

The characters are those of the second century A.D., and the dedication belongs to the time of Kaniṭṭha-Tissa (165–195 A.D.). In an inscription at a monastery at Ussayppu kallu, about nine miles from Marisi-kaṭṭu, and near the Mōdara-gam-oya, this king styles himself 'the Great king Maḷu-Tissa, son of the Great King Nāga.'[1] As Kaniṭṭha-Tissa was the

[1] As this inscription is in a somewhat inaccessible part of the island I have given a facsimile in Fig. No. 153.

The transliteration is:—Siddham. Naka maharajaha puta Maḷu Tisa ma (2) haraji ma gananē kariyihi wawa Luwimitayah(i) Cuḍataka wawiyi ca (3) jabo awiyi ca, mata karawiyi ca, tapawana awiyi ca, me c(e)taka wawiya (4) bojiyapati, Karakaḷaya Kuba wihara kahi paca wata hiti. Ihata mula c(e)ta mawati (5) ya jina paḷisatiriya koṭu dini.

Hail! The Great King Maḷu-Tissa, son of the Great King Nāga, having formed and protected a tank of a great quantity of karīshas (in extent) at Luwimitaya, and the Cuḍataka tank, and (thereby) caused rejoicings; and having protected the Ascetics' Forest; after having assigned the tank belonging to this dāgaba, built the Karakaḷaya Kumbha wihāra, suitable for the observances connected with the

younger son of King Mahallaka-Nāga, this proves that he is the monarch who terms himself Maḷu-Tissa, 'Tissa-the-younger-brother' (*maluwa* in Elu or old Sinhalese) to distinguish his name from that of his elder brother, King Bhātiya-Tissa 'Tissa-the-elder-brother' (141–155 A.D.).[1]

It is clear that a relic-case with a dedicatory inscription of this king of the second century could not be placed in a dāgaba which was not erected until the last years of the third century. Its discovery in the northern dāgaba proves that this structure was in existence a century before Mahā-Sēna built the Jētavana dāgaba, and is quite fatal to the nomenclature commonly accepted.

The dimensions of the bricks in the domes of the two dāgabas also strongly support the identification; and in fact it was the discrepancy in their sizes compared with others of the respective periods which first led me to investigate this subject more than twenty years ago. Those of the dāgaba to the east of the Sēla Caitya have a length of 15·82 inches, a breadth of 8·41 inches, and a thickness of 2·26 inches; Bt. is 19 square inches, and the contents 301 cubic inches. The table of dated bricks already given proves that they must belong to some date from the first to the fourth century A.D., inclusive.

In the northern dāgaba, the bricks measure 18·92 inches in length, 9·62 inches in breadth, and 3·20 inches in thickness;

requisites [clothing, food, bedding, and medicine]. Having constructed the chief dāgaba at this place, he repaired the dilapidated buildings.

This inscription is a duplicate of one copied by Dr. E. Müller at Galkowila (No. 98 in his list), the purport of which his defective copy led him to misapprehend. The meaning of the word *mata*, which I have translated 'rejoicings,' is doubtful. Ḷuwimitaya (Ḷumitiya at Galkowila) = Lōkamita; compare Alu wihāra = Alōka wihāra. 'Protecting' the tank probably means arranging for its maintenance and appointing a Guardian for it.

King Udaya II (952–955) nearly lost his life through his violation of the sanctity of the Ascetics' Forest (Mah., ii, pp. 82, 83). It was a 'Sacred' forest to which ultra-ascetic monks, especially those termed Pansukūlikas, retired, and it was evidently a sanctuary for offenders of all kinds. Its position is not known.

[1] In Dr. Müller's Inscription No. 16, Kaniṭṭha-Tissa describes himself as 'Tissa, the younger brother of the Great King Bhātiya-Tissa, (and) son of the Great King Naga.'

Bt. is 30·7 and the contents 583 cubic inches. The only dated bricks of this type are those in the Miriswaeṭi dāgaba. While they are large even for the time when Waṭṭa-Gāmiṇi was king, it is practically impossible that such extreme dimensions should have been suddenly reverted to nearly four centuries later, as would be the case if this were the Jētavana dāgaba.

So far as I am aware there is only a single line in the Dīpavansa (xix, 17) which can be held to support the common nomenclature. This work says of King Waṭṭa-Gāmiṇi *Abhayagiriṃ patiṭṭhapesi Silāthūpaṃ cetiyamantare,* 'He built Abhaya-giri between the Silāthūpa and the Cētiya.' Mr. Bell understands this to mean 'between the Sēla Caitya and Mihintale' [Cētiya-giri].[1] But Mihintale is eight miles away, and there is no authority for assuming that the old author omitted the word *giri* after *Cētiya.* I suppose that by the word *Cētiya* the author meant the Abhaya-giri dāgaba, and that the Silā-thūpa is the Silā Sobbha Kandaka Thūpa, now called Lankārāma, which the same king built. The line would then mean that 'he built the Abhaya-giri (wihāra) between the Lankārāma dāgaba and the Abhaya-giri dāgaba,' this being the actual position of a great part of the ruins of the monastery.

The Abhaya-giri Dāgaba

Although the histories contain numerous references to the buildings which formed the Abhaya-giri wihāra, little is said respecting the great dāgaba itself. It is recorded of Gaja-Bāhu I (113–135 A.D.) that 'raising the Abhayuttara Thūpa he constructed it of a greater elevation' (Mah., i, p. 132), a result that might naturally be expected if he raised it. Doubtless this refers only to the works above the dome, in the lower part of which no bricks of this period are to be seen.

It is possible that when King Kaṇiṭṭha-Tissa placed his relic-cases there he at the same time built the wāhalkaḍas. The decorative work on their flanking pillars is of a type intermediate between that of the Ruwanwaeli and Miriswaeṭi dāgabas and that of the Jētavana dāgaba, in some details

[1] Annual Report for 1895, p. 2, footnote.

agreeing with the first two and in some with the other.

King Vōhāraka-Tissa (215–237 A.D.) is said to have caused the chatta to be repaired (Mah., i, p. 144) ; the original work in it must have been done by Gaja-Bāhu I. Probably the spire possessed one from the first, resembling in that respect those of the other great dāgabas. Dhātu-Sēna (463–479 A.D.) again repaired this chatta.

Moggallāna presented a new cloth covering to the dāgaba, and Kassapa II (652–661 A.D.) fixed a jewelled pinnacle on the spire, the top of which is thus shown to have passed through the chatta (Mah., ii, p. 32).

Sena III (955–964 A.D.) laid a stone paving round the dāgaba at a cost of forty thousand kahāpanas (Mah., ii, p. 83). It is surprising to find that at this important monastery such a necessary work had been neglected for more than a thousand years. It is safer to assume that the statement refers to some additional work in laying paving than to suppose that all the earlier zealous Buddhist monarchs had omitted to carry out such an obvious improvement. The sum paid for the work also appears to be totally insufficient to cover the cost of laying the whole paving.

The dāgaba was repaired by Parākrama-Bāhu I (1164–1197 A.D.) with the others at Anurādhapura, all, it is stated, having been seriously damaged by South-Indian invaders long antecedent to that period, that is, in the middle of the preceding century, when they held Northern Ceylon.

It is not specially mentioned as having been broken into during the reign of the invader Māgha (1215–1236 A.D.), but as all the other large dāgabas were injured at that time no doubt considerable damage would be done to this one also; and it was one of those repaired in the time of Parākrama-Bāhu II (1240–1275 A.D.), when all are said to have been in a ruinous state and overgrown with jungle.

This was again its condition in the last quarter of the nineteenth century. It was then surrounded by thick jungle and covered by a forest of trees and interlaced undergrowth. This was felled and the re-growth kept under control, but no repairs have been undertaken yet.

X.

The dome of this dāgaba was found by Mr. Smither to be a semi-globe, the centre of which is four feet above the basement or paved court-yard in which the building stands, which is raised six feet above the adjoining ground and is 587 feet square. The diameter of the dome is 310 feet at the top of the basal ledges.

It rests upon the usual three short basal cylinders, which

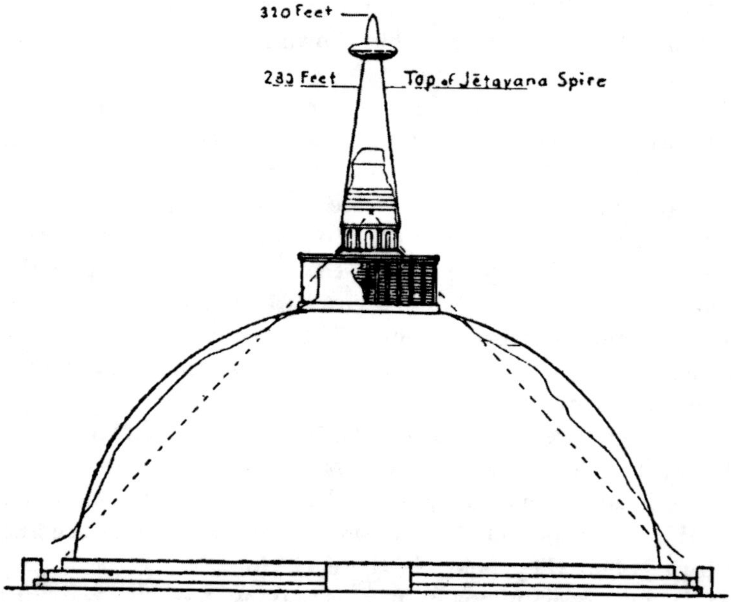

FIG. 85. The Abhaya-giri Dāgaba. $\frac{1}{1100}$.
(The triangle shows the size of the Third Pyramid at Gīzeh.)

have a total height of 16 feet, the lowest one being 6 feet 6 inches high and 355 feet in diameter. The tee is 75 feet square and 33 feet high. It has a plain plinth, and a cornice of three plain overlapping bands. Each face has post-and-rail work in sunk relief, with a disk of the sun in the centre, 6 feet 6 inches in diameter. The railing consists of 12 pilasters each 2 feet 3 inches wide, and 14 flat rails, each 15 inches wide. The spire, which is 30 feet in diameter at the base, springs from a cylinder 15 feet high, and 30 feet in diameter; it is vertical for five feet and above that tapers gradually. Bands of cut stone 6 inches thick are inserted in it, with intervals 2 feet 6 inches high. The face of the cylinder is divided by pilasters into eight compartments, in each of which there is a shallow arched niche. The height from the platform to the top of the tee is 187 feet 6 inches, and the spire, which is broken, now rises 57 feet 6 inches higher.[1]

Four wāhalkaḍas, 45 feet 6 inches long, were built at the cardinal points. Like those at the other great dāgabas, they consist of a series of horizontal cornices or prominent mouldings, separated by plain cut stone-work, and were about 16 feet high. Two square decorated pillars were fixed at each end, carved on the faces with straight-stemmed trees having leaves in pairs, or an ornamental meander springing out of a vase and having animals in its loops. On one pillar the animals are in pairs, one being on each side of the stem of the tree, and are climbing upward. On the side of each outer pillar are two Nāgas, or in some cases other deities, in high false relief, in two panels, one above the other, a male above and a female below. These pillars may have been flanked by a slab carved with a multiple-headed cobra in high false relief.

On the south face of the dāgaba a small building, measuring 24 feet by 15 feet, was constructed, probably to contain relics or statues.

The Jētavana Dāgaba

The Jētavana wihāra is often mentioned in the histories but they rarely allude to the great dāgaba. A reference to the repair of the chatta by King Dhātu-Sēna proves that like similar structures at the old city this one had this form of terminal in early times, and most probably from the date of its erection.

The plaster work on the dome was repaired by King Mahā-Nāga (561–564 A.D.), together with that on the Ruwanwaeli

[1] By the kind permission of the Secretary of State for the Colonies, I am able to give a drawing of this dāgaba, reduced from Mr. Smither's elevation of it, with the exception of the restored spire (see Fig. No. 85).

and Abhaya-giri dāgabas. Moggallāna (608–614 A.D.) presented a new cloth covering for it as well as to these two works, and Kassapa II fixed a jewelled pinnacle on it, as on them.

Although the histories do not mention it, a stone pavement was wholly or partly laid round the structure in the tenth century ; and the record is preserved in some short dedicatory inscriptions cut on several of the slabs presented by private donors. One runs *Kasā himiya taebū pahaṇa,* ' the stone placed by the Lady Kasā.' Another is *Nagā himiya panas pahaṇak,*

FIG. 86. The Jētavana Dāgaba. 1886.

' the Lady Nāgā, fifty stones.' A third states that the cost of two stones given by Kākawannaya was *ran dasa kaḷada,* ' ten kalandas of gold ' ; a fourth inscription records that a stone laid by another person also cost *ran pas kaḷanaek,* ' five kalandas of gold '—the same price.

The dāgaba must have been damaged in the eleventh century, since Parākrama-Bāhu I restored it. In the time of Māgha it suffered like the rest, and was again repaired during the reign of Parākrama-Bāhu II. In the latter part of the nineteenth century it was in nearly the same ruinous state as the other two great dāgabas.

The Jētavana is the widest completed dāgaba in Ceylon,[1] the diameter of the dome at the upper basal ledge being 325 feet. The dome is a semi-globe, or rather part of one, as the centre of the globe was found by Mr. Smither to be 9 feet 6 inches below the base of the lowest of the three cylinders on which it rests. The platform round the dāgaba being raised to this extent, the centre of the globe is at the original ground level.

As at the other large works, the three short basal cylinders rise 16 feet above the surrounding paved platform, and the diameter of the lowest one is 367 feet. They form three steps or ledges round the base of the dome, each 7 feet wide. The lowest one is 6 feet 9 inches high, the middle one 4 feet 9 inches high, and the upper one 4 feet 6 inches high. The paved platform is 590 feet square.

The dome is surmounted by a 'tee,' 76 feet square and 32 feet 6 inches high, the distance from the platform to its top being 183 feet. The spire, 33 feet in diameter at the base, appears to have risen directly from the tee, with possibly at first a slightly narrower neck; it tapered to 24 feet in diameter at 48 feet in height, the point where the top was broken off. The height from the platform to the top of the spire was 232 feet when Mr. Smither measured it. Bands of cut stone 6 inches thick were laid in the spire at intervals of 2 feet 6 inches.

The tee had the usual post-and-rail work on each face, the posts being 11 brick pilasters 2 feet 6 inches wide, while flat horizontal bands 15 inches wide form the rails. A sun-disk occupied the centre of each face.

At the cardinal points there are four wāhalkaḍas, each 48 feet long, flanked by two rectangular pillars at each end; the

[1] A still larger one was commenced at Polannaruwa by Parākrama-Bāhu I, but was not finished. The mound which constitutes its remains, to the north of the other dāgabas there, was about 50 feet high and some 350 feet wide at the top when I examined it many years ago. The Mahāvansa (ii, p. 259) calls it the Damila Thūpa, 'the Tamil Dāgaba,' because it was partly built by Tamil prisoners of war. According to that work it was 'the greatest of all the Thūpas,' and was thirteen hundred cubits in circumference, or about six hundred feet in diameter at the bottom, if the cubit of that time measured 17½ inches in length. The diameter of the dome is not stated.

face work consists of alternate cornices or heavy mouldings and plain stone work. Elephants' heads project above the lowest cornice. The end pillars are decorated in the face by ornamental creepers, or Buddhist emblems or animals placed in the loops of a meander ; and on the outer side of the lower and outer pillar by Nāga princes and princesses in false high relief in two panels, one over the other, the prince being in the upper one and the princess below him in the other [1] (Fig. No. 8). At each end of the wāhalkaḍas, and beyond these pillars, there is a limestone slab carved with a seven-headed cobra in high sunk relief, its body forming two loops on each side ; a chatta or umbrella is usually carved above it. The Nāgas and cobras were expected to act as guards of the relics, or the whole structure ; according to the Dhātuvansa, Buddha on his third visit to Ceylon ordered the Nāgas to protect his relics. A relic-room 26 feet by 18 feet was built at the western wāhalkaḍa.

In 1887 and 1888, the late Mr. R. W. Ievers, at that time the Government Agent of the Province, opened a horizontal tunnel to the centre of this dāgaba, at a level of 33 feet above the surrounding pavement, and at the end of it sunk a shaft in the axis of the structure to a depth of 13 feet below the base. At a depth of 40 feet, or 7 feet below the pavement, a rough stone slab was encountered, under which was a small copper coin, having an animal, apparently a horse, on the obverse. It was stated by Mr. R. S. Poole, of the British Museum, to resemble the coins numbered 55 and 58 of Plate II of Sir Walter Elliott's *Coins of Southern India*, which were attributed to the Korumbars. It must have been placed there when the work was begun. The excavation of the shaft proved that in the centre the foundations only extended to a depth of 3 feet 6 inches below the ground-level. The whole inner work was found to consist of bricks set in a

[1] They are only distinguishable from human beings by the cobras' heads which appear above or at the side of their heads, there being a five-headed cobra with the prince and a single-headed one for the princess. Some figures without these emblems may be intended for other deities (male and female) and one may be Ayiyanār (Fig. No. 37).

FIG. 87. Pillars at Wāhalkaḍa, Jētavana Dāgaba.

To face p. 310.

tenacious clay. No relic-chamber was discovered.[1] A later excavation made by Mr. Bell showed the foundations to be 26 feet deep, in brickwork, underneath which was concrete. This was at the periphery.[2]

The Lankārāma Dāgaba

In addition to the Abhaya-giri it is recorded in the Mahāvansa (i, p. 132) that King Waṭṭa-Gāmiṇi also built a dāgaba to the north of the Ruwanwaeli 'on an eminent place [that is, eminence] which was named Silā-Sobbha-Kandaka.' The only other dāgaba of any importance, now termed the Lankārāma dāgaba, to the north-west of the Ruwanwaeli dāgaba, appears to be the work in question. It seems to have been held in less estimation than the other great structures of the kind, and if it is again mentioned in the histories the monastery at which it was erected was known as the Maṇisōma wihāra, or Sōmārāma, which the same king is stated to have built. (Mah., i, p. 131).

We find the Maṇisōma wihāra mentioned with the Thūpārāma, Miriswaeṭi, and Dakkhiṇa monasteries, this connection indicating that all were at Anurādhapura. Kaniṭṭha-Tissa is said to have constructed an 'edifice' over the Maṇisōma dāgaba (Mah., i, p. 143), and Mēghavaṇṇābhaya I (254–267 A.D.) made some repairs at this 'edifice.'

The length and width of the bricks used in the dome of the Lankārāma dāgaba shows that they are pre-Christian, notwithstanding their reduced thickness. Their length is 17·37 inches, the width is 8·94 inches, and the thickness is 2·62 inches ; Bt. is 23·4, and the volume becomes 407 cubic inches.

It is possible that the original shape of this dāgaba differed from that of nearly all the other early dāgabas in Ceylon, but resembled some early Indian works. In its present state the dome is a segment of a hemisphere 38 feet wide at the point where it leaves the upper cylinder of the three on which it rests, above which it rises 15 feet to the tee. This cylinder, 4

[1] *Manual of the North-central Province*, by R. W. Ievers. 1899, p. 238.

[2] Annual Report for 1894, p. 2.

feet high, is no wider than the dome, and thus does not form a ledge round it as in the other early works, but is in reality a continuation of the dome, with a vertical side. Of the other two cylinders the lowest one is 44 feet 2 inches in diameter and 3 feet 8 inches high, and the middle one 40 feet wide and 4 feet 1 inch high.

The tee was 9 feet 8 inches square without the plinth, and like the others was probably originally faced with post-and-rail work, although in an illustration taken from a photograph, in Fergusson's *History of Indian and Eastern Architecture*, published in 1876 (p. 194), it is shown with only two pilasters at each side of the face and a circular sun emblem in the centre. If its width then was the same as when Mr. Smither measured it in 1877 its total height was some 8 feet. It is not known if the spire had a chatta. As the dāgaba is only twice mentioned after its erection the omission of the historians to refer to such a terminal cannot be taken to prove that it had not this usual ornament, which was also a magical protection from evil. The height of the dāgaba was found by Mr. Smither to be 33 feet 7 inches; he thought it may have been more than 50 feet when complete.

Like the Thūpārāma dāgaba and the Ambatthala dāgaba at Mihintale, this work is surrounded by disengaged thin graceful monolithic pillars, with separate ornamental capitals. While the Thūpārāma dāgaba had four rows of them that at the Lankārāma had only three. The inner row consisted of 20, square at the lower part and octagonal above, each 16 feet 8 inches high; the middle row had 28 similar pillars, 16 feet 11 inches high, their tops being on a level with those of the inner line, on account of a drop in the flooring; and the outer row 40 octagonal pillars, 12 feet 5 inches high. All measure from 11 to 12½ inches across, and they have a general resemblance to those at the Thūpārāma, but they have no tenons at the top. The animals carved on the capitals are horned lions in the inner row, sitting lions in the middle one, and dwarfs in the outer row, some of them playing flutes while others dance.

Although Mr. Smither knew of only the three above-mentioned structures surrounded by stone pillars, there may be a few others in Ceylon, but they are undoubtedly rare. It is possible that some may have had wooden pillars.

The Dakuṇu Dāgaba

There was only one other monastery in Anurādhapura at which a dāgaba of considerable size was built at an early date. This was the Dakuṇu or Dakkhiṇa wihāra, whose dāgaba lay at the southern extremity of a curved north and south line passing from the Abhaya-giri, at the northern end, by the Thūpārāma, and Ruwanwaeli dāgabas. Until Mr. Bell's excavations disclosed its real character it was merely a high tumulus-like mound completely overgrown with bushes and trees, and popularly supposed to mark the grave of the Tamil king Elāra, who was killed by Duṭṭha-Gāmiṇi at the capture of the city; although the Mahāvaṇsa (i, p. 99) says clearly enough that he was cremated and a tomb was built over his ashes at the spot where he fell 'near the southern gate of the city,' the position of which has been already pointed out.

The account of the construction of the monastery is contained in the following words (Mah., i, p. 132), 'Of the eight warriors [chiefs of Waṭṭa-Gāmiṇi] the one named Uttiya built to the southward of the town the wihāra called Dakkhiṇa wihāra.' This statement is repeated in the Dīpavansa (p. 210); and it will be observed that the erection of the dāgaba is not alluded to; but this does not prove that it was not built then, as these two histories similarly do not record the building of the much more important Jētavana dāgaba.

Kaniṭṭha-Tissa (165–193 A.D.) is stated (Mah., i, p. 143) to have constructed a covering for this dāgaba; but in the Dīpavansa he is said to have built the dāgaba. There is thus an element of doubt as to the exact age of the structure, which one would rather expect to have been erected when the wihāra was established.

The other references to it are found in the Mahāvansa. King Vōhāraka-Tissa (215–237 A.D.) is recorded to have caused the chatta of the Dakkhiṇamūla dāgaba, which appears to be this one, to be repaired along with those at some other important structures; and the sub-king Kassapa is stated to have destroyed and rifled the dāgaba during the reign of Aggabōdhi III (624–640 A.D). He appears to have restored it again after he succeeded to the throne.

In such a case as this we must look to the bricks for some light upon the question as to the period when the dāgaba was really built. They average 16·36 inches long, 8·18 inches wide, and 2·31 inches thick; Bt. is 18·9, and the contents 309 cubic inches. It will be seen at once that these dimensions closely agree with those of the Jētavana dāgaba; and they also unmistakably indicate a date after the Christian era. For this reason I accept the statement of the Dīpavansa that the dāgaba was built near the end of the second century A.D. This is the more likely since no dāgabas of any considerable size appear to have been constructed by others than the monarchs of the country.

As to the similarity of the sizes of the bricks at this work and the Jētavana dāgaba, which was erected fully a century later, it may be surmised that the dimensions adopted late in the second century continued to be employed, with slight variations, throughout the third century.

This dāgaba has only been partly excavated by Mr. Bell. In his Report for 1898, p. 5, he refers to three basal platforms round it and mentions that traces of one of the ornamental wāhalkaḍas had been found. A flanking pillar belonging to one of these has the usual male and female guardians on one side in false relief, and on another face a decorative tree surmounted by a bird with a crest and raised wings, like those on the pillars at the Thūpārāma dāgaba. Mr. Bell states that the circumference of the dome, which is bell-shaped, is 464 feet, approximately; thus its diameter was about 148 feet at the top of the basal platforms. At the base of the outermost platform the diameter was about 179 feet 6 inches. There were no detached stone pillars round the dāgaba. The tee was about 38 feet square, or very nearly a quarter of the diameter of the dome.

The Kiribat Dāgaba

At three and a half miles north of the Ruwanwaeli dāgaba, and thus outside the city, there is another now termed the Kiribat, 'Milk-rice,' dāgaba. Although Mr. Bell considered it to be 'one of the oldest of the large dāgabas at Anurādhapura,' [1] the size of the bricks dug out of the shaft that was sunk by him down its axis is conclusive evidence against its early date, if they are similar to those in the rest of the structure. They are 6·80 inches wide and 2·26 thick, Bt. being 15·4. These are the dimensions of bricks used in the repairs of the 'tee' at the little Pabulu dāgaba at Polannaruwa, and they probably belong to nearly the same period as the ruins of the so-called Wijayārāma monastery, which is near the Kiribat dāgaba. Mr Bell has proved that this monastery is a work of the ninth century A.D.[2] The dāgaba is now a mere tumulus. Mr. Bell found that it was built on a raised platform 204 feet square, paved with bricks. It had the usual three basal platforms, each about 2 feet 6 inches high and wide; and it had a diameter of 135 feet.

OTHER EARLY DĀGABAS

The Mahiyangana Dāgaba.

The Mahāvansa (i, p. 5) records that a dāgaba 30 cubits high was constructed by Uddhachūḷābhaya, a younger brother of Dēvānam-piya Tissa, at Mahiyangana, to enclose one 12 cubits high erected there by 'Sarabhū, disciple of the Thēra Sariputta' immediately after the death of Buddha, in which was enshrined a collar bone (*gīvatthi*) of the Teacher. This latter dāgaba was said to be built over one formed of emerald, which was supposed to hold a handful of Buddha's 'pure blue locks,' presented by him to the god Sumana, 'the chief of the devas,' that is, Śakra, on his visit to convert the Yakkhas.

Duṭṭha-Gāmiṇi during the early part of his war against the forces of Elāra enclosed these in a larger dāgaba 80 cubits high. The chatta was repaired by Vohāraka-Tissa (215–237, A.D.).

[1] Annual Report for 1892, p. 5.
[2] Arch. Survey of Ceylon. Sixth Progress Report, p. 9.

I have not visited the place, and the only account which I have of the dāgaba, is the short one given of its state in 1848 by Sir Emerson Tennent, in which he says, 'It is a huge semi-circular mound of brickwork, three hundred and sixty feet in

FIG. 88. The Mahiyangana Dāgaba.
(*From a photograph by* DR. C. G. SELIGMANN.

circumference and still one hundred feet high, but so much decayed at the top that its original outline is no longer ascertainable. When Spilberg, the Dutch admiral, saw it on his way to Kandy in 1602 it was comparatively perfect, as white as marble, and surmounted by a gilded pyramid.'[1]

The Mahāvansa merely states that it was re-plastered by King Parākrama-Bāhu VI (1410–1462 A.D.). Through the kindness of Dr. C. G. Seligmann I am able to give an illustration taken from his photographs of this dāgaba, which shows its present state (Fig. No. 88).

THE KAELAṆIYA DĀGABA

Another very early dāgaba was erected at Kaelaṇiya wihāra by King Yaṭṭhāla-Tissa, nephew of Dēvānam-piya Tissa, probably before the end of the third century B.C. (Rāj., p. 24). It commemorated the site where Buddha was feasted by Maṇi-Akkhika, the Nāga king of Kaelaṇiya.

[1] *Ceylon*, 2nd Ed., Vol. ii, p. 421.

Although the monastery is occasionally mentioned in the histories, I believe the dāgaba is only thrice referred to. The chatta was repaired by Vōhāraka-Tissa (215–237 A.D.). The dāgaba was seriously damaged in the reign of the Tamil king Māgha (1215–1236 A.D.), and was restored by Wijaya-Bāhu III (1236–1240 A.D.). His son Parākrama-Bāhu II (1240–1275 A.D.) then paved the court-yard, or part of it, round the dāgaba.

The only other record with which I am acquainted is contained in Dr. E. Müller's inscription No. 162, in which it is stated that King Dharma Parākrama-Bāhu of Kōṭṭa, who

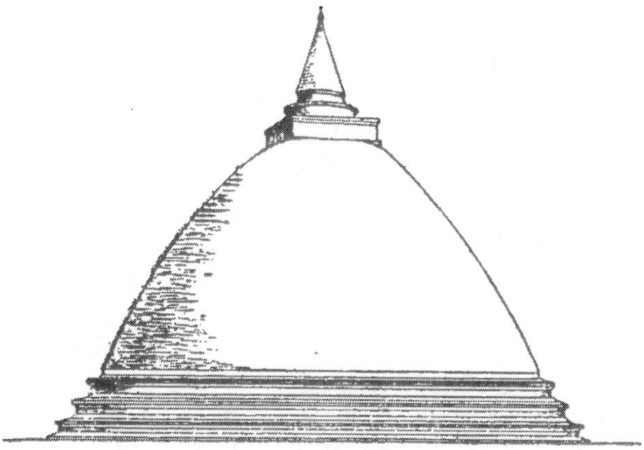

FIG. 89. The Kaelaṇiya Dāgaba. $\frac{1}{480}$.

according to it began his reign in 1508 A.D., caused the dāgaba to be restored and plastered.

The dāgaba was again restored in its present form in 1779, probably, so far as regards the dome, according to its original shape. Its outline is of the type technically known in Ceylon as the 'Heap-of-Paddy' shape. It forms the end section of a wide cone with slightly convex sides, and is perhaps the earliest example of this class of dāgabas. It has no wāhalkaḍas. For the following particulars I am indebted to measurements and photographs which Mr. R. S. MacPhail, of the Irrigation Department, was good enough to obtain for me.

The dāgaba rests on three narrow circular basal platforms, the diameter at the base of the lowest one being 106 feet 10½ inches. The top of this platform is 2 feet 6 inches less in diameter. The top of the middle platform is 98 feet in diameter, and that of the upper one is 92 feet 1½ inches in diameter. The lowest one is 3 feet 5 inches high, the middle one 4 feet 3 inches, and the upper one 4 feet 2 inches.

The total height is 88 or 90 feet,[1] the former being the measurement on a photograph, and the latter being calculated from the shadow of the structure. The dome is 85 feet 7 inches in diameter at the top of its basal moulding, which is 2 feet high; it is 46 feet 8 inches high by the photograph, according to which also the tee is about 19 feet 6 inches wide and 4 feet 9 inches high. The base of the spire, similarly measured, is 3 feet 3 inches high and 13 feet 6 inches wide, above which the spire and its brass pinnacle, which is terminated by a glass point, rise 21 feet 6 inches. The illustration (Fig. No. 89) shows the general shape.

The Dīgha-vāpi Dāgaba

A large dāgaba was built at Dīgha-vāpi by Saddhā-Tissa, the brother of Duṭṭha-Gāmiṇi. This was a very important station in south-eastern Ceylon, where Saddhā-Tissa was stationed for a considerable period before he became king. The dāgaba was built to mark the spot where Buddha seated himself on the occasion of his last visit to Ceylon. It is not mentioned again in the histories.

There is said to be a large dāgaba in the neighbourhood of the tank now called Kandiya-Kaṭṭu, which is almost certainly the ancient Dīgha-vāpi. I have not had an opportunity of visiting the place, which, however, is likely to repay the trouble of an examination.

Major Forbes[2] quoted a note of Bertolacci's regarding it, according to which the ruin was discovered in 1810. 'The size of the building is gigantic . . . the cone forming the

[1] The resident monk stated the height to be 60 *waḍu-riyanas*, or 'carpenter's cubits,' an evident mistake for *riyanas*, or 'cubits.'

[2] *Eleven Years in Ceylon*, Vol. i, p. 153, footnote.

pagoda [dāgaba] is entirely covered with brick and mortar; its basis is about one quarter of a mile in circumference, and the top and side are planted [overgrown] with large trees.'

THE IDIKAṬU DĀGABA

King Kālakaṇṇi-Tissa (40–20 B.C.) constructed 'a beautiful stone Thūpa' in front of a hall which he built 'near the Mihintale monastery.' The structure now called the Idikaṭu ('Needles') dāgaba, at the base of the Mihiṇtale hill, is believed to be this dāgaba, although the upper work is of brick. The

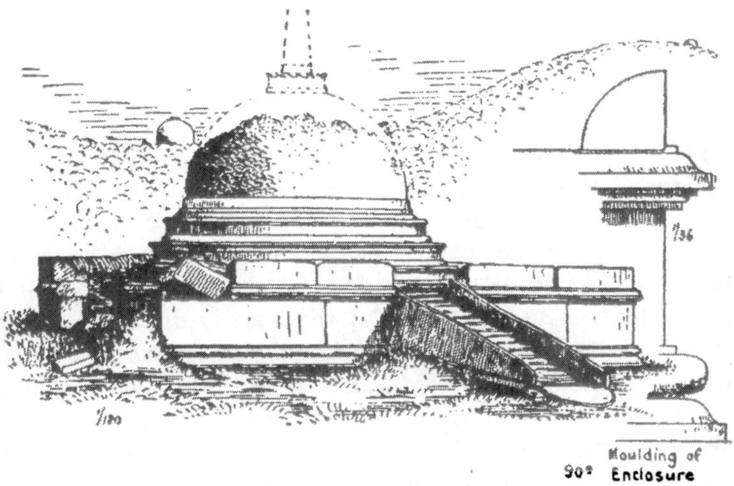

FIG. 90. The Idikaṭu Dāgaba.

historians do not mention its original name, and I believe never afterwards refer to it. In a fine inscription cut on two upright slabs at the side of the great flight of steps[1] which lead up the Mihintale hill, Mahinda IV (975–991 A.D.) termed it the Kaṭu Mahā Sāēya, and ordered its repair.

It is built in a small stone-paved court-yard, measuring about 38 by 40 feet, which is raised five feet above the ground level, and supported at the sides by an excellently cut revet-

[1] Some books state that these steps number 1,500, but this is erroneous. That number is only applicable to the whole of the steps on all parts of the hill, the monks say.

ment wall, with bold mouldings. A quadrantal stone moulding 16½ inches high encloses the floor of this court.

This dāgaba was evidently of the modern bell shape, and it is possibly the earliest one of this form which is known in Ceylon. If, as appears probable, the upper part was hemispherical, the height to the top of the dome may have been 16 feet. For 6 feet 10 inches the face-work consists of a series of well-cut stone mouldings. There are no basal platforms, but three are clearly indicated by mouldings which project beyond the others. Above this the structure is of brick. The diameter at the base is 27 feet 4 inches, and at the top of the mouldings about 18 feet. Nearly all the upper part is broken down, as shown on my sketch. As usual, rectangular stone flowei altars were fixed at the four cardinal points, close to the base of the mouldings. A single flight of steps 6 feet 10 inches wide, on the west side, led to the dāgaba platform.

Around this building there are the remains of a large and very regularly arranged monastery, the dāgaba being near the south-eastern corner of it. The whole is enclosed by a well built wall of uncoursed stone, four feet thick, with a coping of stone laid transversely. All the stones are wedged and slightly cut, the lower ones being squared and dressed on the beds and joints. Such a work as this wall is quite exceptional in Ceylon, nearly all the enclosing walls of monasteries being built of brick. In the illustration the Maha Sāēya and the Aet dāgaba are to be seen on the hill in the background.

The Ambatthala Dāgaba

This dāgaba on the Mihintale hill was erected by King Mahā-dāṭhika Mahā-Nāga (9–21 A.D.), and is believed to mark the spot where the Buddhist apostle Mahinda, the son of the Emperor Aśōka, stood when Dēvānam-piya Tissa first saw him. A headless and armless statue near it, facing the dāgaba, is traditionally said to represent the king and to mark his own position on that occasion. It has no ornaments on the chest or waist, and the sole clothing is a plain cloth from the waist to the ankles. When Mr. Smither examined it the head was there, and he wrote of it (p. 11) that the 'head-dress consists of a plain and slightly elevated pear-shaped cap encircled by a jewelled band or diadem ; the ears are adorned with pendant ear-rings, and the neck with a jewelled neck-piece. The base is carved to represent an expanded lotus flower and it is precisely similar in design to that found at the Thupārāma dāgaba.' Three octagonal pillars round it evidently supported a canopy over it.

FIG. 91.
The Ambatthala Dāgaba. $\frac{1}{120}$.

It is recorded that after building the dāgaba Mahā-Nāga held a great festival at which festoons of lamps were hung round the dāgaba. Twenty-four thousand monks are said to have been present at this great celebration (Mah., i, p. 136).

King Kaniṭṭha-Tissa constructed an 'edifice' over this dāgaba ; possibly this was repaired by Mēghavaṇṇābhaya I (254–267 A.D.). We may assume that the structure was rifled during the Tamil domination in the eleventh and thirteenth centuries, and that it was repaired, like the other principal dāgabas, by the two Parākrama-Bāhus. It is now completely restored, and the early work is covered by a coat of plaster, like that at the Thūpārāma dāgaba. It is said to be built of stone. Its shape is intermediate between the Bell and the Heap-of-Paddy.

According to Mr. Smither its present dimensions are as follows :—The diameter of the dome at the top of the basal platform, or plinth, on which it rests is 23 feet, the plinth being 6 feet wider at its base. The height to the crown of the dome is stated by him to be 20 feet, but it measures only 18 feet on a photograph by Messrs. Skeen and Co., of Colombo, from which Fig. No. 91 is reduced. The height of the square tee is 3 feet in the photograph, and its side, exclusive of mouldings, 6½ feet long. The spire rises about 9½ feet higher, of which its cylindrical base occupies 3 feet 9 inches. The dāgaba rests on a platform 97 feet in diameter, which is raised four feet above the ground level, and is supported by a brick wall. There are no wāhalkaḍas ; these ornamental structures were confined to the five Anurādhapura dāgabas already described.

This dāgaba is surrounded by two circles of slender monolithic octagonal pillars, 12 feet high, the capitals of which are decorated with a procession of lions or hansas marching to the left (which would be their own right when facing front), or a row of dwarfs facing front. They have no tenons on the top ; and whether the roof afterwards raised over the building rested on them or not, they appear to have been erected chiefly in order to carry the festoons of lamps that were hung from them at festivals. In shape they bear a close resemblance to those of the Thūpārāma dāgaba.

The Aet Dāgaba

On the summit of the highest rocky point on the Mihintale hill a small structure, called the Aet (Tusk-elephants) dāgaba was built by an early ruler whose deed is not specially recorded in the histories. There are, however, some references to the dāgaba in inscriptions.

On the side of a slab at the Thūpārāma dāgaba an inscription in letters resembling those used by Wasabha (66–110 A.D.) ends *Ati c(e)tahi paca jara dini*, the meaning of which appears to be ' At the Aet dāgaba he gave (anew) the former decayed (work).' The name of the king is not visible on the stone. The words are quite clear, and the first two prove that this structure was already in existence when the inscription was cut.

Another very much worn inscription on the upright face of a rock near the dāgaba, on the side of the path to it, cut in letters resembling those of the large rock inscription of King Gāmiṇi-Abhaya,[1] the son of a king called Nāga and grandson of one called Tissa, lower down the hill, ends *c(e)ta padaya dini*, ' He gave the dāgaba steps.' It appears to refer to the last flight of steps for ascending to the platform of the dāgaba. The name of the king who made the grant is ' Naka Maharaja ' ; he may be the Siri-Nāga II (245–247 A.D.) who is

[1] Dr. E. Müller's *Ancient Inscriptions in Ceylon*, No. 20.

mentioned as the father of the king in the lower inscription, if Dr. E. Müller's identification of its author as Mēghavaṇṇābhaya I is correct.

The repair of the dāgaba is referred to in the long inscription of Mahinda IV,[1] which was specially devoted to recording the king's orders regarding the management of the services and funds of the Aet wihāra, at that time evidently a very important establishment. We learn from it that the Aet and Idikaṭu monasteries were connected, and were held by monks who belonged to the Abhaya-giri Community. They were independent of the other two large Mihintale wihāras at which were the dāgabas previously described.

On such a high and exposed site the dāgaba would be extremely liable to be damaged by thunderstorms, and it is not surprising to find bricks of three or four periods employed in the lower part of the work. Some are of almost the same size as those in the inner room of the building termed the Daḷadā Māligāwa, 'the Palace of the Tooth-Relic,' at Anurādhapura, and thus may have been burnt early in the fourth century, possibly by Mēghavaṇṇābhaya II, who is described as evincing great interest in the Mihintale monasteries.

I have met with no reference to the construction of this dāgaba, unless it is one of the ten which were built on the hill by Wasabha, according to the Dīpavaṇsa (p. 216). There are a few brick fragments at it which are three inches thick; if they were burnt for it they must indicate that it is of pre-Christian date, but they may have been brought from some ruined building for use in the repairs.

I have no measurements of its dimensions; it is a very small work, and only of interest on account of its situation and Mahinda's inscription.

THE TISSA DĀGABAS

Regarding the group of early works—the Mahānāga, Yaṭṭhāla, Sanda-giri, and Maeṇik dāgabas—built at Tissa, the ancient Māgama, in the Southern Province[2] little definite

[1] Müller, *op. cit.*, No. 121.

[2] See Fig. No. 130 for their positions.

information is available. The original shape of the upper part of their superstructures is lost, but on account of their early date it may be assumed that all, with the exception of the Maeṇik dāgaba, had more or less hemispherical domes, with the usual tee, and a spire with a chatta terminal. All are without wāhalkaḍas or surrounding pillars.

The dimensions of the bricks used in these four dāgabas and another small unnamed one near the high level channel from the tank, throw some light on the period when they were built. They are given in inches in the following table.

	Length.	Width.	Thickness.	Bt.	Contents.
Mahānāga dāgaba .	17·35	8·84	2·83	25	434
Yaṭṭhāla dāgaba .	17·85	8·64	2·90	25	447
Small dāgaba .	17·16	9·11	2·85	26	445
Sanda-giri dāgaba .	17·14	8·67	2·81	24·4	418
Maeṇik dāgaba .	16·57	8·86	2·80	24·8	411

It is clear that the sizes of the early bricks used at Tissa were much more uniform than those at Anurādhapura ; and this being so they may indicate that the Maeṇik or 'Gem' dāgaba was erected by the king who constructed the Sanda-giri, the 'Moon-hill,' or his son ; and that probably both these works are of somewhat later date than the first two in the list. The evidence afforded by the bricks is thus in favour of the statement in the Pūjāvaliya that Sanda-giri dates from the time of Kākavaṇṇa-Tissa, that is, early in the first half of the second century B.C. The Dhātuvansa, however, attributes the construction of the Sanda-giri wihāra to King Mahā-Nāga. The later monarch may have added the dāgaba to it.

The Mahānāga Dāgaba

The first dāgaba constructed there was undoubtedly the largest one, at the Nāga Mahārāma monastery, which was built by King Mahā-Nāga, the brother of Dēvānam-piya Tissa. The Mahāvansa records his founding of this wihāra 'bearing his own name' (i, p, 83) ; it was therefore built early in the second half of the third century B.C. If I remember aright, I was informed that it enshrined the right temple bone of Buddha, but the Dhātuvansa, which gives many particulars of the Tissa works, does not contain this statement.

The superstructure of the dāgaba was repaired or raised by King Iḷa-Naga (38–44 A.D.), who left an inscription recording his work on a stone that is now replaced in the dāgaba, but was previously seen by Dr. Paul Goldschmidt, who copied the inscription.[1]

FIG. 92. The Mahānāga Dāgaba.

King Vōhāraka-Tissa (215–237 A.D.) repaired the chatta on the spire (Mah., i, p. 144). During the Sōla domination in the eleventh century this and the other dāgabas at Tissa 'that belonged to the three Fraternities' were broken into. The next Sinhalese king, Wijaya-Bāhu I (1065–1120 A.D.) restored them.

They all appear to have been rifled again, more thoroughly than on the previous occasion, during the reign of the Indian king Māgha (1215–1236 A.D.), and apparently were not afterwards restored. The tradition of this desecration has been preserved locally.

In 1883, when I first visited Tissa, the restoration of the Mahānāga dāgaba had made considerable progress under the supervision of the incumbent of the wihāra, by means of the subscriptions of the numerous pilgrims who flocked there from the Southern and Western Provinces at the annual festivals;

[1] Dr. E. Müller's *Ancient Inscriptions in Ceylon*, No. 4.

and the outer shell of the dome was already rebuilt. It had three basal ledges, above which it appeared to be nearly vertical for several feet in height, the whole dome being apparently almost a hemisphere. A square tee was afterwards built, and a spire was being added when I last saw the work (see Fig. No. 92). This was subsequently completed.

The method adopted for raising the materials for the superstructure was probably the same primitive one which was employed by the pre-Christian constructors. A long ladder of sticks and bamboos was erected up the surface of the dome, and on this a continuous line of men stood, each receiving the materials—bricks or mortar—from the man below, and handing them to the man above, without moving from his post. At one time about seventy men were employed in this chain, all working without remuneration for the sake of acquiring 'merit' which would beneficially affect their prospects in their next existence. I suggested the use of a winch fixed on the pavement, but the old-fashioned method of their ancestors was adhered to.

On some of the bricks of the largest size I found letters engraved by the brick-makers before they were burnt. These were of the angular type which marks the earliest period of writing in Ceylon.

Through the kindness of Mr. T. Hamer, of the Irrigation Department, I am indebted to the Irrigation Guardian at Tissa for the following dimensions of this dāgaba as now restored.

The diameter at the base is 164·5 feet. Above this there are three cylindrical platforms forming narrow steps round the dome; the lowest step is 6 feet high and 4 feet wide, the second one 4 feet high and 3½ feet wide, and the upper one 2 feet high and 4 feet wide. The diameter of the dome, deduced from the circumference, like other diameters given, is 140·7 feet. The dome is 86 feet high. The tee is very wide, and is 60 feet square, a size which agrees with my own photograph. It is said to be 20 feet high, but in my photograph measures only 15 feet. The base of the spire is 53·4 feet in diameter and 15 feet high. The spire tapers for 41 feet, being 45·8 feet in diameter at the bottom. The gilt finial is 11½ feet high. The total height thus becomes 185½ feet. The height of the dome closely follows the Canon given below, which would require it to be 84·4 feet high.

THE SANDAGIRI DĀGABA, the next in size to the Mahānāga dāgaba, has become a mere high tumulus-like mound partly overgrown with jungle and trees. I have no details of it.

THE YAṬṬHĀLA DĀGABA

I possess no measurements of the Yaṭṭhāla dāgaba, the repair of which was begun when I was at Tissa. It is somewhat larger than the Maeṇik dāgaba. Its construction is credited by the Dhātuvansa to King Mahā-Nāga, and the size of the bricks used in it affords some corroboration of this statement. Possibly it was completed by his son Yaṭṭhāla-Tissa, with whom the name seems to connect it.

This dāgaba had a deep vertical cut made by treasure seekers; it passed entirely through the upper part of the dome, which appeared to be of the usual hemispherical shape. The whole inner work thus disclosed showed no mark of a rebuilding such as is recognised everywhere by the employment of a large proportion of broken bricks, or bricks of a later date than those used in the original work. All were whole bricks of the same large size; and on many of them letters of the very earliest type, with the long attached vowels, some of which perhaps do not occur elsewhere in Ceylon with letters of this early form, were inscribed, or in a few instances impressed by wooden stamps, before they were burnt. A series of these bricks was sent by me to the Colombo Museum.

At first I supposed that these letters were the initials of the various brickmakers; but now I feel little doubt that they were the initials of pious persons who paid for their manufacture and presented them to the builders of the dāgaba, as an act of religious merit. If stamped letters and letters written in quite different styles are the initials of separate names, I found more than eighty persons represented.

When the restoration of the Yaṭṭhāla dāgaba was begun in 1883, the surrounding *débris* was first removed, and in it were found several articles of great interest, which had been taken out of the relic-chamber by the treasure seekers, and had evidently been thrown aside as valueless. That they formed part of the original contents of the relic-room, as it was left by Mahā-Nāga or his son, is rendered most probable by the fact that among them were two small moderately thick Purānas, or silver coins of the early Indian type, one nearly square and the other of a more irregular shape, without punch marks. They resembled some unpunched coins of this kind found in India, which date from a period considerably antecedent to the Christian era. There was also the greater part of an engraved carnelian gem, which had been set in a signet ring, and which is considered at the British Museum to belong possibly to the third century B.C., and to be certainly pre-Christian. I describe and illustrate it below, in a chapter on the earliest coinage of Ceylon (see Fig. 156).

The other articles found at the dāgaba were four small relic-caskets or *karaṇḍuwas,* cut from gems. One (Fig. No. 93) was a chrysoberyl, another (Fig. No. 96) an amethyst or purple crystal, and the other two were of rock crystal, one (Fig. No. 94) being brownish in colour, and the other (Fig. No. 95) quite clear. They are all now replaced in the new relic-chamber, the restoration of this dāgaba having been completed some years ago; but I was able to make drawings of them which are of value as illustrating some of the early types of dāgabas.

Each karaṇḍuwa represented a dāgaba with either one or two basal platforms, but only two were provided with a tee. The smallest one was especially valuable as the only example in Ceylon of a dāgaba with a spire surmounted by a chatta, the horizontal extension of which is of course exaggerated in this stopper. The brown crystal had a lathe-turned stopper forming a plain spire of circular section, tapering so as to fit accurately into the cylindrical hollow which is drilled for receiving the relics. The stoppers of the other two karaṇḍuwas were not discovered.

Each relic-case is provided with a tubular well, drilled into the stone from the top, as shown in dotted lines in the illustrations; and in the smallest one two flakes of gold in which the relics were enveloped, making small packages about the size of a

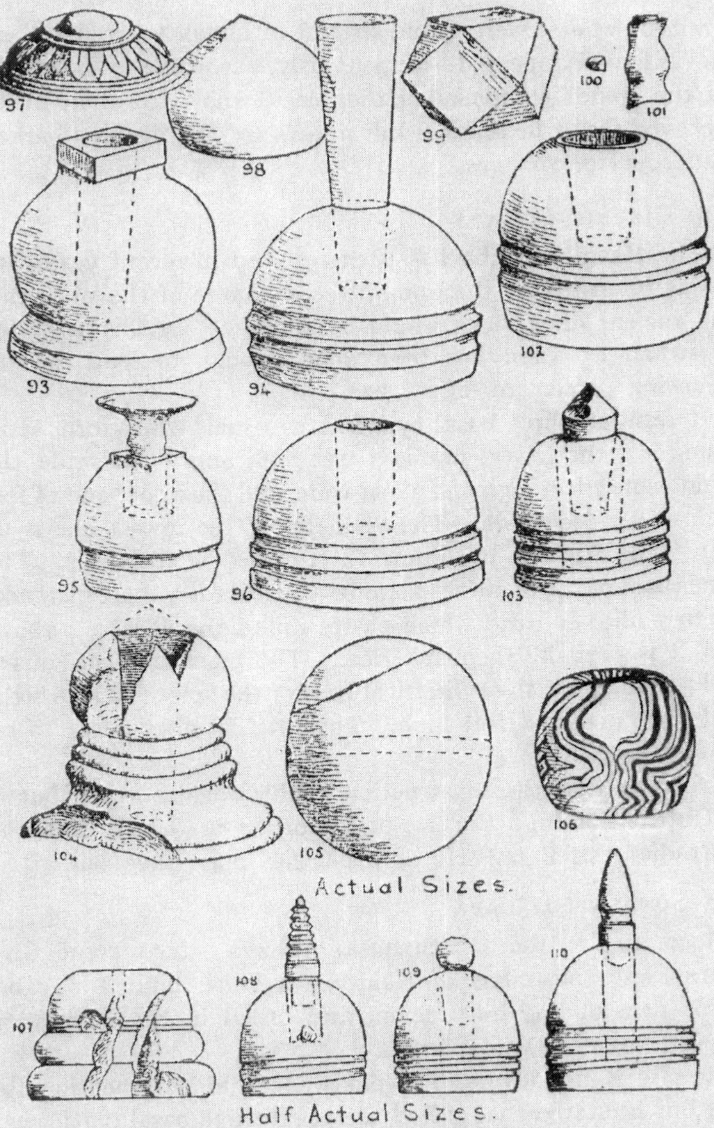

FIGS. 93–110. Articles deposited in Dāgabas.

grain of wheat, were found *in sitū*, although the relics themselves had disappeared—miraculously, according to the opinion of the Buddhist monks of the place, who with many others believed that true relics of this nature are only visible to arhats and royal personages.

The Maeṇik Dāgaba

The Maeṇik dāgaba has been restored in recent years, and I was informed by the Committee in charge of the work that the ancient dimensions would be adhered to. The Irrigation Guardian at Tissa has been good enough to send me the following particulars of its size.

It rests on three basal cylinders as usual, which form steps round it; the lowest one is 3 feet high and 2 feet wide, the middle one 2 feet high and 2 feet wide, and the upper one 1½ feet high and 2 feet wide. The diameter of the lowest one is 60 feet. The base of the dome is 51·9 feet in diameter. The lower part of the dome seems to be vertical for a short distance, up to a fillet or band which passes round the dāgaba; above this it is probably hemispherical. The tee is 12 feet square and 5 feet high; the cylindrical base of the spire is 6 feet high, and the finial is 8 feet high. The total height is said to be 80 feet.

I believe that the construction of this dāgaba is attributed to Duṭṭha-Gāmiṇi; the size of the bricks used in it does not contradict this date. He or his father may have built it.

The Sōmavatī Dāgaba

According to the Dhātuvansa, Abhaya, king of the Giri district and son-in-law of Kākavaṇṇa-Tissa, built a dāgaba in his part of the hill region, and called it the Sōmavatī dāgaba, after his wife Sōmadēvī.

Its site is unknown. The old writer did not mention its size, but he stated that it had the usual three basal platforms, and was of the 'Bubble' shape, that is, hemispherical.

The Sēruvila Dāgaba.

The greater part of the Dhātuvansa is devoted to the history of the relics deposited in this dāgaba, and to an account of its erection, and the ceremonies held in connection with it. It is near the right bank of the Mahawaeliganga, and to the north of the Verukal branch of that river. It was constructed by Kākavaṇṇa-Tissa to enshrine the forehead relic (*lalāṭa*) and a hair relic of Buddha. Although there are now no Buddhists in that district, the inhabitants of which are all Tamils, or the so-called 'Moormen,' [1] some Sinhalese of other parts of the island still make pilgrimages in order to worship at this site.

According to the old work, which no doubt preserves, even although it considerably amplifies, an older account that, from the quotations, was evidently written in the Pāli language, the forehead relic was first brought to Tissa in the reign of Mahā-Nāga, who erected a relic-house for it in the neighbourhood of his palace—'neither near nor far' away. It remained there until the last years of Kākavaṇṇa-Tissa, who was informed that it was his duty to fulfil a prophecy that he would enshrine it in a dāgaba at Sēruvila, then the capital of a subsidiary king—doubtless one of the 'Parumakas' of the early inscriptions.

He and his queen Wihāra-Dēvī proceeded to the spot in a magnificent procession in order to carry out the work, after first handing over the charge of the government to his son Duṭṭha-Gāmiṇi. In order to fix upon the correct position for the structure he resorted to a peculiar device. Two pairs of bulls were decorated with flowers and allowed to proceed alone in the jungle. They were found together in the morning at a rock which was adopted as the site of the dāgaba after the same result had followed similar experiments with a horse and an elephant.

The king found some difficulty in providing all the bricks for the work, but Śakka, that is, Indra, was good enough to relieve him of this trouble by sending Vissakamma, the general builder of the gods, to make them for him.

[1] Although the Moormen of Ceylon have been stated to be descended from Indian Drāvidians who had adopted Muhammadanism, I have the best authority for saying that Arabs from Western Arabia claim a racial affinity with them, and still occasionally settle among them.

When the relic-chamber in the upper part of the structure was ready for the relics, the king carried the forehead relic on his head and deposited it in it, and afterwards the queen similarly placed the hair relic in the room. After every one had put in the relic-room the jewellery and ornaments on his person, the chamber was closed by being covered with a stone slab.

The dāgaba had three basal platforms, and was of the 'Bubble' shape; its dimensions are not stated. A wihāra was also built at the spot and liberally endowed. The book describes its formal gift to the Community of Monks at a great festival at which Abhaya, the king's son-in-law, and other princes were present; and the words doubtless show us the orthodox method of making such grants. A large concourse of monks was there, and before these witnesses the king poured water over the right hand of the superior monk present. Then, in the words of the Dhātuvansa, 'afterwards the king made known (the gift of the temple), saying, " (My) lord, and members of royal families assembled together, in (accordance with) the (usual) arrangement for causing the acceptance of the wihāra, I have poured the water on the right hand"; and the thēra, having heard these words, declared his agreement, saying, "It is good, Maharaja." '

The Nikawāē-kanda Dāgaba

High up on the precipitous eastern side of Nikawāē-kanda, a steep rocky hill in the North-western Province, an early monastery was established at a series of natural caves. Some of these contained statues, and one had also a small dāgaba which had been demolished by treasure seekers, so that only a little of the lower part remained. Local tradition attributed the founding of the monastery to Prince Sāli, the son of King Duṭṭha-Gāmiṇi [1]; in that case it would belong to some date

[1] According to the Mahāvansa, a minister called Sāli, who may have been this prince, built the Sāli wihāra during the reign of Waṭṭa-Gāmiṇi. Its site is unknown; if it was not at Anurādhapura it may be this one.

FIG. 111. Statue of Prince Sāli.
(Nikawāē-kanda Cave Temple.)

To face p. 333.

after the middle of the second century B.C. He appears to have been the chief of this part of the country, and two sites are pointed out as places at which he dwelt, one on a hill near the caves, called Gal-giriya-kanda, and the other to the north-west, called Raja Angana, where remains of various buildings of some importance are to be seen.

The tradition is supported by the sizes of the bricks in the lowest part of the dāgaba. They have an average length of 16·41 inches, and a breadth of 8·16 inches, and a thickness of 3·39 inches; Bt. is 27·6 and the contents 454 cubic inches. The contents indicate a date not later than the first century B.C., while the other dimensions probably belong to the period extending from the accession of Duṭṭha-Gāmiṇi to the early part of the first century, this being evidently a time when larger dimensions than those of either earlier or later bricks were sometimes adopted. These bricks resemble those at some caves at Nuwara-kanda, in the North-western Province, where an inscription was cut which appears to contain a reference to King Duṭṭha-Gāmiṇi.[1] These latter bricks are 16·76 inches long, 8·76 inches wide, and 3·09 thick; Bt. is 27, and the contents 454 cubic inches. On this evidence I conclude that the dāgaba most probably dates from the latter half of the second century B.C., or the first quarter of the next century.

In two of the Nikawāē-kanda caves, which evidently have been abandoned for several centuries, there are two ancient wooden statues, larger than life, protected by a thin coat of plaster, one of which tradition identifies as the figure of Duṭṭha-Gāmiṇi, while the other is believed to be that of his son, the supposed founder of the monastery. The former statue has the high royal crown, resembling in general appearance those represented in reliefs at Anurādhapura, which at least proves that he is a king. A fragment of an inscription of about the eleventh century, which was found on a broken slab in one cave, may belong to the time when works of restoration were carried out at the caves; and possibly these wooden

[1] See *The Earliest Inscriptions*, No. 58.

statues may be assigned to the same period.[1] They tend to show that so long as eight centuries ago the same tradition regarding the founder was current.

About eight years ago, Sēlaratna Thēra, the energetic superior of the monastery now at the foot of the hill, undertook the restoration of the cave wihāra. Among other preliminary work, the heap of bricks in the lower part of the dāgaba was removed, and it was then discovered that the persons who rifled it, possibly the followers of King Māgha, had not found the true relic-chamber, which was covered by a large stone slab in the very bottom of the structure. When this was raised the undisturbed contents of the cavity under it were found to be as follows.

One bead (Fig. No. 106), a little flattened at the ends, belonging to a rosary, ·80 in. long and ·86 in. wide. It resembled porcelain in appearance, but is believed by Mr. C. H. Read, of the British Museum, from my sketch of it, to be of glass. Mr. Read was good enough to write of it,—"Beads of this design were in use in many places, and at several periods. We have some very similar obtained at Akhmīm in Egypt—doubtless Egyptian make—of an uncertain date, but quite old enough to fit in with the date claimed for your Sinhalese dāgaba. Others very like—N. European make—are commonly found in Merovingian graves and in the corresponding English cemeteries which may be dated as sixth century A.D. Of the two the former are more like your description." The ground colour of this bead is white, in which are waving parallel close black lines of varying thickness, except that in two irregular patches the colour is plain deep chrome yellow.

One rounded crystal bead (Fig. 105), 1·32 inches long and 1·12 inches wide. One spherical deep blue glass bead, not measured but like a small 'marble.' One translucent blue glass moulded bead (Fig. 99), ·72 in, square at the top and

[1] In the cave temple at Dambulla a wooden statue of King Nissanka-Malla, which probably dates from the commencement of the thirteenth century, is in better preservation than these, and it proves that in a dry site free from white ants such wooden figures may last a thousand years or more.

bottom, and having similar square faces on the sides at each corner, with the intermediate angles bevelled into triangular facets. All the beads were drilled for stringing.

There were also two pieces of a kind of hard dark brown aromatic composition, cast in moulds, and having a flat bottom and a rounded boss on the top, and blue-lotus petal decoration round the sides (Fig. 97). Numerous tiny specks of gold were to be seen in them, and, strange to state, they distinctly emitted a slight fragrant aroma when I examined them. There were several other persons present at the time, and all noticed and remarked on this long-enduring scent.

Lastly, no less than twelve karaṇḍuwas or relic-cases were there, of which ten were clear crystals and two were formed of glass, one (Fig. 104) being dark green in colour, and the other (Fig. 107) opaque pale green. These were both cast in moulds, and were broken when I saw them. All the glass except the first-mentioned bead exhibited some iridescence on the surface. There was also a clear crystal of a lotus bud form (Fig. 98). The illustrations show the shapes of the articles, and the various types of karaṇḍuwas.

The largest crystal relic-case (Fig. 110) held, it was said, one hundred and twenty minute pearls, all bored, and a tiny fragment of bone wrapped in a piece of thick gold leaf. Each of the others was said to have held a similar relic wrapped in gold leaf, and I have given a figure of one relic (Fig. 100) and a gold leaf package (Fig. 101) containing another, which were produced for my inspection. A much smaller package is visible in Fig. 108. All the cases had stoppers, but I was not shown those of the glass relic-cases. One of the crystal cases (Fig. 103) had a dark blue glass stopper, which was broken when I saw it. All the crystals were admirably cut by the aid of a lathe. There was nothing to indicate whose relics were enclosed in the cases, or by whom they were deposited.

These relic-cases furnish a valuable set of illustrations of some of the early types of dāgabas. The tubular cavities in them are shown by dotted lines.

TYPES OF DĀGABAS

The construction of dāgabas has been practised for so many centuries in Ceylon that it is not surprising to find that there is a recognised Canon which regulates their general proportions, although deviations from it occur in every work. To what date it belongs is unknown ; as it includes the height of the chatta it appears to have been written at some period not much later than 500 A.D., since the histories contain no reference to these terminals after the fifth century.

The Canon is found in a manuscript of which I failed to secure a copy, called the Waiddyānta-pota, and is written in a language which is chiefly Sanskrit, but partly Pāli. It was copied for me in Sinhalese characters as follows :—

Thūpesu tāram kṛiṭa panca bhāgam
Guṇaŋ pamāṇaŋ tribhāga tuŋgam
Ganṭhākāra Ghaṭākāram
Bubbulākāra Dhānyakam
Padmākārāmbala shat vidham

Thūpesu tāram kṛiṭa panca bhāgam
Guṇaŋ pamāṇaŋ catuvīsa bhāgam
Trimāla pancārddhaka garbbham ashṭam
Catussurākoshṭha yugarddha yugmam
Śashṭānta kuntam puṇarddha chatram
Vadanticatah munihih purāṇaih.

'Having divided the width across the dāgaba into five parts, (out of them) three parts are the height (of the dome). Bell-shape, Chatty-shape, Bubble-shape, Heap-of-Paddy, Lotus-shape, and Nelli (fruit) are the six kinds (of dāgabas).

'Having divided the width across the dāgaba into five parts, the length (of the dāgaba) is subdivided into twenty-four parts. For the three stories (or necklaces, take) five and a half ; the chamber (dome) eight ; the four-sided enclosure of the Celestials (dēvatās) a couple and a half; the (other member of the enclosed [1]) pair (one and a half [1]); the last six for the spire; a half more for the chatta. The sage of old prescribed (these proportions) as usually practised.'

The Sinhalese names of the various parts of the dāgaba are, *tun-māl pēsāwa*, or *pēsā-walallu*, 'the three-story ornaments' or 'the ornamental bangles,' the basal platforms; *gaeba*, 'the chamber,' the dome; *hataraes kotuwa*, 'the square enclosure,' or tee; *dēvatā kotuwa*, 'the godlings' enclosure,' or base of the spire; *koṭa*, the spire; *sat*, 'the umbrella' or chatta; *kota kaeraella*, 'the end of the spire,' the pinnacle.

According to these rules, we see that the total height of a dāgaba should be three times the height of the dome, which is three-fifths of its (widest) diameter. The length of the spire is fixed at a quarter of the total height, or three-quarters of the height of the dome. The height of the basal ledges would be eleven-sixteenths of the height of the dome; that of the tee five-sixteenths of it; that of the base of the spire three-sixteenths of it; and that of the chatta one-sixteenth of it. As no chatta is now constructed its part is added to the height of the base of the spire, making it one-quarter of the height of the dome. Modern constructors do not measure these heights vertically on their drawings, but upon a sloping line extending from the centre of the top of the spire to the edge of the lowest basal platform, the outermost line of the circumference. By this means all the heights will be reduced.

Apparently these were the recognised proportions for dāgabas of all the six shapes, and they usually guide modern designers, who, however, I have been informed, commonly add one extra part to the height of their domes, which are now always of the Bell shape, thus making them four-fifths instead of three-fifths of the diameter.

When we apply these proportions to the pre-Christian works there is usually no agreement with them, excepting sometimes in the altitude of the dome.

[1] These words in brackets are necessary to make up the correct number of twenty-four parts.

The chief difficulty in testing the heights lies in the uncertainty regarding the length of the ancient cubit. Dr. Davy (1816–1820) remarked that 'Carpenters and some other artists have measures of their own. The carpenter's *angula* [inch] is equal to the space between the second and third joint of the fore-finger; and his *waḍu-riyana* [carpenter's cubit] is composed of twenty-four *angulas* and is divided into four parts.'[1] In this case the carpenter's cubit would be about two feet long. Twenty years later Major Forbes stated that the carpenter's cubit was two feet three inches in length,[2] but the reputed height of the Kaelaṇiya dāgaba, restored in 1779, does not support this. Captain Robert Knox, writing of the measures used in the middle of the seventeenth century, said, 'A *Rian* is a Cubit, which is with them from the bone on the inside of the Elbow to the tip of the fourth Finger. A *Waddo rian* is the Carpenter's Rule. It is as much as will reach from one Elbow to the other, the Thumbs touching one the other at the tops, and so stretching out both Elbows.'[3] At the present day, Sinhalese artizans make these measures agree with the English scale by using a *riyana* of eighteen inches, subdivided into inches, and eighths of inches called *nūl*, which are again divided into fourths; and a *waḍu-riyana* of three feet, that is, two *riyanas*.

The old Pāli vocabulary, the Abhidhāna-padīpika, has three words, *ratana*, *kukku*, and *hattha*, as synonyms which mean a cubit, or two spans, *vidatthi*. The vidatthi was a measure of twelve *angulas* or fingers; and it will be found on trial that twelve fingers' breadths thus measured by laying the hand flat, the usual method in Ceylon, exactly make up the length of the span from the end of the extended thumb to that of the little finger.[4] In the Pāli edition of the Mahāvansa both *hattha* and *ratana* are employed in stating the heights

[1] *An Account of the Interior of Ceylon*, p. 244. I have corrected his spelling of *waḍu-riyana*.

[2] *Eleven Years in Ceylon*, p. 223.

[3] *An Historical Relation of the Island Ceylon*, p. 98.

[4] According to Winslow's Tamil Dictionary twelve fingers' breadths make one span.

of the dāgabas, these words being alike translated in the Sinhalese edition by the term *riyana*. Thus it would seem that the cubit used in the histories is one of two spans or nearly 18 inches; but this is far from agreement with the actual heights of the dāgabas.

I found that ten men had a mean height of 5 feet 4½ inches, and that their average cubit, measured as described by Knox, the method always used at the present day, was 17·88 inches.

We may obtain a measurement of the ancient cubit by means of the early bricks; the largest ones are always termed *riyan-gaḍol*, 'cubit-bricks,' an expression which indicates that their length was determined by the measure of the ancient cubit.

For ascertaining the length in this manner I have taken all bricks in my tables the volume of which exceeds 400 cubic inches, this being apparently a fairly trustworthy indication that they are pre-Christian, and I find that the length of those used at nineteen different works averages 17·56 inches, or only one-third of an inch less than the length measured on the arm. But bricks shrink considerably in drying, and we do not know whether it was the length of the brick when thus contracted, or the length of the mould in which it was formed, that represented the early cubit. If it was the latter we should require, with the ordinary clay of Ceylon, an addition of at least three-quarters of an inch, or even an inch, to the size of the burnt brick in order to arrive at the true length of the cubit. It is probable, however, that allowance for this shrinkage was made in the size of the mould; at the same ratio as in the men I measured, a cubit of 17·56 inches would be that of men who were 5 feet 3⅜ inches high, which is very nearly the actual height of the present Kandian villagers.

Notwithstanding this contemporary evidence of the length of the early *riyana* used by the brickmakers, a comparison of the heights of the dāgabas given by Mr. Smither with those stated in the histories, shows that another cubit must have been in use from the earliest period. Thus, in the case of the

Ruwanwaeli dāgaba the total height, if the cubit were 17½ inches long, would make the top of the lowest chatta, or of the pinnacle if there was one originally, only eight feet above the tee shown in my restoration; and at the Abhaya-giri the pinnacle would be inside the existing remains of the spire.

Nor is this difference between the existing and the former recorded measurements merely due to the inaccuracy of the latter. When we seek evidence of the length of the other cubit we are confronted by one striking fact. No-one can take many measurements of the ancient works in Ceylon without being astonished at the frequent occasions on which these are found to be an exact number of English feet. For buildings, such sizes as 36 feet by 24 feet, or 18 feet by 12 feet, or measurements of 20[1] or 10 feet, are quite common. The sides of square pillars usually measure 12, or 15, or 18 inches. The culverts of ancient sluices are in most cases exactly 12, or 18, or 24, or 27 inches wide, and some are exactly 2 feet, 2 feet 6 inches, 3 feet, 3 feet 6 inches, and 4 feet high. Mr. Smither's dimensions of the dāgabas are also incontestable evidence which points in the same direction.

These numerous examples indicate that the cubit of the early masons and carpenters was not that which was used by the brickmakers, but was either exactly eighteen inches long, or much more probably exactly two feet long. The recorded heights of the early dāgabas when compared with the existing remains prove that it was considerably greater than eighteen inches long, and it must therefore have been of the other dimension, that is, two feet in length. The ancient cubit was always equal to twenty-four *angulas*; it was the mode of measuring the angula or 'finger' that varied. One trade, the brickmakers, and probably also the general public, employed the width of it, and apparently their cubit was 17½ inches long; other trades, the builders, stone-cutters, and carpenters, had a longitudinal scale, as described by Dr. Davy, and their cubit thus became two feet in length.

[1] I have already stated that the outer shell of the Ruwanwaeli dāgaba is 19 feet 11½ inches thick.

FIG. 112. Miniature Stone Dāgaba.

To face p. 341.

On the whole, it would appear that while definite rules depending on the widest diameter of the dome sometimes regulated the height of the dome, and less commonly the total height also, the early builders allowed themselves considerable latitude in determining the proportions of the various parts which made up the whole dāgaba. The height of the basal platforms was evidently fixed independently of the rest of the structure. In the large Mihintale dāgaba, the Abhayagiri, the Ḷankārāma, the Dakuṇu, and the Jētavana dāgabas, as well as in a later miniature stone dāgaba next described, the breadth of the tee is not far from one quarter of the diameter of the dome. The height of the tee, and the thickness of the lower part of the spire were about one-tenth of the diameter of the dome in very large dāgabas.

Miniature Dāgaba on the Ruwanwaeli Platform

An interesting small limestone dāgaba, cut out of a single stone, was placed on the pavement at the side of the Ruwanwaeli dāgaba; and not being a receptacle for valuables it escaped serious damage by treasure seekers, with the exception of the spire, the upper part of which is broken off.

It appears to be the work referred to by Niśśanka-Malla (1198–1207 A.D.) in his inscription on a large slab called the Galpota, 'the Stone Book,' at Polannaruwa,[1] in which he records that 'he made a stone dāgaba [at Ruwanwaeli] as a worship-place for the Gods.' Excepting in the heights of the dome and the basal platforms, this work partly adheres to the Canon, thus proving that this scale was already in existence.

The diameter of the dome, according to Mr. Smither's measurements, is 38 inches; by the Canon its height should therefore be 22·8 inches, but it is actually only 19 inches. The total height, which is now 4 feet 2½ inches, must have been very nearly according to the Canon. The basal ledges being lower than the Canon requires, the difference has been

[1] Dr. E. Müller. *Ancient Inscriptions*, No. 148.

added equally to the tee and the base of the spire. Round the latter a series of reliefs of standing figures, separated by pilasters, explains why this member is termed the 'enclosure of the dēvatās,' the figures evidently being those of the dēvatās who guard the structure. The series of shallow niches in the base of the spire at Abhaya-giri may have had plaster representations of dēvatās like those on this work, and it may be assumed that the other great dāgabas were all similarly supplied with guardian deities.

The three basal platforms are 10½ inches high, the tee 8 inches, and the base of the spire 6 inches. Elephants' heads project round the base of the dāgaba, and there is a lion looking outward at each corner.

Examples of Types

Of the six kinds of dāgabas, I am acquainted with no pre-Christian example of the modern Bell shape with the exception of the Idikaṭu dāgaba at Mihintale. The primitive type of bell which was usually copied may have been unlike later bells; and it is most probable that the Lankārāma dāgaba, in which a more or less hemispherical dome rested on a short vertical-sided cylinder of the same diameter, may represent the earliest Bell-shaped edifice. If not, we should have in it a seventh type, which the old authority would be unlikely to omit from his list.

In excavating at an early monastic building at Anurādhapura, Mr. Bell found a small copper bell with high vertical sides and a rounded top,[1] which proves that this shape was employed in ancient times for such articles. Ancient Egyptian and some early Indian bells were somewhat similar, with rounded tops. There can be no doubt also that the common wooden bell which is hung on the necks of cattle, and has nearly vertical sides, adheres to a primitive type. The Bell dāgaba of modern times copies the present form of the bell in varying proportions, and is now decidedly the favourite shape with the designers of these structures.

[1] Archaeological Survey of Ceylon. Fourth Progress Report, p. 4.

The 'Chatty' or Water-pot shape has been abandoned, and was never popular. It is formed from the sphere, by fixing the base line at about one-quarter of the height, so that the dome becomes three-fourths of a globe. The only Sinhalese representation of it with which I am acquainted is the Tissa karaṇḍuwa No. 93, in which the greatest diameter is at about one-third of its height. This style of building appears to have been more practised in India[1] than in Ceylon, but not in very early works.

The Bubble, or plain hemisphere, was the favourite design in early times, and it is still found in the case of many small dāgabas reconstructed inside cave temples. Nearly all the very early dāgabas in Ceylon and India followed this type, which with its simple well-rounded outline is perhaps the most effective one for very large structures. A large number of the smaller dāgabas had no tee or base for the spire, which in such a case was in the form of a monolithic stone pillar, usually octagonal in section, with a rounded top ending in a blunt point; it rose directly out of the top of the dome.

The Heap-of-Paddy shape is doubtless a very ancient type of dāgaba, which perhaps represents a form of early eastern tumulus or cairn. It consists of the end portion of a wide cone, with slightly curved sides and a rounded top. The restored Kaelaṇi dāgaba is of this type and the Sēla caitya at Anurādhapura may also have been of this shape. It is not found in Tissa, nor in the karaṇduwas; but a few examples are to be seen at secluded wihāras, and although these have been restored after their original construction it is most unlikely that the form would be changed from another type to this unusual one. The tee in this dāgaba is commonly a very small one, but at the Kaelaṇi structure the length of its side is very nearly equal to a quarter of the width of the dome.

There is a dāgaba of this character at Oṭṭappuwa, in the North-central Province, which is attributed by tradition to Dēvānam-piya Tissa. The bricks in it are 18·60 inches long, 9·52 inches wide, and 3·12 inches thick; Bt. is 29·7 and the contents 552 cubic inches. These dimensions point to some

[1] An example is to be seen in the Amarāvati relief, Fig. No. 81.

time late in the second century, or early in the first century B.C., as the date of the work. An inscription [1] left at it by 'Siri-kaṇa raja' (30–33 A.D.) proves that it was in existence before his time.

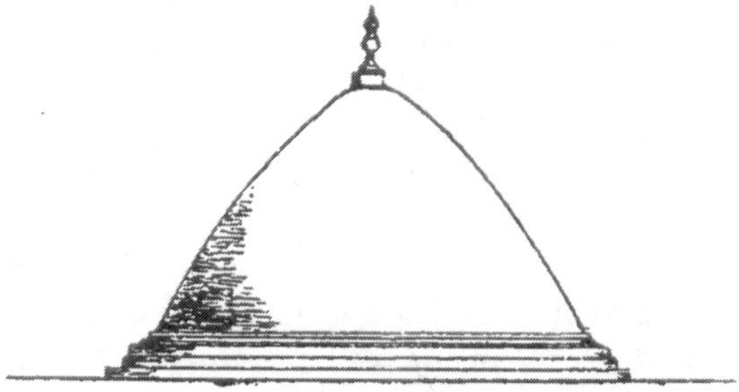

FIG. 113. Oṭṭappuwa Dāgaba. $\frac{1}{240}$.

At a dāgaba of this shape at Wellangolla, in the North-western Province, the bricks are 3 inches thick, a size that belongs to pre-Christian times. At another, at Kahatagaswela, in the same Province, the bricks average 15·22 inches in length, 7·84 inches in breadth, and 2·65 inches in thickness, Bt. being 20·8, and the contents 316 cubic inches. This size indicates that they were burnt in the first three centuries after Christ.

The Lotus (bud) dāgaba might be expected to be of common occurrence, from the popularity of the flower as a decorative 'motive'; but it is one of the rarest forms of dāgaba, and I have not met with a single building of this shape. It is found, however, in the Nikawāē-kanda karaṇḍuwa numbered 104, in which it represents an unopened lotus bud. The crystal numbered 98 may be an unfinished karaṇḍuwa of this type, there being no relic-cavity in it.

The Nelli dāgaba is supposed to represent the form of the fruit of the Nelli tree (*Phyllanthus emblica*), which seems to have been highly esteemed in former times, since it is used as a popular simile in writings and inscriptions. King Niśśanka Malla mentions that he had inspected all Ceylon and 'had as precise a view of the whole as if it were a ripe Nelli fruit in his hand.[2] This is a small round fruit with a green rind,

[1] See the final chapter, and Fig. No. 153 for facsimile.

[2] *Ancient Inscriptions*, No. 143.

growing on a low tree which is abundant in part of the Nilgala district; it is there about the size of the ordinary 'marbles' of schoolboys.

I presume that the round-topped dāgabas in which the curve of the side of the dome is an arc of a circle, the centre of which is beyond the vertical axis, represent this form. This outline is seen in the Tissa karaṇḍuwas numbered 94 and 96 and Nos. 108–110 at Nikawāē-kanda; and possibly such designs as the Tissa karaṇḍuwa No. 95 and the Nikawāē-kanda karaṇḍuwas Nos. 102, 103 and 107 were grouped under this heading. These forms appear to have been rarely adopted in actual construction in Ceylon.

For convenience of reference, I append an amended list of the dimensions of dated bricks, in which I have inserted the sizes of the bricks at the structures to which definite ages have been attributed in this chapter.

AMENDED LIST OF DATED BRICKS.

No	Name of Structure.		Date.	Length in Inches.	Breadth in Inches.	Thickness in Inches.	Breadth x Thickness.	Length x Thickness.	Contents in Cub. Ins.
	Large dāgaba, Sānchi, India		B.C. 3rd Cent.	16·00	10·00	3·00	30	48	480
1	Maha Sāēya, Mihintale	N.C.P.	,,	17·92	8·87	2·91	25·8	52·1	461
2	Mahānāga dāgaba, Tissa	S.P.	,,	17·35	8·84	2·83	25	49·1	434
3	Yaṭṭhāla dāgaba, Tissa	,,	,,	17·85	8·64	2·90	25	51·7	447
4	Sanda-giri dāgaba, Tissa	,,	Early 2nd Cent.	17·14	8·67	2·81	24·4	48·1	418
5	Maeṇik dāgaba, Tissa	,,	2nd Cent.	16·57	8·86	2·80	24·8	46·4	411
6	Miriswaeṭi dāgaba, Anurādhapura .	N.C.P.	,,	—	10·41	3·00	31·2	—	—
7	Ruwanwaeli dāgaba, Anurādhapura (inner work) . .	,,	,,	—	9·67	2·79	27[illegible]	—	—
8	Ruwanwaeli dāgaba, Anurādhapura, (outer work) . .	,,	,,	14·06	8·99	2·90	26·1	40·8	366
9	Ruwanwaeli dāgaba, Anurādhapura, (elephant wall) .	,,	,,	17·00	—	2·85	—	48·4	—
10	Nuwara-kanda . .	N.W.P.	,,	16·76	8·76	3·09	27	52	454
11	Nikawāē-kanda dāgaba	,,	Late 2nd Cent. or early 1st Cent.	16·41	8·16	3·39	27·6	55·6	454
12	Abhaya-giri dāgaba, Anurādhapura .	N.C.P.	Early 1st Cent.	18·92	9·62	3·20	30·7	60·5	583
13	Lankārāma dāgaba, Anurādhapura .	,,	,,	17·37	8·94	2·62	23·4	45·5	407
14	Dambulla cave temple[1]	C.P.	1st Cent.	19·45	—	2·45	—	47·6	—
15	Millāēwa-gala dāgaba	N.C.P.	A.D. 1st or 2nd Cent.	15·57	8·00	2·72	21·7	42·3	339
16	Dakuṇu dāgaba, Anurādhapura .	,,	2nd Cent.	16·36	8·18	2·31	18·9	37·8	309
17	Jētavana dāgaba, Anurādhapura .	,,	Late 3rd Cent.	15·82	8·41	2·26	19	35·7	301
18	Hurulla tank, central sluice	,,	,,	—	8·40	2·70	22·7	—	—
	Hurulla tank, high-level sluice . .	,,	,,	—	8·35	2·51	21	—	—
19	Padawiya sluice .	,,	,,	14·02	8·50	2·46	20·9	34·5	293
20	Vaṇṇāṭṭi Pālama .	,,	,,	13·61	8·48	2·70	22·9	36·7	311
21	Nīrammulla sluice .	N.W.P.	,,	—	8·45	2·70	21·5	—	—
22	Daḷadā Māligāwa (inner room) . .	N.C.P.	Early 4th Cent.	14·10	8·45	2·52	21·3	35·5	300
23	Tōpāwaewa sluice .	,,	Late 4th Cent.	—	7·40	2·43	18	—	—
24	Sīgiriya gallery .	,,	Late 5th Cent.	13·09	7·32	2·31	16·9	30·2	220
25	Rankoṭ dāgaba, Polannaruwa. .	,,	12th Cent.	12·52	8·40	2·00	16·8	25	210
26	Thūpārāma hall (inside)	,,	,,	12·00	8·36	2·00	16·7	24	201
27	Fortification Wall Polannaruwa .	,,	,,	12·63	8·20	2·00	16.4	25·3	207

There is good reason to believe that about the tenth century the breadth was sometimes under 8 inches and the thickness a little less than 2 inches, but I am unable to give the sizes of any dated bricks of that period.

[1] For the age of this temple see *The Earliest Inscriptions*, No. 75.

X

THE EARLIEST IRRIGATION WORKS

THE special feature of the ancient civilisation of Ceylon was its irrigation works, which with the exception of part of the mountain district were made throughout the whole country. Their purpose was to store or convey the water which was required for the rice fields that were formed at every suitable place in the island.

Two different systems of irrigation were adopted, depending on the circumstances of each case. According to one the water was impounded in reservoirs, from which it was gradually passed out, either directly onto the fields where it was wanted, or by means of excavated channels down which it flowed to them.

According to the other system, part of the water flowing down the rivers was turned into longer excavated channels which conveyed it to more distant lands, or reservoirs, temporary dams or permanent masonry dams being constructed across the rivers below the off-takes of the channels, in order to divert into them a larger quantity of water than could be secured without such aid when the flow of the rivers began to diminish after the end of the seasonal rains of the two monsoons. The north-east monsoon lasts from October to March, and its regular rains end in January; the South-west monsoon lasts from April to September, and its rains cease in June.

This latter method of irrigation by means of channels cut from rivers is of the greatest antiquity, having been practised in North-western and Central India, and most probably also Southern India, from immemorial times. It originated in the Euphrates valley, where the cultivation of the fertile lands on both banks of the river was largely dependent on it.

The first record of any irrigation work there is contained in an inscription left by Eannadu, King of Shirpurla in Southern Babylonia, who ruled in about 4000 B.C., and who mentions his construction of several canals, one of them being known as 'Lummadimshar,' at the side of which he made a reservoir, the first on record, 'a basin (containing) 3600 *gur* [each being eight bushels] of water.' Another of these canals is specially stated to have been cut 'from the great river' (Euphrates).

Entemena, nephew of Eannadu, recorded the opening of several fresh canals, and also the prolongation of the Euphrates canal to the river Tigris. Urukagina, King of Shirpurla, who reigned in 3900 B.C., according to the latest conclusions,[1] and not in 4500 B.C. as was supposed by Dr. Radau (*Early Babylonian History*, p. 47), also cut a canal there. His own words regarding it are, 'For Ninā her beloved canal Ninākitum-a he has built.' Ninā was the Goddess Bau, the Great Mother.

In nearly all cases these early canals were distinguished by special names. It is most improbable that this would be the case when irrigation channels were originally made, and as one of the first ones of which a record has been preserved has its own title it may be concluded that the construction of such works dates from nearly 4500 B.C., or possibly an even earlier time.

In India, we find the digging of channels referred to in very early times (Rig Veda, iii, 33, 6; iv, 19, 2), perhaps in the third millennium B.C.; and the benefits derived from them would be so apparent that doubtless many others continued to be opened from that period down to historic times, even although no actual record of them has been preserved.

While it is almost certain, therefore, that the first Gangetic settlers must have been acquainted with this manner of irrigation before they came to Ceylon, there is nothing to indicate that they brought with them a knowledge of the construction of reservoirs, which as a general rule were neither required

[1] King and Hall. *Egypt and Western Asia*, p. 189.

nor made in the districts inhabited by their ancestors in India. Although an inscription at Junāgadh[1] has recorded that one was formed by Pushyagupta, the brother-in-law of the great King Candragupta,[2] and was afterwards repaired by the latter's grandson, the Emperor Aśōka, it appears to have been a comparatively small work, of which little or no trace now remains. It is possible that the Sinhalese acquired a knowledge of the art of reservoir construction in Southern India. In any case, there can be no doubt that the credit of its development and extension in the island is due to some of the first Sinhalese rulers and their responsible advisers.

The nature of the flat plains around the sites of the primitive capitals of Southern India could never have encouraged the construction of reservoirs with high embankments, which, in fact, are still non-existent on them. All that could be attempted there in very early times in the way of making reservoirs would be the formation of shallow village tanks, with embankments from six to ten or twelve feet high, for retaining a supply of rain-water for bathing purposes, and for the irrigation of the adjoining fields attached to each village.

It was only in the districts surrounding the early capitals of Ceylon that the necessary conditions existed for promoting the construction of larger works of this character—a series of shallow valleys down which flowed seasonal streams of moderate size, and a heavy rainfall lasting for only a short period in each monsoon. It may be assumed, therefore, that the formation of all reservoirs of a class with embankments much higher than those of simple village tanks was originally due to the constructive genius of the Sinhalese themselves.

At an early date they undertook the raising of great earthen embankments, often some miles in length, across many suitable valleys, thus intercepting the flow of the streams, and storing up during the rainy seasons, in the reservoirs thus formed, immense sheets of water for the irrigation of large

[1] *The Indian Antiquary*, Vol. vii, p. 257.

[2] According to Mr. V. A. Smith this king reigned from 321 to 297 B.C. (*Early History of India*, p. 44). Sir F. Max Müller's date is 315–291 B.C. (*The Dhammapada*, p. xxxvi).

tracts of land lower down in the valleys, that were found to be suitable for the cultivation of rice, the only culture for which the water was utilised.

In addition to the benefit which the country in general derived from the works, a considerable part of the produce of the irrigated lands was devoted in many instances, after the introduction of Buddhism, to the maintenance of the Buddhist monks. Thus it soon came to be thought an act of great religious merit to construct such reservoirs, and the continuance of the practice by all the pious monarchs of the island was then assured. These were the larger works, such as private enterprise could not attempt to undertake.

In the meantime, the formation of minor works at the villages, by the combined labour of the inhabitants, was doubtless encouraged,[1] until in the end such 'village tanks' were

[1] Moral Suasion, when applied by the district chiefs, must have been an exceedingly effective instrument. Those who possess an intimate acquaintance with the village life of the East will easily understand that in early times the life of the villager who ventured to set his inclinations in opposition to the will of the chiefs would become an extremely uncomfortable one—as is often the case even now. At the present day, in Ceylon it is not necessary that the chief or headman should take any active steps against the recalcitrant person in order to bring this about. In every village there are at least two parties, often bitterly opposed to each other ; usually they consist of the friends and followers of the local headman for the time being, and the adherents to the ex-headman. When a villager is once known to have incurred the displeasure of the local chief, and more especially if he be a man who has played an unpopular rôle in the village for any reason, his enemies proceed to take advantage of the opportunities which this affords them to annoy him. His cattle are stolen, sometimes his corn-stack is burnt down in the night, or his house robbed during his absence. When he appeals to the headman for assistance in apprehending the culprits he is informed that they will be arrested on his discovering them and producing some proof of their guilt ; and there the matter often ends, as the headman is not interested in it, and takes no steps to find out the wrong-doers. In many instances false charges are trumped up against the objectionable person, or false or doubtful claims instituted over his lands, which he often has the greatest difficulty in rebutting, there commonly being some weak points in his own proofs of his ownership. If resort be not made to these extreme measures there are many other ways of inflicting petty annoyances on him the cumulative effect of which almost renders his life a burden to him.

established at practically every little settlement in the drier districts of the island.

The first irrigation works made in Ceylon obviously would be these village tanks, containing sheets of water that covered from two or three acres to one hundred acres or more, the size depending on the amount of the water-supply, the requirements of the village, and the formation of the ground. At first, only the simplest works of the smaller class, with very low embankments, would be undertaken ; but when a better knowledge of the art of raising such banks of earth to hold back greater depths of water was acquired, schemes of a more comprehensive character would be attempted, until at last no reservoir was looked upon as too great to be constructed, and the lengths of the embankments extended for any distance up to a maximum of nine miles, while their heights in a few instances rose to more than fifty feet.

The histories, which were compiled by monks who, especially in early times, were chiefly interested in recording the erection of Buddhistic edifices, and the other religious acts of the various monarchs of Ceylon, contain no reference to the formation of the communal village tanks, and too few notices of the construction of even the larger class of works, some of the most important of which are never mentioned in them, at any rate under names that can be recognised at the present day. In such cases we have nothing to mark the age of the works that cannot be identified in the histories, except the evidence obtainable from the dimensions of the bricks that were commonly used either in some part of them, or in Buddhist monasteries which depended for their existence on the water-supply afforded by the works, and the presence of a considerable population which that ensured. Notwithstanding the possibility of error in fixing the age of a work by such data, the general trustworthiness of these contemporary records is so unmistakable that in the absence of other evidence I shall make full use of them in determining the probable dates of some of the works.

The first notice of the construction of a reservoir in Ceylon is found in the Mahāvansa (i, p. 37), where it is stated that

Prince Anurādha, the brother-in-law of the second king, Paṇḍuwāsa Dēva, made one on the southern side of the capital, Anurādhapura. This was early in the fourth century B.C. It has not been identified, and we may assume that it was merely a small work intended for the use of the village at which the prince resided.

The record, the truth of which there can be no reason for doubting, is interesting as showing that the Sinhalese had already become acquainted with the art of making reservoirs. Considering the intimate connection existing between the first Sinhalese king and the king of Madura—Wijaya having married the latter's daughter—such a knowledge could easily have been acquired from Southern India before this date—perhaps even by the early Nāgas. Wijaya must have obtained his information regarding Madura and its sovereign's family through traders who were visiting the two kingdoms; there could be no other travellers to carry news in those days. Thus there would appear to have been a regular intercourse between the two countries from an early period; it is improbable that it would spring into being simply because Wijaya had become king of Ceylon, since mere settlers from the valley of the Ganges would have no personal acquaintance with Madura, and its ruler, and its trading requirements. They can only have heard of them from traders who had been at Madura. Such persons would doubtless observe the advantages accruing from the presence of village tanks on the line of their journey—dried up as the country becomes when there is no rain—and the knowledge of them would thus be transmitted to Ceylon.

It may appear to be such a simple matter to raise a long bank of earth in order to hold back a certain quantity of rain water for bathing purposes or for watering an adjoining rice field after the rains have ceased, that any people living in hot countries where the rains are only seasonal and are followed by several almost rainless months might be expected to be struck by the idea of making these little reservoirs for themselves, without its transmission from another country; but as a matter of fact the notion of reservoir-making appears to have been originated in only one country, and never to have been invented independently elsewhere, at any rate in the Old World. When I visited West Africa, the natives of the Gambia valley who have cultivated rice for so long a period that they have developed many special varieties of this grain, informed me that such an idea as storing water for its irrigation had never crossed their minds. They had never heard of such a practice, and had no notion regarding the manner in which such works should be constructed, even on the smallest scale. Probably this was the position in other countries.

It is most likely, therefore, that the art of reservoir construction owes its origin to the early peoples of the Euphrates valley, and that it spread westwards and south-eastwards from that centre, reaching the Drāvidian districts of India possibly before the Āryan invasion of the country, and being transmitted thence to Ceylon.

The next work for storing water, of which any information is given in the histories, is of an entirely different class from the village tank of Anurādha. Possibly it was the first reservoir ever made with an embankment of an importance that must have required special acquaintance with the principles of reservoir construction. The honour of occupying this prominent position rests with either Paṇḍā-waewa [1] in the North-western Province, or Abhaya-waewa at Anurādhapura, or possibly another reservoir at that city.

Paṇḍā-waewa

In the North-western Province, near Heṭṭipola, a small village at the junction of two roads, and sixteen miles east of Chilaw, the large deserted tank called Paṇḍā-waewa is found. On its southern side and close to the end of its embankment, there is a fortified site which apparently was once that of a town of considerable size, but is now completely overgrown with forest and jungle. It is known as Paṇḍuwas Nuwara, and is locally believed to have been a city founded by Paṇḍuwāsa

[1] The Sanskrit and Pāli word *vāpi*, the Elu or early Sinhalese words *wawi* and *wiya*, the Sinhalese *waewa*, and the Tamil *kuḷam* have the same meaning, and signify 'tank' or 'reservoir.'

Dêva in the first half of the fourth century B.C., and at one time his capital.

Beyond the name and the tradition, there is no evidence that he actually founded a city at this site; but this at least may be said in favour of the tradition—that it is in the highest degree unlikely that if the town was established by a later monarch he would perpetuate the memory of a much earlier ruler, in preference to his own, in bestowing a name on it.

A long and exaggerated account of the city is given in an old manuscript termed Pradhāna Nuwarawal, 'Principal Cities,' which describes other large towns of this part of the

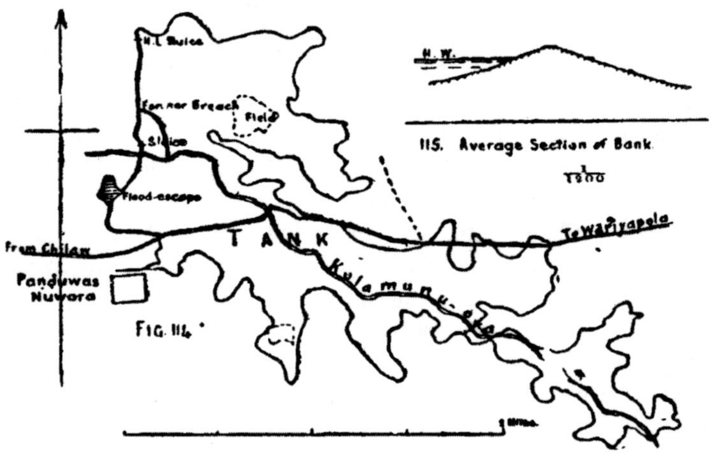

FIGS. 114, 115. Paṇḍā-waewa.

country, such as Kurunāēgala, Yāpahuwa, and Kandy. It proves that the site possessed the same name early in the fourteenth century—when the work appears to have been compiled[1]—and that it was then believed that the city was founded by the same 'Paṇḍuwas Raja,' who, it states, also 'for the support of the city made a great tank.' It mentions that the original city had the honour of being con-

[1] It gives the day and hour, but not the year, of the death of a king called Pandita Parākrama Bāhu, and ends after mentioning the accession of his younger brother, a monk, under the name of Buja Parākrama Bāhu. The former king lived at Dambadeniya, and removed thence to Kandy, which he founded.

structed by Vissakamma, the divine builder, acting under orders issued by Indra.

The fortifications consist of an enclosing wall forty feet thick, faced with brickwork on both sides, and having immediately outside it a ditch which is still some seven feet deep, and more than ten feet wide in the bottom. This wall is well defined and still several feet high; in plan it is a regular rhombus, 1000 feet long on two opposed sides, and 950 feet long on the other two.

Without doubt this fortification is of much later date than the time of the second king of Ceylon, but that is not proof that a settlement did not exist there long prior to its construction. In reality, it shows that some pre-existing station of sufficient importance to be worth strong fortifications was already established there when the wall was built. I possess no measurements of the bricks used in the work. No remains of buildings are known inside this fortified space; this indicates the lapse of several centuries since the place was abandoned.

The connection of the position of the city with the date of the construction of the reservoir lies in the fact that the town was built not only close behind the end of the embankment, but so near the edge of the reservoir that when the latter was quite full the water extended into the ditch which surrounds its wall. This shows that the reservoir was already formed before the exact site of the town was decided upon, so that if the name of the city and the tradition respecting it be regarded as sufficient evidence that it was founded by Paṇḍuwāsa Dēva at this spot, the construction of the reservoir must also be attributed to this monarch, although neither the one nor the other is mentioned in the histories.

The chief difficulty in accepting the identification lies in the area of the reservoir, the water of which would cover no less than 1050 acres when it was full. It was not until at least a century later than the time of Paṇḍuwāsa Dēva that any other reservoir of this size appears to have been made in Ceylon; and on a review of the probabilities of the case I should be inclined to think that a town built there by that king would be nearer the stream across which the embankment of the tank was raised. If the tank was made at a subsequent date, the town, such as it was—probably a mere congeries of wattle-and-daub huts—would be re-constructed in a new position at the edge of the water. If this opinion be not adopted we are driven to the conclusion that this great reservoir was formed in the time when the second king ruled over the country. As evidence in favour of its early date we have the fact that Anurādhapura was established at the distance of nearly a mile from the adjoining river, the Malwatta-oya.

Another difficulty which also throws doubt on such an identification is found in the fact that if the reservoir was made by Paṇḍuwāsa Dēva, we must be prepared to admit that either brick-making or stone-cutting, or both, as well as the art of building with those materials, were sufficiently understood in Ceylon at that early period for the designer to venture to construct a masonry outlet or sluice for the purpose of regulating the flow of the water and passing it out for the use of the rice fields that would be cultivated lower down the valley by its aid. Such a great body of water would never be retained for the mere use of the inhabitants of the city; and the tank must have been originally intended for irrigating rice lands in addition to providing the people with a supply of water for drinking and bathing purposes. For fulfilling such an object some kind of substantially built outlet at a low level would be a necessity.

On the other hand, there can be no doubt that the arts of stone-cutting and brick-burning were well advanced long before the erection of the first dāgabas, and the cutting of the earliest inscriptions and the fronts of the cave shelters of the Buddhist monks, in the third century B.C. No mere learners could have done the works in brick-burning and building, and in stone-cutting, which are still preserved. King Paṇḍukābhaya, who probably became king at about the end of the fourth century B.C. (that is, less than seventy years after Paṇḍuwāsa Dēva), certainly formed a reservoir which had an embankment higher than that of Paṇḍā-waewa. Thus there must always remain a possibility that the tradition regarding the origin of this latter work is correct. I shall therefore give a short account of the works at Paṇḍā-waewa, which *may* be the first great reservoir ever constructed, if we omit from consideration the great lakes of Egypt, since they were merely immense natural hollows into which water was turned.

The histories contain almost no information regarding this reservoir. They state that King Ḍappula II (807–812, A.D.) built a hospital there, 'with a fruitful village attached thereto,' for its support (Mah., ii, p. 57); and it also appears to be mentioned in the same work under the name Seṭṭhivāpi, 'the Heṭṭi(pola) Tank,' as one of the reservoirs repaired by Parākrama-Bāhu I (1164–1197 A.D.). King Niśśanka-Malla (1198–1207 A.D.) left a record of this restoration in an inscription of four lines [1] cut on a stone at the outlet of the low-level sluice. Perhaps the work was only completed in his reign.

The final breach in the embankment was made in the early years of last century, and its history is instructive as showing how many other great reservoirs in Ceylon may have burst. According to the information which I received thirty years ago from persons who had heard the story of the catastrophe related by those who remembered it, a track made by cattle that crossed the embankment had become worn down into a deep hollow which was left unfilled. The natural consequence of such neglect followed. A sudden and extremely high rise of the water (which flooded some of the nearest houses at the side of the reservoir), following a very heavy rainfall, caused its level to mount up during the darkness of a rainy night until it overtopped the low place; and when daylight broke the embankment was found to be completely breached at the spot, and the reservoir was empty.

The last Sinhalese king subsequently entrusted its repair

[1] It begins, *Śrīmat Parākrama Bhussā, Mahā Bhussā, Kālinga Si̥ṅha dapa nerana patetwaṇu*, and the last part is *disa mewara gaḍa waśyam̥*. 'The Prosperous King Parākrama, the Great King, the Kālinga Lion, putting aside and subduing pride . . . the overcoming of the impediment to the work of the country.'

to one of his chiefs, but he was recalled in 1815, before the work was begun, owing to the rebellion which ended in our occupation of the Kandian kingdom at the request of the chiefs; and the reservoir has been left in the same useless state down to the present day, although plans for its restoration were prepared thirty years ago.

The embankment was carried in a north-and-south line nearly straight across the valley of the Koḷamunu-oya—a stream that rises about fifteen miles away—until it passed across this river; it was then turned round to the south-west so as to abut against a large and nearly flat rock, near the southern side of the valley. From the southern side of the rock it then resumed its southward direction for a short distance, after which it was turned up-stream at a right angle for 2100 feet until it ended at high ground not far from the site of the old city, Paṇḍuwas Nuwara. Owing to the configuration of the ground, a considerable amount of earthwork was saved by this sudden alteration in the line of the bank.

The rock, which is about 250 feet across, was utilised as a waste-weir or flood-escape; and it is evident that the valley had been carefully examined, and the site of the embankment chosen with the special view of making use of this rock as a safe place for the escape of floods. It is quite certain that the bank was raised to its full height at the first construction of the reservoir. I made a search in vain for any channel such as the floods must have excavated had they been discharged out of the tank at a lower level; there can be no doubt that from the first they were passed over the rock. That the reservoir remained in working order until perhaps the twelfth century is a proof that the height to which floods would rise over the rock had been correctly estimated.

The embankment is 8400 feet long, or $1\frac{3}{5}$ miles; and is 22 feet high above the sill of the low-level sluice, above which the crest of the rock rose 13 feet. In later years an additional depth of 2 feet of water was retained by means of a temporary dam raised along the front of the rock after the main floods had ceased, by the aid of short rough stone pillars, over which a foot-bridge may have been fixed. The top of the bank was 8 feet wide, and the sides sloped at the rate of 2½ feet horizontal to 1 foot vertical. This section is weaker than that of any other large pre-Christian bank that I have seen. It is almost the only respect in which the bank differs from those of other very early works of a similar size, and it may indicate its greater age; later experience evidently showed the old engineers the advisability of adopting a broader section and flatter slopes. Along the slope facing the water a layer of small boulders is laid as a protection against erosion caused by waves. This may be of later date than the original work; such a protection is found at all the larger embankments in Ceylon, with one or two exceptions.

One sluice, with a rectangular stone culvert for discharging water, was built in the low ground on the northern side of the stream, and another at a high level near the northern end of the embankment. They appeared to differ in no respect from similar structures in other reservoirs in Ceylon; they may have been reconstructed long after the original work was done, as the position of the inscription of Niśśanka-Malla indicates. I shall refer to the question of the type of the Sinhalese sluice in describing one at a somewhat later reservoir where I was able to examine the original work.

When the reservoir retained a depth of 13 feet of water at the low-level sluice the area covered by it was 1050 acres, and its capacity was 311 million cubic feet; the extra depth of two feet increased the area to 1360 acres, and the capacity to 416 million cubic feet.

Although the size of this reservoir was surpassed by other pre-Christian ones, and left far behind by many post-Christian works, we cannot fail to be astonished at the boldness and originality of the early engineer who ventured to construct such an earthen bank across a valley down which floods of considerable volume passed in the rainy seasons. Owing to the heavy rainfall of the gathering ground, which averages about 85 inches per annum, the maximum flood may amount to 12,000 or 14,000 cubic feet per second. Every engineer will recognise that to get rid of this volume of water in safety would be a serious problem; the old designer of the works must have been a highly intelligent man to overcome it so successfully. Besides this he made every effort to reduce the quantity of the earthwork to a minimum; to effect this the line of the bank was twisted about in order to avoid low ground, in a manner never found in later works of large size.

ABHAYA-WAEWA

In about 300 B.C., King Paṇḍukābhaya, the grandson of Paṇḍuwāsa Dēva, made the Abhaya tank at Anurādhapura (Mah., i, p. 43); this is the earliest constructive work which

FIG. 116. Basawak-kuḷam.

can be identified with certainty in Ceylon. Subsequent references to it in the histories, as well as an inscription left at it in the tenth century, containing the orders of King Kassapa IV prohibiting fishing in it, in which it is mentioned by name, prove that it is the existing reservoir at Anurādhapura which is now termed Basawak-kuḷam. The first duty assigned to me on my arrival in the island in 1873 was the survey of this interesting reservoir, at that time almost useless, having a large breach through the embankment, in front of which a low temporary dam of sticks and earth held back a little water; its restoration was undertaken immediately afterwards from the designs then prepared.

It is sometimes mentioned casually in the early part of the histories—in the time of Paṇḍukābhaya and subsequently—but always as a reservoir in working order; and it appears to have remained unbreached as long as Anurādhapura was inhabited—that is, for more than 1500 years, a respectable record for a work of such early date. Of no structures can it be said more truly than of reservoirs, that the most successful works have no history. Decade follows decade, century succeeds century, and while the work is performing its functions satisfactorily there is nothing in its life that is worth recording, except the levels of the water in it year by year. Naturally, therefore, we find nothing noted regarding the state of this tank.

Compared with Paṇḍā-waewa its area is insignificant; when full it only covers 255 acres, although it appears to have been a little larger originally. Yet it was well designed to fulfil its purpose, the storage of rainfall close to the town, for the water-supply of the city and for bathing purposes. It made the best of a very poor catchment area; had it been supplied with a higher embankment it would have failed to secure much more water in years of ordinary rainfall. Owing to the small area from which the surplus rainfall flowed into it there would be no difficulty at it, like that experienced at Paṇḍā-waewa, from very high floods, either during its construction or afterwards.

The plan of the tank on Fig. 70 shows that a much shorter bank might have been carried across the valley in a south-east line from the flood-escape to a projecting point on the opposite side of the reservoir; but this would have removed the water nearly half a mile further from the early city, whereas the evident aim of the designer was to construct the tank as close to the town as possible. He therefore ran the bank to a position lower down, where on the eastern side the ground level was below that of the water to be retained. From this point he turned the line in an up-stream direction, at nearly a rectangle, until higher ground was encountered. This turning of one end of the embankment upstream is a special feature of the Anurādhapura reservoirs, Paṇḍā-waewa, and Sangili-

Kanadara tank, described below, and is not found elsewhere in Ceylon, I believe, excepting in the tanks of the Mannār district, where the configuration of the ground, which is practically a sloping plain, rendered it unavoidable.

The embankment is 5910 feet long, or 1⅛ miles. As now restored, its crest is 22 feet above the sill of the sluice; but originally it appears to have been six feet higher, judging by the levels of its more elevated portions. It was considerably eroded, and for a great part of its length the top was below the level adopted at the restoration. The width of its crest was only from six to eight feet, but the slopes on both sides were flatter than at Paṇḍā-waewa, being at the rate of 3·1 feet horizontal to one foot vertical. The slope adjoining the water was protected by a layer of small boulders (Fig. 138).

A single sluice was built near the western end; it consisted, as usual, of a stone-lined rectangular well near the water-level, and a stone culvert for discharging water. This was a work of later date than the embankment, a number of pillars and other stones removed from pre-existing buildings being used in its construction. After it was built a small rice field was formed on the low side of the embankment.

Floods were allowed to escape round the west end of the embankment, through a slight hollow 22 feet wide, the level of which was 19 feet above the sill of the sluice. The present flood-escape is 3 feet 8 inches lower. The original area of the reservoir was about 330 acres, and its capacity about 133 million cubic feet.

There is nothing in the design of the embankment which is indicative of its antiquity. The slopes of the sides were similar to those of many later works, and the weak section which appears to be a primitive characteristic of Paṇḍā-waewa is thus absent. At a little later date it will be seen that it became the custom to make them still flatter. In view of the general features of the design, I am of opinion that several other embankments of considerable size had been constructed in Ceylon before the works at Abhaya-waewa were undertaken.

JAYA-VĀPI

Another reservoir made by Paṇḍukābhaya at the same city, before Abhaya-waewa was formed, appears to have been a somewhat large one. The Mahāvansa relates of it (i, pp. 42, 43), 'Causing his uncle's canopy of dominion to be brought, and having washed it in the natural tank that was here, this Paṇḍukābhaya caused himself to be anointed king with the water of that very tank. . . . Having deepened the above-mentioned marsh, he made it contain a great body of water. By his having been anointed with that water as a conqueror (Jaya) it obtained the name of Jaya-vāpi.'

The old name having been changed, this reservoir has not been identified. If it had an embankment and was not

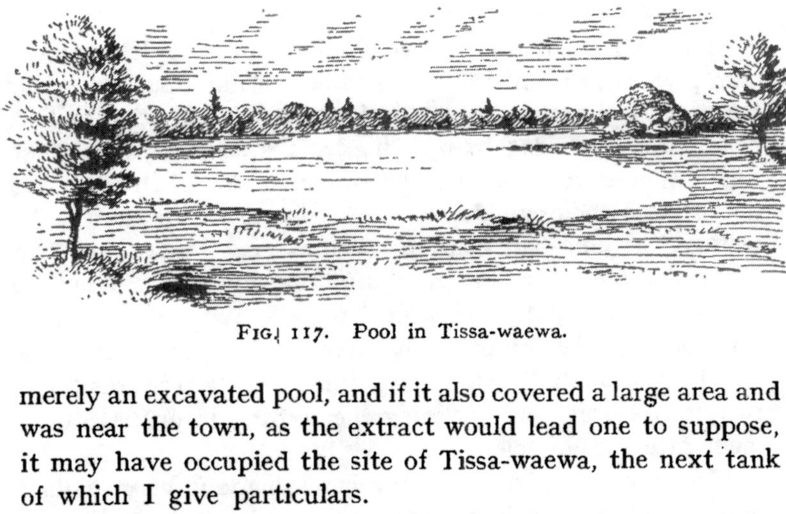

FIG. 117. Pool in Tissa-waewa.

merely an excavated pool, and if it also covered a large area and was near the town, as the extract would lead one to suppose, it may have occupied the site of Tissa-waewa, the next tank of which I give particulars.

The illustration (Fig. No. 117), from a sketch made by me in 1873, shows a large natural pool in the bed of Tissa-waewa. It is not unlikely that an embankment may have been raised on the low side of this sheet of water, along the line of the present embankment of Tissa-waewa, so as to retain a better supply during the dry seasons, before the construction of Abhaya-waewa. There is some evidence of this in the name of a long channel that was subsequently cut in order to lead water from the great Kalā-waewa into Tissa-waewa; it bore the name Jaya-ganga, 'the Jaya river'; this may indicate that it was the channel that conveyed water into the Jaya tank.

A third reservoir at Anurādhapura, termed Gāmani-vāpi, is referred to (Mah., i, p. 43) as being in existence to the northward of Abhaya-waewa during the reign of the same king. The name has been changed, and the tank has not been identified. The time of its construction is uncertain; as the father of Paṇḍukābhaya was named Gāmaṇi the tank may have been constructed by him. According to the Mahāvansa he lived at Anurādhapura. Its winding embankment indicates a possibility that the shallow tank now called Peramiyan-kuḷam is this work.

TISSA-WAEWA.

Soon after the middle of the third century B.C. King Dēvānam-piya Tissa formed the Tissa tank at Anurādhapura (Mah., i, p. 79). The account of the incident which led to the erection of the Miriswaeṭi dāgaba by King Duṭṭha-Gāmiṇi proves that this is the reservoir on the south-western side of the dāgaba; it still bears the original name. According to the story in the history, the king had gone to bathe in Tissa-waewa, and had set up his sceptre in the ground at the side of it. When he had finished his bath and wished to take away the sceptre it was found to be miraculously fixed, and immoveable. The dāgaba was built by the king immediately afterwards, close to this reservoir, and enclosing the sceptre, in order to commemorate the miracle.

The valley in which the reservoir was made is very shallow, and the design took a peculiar form in consequence. A straight bank was raised across the lower part of the ground for nearly three-quarters of a mile, running nearly north and south. From each end of this a long arm was carried in an up-stream direction, forming an obtuse angle with the central part, and being continued until ground was met with sufficiently high to prevent the escape of floods. If Paṇḍukābhaya raised an embankment at this place, it must have occupied the line of the central straight part of this bank.

The embankment of Tissa-waewa is 11,000 feet, or $2\frac{1}{12}$ miles, in length, and about 25 feet high across the bed of the valley, which is flat for a long distance. The width of the crest averages 12 feet, but in parts is 18 feet. The outer side slopes at the rate of 3 feet horizontal to 1 foot vertical; the upper part of the inner slope, adjoining the water, falls at the rate of 2·8 feet horizontal to 1 foot vertical until at the level of the flood escape it reaches the stone facing of boulders and wedged stones which is laid to protect it from erosion by waves; this is at an inclination of $1\frac{1}{2}$ feet horizontal to 1 foot vertical (Fig. 139). The bank is a well made and substantial work, which with a little attention may last practically for ever; it appears to be in its original state, and is a credit to the men who raised it. There is no sign that it has ever given way except at the low-level sluice, where there was a small breach when I first saw the work in 1873.

A low-level sluice was built in the northern arm of the embankment, and a high-level one at about the middle of the southern arm. These had the usual rectangular wells and stone culverts. The well at the low-level sluice was nine feet wide in the line of the culvert.

A place for the escape of floods was left at each end of the bank, unprotected by masonry. The level at both was about 15 feet 4 inches above the sill of the low-level sluice; it is now raised to 17 feet 6 inches. Their total width only amounted to about 50 feet, the catchment basin of this tank being a very small one.

The area of Tissa-waewa was about 396 acres; as now enlarged it may be 550 acres. Its capacity is unknown.

Vavuṇik-kuḷam

The construction of Vavuṇik-kuḷam, a reservoir in the Northern Province, should probably be assigned to nearly the same period. Its original name was Pēli-vāpi, so-called because it was formed by raising a long embankment across the valley of a stream now termed the Pāli river. The single reference to it in the Mahāvansa (i, p. 107) shows that it was in existence before the time of Duṭṭha-Gāmiṇi, and this may carry its construction back to the third century B.C., as the Tamil ruler Elāra, who was killed by that king, and who is stated to have been on the throne for forty-four years, from 205 B.C., to 161 B.C., is not known to have made any reservoirs. Of course there remains a possibility that it was formed during the reign of Elāra, and that the early annalists omitted to record the fact.

The reference to it in the history is as follows: 'To the northward of the capital, at the distance of seven yōjanas, in the sand-banks of the stream flowing into the tank of Pēli vāpi gāma, four superb gems, in size about a small grindstone[1] and of the colour of the Ummā flower, were produced.' The name, the distance from the city, and the reference to a stream with sand-banks render the identification certain, there being no other reservoir on the river, and no other stream with sand-banks at that distance north of Anurādhapura.

According to my hand copy of the inscription left by King Wasabha (66–110 A.D.) at Peramiyan-kuḷam, on the northern side of Anurādhapura—(No. 7 of Dr. E. Müller's *Ancient Inscriptions*)—it appears to have been granted by that king to the Community of Monks. The words in my copy are, *Pali nakaraka wawiya ma tera Majibaka dini.* 'He gave the Pāli-nāgara tank to the great thēra Majjhima.' In the forest near the northern end of the embankment, Mr. C. F. S. Baker, the engineer who surveyed the tank, met with some ruins which may indicate the site of this ancient city, Pāli nāgara.

Detailed surveys have shown that when the reservoir was full the water covered an extent of 1975 acres, and the tank then had a capacity of 596 million cubic feet.

The work was of a different class from those already described its object being solely the storage of water for the irrigation of the rich lands lower down the valley. Thus it may have been the first large reservoir entirely devoted to such a purpose. The fact that some of the most productive land in northern Ceylon would be irrigable by means of it, accounts

[1] I do not know what is meant by this, the grindstone not being an Eastern article.

for the selection of this valley as the site of one of the first large irrigation schemes.

But the provision of water for this purpose would be useless were there not cultivators ready and willing to utilise it; it follows, therefore, that an adequate population who understood rice-growing was already established in this part of the island at this early period. We may safely assume that all could not be the descendants of settlers from the valley of the Ganges; and if not, the others must have been Drāvidians, that is, most probably Nāgas, the Vaeddas being a race who were unacquainted with rice cultivation. The raising of such an embankment as that of Vavuṇik-kuḷam would necessitate the presence of many hundreds of labourers accustomed to earthwork; the amount of work done itself indicates that there was already a large resident population in the district.

We may feel confident that other irrigation reservoirs of considerable size had been formed before the benefits derivable from large schemes of this nature had become sufficiently well known to induce the sovereign, who of course was the moving spirit in such matters, to undertake the construction of the long embankment of this tank solely for the furtherance of agriculture in an outlying part of his dominions.

The design of the work was of a simple character. A straight embankment was carried across the Pāli river, from the northern side of the valley, in a south-south-eastern direction, for a mile and a half. After arriving close to the southern side it was deflected into a south-western line for three-quarters of a mile, so as to include in the reservoir another subsidiary shallow valley, this part of the work being doubtless a subsequent addition to the original scheme. The extended bank ended by being turned round again into a south-eastern curve until it encountered higher ground. The total length is 13,350 feet, or about 2½ miles.

Although the river rises only twenty miles away, and the catchment area has a rainfall which amounts to less than 50 inches per annum, the embankment has been badly breached in five places, and the reservoir has been abandoned for many centuries, and its bed is now overgrown with jungle. There are also unmistakable signs of former breaches that have been repaired.

The only possible natural way in which five breaches can

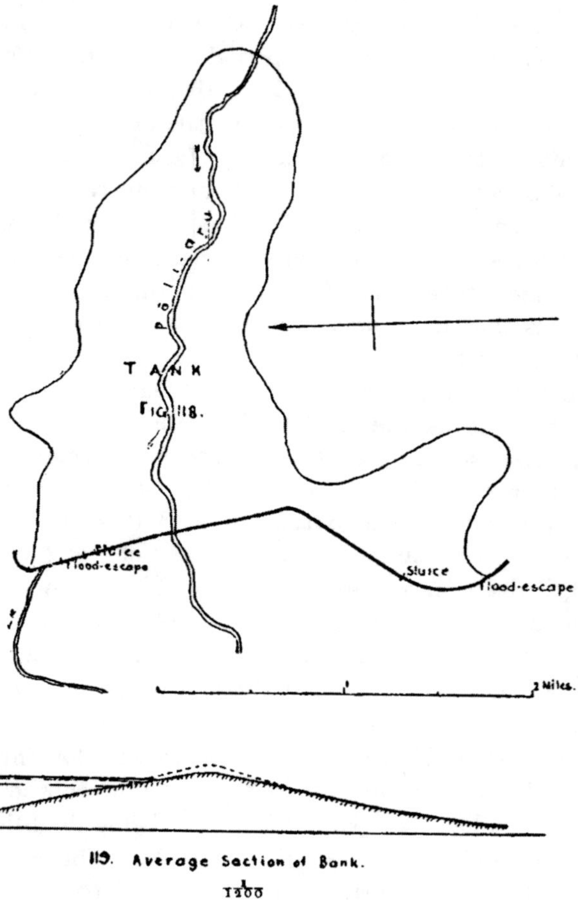

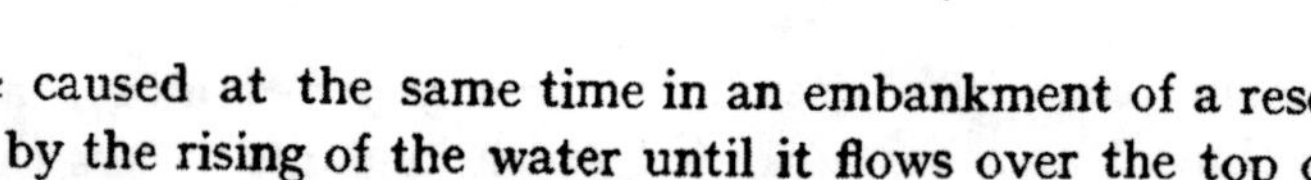

FIGS. 118, 119. Vavuṇik-kuḷam.

be caused at the same time in an embankment of a reservoir is by the rising of the water until it flows over the top of the bank at any points where the earthwork is a trifle lower than elsewhere. This is what must have occurred at Vavuṇik-kuḷam; but it does not indicate, as might appear to be the case, that the space provided for the free escape of all ordinary floods was insufficient. On the contrary it may have been enough, under ordinary conditions, for a reservoir in such a site. In the northern part of the bank a flood-escape at least 80 feet wide, and possibly much more, was left open. At the southern end a width of 450 feet was allowed at the end of the extended bank, and therefore most probably a wide flood-escape existed at the end of the original bank.

The experience of the last twelve years has shown that it may be suggested with confidence that the bursting of the reservoir was due to one of those violent cyclonic rain-storms which sometimes occur in this Province, and against which in most cases it is impossible to make provision, even if it could be foreseen. On the occasion of such a downfall in another part of the Northern Province in December, 1897, the actual depth of rain which fell in 24 hours, as recorded by three observers at Neḍunkēṇi, one being the Medical Officer of the station and another his dispenser, was 31·72 inches. The enquiry which I personally made on the spot regarding the manner in which this fall was gauged satisfied me that it correctly represented the quantity of rain collected in the rain-gauge, and that in addition a small amount must have been intercepted by two high trees as the wind veered round in their direction. The storm began about three hours before this record commenced, and the total amount which fell in twenty-seven or twenty-eight hours must have been 34 or 35 inches deep.

It is almost unnecessary to state that the damage caused throughout the tract which experienced this cyclonic storm was enormous. Roads were washed away, and one iron bridge presented a curious spectacle, standing isolated over the river that it spanned, with the approaches, that is, the road on an embankment at each end of it, more or less carried away. The tanks of the district suffered most; more than 160 were burst, in all cases by the flood-water's pouring in a great volume over the crests of their banks.

One work called Periya-kuḷam, that had been restored by

the Government, and has an embankment half a mile long, with sufficient space at one end for the escape of all ordinary floods, is in a catchment area that extends only some five miles in length above the embankment. The bank is about 20 feet high. The flood rose until it poured over the whole length of this embankment, and when I afterwards visited it there were several small logs and one large one stranded across its crest, left there by the water on their way over its top. Of course a deep breach was made at a place where this bank at last gave way.

All ordinary precautions against floods must be unavailing when such an outburst as this occurs. The design of the Vavuṇik-kuḷam scheme cannot be considered defective if it failed to meet such a contingency. The tank may have been in good working condition for many centuries before the former breaching of the bank took place, and many more may have passed before its final destruction.

The designer did, in reality, take quite unusual steps to ensure the safety of the reservoir. Though the crest of the bank is only ten or twelve feet wide in the better sections, the up-stream side slopes at the rate of 4·8 feet horizontal to 1 foot vertical, and the outer one at the rate of 4·6 feet horizontal to 1 foot vertical. It may be doubted if there are more than three or four other reservoirs in Ceylon with such flat slopes in their embankments. The whole bank is made of good material, and the side adjoining the water is protected up to the ordinary water-level by a layer of small boulders. Under ordinary conditions the work might have survived intact to the present day; but the person responsible for the design could not be aware—as, in fact, no one in the island knew twelve years ago—that this part of Ceylon is liable to experience such frightful rain-storms as that which I have just described—which was perhaps the heaviest that has visited the modern world.

The depth of water retained in the reservoir between the sills of the sluices and the level of the flood-escapes was about 18 feet, and the crest of the bank was 8 feet higher.

Only two sluices were found at this work, one being near each side of the valley. They consisted, as usual, of a rectangular well, and a rectangular stone culvert which passed under the embankment. I did not see them; they were lost in the thorny jungle which enveloped the whole bank, and their sites were unknown when I visited the place. Their wells measured about 10 feet by 15 feet in plan, and were built of brickwork. According to the drawings, the northern one was 80 feet and the southern one 140 feet from the centre of the bank, these being distances that are far greater than those at other similar embankments, in which the well is usually placed near the point where the water-level meets the up-stream slope of the earthwork. This variation from later practice indicates the early date of the works.

Pāvaṭ-kuḷam

On account of the dimensions of the bricks used in one of its sluices, another reservoir in the Northern Province, now called Pāvaṭ-kuḷam, twenty-eight miles south of the last, also appears to be a work of either the third century B.C. or the following century. As its original name is unknown it cannot be traced in the histories, even if it is mentioned in them.

This reservoir was made at the junction of two streams which flow westward through the district to the south of Vavuṇiya, the total length of the catchment area being about 16 miles; the average rainfall amounts to a little more than 50 inches per annum.

Evidently the valley had been well explored before the position of the embankment was decided upon. Advantage was taken of the presence of a long and high rocky ridge which projected into the valley from the northern side, and the embankment was run in a south-south-westerly direction from its end to a continuation of it two miles away, on the opposite side of the valley, meeting on the way two high rocky detached portions of the ridge. There are thus three separate banks which fill up the gaps left in this rocky ridge. The total length from end to end is 9700 feet, or $1\frac{5}{8}$ miles, of which the artificial bank occupies about a mile and a half. The

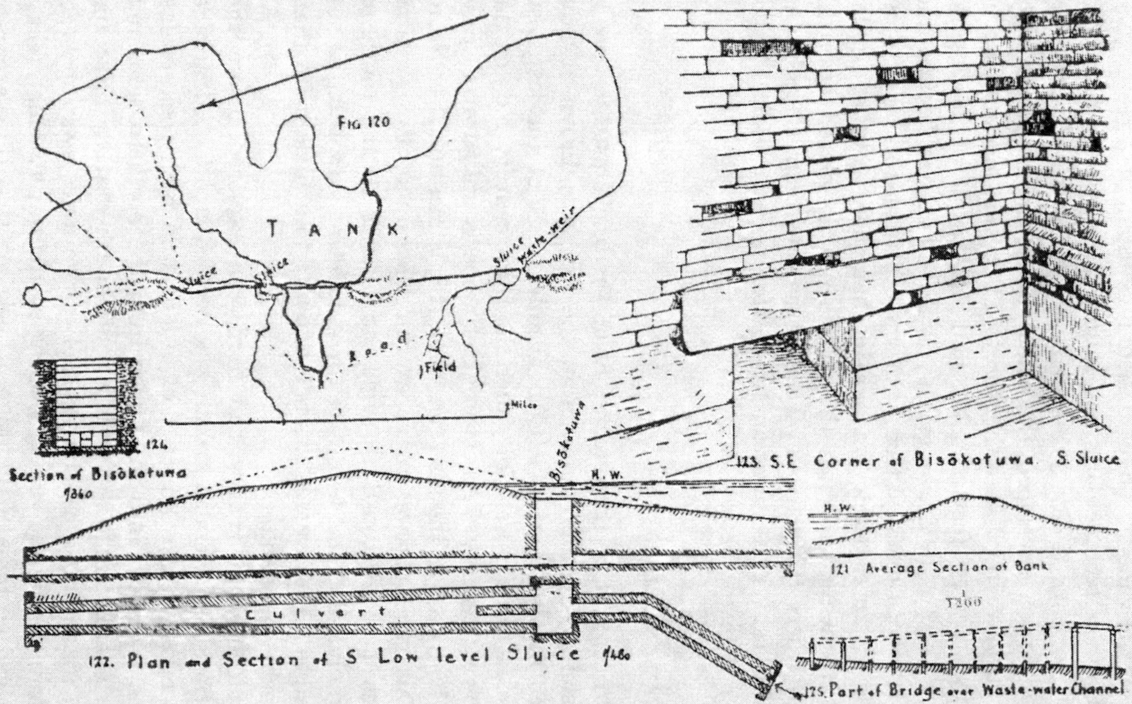

FIGS. 120–125. Pāvaṭ-kuḷam.

site was undoubtedly the best one in the whole valley for the formation of a storage reservoir.

The tank held a depth of 18 feet of water above the sill of the lowest sluice, up to the permanent level of the flood-escape; its area was 2029 acres and its capacity 779 million cubic feet. The scale of the work therefore resembled that of Vavuṇik-kuḷam, but the quantity of earthwork in the bank was much less than at that reservoir. The quality of the soil in the irrigable tract is not so good as at the northern work, and as some difficulty was experienced in providing sufficient space for the passage of floods it is probable that Vavuṇik-kuḷam would be the first to be selected for construction. The sole object of the work was the storage of water for the irrigation of rice fields.

The embankment has a total height of 28 feet in the deeper part of the reservoir; its crest was 8 feet above the permanent water-level. The top is usually about 10 feet wide, but on many sections (at which it may have been worn down) it is from 15 to 25 feet in width. The side-slope on the up-stream face is about 3·2 feet horizontal to 1 foot vertical, and on the outer face 2·6 feet to 1. The engineers were evidently beginning to recognise that it was unnecessary to give the outer face as flat a slope as that of the inner one. The inner slope was protected as usual by a layer of small boulders and wedged rubble stones, extending downwards from the water level. The top has been generally worn down three or four feet below its original level.

In order to allow the passage of floods three places were left open. Owing to the steep ends of the rocky ridges, the designer found it a difficult matter to provide sufficient space for this purpose, and as a matter of fact he must have underestimated the requisite extent; I calculated that with a probable flood of 11,500 cubic feet per second the water would rise within two feet of the crest of the embankment. In such a long bank the settlement or gradual wearing down of the top of the bank to this extent in some places might escape notice, and the result was that the embankment was breached two or three times. The sites of three repaired breaches are visible, one of them being of large size, and at the present day there are two deep ones through which the rivers flow.

At the southern end of the bank there is a flood-escape 125 feet wide in the line of the bank. Its floor and the ends of the embankment at it are covered with large wedged slabs of stone, carefully laid, those on the floor occupying a transverse breadth of 60 feet. This may be a work of later date than the construction of the reservoir.

This 'waste-weir' is provided with a series of pairs of stone pillars, irregular in size and shape, a short one about two feet high being in front of a taller one five or six feet high, and a few inches distant from it. By the aid of these, a temporary dam of sticks and earth could be raised across the waste-weir after the floods had passed, so as to retain an extra depth of two feet of water. This would increase the area of the reservoir to 2400 acres and its capacity to 972 million cubic feet. A road-bridge of stone slabs laid on stone pillars enabled the stream from this flood-escape to be crossed when a considerable volume of water was passing down it (Fig. 125).

The other flood-escapes were simple overflow channels at rocky sites, one being 25 feet and the other 100 feet wide. At the former the ends of the bank are protected by squared stones laid in steps from the floor upwards.

The extent to which the reservoir was utilised may be gauged by its being provided with four sluices, in addition to a high level culvert under the floor of the southern waste-weir. One of these was a high-level sluice near the northern end of the embankment; the others were much lower, one being in the northern bank, another in the southern section, while the remains of the inlet of the third one can be seen near the middle of the work.

The southern sluice was the lowest, and was 18 feet 2½ inches below the level of the waste-weir; the northern low-level sluice was 1 foot 8½ inches higher; the northern high-level sluice was 5 feet 1½ inches above the lowest one; and the culvert at the waste-weir was 9 feet 9 inches above it.

The sizes of the wells at these works were as follows, the longer dimension being the measurement parallel to the line of the bank :—At the southern low-level sluice, 11 feet 2 inches by 8 feet 10 inches ; at the central sluice, about 8 feet square ; at the northern low-level sluice, 8 feet 2½ inches square, and at the northern high-level sluice, 13 feet 8½ inches by 8 feet.

The culvert at the waste-weir was built of stone, and the well of the northern low-level sluice was also lined with stone, with a substantial backing of brickwork. At the others, the well of the central sluice probably, and those of the other two sluices certainly, were built of stone in the lower part,

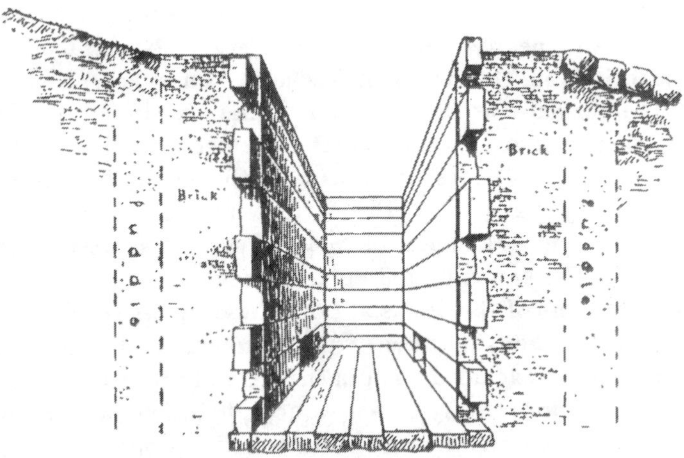

FIG. 126. Bisōkoṭuwa. N. Low-level Sluice.
(One end removed.)

with a backing of brickwork, but after the first two or three courses were finished in brickwork only, the side of the southern low-level sluice adjoining the central line of the embankment being, however, faced throughout with stone slabs (Fig. 124). All the brickwork was laid in excellent mortar made with lime burnt from coral. The stonework in all the sluices is of the type of all later works, and consists of long thin slabs of considerable breadth, passing from one side of the wells to the other when laid in their walls. These slabs were placed on edge when used as linings of the wells, and in all sites they were fitted together with great care. The faces and beds of the stones were well, though not finely, dressed, but the backs were left rough (see Figs. 124 and 126).

The dimensions of the bricks employed in the low-level sluices provide the only clue to the age of the reservoir. At the southern low-level sluice their length was 17·36 inches, the breadth 8·60 inches, and the thickness 2·89 inches; Bt. was 24·8 inches, and the contents 433 cubic inches. The size clearly points to some date not later than the early part of the first century B.C. The figures agree very closely with those of the Sandagiri dāgaba at Tissa, which was built by King Kāka-vaṇṇa-Tissa in the first half of the second century B.C., and they are also nearly those of other very early dāgabas.

The bricks in the northern low-level sluice may be of a slightly later date, as the variations in the length and breadth prove that moulds of a different size were used for them, that is, that they were not burnt at the same time as the others. They have a length of 16·70 inches, a breadth of 8·29 inches, and a thickness of 2·94 inches; Bt. is 24·4 square inches and the contents 408 cubic inches.

The thickness of the bricks at both these sluices is relatively much greater than in those of the Lankārāma dāgaba, and if that work be excluded the dimensions indicate some period either in the third century, or—if we accept the Sandagiri bricks as our guide—in the second century B.C. Considering the advanced type of the designs for the sluices, the latter is the more probable time.

The southern low-level sluice was of special interest. The unbroken state of practically all the bricks used in the face of the well, and the fact that they were all of one size, prove that this part of the work was the original structure, just as it was left by its builders.[1] When I saw it twenty-four years ago, it was still fulfilling the purpose for which it was constructed, although the culvert was damaged; and a small

[1] Mr. R. A. Powell, of the Public Works Department, the engineer who supervised the re-construction of the sluice, has informed me that in the 'backing' of the brickwork he found bricks of several sizes. This must indicate some subsequent repairs to that part of the work, although the lining or face of the walls appeared to be intact.

rice field was supplied with water which passed through it. It is greatly to be regretted that it was taken down and rebuilt according to an 'improved' design a few years afterwards, when the reservoir was partly restored by the Public Works Department. This is the more to be lamented for the reason that in all likelihood it was the only work of the kind of such an age in the island, unless the sluices at Vavuṇik-kuḷam are also in their original state.

As in all later sluices, the work in this one consisted of three parts, (1) a rectangular open well built near the point where the water level met the inner slope of the embankment, (2) an inlet culvert through which the water passed into this well, and (3) a discharging culvert from the well to the foot of the outer slope of the bank.

The well is called in Ceylon a *bisō-koṭuwa*, which literally means 'Queen-enclosure,' but probably would be more correctly termed *bisi-koṭuwa*, 'the enclosure where (the water level) lowers.' The sketch (Fig. No. 123) shows the manner in which the inner work of three of the sides was built at this sluice. The flooring was formed of long well-fitted slabs of cut stone, like those in the walls. I do not know the thickness of the brick walls; at other sluices it is often from five to six feet. Mr. Powell stated that the walls were surrounded by very good clay 'puddle' for a thickness of two feet or more, and that the brickwork was of such excellent quality that he could not avoid regretting that he had been instructed to pull it down. This well was 14 feet deep; originally it was probably built up to the level of the flood escape, that is, a little more than 18 feet above the sill level.

The inlet culvert was 52 feet 6 inches long, and had a peculiar bend in its line, as shown in the plan (Fig. 122). I have seen nothing of the kind elsewhere. Across its entrance there was a block of brick masonry 7 feet thick and 9 feet long, which rose 6 feet high above the sill of the culvert and had foundations 3 feet 6 inches deep. No similar construction has been seen at other works. The culvert was rectangular, 2 feet wide and 2 feet 6 inches high at the inlet, and 2 feet 6 inches wide and 3 feet 6 inches high at its junction with the bisōkoṭuwa or well. It had walls 2 feet thick, and was covered by slabs about 9 inches thick. Its floor was at the level of the bottom of the well.

The outlet or discharging culvert was of a very interesting form. For a length of 14 feet 6 inches it was divided into two culverts, each 2 feet square, separated by a wall 2 feet thick (Fig. 124). From the end of these double passages their outer walls were continued in straight lines to the outside of the embankment, gradually approaching each other until they were 2 feet 6 inches apart at the outer end. The height of the passage for the water was, however, gradually increased from 2 feet until it became 3 feet 6 inches at the end of the culvert. The walls were 2 feet thick, and on them were laid large coverstones of varying thicknesses, from about 9 inches to a foot; these were from 5 feet 9 inches to 8 feet long, or more, and like those of the floor were dressed on the face and sides. Across the outer end of this culvert there was a brick wall like that at the inlet, 6 feet high and 12 feet long. The culvert walls were built throughout of large stones, well dressed on the faces, ends, and beds, and fitted together very carefully. For all these measurements of the culverts I am indebted to the drawings of them made when the new work was about to be built.

When compared with later sluices, practically the only difference occurs in the form of the inlet. In most sluices the inlet channel is a very short one, and in large works its entrance is protected by a high wall across it, with sloping wings built at a batter, to support the soil at each side of the approach to it. The increase in the height of the discharging culvert from the well to the outlet occurs at some large works only; in most cases the section remains the same throughout. It is astonishing to find this early work adhering so closely to the best type of later designs.

No means of regulating the out-flow of the water is visible at any of the ancient sluices in Ceylon, and considerable speculation has arisen regarding the purpose for which the wells were invariably built across the line of the culverts, in the up-stream slope of the embankments. It has been thought that the intelligent engineers who designed these great works may have believed that the culvert was relieved from internal pressure caused by the water in it, when the water was allowed to rise freely in these open wells. This opinion is easily proved to be incorrect. The bisōkoṭuwas, as I prefer to term the wells (the word 'well' usually implying a work with a very different function), are much larger than would be needed for such a purpose, and at the northern high-level sluice at Pāvaṭ-kuḷam we find a larger one than at the low-level sluices. Even when other arrangements were adopted which would really tend to relieve the culvert from excessive pressure—as by enlarging its sectional area from the well to the outlet—we still find the well always present.

As one whose duties permitted him to gain an intimate acquaintance with the ancient works, I have never concealed my admiration of the engineering knowledge of the designers of the great irrigation schemes of Ceylon, and the skill with which they constructed the works; and my friend and predecessor the late Colonel C. Woodward, R.E., expressed the same opinion to me more than thirty years ago, when recommending me to study them thoroughly. When we find, therefore, that the open well is never absent at any sluice in a reservoir, excepting only such works as the culvert under the Pāvaṭ-kuḷam waste-weir, we may safely conclude that it fulfilled a very important function.

Since about the middle of last century, open wells, called 'valve-towers' when they stand clear of the embankment and 'valve-pits' when they are in it, have been built at numerous reservoirs in Europe. Their duty is to hold the valves, and the lifting-gear for working them, by means of which the outward flow of the water is regulated or totally stopped. Such also was the function of the bisōkoṭuwa of the Sinhalese engineers; they were the first inventors of the valve-pit, more than 2100 years ago.

It will be readily understood that in an age when iron-casting was unknown, and even the smallest plates of iron could be heated only with difficulty in the early forges, no iron or iron-bound sluice valves were made, and that it must have been no easy task to control the out-flow of the water at reservoirs which had a depth of thirty or forty feet, as was the case at several of the larger works. Yet the similarity of the designs of the bisōkoṭuwas at all periods proves that the engineers of the third century B.C., if not those of an earlier period, had mastered the problem so successfully that all others were satisfied to copy their designs.

An examination of the bisōkoṭuwas reveals two invariable and peculiar features in them: they are always rectangular, and the faces of their walls are never rough or uncut. The commonest type of them is an oblong enclosure, ten or twelve feet long by eight or ten feet wide, built across the culvert at a short distance nearer the water than the point where the water-level meets the slope of the bank. It has thick walls of brickwork laid in mortar, round which there is an excellent watertight backing of tempered clay, or 'puddle. Where the plan is an oblong the longest sides are always built across the culvert. At most works the brickwork is faced or lined inside the well with admirably cut thin slabs of stone, laid horizontally, and invariably on their edges, which fit closely together. Usually they extend as monoliths along the whole length of each wall, and all have well-cut faces, free from any twist. In some cases there is no facing to the brickwork.

The wedging and accurate cutting of these long stone slabs, which are always of gneiss, must have proved a difficult work in pre-Christian times; we may guess that their preparation was the most arduous part of the construction of the sluices. As they have rarely a greater thickness than ten or twelve inches, even when they are two or three feet broad, and ten or twelve, or more, feet long, while the brick wall behind them is often six feet thick, it is clear that in most cases they were not used merely in order to increase the strength of the wall. They may have been inserted partly to protect the front of the brickwork, but the accurate cutting of their faces shows that this was not their only purpose.

In my opinion they were intended to permit the accurate

fitting, close to the face of the wall, of a further lining of woodwork. This alone will account for the excellent manner in which their faces were cut. It would transform the well into a nearly watertight box.

At a few sluices I have observed indications of the manner in which other woodwork was fixed inside these wells. It was evidently in the form of substantial beams or posts, the duty of which must have been partly to support the wooden lining of the walls, and partly to carry some form of lifting-gear by which a door or valve might be raised or lowered, so as to regulate the discharge of the water.

This part of the woodwork appears to have varied in design at different sluices, but generally there was a vertical post about one foot square on each side of the entrance to the outlet culvert. These must have been supported by horizontal beams which also held up the wooden lining of the walls, some of them probably resting against other wooden posts standing near the corners. At one sluice at Minnēriya tank, a work of the third century A.D., square sockets were cut in the floor in order to receive tenons left at the ends of the vertical posts.

At a bisōkoṭuwa at Kaṭiyāwa, in the North-central Province, which tradition attributes to the time of Duṭṭha-Gāmiṇi, that is, the second century B.C., there are two lateral recesses, two feet square, at the lower corners of the side walls next to the centre of the bank. In this, as at some few other sluices, there is a wide step of ashlar work in the bisōkoṭuwa, at each side of the inlet culvert, extending up to the side walls; its use is unknown. There is also a cut ten inches wide through the projecting coping stone, above the entrance to the outlet culvert. The age of the work is indicated by the bricks at another sluice; these are of the large type which belongs to the second half of the second century B.C., or the first part of the first century.

Wooden doors or valves, which might slide vertically in wide grooves, must have been placed so as to open or close both the culverts leading out of the wells. Most probably these were worked by means of levers supported by upright posts.

It must have been in order to reduce the friction at these valves that, while there was a single inlet culvert at Pāvaṭ-kuḷam, there were two outlets for discharging the water from the bisōkoṭuwa, each having a sectional area rather less than half that of the inlet, and thus permitting the use of a door or valve of much smaller size than would be otherwise necessary. This is unmistakable evidence that difficulty had been experienced in other works, before Pāvaṭ-kuḷam was made, in overcoming the friction due to the pressure of the water on valves of larger area. A similar arrangement is found at many later works.

As no example of the woodwork of the sluices has been preserved, its exact details can only be conjectured; but it is clear from the indications given above that the purpose of these carefully-built bisōkoṭuwas was to act as true valve-pits. Whatever form the design took it was a triumph of the ingenuity of the ancient Sinhalese engineers, and the more surprising when we find one of the earliest sluices furnished with it. Evidently from the first it was a device the general form of which later generations were unable to improve.

It was this invention alone which permitted the Sinhalese to proceed boldly with the construction of reservoirs that still rank among the finest and greatest works of the kind in the world.[1] Without some efficient means of regulating the discharge of the water through the sluices, the provision of reservoirs for storing it could never have extended beyond the minor tanks. Thus, it may be inferred that the bisōkoṭuwa, with its valves, had not only been designed but had been found to work satisfactorily before the engineers would venture to undertake the construction of Pāvaṭ-kuḷam and Vavuṇik-kuḷam, both of which in many years would be of limited use without it. Whether the works of Paṇḍuwāsa Dēva or Paṇḍukābhaya were furnished with this means of

[1] There are eight or nine post-Christian reservoirs in Ceylon which have areas exceeding 4000 acres; detailed surveys have been made of one (Maha Kanadara-waewa) which covered 5670 acres, and of another (The Giant's Tank), which was not completed, that apparently would have had an area of 6400 acres; as now restored, the latter covers 4425 acres with water at a very low level.

regulating the outflow of the water is unknown. In any case it appears to date from either the fourth or the third century B.C.

Every engineer must feel astonishment to observe that the designer of this early sluice enlarged the sectional areas of his inlet and outlet culverts from their entrances to their outlets. He was evidently aware that as the water passed along the culverts the friction of the sides retarded its velocity, and thus rendered an increased space for it necessary in order to avoid undue pressure against the sides and roof. Without such enlargement the resulting increased pressure would tend to force the water through the joints of the masonry, along the back of which it would then flow, gradually removing the soil in suspension until in the end the bursting of the reservoir might be brought about. It is extremely likely that the existing breach at the great Padawiya tank was caused in this manner, and I feel no doubt whatever that other embankments gave way from the same cause; but the designer of Pāvaṭ-kuḷam cannot have had many opportunities of observing such effects, and it is therefore the more surprising to find him taking these precautions against them.

The use of well-tempered clay 'puddle' round masonry that was subject to water-pressure was perfectly understood at the time when Pāvaṭ-kuḷam was constructed. It continued to be employed in similar positions at nearly all later sluices, and sometimes round the culverts also. It was always of excellent quality.

Sangili Kanadara-waewa

A smaller reservoir for storing water for irrigating rice lands was formed at an early date in the valley of the Sangili Kanadara-oya, a small river on the eastern side of the Malwatta-oya valley. It had not special features like the last, but was a good average example of a class of reservoirs made solely for irrigation, and occupying a position between the larger village tanks and the great works like those last described.

The embankment, instead of running straight across the bed of the valley as usual, was raised for a great part of its length in a north-and-south curve, having its convex side facing the reservoir. Its northern end was turned towards the west for 2000 feet, so as to carry part of the flood-waters clear away from the work; its southern end, on the other hand, was deflected sharply eastwards for 1700 feet, to meet high ground.

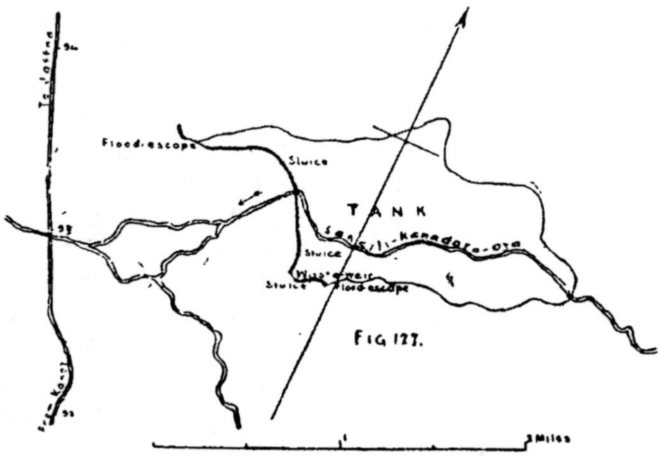

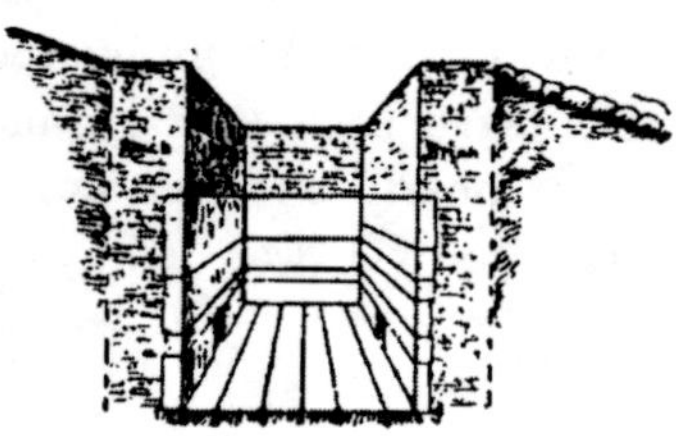

128. Section of Bisokotuwa

129. Section of Waste-weir

FIGS. 127–129. Sangili-kanadara Tank.

The bank has a total length of 8100 feet, or about a mile and a half; and its crest was 17½ feet above the sills of the low-level sluices. Its top was 10 feet wide; and the sides sloped on the up-stream face at about 4 feet horizontal to 1 foot vertical, and on the outer face at 3·5 feet to 1. The slope adjoining the water was protected by small boulders up to a height of one foot above the level of the waste-weir.

There were three sluices,two at about the same level being in the deeper part of the bank, and one at a slightly higher level near the middle of the southern arm. The middle one (Fig. 128), of which only I have particulars, had a rectangular bisōkoṭuwa 10 feet 5 inches long, parallel to the bank, and 6 feet 3½ inches wide. There was a single rectangular stone culvert, 13½ inches wide and 12 inches high in the inlet portion, and 12½ inches wide and 12 inches high in the outlet part, the latter being raised 3½ inches above the floor of the bisōkoṭuwa. The walls, 9 feet 5 inches high, were built of brickwork, and their lower part, for a height of 5 feet 10 inches, was lined with thin monolithic stone slabs, laid on edge.

The brickwork portion of the sluice was repaired or rebuilt several times, there being bricks of four different sizes in it. Some which were 2 inches thick belonged to the tenth or twelfth century A.D., and point to the last restoration of the work.

Others, 17 inches long and 2·33 inches thick, may have been burnt in the first or second century A.D. Those of a third type were 18·18 inches long, 9·12 inches wide, and 3·22 inches thick, Bt. being 29·3 and the contents 534 cubic inches. These belong to the period of very large bricks, extending over the second half of the second century B.C. and the early years of the first century.

The fourth type had a length of 17·75 inches, and a thickness of 2·75 inches, Bt. was 24·4, and if the width was half the length the contents would be 433 cubic inches. Apparently these bricks cannot belong to the same period as the last ones, and if, as is probable, they are of prior date, they may have been burnt in the third century B.C. It is possible, therefore, that the reservoir may have been constructed at that early period. The flat slopes of the bank also indicate a very early date.

Three flood-escapes were provided; one at the northern end of the bank, measuring 450 feet in width, but probably scoured out and much widened by floods; one at the southern end about 80 feet in width, these being on the natural surface of the ground; and a waste-weir of stone masonry built in the angle at the commencement of the southern arm of the bank. Most probably this was of later date than the original formation of the reservoir. It was 270 feet long, and in its form of construction it resembled many subsequent works of the kind (Fig. 129).

In the deepest part it had five courses of wedged and partly-cut stones, the top one being 27 inches deep at the outer face, and the others 18 or 20 inches; each course was set back 3 inches from the face of the course below, and was sunk an inch deep into it. The top of the weir was 17 feet wide, and it had a backing, along the side adjoining the tank, of brickwork apparently laid in mud, to prevent leakage through the stonework. At a distance of 10½ feet from the outer face there was a row of dwarf cut-stone pillars, about 12 inches square and 2 feet 7 inches high, fixed in the top of the weir at irregular distances, which ranged from 10½ feet to 17 feet. These were evidently placed there in order to assist in raising a temporary dam of sticks and earth after the floods had ceased, so as to retain an additional depth of perhaps 2 feet of water in the reservoir, an extremely hazardous proceeding when the level of the crest of the weir was itself dangerously near that of the top of the embankment.

The crest of the weir was 13 feet 6 inches above the sills of the low-level sluices, and the top of the bank was only 4 feet higher. At the weir level the area of the reservoir was 800 acres, and its capacity 200 million cubic feet. With an extra depth of 2 feet of water temporarily retained, the area became 918 acres, and the capacity 275 million cubic feet. The tank has recently been restored with a water-level about 2 feet below the original height of the weir, and an area of 646 acres, which was probably nearly the primitive size of the work.

The Southern Reservoirs

During the third century B.C., King Mahā-Nāga, the brother of Dēvānam-piya Tissa, and tributary king of southern Ceylon, appears to have formed a reservoir called Tissa-vāpi, at his capital, Māgama. He or his immediate successors, in the

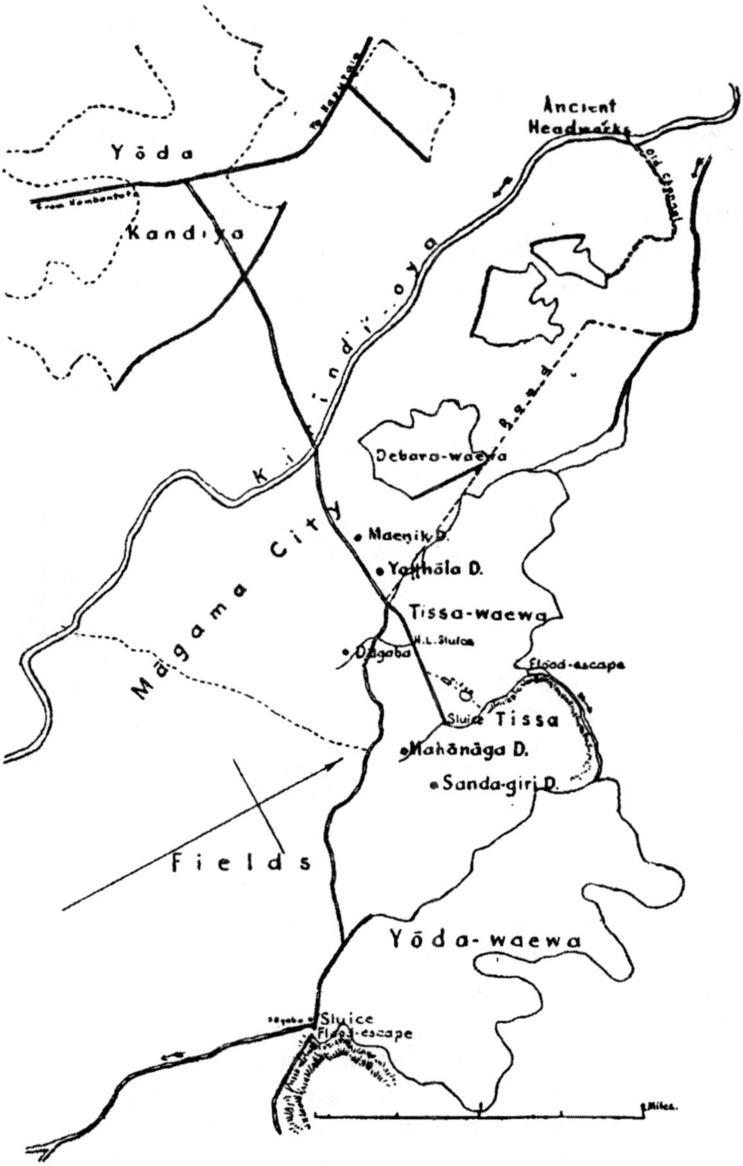

FIG. 130. Tissa, S.P., and its Tanks.

latter part of that century or the first half of the second century B.C., constructed also the Dūratissa-vāpi, 'the Far Tissa' tank, as well as another called Dīgha-vāpi, 'the Long Tank.' To these may probably be added one now termed Yōda-kandiya, 'the Giant Embankment,' the original name of which is unknown.

TISSA-WAEWA

The southern Tissa-waewa was made in a shallow valley about a mile and a half east of the Kirindi river, which flowed

FIG. 131. Tissa-waewa, S.P.

past the capital. The town occupied the ground between the reservoir and the river, and for some distance lower down the valley, and also extended on the eastern side of the tank. The chief purpose of the work was the storage of water for the use of the city; it is not certain that any rice fields were irrigated by means of it, at any rate in very early times.

Although the area from which water flows into the reservoir is very small, being only some five square miles, it is considerably larger than that of Abhaya-waewa, at Anurādhapura. The rainfall amounts to about 47 inches per annum. The early designer of the work evidently gave this matter careful consideration, and decided that under such conditions it would be safe to allow a smaller margin than usual between the water-level and the crest of the bank; he fixed this at 5 feet, and his opinion has been justified by later experience.

The reservoir was formed by raising a straight bank about half-way across the bed of the valley until it met a low ridge with two slight elevations on it. From that point it was deflected slightly up-stream, so as to follow this ridge and save earthwork.

In the first century A.D., King Iḷa-Nāga (38–44 A.D.) improved the appearance of the work by abandoning the ridge, and in place of it continuing the straight portion of the bank in one line to the eastern side of the valley. The mounds on the ridge now form two small islands.

As there is no record of its restoration, the tank may have remained in working order until the end of the twelfth century, beyond which time the histories do not contain any references to Māgama. At last, however, probably owing to continued neglect of the ordinary works of maintenance, it was breached; and the town, which had evidently dwindled into an unimportant settlement, was totally abandoned, the residents being too apathetic to carry out the small and simple work of repair that was necessary. The whole bed of the reservoir, the embankment, and the former rice fields or the lands on the low side of the bank, as well as the site of the old city, then became gradually overspread by a thick forest growth, infested by wild buffaloes, elephants, and bears. It is clear that the breaching of the embankment must have occurred several centuries ago.

The embankment was about three-quarters of a mile long, and after King Iḷa-Nāga's improvements was practically straight from end to end. It had a top which appears to have been always used as a cart-road (as at present), and was from 15 to 20 feet wide, with the flat side slopes that characterise many other early works. The inner slope was at the rate of about 5·1 feet horizontal to one foot vertical, and the outer one 4·4 feet to one. The level of the highest part of the bank was about 18½ feet above the bed of the reservoir, in which apparently a depth of 13½ feet of water was retained, the area covered being 652 acres and the resulting capacity 160 million cubic feet.

I have met with no reference to any sluice at this reservoir. In one built in 1871, and afterwards replaced by a larger one, there were no stones of the kind that one would expect to find if the materials of an old bisōkoṭuwa had been utilised in it. It is possible that a small brick sluice may have been constructed long after the original works were made.

A single escape for floods, about 100 feet wide, was left at the natural ground level on the eastern side, half a mile from the bank, behind some high ground against which the end of the bank abutted. From this, surplus water passed down a depression for three-quarters of a mile, and entered another reservoir now called Yōda-waewa, which appears to be the Dūratissa tank of the histories.

At the restoration of Tissa-waewa in 1871, as a great part of the top was found to be much worn away the higher parts of the bank were cut down to the extent of three feet, and the depth of water retained was ten feet. After more than a quarter of a century, however, it was found necessary to raise the water level once more to what seems to have been the height originally fixed by the old Sinhalese engineers. This is a high mark of appreciation of the excellence of their designs and their suitability under the conditions which control such works.

The reservoir was of such vital necessity to the city that after experience had proved that it often remained unfilled during dry years, important measures were adopted in order to ensure its getting a better supply of water. For this purpose a permanent stone dam was erected across the Kirindi-oya, the river which flowed past the capital, at a distance of two and a half miles from the upper part of the tank. A short shallow channel, with a bed about ten feet wide, was then opened from a point immediately above it in the river, up to a site whence the water conveyed by it could flow into the tank by gravitation, without further works beyond the closing of a hollow which led back to the river. The age of this part of the scheme is unknown, but it must be an extremely early work, and possibly the dam was the first one of the kind built in Ceylon.

The stones of the dam had been removed before I visited the place; but a few notes on it, in a Report written in 1858 by Mr. G. D. B. Harrison,[1] are of interest. It was then altogether broken down by floods. He stated that it had had a height of fifteen feet, and that it 'was built of large roughly-hewn blocks of stone, few of which are less than a ton in weight,

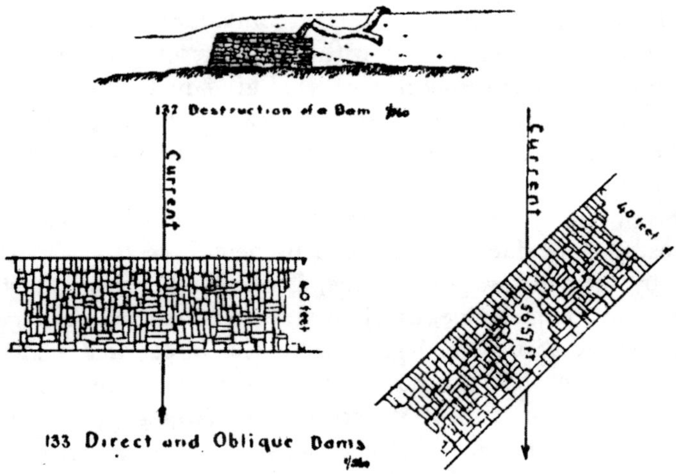

FIGS. 132, 133.

while many are far more. They appear to have been set dry, or without being imbedded in any mortar. . . . A great volume of water must have passed over the anicut [dam] during the rainy season, and carried with it large trunks of trees, with a force sufficient to destroy anything but the most massive masonry.' Floods, or rather the impact of the great tree trunks that they brought down, did, in fact, eventually destroy the dam, as well as nearly every other work of the kind in Ceylon.

The body of water which is approaching a dam built across a river extends considerably below the level of the crest; but

[1] Report of the Irrigation Commission, 1867, p. 229.

immediately before arriving at the up-stream face of the masonry the lower part of the moving water rises so as to pass over it. With it rise any bodies that were being carried near the surface, such as large trunks of dead trees ; these are tilted obliquely upwards, and at that angle may strike the upper stones of the face of the dam. In that case, when the water is moving with great velocity and the tree trunk is very large—(I have seen one of over ten tons stranded on one of these dams)—there is great probability that one of the stones of the top course will be displaced as in Fig. No. 132. It is in this manner that the ancient Sinhalese masonry dams have been breached almost without exception. Among the numerous ancient structures of this kind in Ceylon I have observed all stages of this destruction, from the displacement of the first stone on the up-stream face to the total demolition of the work.

The special point of interest in the Kirindi-oya dam is the astonishing fact that instead of being taken across the river by the shortest possible line, as one would expect, it was built at an oblique angle, which, from the traces I saw, I judged to be nearly forty-five degrees from the direct line. There is a possibility that this does not prove that the principle of the oblique dam, and of its greater discharging power than one built square across a river—the knowledge of which was only acquired in comparatively recent years in Europe—was understood in Ceylon in very early times ; Mr. Harrison, in commenting on this oblique dam, stated that in India there was an idea that one built at such an angle would be less exposed to the action of the current than one built square across the river. The Sinhalese possessed profound practical knowledge of the best methods of dealing with water, and the illustrations in Fig. No. 133, of typical dams 40 feet wide, the usual size of the larger ancient works, show clearly that they were correct if they believed that such a dam must have much greater stability than one of the same width built square across a river ; and especially must be more capable of withstanding violent shocks due to the impact of great tree trunks, than the direct dam. It is evident that in the oblique dam the blow of a log carried by the water would have much less tendency to displace a stone than in the other. Nevertheless nearly all the later dams were built square across the rivers, probably because that was the line of the rocks on which they were founded.

It is certain that the dam and its channel are not of much later date than the Dūratissa tank next described, which in many years could not be expected to fill without their assistance.

The Dūratissa Reservoir

This work is first mentioned in the second century B.C.; it is stated that King Saddhā-Tissa (137–119 B.C.) built a wihāra there (Mah., i, p. 128). The construction of the reservoir is not referred to in the histories; it must have been made by a previous ruler during that century, or late in the third century B.C. Its purpose was chiefly the irrigation of rice lands. There is little doubt that this is the reservoir now called Yōda-waewa.

In the first century A.D., King Iḷa-Nāga is stated to have executed some works of enlargement at it. There are also later references to it, the last one being in the reign of Parākrama-Bāhu I (1164–1197 A.D.), when it is included with other large works which he restored; apparently it was then in a breached state.

The embankment, about 3400 feet long, or nearly two-thirds of a mile, was taken in a north-west and south-eastern direction across the mouth of a subsidiary valley to the south-east of the Tissa tank, its south-eastern end abutting against high rocky ground at the point where the valley joins the low lands that stretch for seven miles between the Tissa tank and the sea. The bank was about 14 feet high above the sill of the sluice, and the depth of water retained by it was about nine feet, at which level the area was 1230 acres, and the capacity 336 million cubic feet. The top of the bank was about 15 feet wide, and was doubtless utilised as a cart-road.

A single sluice was built at the south-eastern end of the bank. It consisted of the usual short inlet culvert, bisōkoṭuwa, and two discharging culverts. As restored, probably according to the original dimensions, the inlet culvert was 3 feet 5 inches wide and 2 feet 8 inches high; the bisōkoṭuwa was 13 feet 2 inches wide, in the line of the bank, and 12 feet 6 inches long, in the line of the culverts; and each outlet culvert was 2 feet 6 inches square. These were separated by a pier 2 feet thick. They passed the water into a channel with a base 10 feet 6 inches wide, excavated in decomposed rock. A small dāgaba was built on a rock at the side of this channel; possibly this was at the monastery founded by Saddhā-Tissa. The work in the sluice and culverts was of the usual type of stonework.

A place for the escape of floods was left open at the side of the sluice, between it and the rocky hill against which the end of the embankment abuts. It was only about 60 feet wide. High floods apparently were allowed to escape round the other end of the bank.

The reservoir received its water-supply partly from some short streams that flowed down from adjoining rocky hills, one being about four miles and another six miles in length; but its chief and unfailing source of supply was from the flood-escape of Tissa-waewa, over which the water brought down from the Kirindi-oya dam flowed into Yōda-waewa. After these head-works had been constructed there was little fear of any loss of crops in the lands to which this reservoir supplied water; and it is evident that the prosperity of Māgama was largely dependent upon them.

Since the restoration of the Tissa tank and Yōda-waewa about 7500 acres of wild forest below them have been converted into rice fields; and the place, instead of possessing, as formerly, one of the most deadly climates of the island, is now fairly healthy. Numbers of healthy-looking children are to be seen about the houses of the cultivators. There is no place in Ceylon where a greater change has been effected by irrigation.

Yōda-kandiya Reservoir

This work was formed in a very shallow valley on the western side of the Kirindi-oya, down which a small stream flowed into that river. It is opposite the Tissa tank, on the other side of the valley. Nothing is known of its history, the ancient name having been lost. Its sole object seems to have been the storage of water for irrigating rice lands.

The embankment runs in a general north-west and south-east line, and is 11,400 feet long, or 2⅛ miles; its line forms a long curve and reverse curve, a shape for which there appears to be no special reason in the contour of the ground. The side slopes are extremely flat, and it is this peculiarity that induces me to include it as one of the very early works. On the inner side the rate of inclination was about 7·4 feet horizontal to 1 foot vertical, and on the other about 6·8 feet to 1. The top seems to have been 15 or 20 feet wide; but all is now very much worn down, and when originally made it may have been higher at these places, and therefore narrower at the top. The depth of water retained in the reservoir if, as at the works on the opposite side of the valley, the flood-escape was at a level of five feet below the crest of the bank, was about 12 feet 6 inches. At this level the area was 1407 acres, and the capacity 380 million cubic feet.

No sluice has been discovered in the embankment,[1] which is also so much worn down, except at a few points, that it is impossible to recognise the ancient flood-escape.

Doubtless the work would be of a little later date than those nearer the capital, which have been described last. It must have been carried out after the population of the neighbourhood had increased, and required facilities for the extension of cultivation. It is almost certain that water was obtained from the Kirindi-oya, for filling the tank; but no direct channel into it has been discovered in the thick forest and jungle which covers the valley, although one was taken off from the river at a distance of some two and a half miles above the dam which diverted water to Tissa-waewa. After flowing some distance in a cut channel, the water may have been

[1] Mr. Hamer, the engineer who has charge of the works of restoration that are now being undertaken, informs me that he has not yet dug out the soil in the bed of the main breach. The sluice may have been at this site.

allowed to find its own way into the reservoir by gravitation.

It was in the lands below this work that Gōna-gama was situated, the village near the site at which Wijaya is supposed by me to have landed. The pool which still preserves the ancient name is four or five miles from the tank.

DĪGHA-VĀPI

This reservoir is mentioned in the Mahāvansa (i, p. 93) as being in existence during the reign of Kākavaṇṇa-Tissa, the father of Duṭṭha-Gāmiṇi, that is, some years prior to 161 B.C. Its importance in those early times may be judged from the fact that the king's second son, Tissa, who succeeded Duṭṭha-Gāmiṇi on the throne, was specially stationed at it 'to superintend the agricultural works in progress,'—possibly a reference to the reclamation of the irrigable lands to which it supplied water.

The place is occasionally mentioned in later times. In the middle of the seventeenth century, at the time of the first arrival of the Dutch in Ceylon, the country about it was termed 'a rich, prosperous, and populous district' (Mah., ii, p. 332).

This reservoir has never been satisfactorily identified; but as it was certainly in south-eastern Ceylon, and a work of great importance, there is every probability that it is the tank now known as Kandiya-kaṭṭu or Maha Kandiya, a reservoir which has been supposed to be capable of irrigating 10,000 or even 20,000 acres of rice fields. The 'prosperous and populous' neighbourhood of the work is totally abandoned, with the exception of two small hamlets; all has relapsed more or less into its original wild forest.

According to the topographical survey, the reservoir is supposed to be narrow, but very long in the direction parallel to the bank. It was formed near the foot of the Kandian mountains, by raising a low embankment across a hollow on each side of a central stretch of high ground, so as to retain a great sheet of water that was perhaps six miles in length parallel to the banks, but possibly less than one mile in width on the average. Although so large, it seems to have had a very limited catchment area, but water may have been diverted into it from an adjoining river. I have not visited the place, and therefore cannot describe the works.

The southern part of what is now the Eastern Province was of so much importance in pre-Christian times that it may be accepted as certain that several other reservoirs were in existence there in the first three centuries before Christ. At present, however, there are no data by which they can be identified,[1] and if they are mentioned in the histories their original names are unknown. Some of the works were among the earliest to be restored in modern times, and their masonry structures were pulled down and rebuilt, leaving no trace of their primitive state, of which also no descriptions were preserved.

Batalagoḍa-waewa

In the account of one of the 'Lost Cities,' Parana Nuwara, I mentioned that the reservoir made at it is of pre-Christian date. Its age is proved by the dimensions of the bricks found at its southern sluice, its flood-escape, and a building which may have been a wihāra, close to the southern end of the embankment. Among the nearest dimensions which I have found elsewhere are those of the bricks used in a ahll at Veḍikkināri Malei, a low hill in the Northern Province, where the inscriptions Nos. 41, 42 and 43 of my list are found at some caves, and may belong to the second century B.C. The breadth and thickness of the bricks in the Ruwanwaeli dāgaba at Anurādhapura are also similar. Thus the reservoir was made when the large bricks were in vogue in the second, or early part of the first century B.C.

These sizes are—

	Breadth.	Thickness.	Bt.	Possible Contents.
Southern Sluice .	9·90 ins.	2·83 ins.	28	476 cubic inches.
Flood-Escape .	9·0 (one only)	2·86	25·7	441 ,, ,,
Wihāra . .	9·50 (one only)	3·0	28·5	513 ,, ,,
Veḍikkināri Malei	9·30	2·90	27	470 ,, ,,

[1] Tradition attributes the construction of one or two of the smaller ones to Duṭṭha-Gāmiṇi.

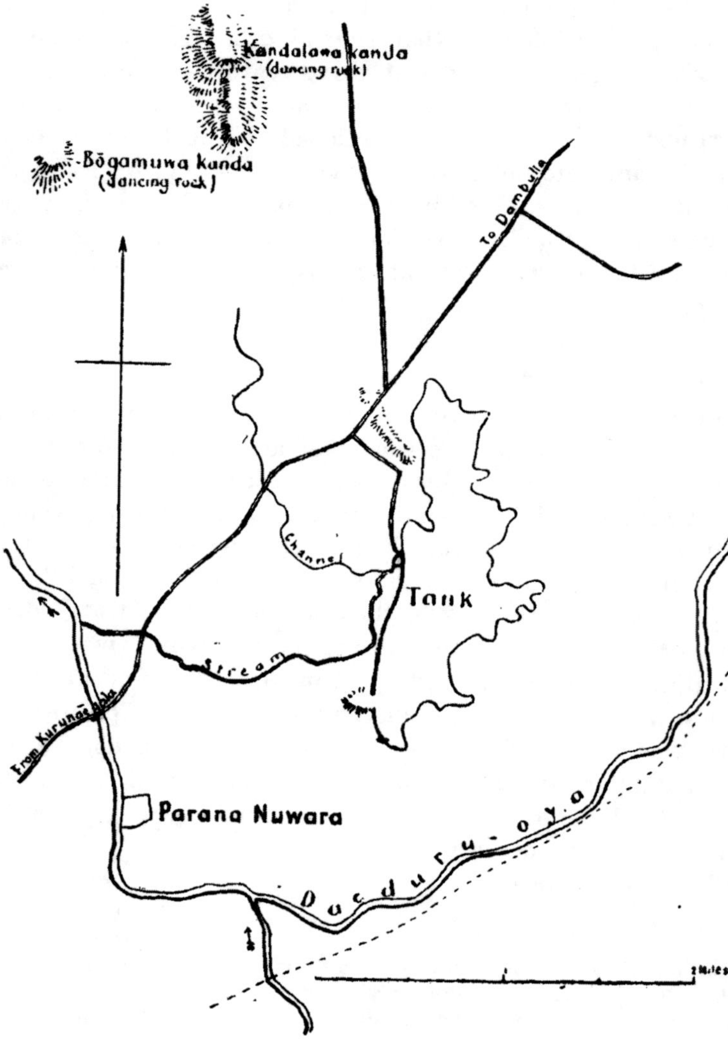

FIG. 134. Plan of Batalagoḍa Tank.

There is a worn inscription in characters of the tenth century on a pillar at the embankment, which indicates that it was then restored, or was in working order; and a longer one on a large slab left there by Queen Kalyānawatī (1202–1208 A.D.), and cut in the third year of her reign, in which she relates that she had examined the sites of 'the known sluices,' and had rebuilt one of them, besides causing three breaches to be filled up.

There is no tradition regarding the date when the tank burst again; possibly it was not very long after the time of its restoration, as part of the embankment was covered with large forest trees when I undertook its repair in 1890.

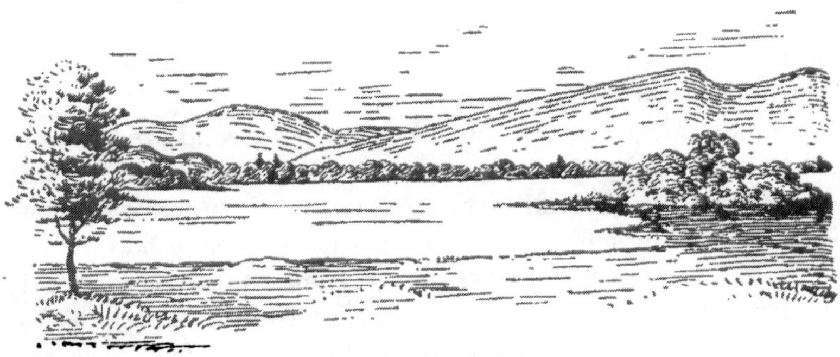

FIG. 135. Batalagoḍa Tank.

The reservoir was doubtless constructed chiefly for the use of the inhabitants of the early city called Paraṇa Nuwara; but partly also for irrigating some adjoining rice fields. The bank blocks up the valley of a minor stream; but instead of taking it square across the stream in the usual way the designer wisely adopted an oblique line, in order to utilise some elevated ground, and effect a saving in earthwork. He merely closed up a hollow on each side of this central high ground, and by doing so made the reservoir of greater capacity than if the direct line across the valley had been followed.

The bank was originally 6000 feet, or about $1\frac{1}{8}$ miles, in length from end to end, but the actual length built was only about 4000 feet. The top was from 10 to 12 feet wide, and the sides sloped at the rate of 3 feet horizontal to one foot vertical in the face adjoining the water, and 2½ feet to one in the outer face. The up-stream face was not protected as usual by a layer of small boulders. The total height was about 30 feet. The top was considerably worn down, so that the original level of the flood-escape was uncertain; if, as is probable, it was 13 feet below the crest, the area of the reservoir was 470 acres, and its capacity 141 million cubic feet. As now restored, the tank covers 635 acres.

The sluices were completely destroyed before the modern restoration. Apparently only the upper eight or ten feet of water were drawn off for irrigating or other purposes. A tradition, to which the inscription of Kalyānavatī appears to contain a reference, states that the reservoir once possessed seven sluices; it seems to have been without any foundation in fact. It is unlikely that there were more than two, one of them being near the southern end.

Floods calculated at 4000 cubic feet per second are expected to be received by the reservoir from a catchment area of only ten square miles, in which the mean rainfall is about 78 inches. The ancient designer of the works, who may have had experience of floods in much drier districts only, must have greatly under-estimated them; and totally inadequate space was left for their escape. The breaching of the embankment on several occasions must have been the result. Bricks of four sizes in the southern sluice show that it had been rebuilt three times, and there were three breaches in the bank at the time of the last restoration, as well as in the thirteenth century. These prove that the floods found their way over the crest of the bank on both occasions.

Nuwara-waewa

It is probably to the early part of the first century B.C. that the construction of Nuwara-waewa, 'The City Tank,' the last of the early reservoirs of Anurādhapura, must be assigned. It is on the east side of the Kadamba river or Malwatta-oya, and a mile and a half distant from the present town, in a shallow flat valley, with a drainage area of about 29 square miles, from which no excessive floods were to be expected, the rainfall amounting to only 55 inches per annum. The work was utilised partly for irrigating rice fields and partly for supplying water to adjoining monasteries and suburbs.

The embankment follows the example of that at Tissa-waewa, Anurādhapura, that is, the higher portion, a mile long, crosses the bed of the valley, while at each side long arms stretch up-stream at obtuse angles, to sufficiently elevated ground to prevent the escape of floods round their ends. At the southern end of the main bank a long mound of high ground rendered any earth-filling unnecessary for three-quarters of a mile; the southern arm began on the opposite side of this. The total length was three miles.

The embankment was 37 feet high in the bed of the valley, above the sill of the low-level sluice, and from 12 to 16 feet wide on the top. The side facing the water sloped downward at the rate of 3 feet horizontal to one foot vertical, to the top of the wedged stonework or 'pitching' that protected the face from erosion; this began at about 4½ feet below the crest of the bank, and was laid at a much steeper inclination, perhaps 1½ or 2 to one. The outer face sloped at about 2½ feet horizontal to one foot vertical. The main bank appears never to have given way excepting at one insignificant breach, which may have been cut, but there is some leakage through the soil under it.

This reservoir was provided with two sluices, one being at a low level, and the other having a sill 3 feet 1 inch higher. At the low-level sluice, the bisōkoṭuwa measured 11 feet in the line of the culvert, and 15 feet in a transverse direction; it had walls 3 feet 6 inches thick, which rose 14 feet above the sill. It was lined with stone slabs.

There were two inlet and two outlet culverts built of stone. The former were only 17 feet 6 inches long, and were separated by a masonry wall 6 feet 6 inches thick; they were 2 feet wide, and 4 feet 2 inches high. An open paved inlet channel, 71 feet 6 inches long and 15 feet wide, led up to them; this had side walls 3 feet 6 inches thick.

The outlet culverts were about 156 feet long, and were separated by a wall 7 feet thick. They rested on a floor 18 inches thick. Each culvert was 2 feet wide and 2 feet 9 inches high; their outer walls were 18 inches thick, and they were covered with large stone slabs.

The bisōkoṭuwa of the high-level sluice was built of brick and not lined with stone; it measured 8 feet 4 inches transversely, and 7 feet 10 inches in the line of the culverts. It was 22 feet high, and had walls 3 feet thick.

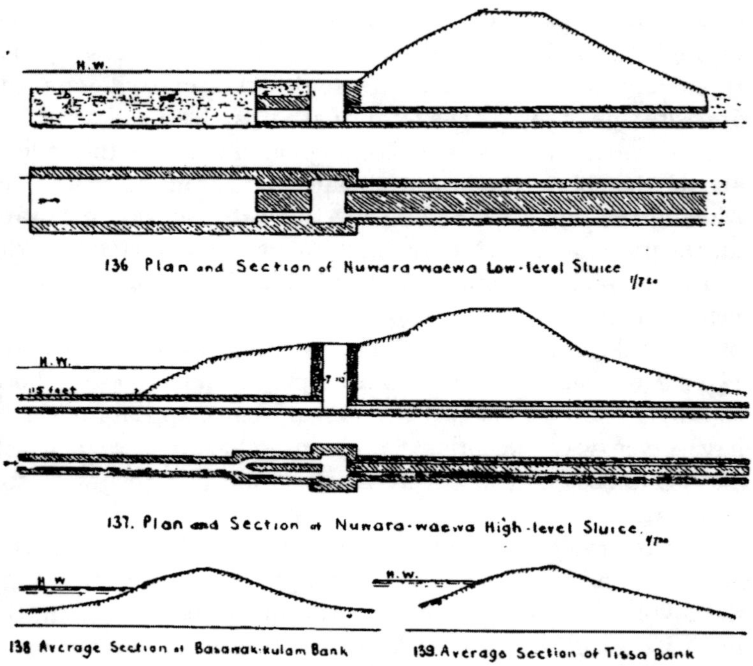

FIGS. 136–139. Nuwara-waewa Sluices, and Anurādhapura Banks.

The inlet culvert was of a peculiar form. It began inside the reservoir, at 115 feet from the toe of the bank, as a single rectangular stone culvert, 2 feet 9 inches high and 2 feet 6 inches wide, with walls and floor 18 inches thick, and cover-stones one foot thick. At 148 feet from its entrance it was converted into two culverts, 2 feet wide and 3 feet high, with the wall between them, the side walls, and floor 2 feet thick, and cover-stones 18 inches thick. These were 25 feet long up to the interior of the bisōkoṭuwa.

There were two outlet culverts, 14 inches wide and 20 inches high, separated by a wall 2 feet 8 inches thick, having side-walls and cover-stones 18 inches thick, and a floor 2 feet thick. They were 154 feet long, and the total length from the entrance of the sluice to the outlet was 335 feet. A thickness of 2 feet of clay puddle was laid round all the masonry. For these particulars I am indebted to drawings of the sluices made by Mr. W. Wrightson, C.M.G., who carried out their restoration.

The bricks used in this sluice afford the only means of fixing the age of the reservoir. I was unable to measure their length; the breadth is 9·85 inches, and the thickness 3·15 inches, Bt. being 31 square inches. If the length was six times the thickness it would be 18·90 inches, making the contents 586 cubic inches. When these dimensions are compared with those of the bricks laid in the Abhaya-giri dāgaba, they are seen to agree extremely closely with them. At the latter structure the length of the bricks is 18·92 inches, the breadth 9·62 inches, and the thickness 3·20 inches; Bt. is 30·7 inches, and the contents becomes 583 cubic inches. I conclude, therefore, that the reservoir was made during the reign of Waṭṭa-Gāmiṇi, in the first twenty years of the first century B.C., or at very nearly that time.

It was repaired at subsequent times. One of these is indicated by bricks which measure 8·48 inches in breadth and 2·64 inches in thickness, to have been about 300 A.D. At a later restoration the bricks were 7·50 inches wide and 2·30 inches thick, a size which points to about the fifth century.

A flood-escape was provided in the high ground to the south of the main bank, at a rocky site. It was 136 feet wide. The sides of the cutting were protected by dry stone walling, probably at a later date than the formation of the reservoir. The permanent depth of water retained appears to have been 17 feet; but it seems probable, as the crest of the embankment was 20 feet higher, that a temporary dam of sticks and earth was raised at the site, so as to hold up a considerably greater depth of water. The top of the stone pitching which protected the slope of the bank is 14 or 15 feet higher than the rock at the flood-escape, a height that would be unnecessary if an additional depth of water had not been retained. Had this not been the case the southern arm of the bank would also not have been required.

With a depth of 17 feet the area was 2160 acres ; at six feet higher, the level now adopted, which appears to have been nearly the former higher level, it became 3180 acres, according to my tracing of the contours. The capacity then was about 1500 million cubic feet.

Immediately after the reservoir was made the flow off the catchment area must have failed to fill it year after year, and an additional supply of water was discovered to be necessary. This was obtained by taking levels—(as we may assume)—up the adjoining Malwatta-oya, until a point was reached sufficiently high to permit water to be diverted from it into the reservoir. Above this spot a ridge of rocky ground approached close to the river, and indicated the most suitable place for the dam which was required. At this site, therefore, a strong masonry dam (Fig. 140) of wedged and more or less cut stones was built across the river.

Nearly all the stones were removed in 1873, for use in a road-bridge that was erected over the river. The remains show that the dam was at least 33 feet wide and nearly 160 feet long ; it was well and solidly built. It rose about 8 feet high above the bed of the river. At the north end, an abutment 10½ feet high, of rough stones, laid in four courses, protected the end of the bank of the channel that was cut for conveying the water to Nuwara-waewa.

From this point a channel about 40 feet wide, capable of passing a depth of four feet of water, was opened till it met with a small stream that flowed into the reservoir, at 5½ miles from the dam. The bed of the channel had a gradient of about one foot in 5000 feet, a slope adopted in several later instances.

At 150 feet from the dam, an escape for floods was provided at a rocky site, in order to pass out surplus water when it entered the channel. This was 44 feet wide, and over it a bridge 12½ feet wide was constructed, supported by two pairs of wooden pillars for which socket-holes were cut in the rock. The ends of the bank at each side were protected by boulders.

At 6 miles, a bridge 154 feet long crossed the stream down which the water flowed. It was carried on three lines of stone posts, fixed in rows of three, which were 6 or 7 feet apart. Over each set of three posts a stone beam about 12 inches square and 10 feet long was placed; on these, longitudinal wooden beams must have been laid, for carrying the planking of the bridge, as shown in my restoration (Fig 141).

The bricks found at the dam are a proof of its age. They are 9·05 inches broad and 3·25 inches thick; Bt. is 30·9, and the length may have been 18 or 19 inches. It is evident that they belong to the period when the larger types of bricks were burnt, that is, that they must belong to the early part of the first century B.C., since they cannot be of earlier date than Nuwara-waewa.

For several centuries the water-supply provided by these works was sufficient for the requirements of the district and the people below them; but at length, as the population increased, it became insufficient in dry years. Doubtless it was observed that in flood times the greater part of the water passed over the dam in the river, and especially that when freshets occurred at times when the water was urgently needed, only a limited part of the flood could be secured.

Nāccādūwa Tank

A careful examination of the valley showed that at 3½ miles below the dam in the river, two ridges projected into it, leaving a gap of only a mile between their ends. In order to increase the water-supply it was then decided to raise an embankment across the valley at this spot, closing up this gap, and impounding the floods in the reservoir thus formed, which is now termed Nāccādūwa. It was a bold scheme, as floods estimated to amount to 14,000 feet per second were to be expected, and there was no suitable rock over which they could be allowed to flow; but it was carried out successfully.

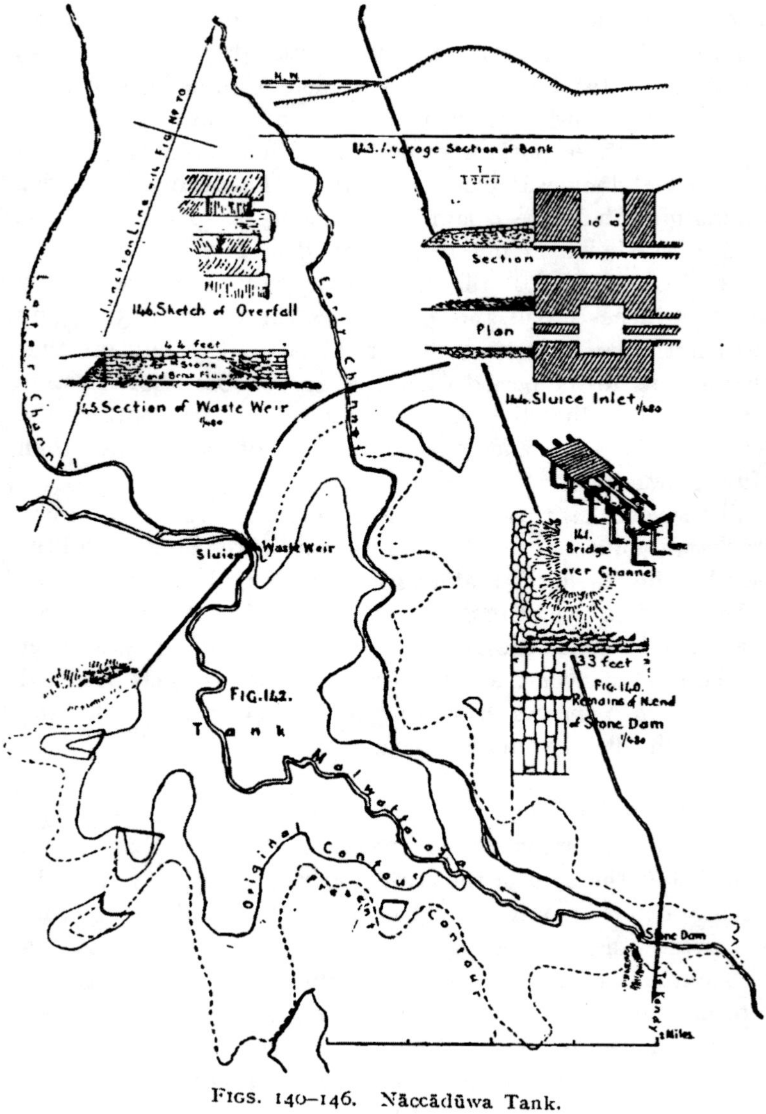

FIGS. 140–146. Nāccādūwa Tank.

The embankment, running nearly north and south, is 5550 feet long, or a little more than a mile. It was 36 feet high above the sill of the sluice, and 55 feet above the bed of the river ; its top was about 20 feet wide, and both the sides sloped at the rate of 2½ feet horizontal to one foot vertical. The slope facing the water was protected by a layer of small boulders.

A single sluice (Fig. 144) was built near the point where the bank crossed the river. It had the usual bisōkoṭuwa, 10 feet 10 inches long in the line of the culverts, and 12 feet 6 inches wide. Its walls were 7 feet thick, but 11 feet thick on the side facing the tank ; they were 16 feet high. The floor, and the walling for a height of 3 feet, were built of stone ; above that level all the work was of brick.

Two inlet culverts, separated by a wall 2 feet thick, passed through the wall of the bisōkoṭuwa. They were 2 feet wide, and according to the drawings under 2 feet high. An inlet channel 9 feet wide, and 27 feet long led up to them. Its sides were protected by sloping walls of rubble stones, built at a batter.

There were two outlet culverts built of stonework, each 22 inches wide and about 18 inches high, separated by a wall 22 inches thick ; they were covered by large thin slabs of stone.

In order to pass out the floods, a fine masonry dam, 44 feet wide at the crest, and 167 feet long (Fig. 145), was built at the point where the embankment abutted against the northern ridge. Its top sloped upward considerably from the back to the overfall, and the back was protected by a mass of brick-work to prevent leakage, although all the inner work of the dam consisted of boulders and wedged stones laid in good lime mortar, as well as brickwork.

In the deeper part, the work in the down-stream face consisted of seven courses of stones from one foot to 19 inches thick, each course projecting two inches beyond the one above it, which was sunk into it for about an inch. The upper course projected six inches, so as to form a coping ; all the stones in it at the overfall were laid as 'headers,' while those at the rear face were 'stretchers.' A peculiar feature, which also occurs at some sluice inlets of stone masonry, was a number of hammer-headed stones laid as headers in the down-stream face, so that the projecting 'head' of the hammer rested against the course above and the course below, to prevent them from moving outward (see Fig. 146).

Stone abutments were built at each end of this dam or waste-weir, with a backing of brickwork laid in lime mortar.

Part of the flood water which escaped over the dam was caught near the point where it rejoined the river, and passed down to Nuwara-waewa, by a channel about 50 feet wide. Possibly other water was permitted to flow down to this channel by a cut opened round the northern end of the waste-weir. Even by this means only limited use can have been made of the reservoir for supplying water to Nuwara-waewa, since only a shallow layer of the upper water can have been drawn off for it; and it is clear that the old channel opened from the dam in the river must have continued to be indispensable. The new tank only supplemented the old works to a small extent; part of its water was used for irrigating the land on the opposite side of the river.

The crest of the flood-escape at Nāccādūwa tank was 21 feet 6 inches below the top of the embankment, and 14 feet 2 inches above the level of the sluice. The tank had an area of 2015 acres, and a capacity of 525 million cubic feet. It is now restored so as to retain an increased depth of 8 feet 5 inches, at which the area is 3920 acres and the capacity 1600 million cubic feet.

The bricks used in the sluice measured 8·50 inches in length and 2·58 inches in thickness, Bt. being 21·8. These are the same dimensions as those of some bricks used in the repairs of the high-level sluice at Nuwara-waewa, and they show that the work at both reservoirs was done at about the same time. According to tradition, Nāccādūwa tank was made by Mahā-Sēna (277–304 A.D.); the bricks strongly support this date.

The upper part of the bisōkoṭuwa was built chiefly of a later type of bricks, which have a length of 12·55 inches, a breadth of 7·40 inches, and a thickness of 2·04 inches; Bt. is 15·1; and the contents 189 cubic inches. They nearly resemble the bricks of the twelfth century found at Polannaruwa, but are not so wide; it is possible that they are of a little earlier date. There are also very large rectangular wedge-holes in some stones of the waste-weir, of a type which I have not found elsewhere excepting in twelfth century work, especially that of the time of Parākrama-Bāhu I. It is probable that he restored the work, and rebuilt the masonry weir.

When we examine the lists of reservoirs constructed by Mahā-Sēna and restored by Parākrama-Bāhu I (Mah., ii, p. 263), we see that if Nāccādūwa be included among them it must be one of two works, (1) the tank called Tissawa, Waḍunnāwa, or Vaḍḍhana, or (2) Mahadāragalla. Of the rest that are found in both lists, I can identify all but the tank called Cīra-vāpi or Walāhassa, the first name of which, meaning 'Small Tank,' shows that it cannot be Nāccādūwa. With another Tissa tank at Anurādhapura, this one is not likely to have been termed Tissawa; thus it may be Mahadāragalla.

How long the reservoir remained in order after the twelfth century is unknown. When the recent restoration was undertaken it had a deep breach at the river, and evidently it had been abandoned for many centuries. The whole bed and the embankment were overgrown with high forest, and I was informed that a year before my first visit two bear cubs were captured inside the bisōkoṭuwa; this will give an idea of the wild state into which the place had relapsed.

Other Early Works

It is stated in the Mahāvansa (i, p. 34) that King Kāla-kaṇṇi-Tissa (42–20 B.C.) 'formed the great canal called Vaṇṇa-kaṇṇa, as well as the great Āmadugga tank,' but neither of these works has been identified, and the history gives no information regarding their position, nor are they again mentioned in it.

A reservoir called Paṇḍa-vāpi is referred to as being in existence during the reign of King Mahā-dāṭhika Mahā-Nāga (9–21 A.D.), and apparently it was made in pre-Christian times; but nothing is known of its construction. The name recurs twice or thrice afterwards in the histories, and especially as that of a reservoir which was greatly enlarged by Parā-krama-Bāhu I, whence it acquired the name Parakkam Samuddā, 'The Parākrama Sea' (Mah., ii, p. 148). As the context shows that it was not in the part of Ceylon over which his cousin Gaja-Bāhu ruled at that time, it may be the great abandoned tank now called Paṇḍik-kuḷam, in the southern part of the Ūva Province, which I have not examined. It is certainly not Paṇḍā-waewa, in the North-western Province.

The measurements of the bricks at some reservoirs of smaller size indicate that they also are of early date; but it is unnecessary in a work of this nature to give a description of such tanks, which cannot be identified in the histories.

Although other works of great interest were constructed at a later period, I include in the present account only the more important schemes which can be shown to have been originated in pre-Christian times.

The Allekaṭṭu Dam

In addition to the Malwatta-oya dam for turning water into Nuwara-waewa, and the Kirindi-oya dam for supplying water to the Māgama tanks, I know of only one other pre-Christian masonry dam across a river in Ceylon. It is termed in Tamil the Allekaṭṭu, and is built across the Kallāṛu, the river that flows from the breaches in Pāvaṭ-kuḷam, and forms the principal feeder of the Malwatta-oya in the Northern Province. The dam is two miles above the road bridge over the Kallāṛu on the road from Mannār to Madawachchiya.

The evidence of its age depends chiefly upon the sizes of the bricks found at it, but partly also on the primitive style of the design. The bricks measure 9·45 inches in breadth, and 3·0 inches in thickness; Bt. is thus 28·3 inches. If the length was 18 inches, the contents would become 510 cubic inches. It is clear that they belong to the period when these large bricks were burnt, in the second half of the second century B.C., or the early part of the first century.

The dam, which is roughly but substantially built, is carried in a north-and-south direction square across the general line of the river, along a ridge of gneiss. It follows the highest line of the rock, and in consequence has two slight bends. Many of the outer stones are roughly dressed, and nearly all are

FIG. 147. The Allekaṭṭu Dam.

wedged into a shape that in section bears at least some affinity to a rectangle. The inner work consists only of round or shapeless boulders, apparently laid without mortar; they may have been embedded in clay, like those at some other works. All the stone was obtained in the bed of the river, close to the site.

The discharging length is 220 feet. The down-stream face is from three to six feet high, and has no batter; it consists of two, three, or four courses. The top of the dam, which is horizontal throughout, is 19 feet wide in the northern part where it is complete, and is formed of six roughly-parallel rows of flat and partly dressed slabs. The northern end has an abutment which is four feet high, and two courses were similarly built at the southern end, with a slight backing of wedged stones and boulders.

Although founded on rock, it was breached by floods in two places, and a third cut was made by them round the southern end.

A small channel was cut on each bank for conveying water to some irrigable land, or perhaps for filling some village tanks lower down the valley.

Four miles higher up the river another early stone dam,

called the Kurinjā-kuḷam Tēkkam, was also built. It is of a rougher type than the last, but may be of later date. Only bricks of a smaller and later size than those at the other work are found at it. A mark of its later date is the upward slope of the top from the up-stream face to the overfall.

This dam is 266 feet long, 20 feet wide at the top, and from 7 to 10 feet high. It consists of roughly-laid gneiss blocks, nearly all being uncut and many being unwedged, which were gathered in the river, close to the work. The down-stream face has a considerable batter. Though rough in construction this dam is still unbreached, but the river has cut a new course for itself down the southern channel that was opened from it, re-entering its former bed after flowing down it for some 800 feet.

Probably there are other works of this kind, of pre-Christian age; but in the absence of bricks of the period of their formation there is no way of identifying them. It is certain that the number is small, since nearly all the river dams of Ceylon exhibit a later type of construction, and consist of masonry laid in lime mortar.

As all the works that I have described are the earliest schemes of the kind, in Ceylon or elsewhere, which can be identified, I have thought it advisable to give exact measurements of them as far as they are available, so as to preserve these in a form suitable for reference by engineers or others who study this subject. The general reader of course cannot be expected to feel much interest in these details, many of which, were they not inserted here, would be lost for ever.

Part III

ARTS, IMPLEMENTS, AND GAMES

XI

THE EARLIEST INSCRIPTIONS

SINCE 1883, when Dr. Edward Müller compiled and published for the Ceylon Government the first complete account of the ancient inscriptions then known in the island, much progress in copying others has been made, especially by Mr. H. C. P. Bell, of the Ceylon Civil Service, the present Government Archaeologist, whose excellent and systematic work is of the greatest antiquarian value in preserving complete records of the constructive and epigraphical work of the ancient Sinhalese. There were numberless sites in the jungle where inscriptions have been cut that neither the lamented Dr. Paul Goldschmidt, who was the first to completely overcome the difficulties attending their decipherment,[1] nor his successor, Dr. E. Müller, had heard of; and up to the present day many fresh inscriptions continue to be discovered, and doubtless others will be found for many years to come. This is especially the case with those inscribed on rocks lying on the slopes of the less known hills isolated in the depths of the wild jungle, and often at considerable distances from any villages. Even where such sites occur in the immediate neighbourhood of the jungle hamlets it is generally found that little is known of them by the inhabitants, who have no inducement to make a systematic search for ancient remains.

It would be easy to mention many instances of the annoying manner in which comparatively long inscriptions elude observation even when in close proximity to others that are well known. On many rocks one may walk over an inscription without suspecting its presence, until some ray of sunlight illuminating one side of the shallow letters and

[1] Translations of some inscriptions had been made by Professor Rhys Davids before that time.

throwing the other into shadow makes the whole stand out in comparative clearness. This fact indicates one of the difficulties of correctly copying the more worn inscriptions. It is often necessary to have light from two different quarters in order to read them; the morning rays to catch one side of some letters, the afternoon rays to display others. It too often happens that the passing archaeologist finds it impossible to devote so much time to the decipherment.

In my own experience an excellent illustration of this difficulty occurred. On two mornings I had examined an inscription (No. **83**) cut on the flat top of a rock at a distance of four miles from my temporary station, and had obtained a satisfactory hand-copy of three lines of it; yet though it was evidently incomplete and I had had considerable practice in copying such letters I failed to see any continuation of it. On paying it a third visit one afternoon I found that the light, falling from a different direction, lit up the whole remaining line in such a manner that it could be copied with ease.

A trained eye is also necessary in order to distinguish slight artificial cuts from the natural markings of weather-worn rocks. On one occasion I pointed out to a friend who had accompanied me a very early shallow inscription about five feet from the ground on a weathered vertical face of a large rock, and proceeded to copy it without difficulty; yet my friend assured me that he was unable to distinguish a single word of it. All appeared to him like the natural hollows in the face of the rock.

Dr. E. Müller ascribed the earliest inscription known in Ceylon up to 1883 to either King Duṭṭha-Gāmiṇi (161–137 B.C.), or to King Waṭṭa-Gāmiṇi (88–76 B.C.); and stated, without giving reasons for his opinion, that the king's title, 'beloved of the Gods,' rather pointed to the latter monarch.[1] The date of the first one known at the present day is certainly the third century B.C., and almost contemporary with those of the celebrated Indian emperor Aśōka.

It is found at a low rocky hill called Nāval Nīrāvi Malei,

[1] *Ancient Inscriptions in Ceylon*, p. 25.

'The Hill of the Jambu Well,' about eight miles north-east of Vilānkuḷam, in the Northern Province. The hill itself is quite inconspicuous and is hidden in the midst of wild thorny

FIG. 148. Tēvāndān Puliyankuḷam Hill.

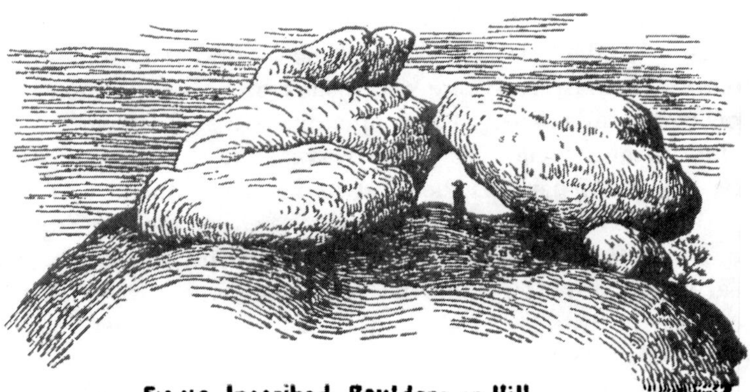

FIG. 149. Inscribed Boulders on Hill.

jungle frequented by bears, three of which, an adult and two cubs, escaped from an open cave at it on the occasion of my first visit to the place. The top of the hill is crowned by rocks and large boulders, a few of which are also on its slopes; the hollows under their sides formed shelters which were improved for the occupation of the monks who took up their residence in them.

There are two other low hills to the south of it, called respectively Tēvāṇḍān Puliyankuḷam Malei, and Ērupotāna-kanda, the three being nearly in a line about one and a half miles long. Ērupotāna-kanda is a hill somewhat like Nīrāvi Malei, but higher, with numerous large boulders on its slopes. The other hill is formed by an immense steep-sided rock, with a high vertical precipice to the east, and a gradual ascent on the north and south-west sides. There are large boulders on its top, which extends in a long north and south line.

On the detached boulders which are scattered about all three hills numerous cave inscriptions are cut, which indicate that this little known part of the island was once the residence of a large community of Buddhist monks. When we seek to learn why such a site should have been selected for cutting what must have been at the time some of the earliest inscriptions in the island, it is found that the explanation seems to lie in the fact that this place was on the line of an early high-road leading from the capital, Anurādhapura, nearly due north-east to the port from which vessels sailed for the eastern coast of India. It is not surprising to find that some of the earliest monasteries were established on this well-known line of communications. The numerous cave shelters and the traditional associations of the Nāval Nīrāvi site caused it to be chosen for perhaps the most important of them. At other rocky hills near the same line there are either early inscriptions or other Buddhist remains; while numerous fragments of an early type of pottery and the early coins found at Mulleittīvu, on the north-east coast, and described in another chapter, prove that this town also was a pre-Christian settlement.

Of the inscription in question fortunately no less than three copies were cut, each over the entrance of a different rock-shelter, or cave, that had been cleared out and prepared for the occupation of the ascetic monks to whose use it was made over. As is seen in other caves that have been used for this

FIG. 150. The Earliest Inscription. (No. 2.)

To face p. 418.

purpose down to the present day, the inside was doubtless whitewashed, or even plastered, and a brick or mud wall was built so as to form a protected or enclosed room under the shelter of the rock. At two of the caves a deep cut, termed a *kaṭāra*, was also made along the rock, above the front of the cave, and for a short distance below this the face of the stone was cut away, as is usual in nearly all such cases, in order to prevent the rain-water that trickled down the front of the upper part of the rock from entering the room. The cave inscriptions are almost always found in this dressed face of the rock, and two of these are also cut in it, each in a single line.

Two copies are cut over caves or recesses at the north side (No. **2**) and south side (No. **3**) of the same rock, a large block standing on the top of the Nāval Nīrāvi hill. Fragments of bricks found at them are of three sizes, 3·10 inches, 2·55 inches, and 2·10 inches thick, indicating the use of the caves and the repair of the brickwork from some pre-Christian date down to the tenth or twelfth century A.D. The third copy (No. **1**) is in a similar position at a cave to the north of the last. Fragments of brick 3 inches thick lie in this cave, which was therefore also occupied in pre-Christian times.

The inscription which I have numbered (**1**) was discovered on a visit that I paid to the hills in 1886 with Mr. G. M. Fowler, who was then the Assistant Government Agent of the district; the other two were found by him on a second examination which he made of the hill in 1887. The hills had been explored some years before our visit by Mr. S. Haughton of the Civil Service, who first drew my attention to the fact that inscriptions were cut at them. He copied a few himself, but was not so fortunate as to discover these earliest ones. I am indebted to him and to Mr. Fowler for copies of all the inscriptions found by them. I have not acknowledged each one separately as I recopied all but one short one myself on subsequent visits.

All the copies of the first inscription made by us were incomplete, owing in two cases to the flaking of the rock, which had destroyed the latter portion of the inscriptions (**1**) and (**3**), this last being cut in the natural face of the rock; and in the other case to the rather faint characters, which were at some height from the ground. At a later date, in 1901, I succeeded in copying these by using a rough ladder in order to reach them.

I give facsimiles of all three from my hand copies, arranged one under the other. The inscription No. **1** is twelve feet long to the point where the stone has given way, and the letters are three inches high. No **2** is fifteen feet long, with letters from two to three inches high, cut about a quarter of an inch deep. No. **3** is fourteen feet long as far as portions of the letters remain, and its full length has been about fifteen feet; the letters in it are four inches high and are a quarter of an inch deep.

(The *e* of *loke* is accidentally missing in the copy.)

The complete inscription is as follows [1]:—

> Raja Naga jita Raja Uti jaya Abi Anuradi ca Raja Uti ca karapitase ima leṇa catu disasa sagaya agatagata na Pasu wiharaye aparim(i)ta loke ditu yasa tana.
>
> Abhī Anurādhī, the wife (of) King Uttiya (and) daughter (of) King Nāga, and King Uttiya have caused this cave to be made for the Community of the four quarters, present or future, at the Pāsu wihāra, an illustrious famous place in the boundless world.

In addition to its age, there are several points of interest in connection with this inscription, the date of which belongs to about the middle of the second half of the third century B.C. In the first place, it confirms the statement of the early annals that King Mahā-Nāga ruled over southern Ceylon with the

[1] In this and other transliterations and names the letter c is pronounced like *ch*, as in 'church'; the vowels *a*, *i*, and *e* have the continental sound; *u* is pronounced as in 'gun'; *ae* represents the sound given to this diphthong in the New Historical Dictionary; *ṭ*, *ḍ*, *ṇ* are hard as in 'dot' and 'ton'; *ḷ* is like *ll* in 'full'; *g* is always hard as in 'gun'; *t* and *d* are distinctly dental; *ś* is very soft, approaching *h*; the other letters are pronounced as in English.

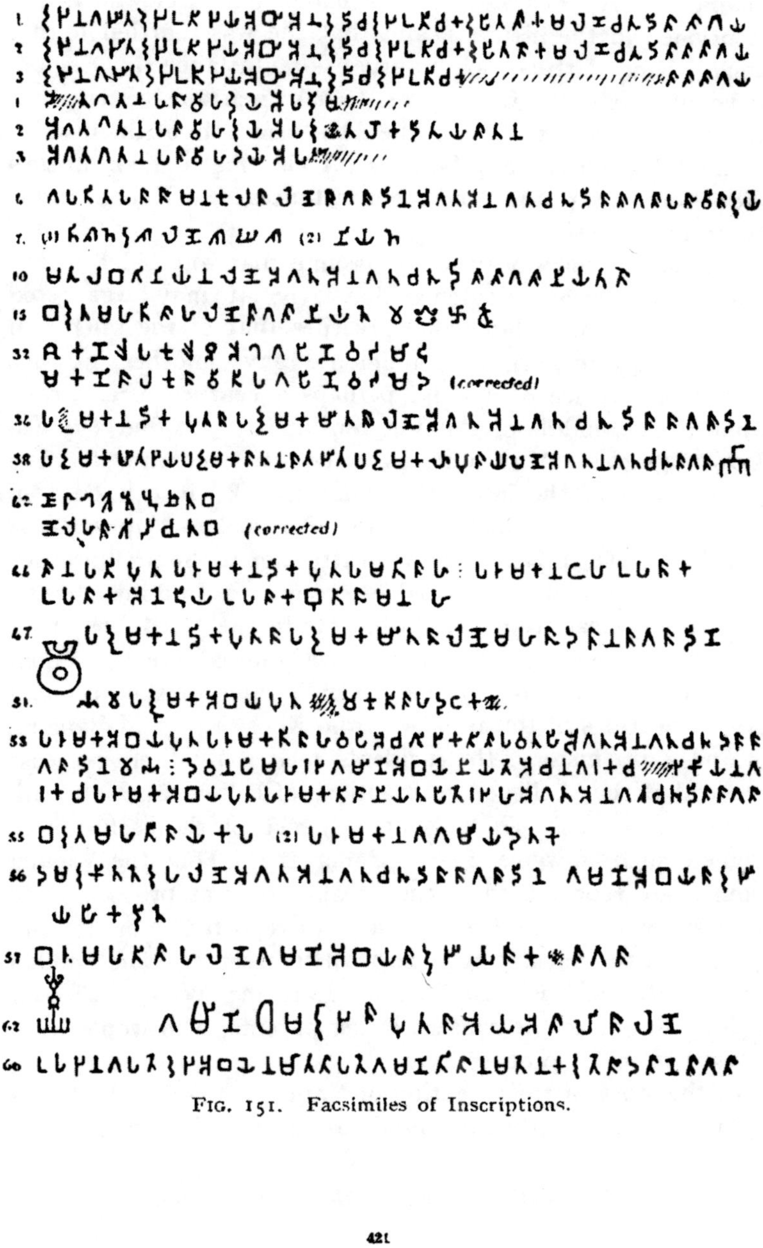

FIG. 151. Facsimiles of Inscriptions.

title of king while his brother was supreme monarch at Anurādhapura. We learn also that he had a daughter who is not mentioned in the histories, and that she was married to her uncle King Uttiya, an unusual circumstance in Ceylon, although Yaṭṭhāla-Tissa appears to have married the daughter of his sister, the latter being the Abhī Anurādhī of the inscription. King Wasabha (66–110 A.D.) also married his uncle's widow (Mah., i, p. 140), and other instances of such connections occur in later times.

We may perhaps venture to assume that some idea of the position of women in Ceylon at that early date may be gathered from the fact that her name precedes that of the king. In dealing with the primitive religion I gave another instance of the precedence of a lady, perhaps a century afterwards; while in the middle of the first century B.C. we find a queen Anuḷā (47–42 B.C.) reigning over the whole country for five years. Also in the inscription numbered **38** it will be seen that the name of a female chieftain, Parumaka Aḷapusayā, is mentioned. Dr. Davids has drawn attention to the circumstance that women are always placed before men in Buddhist texts.[1]

It is also clear from the statements in the Mahāvansa that from the earliest times women were allowed great freedom and independence in Ceylon. Even if some of the accounts are fabrications of the annalists from whose works Mahānāma compiled his history, the incidents related by them at least prove that they believed such actions of ladies of a high rank to be customary. There is no evidence of the seclusion of women, such as we see in the Rāmāyana. Thus the Vaedda women are represented in the Jātaka story as proceeding to meet shipwrecked traders, who are not reported to evince any surprise at their accosting them without reserve. The Vaedda princess Kuwēnī is described as marrying Wijaya without waiting to obtain the consent of her parents, who would have refused it in all probability.

In the story of the reception of Mahinda, the first Buddhist apostle, at the royal palace in about 244 B.C., it is stated that

[1] *The Questions of King Milinda*, p. 83, note.

King Tissa sent for Anuḷā, the wife of his brother, the King Nāga of this inscription, and apparently the mother of Queen Abhī Anurādhī, and probably also Tissa's own sister,[1] to hear him expound the doctrine of Buddha. 'The said princess Anuḷā proceeding thither, together with five hundred women, and having bowed down and made offerings to the thēras [Mahinda and his five companions] placed herself respectfully by the side of them' (Mah., i, p. 53). In the afternoon when Mahinda was about to preach in the royal garden 'innumerable females of the first rank resorted thither, crowding the royal garden, and ranged themselves near the thera' (p. 54). According to the Dīpavansa 'Noble women and maidens, the daughters-in-law and daughters of noble families crowded together in order to see the thēra. While he exchanged greetings with them night had fallen' (p. 175).

The name of the place at which the inscription is cut is repeated at a cave lower down the hill in another inscription cut in similar early letters, as follows :—

(4.) Gapati tapasa Sumana kulasa leṇe sagasa dine agata anagata catu disa sagasa Pasu wisaraye.

The cave of the family (of) the ascetic Sumana, the householder; given to the Community, to the Community of the four quarters, present or future, at the Pāsu tank.

I think that there can be little or no doubt that the monastery was the Pācīna, or Eastern, wihāra which is recorded (Mah., i, p. 79) to have been established by King Dēvānam-piya Tissa, the first Buddhist King, and elder brother of Uttiya, who succeeded him. Pāsu represents the Pāli word Pācī, east; several examples of the change of *c* into *s*, and *i* into *u* might be quoted.

Tissa ascended the throne in 245 B.C., and is said to have reigned forty years; but this cannot be trusted, as the reigns of the kings who lived about that time have been extended by the chroniclers in order to make the supposed arrival of the

[1] I have already pointed out that the Indian Sākyas from whom the royal family were partly descended were accustomed to marry their sisters.

first Magadhese settlers under Wijaya synchronise with the very doubtful date adopted by the Sinhalese historians as the time when Buddha attained Nīrvāna or died, viz. 543 B.C. The real date was 477 B.C. according to Sir F. Max Müller ;[1] but doubts have been expressed regarding even this date, and Dr. Fleet has adopted 482 B.C. as a more satisfactory one.

There are no data for fixing the true lengths of the reigns between 245 and 205 B.C., but apparently all have been doubled in length by the early chroniclers.[2] We shall be nearly correct in assuming that the wihāra was established in about 235 B.C., and that the inscriptions may have been cut ten or fifteen years later.

The reason why King Uttiya used the term 'illustrious famous place' is explained in the Mahāvansa (i, p. 75) in the account of the transportation of the celebrated Bō-tree to Anurādhapura. 'On the tenth day of the month, elevating and placing the Bō-branch in a superb car this sovereign [Dēvānam-piya Tissa] who had by enquiry ascertained the consecrated places, escorting the monarch of the forest, deposited it at the site of the Pācīna wihāra ; and entertained the priesthood [monks], as well as the people, with their morning meal. There (at the spot visited by Buddha's second advent) the chief thēra Mahinda narrated, without the slightest omission, to this monarch, the triumph obtained over the Nāgas (during the voyage of the Bō-branch) by the deity gifted with the ten powers. Having ascertained from the thēra the particular spots on which the divine teacher had rested or taken refreshment, those several spots he marked with monuments.'

The reference to the action of 'the deity gifted with the ten powers,' that is, Buddha, shows that Mahinda was not relating an incident of the voyage of the Bō-branch, but the manner in which he was supposed to have terrified the Nāgas into submission at this place when he came to Ceylon and

[1] *Dhammapada*, p. xxxvi.

[2] See my remarks on the chronology of the early kings of Ceylon at the end of this chapter. In the genealogical table I have allotted those from 245 to 205 B.C. half the time allowed in the Mahāvansa.

visited Nāgadīpa. When the second note which Turnour inserted in brackets is omitted the meaning is quite clear.

Thus the words of the inscription confirm the statement of the history that even at that early date the story of Buddha's visits to Ceylon was currently believed. This monastic establishment evidently marks the place at which he was thought to have suppressed the civil war between the Nāga kings Cūlōdara and Mahōdara, and at which the Rājāyatana tree (*Kiripalu* in Sinhalese, *Buchanania angustifolia*) of Śakra was planted for the Nāgas to worship (Mah., i, p. 6).

There is a discrepancy regarding the site of the Pācīna wihāra as proved by the inscription and that which is mentioned in the history. According to the Mahāvansa, in the quotation just given it would appear to be only half a day's journey from the place at which the Bō-tree was landed, but on p. 79 it is said to be at the port itself. I am unable to explain these conflicting remarks; the record left by King Uttiya must outweigh any ideas regarding the site expressed by a monk of Anurādhapura. A similar mistake is made by the annalist regarding the position of the Piyangala wihāra, which on p. 113 is represented as being less than two days' march for a monk from Anurādhapura, whereas the actual distance in a straight line is some 63 miles, which the windings of the path would make seventy or more. This wihāra was certainly at Kurundan-kuḷam, and an inscription left there refers to it by name as 'this fearless[1] excellent mountain Piyangala' (*me abhaya isirī paw Piyangala*). Until I studied King Uttiya's inscription I believed that the Pācīna wihāra was at Piyangala, which is in the midst of wild forest, about 15 miles south-west of Mulleittīvu.

It is recorded (Mah., ii, p. 58) that Senā, queen of Dappula II (807–812 A.D.), 'repaired the terraced house on [at] the Pācīna wihāra.'

It is surprising to read that King Silākāla (526–539 A.D.) removed the celebrated 'gem-set throne,' over the possession of which the Nāga kings were represented to have quarrelled

[1] The character of the hill shows that in this instance *abhaya* must have been used with the meaning 'not causing fear.'

at the time of Buddha's visit, from the Pācīna wihāra to a house at the foot of the Bō-tree at Anurādhapura. The throne may have been constructed to suit the story related by Mahinda to the credulous Dēvānam-piya Tissa, by way of confirming it.

The tank mentioned in the fourth inscription is a shallow one of eight or ten acres, with a straight low embankment eight or nine feet high, a typical village tank of the smaller kind, having an inferior water-supply provided merely by rainfall flowing into it from the adjoining jungle for a length of about a mile (see Fig. No. 148).

At the Nāval Nīrāvi hill where these inscriptions are cut no remains of a built wihāra or a dāgaba have been discovered. There is an earthen platform which has a supporting wall of stone, at the western side of the hill. As no traces of a building are to be seen on it it may have been the site of the Kiripalu tree of Śakra, or a Bō-tree. At the southern hill a broken statue of Buddha in a cave proves that a wihāra was there at a later time.

As this monastery is of such an early date, and without doubt one of the earliest of which traces have been discovered in Ceylon, I now give the rest of the numerous inscriptions copied by me at the three hills and two others of the neighbourhood, some few being nearly as old as those of the king and queen, according to the indication afforded by the shapes of the letters. Unfortunately all are mere dedications of caves to the use of the Buddhist monks.

Other inscriptions at Nāval Nīrāvi hill.

(5.) To west of the upper royal cave. Bata Sumanasa leṇe sagasa diṇe.

The cave of the workman Sumana; given to the Community.

(6.) To north of the last. Upasaka Nāgaha leṇe sagasa dine.

The cave of the lay devotee Nāga; given to the Community.[1]

[1] In all cases the words 'of Buddhist Monks' are to be understood as following 'Community.'

(**7**.) To west of No. 6. Tisa terasa leṇe saghasa niyate.
The cave of the thēra Tissa is assigned to the Community.

(**8**.) To south-east of the upper royal cave. Damarakita terasa leṇe catu disa sagasa dine.
The cave of the thēra Dhammarakkhita; given to the Community of the four quarters.

(**9**.) To north of the last. Damarakita teraha leṇe sagasa (letters of first century B.C.).
The cave of the thēra Dhammarakkhita; to the Community.

(**10**.) To north of No. 4. Bata Sumanaha leṇe cadu disa sagasa.
The cave of the workman Sumana; to the Community of the four quarters.

(**11**.) To north-west of the upper royal cave. Bata Damagutaha Asatisa putaha Asadamarakita leṇe sagasa agata anagata catu disa.
The cave (of) Āsadhammarakkhita, of the son of Āsatissa, (son) of the workman Dhammagutta; to the Community present or future (of) the four quarters.

(**12**.) Cave full of bats, below royal upper cave. (1) Sagasa; (2) Parumaka Majimaha putasa Parumaka Sidaṭaha Parumaka Cuḍa Sidaha Parumaka Tisaha.
To the Community. (The cave) of the Chief Siddhaṭṭha, of the son of the Chief Majjhima; of the Chief Cuḍa Siddha; of the Chief Tissa.

(**13**.) Above the last. Bata Budarakitaha matuḷaniya upasika Pusaya le (ṇe) saghaye niyate (1st cent. A.D.).
The cave (of) the female devotee Pusayā, the aunt of the workman Buddharakkhita, is assigned for the Community.

The next four are cut over shelters or caves round the overhanging sides of one immense boulder, each in one line. The inscription No. **4** is also cut at this boulder in a similar position.

(14.) Matula baginiyana leṇe agata anagata catu disa sagasa niyatase.

The cave (of) the sisters (of) Mātula; they have assigned (it) to the Community of the four quarters, present or future.

(15.) Barata Mahatisaha leṇe sagasa niyate; followed by the symbols Fish, Trisūla over circle, Swāstika, and Aum monogram.

The cave of the royal messenger Mahātissa is assigned to the Community.

(16.) The cave of the royal messenger Mahātissa is assigned to the Community of the four quarters.

(17.) Parumaka Humaneha leṇe (letters of first cent. A.D.).

The cave of the Chief Sumana.

Inscriptions at Tēvāndān Puliyankuḷam rocks, many of them over the shelters formed under large overhanging boulders that lie on the top of the rock (see Fig. No. 149).

(18.) On west side of southern rock. Gapati Vasali puta Maha Sumanasa.

(The cave) of Mahā Sumana, son (of) the householder Vasali.

(19.) On east side of north-west rock. Parumaka Uti puta Cuḍa Nagasa leṇe.

The cave of Cuḍa Nāga, son (of) the Chief Uttiya.

(20.) On south side of north-east rock. Gapati Damasena puta Sumana Malasa ca Gapati Majima Tisa puta Digat(i)sasa ca leṇe.

The cave of Sumana Malla, son (of) the householder Dhammasena, and of Dīgha-Tissa, son (of) the householder Majjhima-Tissa.

Group to the north of these.

(21.) On south side of southern rock. Tebakaṭa Tisa puta Royogutasa leṇe.

The cave of Royogutta, son (of) Tebakaṭa Tissa.

(22.) On east side of middle rock. Parumaka Sigiṇika T(i)saha leṇe.

The cave of the Chief Singhiṇika Tissa (Tissa of the Nose!).

(23.) Under the last. Barata Utara Kasabaha paṭi ucaya. The dwelling (?) of the royal messenger Uttara Kassapa.

(24.) On south side of north rock. Gapati Pusa..sa Tisasa leṇe.

The cave of the householder Pusa..sa Tissa.

(25.) On east side of north rock. Dame davanipi gapati Visakaha liṇe. The stone-cutter, evidently ignorant of Pāli and therefore possibly a Drāvidian, has omitted the lower parts of the letters *da* and *pi*, and made mistakes in the vowels.

The cave of the devout householder Visākha, beloved of the Gods.

(26.) On south-east side of north rock. Parumaka Āsa Adeka Veḷasa jaya Tisaya leṇe.

The cave (of) Tissayā, wife of the Chief Āsa Adeka Vēḷa.

(27.) At south-east end of north rock. Parumaka Nuguya Veḷa putana Sigara Maḷasava Nuguya Maḷasava leṇe.

The cave (of) Sigāla Maḷasava (and) Nuguya (Nudguhya) Maḷasava, sons (of) the Chief Nuguya Vēḷa.

(28.) Under-side of east rock. Magasa leṇe. The cave of Māgha.

(29.) Western cave on top of rock. Badira Mahatisa puta Maha Sumana leṇe.

The cave (of) Mahā Sumana, son (of) Mahātissa the Deaf.

(30.) West side of eastern cave. Citagutasa ca Baraṇiya cā leṇe.

The cave of Cittagutta and Bharaṇiya.

(31.) Southern cave. Ramasi leṇe.

The cave (of) Rāmāsī.

(32.) At the side of a flight of steps cut in the rock at the north end of the hill there is an inscription in one line which may be the first instance of what is known in Ceylon as Paeraeli Bāsa, or transposition of letters in written or spoken words.

In the facsimile I first give the inscription as it stands, and then a corrected copy, that is, one with the same letters turned round horizontally or vertically or both. It must be read from right to left, and only the consonants in the word *savi* require transposing, making this word *Siva*. When thus corrected the inscription is :—

Meka ni salaku savi tipaga pinuvada meda, or when transposed—Dame davanupi Gapati Siva kulasa nikame.

The work of the family (of) the devout householder Siva, beloved of the Gods.

Inscriptions at Ērupotāna hill.

(33.) South-east cave on south side. Parumaka Ku (4 letters) Siva puta Abayasa leṇe sagasa niyate. Trisūla over circle.

The cave of Abhaya son (of) the Chief Ku . . . . Siva is assigned to the Community.

(34.) South cave on south side. Parumaka Nadika putasa Parumaka Mitasa leṇe agata anagata catu disa sagasa dine.

The cave of the Chief Mitta, of the son (of) the Chief Nandika ; given to the Community of the four quarters, present or future.

(35.) North side of south cave, near the tank. Tisa teraha atevahika Sumana teraha leṇe agata anagata catu disa sagasa.

The cave of the thēra Sumana, pupil of the thēra Tissa ; to the Community of the four quarters, present or future.

(36.) South side of south cave. Damagutaha leṇe sagasa.

The cave of Dhammagutta ; to the Community.

(37.) South-eastern cave, east side. Parumaka Hadaka bariya upasika Nagayą ca puta upasaka Tisaha ca upasaka Deva ca leṇe agata anagata catu disa sagasa niyate.

The cave (of) the female devotee Nāgayā, wife (of) the Chief Saddhaka, and of the lay devotee Tissa (her) son, and (of) the lay devotee Dēva, is assigned to the Community of the four quarters, present or future.

(**38.**) Northern cave, containing a broken statue of Buddha. Fragments of bricks in the brick wall of this cave measure 3 inches, 2·30 inches, and 2 inches in thickness.

Parumaka Pita jaya Parumaka Satanasata jita Parumaka Ḷapusaya leṇe agata anagata catu sagasa. A symbol follows, apparently a flag-staff surrounded by a fence of four uprights and one cross bar at their top. Possibly it represents the Flag of Victory (of Buddhism), supported by the four great Truths.

The cave (of) the (female) Chief Aḷapusayā (?Alaṃbushā), daughter (of) the Chief Santānasatta, wife (of) the Chief Pīta; to the Community of the four (quarters), present or future.

(**39.**) At south end of eastern rock. Tisaguta terasa sadi wiharaya barata Majima. . . Tisaya leṇa sidasano agata anagata catu disa sagasa neyate.

The cave 'Beautiful' (of) the royal messenger Majjhima . . . Tissaya, for the excellent wihāra of the thēra Tissagutta, is assigned to the Community of the four quarters, present or future.

(**40.**) Copied by Mr. Fowler. Barata Tisaha leṇe.

The cave of the royal messenger Tissa.

At Veḍikkināri Malei, a hill some miles to the north, near Āriyamaḍu.

(**41.**) North cave. Parumaka Pusamita puta Ma(jima)ha leṇe agata anāgata cudi sagaha.

The cave of Majjhima, son (of) the Chief Pusamitta; of the Community (of the four quarters), present or future.

(**42.**) South cave (*a*). Maha Samuda puta Gutasa leṇe sagasa. Parumaka Bamaheta putaha Maha Gutahe l(eṇe).

The cave of Gutta, son (of) Mahā Samudda; to the Community. The cave of Mahā Gutta, son (of) the Chief Brahmahatta.

(**43**.) South cave (*b*). This is another example of ' Paeraeli Bāsa.' When the letters are correctly arranged it becomes Ṇele hasati ḍicu taba. It is read from right to left. The Cave of the workman Cuḍi Tissa.

At Kaccatkoḍi, a mile and a half south of Ērupotāna.

(**44**.) (1) Senapati puta Parumaka Nadika 'puta Pamatisaha ; three dots in a vertical line, forming a full stop. Parumaka Naṭaha upasaka, (2) upasaka Anediya, upasaka Buti Sumanaha (see Fig. No. 152).

(The cave) of Pamātissa, son (of) the Chief Nandika son (of) Senāpati. Of the Chief Nāṭa, the lay devotee ; (of) the lay devotee Anediya ; of the lay devotee Bhuti Sumana.

(**45**.) Another example of ' Paeraeli Bāsa.' Hagasa ṇale (Na)la Bati gaba. The inscription is read from the middle outwards, first to the right and then to the left. The room of Nāla Bhātiya, a cave of the Community.

(**46**.) Asadama Gutaha leṇe sagasa.

The cave of Āsadhamma Gutta ; to the Community.

Some of these inscriptions, especially those at Nāval Nīrāvi Malei, may be as old as the last quarter of the third century B.C., while the rest with a very few exceptions belong to the second century and the first half of the first century B.C.

The most interesting inscription after those of the king and queen is No. **34**. Strange to say, apparently the same chief caused a similar one to be cut, letter for letter identical throughout the first portion, at the eastern side of a rock termed Kuḍimbigala, near Haelawa, in the extreme south-east of Ceylon.[1] It runs as follows :—

(**47**.) Parumaka Nadika putasa [2] Ṗarumaka Mitasa leṇe Maha Sudasana sagasa diṇa.[3]

[1] The cave over which it is cut was occupied by a bear at the time of my visit.

[2] It is a distinctive feature of this and No. **34** that this word is in the genitive case.

[3] Most probably the right cut at the top of the *n* was accidental ;

The cave 'Great Beautiful' of the Chief Mitta, of the son (of) the Chief Nandika; a gift to the Community.

(48.) Another on the west side of the same rock is—

Bata Pusagutasa leṇe Ma(ha Su)dasana leṇe sagasa dine.

The cave of the workman Pusagutta, the 'Great Beautiful' cave; given to the Community.

The bricks in a wall at this cave average 17·20 inches in length, 8·90 inches in breadth, and 3·16 inches in thickness; Bt. is 28·1 and the contents 484 inches. The size indicates the second, or early in the first century B.C. as the time when they were burnt.

The inscriptions numbered **34** and **47** are in the earliest characters and appear to date from some time prior to 100 B.C. The most probable explanation of their authorship is that the person who caused them to be cut may be one of the chiefs who accompanied King Duṭṭha-Gāmiṇi from southern Ceylon during his war against the Tamils of northern Ceylon. The name of the chief's father renders it extremely likely, or perhaps certain, that the inscription may be attributed to the famous Nandi-Mitta, or Nandika Mitta, the first of the ten celebrated champions or chieftains of King Duṭṭha-Gāmiṇi. If so, this would provide a satisfactory explanation of his leaving two inscriptions at places so widely separated.

The fanciful derivations in the histories, out of which some of the champions' names have been evolved, are of course ridiculous. In the case of another of them, Gōṭhayimbara, who is said to have been so called because he was short and was strong enough to uproot 'imbara' trees, the writer ignores the fact that Ayimbara was a personal name of the time. An inscription of perhaps 100 B.C. at Nayindanāwa wihāra in the North-western Province runs:—

(49.) Parumaka Mahatisa puta Cuḍa Ayimaraha leṇe Ayimare pavatahi.

the interpretation would then become the usual formula 'given to the Community.'

The cave of Cuḍa Ayimbara, son (of) the Chief Mahātissa, at the Ayimbara mountain.

Thus Gōṭhayimbara may mean either the 'Short Ayimbara,' or Ayimbara son of Gōṭha. Koṭā is a nickname now used in Ceylon for a short person. In the same way the story regarding Nandi-Mitta may be put aside as absurd.

We learn from Mah., i, p. 88, that he belonged to a family of high position. His uncle, whose name (Mitta) he bore, was a general (*cāmupati*) under the Tamil king Elāra, and was a native of a village in the north-eastern part of the island, near a hill called Citta, which has not been identified. Nandi-Mitta lived at his uncle's village as a youth, and afterwards with his uncle at Anurādhapura, eventually proceeding to southern Ceylon to join Duṭṭha-Gāmiṇi. His residence for some years in the south might enable him to dedicate a cave to the Buddhist monks in that part of the island.

After returning to northern Ceylon as one of the Sinhalese king's leading chieftains, if his native village was in the same district as the Pācīna wihāra, which is equally to the north-east of Anurādhapura, he would be predisposed to do the same for the monks connected with that 'illustrious famous' temple. According to the history he was of a pious disposition and a devoted Buddhist. He is expressly stated to have had the furtherance of that religion in view in joining the Sinhalese prince. "I will bring about the revival of the glory of the religion of Buddha," he is reported to have said (Mah., i, p. 89). A chieftain of such influence holding these opinions would be certain to make gifts to the monks, and therefore in the absence of any negative evidence there is good foundation for the opinion that it was he who caused both the inscriptions to be cut.

In the inscriptions at the Kaccatkoḍi caves, No. **44** belongs to a Pamātissa who was also the son of a chief called Nandika. The differences between the forms of the letters in this inscription and that of Nandi-Mitta, as seen in the use of the straight *r* instead of the bent one, and the employment of *ha* instead of *sa* for the genitive case, may perhaps point to some other person than a brother of Nandi-Mitta. There still remains a possibility that this is one belonging to the same family. The father of Nandika is here termed Senāpati, which may be either a personal name, or a title, the General. At this early date one would rather expect it to be the latter, especially as it is not preceded by the word *Parumaka*, Chief, as in the case of that of his son. Thus there is a possibility that he might be the great General of the family, Nandi-Mitta himself, Pamātissa thus being his grandson. Such an identifica-

Fig. 152. Cave Temple, Kaccatkoḍi.

tion would suit the forms of the letters, and would render it unnecessary to assume that there were two chiefs called Nandi, both closely connected with a Senāpati, in the same immediate neighbourhood.

No other names can be identified with those given in the histories. It is surprising to see a female Chieftain mentioned in No. **38**; it is the only example of the kind, I believe, but the names of two female Chiefs of the Vaeddas were given in a previous chapter.

With regard to the characters used, it is interesting to observe in no less than four of these early inscriptions (Nos. **13**, **26**, **27**, and **38**) a letter *ḷ* which in India I believe is only found in southern inscriptions. I am not aware that it occurs in early cave inscriptions in other than the northern parts of the island. It is used in the name of a chief called Paḷikada, written also Palikada, whose son was the donor of a cave at Wessagiri near Anurādhapura. Drāvidian influence appeared to require a letter to represent a cerebral sound of the letter *l* which is not found in Sanskrit.

I am afraid that it would be unsafe to assume that the names given in Nos. **26**, **27**, **28** and **31** may be those of Drāvidians ; there might be such chiefs in northern Ceylon whose families were Buddhists.

Returning to the royal inscription, we already see a great difference between its alphabet and style, and those of Aśōka's inscriptions. There are no duplicated consonants, which I think do not make their appearance in Ceylon before the ninth century A.D., while compound letters, excepting in such words as *Siddham* or *Swasti*, 'Hail,' or 'May it be well (with you),' are not found until a still later date.[1]

The aspirated consonants and long vowels were already practically abandoned, although an occasional long *a* and aspirated *b*, *c*, *d*, or *g* occur in other early inscriptions. The royal grant is, in fact, written in early Elu, or ancient Sinhalese, as much as in the Pāli language.

The letter *j* is already represented by the form employed in India for the aspirated *jh* ; it had nearly disappeared in Ceylon early in the first century B.C. The long initial *ī* is used for the short *i*, as in the Tōnigala inscription No. **54**. A special form of *m* of a deep cup shape with a central horizontal cross bar, differing from the letter generally used in India, and afterwards abandoned in Ceylon by the end of the second century or early in the first century B.C., had already made its appearance. The trifid *s* always takes the place

[1] Sir A. Cunningham found only three compound letters in the early inscriptions at Sānchi. *The Bhilsa Topes*, p. 268.

of the usual curled letter, which in these forty-nine inscriptions only occurs in one word in No. **20**.

These variations in the alphabet prove that writing had already been employed for a considerable period in Ceylon, long enough to allow time for a local development of the letters to take place.

As the bent form of *r* is alone used in the royal inscription, the presence of the straight form may perhaps elsewhere generally be evidence of a later date than that of inscriptions in which the crooked letter occurs.

With regard to the language used by King Uttiya it is interesting to see the word *leṇa*, cave, instead of the usual *leṇe* of practically all later inscriptions. It appears to be confirmed by the last word of the inscription, *tana*. There are only two other special variations from the ordinary language of similar inscriptions found in the island. One is the expression *āgatāgata na* instead of *āgata anāgata*, ' come or come not ' in place of ' come or not come.' The other is the use of *āse*, ' they were,' evidently suffixed to verbs in the sense of ' they have,' both in this inscription and in No. **14**. The object also is placed after a transitive verb, as we see it in Nos. **53** and **54**, below.

In No. **14** the word *bhāginiyāna* is evidently a plural form like *putāna* in No. **27**. I have also met with a form *ditāna* (the last letter being damaged) where the context shows that two daughters are mentioned. The inscription in which it is found is at Kandalawa wihāra, in the Kurunāēgala district, and is as follows :—

(**50**.) Parumaka Majimasa gapati Anu(ra)di puta Gapatiya dita(na) Tisagutasa Cuḍasa leṇe. Tisagutasa Cuḍasa bata Sumanasa leṇe saga(sa).

The cave of Tissaguttā (and) of Cuḍā, daughters (of) Gāpatiya, the son (of) the (female) householder Anurādhī, (daughter) of the Chief Majjhima. The cave of Sumana, brother of Tissaguttā (and) of Cuḍā ; to the Community.

In the other inscriptions *bata* appears to represent *bhatika*, workman ' ; it occurs too often in these and many other inscriptions, and almost always before other names, to be a personal name 'Bhātiya,' which in fact is commonly found in the form *Bati*, as in No. **45**, and later examples. *Paṭi ucaya* in No. **23** may perhaps be derived from √*vas* to dwell.

The next inscriptions known are two which are cut at a wihāra established under an immense towering rock in the Puttalam district, called Paramā-kanda. One of them, No. **51**, is cut on the vertical face of a low rock at one side of a small pool of water, termed in Ceylon a *pōkuna*. The other, No. **52**, is at a considerable height on the face of the precipice, over the entrance to the wihāra. High above it is a nesting place of the Indian Peregrine Falcon (*Falco peregrinator*) which has doubtless bred there for immemorial ages. The whole site is strikingly picturesque. In the case of both inscriptions a close examination of the letters is not possible on a casual visit. My copies of them are as follows :—

(**51**.) Two symbols, the second being the fish. Parumaka Abaya puta Parumaka Tisaha duṭa kaṇa.

The assigned pool of the Chief Tissa, son (of) the Chief Abhaya.

It has been suggested by Dr. E. Müller that the letters *duṭaka* may refer to Duṭṭha-Gāmiṇi, but it is most unlikely that a sovereign would apply a nickname meaning 'Angry' to himself in one of his grants. I prefer to assume that the letter *pu* has been omitted or has been worn away. With it the last word would become *pukaṇa*, pool. *Duṭa* would then be *dishṭa*, assigned or ordered.

(**52**.) A symbol unexplained. Parumaka Abaye puta Parumaka T(isa)ha leṇe agata anagata caya d(i)sa sagasa.

The cave of the Chief Tissa son (of) the Chief Abhaya. To the Community of the (four) quarters, present or future.

The last part is indistinct ; I read it with a field glass in 1876. The word which I copied as *caya*, six, is most probably *catu*, four, as usual.

There are two other inscriptions near the same hill, both on a low rock called Tōnigala, the Boat-rock, at the side of a small tank, Galawaewa, the Rock tank. Their cutting is by far the boldest of any inscriptions in Ceylon. Each is about 100 feet long, with excellently chiselled and quite upright letters a foot high and cut an inch deep in the rock.

(53.) Parumaka Abaya puta Parumaka Tisaha vapi Acagirika Tisa pavatahi agata anagata catu d(i)sa sagasa dine. Two symbols, the first being the fish, followed by three dots in a vertical line as a full stop. Devanapi Maharaja Gāmiṇi Abaya niyate Aca nagaraka ca (Tavi) rikiya nagaraka ca Parumaka Abaya puta Parumaka Tise niyata pite rajaha agata anagata catu disa sagasa.

The tank of the Chief Tissa, son (of) the Chief Abhaya, at the Acagirika Tissa mountain; given to the Community of the four quarters, present or future. (By) the great king Gāmiṇi Abhaya, beloved of the Gods, (are re-) assigned[1] both Aca-nāgara and Tavirikiya-nāgara (which were) assigned by the Chief Tissa son (of) the Chief Abhaya, father of the king, to the Community of the four quarters, present or future.

(54.) Parumaka Abaya puta Parumaka Tise niyate ima vapi Acagirika Tisa pavatahi agata anagata catu d(i)sa sagasa. Emblem and fish, followed by three dots arranged in a vertical line as a full stop. Devanapiya Maharaja Gamiṇi Abaye niyate Aca nagaraka ca Tavirikiya nagaraka ca Acagirika Tisa pavatahi agata anagata catu d(i)sa sagasa Parumaka Abaya puta Parumaka Tisaha visara niyata pite.

By the Chief Tissa son (of) the Chief Abhaya is assigned this tank at the Acagirika Tissa mountain to the Community of the four quarters, present or future. By the great king Gāmiṇi Abhaya, beloved of the Gods, (are re-) assigned

[1] As the property of the Community of monks.

both Aca-nāgara and Tavirikiya-nāgara at the Acagirika Tissa mountain to the Community of the four quarters, present or future. The tank of the Chief Tissa son (of) the Chief Abhaya assigned by (my) father.

I cannot see any reason to doubt that the inscriptions numbered **53** and **54** belong to the only king of an early date called Gāmiṇi Abhaya, who had a father and grandfather named Tissa and Abhaya respectively. They must have been cut by King Duṭṭha-Gāmiṇi, who reigned from 161 to 137 B.C. Before he reconquered northern Ceylon, which had been in the hands of Tamil conquerors for some forty-four years, his father and grandfather ruled over southern Ceylon, after Mahā-Nāga and his son Yaṭṭhāla-Tissa, as tributary sovereigns under the Tamil king, Elāra. The Rājāvaliya says (p. 25), 'In those days King Kāwantissa, residing in Māgama of Ruhuṇa, paid tribute to the Tamil king.' This was also the practice while the previous Sinhalese kings held Ceylon. The same work states, 'The kings of Māgama in Ruhuṇa and of Kaelaṇiya used regularly to pay annual tribute to the king of Anurādhapura' (p. 24).

We now learn from these inscriptions that under the foreign domination they had not even the title of 'king,' like Mahā-Nāga, but were merely termed 'Chief' (*Parumaka*) like numerous others in the country. Although the title commonly indicated that its bearer was a person of importance in the country, some of these Parumakas occupied subordinate posts, and sometimes were even village headmen. An inscription at Gallāēwa wihāra in the North-western Province, which having both the bent and straight forms of *r* and the cup-shaped *m*, probably belongs to the second half of the second century B.C., runs :—

(**55**.) (1) Barata Maha Tisaye kape (2). Parumaka Naga gamiya detake.

Cut by the royal messenger Mahā-Tissa, the Chief Nāga (being) the village headman.

Tissa, the father of Duṭṭha-Gāmiṇi, married the daughter of another subject king or chief who ruled over the district of which Kaelaṇiya, near Colombo, was the headquarters. It would seem that he acquired or succeeded to his father-in-law's territory, which must have extended far up the west coast, so as to embrace the tract of country in which Paramā-kanda is found. At a much later date it is certain that the Kaelaṇiya kingdom included this district and extended many miles to the north of it, up to the Kalā-oya [1]; and this may have been its limit in earlier times also. This will account for Tissa's being able to make grants to this temple while Elāra was ruling at Anurādhapura.

Both the inscriptions at the Paramā-kanda wihāra purport to have been cut to record grants made by this Chieftain Tissa; but the difference in the shapes of the letter *r* in them appears to show that the first is older than the other, which may perhaps have been cut by order of Duṭṭha-Gāmiṇi as a record of his father's work at the cave temple. If both were the work of the same stone-cutters it is not likely that such a variation would be made in the forms of the letters. The older one may date from the first quarter of the second century B.C.

In No. **52** and the two following inscriptions we find the straight *r* always used, and the earliest forms of *m* and *j*. The symbol inserted beside the fish does not appear to occur elsewhere in Ceylon, and I offer no explanation of its presence. It is the letter *m* with a central upright, of the earliest known script, and it occurs in Spain and Egypt (1st Dynasty). I should assign these inscriptions to the middle of the second century B.C.

I place next an inscription over a cave at a large boulder lying on the side of the hill at Dambulla, on the road from Kandy to Anurādhapura. The early shapes of the letters *r*,

[1] This is proved by the list of tanks repaired by Parākrama-Bāhu I at the time when he was ruling over only southern Ceylon and Kaelaṇiya, and Gaja-Bāhu was king at Polannaruwa (Mah., ii, p. 149). Those which can be identified extend through the district immediately south and west of the Kalā-oya, and include Māgalla, Giribāwa, Morawaewa, Maediyāwa, Talagalla, and Siyambalan-gamuwa. On p. 150 the Tabba (Tabbowa) district, which is far north of Paramā-kanda, is referred to as being under him.

m and *j* render it probable that it also dates from the time of Duṭṭha-Gāmiṇi. It is as follows :—

(**56**.) Damarakita teraha leṇe agata anagata catu disa sagasa dine. Gamaṇi Abayasa rajiyahi karite.

The cave of the thēra Dhammarakkhita ; given to the Community of the four quarters, present or future. In the reign of Gāmaṇi Abhaya it is made.

In the Dīpavansa (p. 209) a thēra termed the 'learned Dhammarakkhita' is mentioned among those who came from India at the laying of the foundation bricks of the Ruwanwaeli dāgaba, but there is nothing to prove that he remained in Ceylon, or that this inscription was cut by his orders. The name was not uncommon, and is found in the inscriptions numbered **8** and **9**, and elsewhere.

(**57**.) Of about the same age is one at a dēwāla, or demon temple, on Dēwāla-hīnna, a hill at Tittawaela, in the North-western Province :—

Bata Maha Tisaha leṇe. Gamaṇi Abayasa rajiya sika(ka) sagasa.

The cave of the workman Mahā-Tissa. (In) the reign of Gāmaṇi Abhaya. To the Community who keep the Precepts (*sila*).

Possibly the following inscriptions belong to the same period. They are found at Nuwara-kanda in the Kurunāēgala district, a hill buried in the jungle, on the bank of the Daeduru-oya. Another inscription of later date informs us that its ancient name was the Tissa mountain. The size of the bricks found there has been given previously.

(**58**.) Gamika Siva puta Maharajaha rāmata Kaṇatisaha agata anagata chatu disagasa dine.

(The cave) of Kaṇatissa, devoted to the great King, son (of) the villager (headman) [1] Siva ; given to the Community of the four quarters, present or future.

(**59**.) Gamika Siva puta Gami Kaṇatisaha leṇe.

[1] *Gamika* is probably equivalent to the modern word *Gamarāla*, a village headman or elder. Compare No. **55**.

The cave of the villager (headman) Kaṇatissa, son (of) the villager (headman) Siva.

(60.) Gami Kaṇatisaha Badakajaka Anu(rada) ha leṇe agata anagata catu disagasaga.

The cave of Bhaddakacchaka Anurādha (son) of the villager (headman) Kaṇatissa; to the pre-eminent Community of the four quarters, present or future.

(61.) Tisaguta terasa leṇe.

The cave of the thēra Tissagutta.

I omit many cave inscriptions at places where no reference is made to the king of the period, although the forms of the letters indicate that many of them belong to the second century B.C., or earlier.

The next inscription is cut above a cave on the edge of a deep precipice at Mihintale. I examined the letters closely by the aid of a ladder held back by two men and almost overhanging the precipice, so that there should be no uncertainty regarding them. It belongs to Prince Sāli, the son of Duṭṭha-Gāmiṇi, whose romantic love story is related in the Mahāvansa (i, p. 127), which explains how he abandoned his right to the throne in order to keep his low-caste wife.[1]

The inscription is preceded by a complex symbol which may represent the Flag of Victory of Buddhism, raised high on a pole which rests on a horizontal base-line. Under the flag, on the same staff, is the trisūla resting on the circle, and below this a reversed disk-and-crescent. Four short uprights, two on each side of the pole, which stand on the base-line may indicate the Four Great Truths of Buddhism, or the four-fold

[1] 'He had a son renowned under the designation of the royal prince Sāli, gifted with good fortune in an eminent degree and incessantly devoted to acts of piety. He became enamoured of a lovely female of the Candāla caste. Having been wedded in a former existence also to this maiden,[2] whose name was Aśōkamālā, and who was endowed with exquisite beauty, fascinated therewith he relinquished his right to the sovereignty.' She is said by tradition to have lived at a Duraya village at Hengamuwa, in the North-western Province.

[2] His grandfather was also believed to have been a pious Candāla in his former life.

forces of the sovereign, protecting the symbols. The inscription is very short :—

(62.) Gāmiṇi dhama rājasa putasa Aya Asalisa leṇe.

The cave of the Noble Asāli, of the son of the devout king Gāmiṇi.[1]

Mr. Bell, the Government Archaeologist, met with some cave inscriptions in the North-central Province, left by the sons of Saddhātissa, the brother of Duṭṭha-Gāmiṇi. One of these, at a hill called Kuḍā Arambaedda-hīnna, which is part of Riṭigala, is as follows (Annual Report, 1893, p. 9). The king is of course Lajjitissa (119–109 B.C.).

(63.) (La)jaka Tisa maharaje wihara karawaya Abadaḷuka wawi saga dini.

The great king Lajjaka Tissa caused the wihara to be made (and) gave the Abadaḷuka tank (to) the Community.

(64.) Another at the same place is—Gamani Abayi kubara saga dini.

Gāmaṇi Abhaya gave the field (to) the Community. Apparently this belongs to Waṭṭa-Gāmiṇi before he came to the throne in 104 B.C. ; it is noteworthy that he does not give himself the title 'Noble.'

In his Annual Report for 1897, p. 11, Mr. Bell mentions another inscription by Waṭṭa-Gāmiṇi at Mīn-vila, and at p. 9 one by Lajjitissa at Duwegala, but gives no copy or transliteration of them.

(65.) He records one of nearly the same period over a cave at Saessāēruwa, in the North-western Province, and gives a transliteration of the first part of it as follows :—

Devanapiya Maharajaha Gamaṇi Abayaha jita Abi Anuridiya, etc., the rest probably being merely the usual dedication of the cave to the monks.

Abhī Anuridhiyā, daughter of the great king Gāmaṇi Abhaya, beloved of the Gods, etc.

Mr. Bell attributes it to a daughter of King Waṭṭa-Gāmiṇi ;

[1] I have two other inscriptions of one district in the North-western Province, in which a 'Parumaka Asaliya' is mentioned, but evidently he is some other person, his father being a chief called Nāga.

it may be gathered from Mah., i, p. 129, that this king had one whose name is not given by the annalists.

Through the kindness of my friend Mr. F. Lewis of the Forest Department in Ceylon, I am able to add a recently found inscription cut at a cave at Kusalāna-kanda, near Rūgama, in the Eastern Province. It was discovered and copied by his Forest Ranger, and has not been examined by Mr. Lewis; but it appears to be so important in connection with the identification of the authors of several other inscriptions, that although it may prove to require some correction I now give a facsimile (Fig. No. 151), and a transliteration and tentative translation of it as it stands in the hand-copy sent to me.

(**66**.) Upaja Naga p(u)te Raja Abaye namā tatā-p(u)te Gamaṇi Tisa namate nakarate sudasane sagasa.

Born the son (of) Nāga (and) by King Abhaya named (his) 'own son' (the prince) named Gāmaṇi Tissa has prepared the 'Beautiful' (cave) of the Community.

This agrees so accurately with the account in the Mahāvansa (i, p. 129) of Waṭṭa-Gāmiṇi Abhaya's adoption of the son of his brother, King Khallāta-Nāga, that it appears to settle the question of the identification of the sovereign called Gāmiṇi-Tissa, who is thus Mahācūla Mahā-Tissa.

It still leaves some difficulties. In the first place, the letters are all of the very earliest shapes, with the bent *r*, the angular *s*, and the cup-shaped *m*; one would not expect to find all these forms still in use during the reign of Waṭṭa-Gāmiṇi. Secondly, we have the Gal-lena inscriptions which follow, that appear to belong to the same prince, who calls himself in them merely 'the Noble Tissa,' and uses a decidedly later type of letters. The difficulty in connection with the writing may perhaps be explained by assuming that there was still a retention of the old forms of letters in the beginning of Waṭṭa-Gamiṇi's reign, while an alphabet more in accordance with that used in India was coming into use by the stone-cutters after he had regained the throne in 88 B.C.

With only two exceptions there is a peculiarity observable in Gāmiṇi-Tissa's inscriptions; in six out of the eight that are now known he gives a name to the cave that he dedicates to the monks, while in other cave inscriptions the proportion of the caves so named does not exceed three or four in a hundred.

The following inscription was discovered by Mr. H. Nevill at Henannegala, in the south-eastern part of the Eastern Province, and was published by him in the *Taprobanian* (Vol. i, p. 38, ff.).

(**67**.) Undescribed symbols. Gamiṇi Tisaha pitaha ca Majama Rajaha ca niyata gama nisa paribegani sagasa Giritisa game, Karajinitisa gama, Wila gama, Kasuba nagare Malaga Naka like.

The villages assigned by the father of Gāmiṇi-Tissa and by the Majjhima Raja (King of the Middle Country) as a resource for the food of the Community (are) Giritissa-gama, Karajinitissa-gama, Wiḷa-gama. Written (by) Malaga Nāga of Kassapa nāgara.

It is rather strange that the name of Gāmiṇi-Tissa's father, Khallāta-Nāga, is not inserted in this inscription. The king of the 'Middle' Country, that is, the Malaya or hill district, may have been Waṭṭa-Gāmiṇi, who took refuge there when the Tamil invaders occupied Northern Ceylon in 104 B.C. Possibly this inscription was cut by Gāmiṇi-Tissa during that period.

Following the last we have a series of five inscriptions at Gal-lena wihāra, in the North-western Province, all recording the dedication of caves, four of which are distinguished by special names.

(**68**.) Devānapiya Mahā rāja Gāmaṇi Abhayasa puta Tisayasa Mahā leṇa [1] agatānāgatasa cāt(u) disa sagasa. The 'Great' cave of Tissa the Noble,[2] son of the great king Gāmaṇi Abhaya, beloved of the Gods; to the Community of the four quarters, present or future.

[1] Dr. E. Müller has *leṇe*. *Anc. Inscriptions*, p. 73.

[2] Tisaya = Tissa + Aya, as at Koṭā-daemu-hela below, where both forms occur. See also Dr. Müller's inscription numbered 34 (*a*) in which the son of a King Abhaya is called Tisaya, 'the Noble Tissa.'

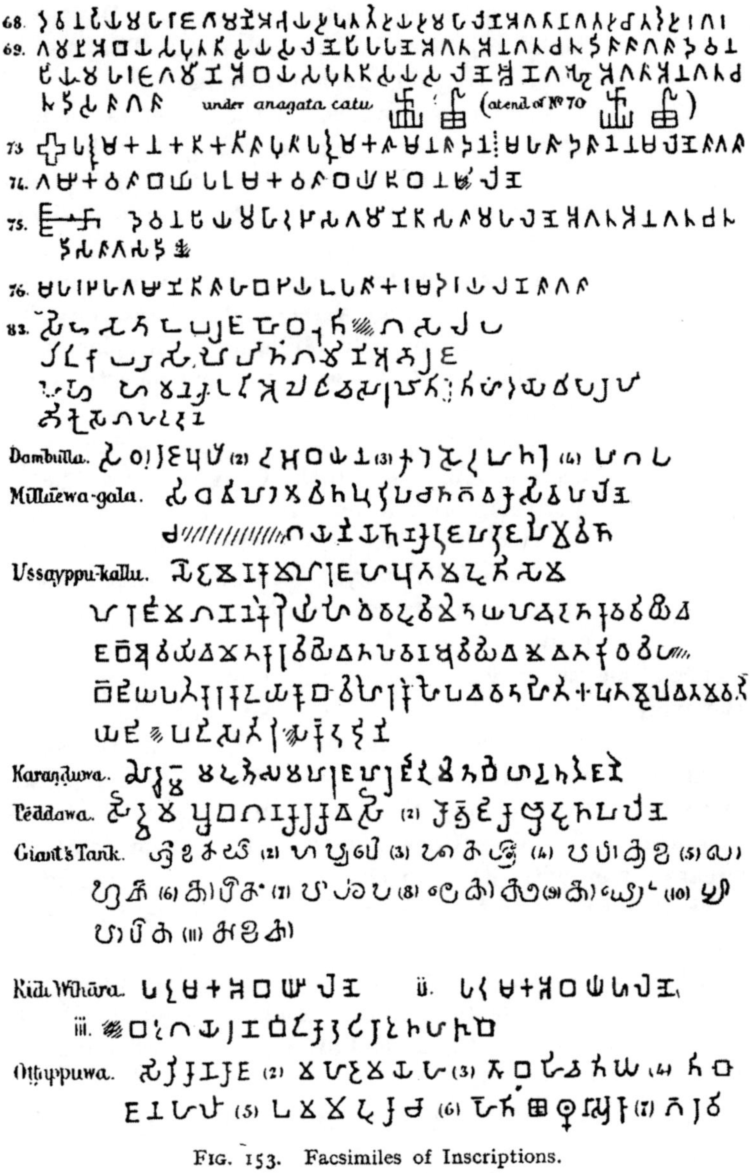

FIG. 153. Facsimiles of Inscriptions.

(**69**.) Gamani Abayasa puta Tisayasa leṇe Sihapaṇe[1] agata anagata catu disa sagasa. Devanapiya Maha raja Gamiṇi Abayasa puta Tisayasa leṇe Ṇaga heṭi agata anagata catu disa sagasa. Under this are two symbols, (1) the Swāstika, or magic cross, raised on a pole standing on a horizontal base line from which rise four short upright lines, two on each side, as in No. **62**, the tops of the two middle ones being joined by a straight line; and (2) a flag on a standard which rests on an upright cross enclosed in a rectangle. This may be a fence round it. Dr. Müller erred in placing this inscription at Giribāwa; it is cut over the wihāra at Gallena.

The cave 'Sihapaṇe' of Tissa the Noble, son of Gāmaṇi Abhaya; to the Community of the four quarters, present or future. The cave 'Under-the-Rock' of Tissa the Noble, son of the great king Gāmiṇi Abhaya, beloved of the Gods; to the Community of the four quarters, present or future.

The stone-cutter was an ignorant man who began to cut the word *aṇagata* in place of *Naga*, and then cancelled the initial *a*. He may have made some mistake in the second word, which I take to be a name of the cave, and possibly intended for *Siha pahaṇe*, 'the Lion Stone.' Compare *Nilapa-ṇataṭa, lit.* 'the Blue Stone plain,' in an inscription at Ridi wihāra, given with others at that place in the account of the Ancient Weapons. *Nila paṇa* is equivalent to the modern *kalu gala*, gneiss.

(**70**.) Devanapiya Maha rajasa Gamiṇi Abhayasa puta Tisayasa leṇe Sita guhe agata anagata catu disa sagasa. At the end are the same two symbols as in No. **69**.

The cave 'Cool Cave' of Tissa the Noble, son of

[1] Dr. Müller informed me that the initial is *S* and not *P* as I copied it in 1878.

Gāmiṇi Abhaya, of the great king beloved of the Gods; to the Community of the four quarters, present or future.

(71.) Devanapiya Maha raja Gamaṇi Abayasa puta Tisayasa leṇe Cuḍa Sudasana agata anagata catu disa sagasa.

The cave 'Small Beautiful' of Tissa the Noble, son of the great King Gāmaṇi Abhaya, beloved of the Gods; to the Community of the four quarters, present or future.

(72.) Devanapiya Maha raja Gamiṇi Abayasa puta Tisayasa leṇe agata anagata catu disa sagasa.

The cave of Tissa the Noble, son of the great king Gāmiṇi Abhaya, beloved of the Gods; to the Community of the four quarters, present or future. Ṭhis is cut over the wihāra.

With regard to the names of these caves, various titles of such dwellings are sometimes met with elsewhere, as in Nos. **47, 48** and **81**. An inscription in letters of the earliest type at Periyakaḍuwa wihāra, in the North-western Province, runs :—

(73.) Symbol, an upright plain cross with wide arms each consisting of two lines joined at the ends by transverse ones. Parumaka Nakatika Tisa puta Parumaka Sumanasa dane. Five dots in a vertical line, making a full-stop. Maha Sudasane nama leṇe sagasa.

The gift of the Chief Sumana, son (of) the Chief Nakatika Tissa. The cave 'Great Beautiful' by name; to the Community. The name of the donor's father may perhaps be Nāga Tikkha Tissa, or he may have belonged to a village of the district now called Naekatta.

Another, in characters of the first century B.C. at Rankirimaḍa wihāra, in the same Province, is :—

(74.) Gamika Wasabayi Parumaka Wasabaya tiba nami leṇe.

The villager (headman) Wasabhaya's cave, which has the name 'the Chief Wasabhaya.'

The shapes of the letters in all the Gal-lena inscriptions are distinctly those of the first century B.C. At that period there was only one king, Waṭṭa-Gāmiṇi, who was called Gāmiṇi Abhaya, and his adopted son Mahācūla Mahā-Tissa must have caused the inscriptions to be cut while the king was still reigning, and probably, as he is entitled 'Dēvānam-piya,' in the latter part of his reign, that is, about 80 B.C. The omission to mark the long *a* or aspirated *b* in some of them is not unusual elsewhere; it is, in fact, the general rule in Ceylon.

(75.) After Gāmiṇi-Tissa succeeded to the throne he made over the great Dambulla cave to the monks, and left there the following inscription :—

> Symbol, a Swāstika elevated on a pole with two short vertical bars on each side of it rising from the base line on which it stands. Devanapiya Mahā rajasa Gāmiṇi Tisasa maha leṇe agata anagata catu disa sagasa dine.
>
> The great cave of the great king Gāmiṇi-Tissa, beloved of the Gods; given to the Community of the four quarters, present or future.

(76.) After this we have one at Mihintale cut by his wife.

> Maha rajaha Gamiṇi Tisaha bariya upasika Ramadaraya l(e)ṇ(e) sagasa.
>
> The cave (of) the female devotee Rāmadharayā, wife of the great king, of Gāmiṇi-Tissa; to the Community.

We learn from the Mahāvansa that Mahācūla had two wives. One was the notorious Anuḷā, the mother of Kuḍā-Tissa, whom his brother married after his death; the other, who became a nun, was the mother of Kālakaṇṇi-Tissa. Evidently it was she who caused this inscription to be cut.

Prince Gāmiṇi-Tissa must have been more than a youth when his uncle Waṭṭa-Gāmiṇi adopted him on his accession, as his son; or the succession would not have been secured to him in preference to the king's own son. It may be conjectured that it was a politic act of the king to pacify the party who supported Tissa's claim to the sovereignty. As the Tamil invaders afterwards held northern Ceylon for fifteen years, he may have been between thirty and forty years old when Waṭṭa-Gāmiṇi regained the throne in 88 B.C. He might possibly cut the Rūgama inscription immediately after his adopted father began to reign, that is, in 104 B.C., before the latter had built the Abhayagiri dāgaba and wihāra and thereby acquired the title Dēvānam-piya. At the latest, it must have been cut soon after 88 B.C. The inscriptions at Gallena may have been cut shortly before Waṭṭa-Gāmiṇi's death, after he had acquired the title.

Next come the inscriptions cut by the sons of Gāmiṇi-Tissa.

(77.) Mr. Bell found an inscription at Āndiya-kanda, another part of Riṭigala, which runs :—

Devanapiya Maha raja Gamani Tisaha puta Devanapiya Tisa A— leṇe agata anagata chadu disa sagasa leṇe.

Mr. Bell fills the blank in the second name by making the word *Abaha*, but the inscriptions which follow indicate the expression *Ayaha*, and the translation would then be :—

The cave of Tissa the Noble, beloved of the Gods, son of Gāmaṇi-Tissa, the great king beloved of the Gods. A cave of the Community of the four quarters, present or future.

This inscription may belong to Prince Kuḍā-Tissa, and the absence of the royal title in his case shows that he had not succeeded to the throne, that is, it must have been cut before 50 B.C., and most probably during his father's lifetime.

Next comes the inscription at Nuwara-gala in the Eastern Province, which was republished in 1907 by Mr. F. Lewis, in the Journal of the Ceylon Branch of the Royal Asiatic Society. It was discovered and first published by Mr. Nevill in the *Taprobanian*, vol. i, p. 150. The forms of the letters *j* and *m* prove that it belongs to the first century B.C.

(78.) Devanapiya maha rājaha Gamiṇi Tisaha puta Maha Tisa Ayaha leṇe sagike.

The cave belonging to the Community, of Mahā-Tissa the Noble, son of the great king beloved of the Gods, Gāmiṇi Tissa.

The son who left this inscription may be the one who became

King Kālakaṇṇi-Tissa (42–20 B.C.). Mahācūla's other son being called Kuḍā-Tissa in the Mahāvansa apparently cannot be the prince here termed Mahā-Tissa.

Kālakaṇṇi-Tissa is mentioned as a devout Buddhist, and for some time he actually became a monk. As he does not term himself king, this record must date from prior to 42 B.C., and probably from his father's reign.

After this we have thirteen inscriptions at Koṭādaemu-hela and neighbouring rocks in the southern part of the Eastern Province which were discovered and published in the *Taprobanian* (vol. i, p. 150) by Mr. H. Nevill. All are described by him as very nearly identical. I therefore give only one transcript, adding the word *jaya*, as found in some others.

(**79**.) Dama raja puta Maha Tisa Ayaha jita Aya Abaya puta Aya Tisaha (jaya) Abisawaraya dana sagasa.

A gift to the Community by Abhisawarā, wife of the Noble Tissa, son (of) the Noble Abhayā, daughter of Mahā-Tissa the Noble, son (of) the devout king.

In some of the inscriptions Mahā-Tissa's daughter is termed Abisawara Ayabaya,' and her son's name is also written Tisa Aya and Tisaya.[1]

As the name of the 'devout king' is not given, and Mr. Nevill did not publish a facsimile of the inscriptions, there is some doubt regarding the identification of his son Mahā-Tissa. At present I can only assume that he is the same person as the Mahā-Tissa, the son of Gāmiṇi-Tissa, who cut the inscription numbered **77**. The fact that he does not receive the title of king indicates that at the time when these were cut he had not succeeded to the throne. For this to be the case it is very evident that early marriages must have been the custom in the royal family, and even in that case Gāmiṇi-Tissa must have been born before 120 B.C. for his great-grandson's wife, whose age would not exceed her husband's, to be

[1] It is uncertain if the expression *sawara* indicates a connection with the Vaeddas. *Sawara* usually stands for *sabara*, 'barbarian,' or in Ceylon, 'Vaedda.'

old enough to cause these inscriptions to be cut before 42 B.C., the year when Kālakaṇṇi became king.

The inscriptions are interesting as showing that at this period all the members of the direct line of the royal family had the title Aya (=Āriya), 'Noble,' instead of Prince and Princess. This title is applied to the princes in Prince Sāli's inscription, those at Gal-lena, probably that at Āndiya-kanda, three others at Bōwata which follow, and No. 34*a* of Dr. Müller's work.

It would seem that Gāmini-Tissa's grand-daughter, Abhayā, had married some local chieftain of south-eastern Ceylon, and that her son, whose wife caused these inscriptions to be cut, continued to reside in that district.

Three inscriptions were cut at some caves at Bōwata, in the extreme south-east of Ceylon. These also were found by Mr. Nevill, and published without facsimiles in the *Taprobanian* (vol. i, p. 52 ff.). They are as follows:—

(80.) Symbols, Sūla and fish. Maraja puṭha Maha Tisa Ayena karite. (This) is made by Mahā-Tissa the Noble, son of the great king.

(81.) Symbols, Fish and sūla. Samaṇaha tedasa Batika Nā puta sawa puṭaha pute dama raja dama raki(ta) ra(ja) Maha Tisa Aye karite (i)ma lēṇa Maha Sudasana sagasa dine.

This cave, 'the Great Beautiful,' is made by Mahā-Tissa the Noble, son (of) the samaṇa (monk), the famous Bhātik a-Nāga, the (best) son of all sons, the devout king, the king who protected the Dhamma (religion); given to the Community.

Without facsimiles of these inscriptions any identification of the prince who caused them to be cut must be tentative. There is only one king called Bhātika in the first century B.C.; he began to reign in 20 B.C., and was apparently the brother of the Princess Abhayā of No. **79.** His name was Abhaya, and as his younger brother was called Nāga there could be no reason for terming him Bhātika (the elder brother) unless his brother's name was also Abhaya in addition to Nāga, or his own name was Nāga in addition to Abhaya. In the same way, two kings called Tissa were discriminated in the second century A.D., the elder one being called Bhātika. Provisionally, therefore, I attribute these inscriptions to a son of Bhātikābhaya (Nāga) who is not mentioned by the historians; the king's title 'Mahāraja' in No. **80** shows that he was the supreme king of Ceylon, and not merely a subordinate ruler of southern Ceylon. The character of the father agrees with that of Bhātikābhaya, who was a most devout king.

The third inscription at Bōwata is:—

(**82.**) Undescribed symbols. Samaṇaha Tedapana Tisa raja Uti puta Aya Abayasa jita Abi Anuradiyā. (The cave of) Abhī Anurādhiyā, daughter of the Noble Abhaya, son (of) King Uttiya, (son of) the samaṇa (monk) Tedapana-Tissa.

This King Uttiya may have been a king of Ruhuṇa or southern Ceylon, there being no ruler among the kings of Anurādhapura who can be identified by this name, except the first one, whose father died before Buddhism was introduced into the island.

With this, my list of the earliest inscriptions is ended. I believe that it includes all royal inscriptions cut prior to the Christian era, so far as they are known at present,[1] unless Mr. Bell has found some that are not yet made public. It is unnecessary to give transcripts of numerous others that merely record the dedication of caves by unknown persons at unknown places. The latest record I have seen, in an inscription, of the grant of caves to the monks is contained in one by King Mēghawaṇṇābhaya II (304–332 A.D.).[2]

I add one other rock inscription of the second century A.D., as it was covered up when the embankment of Iratperiya-kuḷam, a reservoir near Vavuṇiya in the Northern Province,

[1] Dr. Müller has one (No. 34a) of a prince who cannot be identified. It is:—Pacina raja puta raja Abayaha puta Tisayaha leṇe agata, etc. 'The cave of Tissa the Noble, son of King Abhaya, son (of) the King of the East (or Pāsu country); to the Community, etc.' It appears to be of early date.

[2] Mr. Bell found one record of the twelfth century. (Arch. Survey, Annual Report for 1897, p. 9.)

was restored, and therefore will not be seen when the inscriptions of that Province come to be copied.

(83.) (1) Sida. Sata uparaja bare Ti(ya)gasala pa (2) rinika parasiha pite Gamiṇi Abha raja (3) ha hamaneka udi Aḷavicaka haraha tire Tihadaya wiharahi (4) bhiku sagahaṭa dine.

Hail! The son-in-law (of) the wise sub-king (and) father (of) Tiyāgasāla, the pre-eminent hero, the Crown-prince, King Gāmiṇi-Abhaya has given six amunas of undi (pulse) to the Community of monks at the Tihadaya wihāra, on the shore of the Aḷaviccha Lake.

This inscription belongs to Gaja-Bāhu I (113–135 A.D.) whose father-in-law, Mahallaka-Nāga, succeeded him. The prince who is referred to in such unusual terms is not mentioned in the histories by this name. He would appear to have greatly distinguished himself in the invasion of Madura,[1] the only war in which Gaja-Bāhu is known to have been engaged. He may have died while his grandfather or uncles held the throne, as the prince who succeeded them, from 193 to 195 A.D., was called Cūlanāga. From this record we learn that the ancient name of the tank was the 'Scorpion Lake,' and this enables the Gōnusu (Scorpion) district which is mentioned in later times to be identified as this part of the island.

I annex a genealogical table of the early kings of Ceylon. The date when Dēvānam-piya Tissa ascended the throne is practically certain within a few years. The Dīpavansa states that it occurred seventeen and a half years after the accession of the Indian emperor Aśōka, which may lie within four years of 263 B.C. Dr. Duncker, in his *History of Antiquity*, vol. ii, p. 525, has fixed it at 263 B.C. Sir F. Max Müller, in the Introduction to the *Dhammapada*, p. xxxvi, by entirely different reasoning arrived at the year 259 B.C. Professor Rhys Davids

[1] He must have been a youth at the time; his brothers died in 195 and 196 A.D. The manuscript 'Pradhāna Nuwarawal' states that Gaja-Bāhu was only 16 when he became king. I suggest that Mahallaka Nāga was probably a son of Wasabha.

states in his *Buddhist Suttas*, p. xlvi, that it must be within a year or two of 267 B.C. I adopt 263 B.C. as a mean date;[1] the accession of Dēvānam-piya Tissa would thus take place in 245 B.C., and in any case not more than ten years earlier than that date.

In the Mahāvansa, Tissa's father, Muta-Sīva, is stated to have reigned 60 years, and the latter's father, Paṇḍukābhaya, 70 years. The same work also records that Paṇḍukābhaya was born in the year in which his grandfather, Paṇḍuwāsa-Dēva, died. Paṇḍuwāsa-Dēva was succeeded by his eldest son Abhaya, who after reigning 20 years was deposed by his brother Tissa.

Before Abhaya's deposition his nephew Paṇḍukābhaya had taken the field against him, and had also married his niece Suvaṇṇa-Pālī. It may therefore be assumed that Paṇḍukābhaya's son, Muta-Sīva, was born about the time when Abhaya was deposed, which was 17 years before Paṇḍukābhaya succeeded in acquiring the sovereignty. According to Sinhalese chronology, the age attained by Muta-Sīva would thus be the length of his own and his father's reigns, plus this 17 years, or a total life of 147 years. Even if we allow him an extremely long life we cannot accept more than 90 years as his age when he died; but as a more probable lifetime I take 80 years. This would fix the deposition of Abhaya at 325 B.C. as the earliest reasonable date, if the accession of Dēvānampiya Tissa took place in 263 B.C.

The lengths of the reigns of the two preceding kings, Wijaya and Paṇḍuwāsa-Dēva, given in the table, are those of the Mahāvansa. As it is unlikely that both Muta-Sīva and his father lived exactly 80 years, I have apportioned 70 years to the latter, whose life would then terminate in 275 B.C. This does not affect the total length of their two reigns.

What I wish to emphasise is that if the lengths of the reigns of Wijaya, Paṇḍuwāsa-Dēva, and Abhaya are correctly given by the annalists, and no kings are omitted by them, Wijaya

[1] In his *Early History of India*, p. 145, Mr. V. A. Smith makes the date 272 or 273 B.C.

cannot possibly have become king more than a few years prior to the date, 414 B.C., given by me as the earliest reasonable one for his accession.

Although it has been suggested that the names of some Sinhalese kings may have been dropped by the historians, it appears to me clear that all probabilities are strongly against the omission of the names of any other early sovereigns. By omitting them the chroniclers would be merely intensifying the difficulty which they experienced in stretching back their chronology so as to make it extend to 543 B.C., the assumed date of the death of Buddha. Being left without other kings to fill up the gap, they were obliged to double the lengths of the reigns between 205 and 245 B.C., and also those of Paṇḍukābhaya and Muta-Sīva, thus making these two last stretch to a ridiculous and impossible extent. As the existence of other kings would have relieved them from this necessity of falsifying the chronology they would be most unlikely to omit their reigns.

It is much more probable that fictitious names would be inserted in order to span the gap up to 543 B.C. than that the names of actual rulers of Ceylon would be struck out of the list.

If there is any additional error, therefore, it must be looked for in the lengths of the first three reigns. But it is evident that in any case these cannot be lengthened more than a very few years. The historians allow a reign of 38 years to Wijaya, 30 to Paṇḍuwāsa-Dēva, and 20 to Abhaya, who however was alive for more than 17 years later, since it is recorded that his nephew Paṇḍukābhaya appointed him after that period City Conservator of Anurādhapura. As Paṇḍuwāsa-Dēva was married immediately after he came to the throne, we may assume the age of Abhaya, his eldest son, to have been 66 [1] when he was appointed to this office. There is nothing to show that he died immediately afterwards, and he may have survived for several years. Thus it is clear that no addition can be made to the length of reign allotted to him by the

[1] Made up by 29 years of his father's reign, 20 of his own, and 17 years of his life after his deposition.

historians, since a service of only four years as Conservator would bring his age to 70 years.

We are therefore left with only Wijaya and Paṇḍuwāsa-Dēva as the sole kings whose reigns might have lasted a little longer than the time stated in the histories. If it be permissible to assume that both were not more than 25 when they became kings, Wijaya's age would become 63 at his death, and Paṇḍuwāsa-Dēva's 55. Even if we extend both up to 70 years it would carry the beginning of Wijaya's reign only 22 years further back. But the probabilities are overwhelmingly against such an addition to their ages. It would show, as a result, that in the case of five legitimate consecutive rulers (omitting Tissa, the brother of Abhaya, as a usurper), not one died under the age of 70 years. Such a chain of long-lived monarchs is unheard of, and is manifestly inadmissible.

I am not concerned in attempting to reconcile the date of Gōtama Buddha with that of Wijaya, who is stated to have arrived in Ceylon and become the first Sinhalese king in the year when Buddha died.[1] According to the genealogical table of Buddha's relatives they appear to have been contemporaries, as the queen of Paṇḍuwāsa-Dēva, the nephew of Wijaya, was the daughter of Buddha's cousin, if the Sinhalese histories are correct. Any error in the chronology is likely to be found among this queen's ancestors; it is possible that two or three names have been omitted between her and Amitōdana, the uncle of Buddha. Such an omission would account for the discrepancy in the dates of Buddha and Wijaya, without its being necessary to assume that the list of Sinhalese kings is at fault. I have shown this in the table, therefore.

[1] Mr. V. A. Smith, in his *Early History of India*, 1908, p. 42, states that Dr. Fleet now considers 482 B.C. the most probable and satisfactory date of the death of Buddha.

XII

THE EARLIEST COINS

THERE is nothing to indicate the date when the first coinage was introduced into Ceylon from India; all that can be said regarding it is that coins were in the country in the second half of the third century B.C. I myself saw two silver Purānas or Salākas, nearly square but rather thick coins without any punch-marks, resembling the copper coin numbered 20 on Plate I of Sir A. Cunningham's *Coins of Ancient India*, which were found in 1884 with the four relic-receptacles that had evidently been deposited in the relic-chamber of the Yaṭṭhāla dāgaba, built by King Mahā-Nāga or his son in the third century B.C. at Tissa or Māgama, the ancient capital of southern Ceylon. I have already described the relic-cases in the chapter which deals with the ancient dāgabas.

The Buddhist monk who was in charge of the largest dāgaba at Tissa, which was undoubtedly built by Mahā-Nāga, informed me in 1884 that some similar coins made of copper, with small punch-marks on their surface, the shapes of which he could not describe, were also found in the débris thrown round its base by its despoilers. They were all replaced in the relic-chamber when it was closed during the restoration of the structure, but the description that was given of them leaves no doubt as to their presence at that work also.

The histories of Ceylon contain no statement that invaders held the southern part of the island before the eleventh century, in the early half of which it is recorded in the Mahāvansa (ii, p. 90) that the forces of the King of Sōla occupied that part of the country and despoiled many wihāras. Even if the relic-chambers of these two dāgabas had been broken into at that time (of which, however, there is no record) it is improbable that any Sinhalese king who restored them afterwards would think it necessary to place such early coins in the new relic-rooms. The presence of the coins therefore is very strong evidence that it was only at the spoliation in the time of the Pāndian king Māgha (1215–1236 A.D.) that the relic-chambers were rifled. The finding of the carnelian gem belonging to the royal seal, to which allusion has been made in a former chapter, is a further proof that this was the case. At the Yaṭṭhāla dāgaba, which I often saw before its restoration, I could not observe the slightest evidence of any restoration or rebuilding of the dome, though I looked carefully for it; only one size of bricks was used in it, and those in the dome were all unbroken and evidently undisturbed ones. It may be concluded, therefore, that the relic-chambers remained intact until the thirteenth century; and that the Purānas were placed in these dāgabas in the third century B.C., and were lost or thrown away by the persons who broke into the structures in the time of the Tamil king Māgha.

In 1885, several of these coins were discovered at Mulleittīvu under circumstances that gave them a special interest. A man who was in charge of a small coconut garden on the north side of the town, where the soil all around is full of fragments of a rough type of pottery, as the result of an unusual fit of energy determined to level a mound of sandy material, and to utilise the soil for filling up some hollows near it. When he reached the level of the adjoining ground he was surprised to meet with the top of a large ring of coarse earthenware such as is used in Ceylon by some of the Kandian Sinhalese for lining wells at their houses. On clearing the sandy soil out of the inside of this ring he found others below it, and discovered that he had unearthed an ancient shallow well at the bottom of which there was fresh water. The rings were 3 feet in internal diameter; the top one was 6½ inches deep and the others about 8 inches. At the present day such well-linings are from 2 feet to 2½ feet in diameter, and about an inch thick.

At a short distance above the water-level, and embedded in the sand, he obtained a number of silver Purānas, and some thin oblong copper plaques which proved to be an entirely new type of money [1] described by me in the previous year from specimens obtained at Tissa. The total number of Purānas was 51, and of the plaques 16. The late Mr. R. Massie, the Assistant Government Agent of the district, obtained nine of the plaques, out of which he presented four to the Colombo Museum, two to me, and at a later date two to the British Museum. I got the other seven when I visited the place shortly afterwards.

It would appear that the original owner of this money, possibly fearing the result of some disturbance or war, first threw some sand into his well and placed his small stock of cash on it; he then filled up the well and to mark the spot raised over it the mound to which its modern discovery was due, little expecting that more than two thousand years would elapse before it would be disinterred.

In addition to these coins four other oblong plaques were found by me at Tissa in 1883, in excavating channels from two sluices at the Tissa tank, and I obtained two halves of others from a neighbouring village. The position of these coins enables us to fix the date of the earliest type of this money as yet discovered.

At the end of the embankment of the Tissa tank, on the high side of a hollow or small water-course, there had been a village of potters and other artizans who were accustomed to throw the ashes and rubbish from their houses and furnaces into the hollow, which thus became a kind of 'Kjökken-mödding.' Afterwards, soil carried down by rains covered up this deposit, and eventually filled all the hollow to the depth of eighteen feet at the deepest part. By a lucky accident, a channel from a new sluice was cut by me through this very site, and numerous articles belonging to the ancient work-people were met with, including thousands of fragments of pottery, some few of which were inscribed with letters of the

[1] Doubts have been expressed as to whether the plaques were coins or votive offerings, but I was led to understand that the authorities of the British Museum do not share them. I have shown below that all the early Indian and Ceylon coins were amulets as well as money.

earliest angular type which is certainly of pre-Christian date. In two instances there are words on the upturned sides of rice-plates, which appear to be the names of the persons for whom they were made. One was inscribed *Gapati Sivasa*, 'the householder Siva's'; the last letter is near the broken edge of the fragment of earthenware, and possibly the name of this person's son followed it. The other, which is also incomplete, is ——*ke Dayapusaha Aba*, 'Abhaya, (son) of —— Dayapusa'; the missing word may have been *gamike*, 'the villager,' or *bojike*, 'the headman.' On all other fragments only one or two letters were found.

From the primitive forms of the letters, which do not include a single round *s*, or the rounded vowels or lengthened *k* or *r*, which stamp the date on post-Christian writing, it appears certain that the letters on the pottery in the upper part of this stratum, which were all written on the earthenware before it was baked, were inscribed at the latest three-quarters of a century before the Christian era, while those in the lowest part most probably date from the second and third centuries B.C., when the construction of the large dāgabas and other important monastic edifices must have necessitated the presence of a large force of workmen. On many of the bricks laid in the Yaṭṭhāla and Mahānāga dāgabas similar letters were written or stamped before they were burnt.

The lowest stratum of remains was four feet thick in its lowest part, which was eighteen feet below the surface of the ground. In the very bottom of this layer one of the oblong coins (No. **1**) was unearthed in 1883 in my presence, and it must, I believe, belong to the third century B.C. A second (No. **2**) was taken out of another part of the same stratum, and therefore probably belongs to either the second or third century B.C. A third (No. **3**) was found slightly above the pottery layer, and may be a century or perhaps two later than these. A fourth (No. **4**) was met with at the remains of some early dwellings that were cut through in opening a channel from another sluice at this tank. The fragments of pottery which were found there were similar to those at the former cutting, and some bricks were of the same dimensions as those used in the great dāgaba of Mahā-Naga and appeared to have been made in the very same moulds. This coin, therefore, may also possibly date from the first, second, or third century B.C.

At the excavations made subsequently at Anurādhapura, twelve specimens of the oblong coins were found by Mr. S. M. Burrows, late of the Ceylon Civil Service, behind the northern wāhalkaḍa at the Abhayagiri dāgaba,[1] and others were discovered by Mr. Bell, near the Jētawanārāma,[2] but so far as I am aware not under circumstances which afford a clue to their age. It may be assumed that those having the simpler designs on them are of pre-Christian manufacture, while others are of later date, and one at least is proved by the Aum monogram on it to belong to about the third or fourth century A.D. I am indebted to the courtesy of Mr. Bell for permission to include descriptions of these coins with the rest.

THE PURĀNAS, OR DHARANAS, OR SĀLĀKAS

Many of these coins have been discovered in India, and Sir Alexander Cunningham estimated that he had seen between four thousand and five thousand specimens.[3] They have been figured and described on several occasions, but I think that no account has been given of any from Ceylon, except nine much worn examples found by Mr. Bell among the débris at an early monastic site in Anurādhapura, which was surrounded by a 'Buddhist Railing.' These were described and figured by him in 1892.[4]

All the Purānas found in the island have been imported from India. The punch-marks on them, each impressed by a separate small punch, and almost all near the sides of the coins, are, with perhaps two or three exceptions, identical with those on Indian coins; and silver and copper, the materials of which they seem to be composed, are not products of Ceylon.

[1] Ievers, *Manual of the North-Central Province*, p. 234.
[2] Arch. Survey of Ceylon. Fourth Progress Report, p. 13.
[3] *Coins of Ancient India*, p. 42.
[4] Arch. Survey of Ceylon. Fourth Progress Report, pp. 4 and 12.

These coins are thus a proof of the early trade with India. The majority are so much worn that any symbols that may have been impressed on them have almost disappeared.

The common designs that can be recognised on the obverse of this money are the rayed sun-symbol, a circle with six emblems round it, the dog, the elephant, the bull, fishes (some of them in tanks), the turtle, forms of trees, and a three-arched structure, surmounted in one case by a crescent. All the mammals face towards the right. The usual emblems that are absent from the coins which I have seen are the human figure, the bow and arrow, the caduceus, the Swāstika, and birds.

On the reverse side some coins have several symbols which are generally nearly worn away, but as a rule there are few marks on that face, among which are the rayed sun, the tree, and the structure with three arches. In one case a person has engraved a design which perhaps was intended for the early cup-shaped letter *m*, with a cross-bar in the middle, as it occurs in local inscriptions of earlier date than 100 B.C. Another has a punched symbol which resembles an early letter, but may be part of an animal design.

The shapes vary as in India, about one-third of the coins being round in outline, while the others are more or less rectangular, and occasionally have one corner or two adjoining ones cut away. According to Indian authorities this indicates that when first cut off the strip of beaten silver hardened by an alloy of copper, from which it was taken, the coin was found to be too heavy and was therefore reduced in weight in this manner. It is obvious that it might still vary from the correct weight to the extent of some grains.

The full weight of such coins as these has been shown by Sir A. Cunningham to be about 57·6 grains.[1] If this was the original weight of those found at Mulleittīvu all must have been subjected to wear for an extended period, since the average of thirty-three[2] is only 33·8 grains, and runs from 28 to

[1] Is it more than a coincidence that an early silver coin found in Crete weighs 56·4 grains?

[2] The rest, which were extremely worn and unfortunately were unweighed, were 'acquired' by an inquisitive servant.

39 grains; the heaviest weigh 38½ and 39 grains, and the lighter ones from 28 to 30 grains. That these very low figures are due chiefly to wear and not merely to original short weight appears to be confirmed by the well-rounded corners of all the rectangular coins, and the indistinct or fragmentary state of the punch marks on all but four or five.

There are no sharp angles like those in the examples illustrated in the *Coins of Ancient India.* Some from which one or two corners have been cut are now among the lightest; it is to be presumed that these have lost half their original weight while in circulation, as they are too much worn to be coins that were at first of half the full weight. In Mr. V. A. Smith's *Catalogue of the Coins in the Indian Museum, Calcutta,* the weights of 108 selected out of about 300 range from 35·7 grains to 55·6 grains.

The late Sir Alexander Cunningham, who was for many years the Director-General of the Archaeological Survey of India, and was the greatest authority on these coins, stated the mean weight of 800 to be 47 grains,[1] and the average loss to have been one and a half grains per century of their age. He characterised a loss of 19 grains in a presumed age of 600 years as 'very exceptional' (*C. A. I.*, p. 55), and he referred to a coin weighing 34 grains as an example of long wear.

If the loss of weight of the lighter coins found at Mulleittīvu has been at this average Indian rate it would remove the date of issue of several of them to about 2000 B.C. At the 'very exceptional' rate the date would still be carried back to the eleventh century B.C.; and in the case of even the heavier ones it would extend to the eighth century.

I express no opinion on these ages; I merely point out the times to which Sir A. Cunningham's data would remove their origin if my belief regarding the date of their deposition is correct, leaving those with a knowledge of the subject to draw their own conclusions. Sir A. Cunningham thought that Purānas were issued by 1000 B.C., but Mr. V. A. Smith, in the Introduction to his Catalogue (p. 135), remarks that this estimate 'almost certainly is much in excess of the truth.'

[1] *C. A. I.*, p. 55.

As he states that it is well established that the full normal weight was 'about 58 grains,' it is to be presumed that he considers the rate of their erosion which was accepted by that distinguished archaeologist to be too low, although he states (p. 1) that 'Sir Alexander's unique experience extending over considerably more than half a century enabled him to accumulate a mass of knowledge, both general and special, concerning all classes of Indian coins, which nobody can hope to rival.'

The date when the Purānas were buried at Mulleittīvu is approximately fixed, as will be shown below, by the type of the oblong coins found with them as probably in the first half of the second century B.C., and it is extremely unlikely to be later than the first years of the first century B.C.

Since the amount of the loss of weight of these Purānas must be accepted as proof that they were in circulation for a period amounting to at least several centuries, it is apparent, if that date be correct, that they all belong to a time prior to the introduction of Greek coinage into India.

They are of two general types, with some intermediate gradations, a larger thin coin of which both nearly square and rounded specimens occur as in India, and a much smaller but thicker coin which is usually oblong in shape, although both rounded and square examples occur. The larger coins have numerous punch marks on them, in several cases on both sides; the smaller specimens have few marks and those almost worn away. On some faces no marks are visible. The general appearance of the small coins, the surface of which is of a rougher texture than that of the others, and the extremely worn condition of their marks, a few of which can only be faintly seen in a strong light, lead me to suppose that they are considerably older than the larger coins; but there is not much difference in the weights of the two varieties, since although several of the lightest coins are of the smaller type other small ones are as heavy as many of the larger variety. It is important to note, however, that in the smaller coins the surface exposed to wear is little more than half that of the larger ones, and therefore an equal loss of weight in their case must indicate a far greater age.

The different shapes are all visible in the illustration in *C. A. I.*, from a photograph, of the early carving (B.C. 250) found at Gayā, which represents the purchase of the garden for the celebrated Jētavana monastery at Srāvasti. The small coins are few in number in that relief. In the later one at Bharhut (150 B.C.) only the larger coins, both rectangular and round, appear to be shown.

Copper, which was used in the coins, is found sparingly in Northern India, but I think is not mentioned in the Vedas. Silver certainly was known in India at that early period, the moon being described as 'Silvery' (R.V., ix, 79, 9).

Although wealth is everywhere defined in the Vedic prayers as consisting of cattle, horses, and gold, it is to be remembered that the authors of the hymns were priests who always demanded the most valuable things, and that even if there was a gold coinage of some kind there would be few gold coins to pray for. As Mr. Del Mar remarks in his *History of Money*, they could only be required as multiples of a coinage of lower values. The omission to mention gold coinage in the hymns is therefore not a definite proof of its non-existence.

Mr. Del Mar has pointed out that the state of society and civilisation in India in the [later] Vedic age was one that apparently necessitated the use of some kind of money; and if the reference to a gift of the value of a thousand or ten thousand pieces in the Sāma Veda (Prapathaka, iii, 10, 9) is correctly translated by Stevenson it is clear that coins were numerous in the second millennium before Christ. The extract is as follows :—'O Wielder of the Thunderbolt, thou art not impoverished by a noble and surpassingly splendid gift, not by one of a thousand pieces' value, no, nor by one of ten thousand, not even, Possessor of Wealth, by such a gift a hundred times repeated.'

In the Rig Veda (Griffiths) viii, 1, 5, the words are, 'O Caster of the Stone, I would not sell thee for a mighty price, not for a thousand, Thunderer! not for ten thousand, nor a hundred, Lord of Countless Wealth.'

As in early times there was usually only one coin which

was found in great numbers in a country, it was a common practice to omit specifying any special coin, or even money, when mentioning large sums; only the number of the coins was given. Thus the pre-Christian annalists from whom the author of the first part of the Mahāvansa borrowed his historical facts stated that at the building of the so-called 'Brazen Palace' at Anurādhapura King Duṭṭha-Gāmiṇi, in order to provide for the wages of the workpeople, deposited 'eight hundred thousand' at each of the four entrances. It is also recorded that in offerings at a festival at the Bō-tree he expended 'one hundred thousand,' and that he rewarded the architect of the Ruwanwaeli dāgaba, for his lucid explanation of his design, with a suit of clothes—a Robe of Honour—worth 'a thousand'; and other similar examples might be quoted.

Of such statements there are several instances in the Rig Veda. In Book x, 17, 9, the line occurs, 'Give food and wealth to present sacrificers, a portion, worth a thousand, of refreshment.' In x, 102, 2 we find 'Loose in the wind the woman's robe was streaming what time she won a car load worth a thousand'; and in verse 9 of the same hymn, 'Therewith hath Mudgala in ordered contest won for cattle for himself a hundred thousand.'

I have not searched for earlier examples. Those which I have quoted appear to be quite as unmistakable references to money as the instances from the Mahāvansa. Since gold and silver money, which must have been preceded by a currency of lower value, is mentioned in the early part of the Rāmāyana as being well known (Book i, 13; ii, 32), I accept these references in the Rig Veda as clear proofs of the existence of some form of money that was in extensive use in later Vedic times.

We cannot expect ever to see many examples dating from such a far-distant period. Although, thanks to the early annalists, it is certain that numberless coins, which in some instances were stated to be termed *Kahāpana*, were in use in Ceylon in early times, not one specimen of them had been seen twenty-seven years ago; and even now few have been

FIG. 154. Mulleittivu and Tissa Coins.

To face p. 469

discovered, notwithstanding Mr. Bell's excavations throughout the ruins of the ancient capital, Anurādhapura. When that is the case with coins of such comparatively recent date, little surprise should be felt that the money of Vedic times has remained so long unknown. Its absence is not a proof that such a coinage did not exist.

I mention this because it appears to be probable that the oldest examples of the Mulleittīvu money, and also some of the Purānas found by Mr. Bell, may date from an extremely early time, and though later than the Vedic age may have preserved the type of a coinage which may have been current in that period, or shortly afterwards.

I give illustrations of the best specimens found at Mulleittīvu, together with typical examples of the smaller variety (Fig. No. 154). Some of the symbols on the former coins are clearly defined; it must be presumed that these were impressed long after the money was issued, the reduced weights of the coins on which they occur plainly showing that they have been in circulation for a period long enough to have nearly or totally worn them away had they been stamped soon after the coins were made.

Beginning at the top and proceeding down the left side in the direction taken by the quadrupeds, the emblems on the coins which are illustrated are as follows:—

(**a**.) Rectangular, with two corners cut off; ·72 in. by ·68 in.; weight 37 grains.

Obverse. Standing Humped Bull, wearing a collar, which is indicated by a projection on the nape and throat; Wheel or Sun symbol; Dog; Symbol composed of two concentric circles—that is, a disk with a circular band round it—from the outer circumference of which project six emblems (parts of three only can be seen); Tree.

Reverse. A straight leafy Branch in centre, in a very narrow ellipse; and remains of other symbols, among them apparently a Fish, a Structure of five or six arches, a 'Taurine' emblem, and possibly another form of Tree.

(**b**.) Rectangular, with corners rounded by wear; ·66 in. by ·61 in.; weight 39 grains.

O. Dog with raised tail and forequarters lowered as though about to spring forward, standing on two arches, the tops of which are visible; Tusk Elephant; Circle with emblems; two Arches of a structure of which probably a third one has been destroyed by being over-stamped with the Elephant; Humped Bull with collar; Sun emblem.

R. Broad plain cross in a circular punch-mark; Tree (inverted) and remains of other symbols among which may be the three-arched Structure.

(**c.**) Rectangular, with corners rounded by wear; ·68 in. by ·62 in; weight 38 grains.

O. Bull; Circle with six emblems; a form of Tree punched over one of the last emblems; three arches of a Structure which probably had five, three in the lower row and two above them; these last are separated by a central space over which stands a Dog, with its hind feet on one arch and fore-feet on the other; Sun emblem, the inner disk of which is connected with the outer ring by tiny spokes.

R. (not illustrated). Upright Axe with handle, or part of a Steel-yard, the whole punch-mark being a half ellipse; three Beads attached to the sides of a sector-shaped punch-mark; Tree, and fragment of a symbol.

(**d.**) Irregular oval in shape; ·87 in. by ·72 in.; weight 30 grains.

O. Dog; an uncertain symbol; Sun emblem; uncertain Quadruped behind with thick legs; a figure from the five angles of which rise twigs with three leaves which form crosses, a flower or fruit on a short stem being in each intermediate space (only half the figure is on this coin); concentric Circles with six emblems. Quadruped wearing a broad collar and having two cuts above the tail.

R. Symbol which is possibly a Yak-tail Fly-whisk; Sun emblem; Fish; above these the Structure with three arches, surmounted by a crescent; above this a fragmentary symbol; part of uncertain symbol; a long punch-mark in which are a 'Taurine' symbol and two concentric circles without surrounding emblems; two uncertain symbols; an oblong punch-mark, inside which is a transverse bar near each end and a minute emblem between these.

(e.) Irregular oblong; 1·02 in. by ·44 in.; weight 37½ grains.

O. Symbol resembling three or four leaves (not beads) projecting from the sides of a hollow, towards its centre; traces of a symbol above it; a long elliptical punch-mark, the symbol in which is partly destroyed by the next one; the upper part of it may be a form of Trisūla and when the coin is turned round the other part resembles a Bull; Sun emblem; large 'Taurine' emblem; remains of another symbol above it.

R. Circles with surrounding emblems; Sun emblem, about 16 rays.

(f.) Rounded; ·76 in. by ·63 in; weight 37 grains.

O. Structure of three arches resting on vertical walls, the central arch rising half as high again as the others. Over it a snake formed by a deeply-waved line; it resembles the conventional clouds of temple artists, but possibly was not impressed by the same punch as the arched structure; worn symbol, apparently an animal and possibly a lion; Sun emblem, 16 rays; a design like a Palmira tree, but apparently a Flower with a circular centre and five petals, on a stem, perhaps stamped over the head of an Elephant.

R. Symbol like an upright Axe with short handle, punched over part of another emblem with a straight bar beneath it and possibly an arched Structure; traces of two other emblems.

(g.) Nearly circular; ·58 in. by ·58 in.; weight 34½ grains.

O. Dog (?); Circle surrounded by emblems; Fish, partly over-stamped by another design; Sun emblem, and others.

R. Traces of emblems.

(h.) Oblong, one corner cut off, ·55 in. by ·34 in.; weight 29½ grains.

O. Rude punch-mark, shaped like a Quadruped but turned to left.

R. Blank.

(i.) Oblong, one corner cut off; ·56 in. by ·45 in; weight 34½ grains.

O. Punch-mark, resembling a letter, but possibly part of a symbol.

R. Traces of symbols.

(**k.**) Oblong, two corners cut off ; ·56 in. by ·44 in ; weight 29 grains.

O. Trace of part of concentric Circles with surrounding emblems ; trace of Sun emblem.

R. Blank.

Three other small coins are as follows :—

(**l.**) oblong ; ·57 in. by ·44 in.; weight 28½ grains.

O. Fragments of Circle with surrounding emblems, and traces of three other symbols. R. Faint traces of two symbols.

(**m.**) short oblong, one corner cut off ; ·57 in. by ·50 in. ; weight 29½ grains.

Only indistinct crescentic symbol with straight back.

(**n.**) oblong ; ·55 in. by ·44 in.; weight 30½ grains.

Traces of two symbols on one side, and of one on the other.

The average weight of thirteen coins of the smaller variety is 32·9 grains, the heaviest weighing 38½ grains.

(**o.**) The lightest coin weighs 28 grains, and is a little larger than these. It measures ·59 in. by ·56 in., and is thus almost square, with rounded corners ; one corner is cut off.

There are four or five very faint punch-marks on O. One is a Structure of three arches with a channel below it ; another appears to be the fore-quarters of an Elephant ; between these is part of a Sun-emblem ; there are also faint traces like part of the Circle with six emblems, and of two other symbols. On R. all that can be seen is a worn punch-mark of a narrow Leaf-shape, and perhaps the trace of another symbol.

In the case of the nine Purānas discovered at Anurādhapura by Mr. Bell, in 1891,[1] the antiquity of the building at which they were disinterred is proved by the size of the bricks employed in the lower part of the walls. These measured 18 inches by 9 inches by 3 inches, Bt. being thus 27 square inches and the contents 486 cubic inches. My 'Amended List' of bricks shows that these dimensions probably belong to the latter part of the second century or the early part of the first century B.C. Unfortunately there is nothing to indicate the period when the coins were deposited there ; judging by their extremely worn state it may have occurred at some date con-

[1] Arch. Survey of Ceylon. Fourth Progress Report, pp. 4 and 13.

siderably after Christ, as other money, both South Indian (Kurumbar and Pallava) and Roman (Theodosius), was also found at the site.

Three of the Purānas were apparently spurious imitations of silver coins, being made of copper and having still traces of the silver coating which had been applied to them. Two of these were square, with half inch sides and weighed 24 and 29 grains. The third was an oblong, ·7 in. by ·37 in., weighing 40 grains. On its obverse was a standing figure unlike those of the true Purānas, and perhaps copied from an oblong coin like those described below, with a length amounting to three-quarters of the coin ; on the reverse appeared a chequer pattern.

The other six were silver coins, three being more or less oblong, and three nearly square. Of the former variety, one coin measured ·56 in. by ·44 in., and weighed only 16 grains. It had the Sun emblem, and the remains of another. Each of the others weighed 19 grains, and was a broad oblong, with one corner cut off. Both had traces of symbols.

Of the square coins, two had sides of half an inch ; one with a corner cut off weighed 30 grains, and the other 42 grains ; these also showed traces of symbols. The third one, of an irregular shape, had a length of ·75 in., and weighed only 17 grains. On its obverse was a Sun symbol, a Tree, and other worn punch-marks, one of them appearing in the figure to be the three beads projecting into a hollow. It may represent pearls in the shell, a powerful amulet in Vedic times (Ath. Veda, iv, 10).

It is noticeable that on nearly all the Purānas of apparently the earliest date traces are visible of some of the same punch-marks as those on the coins of the latest type. Among these the wheel-like Sun symbol was the emblem most generally employed.

The symbol consisting of two concentric circles from which project six emblems is common on Indian coins. In the Mulleittīvu coins the emblems usually are a 'Taurine' or bull's-head symbol enclosed in a semi-ellipse, and another which has been termed a Chatta or umbrella, but which may be a form of Axe-head with a narrow stem and a semi-circular cutting edge. These occur alternately, being three times repeated. On another Mulleittīvu coin a Fish is placed between them, the three emblems being twice repeated.

The meanings of the symbols will be considered after the other coins have been described.

THE OBLONG COPPER COINS

The Tissa Coins

These coins are all thin copper oblongs of one type, cut off strips of beaten copper which were themselves cut off a larger sheet. The designs on both faces were impressed simultaneously by means of two dies that were nearly as large as the coins. On the obverse, which has a flat border, a person is represented, standing facing front, and holding an upright object, apparently a flower stem, at each side of the coin. On the reverse the Swāstika appears, exactly resembling those cut at some pre-Christian inscriptions, being raised high on a central pole which rests on a transverse base line from which rise two short upright bars at each side of the central post. This symbol is found on all the oblong copper coins of the island, and also on a large circular copper coin which supplanted them. As a typical emblem of ancient Ceylon it is stamped on the cover of this work.

In the following descriptions of the coins the letter f. is 'front,' and r. and l. are 'right' and 'left' respectively.

1. 1·14 in. by ·46 in.; weight 52½ grains.

O. A figure of a deity, facing f. Over and round the head runs a slightly waved line or circlet. The l. hand appears to rest on something represented by three upright lines; the r. fore-arm apparently turned upwards. Legs slightly apart and feet turned outwards. There may be a tunic or cloth extending onto the thighs. The figure is well proportioned and even somewhat graceful.

R. Indistinct. Part of the Swāstika symbol visible with its arms turned r. To l. under arm of cross there are indistinct marks in relief.

Colombo Museum.

2. 1·18 in. by ·46 in.; weight 44 grains.

O. Within a flat border, above the level of which the design does not rise,[1] a full-length figure of deity, wider at the hips than shoulders, facing f. A thin oval circlet round and over head, springing from the shoulders. Feet turned half outwards. The arms hang down, l. hand appearing to grasp an upright bar at border, and r. holding a curved stem, at the top of which is a trumpet-shaped flower or a cornucopia with a circular flower over it, and leaves or buds above. At each side, near border, is a thin upright line. One anklet on each leg and a bangle above r. wrist.

R. In the upper third a Swāstika, turned r. with stem prolonged downwards to middle of lowest third of coin, where it springs from a slightly curved horizontal line. Two short equidistant vertical lines of the length of the arms of the Swāstika rise from the base line, on each side of central stem. Below base line and separated from it by a well-marked channel there is a parallel line, beneath which is a broad flat border line. Between the Swāstika and basal uprights there are raised marks on each side of the central stem, but what they represent is uncertain. Col. Mus.

3. 1·22 in. by ·50 in.; weight 41 grains.

O. Below a flat border line outside which is a sunk channel, a standing deity, facing f. Thick circlet from shoulders round head. Four anklets on each leg and perhaps bangle on r. wrist. Arms hang down, hands grasping on each side a curved line which may be a flower-stem, that on r. having a side view of a trumpet-mouth at level of shoulder, above which may be an open flower and buds, as in No. 2. Stem on l. may also end in flowers and leaves. Below the feet a horizontal row of beads consisting of three thin upright ones in the centre and two larger round ones at each side.

R. The same Swāstika, with thick lines, turned r.; base

[1] This style of false relief is a distinct characteristic of Sinhalese art, whether of early or later date, and is also seen in Southern India. Dr. Dresser, unaware of this, stated his belief that it was 'not practised by any other peoples than the Egyptians and the Japanese.' *Japan, its Architecture, Art, and Art Manufactures*, p. 341.

line nearly straight. Below it two slightly bent flat parallel bars separated from each other and the base by deep wide flat-bottomed channels. At sides of central pole are raised marks of uncertain character. Col. Mus.

4. 1·20 in. by ·55 in.; weight 35 grains.

O. Broad flat border along top and upper part of r. side. Standing deity, facing f., with irregular circlet over head and resting on shoulders; above the head a flat horizontal bar separated by a channel from the border. Feet turned half-outwards, and clearly and accurately represented, with heel, instep, and side view of toes. A large anklet on each leg. Arms hang down, and hold at each side near border a thin curved line which may be a flower stem, ending at shoulder level in indistinct flowers and leaves. Above them two beads on each side, near circlet.

R. Swāstika as before, turned l., on thick winding base, below which and separated from it by a wide flat channel are two similar raised parallel bars, with narrow channel between them. On both sides of central pole are faint raised designs, that on l. resembling an early letter *Ke*. Col. Mus.

5. About half only, from Sittrawila near Tissa, ·54 in. by ·49 in. wide.

O. Lower half of standing deity. An upright line to r.

R. In opposite direction to O. Swāstika, turned r.

H. Parker.

6. Over half, from Sittrawila, ·66 in. by ·50 in. wide.

O. Flat border at bottom. Lower half of standing deity with hanging arms; l. hand grasps an upright line.

R. Indistinct. Lower part of Swāstika symbol, with raised marks in side spaces. H. P.

THE MULLEITTĪVU COINS

These coins are also oblongs of beaten copper, wider than those of Tissa; they are all of one type which differs in some respects from that of the Tissa coins. Each has the standing deity on O., and the peculiar Swāstika symbol on R.; but all are characterised by having in the space under the arm of the Swāstika and usually on the right side of the central pole, a recumbent humped bull, sometimes kneeling on one knee, and on the opposite side a vase out of which grows a plant. The flat border of the Tissa coins is absent, as well as the line under the base of the Swāstika, and sometimes the circlet over the head of the deity. These coins cannot have been long in circulation, the edges being sharp as though freshly cut; but on several of them the design is quite faint.

7. 1·16 in. by ·64 in.; weight 49 grains.

O. Standing deity, facing f., with legs slightly apart. Arms hang down, and hands grasp two upright lines at level of hips. That on l. has a boss on it below shoulder level; opposite the neck it divides into two arms which are at first horizontal and then vertical, forming a bident. The other seems to be similar. From top of inner prongs of bident an arched band rises over the head. Beginning above the shoulders and extending round the head are seven clearly defined beads, and another is on each side close to the hips. Bangles on both wrists and an anklet on l. leg; the other ankle and both feet cannot be distinguished.

R. Opposed to O. Swāstika symbol, turned r., on straight base. In space to r. of central pole and facing Swāstika a recumbent humped bull. In space to l. a round-bodied object, a vase with plant; one stem has three leaves. Mouth of vase faces Swāstika. H. P.

8. 1·03 in. by ·61 in.; weight 44½ grains.

O. Narrow-waisted standing deity, facing f., with legs well apart and arms hanging down. The l. one grasps a strong upright pole, which at level of neck becomes a bident or trident, only one prong being recognisable. A bead above each shoulder and traces of two others above them. If a circlet of beads passed round head they may have been only five in number. Feet and r. hand indistinguishable.

R. Opposed to O. Broad-stemmed Swāstika symbol, turned r., with pointed arms. Recumbent humped bull facing it on r.; a vase with indistinct plant on l., turned towards Swāstika. H. P.

9. 1·12 in. by ·72 in.; weight 32¼ grains.

O. Standing deity, facing f., with two large anklets on each leg. Arms hang down and hands grasp two upright poles near sides of coin, of which that on l. becomes a wide bident above level of neck, l. prong ending in a barbed point. A bead above each shoulder, and some kind of covering or head-dress on head, extending beyond it laterally.

R. Opposed to O. Raised Swāstika, turned l. Facing it on r., the recumbent humped bull. Vase on l. with plant, facing Swāstika. H. P.

10. 1·20 in. by ·70 in.; weight 38½ grains.

O. Standing deity, facing f., very narrow-waisted, with bangle on l. wrist. Side uprights barely distinguishable; that on r. appears to end in bident opposite neck. A circlet of beads extends from shoulders and round head, on each side of which three are visible.

R. Opposed to O. Raised Swāstika, turned l., with arms and basal uprights pointed. Indistinct symbols below it; that on r. may be the recumbent bull facing it. H. P.

11. 1·14 in. by ·66 in.; weight 46¼ grains. About one-tenth of the coin has been cut off r. upper corner; allowing for this, the full weight would be about 50½ grains. Design is in higher relief.

O. Standing deity, facing f., with wider waist. Hands hold upright poles or stems near sides of coin. Arched line over head with lower edge scalloped. A bead above each shoulder, and another over it on l.; there may have been seven round the head. There are indications of flowers on stems on each side of the legs.

R. Raised Swāstika, turned r. Base straight; short side uprights resting on it are pointed at ends. In space to r. a kneeling humped bull, with r. fore-foot on ground. Tail is curled back on l. quarter, its end being on the ground. The bull is tied to the Swāstika by a halter. Two points on its neck may indicate two collars. On l. a wide vase on a flat base; tree grows out of it, an upright stem, from which branch four side shoots, ending in leaves or flowers. H. P.

12. 1·12 in. by ·65 in.; weight 51 grains.

O. Standing deity, facing f., indistinct. Hands hold uprights near edge; that on r. may end in bident. A bead on each side above shoulders, and anklet on r. leg. Transverse bar below feet bent downward in middle.

R. Opposed to O. Raised Swāstika on strong stem, turned r. Recumbent humped bull on l. facing Swāstika, with hanging ears and dewlap. On r. a round-bodied vase out of which grow probably three stems, two only being visible, each ending in a leaf or flower. H. P.

13. 1·04 in. by 60 in.; weight 29¾ grains.

O. Standing deity, facing f. Anklet on left leg; lower part of other leg indistinguishable. Upright pole on r. appears above shoulder to curl round towards head in a rough circle, which may possibly be a large trumpet-mouthed flower.

R. Opposed to O. Raised Swāstika, turned l. The only two basal uprights which are distinguishable end in points. To r., recumbent humped bull facing Swāstika. To l., vase with wide mouth facing Swāstika; r. shoot from it ends in a broad pointed leaf. No transverse bar under base line of Swāstika, this being the only coin which shows clearly that this special feature of the Tissa coins is omitted from those found at Mulleittīvu. H. P.

14. 1·18 in. by ·66 in.; weight 56 grains.

O. Standing deity in relief, facing f., feet turned half outwards; holds upright pole at each side. That on r. becomes a bident at level of chin, with horizontal base and prongs sloping slightly outwards. A broad circlet passes from inner prongs over the head, and on the under side has a scalloped edge. There are seven beads round the head, the two lowest being close to shoulders. On r. wrist two bangles, and anklet on r. leg. To l. between leg and pole, a raised symbol, the side view of a lotus leaf on an upright stem. To r. a thin curved stem ending in large flower. A fold of the dress hangs down between the legs. Three cuts across r. foot indicate a shoe or slipper.

R. Opposed to O. Raised Swāstika, with thick arms turned r., two short thin bars cross the ends of its arms and of the basal uprights. To r. recumbent humped bull facing Swāstika, to which it is tied by a halter. To l., a wide heart-shaped vase, pointed at bottom and having a high neck and lip, with upright plant ending in one leaf; it has a r. and l. branch, former ending in a large leaf. H. P.

15. 1·04 in. by ·66 in.; weight 51 grains.

O. Standing deity, facing f., holding upright poles at sides; bangles on wrists. A flattened circlet passes over head, from uprights. Traces of beads round head.

R. Opposed to O. Raised Swāstika, appearing to turn r, with pointed basal uprights. End of central arm on r., the only one distinguishable, seems to be bent horizontally towards the stem and to end in a fork. To r., recumbent humped bull, facing Swāstika. To l., a vase out of which grows an upright tree, perhaps ending in three large leaves. H. P.

16. 1·20 in. by ·66 in.; weight 54 grains.

O. Standing deity (goddess) with small waist, facing f., and grasping a thick pole at each side of coin. Two bangles on r. wrist, and one or more on l.; anklets on legs. A broad bead on each side of neck.

R. Raised Swāstika, the side uprights end in points; ends of arms are not visible. Bull and vase as usual.

Col. Mus.

17. 1·21 in. by ·74 in.; weight 52 grains.

O. Vigorous figure of deity (goddess) with very narrow waist, facing f.; apparently an anklet on each leg. A raised bead on each side of neck. Hands seem to hold usual upright poles.

R. Opposed to O. Raised Swāstika, turned r. Basal uprights end in points; ends of arms not distinguishable. Usual bull and vase, transposed to l. and r. respectively. Vase has flat base, very narrow mouth, out of which grows a plant of three shoots each ending in one leaf. Col. Mus.

18. 1·20 in. by ·68 in.; weight 51 grains.

O. Standing deity, facing f.; one or two anklets on each leg. Upright pole on r., at edge of coin.

R. Raised Swāstika, turned l., on wide stem, with very short basal uprights. To l., recumbent humped bull facing base line; the only instance in which it does not face the Swāstika. To r. the vase also inverted, with plant of three shoots each ending in a leaf. Col. Mus.

19. 1·20 in. by ·71 in.; weight 29 grains.

O. Standing deity with wider waist, facing f.; two bangles on r. wrist, and a bead above each shoulder. Feet and other hand not visible. Upright pole to r. appears to end in bident with prongs inclined outwards. Portion of arched line over head is visible. On each side of legs are reliefs that I cannot identify.

R. Opposed to O. Swāstika turned r. Bull with curled tail; two shoots of plant visible. Col. Mus.

20. A portion only. ·97 in. by ·76 in.; weight 19½ grains.

O. Standing deity, facing f.

R. Recumbent bull, repunched from O. R. Massie.

21. A portion only. ·92 in. by ·56 to ·64 in.; weight 42 grains.

O. Standing deity, perhaps facing half l. Bangles and anklets as usual, and upright poles at sides; the pointed head of one, at shoulder-level, appears to show that they are javelins. A bead on each side of neck.

R. Opposed to O. Swāstika, turned r. Design to r. indistinct; to l. a full-bodied vase in good relief, with small mouth and distinct lip. Parts of three shoots each terminated by a leaf. ? Brit. Mus.

22. 1·10 in. by ·68 to ·73 in.; weight 47½ grains.

O. Standing deity with narrow waist, facing f. Each hand holds upright pole at side of coin, that to r. having a square knob at its base. Bangles and anklets as usual, and a bead on each side of neck. Circlet passes over head, appearing to rest at each end on the side poles.

R. Indistinct; part of Swāstika. Usual bull and vase; plant of two shoots each branching into two. ? Brit. Mus.

23. To these I add one coin purchased for me at Anurādhapura by my friend Mr. Balfour of the Irrigation Department, as it is of the same type as the foregoing, and unlike others dug up at that town which are described below.

1·09 in. by ·62 in.; weight 41 grains.

O. Standing deity with narrow waist, facing f. Anklet on l. leg. Arms as usual; l. one holds an upright pole which appears to become a bident at level of neck.

R. Raised Swāstika turned r. Bull as usual; one stem of plant on l., ending in a leaf. H. P.

24. Another of this type found by Mr. Bell at Anurādhapura,[1] at the structure surrounded by a 'Buddhist railing,' measured 1·12 in. by ·7 in., and weighed 51½ grains.

O. Standing deity, facing f. holding the shaft of a trident in each hand.

The raised Swastika, turned r. Recumbent bull on r., and plant of three stems on l., each ending in a leaf, and springing from a cross-bar. Col. Mus.

The Anurādhapura Coins

These coins, with the exceptions of the two last described, represent a type which in some instances differs in important respects from either the Tissa or Mulleittīvu coins. In the case of at least seven of them the figure is seated, with the leg doubled up so that the heel approaches the body; the right leg hangs down. In each of the seven the l. hand rests upon the l. thigh, and r. arm is bent upward, the hand being raised to the level of the shoulder, and probably holding a flower. The other coins have standing figures on O.

On R., the humped bull does not appear to occur on the coins I have seen, except on **23** and **24**, its place being taken by other symbols and marks which are usually indistinct; in one instance the Aum monogram is present, and probably in another the Swāstika. The Vase is visible on some coins, and may have been on all originally. In all the specimens the workmanship differs from that of the Tissa coins, and the die for the O. was often not much larger than the figure. I believe that all these coins are now in the Colombo Museum, with the exception of one which is in my own collection.

25. 1·06 in. by ·56 in.; weight 49½ grains.

O. Standing goddess with small waist, facing f., holding upright pole at each side of coin, that on r. possibly ending in trident at level of chin. A bead above each shoulder, and apparently anklets. To r. of legs a symbol resembling an

[1] Arch. Survey of Ceylon. Fourth Progress Report, pp. 4 and 13.

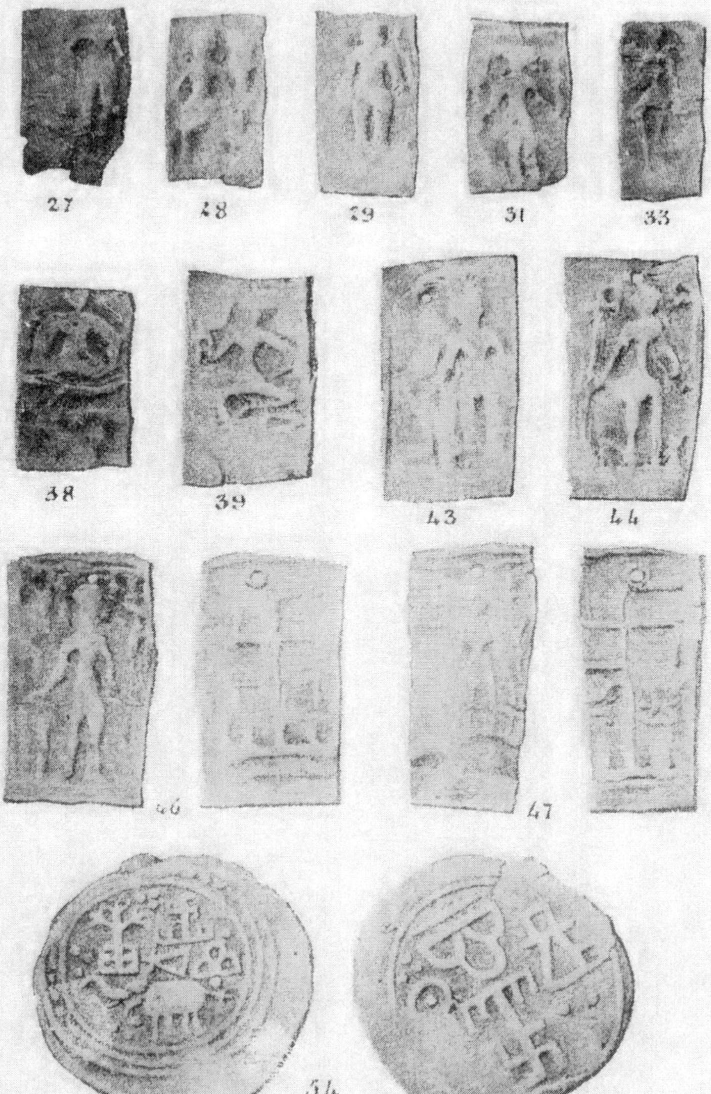

FIG. 155. Anuradhapura Coins.

To face p. 482

upright post with its top turned towards legs. To l. a symbol like the supposed lotus leaf of No. **14,** but smaller.

R. Opposed to O. Raised Swāstika turned r., with very broad arms, the ends of which, as well as those of the basal uprights, are pointed. Indistinct symbols to r. and l., that on l. being forked and somewhat like a 'taurine' emblem.

26. 1·02 in. by ·56 in.; weight 13 grains.

O. Standing deity, facing f., with arms as usual. Two bangles on l. wrist, and anklets high on legs.

R. Opposed to O. Raised Swāstika turned l. A round elevation to r. may be a vase.

27. 1·06 in. by ·56 in.; weight 24 grains; lower edge irregular.

O. Standing figure of deity with very narrow waist, facing f. Arms as usual, two bangles being on l. one. Two anklets on l. leg; perhaps a third above calf. To r. of legs a raised bead opposite the knee, resting on an upright post, the top of which is pointed.

R. Raised Swāstika. Little to be seen.

28. 1·01 in. by ·52 in.; weight unknown.

O. Standing deity as usual; two bangles on l. wrist. A cloth from waist nearly to knees. Upright pole on r. may end in bident at shoulder level. A bead above each shoulder.

R. Raised Swāstika. Indistinct.

29. 1·04 in. by ·54 in.; weight unknown.

O. Standing deity, stouter than usual, facing f., with two bangles on l. wrist; hand holds upright pole which may end in bident at level of neck.

R. Indistinct.

30. 1·07 in. by ·43 in.; weight unknown.

Both faces indistinct, but part of standing figure visible.

31. 1·01 in. by ·53 in.; weight 17 grains.

O. Standing deity facing f., and holding poles as usual. Two anklets on each leg and a bangle on each wrist. Circle of beads may have passed over head, two being visible on each side. Upright poles may have ended in bidents.

R. Very faint, but part of stem of Swāstika can be seen perhaps part of vase to r.

32. 1·17 in. by ·51 ; weight 22 grains.

O. The die has moved and rendered design blurred. A goddess standing facing f., holds on r. a bident. Bead on each side of neck. To l. of r. ankle a large bead rests upon a thick upright stem which is widened out at the top ; this resembles the 'disk on the altar.' To r. of legs, an upright bar with upper part turned r.

R. Opposed to O. Raised Swāstika, turned r. On l. a raised oval may be the vase.

33. 1·04 in. by ·43 in. ; weight 17½ grains.

O. Standing goddess (? Muktakēsī, a form of Durgā, with loose hair) thin, with wasp-like waist, facing f. Short skirt from waist to mid-thigh. Long loose hair incised after stamping, in fine lines, hangs down on l., reaching below waist. A bead above l. shoulder. Side poles not visible. Mark of top of die extends in an arc over the head.

R. Opposed to O. Part of raised Swāstika.

34. 1·17 in. by ·62 in. ; weight 45½ grains.

O. Standing deity, facing f., with cloth apparently folded round the hips. Arms hang down as usual. Trace of top of bident on l.

R. Raised Swāstika, turned l. To r., large round-bodied vase, with lip. To l., a symbol resembling an early letter *n*.

35. 1·10 in. by ·46 in. ; weight 30 grains. Purchased for me in Anurādhapura.

O. Standing goddess, facing f., and holding poles as usual. The head is gone ; navel distinctly marked. Two bangles and an armlet on r. arm ; anklets on both legs. A row of five or seven beads round head, and perhaps a horizontal row above them. Under the feet three short vertical raised lines. Upright on l. widens out at shoulder level ; both are too much worn for tops to be discriminated. A line on l. between the leg and side pole may be the edge of her dress.

R. Raised Swāstika, turned r. ; the lower arm appears to be straight and extends horizontally to r. and l. of centre line. Two narrow parallel waved lines below base line.

H. P.

36. 1·25 in. by ·76 in. ; weight unknown.

O. Seated figure, turned f., with face to l. Two anklets on r. leg, and one or two on the other. The l. leg doubled under body ; r. leg hangs down from knee. The l. arm hangs down and hand rests on l. thigh. The r. upper arm hangs down and fore-arm bends out horizontally. Hair-knot, or head-dress, or helmet extends at back of head. Raised work in front of face, some of it being part of an arched band that passes round and over head.

R. Swāstika, turned l. No bar below its base line. To l., a symbol which may be the vase ; to r., a small symbol indistinct.

37. 1·20 in. by ·82 in. ; weight 74 grains.

O. The die merely includes a sitting figure (? female) in the same posture as last. Two armlets on l. upper arm, and an anklet on l. leg. Hand on r. holds a flower on its stem before the face. One bead above l. shoulder. A head-dress, or crown, or helmet on head, above which the die ended in a point.

R. Opposed to O. Indistinct. Swāstika, and symbol on r.

38. 1·09 in. by ·62 in. ; weight 40 grains.

O. Lower third of coin untouched by die. Seated figure (? female) in the same attitude, with one bangle on l. wrist, and two anklets on l. leg. The arm bent up near shoulder on r., and flower held at shoulder level. A bead on r. of head.

R. Opposed to O. Swāstika turned l., with thick base line. To l., vase with three shoots ; to r., a symbol indefinable.

39. 1·21 in. by ·71 in. ; weight unknown.

O. Seated figure (? female) in same attitude, bangles on wrist, two armlets on l. upper arm, two anklets on l. leg, perhaps only one on r. leg. Fore-arm on r. raised to shoulder level. The die did not include more.

R. Very indistinct.

40. 1·24 in. by ·75 in. ; weight unknown.

O. Seated figure in same attitude ; bead over l. shoulder. Five nearly upright short lines below l. foot and calf, rising from a horizontal one which turns down on l. close to r. foot, may indicate a seat or throne. Hand raised to level of head on r. A bead between l. arm and waist.

R. Raised Swāstika. Vase to r., with shoots each ending in a flower or leaf.

41. 1·31 in. by ·74 in.; weight unknown.

O. Seated figure in same attitude, but r. leg doubled under body, and l. leg doubled under r. one. Two bangles on l. wrist, and one or two on r. one. A bead on each side of waist. Hand raised to shoulder level on r. A curved band seems to pass round head. Upright pole near l. edge of coin, ends invisible.

42. 1·50 in. by ·79 in.; weight 74 grains.

O. Seated figure with wider waist, in usual attitude. Hand on r. holds flower at shoulder level. A bar passes down from l. knee and is then turned horizontally to r. toes; it may represent the outer side of a throne, or the side of the dress.

R. Opposed to O. Raised Swāstika, turning l., rising from a waved base line, below which, and separated from it by a wide channel, is a straight horizontal band. To l., the vase with two round flowers or leaves above it. An emblem to r., like a bull's head looking downwards.

43. 1·43 in. by ·72 in.; weight 75 grains.

O. Standing deity, facing f., as usual; one or two bangles on r. wrist, and anklets on r. leg; other hand and foot not visible. Upright pole on r. Lines are incised, curling from the top of the head upward and outward, evidently to indicate loose hair.

R. Raised Swāstika, turned l., on strong stem which springs from a wide straight base line, below which is a flat channel. The short basal uprights are pointed. To l. the vase. To r. no emblem visible.

44. 1·42 in. by ·72 in.; weight 64 grains. A hole is drilled near the top for suspending the coin on a string.

O. Standing deity, with very long narrow waist, facing f. An armlet on r. upper arm, bangles on each wrist, and anklets on legs, two being on l. leg. Opposite the hips the hands grasp two upright poles; that on l. ends at level of head, apparently in a trident. Top of the other uncertain. A symbol on each side of legs; that on l. may have been a bead or disk on a post, but the bead is not now visible.

R. Raised Swāstika, turned r. The short basal uprights on l. are pointed; those on l. have square ends. Vase to r., out of which grow incised leaves on stems, one having shape of a Bō-leaf. Under the vase is a wide bar curved into an arch. To l., an indistinct symbol, resembling a bird with raised wing,[1] facing Swāstika.

45. 1·21 in. by ·70 in.; weight 58 grains.

O. Middle part of design gone, and rest fragmentary. The details appear to differ from those on other coins, and it is doubtful if a deity was represented. Two curved bands ending in curls are on l., and perhaps a vase below them.

R. Raised Swāstika, turned l.

46. 1·45 in. by ·76 in.; weight 82½ grains. A hole is drilled near the top for suspending the coin on a thread or fine string.

O. Standing deity, facing f. There may be a helmet, or crown, or raised cover on head. A wide broken line passes over head from shoulders. On each side the hands hold an upright pole which appears to end in a bident or trident. On l. of legs an upright design.

R. A raised border, excepting on r. Swāstika turned r. A horizontal bar separated from base line of Swāstika and border by two channels. To r., probably a smaller Swāstika turned r.; to l., a rectangular raised line like early letter *u*.

47. 1·53 in. by ·65 in.; weight 126 grains. A hole is drilled near the top for suspending the coin on a thin string.

O. Standing deity (? female) with wasp-like waist and hanging arms; hands hold upright pole at each side of coin. That on l. ends in cross-bar at level of shoulder, above which are four flowers, lower two being circular and upper two trumpet-mouthed. The pole on r. winds slightly and ends in a thick curl at level of neck. Above this a relief like a standing deer; but lower part may be intended for a flower and the rest part of a band passing over head. Thin transverse bar above it, separated from border by a channel.

R. Large raised Swāstika, turned r. Under its base line a transverse band separated from border by a narrow channel.

[1] A bird with raised wings is carved in false relief on a pillar at the Abhayagiri dāgaba, and on one at the Dakuṇu dāgaba.

To r. a clear Aum monogram, with straight sides. To l. side view of flower resting on a thick cross-bar, bud on r. of it.

48 to **51.** Four other thin coins, averaging 13½ grains in weight, have the following dimensions:—1·01 in. by ·45 in.; 1·05 in. by ·50 in.; 1·05 in. by ·50 in.; and 1·10 in. by ·50 in. All much worn on both sides.

52. An additional coin of this type found by Mr. Bell at Anurādhapura,[1] at the site with the 'Buddhist railing,' measured ·80 in. by ·62 in., and weighed 44 grains.

O. Standing deity, facing f., holding shaft of trident in his r. hand, and perhaps another in l. hand, which is indistinct. Mr. Bell thought that irregular upright lines near these were the edges of his dress.

R. Raised Swāstika, turned r.; plant on l., of three stems, springing from a cross bar. Indistinct marks on r.

The mean dimensions of the Tissa and heavier Mulleittīvu coins are:

Tissa coins, 1·18 in. by ·49 in.; weight 46 grains (mean of 3). Mulleittīvu coins. 1·13 in. by ·67 in.; weight 50 grains (mean of 11).

The Anurādhapura coins differ greatly in weight, which varies from 13 grains to 126 grains.

Sir A. Cunningham has given two scales of the weights of ancient Indian money, one for copper coins and the other for silver coins.[2] These are as follows:—

Scale of Copper Coins.		Scale of Silver Coins.	
1 Kahāpana . .	144 grains.	2½ Kahāpanas . .	144 grains.
¾ „ . .	108 „	1½ „ . .	86·4 „
½ „ . .	72 „	1 „ . .	57·6 „
¼ „ . .	36 „	½ „ . .	28·8 „
⅛ „ . .	18 „	¼ „ . .	14·4 „

In the later Sinhalese coins we find both the copper and silver coinage following the same copper scale. This is seen in the following table, which gives the mean weights of some of the ordinary 'Massa' coins in my possession, taken

[1] *Arch. Survey of Ceylon.* Fourth Progress Report, pp. 4 and 13.
[2] *Coins of Ancient India,* pp. 46 and 47.

without selection. I annex for comparison the weight of some coins of the south Indian king Raja-Raja, purchased by me in Madura, from which I have excluded only coins that are evidently cut away at the edges.

Date.	Name.	Number of Coins.	Mean Weight. Grains.	Material.
1153–1186	Parākrama-Bāhu . . .	25	62·5	Copper
1186–1187	Wijaya-Bāhu	14	55·6	,,
1197–1200 1209–	Lilāwatī	50	65·4	,,
1200–1202	Sāhasa-Malla	50	63·1	,,
1208–1209	Dharmmāsōka-Dēva . .	14	64·3	,,
1296–	Bhuvanaika-Bāhu . . .	25	65·3	,,
1186–1187	Wijaya-Bāhu	10	64·1	Silver
985–1011	Raja-Raja (Indian) . .	25	63·4	Copper

The oblong money can be divided only into a larger and a smaller type, as shown in Fig. 155. The former includes the Mulleittīvu and the larger Anurādhapura coins, and has a mean width of ·70 in.; the rest of the coins average ·50 in. in width. Whether these sizes indicated different values is doubtful.

The great variation in the weights proves that no special scale was followed in them; the plaques were tokens rather than money. Yet they may have answered all the purposes of money in being used as mediums of exchange which probably had fixed values in the country.

Histories and inscriptions alike prove that coins called kahāpanas existed in countless numbers in Ceylon in very early times; yet no other coin which could possibly represent this money has been discovered. That such coins were made of copper is rendered certain by the discovery of the circular coin described below (p. 503), which appears to be a double kahāpana, as Mr. Still stated. Necessarily, this must have been preceded by the single kahāpana and its subdivisions, which could not be formed of a more valuable metal than the money of higher value, and therefore must have been copper coins. Thus, until some other form of copper money of suitable weights has been found it appears to me that these oblong plaques must be accepted as partly filling the gap. Mr. Bell's spurious oblong Purāna, with a figure on the obverse like those on the plaques, strongly supports this view.

Cast coins of the same size and shape occur in southern India (see p. 506). The slight amount of wear in most of the plaques may be due to their being hoarded as amulets; some are considerably eroded on their faces. In the irregularity of the weights the coins only followed the example of the Purānas found in Ceylon, the weights of which show that while all probably had the same value as mediums of exchange they were in reality tokens, that is, they did not circulate in Ceylon at their intrinsic value. The surprise which the Sinhalese king expressed to the freedman of Annius Plocamus at the exact weights of the Roman coinage is a proof that all the local money varied greatly in this respect.

That the oblong type of coin continued to be issued up to the third or fourth century A.D. is clearly proved by the form of the 'Aum' monogram on the coin numbered **47**, the *m* of which is of a type which is found in some inscriptions of that period. I met with a similar letter cut on the faces of two stones inside the valve-pit or 'bisōkoṭuwa' of a sluice at Hurulla, a tank constructed by King Mahā-Sēna (277–304 A.D.). Large coins of a circular shape made their appearance at about this time, having a similar 'Aum' monogram on them, and it may be assumed that the issue of the oblong money then either ceased or was of less importance than before.

As all probably had a two-fold value as coins and also as protective amulets the discovery of a few isolated specimens about religious edifices of a later date does not quite prove that they continued to be issued up to that time.

Two years ago Mr. Still mentioned that he had examined some 200 specimens, among which were three cast ones with outward-curving sides, found near the Thūpārāma. Another cast one was found in the excavation inside the Kiribat dāgaba, and a fourth near the Thūpārāma. (Journal, R.A.S., Ceylon, 1907, p. 199 ff.).

The special Swāstika symbol of all the early Sinhalese coins, including also the large circular coin just mentioned, which will be described later on, is cut at the beginning or end of three pre-Christian inscriptions in Ceylon, and it was also discovered by me engraved on the outside of pottery taken out of the lowest stratum of the remains at Tissa. Its occurrence there proves that it had been adopted in Ceylon as early as the second or third century B.C. It is cut at the beginning or end of the inscriptions numbered **69, 70,** and **75,** which belong to the first century B.C. The central bar and four side uprights are found in the symbol which precedes the inscription numbered **62,** by Prince Sāli, which dates from about the middle of the second century B.C. Although I believe it does not occur at any inscription of post-Christian date, its presence on the oblong coin No. **47** and the large circular coins shows that it continued to be employed as a local symbol until the fourth century A.D., or later. It appears to be unknown in India.

The Indian meaning of the Swāstika, the cross with bent arms, is *Su* + *asti*, 'it is well,' that is, 'may it be well.' It indicates its luck-bringing power as an auspicious wish, and the words themselves in the form *Swasti* are cut at the commencement of numerous later inscriptions in Ceylon. But the symbol goes back to a date that is far anterior to any such interpretation. Its earliest occurrence is, I believe, at the first city on the site of Troy, the inhabitants of which are considered by Mr. R. H. Hall to have been 'just on the border between the Age of Stone and the Age of Metal'[1]; and their latest date is stated by this authority to be about 2500 B.C. (*op. cit.* p. 49). As the Swāstika was found by Dr. Schliemann on pottery at the bottom of the stratum belonging to this early race it may belong to the fourth millennium B.C. It also occurs in Egypt as a decorative motive in the ceilings of the Theban tombs of the eighteenth dynasty (1700–1400, B.C.).[2] Its

[1] *The Oldest Civilization of Greece*, p. 23.

[2] Perrot and Chipiez, *Hist. of Art in Ancient Egypt*. Vol. ii, p. 359 (from Prisse); Prof. Maspero, *Egyptian Archaeology*, p. 16; Erman, *Life in Ancient Egypt*, pp. 102, 397, and 479.

highly developed form in that country proves that it was known there long prior to its use in these tombs.

It may have been carved at the inscriptions, and may also be placed on the coins, as a special emblem of Good Luck or Prosperity, which acts as a protection from evil influences.

In describing the inscriptions I have already suggested that the four short basal uprights may typify the Four Great Buddhist Truths, as supporters, or more probably, especially on the coins, the four-fold forces—chariots, elephants, cavalry, and foot-soldiers—of the sovereign protecting the emblem, the prosperity of the country being supposed to depend largely on its ruler. In that case the central pole on which the Swāstika is elevated might represent the sovereign as upholder of the prosperity of the country.

In other countries the Cross is sometimes drawn with a short bar across or near the end of each arm, and it is of interest to observe that in the case of the Swāstika on coin No. **14** two thin bars are thus shown across the terminal parts of each of the two arms the ends of which are visible, as well as across the ends of the short uprights. A Swāstika with one bar of this kind is also represented on coin No. 11 of Plate X in Cunningham's *Coins of Ancient India*. As every line in ancient symbolism has its own meaning there must be a special reason for inserting these peculiar cross-bars.

The only explanation with which I am acquainted, of this barred, or as he terms it 'guarded' Swāstika, is that given by Mr. J. M. Campbell, of the Indian Civil Service, in Vol. 24 of the *Indian Antiquary* (1895)[1]—that such lines are due to a belief that any cross, or, in its usual Indian form, the Swāstika, is a favourite house for spirits. He supposed that the cross-bars at the ends of the arms were intended to prevent the ready egress of good spirits who might have been induced to reside in it, and thus to ensure its beneficial or protective action. It is evident that, as he also remarked, they might equally be drawn to prevent the entry of evil spirits who might desire to take up an unauthorised abode in it, and this is the more

[1] *On the Spirit Basis of Belief and Custom*, p. 164.

probable explanation of the cross-bars, as I shall endeavour to show in a subsequent chapter.

The guarding power of labyrinthine and spiral and meander designs, or zig-zag or crossed lines is, as Mr. Campbell pointed out (*loc. cit.* p. 161), the cause of their constant employment in charms against evil spirits at the present day, both in Ceylon and elsewhere.[1] Thus the partiality which the people of the East as well as those of the West and America, have exhibited for the Swāstika is doubtless largely based on the belief in its defensive properties against these malignant beings.

In addition, therefore, to its symbolic aspect as an emblem of Prosperity, these cross-bars prove that the Swāstika was placed on the coins to fulfil another function, that is, to be a protective charm against the malevolent actions of evil spirits. The pointed ends of some of the arms and short basal uprights may be also due to a similar idea—that of closing them against the ingress of hurtful spirits who might neutralise the omen. A fuller elucidation of the probable origin of the Swāstika will be found in a later chapter.

If this was the ancient notion regarding the powers of the Swāstika, it will be understood that apart from the general belief in the luck-bringing properties of everything that turned to the right and followed the course of the sun, it would be a matter of comparative indifference, as regards its spiritual aspect, whether its arms turned to the right or the left. In either direction they would equally act as a check to spirit progress. Thus, out of the 52 coins described above, in 18 cases the symbol is indistinct; on the remaining 34 coins the arms turn to the right in 22 instances, and to the left in 12.

The line or two lines, which are sometimes waved, below the base line of the Swāstika may represent a snake or snakes, which also have guardian powers against evil spirits, especially in the East.

The other designs on the reverse of the Mulleittīvu coins admit of simple explanations. The plant growing out of a

[1] I have a Sinhalese MS. book of charms and spells against sickness and evil spirits and planets, in which designs of crossed and complicated lines constantly occur.

vase indicates that the latter is filled with water; and the full vase is well known to be a general emblem of Good-luck which is much employed in the East, the reason being, as may be gathered from the Vidhura-paṇḍita Jātaka,[1] that if the vase be full it cannot be imperfect. It is thus an emblem of Perfection, and therefore most auspicious. It is not a special symbol of Buddhism.

The recumbent humped bull is the special emblem of the Sōlian kings of southern India, and its appearance on these coins of Ceylon must point to Sōlian influence in the country. The coins which have this symbol may thus have been issued in the first half of the second century B.C., by the only Sōlian King who reigned in Ceylon for a considerable period at an early date, that is, Elāra, whose rule is alluded to in very favourable terms by the pre-Christian Buddhist annalists, and who occupied the throne from 205 to 161 B.C. There is no probability that an early Sinhalese king would insert this South-Indian symbol on his coinage, and it is not found on the Tissa nor, with two exceptions,[2] the Anurādhapura money which I have seen, that must have been issued by native rulers.

Even if the coins of this type were issued by the Indian usurpers who ruled the country from 104 to 88 B.C., those found at Mulleittīvu appear to have been buried in the first century B.C.

If it be held, however, that the mark on the Purāna (i) is the letter *hu* its shape must prove that the Mulleittīvu coins were buried in post-Christian times; but the good state of many of the symbols on the Purānas does not support this conclusion.

On the Obverse I take first the seated figure on the Anurādhapura coins, which can be explained without difficulty.

Among the articles found in removing the débris left round the Yaṭṭhāla dāgaba at Tissa, which, it may be repeated, dates from the third century B.C., there was, by extreme good-luck, a little more than the half of an admirably cut and polished

[1] *The Jātaka.* No. 545. Translation, p. 152.

[2] If Elāra issued this coinage some examples of his coins would occur among later hoards, of course.

FIG. 156. Seal from Yaṭṭhāla Dāgaba.

To face p. 495

thin carnelian of an elliptical shape and perfect colour, which had evidently been the stone set in a seal-ring. The persons who rifled the relic-chamber of the dāgaba apparently wanted only the gold setting, and broke and rejected the stone, which remained buried among the brick rubbish thrown out of their cutting. It was discovered when the recent restoration was begun in 1884, and the Buddhist Committee who supervised the work were so good as to present it to me. The other half of the stone was not found. The portion in my possession is a regular ellipse, measuring ·80 in. in width, and probably 1·20 ins. in length when perfect. Its present length is ·64 in., and the middle thickness is ·13 in. An impression of it is shown, considerably enlarged, in Fig. No. 156. I am indebted to the skill of Mr. Norman May, of Malvern, for this admirable reproduction of this interesting seal, in the exact state in which it was left by the camera.

On this portion there is excellently engraved in intaglio the figure of a person sitting upon an ornamental chair, which can be no other than a royal throne. In the impression taken from it the face is turned to the right and the body half right. The king is leaning slightly backward in an easy attitude with his right foot hanging down from the throne and his left leg doubled so that the foot is placed on the chair. His left arm rests above the elbow on the raised left knee, and the fore-arm and hand are elevated, and hold a flat object, at which he is looking, in front of his left shoulder. His right arm hangs down and grasps near his hip a thin sash which passes over the right shoulder and back round his left side, the two ends, which appear to be fringed, standing out at the back of the chair.

He is very simply dressed in a cloth from the waist downward; the top of it is shown passing round the waist, and its edge hangs down from the left knee, while its folds are clearly seen on both thighs. Round the base of his neck is a thin necklet, and a plain armlet passes once round the arm above each elbow. No bangles are on the wrists; his ankles are not visible, having been on the missing portion of the stone. No hair is represented on the face; that on his head is cut short, and simply thrown back from the face in loose masses, without reaching the neck. There is no hair-knot. His nose is prominent and quite straight, and his forehead rather high.

The throne is of a very interesting shape. The side is an oblong; enclosed in a plain frame there are four horizontal rows of square hollows, each row now consisting of seven, but apparently nine on the full design, separated by raised bars; this represents very open basket-work. The right corner rests upon two feet,[1] which are formed of round balls placed upon flat bases. The whole back of the chair winds backward, and the end of the upright bar at the side curls over above the transverse bar, which passes quite through this upright and across to the other rear upright, immediately below the level of the shoulder.

The engraver has taken great pains to make it perfectly clear that this side upright of the back is a rustic one, and he has shown five short branches projecting from it and cut off at a distance from it equal to about its thickness. This rustic post passes down to the feet of the throne, and into the lower horizontal bar of the frame of the basket-work. From the points where the branches unite with the stem three curled ornaments spring upward on the outer side, the two lower ones ending in a curl which turns inward to the upright, and the top one curling outward below the level of the cross-bar at the back of the throne, and terminating in two tassels which hang from its end.

At the level of the king's face the tip of another design appears at the fractured edge of the stone; it consists of four leaf-like projections in close contact.

There can be no reasonable doubt that this gem was deposited in the relic-chamber of the dāgaba along with the relic-receptacles which have been described in a previous chapter, and it may be assumed that it dates from some time prior to the original construction of the dāgaba. When it was submitted twenty-four years ago for the inspection of the

[1] We learn from the Mahā Hansa Jātaka, No. 534, that one royal throne had eight feet.

authorities of the British Museum, the opinion expressed regarding it was that it is of Indian origin and workmanship, and that it might perhaps belong to the seventh century A.D.; but on its being re-examined in 1903 in the light which increased knowledge of early Indian art throws upon such designs, it was considered to be of pre-Christian date, and perhaps to go back to the third century B.C. but to no earlier period. This authoritative opinion is therefore entirely in favour of the arguments previously advanced regarding the age of the gem and relic receptacles, since all probabilities forbid the assumption that the dāgaba was re-opened, and these articles and especially the two Purānas also found with them were afterwards placed in it in either pre-Christian or early post-Christian times.

In the Mahāvansa we read of numerous presents passing between the great Indian Emperor Aśōka and the Sinhalese monarch Dēvānam-piya Tissa, the brother of Mahā-Nāga; and there are accounts of at least two embassies that Tissa sent to Aśōka's capital, Pāṭaliputta, on both occasions the king's nephew, Mahā Ariṭṭha, being the ambassador. This prince afterwards became a monk, and according to the Dhātuvansa resided at Tissa. Thus we get a direct communication between Tissa and Aśōka's capital.

It may be surmised that either the Prince-monk, or much more probably King Mahā-Nāga or his son Yaṭṭhāla-Tissa, deposited this finger-ring in the relic-chamber on the occasion of the festival that would be held at the time when it was closed. In the next century, at the closing of the relic-room in the Ruwanwaeli dāgaba at Anurādhapura we read (Mah., i, p. 122) of King Duṭṭha-Gāmiṇi that 'while [he was] within the [relic] receptacle he made an offering of all the regal ornaments he had on his person.' The Dhātuvansa, in relating the account of the deposition of relics in the Sēruvil or Sēruwāvila dāgaba by King Kākavaṇṇa-Tissa, doubtless describes what usually occurred at important structures of the kind. It says, 'All the dancing women offered the ornaments that each one was wearing. Then the king and the great ministers, etc., having taken off the ornaments that each one was wearing offered them in the relic chamber.' Mahā-Nāga or his son may have acted in a similar manner at the Yaṭṭhāla dāgaba.

As the gem is an early Indian work, exhibiting strong Greek influence and therefore probably not of south Indian origin, and as it seems certain that it represents a king on his throne, it is quite possible—one might even say probable—that the figure is that of Aśōka himself, or is copied from representations of him.

The nearest approach to the attitude of the king which I have found on early Indian coins is that of the sitting Herakles on the coins of Euthydemos, King of Baktria (*circa* 230–200 B.C.), as he appears in Plate I, Nos. 3 and 5, of Mr. V. A. Smith's 'Catalogue of the Coins in the Indian Museum, Calcutta.' The Indian engraver took a nearly similar design, and adapted it to Indian requirements by raising the bent leg till the foot rested on the throne, and giving the raised hand a small object, possibly a flower but not recognisable as such in this example, to hold in place of a club.

The sitting figure on several of the oblong coins is in the same attitude as the king in the gem, with the exception that one hand rests on the thigh instead of holding a scarf or sash. On both gem and coins one leg hangs down while the other is doubled up; and one hand holds a flower or other object near the level of the shoulder, while the other hangs down to the level of the thigh. In the figure on this gem, therefore, we have the original Indian design of the sitting figure on the oblong coins, as well as the original type of the sitting king on the later coinage of Parākrama-Bāhu I and his successors. On these last the throne has degenerated into one or two horizontal lines with short vertical lines crossing them—the basket-work on the gem.

The similarity of the design on the gem and the later coins, where the monarch's name at his side leaves no doubt that the figure is intended for him, renders it most probable that the sitting figure on the oblong coins is also intended for a representation of the ruler of the time. The monarch is placed in nearly the same position on many Indian coins; it was the conventional attitude in delineations of the seated kings.

FIG. 157. Guard-stone (Anurādhapura).

To face p. 499.

In the case of the standing personage on the oblong coins the identification is less obvious. Notwithstanding the fact that the upright figure on the later Sinhalese coins has always been termed a king in the descriptions of them, all the available evidence shows that the design is intended to represent a guardian deity, and not always the same one.

It is certain from the distinctly marked breasts that the standing figures in the coins numbered **25, 33,** and **35** are those of females; and not unlikely that the figure is intended for that of a female on several other coins on which the wide bust and hips and the extremely narrow waist are the characteristics of female rather than male forms.

The winding stems ending in flowers which some of the more masculine figures hold are special characteristics of the Guardian Deities or Dwārpal who are carved on slabs erected on each side of the steps at the entrances of numerous Buddhist buildings at Anurādhapura and elsewhere. In their case, in one hand a curved stem is held which ends in a high cluster of flowers, while the other supports a vase out of which several flowers rise [1]; but there is (or was in 1873) one example in which a curved stem ending in a flower (lotus) or bud is held in each hand. Thus, on the coins on which this special design is found the figure seems to be that of a Guardian Deity rather than the Monarch. If so, it is most probably that of a deity on the other oblong coins, and also on the later coins.

This view is strongly supported by the design on the coins which I have numbered **24, 44,** and **52,** where the article held is a trident, the symbol of Śiva and his wife, and of his son Gaṇēsa,[2] and perhaps also of his other sons, Skanda, the God of Kataragama, who is now considered to be one of the Four Guardian Deities of Ceylon, and Ayiyanār, the Guardian

[1] The illustration (Fig. No. 157) shows one of these Dwārpal of an early type, near the Thūpārāma dāgaba. The animal on the side pilaster is a horse, for which, curiously enough, a heap of provender is provided; he appears to be eating it.

[2] In an ancient temple of this deity at Ōmantan in the Northern Province, a stone trident stands on an altar as the God's emblem, the central prong representing a lingam.

Forest Deity of Ceylon. The javelin and the apparent bident which appear on several coins also point to the latter gods or Durgā as being the deity who is commonly represented. In some unworn coins of Wijaya-Bāhu, also, a weapon with a long sharp-pointed head is distinctly shown at the side of the article held in the right hand of the standing figure; it resembles the weapon at the side of Skanda on coin No. 9 of Plate VI, *C. A. I.*, and No. 15 of Plate XXI, Ind. Mus. Cat. In the Pāndiyan coin No. 143, Plate IV, of Elliot's *Coins of S. India* a similar figure who has the trident at his side must be Śiva or one of his sons.

In the same manner as in the later Sinhalese coinage, the king is delineated on one face of many Indian coins, and a deity on the other. In the Gupta coinage the latter is often Śiva or a goddess; but Skanda also appears in other coins, and he would be specially appropriate for the Ceylon money on account of his local connection with the island. As for the bangles and anklets, all the Dwārpal in Ceylon have them.

That the figure is a deity is also indicated by the presence of the arched line or circlet of 5, 7, or 9 beads which in some cases passes round and over the head of the standing figure, but not over the head of the seated person. Each of the Dwārpal in Ceylon, with the exception of figures of Bhairava, is protected by the expanded hoods of a Cobra which has 5, 7, 9, 11, or in one instance 13 heads; and in several of these carvings which are somewhat worn the heads stand out from the arched line of the hoods like large beads. Thus it is possible that the beads round the head of the standing figure symbolise, if they do not actually represent, the many-headed cobra guarding or sheltering him.

Where one bead is shown on each side of the neck it is merely the ear-pendant. When near the waist it is the fold of the sash which holds up the cloth. The arched line which passes overhead in some coins may be a 'chatta' or umbrella, with a scalloped fringe in some instances.

I conclude, therefore, that in all cases the standing figure shown on the Sinhalese coinage, whether ancient or more recent, is a guardian deity and not the king.

FIG. 158. Durgā, as Kālī, destroying the Asuras (Tanjore Temple).

To face p. 501

In the later coinage the peculiar article held by him, which some have supposed to be a weapon, is a double 'trisūla' resting on a circle or lotus that is represented by the bead under it, exactly as it is seen in the post-Christian Ajōdyā coin No. 15, on Plate XIX of the Indian Museum Catalogue. The double trisūla is also found on the early Yaudeya coin No. 1 of Plate VI of *C. A. I.*, which is said by Sir A. Cunningham (p. 76) to date from about the first century B.C.; and on the Eran coin No. 19 of Plate XI of that work. It also appears on the Andra coin numbered 14, in Plate II of Sir W. Elliott's *Coins of Southern India.* This design is not recognisable on the oblong coins that I have seen.

Whether it was developed from the Greek caduceus, which occurs (or a symbol like it) on some Indian punch-marked coins, is uncertain; whatever its origin, it may have been perpetuated in its present form not only as a lucky emblem, a form of trident, a weapon greatly feared by demons, but also as a monogram that might be interpreted *jaya*, 'victory,' if the lower part be read as the letter *ja* and the upper part as *ya*—as its shape on the Ajōdhyā coin seems to indicate. In the latter meaning it would be a particularly appropriate emblem for any guardian deity. The word *jaya* itself is found on coin No. 14 of Plate XX of the Ind. Mus. Cat.

With respect to the female deities who appear on the oblong coins, the weapons which some hold must identify them with some form of Durgā, as the slayer of the Asuras or demons. Skanda was also the later champion and leader of the Gods against the demons.

The standing figure, whether male or female, would thus, like the Swāstika, be thought to have special protective power against all classes of evil spirits; and that the oblong coins were credited with the possession of beneficial qualities is proved by finding some that were drilled for suspension on the neck as amulets.

The only other distinct symbol on the obverse of these coins is that on Nos. **27** and **32**, and perhaps **44**, the bead on the post, which has been sometimes termed the disk on the altar. It is found in the reliefs carved on a pillar at the side of one of the wāhalkaḍas at the Jētawana dāgaba (of the Nandana garden) at Anurādhapúra. The other designs included with it there in the spaces of a leafy meander pattern are all emblems that are not exclusively Buddhist, such as the Trisūla, the Swāstika, the Chank, the Five-headed Cobra, and the Yak-tail Fly-whisk; on other pillars the Elephant, Lion, Bull, the Structure with three arches, and Nondescript animals are carved. Considering the unimportant position which it holds on the pillar, and its small size, it cannot be a Dhamma-Chakka, or 'Wheel of the Law,' such as is worshipped in the Amarāvati carvings, and it is not a fan, the circle being little wider than the post in one instance.

A circular fan, with a straight handle, is often carved after pillar inscriptions of the tenth century A.D. in Ceylon, when they contain grants of privileges in connection with monasteries, as one of the common emblems of the Community of Buddhist monks. In the case of the oblong coins, however, it is not probable that this meaning can be attached to a symbol at the side of an Indian deity, where it is much more likely to have some protective function, or to be an emblem of the god. It may be the sun-emblem or discus of Vishnu; if so, the person at whose side it stands may be that god or his 'śakti' or female manifestation, Lakshmī, the Goddess of Prosperity.

This symbol appears to be a relic of the early Indian Sun-worship; it represents the sun as it would appear when it rose due east of the pointer-stone of a sun-temple, on which occasion it would be visible for a moment from the centre of the circle, as a full disk resting on the summit of the stone. In the case of perhaps the earliest existing representation of a pointer-stone, the sun, as an eight-pointed star (with eight intermediate rays of light radiating from a central ball), is delineated as resting on the rounded apex of a tall cone which is carved in relief on the 'Stele of Victory' of Narāmsin, King of Agadē in the Euphrates valley (3750 B.C.).[1]

In the coin No. 27 it is clear that the post or column at

[1] See the Plate facing p. 160 in Messrs. King and Hall's *Egypt and Western Asia*, 1907.

the top of which the disk is placed is terminated in a blunt point, like a pointer-stone. There is a round column of nearly the same shape, with a rounded apex, but without the disk, at the side of a three-arched structure surmounted by a crescent, on the Taxila coin No. 6 of Plate II of Cunningham's *Coins of Ancient India*; and I have seen quite similar cut pointer-stones, like circular obelisks, on the eastern side of stone circles in the Gambia valley in West Africa.

The learned authors who have described the coins termed Purānas agree that the wheel with straight spokes is a sun emblem and not a Dhamma-chakka; and we know that on each of the faces of the 'tees' of the early dāgabas of Anurādhapura there was a representation of the sun in relief, which is still to be seen on one of them. A disk with a central flat boss and a circle round it, similarly raised on a pillar which has a base and capital, is carved in relief at the top of the face of each engaged pillar at the sides of the wāhalkaḍas at the Miriswaeṭi dāgaba at Anurādhapura. It has a chatta above it. It appears to be the same sun-emblem, perhaps converted into a Dhamma-chakka (Fig. No. 84).

In these notes on the symbōls I have referred to a large circular coin of Ceylon. The first specimen was discovered by me at the Tissa excavations, in digging a channel; it is in the Colombo Museum. Several others have been obtained at Anurādhapura and one at Mihintale. In his Annual Report for 1900, p. 5, Mr. Bell records his finding one in a peculiar brick-lined pit at Anurādhapura, and mentions that about fifty of these coins were discovered at one site on private land at that town; of these some selected examples were sent to the Colombo Museum. The three which I have seen appeared to belong to the third or fourth century A.D. I append descriptions of the Tissa coin and two others kindly submitted to me by the late Mr. Ievers when Government Agent of Anurādhapura.

53. A roughly circular copper coin with a mean diameter of 1·27 inches; weight 220 grains. Found in digging a channel at Tissa. The designs on it and the others were impressed by two dies, the marks of which are visible; they do not rise above the level of the border. Those on the reverse side were afterwards cut more deeply by hand on this coin.

O. The design is surrounded by two parallel circular lines, ·10 in. apart, having between them an intermediate line, broken in one part into a series of dots, and perhaps similarly broken on the opposite side. Owing to the erroneous position of the die only three-fourths of the design is on this face.

In the right lower corner is a well-shaped elephant, facing l., with extended tail. Above it, but to l., a tree standing on a cross enclosed in a square, or surrounded by a fence. On each of the upper corners of the enclosure is a bead or disk surmounted by a crescent, like some so-called 'Taurine' symbols on Indian coins. The tree has an upright stem from which grow two alternate lateral branches, each, as well as the stem, ending in three leaves, one terminal and the others lateral. At the top of the coin and to r. of the tree, the Swāstika symbol raised as before and turned r., with four basal supporters. Between it and the tree are three beads, and another is near the rim at the r. lower corner. Between the base of the Swāstika and the back of the Elephant is an isosceles triangle lying on its side and pointing l., with a cross-bar at the apex; to the r. a structure of three arches.

R. A single flat rim. There are three symbols in the upper half of this face and one in the lower half. In the middle of the upper half the Swāstika as before, of broad lines, turned r.; near its r. upper corner three beads arranged in a triangle. To l., an indistinct symbol. To r., an Aum monogram of two triangles meeting at their apices, with a cross-bar there and a shorter one projecting on r. of lower triangle. In the middle of the lower half a structure of three arches on each side of which are three beads arranged in a triangle.

54. A roughly circular coin, 1·47 inches in diameter; weight 223 grains. It was found on the bank of the Malwatta-oya at Anurādhapura.

O. Two raised circular bands enclose the design, with a third between them broken into three beads near the top and on the l. side. In the middle, at the base, a tusk elephant with raised trunk and extended tail which branches into three at the end. Below its mouth are three beads arranged in a triangle. Above its tail a structure of three arches under the base line of which is a bead. Above the elephant's back is the isosceles triangle, pointing l., with an upright cross-bar below its apex. To l. of this a tree fenced by or standing on an enclosed cross as before, with opposed branches. There are no symbols on the corners of the enclosure. To l. of this, near the border, three beads arranged in a triangle. Above the arched structure and the triangle the raised Swāstika turned r., with one bead near r. end of its base, and three arranged triangularly between its upper part and the top of the tree. Eleven beads in all.

R. opposed to O. Emblems larger and formed with bolder lines. In the middle, at the bottom, the three-arched structure, below the base line of which is a straight raised line. To r., three beads arranged triangularly. Above the arches the raised Swāstika, turned r., with three beads on each side of the upper part. In the space to l. of its basal uprights the Aum monogram. To r. of Swāstika and arches, a symbol, part of which only is visible, consisting of a circular band with central bead. Mr. Still has pointed out that when seen in its complete form on other coins this is a trisūla resting on a disk or bead.[1]

55. A roughly circular coin, 1·27 inches by 1·31 inches; weight 264 grains. Found at Mihintale.

O. One circular band encloses the design; in one part an outer one is visible. Designs are like No. **54,** but elephant's tail has only one end. The beads below its head are absent, but there are two to r. of arches and two to l. of the fence, a total of ten.

R. Opposed to O., and indistinct on r. The design re-

[1] *Journal R.A.S.*, Ceylon, 1907, p. 201 ff. Mr. Still stated that the weights of twenty examples varied from 197 to 275 grains, the average being 242·75 grains. He considered that they represent a double copper kahāpana of 288 grains. All the specimens had the same symbols, arranged in the same manner, on the two faces, the only variation being the transposition of the double-triangle or Aum monogram and the Trisūla on the reverse of a few coins.

sembles No. **54**. Three beads to l. of arches, instead of r., and one above them.

Although the Elephant, the Tree, and the Structure with three arches might be thought to be connected with Buddhism, it is extremely doubtful if they have such a signification on these coins. All three emblems occur on the Purānas, which date from an age anterior to Buddhism. They may have been merely copied from the earlier coinage, seeing that there is not another exclusively Buddhist emblem on either the earlier or later coinage of Ceylon. The probability of such borrowing of the symbols will appear more evident after the following remarks have been read.

The isosceles triangle appears on several early Indian coins reproduced in Cunningham's *Coins of Ancient India*, especially those of Eran, where in two instances it is elevated on a pole at the base of which in one case there is a cross enclosed in a square (Plate XI). It is also found on a coin of Ujjain (No. 14, Plate X), where Cunningham calls it a 'sun-standard'; on a Yaudeya coin (No. 5, Plate VI); and on several Kuninda coins in Plate V. These examples show that in its correct position the apex of the triangle is at the bottom.

I suggest that the middle cross-bar, which is sometimes on one side of the triangle and sometimes on the other, indicates that it symbolises a sistrum, an identification that is strongly supported by the form illustrated in Plate XXXIX, Fig. No. 14, of General Maisey's *Sānchi and its Remains*, in which the side bar ends in a hook. The sistrum is not found in the carvings in Ceylon. This instrument is clearly and unmistakably pourtrayed on an oblong cast coin which Dr. J. R. Henderson of Madras was good enough to forward for my examination. It was found in the bed of the Vaigei river at Madura, and has the elephant in high relief on the obverse, with the sistrum and several other symbols, such as the vase, trisūla, crescent, and double trident in a line near the upper edge. The sistrum is a well-known demon-frightener, and therefore would increase the protective power of the coins on which it occurs.

The line below the arched structure may represent a snake, as a guardian deity.

It would appear that at the time when these large circular coins were issued the same confidence was still reposed in the protective powers of the emblems. The sistrum, if it is one, takes its place among them for the first time in Ceylon. We still find the same raised Swāstika symbol repeated exactly as in the oblong coins, a proof of the firm belief in its luck-bringing virtues. It is strange that it is now unknown in the island; it is perhaps impossible to meet with ten persons there who are acquainted with either the name or shape of any form of Swāstika.

The meaning of the numerous beads on these coins is unknown. The five beads on the later Sinhalese coins afford no assistance in elucidating it, their own meaning being equally unknown. Probably the latter have some reference to the guardian deity at whose side they are represented; on some specimens the uppermost of the five is a lotus bud.

With regard to the structures of three or more arches commonly, when shown on the Purānas, termed 'Chaityas,' that is, dāgabas, I am not satisfied that this title furnishes a correct interpretation of their meaning. In fact, I can see little reason to apply this term to them. The designs with three and five arches appear to be representations of the domed roofs of buildings which originally may have been Hindu temples as in the Kosambi coin No. 11 of Plate V of *Coins of Ancient India,* where the nature of the edifice is indicated by the bull standing at its side. The character of some is also clearly expressed on several coins described on pp. 137 and 138 of the Indian Museum Catalogue, by the peacock on the summit of the central arch, which denotes that the building is a temple devoted to Skanda, or is under his protection. Figures of peacocks are still placed on the outsides of his temples, and the bird itself and its feathers are considered to be emblems of good luck in India[1] and Ceylon. If in later instances in Ceylon the arched structures were intended for Buddhist

[1] Crookes. *Popular Religion and Folklore of Northern India,* Vol. ii, pp. 233, 250.

wihāras, it was probably as places to be avoided by evil spirits that they were delineated among other demon-frightening emblems. That such buildings sometimes had domed roofs is proved by the names Ganthākāra (Bell) Wihāra and Piriwena which occur in the Mahāvansa.

Somewhat similar domed buildings are illustrated among the Amarāvati reliefs.[1] The central roof, like that of the structures on the coins, is at a much higher level than the two

FIG. 159. Relief near Ruwanwaeli Dāgaba.

lateral ones. There are also two reliefs of unknown age at Anurādhapura which show domed roofs of wihāras rising one behind another in nearly the same way, in one instance five roofs being visible (Fig. No. 159), and in the other three roofs, as on most of the coins.

On one of the Purānas from Mulleittīvu the structure is evidently a temple or palace, the central arch rising from the

[1] *Archaeological Survey of Southern India*, Vol. i, Plate XLII, Fig. 9.

ground-level, with high vertical sides. A similar design occurs on Indian coins, and is illustrated by Mr. Theobald in his essay on the symbols. In the Taxila coin No. 5 of Plate III, *C.A.I.* (No. 34, p. 158, Ind. Mus. Cat.) one of these structures is shown with only two arches side by side; this cannot be a dāgaba. In the third Purāna illustrated by me the building is also not a dāgaba.

An undoubted dāgaba appears on the Andhra coins 41 and 42 of Plate II of Sir Walter Elliott's *Coins of Southern India.* It is a building of a different type, having a single dome, with two rows of niches for lamps below it, just as they are to be seen in walls about some of these buildings in Ceylon. There must have been few dāgabas, and those only small ones, in India before the middle of the third century B.C., whereas the arched symbol on the Purānas appears to be of much earlier date. It is interesting as being probably the first illustration of an Indian roofed building.

The crescent which often crowns the top of the uppermost dome of these arched edifices has not been satisfactorily explained. It is not a Būddhist emblem, and is never seen as an independent emblem on the coins or early sculptures of Ceylon, but it is on a punch-marked Purāna from Mulleittīvu.

In the Taxila coin No. 17, of Plate II, *C.A.I.* (No. 13, p. 157, Ind. Mus. Cat.) a person is paying reverence to this symbol fixed on the summit of a three-domed building, below which is a mound of seven beads, which may be a tumulus or a sacred hill. On coin No. 14 of the same Plate (No. 9, p. 157, Ind. Mus. Cat.) the worshipper has turned his back on the so-called 'Chaitya' and its crescent finial, in order to adore a similar mound of seven beads, which in this case is evidently a sacred hill or tumulus. It is significant that the crescent is never seen on these mounds, but only on the arched buildings.

On the coins of Rudradāman (150 A.D.) and his successors, the crescent appears on the top of the three-domed building; while a symbol of the sun, a bead with six, seven, or eight rays, is on the right of the arches, and one of the moon, in the form of a crescent, on the left of them (Plate XVIII, Ind. Mus. Cat.). It is clear that the upper crescent in this and other instances has some symbolical meaning which the lower one, treated simply as the partner of the sun, does not express.

What this is, may be learnt from the Atharva Veda (ix, 6), which mentions 'Sōma, the God who is called Chandramas' [the moon]. Sōma is still one of the synonyms meaning the moon. The Rig Veda is in agreement with this, and also refers to Sōma as the moon. It says of Sōma, 'He follows the Wide-strider's [the sun's] rapid movement. . . . He with the sharpened horns brings forth abundance ; the Silvery shines by night, by day the Golden' (ix, 79, 9). Sōma is also referred to as 'Subduing our assailants, chasing the demons hard to be encountered' (ix, 110, 12). We also expressly learn of him that 'The mighty takes his seat, and Sōma, ever watchful, guards from fiend and evil sprite. Gold-hued he makes the cloud his diadem, the milk his carpet in both worlds, and prayer his robe of state' (ix, 71, 1). One hymn which is addressed to Sōma ends with the words 'Those awful weapons that thou hast, sharpened at point to strike men down—guard us therewith from every foe' (ix, 61, 30). Sōma is also identified with the great demon-slayer Indra :—'Indra's self is Pavamāna [Sōma], yea, the Bull' (ix, 5, 7). 'Indu [Sōma] is Indra' (ix, 5, 9).

It is most probably in this aspect, as Sōma, the 'ever-watchful' protector from demoniacal interference, that the crescent is so often placed on the arched buildings represented on the coins, whether they are temples or palaces.

Thus it is seen that in the case of most of the early coins of the East, with its elaborate symbolism (excluding those which were mere imitations of Greek models) care was taken to insert on them emblems, or figures of deities, which were believed to have protective powers against evil spirits, as well as others that were thought to be especially luck-bringing.

This may furnish the explanation of the other strange punch-marks of the Purānas, the early signification of many of which is known, while that of some is difficult to understand. For instance, there can be little doubt as to the purpose of the following figures on the coins.

The Elephant is at once recognised both as the 'Vāhana

or riding-animal, of Indra, a persistent enemy of the demons, and as a lucky emblem.[1] It is also the Vāhana of Ayiyanār, who in India protects villages from nocturnal spirits. The dream of a white elephant was the omen of the birth of the Buddha, Gōtama ; and in Ceylon it is still thought to prognosticate the birth of a son, which in India is one of the most fortunate of all occurrences. Miniature elephants of ivory are still sold largely in Ceylon as lucky charms. As I have already mentioned, the elephants' heads projecting from the walling and wāhalkaḍas at the Anurādhapura dāgabas were most probably placed there as a protection against evil spiritual influences, and not as mere ornaments.

Indra, the 'terrific wielder of the ancient thunder'[2] which was a favourite weapon of the Gods in their wars with evil spirits, whether Titans or others ; and Agni, 'the master of all wealth' ; and the Sun—all, according to the Vedas, noted slayers of demons, and those who practised evil magic —were all, but especially the first one, termed 'Bulls' in Vedic times, perhaps because of their irresistible power, which the Bull also symbolised in the Euphrates valley and Egypt. This animal afterwards became the Vāhana of Ṡiva, who through his Ṡakti, or female manifestation, slew the demons called Asuras.

The 'Taurine' symbol, which is in the form of the skull of a bull, perhaps also signifies these Bulls. Such skulls are everywhere employed in Ceylon as potent guards against the Evil Eye, that bug-bear of all people, and the Bull's head or skull was an amulet in Egypt from prehistoric times, as also in early Greece. It is extremely doubtful if this design has, as some have supposed, an astrological signification ; when placed on the corners of the fence or enclosure at the tree its position proves that it was thought to be an additional protection.

The Sun was the luminary whose rays, shown on most of the early Indian coins as straight lines or arrow-heads radiating

[1] *The Jātaka* ' (Translation), Vol. vi, p. 251.

[2] Rig Veda, iv, 20, 6 ; in x, 92, 8, it is stated of him 'Unhindered, from the air's vault thunders day by day the loud triumphant breathing of the fearful Bull.'

outwards from a central circle,—the 'arrowy beams' (ix, 76, 4), or the 'long loose locks' (x, 136, 1) of the Rig Veda—every day discomfited the demons, and dispelled the darkness under cover of which they exerted their powers. Naturally, according to this view of the purpose of the emblems, this is the commonest of all designs on the earliest money. The circle with many internal radial lines proceeding from a central ring represents its single wheel, with which Indra destroyed the Asuras.[1]

The Sacred Tree, of whatever kind, owes its position to its guardian properties against demons; and according to the Atharva Veda amulets against them were made from many different species. From some kinds the wood of the fire-drill was taken, by means of which the presence of Agni, the Fire Deity, the chief demon-slayer of Vedic times, was secured. In the Atharva Veda, the Bō-tree, the Pipal of India, is called 'the Seat of the Gods,'[2] and thus was a place to be avoided by the demons. It will be seen, therefore, that the Bō-tree or a Bō-branch is not necessarily a Buddhist emblem when it appears on these early coins.

The defensive value of the Cross is explained in a later chapter on the Swāstika.

The Snake is a well-known protector against demons. In the Rig Veda (vii, 104, 9) Sōma is prayed to hand over the evil demons to the Serpent. In the Atharva Veda (xii, 3, 55–60) Serpents are mentioned as Guardians of the Four Quarters and the Zenith. Representations of five-headed or seven-headed Cobras carved in high relief are placed at the sides of some of the dāgabas at Anurādhapura and elsewhere, as guardians of the relics deposited in them. Similar carvings are also fixed as defenders at the outlets of the sluices and sometimes on the embankments, at the larger reservoirs in Ceylon. In the manuscript which I possess, containing magical formulae and diagrams, the Snake is included as a protector against illness caused by demons (Yakshas). The Snake is also everywhere believed to guard hidden treasures, and even to be

[1] Rig Veda, i, 130, 9; iv, 30, 4.

[2] *Sacred Books of the East*, Vol. xlii, p. 4.

a manifestation of the household guardian spirit. In China it is an emblem of the God who controls thunderstorms, rain, wind, and fire, all powerful weapons against demons, and used by Buddha against the Yakshas of Ceylon. In China its figure is also employed as a charm against evil influences.[1]

The Dog is also a demon-frightener. According to Sinhalese beliefs he howls at night when he sees them, and in the jungle dialect he is called Ædurā, 'the demon-expeller.' In some parts of India he is a sacred animal; and he still protects the household from evil spirits.[2] In the Atharva Veda (xlii, 13) the Sun is termed the 'Heavenly Dog,' probably because he was constantly acting as a guardian against the demons, A 'Heavenly Dog' is an evil deity in China; but other dogs are worshipped as beneficent deities, while a dog's head drawn upon yellow paper is a protective charm.[3]

It is among the Āryans of Persia that we find the most decided evidence of the power of the Dog over demons. In the Vendīdād (Fargard xiii) Ahura-Mazda says of one species, "This is the good creature among the good creatures of the Good Spirit that from midnight till the sun is up goes and kills thousands of the creatures of the Evil Spirit." He also tells Zarathrustra regarding it that when Ahriman, the Evil Spirit, tried to kill Gayōmart, the first man, 'Ormazd [the Good Spirit] cried out "O thou yellow-eared dog, arise!" And directly the dog barked and shook his two ears; and the unclean Satan and the fiends when they saw the dreadful looks of the yellow-eared dog, and heard his barking, were sore afraid and fled down to hell.'[4] In Fargard viii, (*S.B. of E.*, iv, p. 99), such a dog is commanded to be brought to look at a dead body in order to scare away the Death Fiend. This is still done. At a Parsi funeral which he attended in 1875, Sir Monier Williams saw a white dog led in the procession; at a distance of thirty yards

[1] Doolittle. *Social Life of the Chinese*, Paxton Hood's Revision, pp. 204, 566.

[2] Crookes. *Popular Religion and Folklore of Northern India*, Vol. ii, pp. 218, 222.

[3] Doolittle, *op. cit.* pp. 230 ff., 567.

[4] S.B. of E. *The Zend Avesta*, Vol. iv, p. 156; Introduction, p. lxxiv.

from the Tower of Silence to which it was going 'the dog was brought towards the corpse, made to look at the features of the dead man, and then fed with bread.' [1] Thus it is not surprising to find the figure of this powerful demon-scarer placed on the summit of the five-arched structures, if not as an independent emblem on the Purānas.

The Fish in the tank signified that it was full of water, and this betokened a good agricultural season for those whose crops depended on the water-supply derived from it.

Of the River, the winding design in which fish are pourtrayed in order to show its nature, the Rig Veda (x, 30, 2) says, 'Wealthy Waters, ye control all treasures, ye bring auspicious intellect and Amrit' [the water of immortality]. Thus both the Tank and the River were emblems, and therefore omens, of coming prosperity and wealth.

The Fish and the Turtle were incarnations of Vishnu, a well-known enemy of demons. Crookes states that drawings of fish on the walls of houses are still a charm against demoniacal influence in India.[2]

According to the Rig Veda (vii, 103, 10) the Frogs granted riches and 'cows in hundreds,' besides lengthening the lives of the Āryans.

The Horse was a Vāhana of Indra, of Ayiyanār, and of Vaisravana or Kuvēra, the Overlord of the Yakshas, and the God of Wealth; it was also identified with the sun (R. V. i, 163, 2). It is still a demon-scarer and a guardian animal in some parts of India, where it is commonly worshipped.[3] It is also carved in relief at the entrances of monastic buildings at Anurādhapura, on the top of a pilaster (see Fig. 157), as well as on 'moonstones' at the base of steps, doubtless as a guardian animal.

I have little information about the Rhinoceros, which is sometimes represented on Purānas; but scrapings from its horn are still thought to be a most valuable and powerful antidote in certain diseases in India and Ceylon. This may

[1] *Modern India and the Indians*, p. 173.
[2] *Op. cit.*, Vol. ii, p. 254.
[3] Crookes. *Op. cit.*, Vol. ii, pp. 207, 208.

FIG. 160. Bhairava as Guardian.

To face p. 515

account for its presence, since in R. V. x, 97, 6, a physician, 'chaser of disease,' is termed a fiend slayer. Water drunk out of a cup made of Rhinoceros horn is stated by Lane to be thought a cure for poison in Egypt (*Manners and Customs of the Modern Egyptians*, 1896, p. 268).

The Goat which appears on some Indian examples may be inserted as an emblem of Pūshan, who was especially the God who was the 'Giver of blessings, the conductor by ways free from fear and danger' (R. V. x, 17, 5); while in R. V. x, 26, 7, he is termed 'the Strong Friend of all prosperity.'

The Lion was a Vāhana of Lakshmī, the Goddess of Prosperity,[1] and of Parvatī, the wife of Śiva. Reliefs of lions are numerous at Anurādhapura and elsewhere, at the entrances of monastic buildings; and a lion's face with open mouth is also carved in the front of the crowns of most of the Dwārpal or Guardian Deities at these edifices. Lion statues were set on the tops of the high side pillars at the Ruwanwaeli and Miriswaeṭi wāhalkaḍas, with open mouths as though roaring. It is evident that in these sites they were thought to have protective powers against evil spirits. This notion will account for the lions on a royal throne, the *Sinhāsana*, or 'Lion throne.' The claws are also amulets. (See Fig. No. 217.)

No clearer proof can be desired that the symbols on the early coins were inserted because of their defensive powers, than the little figure holding an object like a staff which is curled over his head, on the early coin No. 12, Plate XIX of Smith's Catalogue. The same figure is found carved in stone on a slab, and placed as a door guardian at Anurādhapura, near the Ruwanwaeli dāgaba. It is there said to represent Bhairava, as the defender of temples and treasures. Being the master of all demons he would be expected to protect the owner of the coin from them. At Benares he guards Saivite temples, and 'saves his votaries from demons.'[2]

[1] In Egypt it was identified with the Sun. Nebseni is represented as saying, "I am the Lion-god Rā [the Sun]." Dr. Budge, *The Book of the Dead*, p. 110.

[2] Sherring, *The Sacred City of the Hindus*, p. 119. (Quoted by

The carving at Anurādhapura (Fig. No. 160), shows plainly that the thing which he holds is a snake; its scales and head are distinctly visible, though unfortunately the latter is not fully included in my photograph. It passes under his feet both there and on the coin. All the other fat figures on the Anurādhapura guard-stones are nearly similar representations of this deity, but I believe that only in this one is the nature of the snake evident. In nearly all cases he is there represented standing on it and holding it by one hand. At Maḍukanda wihāra, in the Northern Province, it encircles the body of a personage who may be the same god, and he is carved in a dancing attitude; this appears to render the identity of the deity certain.

The Bow with an arrow may indicate the crescent moon as Sōma. In the Rig Veda, ix, 50, 1, Sōma is prayed, 'Urge on thine arrow's sharpened point,' and at ix, 90, 3 it is likened to a warrior 'with sharpened arms, with swift bow, never vanquished in battle.' If it be not indicative of Sōma, it may be as an emblem of either Indra or Rudra that it is present on the coins. The Sāma Veda terms Indra 'the most excellent handler of the bow-string' (Adhyaya, xiv, 2); while Rudra is called in the Atharva Veda, xi, 2, 'the Archer with the dark crest,' his symbol being a bow and arrow in Vedic times.

The Circle or bead surmounted by the Crescent is one of the commonest symbols on these early coins. We find it on the corners of the fence or enclosure of the Sacred Tree on the large Sinhalese coin numbered **53**, as well as in a similar position on an Indian coin.[1] It also appears, reversed, on the stem of the elevated symbol which is cut at the beginning of inscription No. **62.** At the side of the inscription left by Nandimitta (No. **47**), it is very clearly cut in a form that differs from some of the others, the wings of the crescent ending in broad flat tops, instead of points, while the circle or disk has a smaller

Crookes, *op. cit.*, ii, p. 110.) Hence one of his titles in Tamil is *Kēttira-pālaṇ*, 'Protector of sacred places.'

[1] 'Notes on some of the Symbols found on the Punch-marked Coins,' by W. Theobald, in the *Journal of the Asiatic Society of Bengal*, 1890, pp. 181 ff.

one at its centre. It is noteworthy that in this symbol these circles never have rays.

At present I am unable to suggest a satisfactory explanation of it, the last-mentioned example, as well as its position on the fence at the tree, being against its identification either as a combination of the sun and moon, or as an astrological symbol. This design sometimes takes the place of the 'Taurine' emblem on the early coins.

Its place appears to be filled among modern Sinhalese magical diagrams against evil spirits by a design  which is repeated constantly in them and round them with or without a longer vertical line, and is called a *sula*, or torch. It may have been developed from the symbol in question, in which I think it probable that we have the original figure from which the single 'trisūla,' with a bead below it, is derived. This, however, still leaves the original signification of the Circle-and-Crescent without a complete explanation, even if it be a form of the 'Taurine' symbol, as is not unlikely.

The figures of two concentric circles, or a disk with an encircling band, round which are arranged six emblems, is most probably not a sun-symbol, but a protective magical diagram, the Axe which is part of it being a well-known magical and auspicious emblem. Even if the object be not an Axe but a Chatta, the magical nature of the design will still remain, as the Chatta itself has magical defensive powers against evil influences. The Mahāvansa (i, p. 121) states that at the laying of the foundation bricks at the Ruwanwaeli dāgaba 'a magical chatta,' was erected in order 'to prevent the interference of Māra' (death personified).

When the figure of a person was stamped upon the coins it would be appropriately that of a deity who was a noted demon-slayer, such as Skanda with his two wives, or Durgā, or sometimes Lakshmī, the Goddess of Prosperity, against whose influence the evil spirits were powerless.

Some of the other emblems on the early coins can be accounted for in a similar manner. Thus the Pentacle was and is still believed to possess power over evil spirits, and Crosses, Squares, and Circles, and a figure composed of two opposed Triangles meeting at their apices (? the Double-Axe, or perhaps the small hand drum called in Sinhalese Uḍakkiya) are exceedingly common among Sinhalese magical diagrams which afford protection from sickness, evil spirits, and planets.

Regarding the cause of the insertion of these symbols on the coins various hypotheses have been propounded. Some have supposed them to be mint marks, but the mere number of them sufficiently disproves this notion. Mr. Theobald illustrated three hundred of them, and doubtless there are many others, as we see in even the few specimens from Ceylon.

Sir A. Cunningham stated [1]: 'I have a suspicion that several of the symbols may have been the private marks of ancient money-changers. . . . The number of these symbols is so great, nearly three hundred, that their origin was probably due to several different causes.' Mr. V. A. Smith's opinion coincides with that expressed in the first of these sentences.[2]

For all to be the marks of money-changers it would be necessary to admit that there were persons who earned a living in this manner in the early days when the oldest Purānas were made, and that nearly all the coins which were issued passed through the hands of some ten or a dozen men or their representatives, one or more of this number of emblems appearing on nearly every coin. It is evident, also, that this theory does not explain the presence of many of the same symbols on the later coins.

Although I also believe that some few of the later symbols on the Purānas may possibly be those of money-changers, I venture to hold that this theory is inapplicable to such early marks as the Sun emblem, the Crescent on the arched structure, the Dog, the Bull, and several others, traces of which are found on even the lightest and most worn examples. The opinion which a study of the symbols has led me to adopt is as follows.

Of the early period at which the first Purānas were issued, there is evidence in the fact that it would be difficult, if not impossible, to explain some of the emblems—such as the Cres-

[1] *Coins of Ancient India*, p. 158.
[2] Catalogue. Introduction, p. 133.

cent, the Frog, and the River—without the assistance of the Vedas. It is to be found also in the almost entire absence of the Trident of Siva and of the Lingam from the punch-marks ; while we see constant indications of the worship of the Sun and Indra, and numerous references to some of the incarnations of Vishnu. The Rākshasas had not become protecting spirits, therefore they were still enemies to be guarded against.

Of Buddhism I cannot discover a trace on the Purānas.[1] Every symbol which might be claimed as embodying some allusion to that religion can be shown with greater probability to be of anterior date, according to the evidence of Mr. Theobald's illustrations. There is not a single unmistakable dāgaba on the Purānas, and with the exception of this design, and the three bars of the railing, and the fan-shaped sun-shade of Buddhist mendicants—both of which are also absent—Buddhism merely borrowed pre-existing symbols. Even the two foot-prints which came to represent Buddha are shown in a later chapter to have been known in Egypt as magical diagrams in the fourteenth century B.C.

However much the designs on the early coinage vary in age and character, I have demonstrated that practically all to which an Indian meaning can be assigned possess one of two attributes in common. They have the power either to scare away evil spirits, or to bring prosperity and good-luck. Considering the amount of variation in the marks, this fact is so striking that it suggests at once that it was solely because of these useful qualities that such designs were placed upon the coins. If not, why were only those quadrupeds depicted which possessed these powers ? Why not also the tiger, the bear, and the buffalo ?

As all sickness of man or beast, all bad luck of any kind, all want of success in trade, all the hurtful results that followed evil magic, and even errors in sacrificial ritual were believed to be due to the malevolent actions of evil spirits, it cannot be doubted that the insertion of symbols which had powers of terrifying them, or counteracting their evil influence, would

[1] Unless the supposed plan of a monastery be a Buddhist emblem.

be thought to conduce to the prosperity of the early traders for whose use the coins were issued.

In the period when the Purānas were being made there was probably no state monopoly of coinage, nor even a state issue of money.[1] Every person would thus be at liberty to stamp it with his own mark. Thus if a trader had formed an opinion that a particular emblem of this kind was a specially lucky one for him, it may be surmised that he would take care to get it impressed—sometimes destroying an earlier punch-mark by it—on many of the coins which came into his hands. This will account for the presence of some of the best known demon-frightening symbols on almost all the Purānas. Having this bad-luck-preventing and good-luck-bringing money, the traders and all who carried the coins would believe that they would have increased prospects of success in their undertakings. It was at the same time a medium of exchange and a powerful preservative and auspicious amulet.

At a later date in both India and Ceylon, when the coins were issued by state authority, and either cast, or marked by a single die on one face, or two dies, one on each face, some of the same emblems which had proved so effectual in early times were still retained for the reasons which induced the earlier people to impress them.

In the East, and probably everywhere, it was—and still is in most countries—at least quite as necessary to guard one's-self against the malevolence of evil spirits in the affairs of every-day life as to pay worship to the Gods. The amulets of the Neolithic and later Lake Dwellings, the primitive charms of Egypt, the Assyrian writings and carvings, and the Hymns of the Vedas afford abundant proof of this.

The constant use of the emblems of the deities was not intended for the satisfaction of the Gods; this was provided for by the offerings presented to them. The symbols, whether carved or drawn, were thought to be the most effectual guards

[1] Mr. V. A. Smith states (Cat. p. 133), 'It is clear that the punch-marked coinage was a private coinage issued by guilds and silver-smiths with the permission of the ruling powers.'

against all kinds of injuries inflicted by the evil spirits,[1] who were both vindictive and numberless.[2] How much impressed the ancient peoples were by this idea is evident from the strength in which such notions have been handed down to the present day. It is in this fact alone that any satisfactory explanation of the early mystic symbolism of the East, and of a great part of all the early symbolism, can be found.

[1] Exactly like the sign of the Cross in Christianity.

[2] A Sinhalese estimate makes the number in Ceylon two millions.

XIII

THE ANCIENT WEAPONS AND TOOLS

THE ANCIENT WEAPONS

FROM the occasional references in the histories to the weapons of the ancient Sinhalese, it can be gathered that the Sword and the Bow were the ordinary arms of the people, and were often carried by the chiefs and sovereigns, at any rate when they were engaged on warlike expeditions. When the Javelin or short throwing-Spear is added the list of primitive weapons mentioned separately by these authorities is nearly exhausted. Yet there is very good reason for believing that they possessed other arms even in early times, and 'the five weapons of war,' which according to Clough's Dictionary were the sword, spear, bow, battle-axe, and shield, are once alluded to collectively in the Mahāvansa.

Prince Wijaya, who became the first sovereign, is represented as being armed with both a sword and a bow when he landed in Ceylon (Mah., i, p. 32). A sword of state was also included among the presents sent by the Indian Emperor Aśōka to Dēvānam-piya Tissa in the third century B.C., and we are told that this king carried a bow when hunting Sambar deer (Mah., i, p. 50).

In the second century B.C., Phussadēva, one of the champions or generals of Duṭṭha-Gāmiṇi, is described as being an extraordinarily expert archer, who shot 'by a flash of lightning,' or 'through a horse-hair,' or 'a cart filled with sand, as well as through hides a hundred-fold thick; through an Asōka plank eight inches, an Udumbara plank sixteen inches thick, as well as a plate of iron, too, and a plate of brass four inches thick. On land his arrow would fly the distance of eight usabhas and through water one usabha' (Mah. i, p. 92). An usabha is 140 cubits, or about 204 feet.

In his fight with his brother Tissa, Duṭṭha-Gāmiṇi is mentioned as using a javelin while on horse-back; Prince Tissa, who was mounted on an elephant, wore armour on this occasion, that is, in the first half of the second century B.C. (Mah., i, p. 94). In Duṭṭha-Gāmiṇi's battle with Elāra the Tamil king, the Chiefs on both sides, who fought on foot, had swords and shields, while the two kings, who were on elephants, were armed with javelins(Mah., i, p. 99). In his battle with Elāra's nephew Bhalluka, the same king, who was on an elephant, is described as guarding his mouth with the handle of his sword when Bhalluka threw a javelin at him. One of Duṭṭha-Gāmiṇi's chiefs, who was seated behind the king on the elephant, also carried a javelin, but later on it is termed an arrow (Mah., i, p. 100, 101). King Waṭṭa-Gāmiṇi is stated to have been armed with a bow while awaiting an opportunity to regain the throne, at the beginning of the first century B.C.

With the exception of the State Sword carried by an official who was termed the Sword Bearer, and who ranked as one of the Great Officers of State, as in India,[1] weapons are not again mentioned in the history until the twelfth century A.D., when we find Prince Parākrama-Bāhu I described as being armed with a sword and shield; an attendant also bore an umbrella for him, and the general opposed to him was similarly provided with one. When the house occupied by the Prince was surrounded by the enemy at night, he is said to have wrapped himself in his blanket, and to have fought with his sword (Mah., ii, p. 137). Also when he escaped from Polannaruwa at night he carried a shield and a sword with which he killed a bear that attacked him in the path (Mah., ii, 143).

He armed some of his men with 'swords, lances, darts, and other weapons of war,' and we learn that one party of them also had clubs (Mah., ii, p. 151). In these wars we read for the first time of chariots used in battle in Ceylon; and the leader of the enemy's troops went to battle in one instead of riding on an elephant according to the custom of earlier times (p. 157). The men wore 'armour that could not be pierced through';

[1] *Questions of King Milinda*, p. 171.

what this was is evident from references to 'coats of mail of buffalo hides' (p. 207), and 'coats wrought of iron and skins of deer to keep the sharp-pointed arrows from piercing them' (p. 231). Other kinds of protective covering were also employed, and some of the enemy were 'clad in ten kinds of armour' (p. 165). 'Showers of arrows' are mentioned; and 'stones without number hurled from engines flew about on every side' (p. 186). In one fight 'burning javelins bound with chains' are referred to. In the account of the Sinhalese invasion of Southern India during this king's reign only swords and arrows are mentioned.

When Ceylon was invaded by Malays in 1251 A.D., it is stated that poisoned arrows were used by the invaders; they were 'shot quickly from engines' (p. 282), which must have been cross-bows. But 'the Sinhalese, who were skilful marksmen, broke them in pieces with their sharp broad arrows'—like Rāma in his wonderful battles with the Rākshasas. There is no indication of the use of poisoned arrows by the Sinhalese, nor are crossbows ever mentioned in the histories as employed by them, although they were used in Captain Robert Knox's time (seventeenth century). They were known in India in early times, and are mentioned in *The Questions of King Milinda*, p. 159. They do not appear in early Indian carvings. It is possible that the 'engines' by means of which stones were thrown were merely enlarged stone-bows with two strings, of the type now made by children. The desultory fighting of the Sinhalese would not permit them to carry about with them such elaborate stone-throwing appliances as those figured by Sir R. Payne-Gallwey in his work on *The Projectile-Throwing Engines of the Ancients.*

The above-quoted notices comprise practically all that is to be learnt in the histories regarding the weapons of the ancient Sinhalese.

Among the insignia carried by the deities of the Dēwālas,—the temples devoted to some Indian gods, and the godlings (Dēvatās), demons, and deified chiefs of the Sinhalese—an additional list of the ancient weapons can be compiled, and in them doubtless the traditional forms of some of them have been preserved. They include the Sword, both straight and curved, the Trident, the Billhook, the Krīs, the Iron Club, and a weapon called Ītiya, a variety of Assegai.

The list is still incomplete, as there can be no doubt that Battle-axes were used in war, in addition to the common Kandian Knife, and a Dagger.

The Sword, *Kaḍuwa*, is almost the sole weapon represented in ancient carvings in Ceylon, and even that is only occasionally met with. The earliest representation of one was discovered by me in the excavations at Tissa, engraved on a fragment of pottery which probably dated from pre-Christian times. The illustration (Fig. 161) shows that it had a long handle with a substantial cross-hilt, but no other guard; and a broad and slightly curved blade, wider at a short distance from the end than near the hilt. It would be a formidable cutting weapon.

Others illustrated on a very small scale in reliefs on a pillar at the Jētavana Dāgaba at Anurādhapura (Fig. 87), and in some places in the hands of armed men who were represented as springing out of the open mouths of nondescript monsters called Makaras, are all straight-edged, somewhat short, pointed weapons, apparently without cross-hilts or guards. The men who hold them in the latter examples carry a small circular buckler in their left hands.

Some interesting panels are carved in the sides of the stone pillars that support the elongated porch (*Dig-gē*) of the Warakā Wihāra, the oldest cave temple, according to tradition, at the Ridi Wihāra, the Silver Monastery, in the Kurunāēgala district. In the panels, which are at the base of each pillar, a dance of soldiers is represented, one figure being in each panel. Some of them carry swords and shields, the only type of the former being the straight pointed sword with and without a straight cross-hilt, but in either case having no guard (Fig. 170).

The temple itself was founded in pre-Christian times, and the name *Paramaka Abayaha leṇe*, 'the cave of the Chief Abhaya,' in the earliest characters of the second or third century B.C., with the bent *r* and the cup-shaped *m*, is inscribed

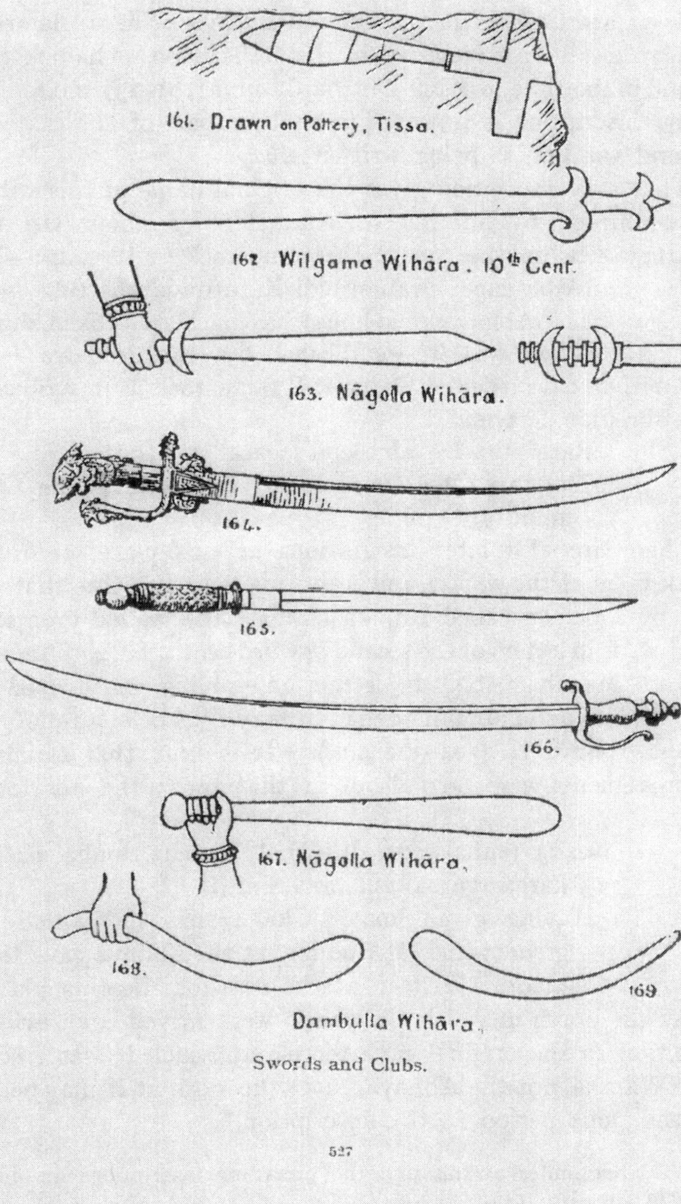

Swords and Clubs.

in another cave there which now contains the principal temple, the Rājata Lena Wihāra, 'the Silver Cave Wihāra,' in which a heap of silver is recorded in the Mahāvansa as having been found in the time of King Duṭṭha-Gāmiṇi (161–137 B.C.). The same inscription is repeated in another part of the cave, the second word in it being written *Abayi*.

That this inscription gives the original name of this wihāra is confirmed by another in characters of about the first century A.D. on the top of the same rock.[1] It runs:—

> (A)ba dagaya raṇ(e) biḍi Karaṭiradataha tube.
>
> The Abhaya relic-house having been broken during war was (re-)established by Karaṭiradatta.

Another cave shelter under the same rock is inscribed in pre-Christian letters,

> Bata puta Devaha leṇe sagasa.
>
> The cave of Dēva, son (of) Bhātiya; to the Community.

There are also later inscriptions at this place, recording work done at the wihāra and grants made to it. One that was left by a person called Bujaka Utaya, 'the landed proprietor Uttiya,' is in letters of the second or third century A.D. Another is by 'Mekaha Aba,' in letters resembling those used by Jeṭṭha-Tissa, son of Mahā-Sēna; it may thus belong to Mēghavaṇṇa-Abhaya II (304–322 A.D.). It is clear that extensive improvements were carried out at that time; the inscription ends,

> Laka (kaha)wana di (Aba) ka leṇa maha paṭima karawaya savasa taṇaṭa lit(i).
>
> Having given 100,000 kahāpanas he caused the great statue (of Buddha) at the Abhaya cave to be made. Written at the tom-tom beating place.

As the porch in which the panels were carved is an evident addition to the original cave temple at which it was erected (the Warakā, not the Abhaya, cave) the work at it may belong to the same period as this inscription.[2]

[1] The facsimiles of this and the preceding inscriptions are to be seen in Fig. No. 153.

[2] I may note that there is no reference in any of the inscriptions

170.

171.

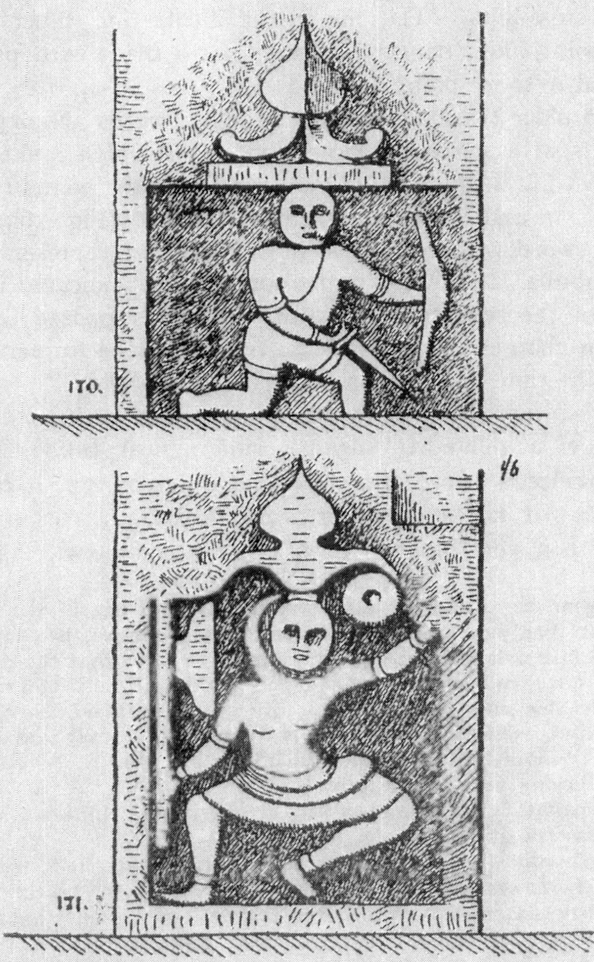

FIGS. 170, 171. Panels at Ridí Wihāra.

Some of the long straight swords carved in these panels follow the type of Indian weapons represented in the Amarāvati carvings (late second century A.D.), which, however, had no cross-hilts. The one in the illustration tapers from hilt to point, like a dagger; another has a blade with parallel sides and a short point.

In the older temple paintings straight swords are depicted with hilts of a shape not now seen. One which I sketched has a cross-hilt in the form of a crescent with the points turned forward; in another the crescent is reversed (Fig. 163). A straight sword without a cross-hilt or guard is represented in the Dambulla Cave temple; the painting was executed in the middle of the seventeenth century, and is supposed by the monks in charge of the temple to reproduce the former work done in the time of Niśśanka-Malla (1198–1207 A.D.).

Below an inscription of the ninth or tenth century, cut on the face of a pillar at Wilgama wihāra, near Bibile, in the Ūva Province, a sword of a somewhat different type is carved (Fig. 162); it has a cross-hilt which ends in a curl on one side, and is a very long narrow straight weapon, twice as wide

to the legend regarding the discovery of silver in one of the caves. Some short badly-cut records of grants to the temple, belonging to about the fifth or sixth century A.D., appear to show that the modern name had not then been adopted. Three contain the name of a temple, apparently this one, which is variously spelt Havidavi, Havadava, and Hividivi, while in another it is Divegala. It may have been Havidiva Wihāra, 'the splendid wihāra on the hill.'

The following are specimens of these records:—

i. Nilapaṇataṭa ca Jalanalana kita ca Havadava w(i)hara ca savisa taṇaṭa liti.

Nilapāṇataṭa (now Nilantaṭṭuwa), and Jalanalaṇa field, with the Havadava wihāra; written at the tom-tom beating place (the flat rock on which the inscriptions are cut).

ii. Uḍabagaṇu Hividivi wihari ca savisa taṇaṭa liti.

iii. Haga sala Divegala w(i)hara ca la sevasa taṇaṭa liti.

A hall for the Community is placed with the Divegala wihāra, etc.

The meaning of the formula seems to be that the names of the places are coupled with the wihāra as part of its property, which once covered a large tract around it. The old name of the adjoining district is said to be Entoṭa Danawwa. A long covered shed was built for the tom-tom beaters by King Kirti Śri (1747–1780 A.D.); it is termed the Hēvisi Maṇḍapa.

towards the point as it is near the hilt. The blade is contracted sharply up to the point, which is extremely short.

In no case, so far as I am aware, is the small modern curved, one-edged Sabre, termed a *Kastānē* (Fig. 164), found in any Sinhalese carvings. In the temple paintings of the contest between Buddha and the demons, which, however, are all comparatively recent restorations, very rarely, in their present state, belonging to an earlier date than the seventeenth century, this is the favourite type of the artists, practically differing in no way from the Kandian ceremonial sabres worn by the chiefs of the present time. These have curved hilts made of buffalo horn, ending in a lion's head, and inlaid with brass, silver, or gold, with usually some work of the same kind fixed or inlaid on the lower part of the blade. All have guards, and there is a half cross-hilt on the opposite side.

I give also drawings of two swords in my possession, from villages in the interior of the North-western Province. The smaller one (Fig. 165) is two-edged, and without guard or cross-hilt; it appears to be a specimen of the short straight Indian type of early post-Christian times. The other (Fig. 166) which is one-edged except at the point, and is curved and has a guard, is a much longer weapon; most probably it is copied from European hangers, if it is not actually of European manufacture. Both these weapons have pommels. The only Scabbards that I have seen were made of two wooden plates held together by bands of silver or brass.[1]

I have seen no Daggers that appeared to be of an early type, but Mr. Bell has illustrated one carved in outline on a rock at Anurādhapura[2] (Fig. 181). One of peculiar shape in the British Museum is doubtless of late date (Fig. 179).

Although the Kandian Knife, *Pihā-Kaetta*, must always have been utilised as an ornamental appendage and as an instrument of daily use rather than as a warlike weapon, its employment in the latter capacity on suitable occasions

[1] Captain Robert Knox says of those used by the better classes, 'The Scabbard most part covered with Silver, bravely ingraven.'

[2] Archaeological Survey of Ceylon. Third Progress Report, Plate VIII.

cannot be doubted. When we read of murders committed by 'plunging a weapon' into the victims we may be certain that the Knife was resorted to in many a fight with the enemy. It does not appear in any carvings.

Its shape varies considerably. The largest type (Fig. No. 172) follows the curve of the short Southern Indian sword (see Fig. No. 158), and has a wide blade; others are much narrower and straighter. The better sorts of knives had carved ivory hafts inlaid with brass, silver, or gold; a thin narrow plate of the same material, with raised conventional decorations, which were usually meanders or simple four-pointed stars, was also attached to each side of the lower part of the blade, the surface of which was sunk at the spot to receive it. Some had carved handles of rock-crystal, a custom which appears to have been common in former times, since it has caused a general expression 'Stone-handled knife' (*Gal-mita pihē*) to be applied to all weapons of the same shape, whatever material be used in the haft. Common knives of course had wooden handles (Fig. No. 177). The usual forms are shown in the illustrations (Figs. 172–178). All appear to have had thin wooden sheaths formed of two hollowed strips tied or pegged together near the point, and bound by a thin plate of brass or silver at the mouth.

The Kris, *Kriciya* (*c* pronounced as *ch*), is shown by its name to be borrowed from Malaya. It is rarely seen, and does not often appear in the wihāra paintings; but it is represented at the Dambulla wihāra, where it is held as a dagger. The fact that a broken blade which appeared to belong to this weapon, with at least three bends, was discovered in the Tissa excavations, in the lowest pottery stratum, proves that it had been introduced into the island in very early times. Unfortunately I preserved no drawing of the blade, which is now in the Colombo Museum.

The *Ītiya* is the true Sinhalese form of a weapon of this type. It is a narrow-bladed short stabbing spear or assegai, but it is also held like a sword. It is described as having a thin blade eighteen inches long, with bends resembling those of the Kris, and two cutting edges. It is found in the Dēwālas,

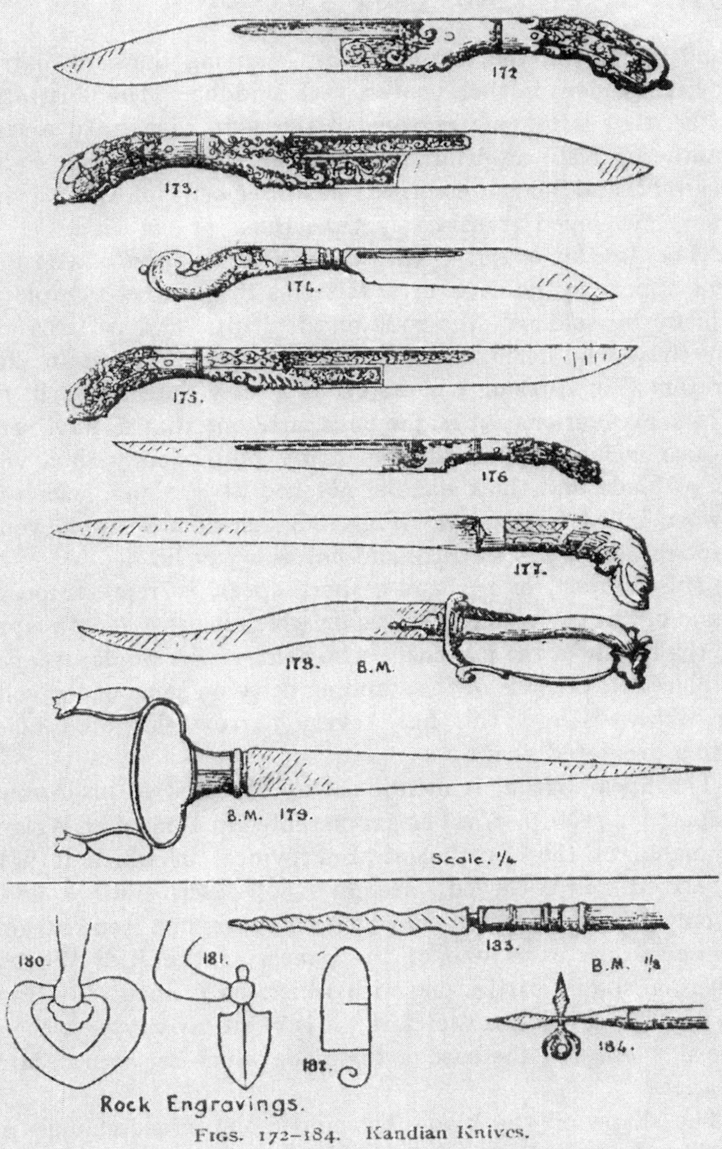

FIGS. 172–184. Kandian Knives.

and appears in the temple paintings among the arms carried by the demons in their contest with Buddha. The illustration (Fig. 187) is taken from one of these drawings. In a large statue of Kālī, at Anurādhapura, this goddess grasps it like a sword, and holds it erect. It has three bends in this carving, more developed transversely than those of the Krīs.

The Javelin or short Throwing-Spear, *Vīsi-hella,* also does not appear in the carvings. It seems to have been employed chiefly by soldiers who rode on elephants, and perhaps also by those who defended city walls and forts. I give an illustration (Fig. 191) of a blade of very early date found in the Tissa excavations; it is the only early one that I have seen. I also include a modern one in my possession with a very large blade and thick handle, notched at the end, which its owner called an 'arrow' (Fig. 186); such a weapon would probably be used as a Pike and not as a Javelin.

This weapon, or perhaps a short spear, is represented on some of the early oblong coins, on which it has a length equal to the height of the personage who holds it. A similar weapon is placed at the side of the standing deity on some of the coins of Wijaya-Bāhu; this has a very narrow elongated blade and a decorated shaft.

The Spear, *Hella,* is mentioned by Mr. Bell in his Annual Report for 1896, p. 7, as being represented in a panel at Welana Damana, in the North-central Province, in which a fight of armed men is carved. He does not describe it. I know of only one other instance in which it appears in a stone carving in Ceylon; this is one of the panels at the Ridi Wihāra, where a soldier carries one with which he is about to attack an enemy. I did not sketch it; it is of an early type, without the side wings at the base of the blade which are seen in later weapons.

The shape of the blade has undergone great changes in Ceylon. In the earliest specimens, obtained from my excavations at Tissa, and apparently pre-Christian, it is thick and nearly straight, one being about two inches wide and seven and a half long, with a somewhat broad rounded point; this form has a half-socket at the base, formed by widening out the stem and

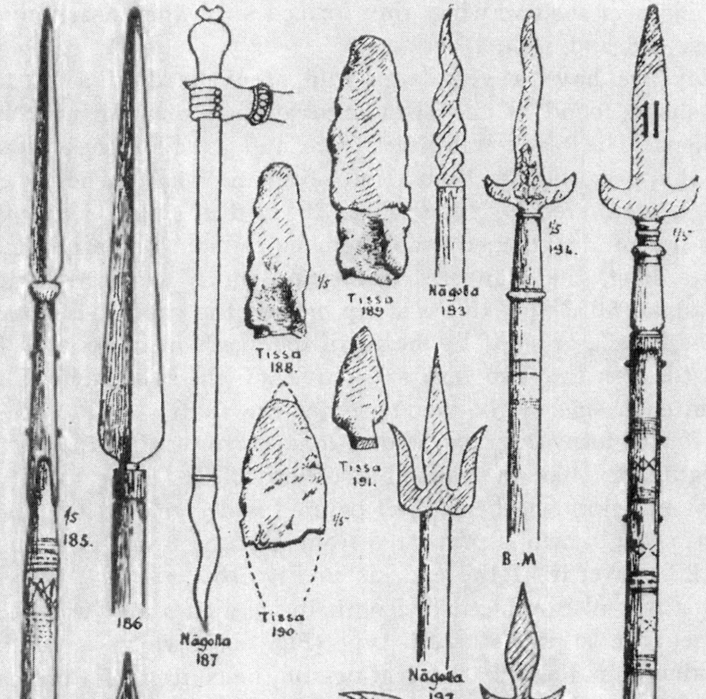

FIGS. 185–200. Sinhalese Weapons.

turning over the two wings thus formed until they nearly met (Figs. 188 and 189).

Next we have a very large thin spear head of a broad leaf shape, found at the Tissa excavations, but unfortunately broken. The blade was nearly two and a half inches wide, and it appears to have been about seven and a half inches long.

A later interesting type (Figs. 185 and 201) has a strong, very narrow, lengthened head, from six to eight and a quarter inches long, the tranverse section of which is a cross with the angles filled up ; this is sharp only at the tip. It is fitted to the handle or shaft by means of four nails or rivets, which pass through the two hollowed halves of the split stem that fit on each side of the woodwork of the shaft.

A fourth form (Fig. 197) is of a long narrow leaf shape, with straight sides, like an enlarged arrow-head. It has no socket ; the stem being lengthened and pointed is driven into the end of the shaft, which is prevented from splitting by an iron ring which fits over it at the end, as in Fig. 186.

This was also reduced in length to 3½ inches and widened at the base to make a fifth type (Fig. 200), which is often introduced in the wihāra paintings of the contest of Buddha with Māra and his demons. It is now commonly employed for keeping in check the wild elephants at Elephant Kraals when they attempt to break through the palisades of the enclosure into which they are driven. In this form there is a round socket at the end of the stem, into which the shaft is driven, being held in place by a nail.

Another type of spear-head was narrow and elongated, with waved edges. Some had no socket to receive the shaft. There is an example in the British Museum, and drawings of it are to be seen in the wihāras (Figs Nos. 183 and 193).

Although the common winged spear-head of recent times seems to be copied from weapons carried by the early European invaders it is certainly of much more ancient date. On the side of the crown of a wooden statue which is supposed to be that of Duṭṭha-Gāmiṇi, at the Nikawaewa Cave wihāra, there are carved reliefs (Fig. 217) which evidently represent spears with winged heads like those now in use, as well as others

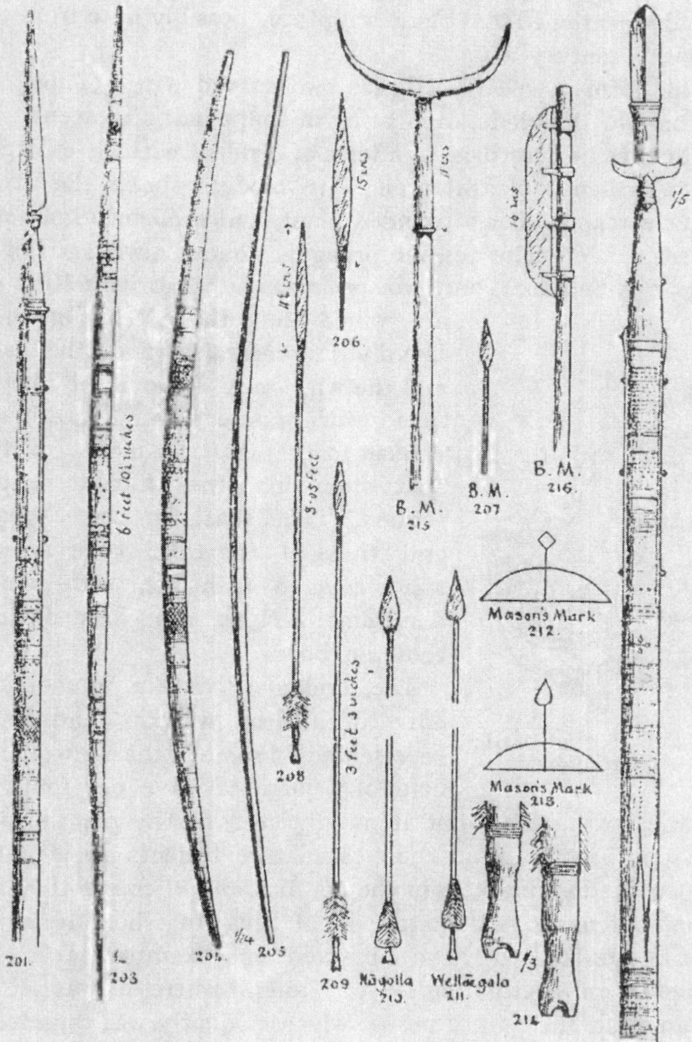

FIGS. 201–216. Sinhalese Weapons.

resembling the fourth and fifth types just described.[1] I have already mentioned that these sculptures possibly date from the eleventh century A.D.

This form of spear-head has two curved wings (*Tattu*) at the base of the blade, each being in shape half a crescent. It might thus be described as a form of Trident with an enlarged and lengthened central prong. In modern spears the blade of such weapons has a rounded point, and is slightly hollowed on each side. The central prong is almost always straight (Figs. 195 and 202), but two specimens in the British Museum are waved along the edges (Fig. 194). Usually the central parts of the blade and the wings are decorated by being inlaid with brass or silver. The blade is fixed to the shaft by means of the split stem, like the third form described. The shafts of these spears and those of the third type are always covered with lac, with which handsome designs are formed, like those on bows.

FIG. 217. Side of Duṭṭha-Gāmiṇi's Crown.

The Trident, *Patistāna*, is undoubtedly an ancient weapon, and it is represented on some of the early oblong coins of Ceylon. I have not found it in any local reliefs, but it is depicted in the paintings in wihāras (Figs. 192 and 196.) Miniature tridents are included among the insignia kept in the dēwālas, and of course they are seen in temple representations of Śiva, of whom it is the special symbol. I have observed one example carved in stone in an ancient temple of Gaṇēsa, where it was set up on an altar, the central prong, which evidently was considered to be a Lingam, and had that shape, being black with the oil poured over it.

[1] We learn from the Commentary on the Hymn vi, 90 of the Atharva Veda (Bloomfield's Translation, p. 506) that the spear was an amulet; this explains the presence of these spear-heads on the King's crown, as well as on the coins.

The Bident has fallen into complete disuse in Ceylon, but according to the evidence of the oblong coins it must have been a common weapon in the island in early times. It is also carved in the reliefs from Amarāvati which are preserved in the British Museum (slab No. 77). The only local stone carving of one with which I am acquainted is a slab of earlier date than the twelfth century, found at the Giant's Tank, where it appears at the side of a rude figure cut in low relief (Fig. 218).

FIG. 218. Pillar at the Giant's Tank.

Although the Bow, *Dunna*, and Arrow, *Īya* or *Īgaha*, were the most important weapons of the ancient Sinhalese, as well as in Vedic times,[1] I have not met with a single illustration of them in Sinhalese stone carvings ; but Mr. Bell found in the panel at Welana Damana, in the North-central Province, to which allusion has been already made, four men armed with them and engaged in a fight with a giant who carried a sword and shield, aided by a kneeling spearman. They are always depicted in the representations of the Māra contest in the wihāras, and I have seen them carried many years ago by Sinhalese hunting parties, as well as by the Vaeddas and Wanniyas.

The correct length for a bow is commonly considered to be a few inches more than the height of the man who carries it. According to this, its length would be about 5 feet 6 inches ; but some are much longer, and two in the British Museum are about 7 feet 6 inches and 8 feet long. According to Dr. Davy the usual length in the early part of last century was 9 feet,[2] but no bows that I have seen were of this size. The expression *Maha Dunna*, 'Large Bow,' as a fixed measure

[1] Rig Veda, vi, 75, 2.

[2] *An Account of the Interior of Ceylon*, p. 244, foot-note.

of length, possibly the nine feet of Dr. Davy, shows that some were of more than the average length. The Mahā Bhārata mentions one four cubits long (*Adi Parva*, 191, 20).

The strongest bows (Fig. 204) are made from a large thorny creeper termed the Mā Wēvael (*Calamus rudentum*); these are much thicker than the bows made from other kinds of wood (Fig. 203), or the strong tough ribs of the leaves of the Talipat palm which are sometimes used. Common bows have plain and rather rough surfaces, and are undecorated. Talipat leaf bows (Fig. 205) are slightly flattened on the outer side; all the rest are of a circular section throughout. The better kinds are highly decorated, being covered with effective patterns in stick lac of various colours, chiefly red, yellow and black, and in early designs also green. They have no notches; the string, *Dunu-ḍiya* or *Dunu-lanuwa*, made of the inner bark of trees or the fibres of the Niyanda plant (*Sansievera zeylanica*), is merely tied permanently at one end and looped over the other when the bow is about to be used.

The Arrows are from about 3 feet to 4 feet in length, and have shafts half an inch thick; they vary greatly in the size of their steel heads (*Italē*), which are from 2½ inches up to almost 18 inches in length, the usual size being 4 or 5 inches. All the more modern heads are practically of one type (Fig. 208), a thin narrow leaf shape, supposed to represent a leaf of growing rice; they have distinct rounded butts, with a narrow stem or tang which is driven into the shaft, and they are invariably unbarbed. The sides of the blade are usually nearly parallel in the central part; the tip is more or less rounded, and the sides converge to it in straight lines (Figs. 206, 208 and 209). The British Museum has one of a slightly different shape (Fig. 207), with a blade wider near the stem, like those of the Vaeddas. A similar form is seen in some wihāra paintings (Figs. 210 and 211), and arrow-heads of this type are clearly indicated in two mason's marks of the twelfth century (Figs. 212 and 213), the date being determined by the shapes of letters cut by other masons on adjoining stones. I have already given a reference in the Mahāvansa to the 'broad arrows' of the Sinhalese in the twelfth century.

The arrows have usually four feathers of the pea-hen's wing, but sometimes only three. As I possess one with six feathers it is clear that the number varied according to the owner's fancy. Hard gum or lac is occasionally placed, as a protection from fraying, over the fine string which is used for tying them on the shaft. The shaft is slightly narrowed between the notch and the feathers (Fig. 214); in this respect it differs from the Vaedda shaft.

I have not seen a crescent-headed arrow, such as Rāma and his brother are described as using against the Rākshasas; it is an extremely ancient form of the weapon, and is mentioned in the Rig Veda (vi, 75, 5) as 'the shaft with venom smeared, tipped with deer-horn, with iron mouth.' It is, however, of far greater age than Vedic times, and long and most beautifully chipped flint specimens, some of the finest examples of chipped flint work ever executed, having a wide V-shaped cutting edge, with extremely fine and regular serrations, of pre-dynastic date, that is, dating from prior to 4500 B.C., have been obtained in Egypt, and are to be seen in the British Museum.

The illustration of a Yaksha given already (Fig. 9), which is copied from a painting of uncertain date in a wihāra of the North-western Province, shows the manner of holding the arrow and string, which is drawn by the first and second fingers, one being on each side of the arrow. The same figure also contains an illustration of a form of Quiver, *Hī-kopuwa*, which in this instance holds seven arrows. It is slung at the side, but the usual position may have been on the back, as in early Indian reliefs.

The Stone-Bow, *Gal-dunna*, of village youths is merely a weak bow with two strings, which half-way from the tips have some cross net-work or are attached to the ends of a small piece of hide used for holding the stone. The strings are kept apart by means of short sticks fixed transversely between them, one being near each end. Small birds are sometimes killed with this bow. A more powerful weapon of this type may have been used in early fighting, but it appears never to be delineated in the wihāra paintings.

The Axe, *Porawa*, is met with in four forms, of which two were Battle-axes, while the others were employed only as tools. One of the former kinds, the *Ketēriya* (Figs. 198 and 199) is still carried by villagers in the interior for protection against bears, and possibly also against demons, since the axe was a powerful amulet even in Vedic times. It has a narrow stem, and a blade which ends in a broad crescent, the convex curve of which is the cutting edge. The handle passes through a socket made in the stem, which in some cases projects slightly as a small hammer-head, termed a *kondē*, on the opposite side of the handle. This weapon occurs once in the hands of a soldier in a panel at Ridi Wihāra; it has there a wide blade which extends up to the handle without diminution of the breadth. It is also included in wihāra paintings of the Māra contest, as a weapon carried by some of the demons. Although its shape is of great antiquity and its use was widespread, it is not mentioned in the histories, nor is it carried by the Vaeddas. It was used in pre-dynastic times in Egypt. At Sānchi, in India, it is represented at the north gateway of the central and earliest dāgaba, which dates from the third century B.C., as being without a socket, the pointed stem of the blade evidently passing through a hole bored in the handle.[1]

The Broad Axe is apparently the true fighting Axe of Ceylon, as its name *Yuddha Porawa*, 'Battle Axe,' shows. As used in the island it was a much heavier weapon than the last, and had a straight cutting edge. It is not once referred to in the histories, and I have not seen an example; but it is very clearly carved in the panels at Ridi Wihāra, where two of the soldiers are armed with this formidable weapon (Fig. No. 171). According to these reliefs it had no socket; but as no diagonal lashings are shown this may be only due to a mistake of the carver.

The Indian Axe carried by attendants in the Amarāvati

[1] General Maisey. *Sānchi and its Remains*, Plates V and XXXIX.

carvings is of an entirely different type, with an extremely long blade, rather narrow at the stem ; towards the cutting edge, which is straight, it widens out considerably to an equal extent at the upper and lower edges, which are slightly curved. In the Badāmi carvings it is the Ketēriya of Ceylon which is represented, and this form is shown in the modern figure of Parasu-Rāma, ' Rāma of the Axe,' one of the Avatāras of Vishnu, in Sir George Birdwood's *Industrial Arts of India.*

The Club, ***Mugura***, is described as being made of iron ; it is usually drawn in the wihāras (Fig. 167) as a thick heavy straight weapon, and is always painted with a grey colour that is used to denote iron. The two Rākshasa guards in Fig. 159 are armed with this weapon, like those on the South Indian gōpuras. Doubtless some were made of wood.

Specimens of a simple form of Mace, with a plain straight handle or staff, on which thick iron rings are fixed at one end, are to be seen occasionally. Such a weapon is certain to be of early date. A club or mace was used in Vedic times (Rig Veda, x, 102, 9).

A curved form of Iron Club is also illustrated in two shapes in wihāra paintings (Figs. 168 and 169). One type slightly resembles a boomerang in its curvature. As a throwing weapon of this shape is known in Southern India such a club may have been used in Ceylon in former times. In the ancient Tamil poem from which extracts were given at the end of Chapter IV, Ayiyanār is described as being ' girt with a curved club.'

The common Shield, *Palisa*, was of the Buckler form, a segment of a hollow sphere, circular in outline, and having considerable convexity, and no boss. In all examples in the wihāra paintings it is shown with only one looped handle in the middle, to enable it to be held by the left hand. This type is also carved in the reliefs at the Tanjore Temple, and at other South Indian temples (see Fig. No. 158).

A very fine specimen in the possession of the late Mr. Philip Templer of the Ceylon Civil Service, afterwards Administrator of St. Lucia, was made of one piece of bark. It had a large boss in the centre, with a hole in the middle, apparently for fixing a spike, round which four small bell-metal disks were placed, making with it the arms of a cross; there was also a circle of round-headed studs near the border. The shield was nearly black in colour, and was decorated with figures of two soldiers in thin metal, fixed on its outer surface, on opposite sides of the boss. Each held a buckler in the left hand and a Kastānē in the right; their sole dress was a cloth from the waist to the knees, and a skull-cap. All the metal work consisted of bell-metal (*lōkaḍa*), with a brassy appearance. This shield was about two feet in diameter; it had two flexible leather handles in the middle, fixed close together, so as to be grasped by one hand. According to the information supplied to me by villagers, many shields had a covering of tin; others probably had a covering of leather nailed on a light wooden or bark frame.

In the Ridi Wihāra panels, the shields, of which only side views are given, may possibly be elongated; and the concavity is of two peculiar types, one shield having on its outer side two straight lines converging to a point in the middle, while the other (Fig. 170), which is shown in two panels, bulges out there into a rounded outline, which perhaps indicates a large high boss. As it would have been at least as easy for the carvers to represent the simple curve of the common buckler in all cases as to cut these peculiar forms, these reliefs apparently illustrate different shapes of shields from the usual one.

In the rough carving on a stone dug up with others at the Giant's Tank, and evidently taken there in the twelfth century A.D. from some pre-existing structure, a shield of another kind is delineated, nearly resembling a form that was once used in Europe. It has a straight horizontal top, and the sides are almost parallel, and make right angles with it in the middle part, ending in the lower part, which is rounded, in arcs of circles (Fig. 218). A shield of this type is illustrated by General Maisey in his *Sanchi and its Remains*, Plate XXXV, Fig. No. 30.

In his Third Progress Report Mr. Bell has figured another form which is cut in outline on a rock at Anurādhapura. It bears some slight resemblance to the carvings of shields at Sānchi, and is small and heart-shaped (Fig. 180).

No Helmets are drawn in the wihāras ; but in an interesting rock carving at the side of the Isurumuniya Temple at Anurādhapura (Fig. 219) a seated warrior is represented in the round, wearing a helmet which from its shape appears to be made of metal. A thick plume forms a crest on the top and hangs down the soldier's back. The horse's head appearing out

FIG. 219. Rock Carving at Isurumuniya.

of the rock behind him shows that the person was a cavalry soldier.

The date of the carving is uncertain. The peculiar arch of the eyebrows is like that of the rock-cut sedent Buddha at Tantiri-malei, the bricks at which may belong to the first century after Christ, and the figure may be of the same age. The representation of the horse's head looking out of the rock is a feature characteristic of Phoenician sculpture. On a slab dug up at Tissa on which a cow and calf were carved in relief, the head of a bull was represented looking out of the stone above the cow's back ; and with this may be also compared a lion's head similarly carved in two reliefs at a building between the Ruwanwaeli and Thūpārāma dāgabas, and the elephants' heads which project at the Anurādhapura dāgabas. The most ancient of these are works of the second century B.C., a date which proves the possibility of the early age of the carving of the soldier. Metallic armour was used in India in the Vedic period and is several times mentioned in the Rig Veda. It is not unlikely, therefore, that it was employed in Ceylon in late pre-Christian or early post-Christian times by those who could afford to purchase it, or to whom it was supplied by the sovereign. The Helmet is mentioned in the Rig Veda (x, 105, 5).

There are some weapons in the British Museum which I have not seen in Ceylon. One (Fig. 215) is a form of Bident, having a wide crescent-shaped iron head with sharp points but no cutting edge, fitted by a long socket onto the end of a shaft about seven feet in length, which is thicker towards the base than at the head.

Another (Fig. 216) has a narrow blade about sixteen inches long, fixed at the side of a shaft or staff four feet six inches long, which passes through four projecting sockets or rings that are welded to the back of the blade at equal distances. The blade ends in two points which are turned back against the handle. It may have been copied from weapons used by the Portuguese soldiers.

A third weapon (Fig. 184) ends in a sharp-pointed head below which is a transverse spike that forms a cross with it and the round socket into which the shaft, about six feet long, is fitted. The shaft is decorated with coloured lac. A similar weapon was used in Europe in the Middle Ages, and was termed a Marteau, according to M. Lacombe (Boutell, *Arms and Armour*).

As I could obtain no description of two ancient weapons that are said to have been employed in former times in Ceylon, I am unable to say if any of these arms are referred to under their names. One is the *Baendi-wāla*, which is perhaps connected with the Tamil word for a sword or saw, *vāl,* though an implement called a Beṇḍuwala is described in Clough's Dictionary as a spear or priest's razor. By some persons Vishnu is said to be armed with a weapon of the former name, which is shown in a rude drawing of him made on Talipat leaf for me by a 'Bali-tiyannā,' or priest who officiates against planetary influences, as being of a meander shape with two curls.

The other is the *Tōmara*, apparently a sort of Javelin; in Sanskrit the word means a javelin, and in Tamil a javelin or club, according to Winslow. It is stated that steel or iron filings were used in some way in their manufacture.

The Billhook is described among the articles included in the next category.

With the aid of references in Indian and Greek works to the soldiers employed in early India, we may form some idea of the armament and organisation of the military forces of Ancient Ceylon. The regular troops were probably very far from being an undisciplined body. Although the wooded nature of the country did not lend itself to the free use of either chariots or cavalry, there can be no doubt that the services of both were utilised to some extent. Elephants were also employed, and there were several classes of foot-soldiers.

The chariots used in war were probably drawn by two horses, like those illustrated in the Sānchi carvings; three or four-horse chariots were, however, to be found in India, and may have been used by the richer classes in Ceylon, though perhaps not in battle. Following the Indian fashion, some may have been decorated with leopard skins. Each chariot carried a driver, and one or two [1] combatants who were armed with bows [2] and swords, and had bucklers. All the occupants, and possibly to some extent the horses, were protected by mail[2] or leather armour. We have no representation of the appearance of these cars of Ceylon; according to the Greek description, those used in India had sitting accommodation for their occupants [1] but at Sānchi the persons shown in them are standing. King Mahā-Nāga of Tissa is described in the Dhātuvansa as presenting Mahākāla, the

[1] Rig Veda, vi, 20, 9. *Ancient India as described by Megasthenes and Arrian*, by McCrindle, pp. 89, 90.

[2] *The Jātaka*, No. 529 (Translation, Vol. v, p. 133).

son of a wealthy man, with a car suitable for four persons, *satara deneku yedu rathayak.* There must have been seats in such a carriage.

The carving at the Isurumuniya temple proves conclusively that in early and possibly pre-Christian times an organised force of cavalry was in existence, the men having a showy helmet with long plumes which hung down the back like those of the Greeks. Some also may have worn the 'shining armour,' or breast-plate that was used in India.[1] Leather armour was provided for the horses,[2] and in India a high hair plume was fixed on the head of each, between the ears.[3] In the second or third century B.C. the men rode without saddles,[4] a skin rug being perhaps employed instead; one person at Amarāvati is riding bare-back, however (Slab No. 41). In the second century A.D. padded saddles were clearly represented at Amarāvati, and probably would be used in Ceylon.

The horse was controlled by single reins held by the left hand, and fastened to a head-stall to which an iron bit was attached, having in the time of Arrian short spikes fitted in a disk at each end outside the lips,[4] but not so delineated at Sānchi or Amarāvati, or Anurādhapura. The riders apparently carried bucklers, and were armed with a sword and bow;[5] some may have been lancers, as in India.[4] Part of this cavalry force doubtless constituted the king's bodyguard.

The Archers formed the chief branch of the regular foot-soldiers and the mainstay of the army. In India their bodies were protected by mail or leather armour, and some at least carried a straight sword at their left side,[6] enclosed in a leather scabbard, and slung by a scarf or belt which passed round the right shoulder.[7] They also had shields, some of which, like

[1] *The Jātaka*, No. 233 (Vol. ii, p. 232).
[2] *The Jātaka*, No. 23 (Vol. i, p. 61).
[3] Amarāvati carvings.
[4] McCrindle, *Ancient India*, p. 221.
[5] *The Jātaka*, No. 529 (Vol. v, p. 132).
[6] *The Jātaka*, No. 522 (Vol. v, p. 67).
[7] Amarāvati carvings.

those in India, may have been narrow and elongated.[1] The Sākya kings would be likely to give special attention to the archery, and Arrian's remarks on the efficiency of the Indian bow-men may have been to some extent applicable to those of Ceylon, as we see by the account in the Mahāvansa of the prowess of Phussa-dēva, the champion archer of Duṭṭha-Gāmiṇi. Arrian said, 'there is nothing which can resist an Indian archer's shot—neither shield nor breast-plate, nor any stronger defence if such there be.'[1]

In Ceylon this force probably consisted chiefly of Vaeddas. As they lived at Anurādhapura in such numbers that the early annalist made special reference to their share in the residential arrangements of the city, it is extremely likely that their services as archers would be utilised by the early Sinhalese sovereigns in their military forces, just as at a later time Parākrama-Bāhu I employed them. They must have formed a great part of the army with which Paṇḍukābhaya gained the throne, or their chiefs would not have afterwards occupied the prominent position accorded to them by that monarch. Malalu Vaeddan, 'Archer Vaeddas' are mentioned in the fifteenth century.

Other foot-soldiers were Spear-men, some of whom also carried swords; a third branch of the infantry consisted of those who were armed only with the Ketēriya, or the Broad Axe;[2] and a fourth was formed of men who carried a straight sword and a buckler or shield.[2]

We may picture to ourselves regiments of each of these four classes of foot-men, each bearing its distinctive banner, and possibly even trained to march in step in regular ranks, and perform evolutions, like the Egyptian, and Assyrian, and Greek infantry; they would be commanded by the young chiefs of the country. In later times, and perhaps early times also, the Sinhalese national flag bore the device of a standing lion with its near fore-leg raised[3]; that of Madura, according to temple artists, was a cock.

[1] McCrindle. *Ancient India*, p. 221. Ridi Wihāra panels.

[2] Ridi Wihāra panels and Welana Damana relief.

[3] I have seen a photograph of a carved stone at Buddha Gayā with a similar lion on it; I do not know its age.

Arrian described the state of the regular soldiers in India as follows; and it is to be remembered that the remarks refer to the very district from which the Gangetic settlers came to Ceylon: 'The fifth caste among the Indians consists of the warriors, who are second in point of numbers to the husbandmen, but lead a life of supreme freedom and enjoyment. They have only military duties to perform. Others make their arms, and others supply them with horses, and they have others to attend on them in the camp, who take care of their horses, clean their arms, drive their elephants, prepare their chariots, and act as their charioteers. As long as they are required to fight they fight, and when peace returns they abandon themselves to enjoyment—the pay which they receive from the state being so liberal that they can with ease maintain themselves and others besides.' [1]

The Elephants constituted a valuable portion of the Sinhalese army. They were carefully protected by leather armour,[2] and carried two or three [3] combatants in addition to the driver. These appear to have been armed with the bow and the sword, and sometimes the javelin. They wore either mail or leather armour. There is no statement of the number of elephants employed for warlike purposes in Ceylon; it must have been small compared with the immense herds of the Indian armies, in one of which, that of Magadha, Megasthenēs reported that nine thousand were used.

The animals were so numerous in Ceylon that in time of war every chief would be called upon to send some to the king for transport purposes, if not for actual fighting. The king himself would certainly maintain a large trained force of them in connection with his standing army, as well as for ceremonial use in processions, and we find the royal elephant stables of the third century B.C. referred to in the Mahāvansa.

While all the foregoing branches of the permanent army must have practised a regular drill and been kept in a state of some degree of efficiency, the untrained levies of villagers

[1] McCrindle. *Ancient India*, p. 221.
[2] *The Jātaka*, No. 80 (Vol. i, p. 205).
[3] McCrindle, *loc. cit.* pp. 89, 90.

who were called out by the local chiefs in case of war were doubtless a more or less undisciplined horde, armed with a miscellaneous collection of weapons, such as bows, pikes, billhooks, wooden clubs, and stone-bows.

In the Mahā Ummagga Jātaka (No. 546) we have a vivid picture of some of the regular troops of early times. Cūḷanī, King of Mithilā, is represented as being clothed in jewelled armour. He held an arrow in his hand as his symbol of authority (like the Vaeddas of Ceylon) while he made a spirited address to his army, and issued his orders from the back of his elephant for the capture of his enemy in the battle that was about to commence :—

"Send the tusked elephants, mighty, sixty years old, let them trample down the city which Vedeha has nobly built. Let the arrows fly this way and that way, sped by the bow, arrows like the teeth of calves, sharp-pointed, piercing the very bones. Let heroes come forth in armour clad, with weapons finely decorated, bold and heroic, ready to face an elephant. Spears bathed in oil, their points glittering like fire, stand gleaming like the constellation of a hundred stars. At the onset of such heroes, with mighty weapons, clad in mail and armour, who never run away, how shall Vedeha escape, even if he fly like a bird ? My thirty and nine thousand warriors, all picked men, whose like I never saw, all my mighty host." He referred to the "golden trappings and blood-red girths" and the "mailed heroes with banners waving, skilled in the use of sword and shield, grasping the hilt, accomplished soldiers."

THE ANCIENT TOOLS

In addition to the Kandian Knife which has been described, other kinds were used for household work. One of these of which an early example was obtained at Tissa, has a straight blade cut off diagonally at the end from the cutting edge to the back. This form was and still is employed for cutting up vegetables and fish, the stem being fixed in a sloping position in a piece of board on which the person using the knife squats, so that the edge of the blade is upward. Another form also found at Tissa has a curved blade with a concave cutting edge. I give an illustration (Fig. 182) of what appears to have been a different kind of knife that was used in ancient times; it was cut in outline on the steps leading up the Mihintale hill, evidently by the masons who laid them, and it may thus belong to the first century A.D.

The Billhook, *Kaetta*, has doubtless always been one of the most necessary tools of the inhabitants of Ceylon, and its antiquity is proved by its being the emblem of the earliest deity, the God of the Rock. The fact that it is not employed by the wildest Vaeddas is probably merely due to their not requiring such an article in their hunting life; the Vaeddas who lead a more settled existence always make use of it for cutting down jungle. Without it or some similar tool it would have been quite impossible to reclaim land that was thickly overspread, like practically the whole of Ceylon, with a dense and often thorny undergrowth.

For general use it has only one shape among the Kandians, with a concave cutting edge (Fig. 221), but in the mountainous tracts a form (Fig. 220) with a returned point not made elsewhere is found useful in thorny jungle and stony ground, as it enables the branches to be dragged out by it after being cut, while small shoots can be removed by an upward cut near their base, thus avoiding damage to the tool by striking stones. The emblem of the God of the Rock differs from the ordinary Billhook in common use, and approaches the shape of the sickle (see Frontispiece).

The Billhook is represented in wihāra paintings among the arms carried by the demons in the Māra Contest, and it must therefore be included as a warlike weapon, though probably not one with which the regular troops were armed.

The Kandian Billhook has no socket; the stem is lengthened to a blunt chisel point, and is driven into the split end of the handle, a broad band of iron with a thicker ring below it being first fitted on the end of the shaft to prevent further splitting. The handles vary in length from 18 inches to 6

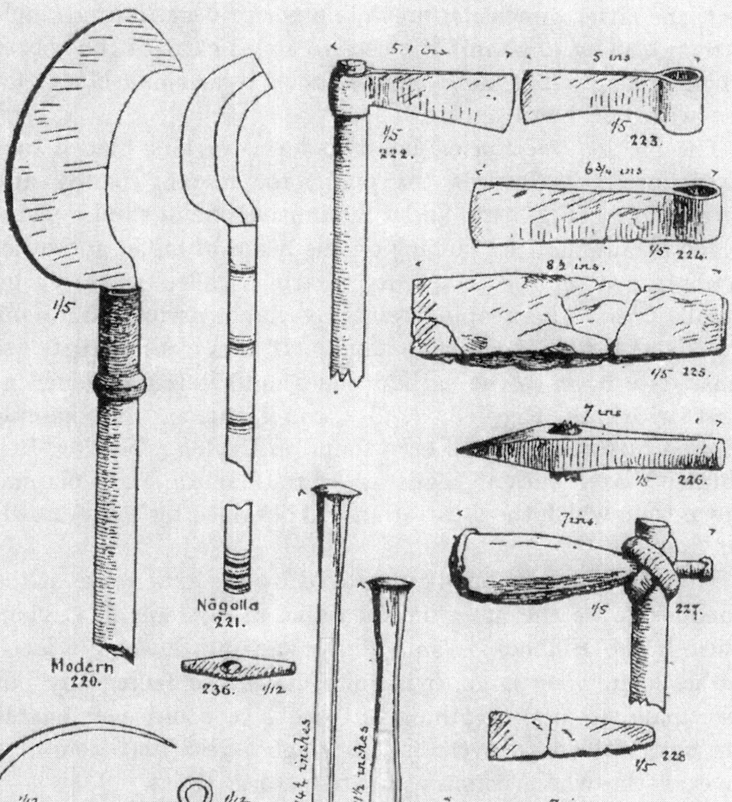

FIGS. 220–239. Sinhalese Tools.

feet, the latter dimension prevailing where very thorny jungle is found, so as to permit the user to stand clear of the thorns while cutting. The short-handled tools have small blades for use with one hand only.

The Sickle, *Dāē-Kaetta,* has two forms, a long-bladed one, nearly straight towards the point, for reaping paddy and cutting grass (Fig. 237), and a diminutive one of similar shape which is only used for cutting off the heads of millet and other grains grown in the temporary clearings called *Hēna,* or by Tamils *Chēna,* this reaping being invariably performed among the Kandians by the women alone. It is evident that its use must date back to the earliest times, and it is mentioned at least twice in the Rig Veda (i, 58, 4, and x, 101, 3). No example of pre-Christian date has been found in Ceylon; but Mr. Bell obtained later ones at Sīgiriya, Anurādhapura, and Polannaruwa, from which the illustration was obtained by Mr. F. Lewis for me.

The Axe, *Porawa,* has been proved by the experience of the Vaeddas to be the most indispensable of all tools in Ceylon. Though the Billhook is suitable for cutting down interlaced bushes even when large, it is quite useless for felling any but the smallest trees. Nothing but the Axe could ever enable the first settlers to overcome the high forest that doubtless covered the whole country in pre-historic times.

At the present day the Kandian Axe has usually only one shape as a tool. The blade is almost straight along the upper edge, rising slightly near the cutting edge, and commonly curved downwards along the lower edge, so that at the end the blade is considerably wider than at the stem (see Fig. 223, of one dug up at Anurādhapura by Mr. Burrows). Of this kind there is a large and a small form; both have a socket hole through the stem. Axes slightly varying from this type were found in the excavations at Anurādhapura by Mr. S. Burrows (Fig. 224).

I have been assured by a Kandian smith of one of the villages of the interior that in its correct shape the blade of the true Kandian Axe should be quite straight on both the upper and lower edges, and a modern one of this form is illustrated

(Fig. 222). In this, the upper edge stands out from the shaft at a right angle, and the cutting edge has a slight convex curve.

At Tissa, two examples of an earlier and different type were met with, in which the edges of the blade are nearly straight, but slightly narrower at the cutting end than in the middle. They bear a close resemblance to a form of polished 'Celt' of the Neolithic age. They are much greater and heavier than the largest axes now made in the island, one (Fig. 225) being 8½ inches long, 3 inches broad at its widest part and three-quarters of an inch thick there, while the other is 2½ inches wide. The cutting edge is straight, and they have no socket; the stem must have passed through the handle, which would be prevented from splitting by being wrapped diagonally at it with cross strips of hide or bark cord, or possibly be fitted with two diagonal iron rings such as those used for fixing the primitive Kandian hammer to its handle. Such an axe is illustrated in General Maisey's work on Sānchi, Plate XIII. These large axes were made by welding together several thinner plates of iron or steel until the required thickness was obtained.

The Adze, *Wāēya*, has not been found among the ancient tools, I think, although it must have been known and used in Ceylon in pre-Christian times. The earliest type may have resembled the African tool, which is without a socket and is almost a straight axe turned sideways, with a cutting edge wider than the stem.

The Digging Hoe, *Udaella*, commonly called by Europeans a 'Mamoty,' from the Tamil word *Man-veṭṭci*, Earth-cutter, is also a tool of early date, but no example of it was obtained at Tissa. The only ancient ones that I have seen were found by Mr. S. Burrows at Anurādhapura; their age is uncertain, but probably they belong to some time earlier than the eleventh century A.D. Through the kindness of my friend Mr. F. Lewis I am able to give an illustration (Fig. 238) of a type which was discovered by Mr. Bell at Sīgiriya and Polannaruwa. Another found by him had a much longer stem and a rather narrow blade. According to my recollection, the Anurādhapura tool was of an earlier type, the socket being formed by widening out the stem and turning over the two wings thus formed. It thus bore some resemblance to the early Egyptian digging tool. It is possible that the earliest form used in Ceylon had no socket, but in its mode of attachment to the handle resembled the African implement, the pointed stem of which passes through the shaft. The correct modern Sinhalese shape is shown in Fig. 239.

I have met with no example of a Sinhalese Pickaxe, *Yawula*. It is certain that as it is constantly employed in Southern India some form of this implement was made in the island at an early date for excavating hard soil. Those used by the Oṭṭas or South Indian Telugu excavators are thick and very heavy tools, with rectangular arms.

A Mason's Pick-Hammer of uncertain age was found by Mr. S. Burrows in his excavations at Anurādhapura (Fig. 226). The modern form of the socket shows that this example is not a tool of extremely early date. Its use has been discontinued by the masons of modern times.

Worn examples of the small Trowel, *Henda* (Spoon), used for pointing the joints in masonry have been found both at Tissa (Fig. 235) and Anurādhapura. They have a general resemblance to the tools now used in Ceylon for the purpose, being much narrower near the stem than European tools.

The Jumper, or Hand-drill for boring holes in rock, with a cutting edge slightly wider than the stem, is a tool of pre-Christian times, and a well-used example of it (Fig. 232) was found at Tissa, with a stem 1·20 inches thick. This implement was employed for cutting the earliest type of wedge-holes, which have a cross section in the form of a pointed ellipse, and a rounded bottom. I have not succeeded in fixing the period when they were abandoned in favour of rectangular holes; it was during very early post-Christian times.

The Mason's Chisel, *Gal-Kaṭuwa*, as well as the pointed Punch, must be equally old, and a short and worn specimen of the latter tool was obtained at Tissa (Fig. 233), as well as a chisel (Fig. 234). In addition to their use in actual stone cutting these tools were employed in making the rectangular wedge-holes that were adopted in place of the early elliptical ones.

The Carpenter's Chisel, *Niyan-Kaṭuwa,* must have been used at a very early date, possibly even before the mason's tools were introduced into the island. Examples of it found at Tissa (Figs. 228 and 229) were flat and thin, and were evidently employed without handles. At a later date the form slightly changed, and the chisels, though still without handles, were much thickened and had square heads for receiving the blows of the mallet. The cross section of their upper part is a square with rounded angles, changing into a flat form as the cutting edge is approached. The illustrations (Figs. 230 and 231) show two in my possession of the type still occasionally found in remote villages of the interior.

Smith's Chisels (*Yakaḍa-Kaṭuwa*) for cutting iron or other metals were also met with at Tissa. They were of a square section excepting at the cutting edge.

No ancient example of a Saw, *Kiyata,* has been discovered yet, so far as I am aware, although it is a tool of very early date. A saw for cutting ivory is mentioned in the Jātaka story No. 545 (Vol. vi, p. 129). The ordinary tool now used by carpenters is a Frame-Saw resembling a fret-saw, the cutting part being made from a narrow strip of thin steel. When in use it is held by the upright end nearest the workman. Primitive saws were of course of a much simpler shape, and some of them probably resembled a form which is still, I believe, sometimes used, of a curved leaf shape with the teeth on the concave edge. No trace of the employment of any kind of saw for cutting stone has been observed by me.

No early specimen of a Smith's Hammer, *Miṭiya,* was discovered at Tissa, but one (Fig. 227) that I obtained in a village in the North-western Province is evidently of the primitive form, and is a very interesting relic of the artificers of old. It has a peculiar shape, with a thick elongated head which tapers at the stem nearly to a point. The section of the head is square with the angles bevelled off, so that at the end it becomes nearly a circle. There is no socket; the narrow stem is passed through a hole bored in the handle, which is prevented from splitting by two flat wrought-iron rings that are shaped to fit close on the handle, and are crossed over diagonally from opposite sides of the stem, as shown in the illustration. This way of fixing the handle copies the method of attaching the socketless 'Celt' to its shaft. A tool of the same shape would doubtless be used as a Sledge-hammer by the early stone-cutters, for breaking large stones. Mr. F. Lewis has kindly sent me a sketch of a hammer head of a shape still in use, found by Mr. Bell in his excavations at Polannaruwa (Fig. 236).

From the Fire Drill, by means of which fire was obtained from two pieces of wood, and which may date from Neolithic times, were developed the other forms of drills for boring holes through wood, stone and metals.

The common Bow-drill, *Dunu-Buruma,* is the simplest tool of this type, being merely the Fire-drill fitted with a steel point or 'bit.' It is worked by a bow with a slack string which is turned once round the shaft of the drill. Usually there is a small bobbin-shaped drum fixed on the shaft, round which the bow-string runs, the necessary downward pressure being applied to the end of the shaft by the left hand, with some protecting material such as a half coconut shell intervening between the palm and the shaft.

The Fixed Drill, *At-Buruma* ('Hand Drill'), is worked by two cords pulled by the right and left hand alternately, one being wound on the axle or drum as the other is unwound. In this form it is used by smiths for drilling holes in iron.

The Pump Drill, *Tarapane,* is also probably an early tool, though no very ancient example of it has been discovered. An important desideratum to make it effective is a substantial weight attached to the shaft of the bit. The illustration (Figs. 240 and 241) shows one in my possession, with an admirably cut stone weight of 3¼ lbs., which was prepared for this purpose apparently many centuries ago. It was obtained in a village of the North-western Province. With such a load fixed on the shaft the drill becomes a most effective tool. The cord is a narrow strip of deer-skin or goat-skin, passing through a hole at the top of the drill shaft, and knotted through others bored near the ends of the transverse bar. The bar is held at each end, and works the drill as it is lowered rapidly. When the turning of the drill has all but unwound the cords, the pressure on the cross-bar is suddenly relaxed, and the momentum then carries on the movement, and re-winds the cords in the opposite direction, ready for another quick lowering of the bar. The length of the cord is just sufficient to allow the cross-bar to reach the weight when lowered.

From the accurate shapes of the crystal and other relic-receptacles which have been described in a former chapter,

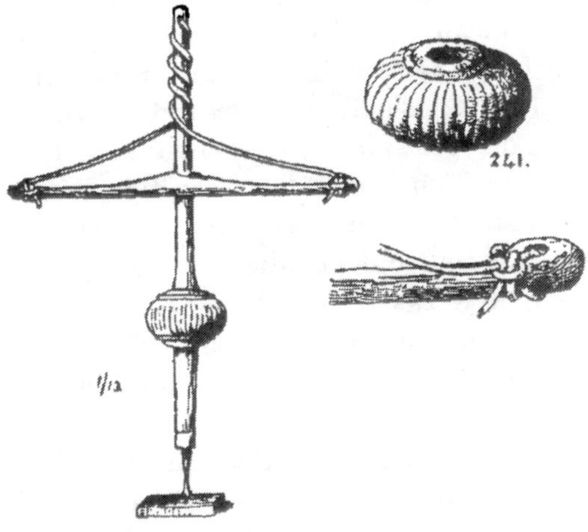

FIGS. 240, 241. The Pump Drill.

it cannot be doubted that the ancient Sinhalese were well acquainted in the third century B.C. with the use of a Fixed Drill and also of some form of Lathe. There are references at the middle of the second century B.C. to pearls and gems which were hung in festoons, for drilling which the former tool would be indispensable. A large Lathe must also have been employed in pre-Christian times, for cutting the larger relic-cases of gneiss and limestone which were found at the early dāgabas at Anurādhapura.

The Bellows, *Mayina-Hama*, employed in early times would be of the kind still used by some of the village smiths, it being impossible to make one of a simpler form. It is constructed out of two skins, which at the present day are those of goats, but originally would be small deer-skins, to the neck of each of which a tube is attached, the other ends of both tubes passing on the ground into a single much thicker and shorter tube of hardened clay which leads the air into the back of the furnace of the forge. A thin piece of wattle-and-daub walling intervenes in order to shield the bellows-man from the heat. At the upper and lower lips of the mouth at the outer end of each skin a strip of smooth wood is attached, having a length nearly equal to the width of the mouth. The person who works the bellows squats or sits down at the end of it or between the skins, and by means of a loop on each upper strip of wood, through which his hand is half passed, raises and then closes the mouths of the skins with his right and left hands alternately, pressing down on each skin after closing it so as to force through its pipe the air which it contains. In this simple manner an intermittent current of air is sent into the fire, the efficiency of the bellows of course depending on the rapidity with which the bellows-man works.

The use of this primitive form of bellows is widespread; it was employed in Ancient Egypt, and is found in India and Africa at the present day. In West Africa the bellows-man sits on a log, and opens and shuts the mouths of the skins with his feet, the toes being passed through the loops for the purpose. I have often utilised the skin-bellows on small works in the jungle when an additional forge was needed for a short time for repairing miners' or masons' tools, and I found it fairly effective for heating such small pieces of steel; but it is not of much utility for any welding purposes.

The early smiths experienced the same difficulty; to make the thicker kinds of tools they built up the shape by welding thinner plates together, but they were not able to do it so thoroughly as to render the junction lines indistinguishable. The thicker kinds of chisels were made by wrapping a piece of flat iron round a central rod or core, and welding all together.

Captain Robert Knox described a different form of bellows which was employed down to about the middle of last century for smelting furnaces. This consisted of two upright hollow wooden cylinders fixed in the ground, across the top of each of which a piece of deer-skin was fastened, having a hole in it of the diameter of a man's finger. Two strings attached to each skin near this central hole were tied to two bent springs of elastic wood fixed in the ground near each cylinder.

Knox describes the action as follows :—' The man that blows stands with his feet, one on each pot, covering each hole with the soles of his feet. And as he treads on one pot, and presseth the skin down, he takes his foot off the other, which presently by the help of the Spring riseth ; and the doing so alternately conveys a great quantity of wind through the Pipes into the Furnace. For there are also two Pipes made of hollow reed [bamboo] let in to the sides of the Pots, that are to conduct the wind, like the nose of a Bellows, into the Furnace.

' For the ease of the Blower, there is a strap, that is fastned to two posts, and comes round behind him, on which he leans his back : and he has a stick laid cross-ways before him on which he lays both his hands, and so he blows with greater ease.' [1]

Early in last century Dr. Davy saw the common form of skin bellows, made from two bullock's skins, employed at such furnaces in the Nuwara Eliya district. Iron smelting has now ceased in Ceylon. I may note that the iron from the furnaces is termed either *Yakaḍa* or *Yabora*, and the scoriae or ' clinkers ' are *Yakaḍa bora*.

OTHER IMPLEMENTS

From its simple form it may be assumed that the Plough, *Nagula*, has been used in Ceylon from the time of the Gangetic settlers, and possibly from the earlier period when the Nāgas came to the island, without any change of shape. Ploughs were used in India in Vedic times. Buffaloes, which

[1] *An Historical Relation of the Island Ceylon*, 1681, p. 97.

were most probably brought over for ploughing or for trampling the soil into mud after the method still practised in the east and south of the island, and everywhere in newly-reclaimed land full of roots, are stated in the manuscript 'Pradhāna Nuwarawal' to have been first introduced into Ceylon in the reign of Dēvānam-piya Tissa, that is, soon after the middle of the third century B.C.; but the plough would be known in the island before that date.

The only early example of the plough which I have seen was a piece of wood evidently cut for one, that was found in the sand of an ancient stream, in a puddle trench, under the embankment of the Batalagoḍa tank. There had been a breach at the site in former times, and the plough may have been washed down by the stream at a much later date than the construction of the reservoir. It had the shape of the modern implement, but was larger than those now used.

The plough share is a thin plate of iron fixed on the sloping end of the plough; its outline is a high arch, a vertical semi-ellipse, resting on nearly upright walls and having a flat base. It has little or no cutting action, its chief function being the protection of the end of the plough; hence, possibly, its employment as an amulet in ancient times. The plough does not cut its way, but is simply pulled through the ground, tearing up clods of turf, which find their way to one side or the other. The plougher raises or depresses the handle, which he holds by one hand only, so as to keep the base of the share about three inches below the surface.

The Potter's Wheel is of equally early occurrence in Ceylon, and numerous fragments of wheel-made pottery were found in the lowest part of the early stratum at Tissa. It is balanced on a smooth boss cut on the top of a block of hard stone fixed firmly in the ground.

The origin of the Cotton Spinning Wheel, *Kapu Katına Yantra*, and Cotton Gin, *Kapu Kapana Yantra*, is doubtless much more recent; there is nothing to show the date of their introduction into Ceylon. Early spinning would be done by hand like that of the Kinnaras at the present day, by means of a whorl fitted on a wooden pin, which at a later date was replaced by an iron one. Perforated whorls of earthenware, with a broad groove round the middle, were found in the lowest stratum at Tissa. The disk-like seeds of a large creeper are now used by the Kinnaras as weights for their spindles, which are sometimes made from the ribs of the side leaves of coconut fronds; and are 12 inches long.

The use of the Spinning Wheel seems to have been practically abandoned during the first half of last century, after cotton yarn and cotton goods of foreign manufacture became obtainable at a cheap rate; but a few persons in the interior still

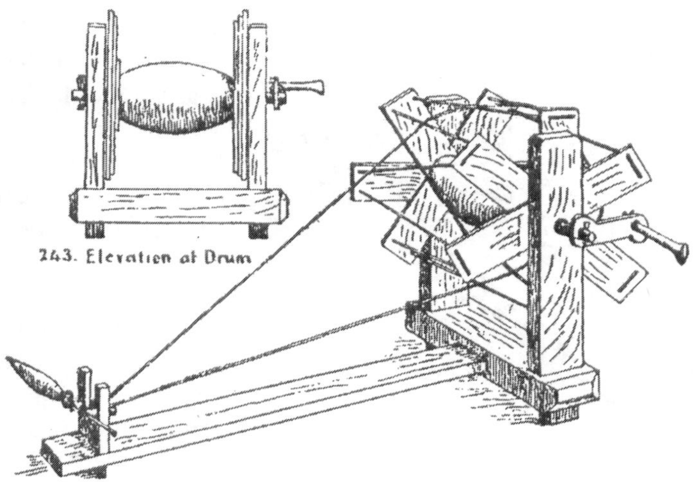

FIGS. 242, 243. The Spinning Wheel.

employ it. Its shape (Figs. 242 and 243) was like that of the rough home-made type of wheel constructed in some Indian villages, having three flat boards, 2½ inches wide, with two holes near each extremity, as spokes at each end of the axle, which was made of great thickness so as to support them firmly. A continuous cord wrapped with calico to prevent the slipping of the driving cord, was carried across from each hole to the nearest one of the next spoke at the other end of the axle, thus forming a flexible skeleton drum. The spokes at one end of it were opposite the spaces at the other end. A Spindle, *Idda*, on to which the cotton was fed by hand, was held in two bird-mouth rests fixed in an upright in front of the drum.

At the beginning, the operator, who was always a woman, commenced by drawing out from a heap of cleaned cotton a band of sufficient thickness which she twisted by rolling it on her thigh until it became as thick as the finger. From this a thread was drawn out, and after being twisted in the same manner on the thigh was wound on the spool or spindle while additional thread was being drawn out and twisted. To wind it on the spool the latter was placed in the bird-mouth rests, and a cord was passed round the drum and back round a reel fixed on the lower half of the spindle. When the loose handle at one end of the axle was turned the friction of the cord on the covered strings of the skeleton drum caused the spindle to revolve, winding the yarn on its upper half, and stretching it to nearly equal thickness. After as much yarn as it would hold had been thus passed on to the spindle, it was removed, and the yarn was wound off it in hanks from the fork of the hand round the back of the upper arm near the elbow. From the hanks it was again wound round short sticks fixed in the ground thirty feet apart, for drying, after which it was ready for the weaver.

FIG. 244. The Cotton Gin.

The Cotton Gin (Fig. 244), which must be of much later date, consisted of two horizontal wooden rollers (*Kambaranga*) placed one above the other between two uprights (*Kakul*) that were fixed in a stand or board. Both rollers were round bars; they passed through the uprights, outside one of which they terminated in endless wooden screws. A loose handle passed through a hole in one roller, at the opposite end. When this was turned the screw on it working on the screw of the other roller caused both to revolve in opposite directions. The space between the rollers was adjusted by means of a plug of wood inserted under the lower one.

While the handle was turned by the left hand (the operator sitting on the long rest which projects at a right angle), the cotton was fed by the right hand between the plain parts of the rollers, which drew it off the seeds; but the action as I have seen it performed was extremely slow. In early times of course the cotton cleaning was done by hand.

I have no notes of the Kandian Weaving Frames, *Accuwa*. They were large rectangular frames, some being 20 feet long and 4 feet 6 inches wide, fixed horizontally near the ground. The Shuttle, *Nadāwa*, made of Tamarind wood, 11½ inches long 1½ inches wide and 1 inch deep, was of the European type, which is also used in West Africa, where the frame is nine inches wide, and is hung from a branch of a tree.

Although some cloth weaving was done by Potters, the principal weavers who worked for hire were men of the Berawa caste, the present tom-tom beaters, to whom the people of better castes were accustomed to hand their yarn for the purpose. Coloured cloth of various interlacing patterns, as well as white cloth, was made in the villages by these people.

Indian weavers formerly settled on the west coast at Chilaw and elsewhere, but I am not aware that cotton cloth is now manufactured in the villages of the interior, although many people understand the work. It is still made at Batticaloa to a very small extent.

For Mat-weaving a long frame is used by the men of the Kinnara caste only, and the work performed by them is slow and laborious. No shuttle is used for it, but each strand, consisting of three or four fine strips of grass or fibre, is drawn towards the operator across the Niyanda strings of the warp at the end of a long thin flat stick, which is pointed at the end and has a hole there through which the grass is threaded after the stick has been pushed through the warp. The stick is then used for pressing it tight against the previous strand. This may be a relic of the original method of cloth weaving. A clue to the district from which these people came may perhaps be found by ascertaining what races employ this mode of mat weaving in India.

The Kinnaras make two kinds of mats in their frames. One is a very durable and flexible mat composed entirely of Niyanda fibre, and is called *Hak-Kalāl*; it is from two feet to two feet three inches wide, and is always ornamented by lines or patterns in dyed thread of red, yellow, and black colours. The other, called *Kalāl*, is made of aquatic grass on a warp of Niyanda fibre. The women usually take no part in the weaving, but assist in collecting the materials and preparing them for the work. A few, however, are able to weave.

Sinhalese of other castes never weave these two kinds of mats, although all, including even the highest castes, are accustomed to make and sell other mats which are plaited on the ground without a frame, and are termed *Paedura*.

For the mats made on the ground three kinds of aquatic grasses are employed. These are called *Haewan* (*Cyperus dehiscens*) or *Gal-laehae Paṇ*, the best, with a soft round dark green stem, and a long grass-like flower spike; *Telhiriya* (*Colubrina asiatica*), somewhat like the last, but much less durable; and *Tun-hiriya*, with a tall coarse broad triangular stem, and a short head of flowers. These are all cut into regular sizes, usually about two and a half feet in length, spread out in the sun on the ground near the houses, and thoroughly dried. Narrow strips of the leaves of *Dunukāēya* (*Pandanus foetidus*), *Indi* (*Phœnix zeylanica*, the Wild Date), and Palmira and Talipat Palms are also used. Mats of all but the last material are termed *Paedura*; Kandian mats made of wider strips of Talipat leaves are called *Māgal*, and are much larger than the others, and only used for covering floors and lining the walls of temporary buildings.

In making all these Kandian mats the women alone undertake the whole labour, which is performed in the verandas of their houses. The weaver commences the work at the near right-hand corner, and holds the strands down with the feet, squatting close to the ground. Patterns, each having a distinctive name, are often plaited in such mats, with strands dyed red, yellow, and black. Many of them are survivals of very early designs, each family preserving and handing down to the next generation its own special set of designs, which the young girls learn by long practice under their mothers' tuition.

The water-tight plaited flat-bottomed baskets prepared in the Jaffna district from wide strips of Palmira leaf are well known to all those who have seen Jaffnese carters feeding their bulls out of them with liquid 'poonac,' the refuse coconut after the oil has been extracted. I am not aware that Sinhalese make any baskets that will hold water.

XIV

THE ANCIENT GAMES

THE games played by a people are usually either almost ignored by travellers and foreign residents alike, or are dismissed with a far too meagre description. Yet it must be evident that any account of a race which omits to notice its amusements cannot be considered a complete or satisfactory one. What should we think of a relation of the customs and habits and characteristics of the residents of Britain which contained hardly any reference to such games as cricket, football, golf, and tennis, or even billiards, bridge, and chess? Such a work would enable no one who was unacquainted with us to form an accurate opinion regarding an important part of our national traits. And although in the case of the Eastern races and those of inferior civilisation the games of their countries occupy a much less commanding position than with us, a knowledge of these amusements is absolutely necessary for forming a satisfactory estimate of the national characteristics.

It is often stated that the Western mind cannot comprehend the thoughts of the East. How can it be otherwise when not one European out of a hundred living in the East has more than the vaguest notion of the universal belief regarding the effect of magic and spells and the far-reaching powers of evil spirits, or the folk-lore and folk-stories, the prejudices, and the amusements of the people among whom he dwells? Without a more or less thorough knowledge of the details of these subjects it is impossible for any real acquaintance with the inner mind of a people to be attained. However humanely a country may be governed, however impartially justice may be administered, however honestly the inhabitants may be treated in all their dealings with the ruling race, the certainty will always remain that without this knowledge we must continue to be strangers, that we must fail to comprehend their inmost thoughts and real life, and that in consequence there can never be any truly sympathetic appreciation of their ideas.

In the present chapter I have endeavoured to present a description of the ordinary games of the villagers of Ceylon, as a first step towards the construction of a bridge across the chasm that now intervenes on the way towards an understanding of the actual feelings and opinions of the people. It will be found to contain also particulars of most of the village indoor games of skill of India, Arabia, and Africa, with some of which those of Ceylon are closely allied.

Although the majority of the types of these games are of great antiquity, it has been feasible in only a few instances to furnish any information regarding their actual age, and this sometimes only in the form of a statement of their presence in the island at some early and more or less uncertain date. Perhaps some future investigator may discover further evidence of the times of their origin and of the countries in which they were invented.

There can be no doubt that some of the simpler games played in Ceylon date from immemorial ages, but the earliest local trace of any games goes back only to the second or third century B.C. In describing the games I shall proceed from the simpler ones to those which are more complex, this being probably also an arrangement that coincides, in some measure, with the order in which they were originated. They may be divided into three classes :—(1) Indoor Games ; (2) Outdoor Games ; and (3) Religious Games.

THE INDOOR GAMES

OTTĒ—IRATTĒ, 'Odd or Even.'

This is the simplest game of all, and certainly one of the earliest of all games. As it postulates an acquaintance with numbers to the extent of a capability of counting and of recognising the difference between odd ones and even ones, this may be doubted. But there is distinct evidence in the carvings on pieces of reindeer horn that the Palaeolithic inhabitants of Europe possessed this knowledge in the 'Madeleine' period.

It is especially played by village girls and women in the interior of Ceylon at the time when they collect the fallen almond-like seeds of the Mī-tree (*Bassia longifolia*), from which oil is expressed for many household purposes.

One of the players takes in her hand an uncertain quantity of the seeds and requests another to guess whether the number is odd or even. The seeds are not counted, but taken out of the hand by pairs. Often there is a small wager in seeds over the result, sometimes amounting to the number of seeds in the hand; and occasionally an unlucky individual loses a day's collection of seeds in this manner.

This was a common game among the Greeks and Romans, the latter people reversing the name by which it is now known, and calling it Par—impar, 'Even—uneven.' It was also played by the ancient Egyptians, and is illustrated in the paintings on the walls of their tombs.

Aembaruṇ̥ Keliya.

This game is played by two or more girls. Each requires five or more small stones for it, all of course having the same number. Any player begins by taking all the stones between her palms, in her doubled hands, and gradually dropping them on the floor by rubbing her palms together. The expression for this action, *ambaranawā*, has given the name to the game.

With a twig or her forefinger she then draws a short transverse line between any two stones, and proceeds to make one of them strike the other by propelling it along the ground from the nail of the fore-finger, as the end of the bent and doubled-back finger springs from the side of the thumb. This wins both the stones provided no other is touched by them. The play is repeated with each pair until all are won, or another stone is struck, or a miss occurs. In either of the latter cases the player stops, and another takes up all the stones that have not been won, and repeats the performance. The play goes round the party in this manner until all the stones have been won. If there be an odd one at the last the person who is playing puts down one of the stones previously won by her, and plays as before. After all have been won, those who have failed to get back their original number of stones are beaten in fun by those who have more than that number.

GAL KELIYA, 'The Stone Game.'

This is known as *Indi Keliya*, 'the Date Game,' in Colombo, a name that indicates its transmission to Ceylon from a country in which dates grow. In Southern India the Tamils term it *Puliyan Koṭṭei*, 'the Tamarind Stones' Game. In Bengal it is called *Dhappā*, and its Japanese name is *Ōtēdama*, 'Hand-ball.' It is played in Egypt, where the Arabic name for it is *Hel*; but I was informed that it is unknown in Senegambia. It was a favourite game in Rome and Greece, where it was played with five stones, and was called *Pentalithos*. In its simplest original form this is probably one of the earliest games invented. Possibly it is the only game of this type which is common to Europe and the Far East.

In Ceylon, Gal Keliya is almost always played only by girls; it requires two or more players, who may be any number up to about ten. Each player provides herself with not less than five small stones, nor more than eight, the smaller number being usually chosen; all the players must have the same number. The players are all seated or kneeling on the ground.

At the beginning a player tosses up all her stones and catches them on the back of her hand and fingers held out horizontally to receive them. She then tosses them up again as they lie on her hand and catches them in her palm. If she fail in either of these acts and allow a stone to fall, the play passes to the next person according to the hand used by the first one, that is, if she used her left hand the turn would go round to the left; if her right hand it would pass round to the right. This next player in her turn tosses up and catches all her stones; and in case of her failure the following one repeats the performance until one player has caught all her stones both on the back of the hand and in the palm. This is a preliminary test, a sort of entrance examination, which in the case of each player precedes the regular play, and all who fail in it receive punishment at the end of the game.

The real game is now commenced. The first one who succeeded in catching all the stones takes in her hand the stones of all the players, tosses the whole up, and as in the first play, catches as many as possible on the back of her hand and fingers. These she tosses up again and catches on her palm. There are so many that in all cases some fall on the ground. The number caught must be three or more ; if it be less her turn is ended and the next player begins in the same way.

When the number is not under three the stones thus caught are tossed up together and allowed to fall on the palm, one of the stones which fell on the ground being picked up by the same hand while they are in the air. If this be done successfully without allowing a stone to drop, the player puts one stone aside as won.

Then all the other stones but one are placed on the ground indiscriminately near the player, who now tosses up the surplus one and catches it in her palm, picking up, while it is in the air, one of those on the ground, with the same hand. One of the two is laid aside on the ground, and the procedure is repeated time after time, until all on the ground have been picked up, or a miss has been made, allowing one to fall down. If all be caught the player puts aside a second stone as won. If a miss be made the play passes to the next person ; otherwise the first player continues to repeat the process with the remaining stones, each time putting aside one as gained, after all have been picked up successfully. A very skilful player may thus win all the stones before a second person has an opportunity of playing ; I have seen this done.

When the number of stones becomes reduced to five, of which four are on the ground and one in the player's hand, the player must pick up two at once while the other is in the air, and repeat this feat with the last two. On this being done, a stone is put aside each time as won. In case of failure the next player endeavours to do it, and the play passes round until some one succeeds.

After two of the last five stones have been won in this manner, one of the remaining three stones is placed on the upturned palm, at the end of the doubled-back fingers ; one near the elbow, at the end of the fore-arm ; and the third halfway between them. The other players then decide which of these is to be caught when all are tossed up together by a sharp upward and forward jerk of the arm. If the player can catch it, first on the back of her fingers and then in her palm, she lays it aside as won. She now tosses up the remaining two from the end positions. If she catch both at once in her palm—not on the back of the fingers this time—she wins one of them. The last stone, which is called *Pedissā*, is then tossed up, and caught. While it is in the air the player must touch with the tip of her middle finger, the ground, her chest, and the tip of her tongue. If this be repeated successfully six times consecutively the stone is won and the player escapes all punishment even if she had won no other stone.

When a stone which ought to be caught falls to the ground for any reason whatever it is a miss, and the play passes to the next person.

At the end of the game, the winners, that is, those who have won the original number of stones or more, punish the others, with the exception of the winner of the Pedissā. Each loser in turn must hold the hands over a stone which is placed on the ground, with the palms joined and fingers pointing downward, rubbing the palms together, while a winner who sits in front of her endeavours by a sharp blow with the flat of one hand or the other to strike the hands of the loser, the loser withdrawing her hands sharply so as to make the striker miss them. This punishment is inflicted for each stone short, and is continued until the striker misses the hands. It goes all round the circle, all the winners punishing all the losers.

The game called 'Checks' or 'Five-Jacks,' which is played in England by girls, is simpler than this Eastern one, and is played differently in the northern counties and in the Midlands.

In the north it is played on a stone pavement. The players have flat counters called 'Checks,' usually four in number, and not exceeding eight for each player. They are scattered on the pavement in front of a kneeling player. A small marble ball is then tossed in the air by the player, and after it has fallen and while it is in the air on the rebound, she picks up one of the checks and with it in her hand catches the ball before it falls to the ground again. After each check has been taken up in turn singly in this manner, the player proceeds to pick them up in the same way, first in pairs, then in threes, fours, and so on, until at last all are picked up at one rapid grab before the stone falls after its rebound. There is no penalty for failure; the play merely passes to the next player.

In the Midland counties five stones called ' Jacks ' are used. Five different rounds are played with them, at the beginning of each of which all the stones are placed on the ground near each other. The player kneels beside them.

First round. A stone is tossed up and while it is in the air another is picked up and the falling stone is caught in the same hand. One of them is put aside, and the proceeding is repeated until all are taken in this way. Next, two stones are picked up before the falling stone is caught, and this is repeated with the other two. After this, one stone is picked up in the same way, and then three stones. Lastly, all four are picked up at once while the stone which is tossed up is in the air; this must of course be caught in the same hand.

Second round. A stone is tossed up, one stone is picked up and the falling stone is caught in the same hand as before. Then one of these two is tossed up, and while it is in the air the other is placed on the ground and a third stone is picked up before the falling stone is caught. The procedure is then repeated until four have been placed on the ground. Finally the stone remaining in the hand is tossed up and all four on the ground are picked up together before the other is caught.

Third round. This begins in the same way as the others, and is like the first round, with the exception that the stones when picked up are retained in the hand.

Fourth round. After picking up the first stone as before and catching the tossed up stone, the two are tossed up together. While they are in the air another is picked up and the falling two are caught in the same hand. All three are now tossed up and a fourth one picked up in the same way. The four are then tossed up and caught, the fifth stone being picked up while they are in the air.

Fifth round. One stone is placed on the back of the outstretched hand. It is then tossed up and another is picked up before it is caught in the palm. While this is held in the palm, the other is tossed up from the back of the hand and a third one picked up, the falling stone being caught in the same palm. This is repeated with the other stones, those previously picked up being retained in the hand.

A variant is played by tossing up a marble each time instead of one of the stones, and catching it after its rebound from the stone pavement. This use of the marble resembles the northern practice, but of course cannot have been the original mode of playing the game.

I did not learn the Arab or Indian game.

Pol-kūru Keliya, 'The Coconut-pins Game.'

This is the game called Spelicans in England, into which country it was imported from Holland, according to Skeat's Etymological Dictionary. The Dutch may have learnt it in India, where it is well known. The thin splinters or 'spells' of ivory or bone with which it is sometimes played are carved in the form of various Eastern weapons—swords, bows, arrows, spears, as well as saws, trumpets, and some ancient military standards. These are dropped on a table in a promiscuous heap, crossing each other as much as possible, and are removed one by one by means of a small ivory hook, the aim of each player being to take out as many as possible without the slightest movement of the others, which disqualifies the player for that turn.

The Sinhalese game is played in exactly the same manner. As the name implies, short lengths of the rib of the side leaf of the coconut, 6½ or 7 inches long, thinned down and well smoothed, are used instead of splinters of bone or ivory. Their number varies. One set made for me numbers about 120, but I was informed that a full set should number 240 or 300, although so many are not often employed. On every tenth stick notches are cut on one edge according to the number of tens, one at the tenth stick, two at the twentieth, and so on. For drawing out the sticks a small hook is cut at the end of one of them, or the end is bent sharply round for the purpose.

The turn to draw out the sticks passes round the players consecutively to the right, each one stopping when some movement is observed among the other sticks. When a stick is once touched by the hook, even by accident, the player must draw out that one, or attempt to do it.

The game ends when all the sticks have been drawn out; and the winner is the player who can count the highest score. In this, one is counted for each notch on the sticks drawn out by the player, as well as for each unnotched stick. The aim of the players is therefore to acquire the sticks with the highest numbers of notches.

NERENCHI KELIYA, written 'Niranchy' by Ludovisi.[1] The meaning appears to be connected with the Tamil verb *nirei*, 'to fill up,' or 'become full,' and *āṇsi* (pronounced *ānchi*), 'play.'

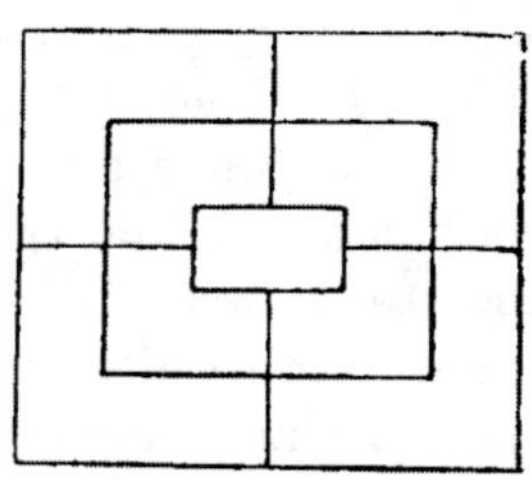

FIG. 245. Nerenchi Diagram (Mihintale).

This is undoubtedly a very ancient game, the age of which is unknown. Perhaps the earliest evidence of it in Ceylon occurs at Mihintale, where two diagrams for playing it, called *Nerenchi-peta*, were cut on the great flight of steps, thirty feet wide, for ascending the lower part of the hill, by the masons who laid them. I have not met with any record of the construction of these steps. Tennent states that the monks at Mihintale informed him that the work is attributed to Mahādāṭhika Mahā-Nāga (9–21 A.D.).[2] Forbes says the same.

In the much worn inscription left by a King Nāga on a vertical rock near the Aet dāgaba, on the crest of the hill,

[1] 'The Sports and Games of the Sinhalese,' by L. Ludovisi. (*Journal of the Ceylon Branch of the Royal Asiatic Society* for 1873, p. 17.)

[2] *Ceylon*, 2nd ed., Vol. ii, p. 606, foot-note.

already mentioned in the account of that structure, the reference to the gift of the steps at the dāgaba may be taken to prove that the much more needed flight at the lower part of the hill was already built by 245 A.D. In that case the most probable time for their construction was during the second century or at the beginning of the first century A.D., when extensive works were undertaken there.

Two other diagrams cut on a rock near the Lankārāma dāgaba are illustrated by Mr. Bell; near them are some letters in 'rock character,' but whether pre-Christian or later Mr. Bell does not state.[1] One diagram which measures 8 inches by 7 inches, is of the usual form the other consists of two crosses, one vertical and one oblique, inside an oblong measuring 5½ inches by 5 inches.

A similar design to the illustration, 15½ inches square, is also cut on one of the great slabs which roofed part of the temple begun by Rameses I (1400–1366, B.C.) and completed by Seti I (1366–1333 B.C.) at Kūrna, in Upper Egypt, on the western side of the Nile valley. Many other designs, which are illustrated in connection with the next chapter (Fig. 273), are on the same roof, and three of them certainly were incised before the stones were finally laid, since in trimming the edges of the slabs on which they occur so as to make them fit against the adjoining ones, the masons cut away part of these diagrams.

If, as appears most probable, the persons who cut these damaged designs also made the rest, it is evident that the knowledge of this game must have been possessed by the ancient Egyptians in the fourteenth century B.C. This is the more likely since among the other diagrams on the same slabs there is an upright cross enclosed in a square, which the small holes marked at the angles and intersections of lines appear to show was used for playing a still simpler form of the game, that was like the 'Noughts and Crosses' of English children. Both in Cairo and at Luxor I was informed that the Nerenchi game is not known at the present day in Egypt, which is equivalent

[1] Arch. Survey of Ceylon, Third Progress Report, p. 5, foot-note.

to saying that it is not an Arabic game. Thus the diagram was not cut by modern Arabs.

The diagram for the Nerenchi game in its simplest form consists of a plain cross enclosed in a square, or an open cross of double lines enclosed in a square or circle. Next, we have two intermingled crosses in a square,[1] one being upright and the other diagonal. In Ceylon all these are favourite designs as charms against planetary and demoniacal influences. Lastly, there is the full design, which consists of a small central square resting on a cross, with two enclosing squares, the central square being further protected against evil influences by having a 'guarded' cross inside it. In the Sinhalese diagram for the game given by Mr. Ludovisi it is interesting to find a small plain cross drawn inside the central square, as in Egypt, where however the cross is a 'guarded' one, having a cross-bar at the end of each arm. The three parallel-sided squares, one inside the other, are also found on articles taken from European Lake Dwellings, where a cross is placed in the centre. They occur at the first city at Troy, without the central cross, and are to be seen on Indian punch-marked coins. They are included in my Sinhalese manuscript book of magical formulas as a diagram which guards against evil caused by planets and demons.

It is probable that in early times this game may have been thought to have some mystical or magical significance. The mystical number three which recurs so often in it was connected with the early deities of Egypt and the Euphrates valley. The number three was also reckoned the first of the odd, or lucky, numbers[2]; therefore to win a game in which victory went to the player who obtained the greatest number of this lucky figure may have been thought an auspicious omen. All idea of such a meaning is now unknown to those who play the modern game.

[1] This form of board was employed for the game in Ireland in the early part of the 18th century, according to Col. Wood-Martin (*Pagan Ireland*, p. 536); and a stone counter and several bone disks which are thought to have been used for such a game have been found in Irish Lake Dwellings (*op. cit.* p. 534).

[2] Plutarch's *Morals*. On the E at Delphi, viii.

The simplest form of the game, the familiar 'Noughts and Crosses,' is not, I think, found in the interior of Ceylon, but the complete game is well known there and is also played in India, as well as in Europe. It is not known in Western Africa, nor have I found any references to it by African travellers. I have also been informed that it is unknown in Japan. In Ceylon the diagram for it is drawn on the ground.

The game requires two players who alternately lay down a small counter—usually a stone or fragment of earthenware—at one of the angles, or the points where the arms of the cross meet the sides of the squares. While doing so, on each occasion when a player forms a row of three of his own pieces, which is termed 'Nerenchi,' he lays down an additional piece.

When only two places remain unfilled the next player moves one of his pieces into one of the vacant points, and the play is continued by the two players, who move their pieces alternately, each one endeavouring to form a row of three of his own pieces, which the other tries to prevent. Whenever a row is so formed the player who has obtained the Nerenchi removes an opposition piece from the board and has an additional move. The play ends when one player has lost all his pieces.

HAT DIVIYAN KELIYA, 'The Game of the Seven Leopards.'

This game is mentioned by Ludovisi, who gives a copy of the diagram on which it is played. This is an isosceles triangle with a central upright from the middle of the base to the apex, and two other lines across it parallel to the base and ending at the sides of the triangle.

It is played by two persons, one of whom has one piece called, according to Ludovisi, the 'Tiger,' while the other has seven pieces called 'Leopards,' which are captured and removed off the board when the Tiger jumps over them one at a time, into an empty place. The Leopards win the game if they can shut him up or 'imprison' him so that he cannot move.

The pieces move along the lines of the figure to all junctions of lines, going one step at a time except when the Tiger is making a capture. The Tiger is first placed at the apex of the triangle. The owner of the Leopards then deposits one of them at any point where two lines meet, and lays down an additional one after each move of the Tiger until all are on the board. The opponents continue to play alternately afterwards. It is evident that the game is a very simple one. I am not aware that it is known in the interior of Ceylon.

DEMALA DIVIYAN KELIYA, or KOṬI SELLAMA. 'The Tamil Leopards' Game.'

The board is an enlarged form of that of the preceding game, all the lines being extended so as to provide an additional set of positions for the pieces on the three sides of the triangle.

Three 'Leopards' and fifteen pieces called 'Dogs' are required for this game, which is played exactly like the last one. Capturing the Dogs is termed 'chopping' them (*v. koṭanawā*). This game is well known in southern India, from which country it was doubtless imported into Ceylon, as its name indicates. Its Hindustāni name is *Rafāya.* Some extend the lines so as to make an extra set of positions for the pieces outside those described above.

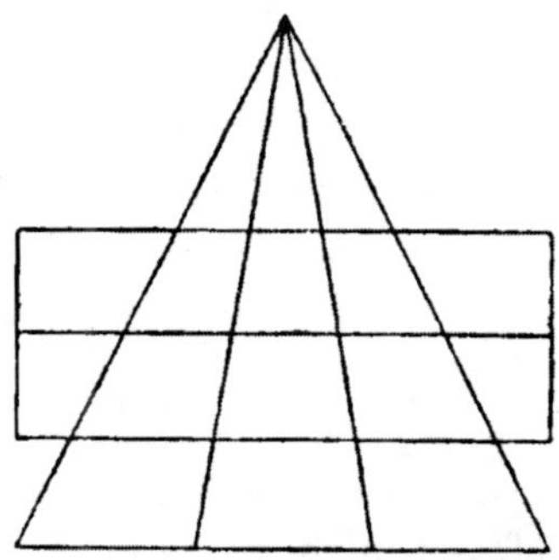

FIG. 246. Indian Diviyan Keliya Diagram.

DIVIYAN KELIYA, 'The Leopards' Game'; or *Diviyalliya,* 'the Leopards' Square'; or *Koṭiyō saha Harak,* 'the Leopards and Cattle.'

This form of board is closely allied to the Kūrna diagrams illustrated in the next chapter. The board is a square with five lines passing across from each face, including the two outer ones; the diagonals which run into the angles of the square and through the middle of each of its sides are also drawn. A triangle of six places for the pieces, enclosed by two extended diagonals, projects at the middle of each face, in addition.

This game is played by two persons, one of whom has two

pieces called 'Leopards,' while the other has twenty-four pieces called 'Cattle,' with which he endeavours to shut up

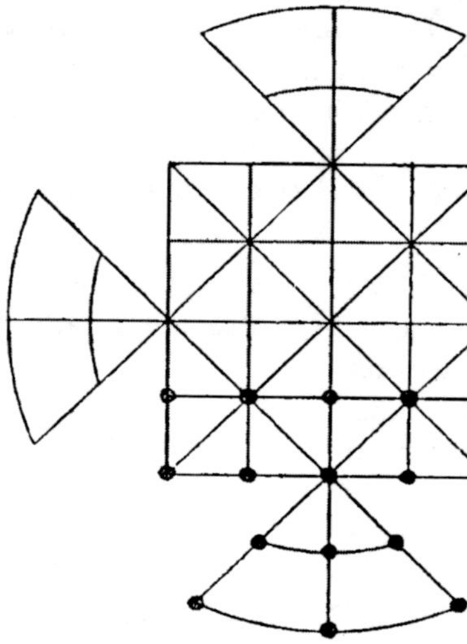

FIG. 247. Diagram for Hĕwākam and Diviyan Keliya.

the Leopards, which are then said to be 'imprisoned.' It is played in the same manner as the last games, the Leopards 'eating' the Cattle one at a time, by jumping over them into a vacant place. The stations for the pieces are at all meeting places of lines, and the pieces move along the lines, both at right angles and along the diagonals, going one step each time, excepting when the Leopard is making a capture. Small stones and fragments of earthenware are used as pieces.

The owner of the Leopards begins the game by placing one of them at the centre of the board, but any other place may be selected for it. One of the Cattle is next put down by the other player at any meeting-point of two or more lines where it will be safe from immediate attack, and his opponent then deposits the second Leopard at any other place which he prefers. Another of the Cattle is then placed on the board, and the rest follow after each move of a Leopard until all are in play, up to which time they cannot be moved on the board. In the meantime some of them will have been 'eaten'; and notwithstanding the large number of them they are almost certain to lose the game if the Leopards can capture eight. With careful play the Cattle always win. This is probably the most developed and best of all shutting-up games.

HĒWĀKAM KELIYA, 'the War Game.'

This is also a game for two players, and the same diagram as for Diviyan Keliya is employed for it, with the exception that the two triangular 'rooms' at the right and left sides are not required.

Each player has sixteen pieces called 'Soldiers,' and these are said to be 'chopped' when captured. All move along the lines of the board, whether diagonals or otherwise, and capture the opponents by jumping over them exactly like kings at Draughts, that is, there is no limit to the number which may be captured at one move. At the same time the player has the option of refusing to capture the men of the other side. Small stones or pieces of earthenware form the Soldiers.

At the commencement, the Soldiers of each opponent are arranged in an orderly manner on the opposite sides of the board, as shown by those of one player in the illustration, leaving only the transverse central line clear of them. The players move the men alternately, taking one step at a time in any direction when not capturing an opponent's pieces. The player who captures all the Soldiers of the other side is the winner.

This game is known in India, and in Bengal is termed *Sōlah Guttiya*, 'Sixteen Balls.'

PERALI KOṬUWA, 'the War Enclosure.'

This is merely a variety of the last game, in which the two side rooms are retained, the board being thus the same as for Diviyan Keliya. Each player has seven more soldiers than in the last game, and in each case these fill up the outer room on his left hand, and three empty places are then left along the central transverse line.

The game is also played in India. Ludovisi mentions a variant called *Koṭu Ellīma*, in which each player has one more

'Soldier,' making a total of forty-eight, so that only the central place on the board is vacant when the play begins. The mode of playing is evidently the same in all these games.

DĀM, Draughts; or literally 'The Net.'

This game, which is known in India also, is closely allied to Polish Draughts.[1] The pieces move in the squares instead of going along the lines. It requires two players, who have a rectangular board of 144 squares, twelve being on each side, alternately coloured red (or black) and white. Each player has thirty pieces called *Ittā* (pl. *Ittō*), which are placed on the white squares at each end of the board, as in Draughts, that is, in six out of each row of twelve squares, thus leaving only the two central rows vacant. The Ittō move only diagonally, and capture or 'chop' the opposing pieces by jumping over them, and taking several consecutively if possible. They can move backwards as well as forwards from the beginning, thus having the powers of Kings in the ordinary English game. Excepting when capturing the opposing Ittō, the ordinary pieces move to the distance of only one square at a time.

Every Ittā which succeeds in reaching the last square on the opponent's side of the board is doubled, and is termed a 'King.' With this increase in rank it acquires additional powers, and it may proceed to the end of each diagonal at one move, if the end square be empty and the way be open, or to any intermediate square, as in Polish Draughts, jumping over and capturing any opponent's pieces on the way if there be any in suitable positions on that diagonal. It cannot pass over Ittō or Kings of its own side, and only over opposing ones if the next square to them be empty.

If any of the opponent's pieces be captured on this diagonal and the king can enter the end square, it may continue its course in the same manner, as part of the same move, to the end or to an intermediate square of the second diagonal, at a right angle from the last one, and so on over a third or more. To be permitted to do this, however, t must capture one or

[1] Falkener, *Games Ancient and Oriental*, p. 236.

more pieces on each diagonal passed over, and there must always be an empty square for it to enter in the diagonal. If the King take no pieces, whether Ittō or Kings, on the first diagonal, he cannot proceed further than its end at one move. He has the option of remaining at any empty intermediate square before reaching the end of a diagonal. All pieces must jump over every opposing piece which they capture ; they cannot stop in its square, or jump over it unless the next square be empty.

In other respects the play is the same as in English Draughts, the game being won by the player who captures all the pieces of his opponent.

The Ittō are flat disks, half being coloured black and half white ; they are made of wood or of shark's bone.

A game of Draughts called Dāma is played in Egypt, and as the name shows is perhaps descended from the original form of the Eastern game. As the boards which I saw resembled those used in England I did not enquire into the manner in which it is played. It is not described by Lane, who merely mentions it as a favourite game there. On some boards the pieces are flat disks like those used in England, while on others they are short cylinders with flat tops.

KOṬI KELIYA, 'the Leopard Game.'

This is played on the same board of 144 squares, and is a form of 'Fox and Geese.' It requires one piece called a 'Leopard,' and six others termed 'Cattle,' or 'Dogs,' which all move diagonally along the squares. The Cattle only move in a forward oblique direction and to the extent of one square at a time, and cannot be captured ; but the Leopard has the option of going double the distance in any oblique direction if the course be unobstructed. He cannot pass over the Cattle.

The Cattle are set on the white squares along one side of the board ; while the Leopard may be placed anywhere on a square of the same colour. As in the English game, the Leopard wins if it can pass through or round the Cattle, whose aim is to enclose or 'imprison' him. Neither this nor the previous game is played in the villages of the interior.

CHESS.

The game is practically unknown to the Sinhalese, and is never played in the villages; but some of the Tamil and other Indian residents in Colombo understand it well, and possibly a few Sinhalese of that city are acquainted with it. The only form of it which I have seen is the one known in Upper India by the Arabic name *Shatreṇ* (with the accent on the lạst syllable and a nasal *n*). It is allied to the Turkish game, and is played without dice. The old Indian name *Chaturanga* does not appear to be used for it in Ceylon, notwithstanding the fact that Ludovisi mentions it by this title, which is applied there to a very different game.

Shatreṇ is played by two persons on a diagram of sixty-four squares, alternately red and white, embroidered on cloth or velvet. The pieces are cylindrical, plain green and red in colour, and of different heights and thicknesses. They are so made in accordance with Muhammad's prohibition of the use of human or animal figures.[1] They are made of ivory or wood.

The only variations from the English game are, (1) the absence of 'Castling'; (2) the additional power of the King to jump at any time as a Knight, until he has been once in check; (3) the limitation of the first move of the Pawns to a single square; and (4) when any Pawns reach one of the last squares they can become only the piece that was in the same column or line of squares originally, provided such piece has been previously captured by the enemy, so as to be available for replacing on the board.

The pieces and their Indian colloquial names are as follows[2]:—The King is Shāh; the Queen is Farthīr (Persian *Farzin*); two Elephants, Fīl; two Horses, Ghōdā; two Castles, Rūkh; and eight Pawns called Piyātha (Persian *Piyāda*, foot-soldier) or Paithal, 'Footman.'

[1] 'O true believers, surely wine, and lots, and images, and divining arrows are an abomination of the work of Satan.' Sale's *Qurān*, Chapter v. Sale states that the word 'images' is believed by commentators to refer especially to the carved figures of chess-men.

[2] In these words *th* is pronounced as in the English word *then*.

Check is Kisht ; Check to the King, Shāh-kō-kisht ; Check to the Queen, Farthī-kō-kisht ; Stalemate is Burad, and Checkmate, Māt. To capture the pieces or pawns is to 'kill' them, as in Paithal-kō-marnā, 'to kill the Footman.' A square is ek Ghar or ek Khāna, 'a house' ; and to move the pieces is Chalnā.

OLINDA KELIYA, 'Tne Olinda Game.'

This is the game called by the Arabs *Mankala*, or as it is pronounced in Egypt *Manala* (with a nasal *n*, and the accent on the first syllable). It obtained the name which it bears in the interior of Ceylon from the small red seeds of the Olinda creeper (*Abrus precatorius*), the Tamil *Kuṇḍumani* or *Kunṛimani*, and Hindustāni *Rati*, which are used for playing it there (Fig. 248).

In Ceylon, the board, Olinda-pōruwa, on which it is played has fourteen little shallow cup-shaped hollows, each, among the Kandians, about an inch in diameter, arranged in two rows at the sides, each containing seven hollows. There are two rectangular hollows between them, near the ends, or projecting at the ends or sides ; it is usually decorated with tracery or other carvings, and is from 10 to 14 inches long. Some boards are made in one piece and often rest on four short legs ; others are formed in two halves joined by hinges, so as to fold up. The rectangular hollows hold the captured seeds. (Figs. 249, 251 and 252.)

In Colombo, where a much larger board is used, with cups two inches wide (Fig. 250) the game is called by the Low-Country Sinhalese *Chōnka* or *Chōnku*, and is there played with cowries, the board, 17 inches long and 6 inches wide, being known as the *Chōnku-lāēlla*, 'the Chōnku plank.' Chōnku is not a Sinhalese word ; it appears to be merely the Malay name for the game, *Chonkak*. Among the Tamils the name is *Pallankuli*, and the board is called *Pallankuli-palakei*, 'the Pallankuli plank' ; either cowries or Tamarind seeds are used as counters in it. In Southern India I have seen some neat ones made of plain polished brass, with sunk cup-holes. Some Tamil boards in the British Museum

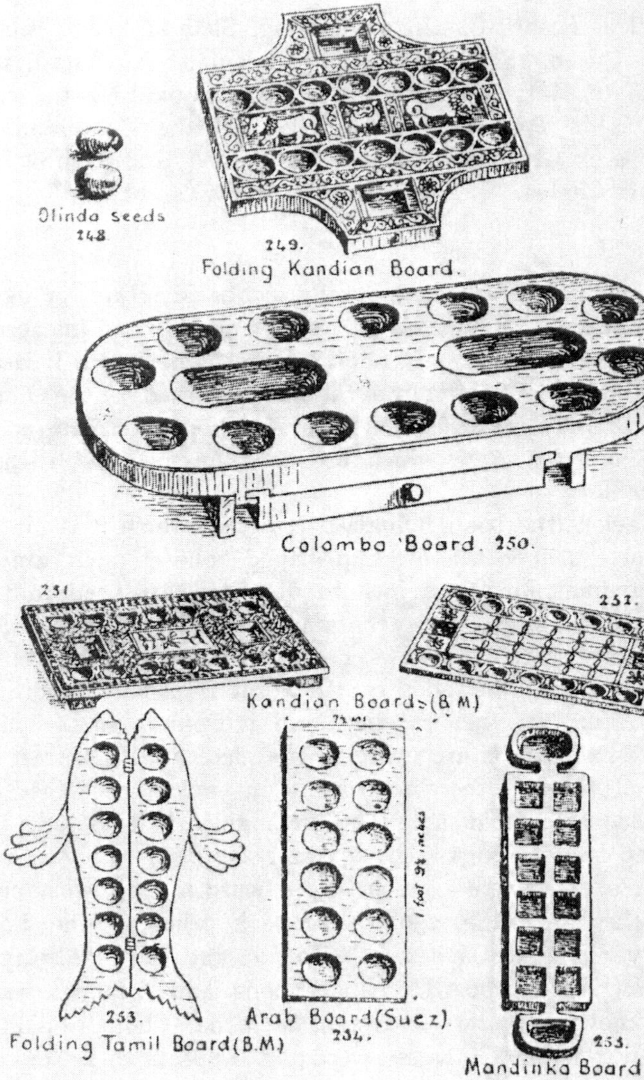

FIGS. 248–255. Olinda (Mancala) Boards.

are of the shape of a fish; they consist of two halves joined by hinges (Fig. 253).

In the account of the ancient Cup-markings I have noted particulars of early sets of cup-holes cut in rocks for this game; they appear to be of not later date than the fourth century A.D., and in one instance may be still older. So far as is known, they are some centuries older than the time of the first influx of Arab settlers from India. The game may thus have been introduced into the island by early Indian traders.

Its antiquity in Ceylon is proved by the variations in the numbers of the holes cut for it. At Pallibaedda there are 18 holes each 1½ inches in diameter, 9 being in each row, with an additional larger one at one end for holding captured seeds. At Galmediyāgala the holes are 12 and 14 in number; they are now only one inch wide and a quarter of an inch deep, but the weathering of the rock may have made them shallower than when first cut. At this site there are no less than five sets of holes side by side. Although it is thus evident that in early times the number of holes was variable in Ceylon, at present the boards used there and in Southern India have invariably 14 holes.

Several well-cut sets of similar holes are to be seen on the roof-slabs of the Kūrna temple in Upper Egypt, and on the summit of the damaged portion of the great pylon built in Ptolemaic times at the entrance to the temple of Karnak, as well as on the tops of the walls there and at the Luxor temple. The rows consist of 6, 7, and 8 saucer-shaped holes on each side, the largest ones being 3½ inches wide and one inch deep. The finest set at Kūrna has 16 holes and is 2 feet long; the holes, which are admirably cut and finished, are 2¾ inches wide and one inch deep. Another excellently cut set of 14 holes on the top of the wall of the first or entrance court-yard at Karnak is also 2 feet long, the holes being 2½ inches wide and one inch deep. In both these instances the centre lines of the cups are from 5 to 6 inches apart. On the Karnak pylon I also saw some holes, perhaps intended for this game, which consisted of two rows with only 4 and 5 cups in each. In all these instances there are no surplus holes for the captured pieces.

Another set of 12 cups, 2 feet long, consisting of two rows from 4 to 7½ inches apart, is cut at the south-east corner of the rock that forms the base of the Pyramid of Menkaurā, at Gīzeh, on a large block of the rock which has since fallen over on its side (Fig. 256). The cups are from 2 to 2¼ inches wide, and from 1 to 1½ inches deep, with a large one at the side, 2¾ inches wide, for holding captured pieces. These holes are much weather-worn, and are quite different in character from the shallow saucers cut by the modern Arab guides at the Great Pyramid of Khufu, for playing the game called Sīga; and they have every appearance of a much greater age. The Sheik of the Pyramids informed me that they had not been observed before I discovered them after a long search for such holes; he stated that no others are known there. It is possible that they were cut by the masons who were engaged in the construction of the Pyramid or some of the tombs near it, since in Muhammedan times there could be no reason why they should not be cut on the stones of the Pyramid, like the modern ones, rather than on a distant part of the rough basal rock. Holes cut in the rock for this game have also been found in Angola,[1] and in the Ussindja district on the southern side of the Victoria Nyanza.[2]

At the present day the number of holes used in different countries varies greatly. In Egypt, and among the Bedwān and the Arabs of Suez, 12 holes are always used. An Asante board in the British Museum has the same number, and this is the number employed by the Mandinkō (Mandingoes), the Fulas, and the Wolofs, of Western Africa (Fig. 255), and also, according to Mr. Culin, in Liberia, in Benin, in the Gabūn, and among the Negroes in the West India Islands.[3]

In Syria, and the Philippines,[4] and among the Malays generally, as well as in India, the number is 14. In the Māldive

[1] S. Culin. 'Mancala, the National Game of Africa.' *Report of the U.S. National Museum*, 1893-4, p. 602.

[2] Kollmann. *The Victoria Nyanza*, p. 108.

[3] Culin, *op. cit.* pp. 600, 601, 603.

[4] Gulin, *op. cit.* Plate 2.

FIG. 256. Mancala Holes at Third Pyramid, Gizeh.

To face p. 590

rocks in Ceylon, that is, 12 holes, which is also the most widely-spread number in Africa, was employed in the game when it was first played there, and probably also in India; and that in the early centuries after Christ, although the number was being increased it was still in a state of transition. The 14 holes that are now always used in both these countries evidently had not then been accepted as the definite figure for it.

Like other things, games doubtless advance from the simple to the complex; the smaller number of holes found at Karnak cannot have been derived from the early 12 holes of India and Ceylon. They appear to indicate a local and simpler form of the game of Egyptian origin, whether the holes at Kūrna and Gīzeh are of very early date or not.

Judging by the name given to the game in Colombo, it appears to have been re-introduced on the western coast of Ceylon by Malay immigrants, possibly at a time when a considerable force of Malays invaded the country and occupied that part of the coast in the thirteenth century A.D.

The native expressions used for the game are peculiar, and they also afford some evidence of its spread into Ceylon from a country where it was played with date-stones. In Ceylon each cup is called a 'hole' (*wala*), or 'enclosure' (*koṭuwa*); the set of seven on each side being a 'row' (*pila*); and the seeds, although their real name is Olinda, are always termed 'Date' (*indiya*, pl. *indi*) while they are being used in the game. The verb which expresses their distribution along the holes is 'to sow' (*ihinawā*), and when they are captured they are said to be 'eaten.' The verb (*innawā*) used to indicate their presence in the holes is only applied in other circumstances to living beings, and appears to be connected with the Arabic and Egyptian name for the shells that are used in place of seeds, viz. 'Dogs.' Holes into which seeds must not be played are said to be 'blind.' Among the Tamils and the Low-country Sinhalese the cowry shells that are used are termed 'Dogs'; they are 'sown' in the holes, and capturing them is 'eating' them.

Similarly, in West Africa I found that among the Mandinkō, although the name of the seeds used in the game is Lenkō, this expression is not applied to them while playing, but they are then known as Worō, which is also the name of the game. Placing them in the holes is 'sowing' them, and capturing them is called 'eating' them.

By the Egyptians and Arabs the cowry shells with which the game is played are known as 'Dogs' (*kelāb*); yet as in Ceylon and West Africa, placing them in the holes is termed 'sowing' them, and when captured they are said to be 'eaten (*akalto*). These facts support the opinion as to the derivation of the game from Egypt or Arabia. The question as to which of the two countries originated it will be considered after it has been described.

It is surprising to find that almost every country where the game is known has its own special mode of playing it, an additional proof of its antiquity. Ceylon is no exception to this rule; and among the Sinhalese there are no less than five different methods, four of which are found in the interior among the Kandians, and one on the western coast. The favourite game of the Kandian Sinhalese is called *Puhulmutu*; the others are *Walak-pussa*, *Koṭu-baendum*, and *Daramutu*. Each requires two players, who sit on mats on opposite sides of the board, which is always placed on the ground or on a mat, and in each game the person who captures all the seeds is the victor.

The games are especially played at the season of the New Year, with which they appear to have some connection that I have been unable to ascertain. At that season Olinda boards that have never seen the light during the previous twelve months are invariably brought out of their hiding places on some dark dust-covered and smoke-begrimed shelf, and hour after hour is devoted to the game for several nights in succession. It is almost a monopoly of the women. According to their own expression some of them play it 'until they are blind.' The boards are then put away carefully, and often are not used again for another year, though there is no feeling of any prohibition against playing it at other times, and occasional games are sometimes indulged in.

In all four games four seeds are first placed in each of the 14 holes; and the game is finished if it end in a 'draw,' or when a player has captured all his opponent's seeds. The play proceeds either towards the right or the left, the direction taken by the first player at the commencement being adhered to throughout the game by both players. The first player begins by taking the four seeds out of a hole on his side of the board, usually the penultimate one, and distributing or 'sowing' them one by one into the next holes consecutively. I shall term the play until one player has no seeds on his side of the board when his turn comes to play, a 'round.'

PUHULMUTU, 'Ash-pumpkin Pearls.'

In this game the player takes the five seeds out of the hole into which the last one fell, and in the same way as before sows them one by one in the next and the following holes, going on round the board in this manner until the final seed falls into an empty hole, called *puhuwala*, or *pussa*, on which the player stops, or 'sits down.' His opponent then begins at any hole on his own side, and plays in exactly the same manner until the last seed of those which he is sowing also falls into an empty hole, after which the first player begins afresh at any hole on his own side of the board, and repeats the sowing.

When a hole has three seeds in it, it must be passed over without receiving any seeds, excepting, in its proper order, the last seed of the set which a player is sowing. When this falls into such a hole he captures the four which are now in that hole (*tun-indin kanawā*, 'eats (them) because of the three dates'), and puts them aside in his separate enclosure provided for them at one end or side of the board. He then takes the seeds of the next hole, if there be any, and sows them as before, and continues his play round the board; but if the next hole to that at which he effected the capture be empty his turn is ended, and he 'sits down.' The opponent now resumes his play, beginning at any hole on his own side, and plays in the same way. Towards the latter part of the round a single seed in the last hole on a player's side cannot be taken as the starting-point if any other hole on his side of the board contain one, or more than one. When all the seeds on one player's side of the board have been captured, or more correctly when a player is left without seeds in his row of holes on his turn's coming to play, the round is ended.

Each player then again arranges his seeds in fours in the cup-holes, taking for the purpose any that were left in the holes on his side of the board, together with those captured by him. Any surplus ones are left in the rectangular hole belonging to him. It will almost always be found that one player possesses fewer seeds than the other. If they have equal numbers (termed *hari mutu*, 'equal pearls'), it is optional to consider the game ended in a 'draw.' But if one player have fewer than the other the game must be continued.

After they are replaced in the holes, in case a player be without seeds at only one hole he is said to be a 'person blind of one eye' (*ekas kanā*) ; if at two holes, a 'person blind of two eyes' (*dāēs kanā*) ; if at three holes, he has no special name, but his side of the board is described as 'four-eye,' referring to the four cups which alone contain seeds ; if there are only seeds for three holes it is 'three-eye' ; if for two holes, 'two-eye' ; if for one hole, 'one-eye.' The player whose seeds are deficient is said to have 'become blind' (*kana welā*). This nomenclature is applied in all the four games.

The 'blind' person must now commence the play, sowing the seeds in the direction of his empty holes, which are left at one end of his row, and are marked by bits of twig or straw being placed across them to indicate that they are 'blind.' During the whole of the round no seeds can be placed in the 'blind' holes by either player. In other respects the procedure in this and subsequent rounds is exactly the same as in the first one, with the exceptions to be now noted.

In all the four Kandian forms of the Olinda game, when the player whose seeds are deficient finds on placing the usual four seeds in the holes at a fresh 'round' that he ends with only one seed for the last hole, this seed is termed his 'son' (*putā*) ; if he have two seeds for it they are called 'younger sister' (*nagā*) ; if three seeds they are his 'slave' (*wālā*). Although seeds are sown as usual, by both players, into these three holes those in the first two, containing a putā or nagā, cannot be taken out and sown, and are also free from capture throughout all that round, and continue to accumulate for the benefit of their owner ; but those in the wālā hole have not this privilege, and are sown and captured as usual. In its case the name is only a descriptive expression, and does not affect the play.

To balance these privileged holes the opponent removes one, two, or three seeds respectively from his last hole before the play begins afresh, so as to make up the sum of four when those left in the hole are added to the seeds in the 'blind' person's last hole. Thus, if the latter player have a putā, his opponent must end with a wālā, or *vice versâ* ; and if he have a nagā the other must also have a nagā. The same names and privileges apply to these holes on both sides of the board. The putā and nagā holes are distinguished from the rest by having some mark, such as a bit of paper or straw, placed in them. As the seeds in these cups cannot be taken out and sown, the turn of the player whose last one falls into either of them comes to an end.

When a player finds himself left with less than twelve seeds at the beginning of a round, he has the option of arranging them among the holes in his row in a different manner. He may place two seeds, or only one seed, in each hole, beginning from one end of the row of holes, the last hole on his side in that case receiving any surplus seeds, not exceeding four. For instance, if he have nine seeds, and if, as is usually the case, they be playing to the right, he will place two in each of the four holes on the left ; the next two holes will be left empty, and are 'blind' and cannot be played into ; and the ninth seed will be placed in the last hole on the right. The opponent's distribution is unaffected by this, and he places the usual four seeds in the holes in his row.

The game now becomes rather complicated, as the two persons play in different ways. The opponent plays and effects captures in the usual manner ; but the 'blind' player only makes a capture when his last seed falls into a hole containing two seeds, whether on his own or the opposite side of the board, in which case he takes the three. If he placed one seed in each hole at the commencement of the round he would make captures when his last seed fell into a hole which contained only one. Otherwise, excepting when playing his last seed, all such holes on both sides of the board with two seeds or one seed, respectively, are passed over by him and do not receive seeds from him when sowing, although his opponent sows into them. On the other hand, the 'blind' player no longer passes over the holes with three seeds, but sows his seeds into each of them. As a general result of this mode of playing, the person who was 'blind' often regains his lost seeds, even when he has been reduced to one seed at the beginning of a round, and the game becomes nearly interminable, and may last for hours.

In order to bring it to an end quickly, a method termed 'Cutting Ash-pumpkins' (*puhul kapanawā*) is sometimes adopted. According to it the player who is deficient borrows a seed out of each of the last two holes on his opponent's side, and places these in the adjoining two holes on his own side. He must then begin his play at the next or third hole; and the borrowed seeds are returned when his opponent is about to commence sowing. There is another method of cutting short the game by a player's moving a seed, or two, on the opponent's side, and then commencing to sow from other holes than the first three on his own side.

WALAK-PUSSA, 'A Hole Empty.'

This game is begun like the last, but when the last seed of the set which is being sown has been placed in a hole he does not remove and re-sow the seeds out of that hole, but always takes those in the next one for the purpose. If this next hole be empty, the seeds in the following one, that is, the second one after that in which he placed his last seed, are captured or 'eaten,' the verb which expresses it being *pussa kanawā*, 'eating because of the empty (hole).' If the following or third hole be empty, the seeds in the one after it are also captured, and so on as long as there is a sequence of alternate empty and full holes. This is termed *wael mutu ekilenawā*.

'picking out the pearls of the necklaces.' He then stops playing and the opponent begins.

At the commencement of the next or succeeding rounds the same arrangements as in Puhulmutu are necessary in case there be a putā, nagā, wālā, or 'blind' holes. In this and all the games, the player with the fewest seeds always begins the play after the first round, and it must go in the direction of the empty or deficient holes.

When the last seed of the set which is being sown falls into an empty hole immediately preceding one containing a putā or nagā, (which is considered to be *pussa*, 'empty,' and the seeds in which cannot be captured) these are passed over as though non-existent, and the seeds in the next hole to them are 'eaten.'

Like the last, this game is almost interminable, and there is no 'Cutting Ash-pumpkins' to curtail it.

KOṬU-BAENDUM, 'Tying up the Enclosures.'

This game is begun and played like Puhulmutu, excepting that it must be commenced from either of the two end holes in each player's row. During the rest of the game the players may begin each turn at any hole on their own side of the board. For re-sowing, the seeds are taken as in Puhulmutu, out of the hole in which the last seed was placed; but if this previously held three seeds the four now in it are 'eaten,' and the next player then begins.

When the last seed falls into an end hole in which there ere three seeds, thus making four, that hole is said to be ed (*baendā*); it becomes like a putā or nagā hole, and the seeds in it cannot be captured, although others continue to be sown in it by both players, as usual. Such holes belong to the person who puts the fourth seed in them, whether they be on his own or his opponent's side of the board; and they receive a distinctive mark like the nagā or putā. All four end holes may thus become 'tied.' When the last seed is sown in a 'tied' hole the player stops or 'sits down,' and the opponent begins, since the seeds in it cannot be taken out and played This game is also a very long one, like the others.

DARAMUTU, or ELLAEWALA-KAṆḌA.[1]

Play begins at any hole of the player's row. When the last seed of the set which is being sown falls in any empty hole the seeds in the opposite hole on the other side of the board are 'eaten.' The player then stops, and the opponent begins. If the last seed fall in a hole containing a putā or nagā it is treated as an empty one, and those in the opposite hole are eaten. In other respects the game resembles Puhulmutu.

The village women play all these games with astonishing rapidity. Without counting the seeds they are about to 'sow' they seem to know instinctively, perhaps as the result of long practice, at which hole it is best to begin in order to effect captures. An inexperienced person has no chance of beating them.

PALLANKULI or CHŌNKA.

This game, as played in Colombo by Sinhalese, Tamils, and Muhammadans is a very different one from those just described. Seven cowry shells, termed 'Dogs,' are placed in each hole as a preliminary, or 98 in all. Play may begin at any hole on a player's own side of the board, and may go round either to the right or left, the same direction being maintained throughout the game. The shells are 'sown' as usual, but the play differs from all the Kandian games in this—that each player after placing a shell in the last hole of his own row, puts the next one in his surplus hole for captured shells, called 'Tāchi,' and then continues to 'sow' in the same manner as before, along the holes on his opponent's side of the board. He does not place any shells in the opponent's tāchi. The shells in both the tāchi cannot be captured. If his last shell fall in an empty hole, he captures both that shell and those in the opposite hole on the other side of the board. In this case, and also when the last one falls in his own tāchi, his turn is ended, and the opponent then plays in the same way. When the last

[1] The meanings of these terms are doubtful.

shell falls into a hole containing others, all, unless it be the tāchi, are taken out and sown as before.

The game ends in one round, and the winner is the person who first finishes his shells.

WORŌ, the game in Senegambia.

In some respects this game exhibits a closer resemblance to the Kandian game than to the Egyptian or Arabic one. Four disk-like Lenkō seeds of a dark colour, with rather flat sides, are first placed in each of the twelve holes, or 48 in all. The play always goes round to the right, and each player may begin at any hole on his own side of the board. He 'sows' the seeds now called Worō, and not Dogs or Lenkō, in the same way as in the Puhulmutu game; but only captures or 'eats' those on the opponent's side of the board. This occurs when the last seed falls into a hole on that side which contains either one or two seeds. He then captures not only the seeds in that hole, but also those in other holes which have the same number on that side of the board, provided they follow each other consecutively, without the intervention of holes containing other numbers.

The play is very simple, and ends with the first round, the loser being the player who has no seed on his side of the board when his turn comes to play. All the captured seeds are deposited in the two end holes, each of which is called a 'Worō-house' (*Worō buṉō*), and are then finally out of play. The cups are called 'Worō-holes.' Both men and women are accustomed to amuse themselves with this game, and I was informed that no other variety of it is known in that part of Africa.

Richard Jobson saw this game played in the Gambia territory early in the seventeenth century. He remarked concerning it, 'In the heat of the day, the men will come forth, and sit themselves in companies, under the shady trees, to receive the fresh aire, and there passe the time in communication, having only one kind of game to recreate themselves withall, and that is in a peece of wood, certaine great holes cut, which they set upon the ground betwixt two of them, and with a number of some thirty pibble stones, after a manner of counting, they take one from the other, untill one is possessed of all, whereat some of them are wondrous nimble.' [1]

MAṆALA (Suez).

The Arabian game differs greatly. As a preliminary, any two holes on one side and one hole on the other are left empty; in each of the other nine holes are placed eight cowry shells, which are termed 'Dogs.' Play begins anywhere on the player's own side of the board, and always goes to the right. 'Sowing' is effected as in Puhulmutu, until the last shell drops into an empty hole. If this occur during the first two sowings round the board, in which no captures are made, the player stops, and the opponent begins to play; but on subsequent occasions he 'eats' the Dogs in the opposite hole, whether on his own or his opponent's side of the board, as in the Daramutu game. He then continues his play, moving into the next hole the last shell which he had just put down, and sowing the shells out of that one, and so on, until his last shell falls into an empty hole opposite which there are no Dogs to be eaten. The other player then commences, and plays in the same way. After each player has once sown the shells, the succeeding player must always begin at the next hole to that at which his opponent ended, unless it be empty, in which case he begins at the following one containing shells.

The game is a rapid one, and ends with the first round, the winner being the person who has 'eaten' most Dogs.

MAṆALA (Bedawi).

This game is played with 70 cowry shells, called 'Dogs. At first all the shells are deposited by one of the players, without counting them, in the four middle holes, the eight end ones being left empty. His opponent feels them with the backs of the fingers of his closed fist, and if he be satisfied with their distribution he begins to play. In case the arrangement be not to his liking he turns the board round and tells the other player to begin.

[1] *The Golden Trade*, 1623. Reprint, p. 48.

Play commences on the player's own side of the board, at the right-hand filled hole, and always passes to the left. The shells are 'sown' as in Puhulmutu, but each player stops when his last shell falls into a hole in which it makes an odd number. But in the early part of the game if it fall into one of the holes full of shells they are not counted; it is assumed that the number is an even one, and the player takes all out and continues to sow them round the holes, commencing at the next one. After both players have had one turn at sowing they begin subsequent sowings at any hole on their own side of the board.

If, when a player has dropped each last shell, there be any even pairs of shells in opposite holes on the two sides of the board, whether twos, fours, sixes, eights, or tens, beyond which they are said not to run, he 'eats' the whole of these pairs. This is the only way in which the shells are captured.

The game ends in one round, when one of the players has no shells on his side of the board after his opponent stops playing; and the winner is he who has captured or 'eaten' the greatest number. The Bedawi who showed me the game assured me that his people knew no other way of playing, but Lane describes slightly different methods as practised by the Egyptians.[1]

As to the country in which this widely-diffused and most popular of all indoor games was invented, the manner of beginning the Arabian and Egyptian games exhibits such a radical difference from the Senegambian and Indian or Kandian-Sinhalese games, with their simple and natural mode of distributing the seeds in the cup-holes, that it is difficult to believe that these last can have been derived from them. It is much more probable that the Indian and Senegambian variants were borrowed directly, or through their introduction by traders, from an original form of the game as practised in Ancient Egypt, and perhaps developed from a simple type in which only eight or ten holes were used. The Arabian games may have been evolved independently from one of the same

[1] *Manners and Customs of the Modern Egyptians*, 1896, p. 357.

early Egyptian forms. Only in this way does it seem possible to account for the close similarity between the Sinhalese and the West African games, and their variation from the Arabian game.

THE ARABIAN AND AFRICAN SĪGA

This game, in which a player captures an opponent's pieces by enclosing them between two of his own, appears to be unknown in Ceylon, and, so far as I could learn, also in India. As another game also termed 'Sīga' is played in Ceylon and India, I first give an account of the Arabian and West African games.

Lane has described the manner of playing Sīga in Egypt, on square diagrams of 25, 49 or 81 compartments, each player having respectively 12, 24, or 40 counters called Dogs,[1] so that when all are placed on the diagram only one square in the centre is vacant. According to Falkener, this is a modification of one of the oldest games known, the 'Senat' of the Ancient Egyptians.[2]

There are several Sīga 'boards' of shallow saucers cut upon the roof slabs of the Kūrna temple,[3] the numbers of the holes being 25 and 49; and the game played at Luxor is exactly the same as that in Cairo described by Lane, the number of holes being commonly 25.

Each player in turn puts down two counters anywhere on the board excepting in the central hole, which is left unfilled. When all have been put down the next person to play moves a counter into the vacant hole, and if on doing so he can enclose one of his opponent's pieces between it and another of his own pieces, he captures the piece so enclosed, and removes it from the board. All pieces are taken in this manner; in each case one of the capturing pieces must be moved horizontally or vertically, and not diagonally, out of an adjoining hole for the purpose of enclosing it. The counters which enclosed the captured piece do not take its place. After capturing one

[1] *Manners and Customs of the Modern Egyptians*, 1896, p. 361.

[2] *Games—Ancient and Oriental*, 1892, p. 71.

[3] These holes are perhaps of much later date than the early diagrams already mentioned as being on the same roof, but they were certainly made by men who were excellent stone-cutters.

counter the same player has another move if by it he can effect another capture ; and he may continue to do this as long as he can enclose and capture an opponent's piece at each move. The winner is the player who captures all his opponent's counters.

CHOKŌ is the only form of the game found in the Gambia Valley.

This game is played on sand or loose earth by the Mandinkō and Fulas, on diagrams of 25 holes made with the finger; bits of stick about five inches long called *Kala*, and others three inches long called *Boṇō* are used as counters. It differs slightly from the Egyptian game.

The sticks are set upright in the loose soil of the holes, one at a time, by the two players alternately, and play usually begins before the last two sticks have been put down. In that case either player may put this last stick into a hole at any stage of the game, the opponent putting down his own last one immediately afterwards. Sometimes play is begun while each player has two or more sticks in his hand ; it may be commenced at any time.

The players have only one move at a time, and capture the opponent's sticks by jumping over them, and not by enclosing them. At each jump over the enemy's stick they remove both that and a second stick belonging to him, selecting one that will most benefit their own play. This soon ends the game, which only lasts for a quarter of an hour or less. The winner is he who captures all his opponent's sticks.

A similar form of Sīga is played in Cairo, on a 'board' of 25 holes made in the ground. The players lay down their pieces called 'Dogs' alternately, two at a time, until only the central hole is unfilled. They then play as in the Senegambian game, capturing those of the opponent by jumping over them, and continuing to capture at one move as many as the 'Dog' can jump over, like Kings at Draughts. This form of capture shows that the game is allied to the Ceylon and Indian game already described as Hēwākam Keliya, which may have been developed from it, or a game resembling it.

A diagram of 25 squares is drawn on the side stone of a cist at Aspatria, near St. Bees, Cumberland.[1] Fergusson attributed the articles found in the cist to 'at least the Viking Age'; but the diagram being on the side of the stone may have been cut at an earlier date, and may have been intended for some form of Sīga game.

Games with Dice.

Saturankam or Chaturanga.

This game as played in Ceylon and Southern India is called Sīga by the Indian Arabs and Muhammadans; but it is a totally different game from the Sīga of Arabia. It is played by Sinhalese and Tamils on a board of 81 squares, 9 being on each side. The middle square (*kaṭṭi*) of each side, and the central square (*tāchi*) are marked by two diagonal lines. The plain squares are called *kōḍu* in Tamil or *gaeta* in Sinhalese.

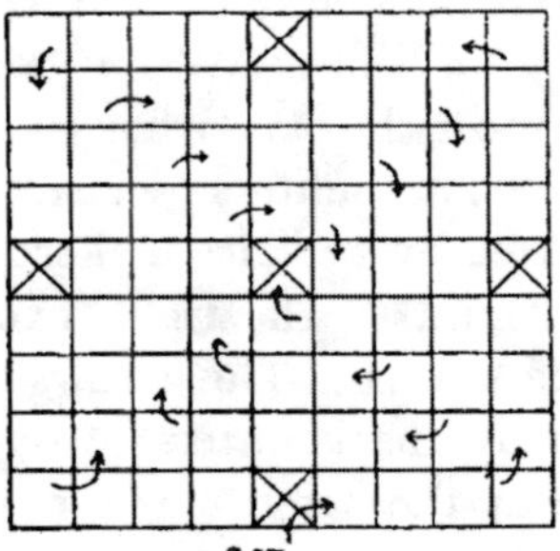

257.

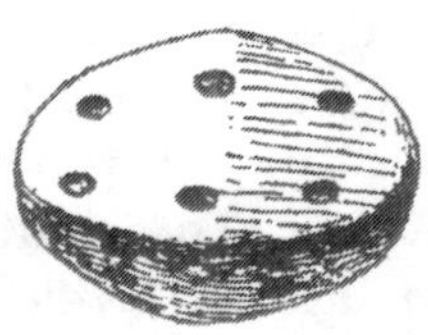

258. Kemadi Dice ½

259. Toppare

Figs. 257–259. Saturankam Diagram.

Two enormous hollow brass dice termed *Kemadi*[2] are used for it; they have rounded edges and are of a peculiar shape, being 2¼ inches long, 1¼ inches wide in the middle, and narrow at each end, where they are less than half an inch wide. They are rolled between the palms and then along the table or floor. Each is marked thus, by holes through the shell, on the four sides :— ·, ⁝, ⁙, ∷. Each player has two nearly barrel-shaped counters, called *Top-*

[1] Fergusson, *Rude Stone Monuments*, p. 157. Col. Wood-Martin, *Pagan Ireland*, p. 569.

[2] From Skt. *kshema*, 'prosperity' + *dita*, pp. of $\sqrt{da}$, 'to give or bestow.'

parei, with round tops on which is a little knob, one pair being coloured red and the other black.

The game may be played by two, three, or four persons, each one playing for himself, and beginning at one of the Kaṭṭi if there be two they sit on opposite sides of the board. The aim of each player is to get his counters into the central square.

At the commencement, each player's counters are placed in the Kaṭṭi on his side of the board. The players then roll the dice in turn. The numbers uppermost are added together, and the sum may be used as the distance for moving one counter, or it may be divided in any way for securing suitable moves for both. When both dice show the same number uppermost the player has an additional roll. No one can refuse to move his counters ; one or both must be moved to the extent regulated by the dice if there be room for them. The counting goes round to the right, excluding the Kaṭṭi from which the counters start. The arrows on the diagram show the direction taken by the counters of one side ; those on the other sides move in the same manner.

While in the crossed squares they are safe from attack, but in the plain ones it is the aim of the opponent to 'chop' them, as it is termed. This is done by passing one of his counters into or over their square, upon which they must begin afresh from the first Kaṭṭi. To permit them to do this their owner must obtain two ones on the dice, even when only one counter is required to enter. This puts them into the first Kaṭṭi, ready for moving onward at his next throw.

For getting into the central Tāchi, the exact number of pips required must be obtained ; therefore it is advisable to bring the two counters up to it together, and not to pass one out before the other is close to it. When both are near it any score on the dice can be divided, so as possibly to enable both counters to pass out together, or one can be passed out alone, if necessary. A further difficulty arises owing to a rule that if the number required be 1 this figure must be obtained on both the dice at one roll, even when there is only one counter left. In the same manner both dice must show threes or fours for passing out either a single counter or both if they be only three or four squares off the centre. Up to this distance both counters pass out as easily as one. Of course any considerable delay in getting into the Tāchi gives the opponent an opportunity, which is almost certain to be utilised, of 'chopping' the player's counters.

THE INDIAN SĪGA.

As played in Colombo by two persons on a diagram marked on the ground, or worked on a piece of cloth which is laid on a mat placed on the ground, this is a similar game to the last; but only 25 squares are employed, 5 being on each side. The middle square of each side and the central square are marked by two diagonals, and when in these positions the counters cannot be attacked. The arrows show the direction of the moves from one Kaṭṭi.

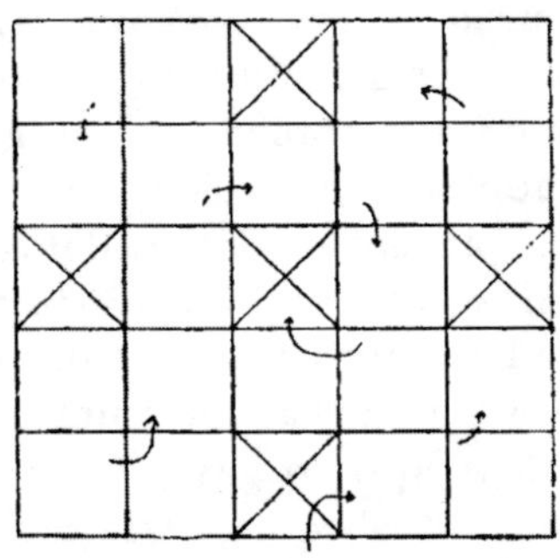

FIG. 260. Sīga Diagram.

When the game is played on a cloth diagram, each player has two counters like the Topparei of the last game; but if it be played on a diagram drawn on the ground he has two distinctive pieces of stick, of a different length or colour from those of his opponent, which are set upright in the square as counters.

Instead of dice, four cowries are thrown down on a mat or on the ground, after being shaken in the closed hands. They are counted as follows:—When all the mouths are upward they count 4; for three, two or one mouth upward, 3, 2, or 1 is counted; and no mouth upward counts 8.

No throw counts until the player has thrown 1; this permits one counter to be placed in the first Kaṭṭi, ready for moving forward at the next throw. The second counter may be put on the same square after another 1 has been thrown. In this game the numbers thrown are neither subdivided nor added together excepting as stated below; each throw gives the length of the move of one of the counters. Each player has an additional throw and move of either counter on throwing 1 or 8, or on cutting out or 'chopping' an opponent's counter. When 'chopped,' the counters must begin afresh and cannot re-enter until the player has again thrown 1.

On coming up to the central square the exact number required to bring one or both counters into it must be thrown; and at this point, only, it is permissible to divide the amount of the throw, so as to bring one or both counters into the centre.

Caillié described, but not very clearly, a completely different form of Sīga which he saw played with dice by the Moors of Senegal. The dice were six flat oval pieces of wood, black on one side, and white on the other; they were shaken in the hand and thrown on the ground. When all, or all but one, had the same colour upward the throw was called 'Sīga'; the player who obtained it counted a score of 1, and had another throw after each Sīga. In all other cases nothing was counted and the turn was ended. One colour belonged to each side; it is stated that the number of dice which fell with the player's colour upward gave the score for each throw, this being only counted when Sīga was thrown.

The players may number two, four, or six persons, who form two opposing sides. Seventy-two holes in three rows, each consisting of twenty-four, are made in the sand. Each party owns one outside row; across these holes straws of distinctive colours are deposited by the players. At each score of Sīga the player who threw it moves forward a mark or straw along the central row of holes, beginning at one end; on reaching the other end he moves it along the opponent's outer row, taking away the opposition straws as he captures the holes across which they were placed. The winner is the side or person who first captures all the holes. Holes are recaptured when the opponent's throw of the dice brings his straw into them.[1]

Early Indian Game.

In the gambling scene inscribed *Citupāda Sila*, which is illustrated in Plate XLV of Sir A. Cunningham's *The Stūpa of*

[1] *Travels through Central Africa to Timbuctoo*, 1830, Vol. i, p. 12.

Bharhut, a square of 36 compartments or rooms, 6 being on each side, is drawn on the ground, with two players, or perhaps four, sitting on opposite sides of it. In the second room from the left, in the second row, one player has set up a twig like those used in the last Indian game. The even number of compartments shows, however, that the game cannot be one of the present class, which requires a central room ; and there is nothing else to indicate the mode of playing it. The absence of shells or dice may point to a game resembling the Mandinka Chokō ; if so, it is unknown in Ceylon at the present day, and in India also, as far as I could ascertain.

PANCHA KELIYA, 'The Five Game.'

This game is played on a peculiar bent diagram, only one compartment in width, which is cut on a board. The illustration

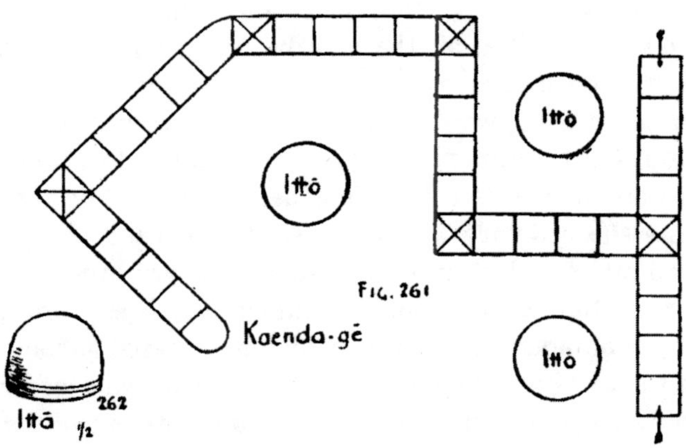

FIGS. 261, 262. Pancha Keliya Diagram.

shows its shape. The name may be derived from one of the numbers thrown by the shells, or from the five Houses of Safety on it in which the counters cannot be attacked ; but the Sīga games just described also possess them. The main part of the diagram rises vertically from a horizontal base. At the point of junction there is a square marked by diagonals and termed a House (*Gē*) ; four others occur at bends in the diagram.

In any of these squares the counters are safe from attack. Each of the other plain squares is a Room (*Kāmara*), or *Kaṭṭiya*. The terminal square is known as *Kenda-gē*. The stations for counters not in play are marked by circles.

The game may be played by two, four, six, or eight players, but there are only two opposing sides, half the players being on each side. The play of both sides commences from opposite ends of the base line. Six counters termed *Ittā*, pl. *Ittō*, are used, three for each side, whatever the number of players may be. They are of a dāgaba shape, without tee or spire; and have grooves to represent the basal platforms. They are made of wood and covered with lac.

Six yellow cowries, usually filled with lead, are used as dice. They are placed in a half-coconut shell, the mouth is covered by the hand, and after a slight shaking they are emptied out onto a mat without reversing the coconut-shell. The counting is as follows :—When all the mouths are upward it counts 6; if five be upward it counts 5, and is called *Pancha*; two, three, or four mouths upward count 2, 3, or 4, respectively; one mouth upward counts 1, called *Oṇḍuwa*; and when no mouths are upward it counts 0, and is called *Bokka*. For the other numbers the ordinary Sinhalese words are used.

To admit each Ittā into the board a player must throw 6, 5, or 1. After each of these numbers has been thrown the player has an additional throw, which is repeated as long as he continues to throw any one of them. The counter or Ittā then moves up the line of squares to the full extent of the total throws; or the score of each throw may be used for each Ittā of that player; it cannot be subdivided. To go out of the last square, termed to 'land' (*goḍa-yanawā*), exactly one more than the number of squares up to and including the Kenda-gē, must be thrown. An Ittā is 'cut' out only when the opponent's Ittā enters the same Kāmara or blank square.

Sometimes the Ittō are made of pieces of coconut, kaju-nut, or areka-nut, and are eaten at the conclusion of the game, being then termed 'Dogs'; they do not receive this name while they are used in the game.

PAHAḌA KELIYA, 'the Race Game' (from Skt. *pra*, 'forward' + *syad*, 'running').

This is the Sinhalese form of the Indian game called *Pachīs*, 'twenty-five.' It is always played on a diagram worked on a cloth, and known as *Pahaḍa–peta*, which closely resembles that employed in Pachīs (Fig. 264). It consists of a central blank square from the sides of which four arms forming a cross extend at right-angles, each having three rows of eight squares. Every square is called a 'House,' *Gē*, and those in the central rows are specially distinguished as Kāmara, 'room.' In all the squares the counters, which are termed *Ittā*, pl. *Ittō*, and are like those used in the last game, may be cut out or 'chopped,' excepting during their progress down the last central row, into the middle enclosure. To assist in counting the squares, little open crosses are marked on each outer corner square, and on the third and sixth from those, in the outer rows.

Two long dice called *Kawaru* or *Kahuru*, or sometimes incorrectly *Pahaḍa lanu*, 'the Pahada Strings,' are used; they are made of bone or ivory, and are 2¼ inches long and $\frac{3}{16}$ in. wide on each of the four sides. Both are marked alike, with small red circles having a central spot, arranged in the following order:—A cross formed of four or seven circles in the middle counts 1; three equidistant circles count 3; three equidistant pairs of circles count 6; and two pairs, one being near each end, count 4.

Some of the names of the numbers shown by the two dice when thrown are peculiar compounds of Sinhalese and Tamil. Thus 1 + 1 is *dugā-deka*; 1 + 3 is *mūṇḍu-oṇḍuwa*, 'three-one' or *nāḷu-hatara*, 'four-four'; 1 + 4 is *anji-paha*, 'five-five,' or *paha-anjiya*; 1 + 6 is *āru-oṇḍu-hata*, 'six-one-seven'; 3 + 3 is *iri-haya*, 'six-lines'; and 4 + 3 is *nāḷu-hata*, 'four-seven.' For the other scores the ordinary Sinhalese words are used.

Casting the dice, termed 'putting down' (*damanawā*), is done in a special manner. They are laid side by side across the fingers of the open hand, one end resting on the fore-finger, beyond the last joint, and are held in place by the thumb. The hand is then reversed, and they are thrown down sharply in the angle between the player's partner and the latter's right-hand opponent.

There are two sides in the game, each having two or four players, who throw the dice, and score, in turn, towards the right. When four play, each person has four dāgaba-shaped counters, eight belonging to each side ; if eight play each has two of the counters. They are coloured red, yellow, black and green.

Pahaḍa Keliya differs from other similar games in having no senseless delay in getting the counters into play. As a preliminary, each player places a counter on the sixth and the seventh squares of the central row at his side of the board, when there are two or four players, and two others on the fifth square of the outer row on his right, on which one of the crosses [1] is marked ; one of the last two stands outside the square. I have not seen a game played by eight persons ; probably in that case the counters are deposited on the board in the same positions, one belonging to each person being in the central row, and one in the outer row. From these points they move forward at the commencement of the play. The outer counters are always moved first, in order to avoid being caught by the enemy, and also in order, if possible, to attack the enemy in front of them ; the other two in the central row are safe from attack, and can wait there if necessary.

The scores of the two dice may be used separately for moving two counters at once ; they cannot be subdivided, but they may be added together so as to bring a single counter out of the opponent's way, or attack him. There is no delay or payment at the re-entry of a 'chopped' counter ; it moves at once from the central square up the middle row and onward to the right round the outer rows, to the full extent of any throw of one or both dice. There are no double throws of the dice, whatever number fall.

The opponent's counters are 'chopped' when the score of a player's throw brings his counter or counters into their squares. They may jump over the enemy's counters—though this is inadvisable, as it renders them liable to be 'chopped' at his next move—or over the other counters belonging to their own side, with the exception mentioned below when in

[1] Of this game ; not those on the Pachīs diagram.

the last outer row of squares, and several may enter the same square.

The counters move to the right of the players, who are seated at the ends of the arms of the board, along the outer rows of squares, and finally down the middle row from which they started, being then placed on their sides. To enable them to enter the central space the exact number required must be thrown, that is, one more than the number necessary to bring the counter into the last kāmara. When once inside this last row they are safe, but getting into it is often difficult.

I now come to the special feature of the Sinhalese game. I shall assume that, as usual, there are four players. When the first of the two partners has got his counters up to the last three squares in which they can be attacked by the enemy, prior to moving down the final central row, he cannot proceed any further if his partner have any counters following him until two of these are brought up to his assistance. It is evident that for this to happen his counters must have got in front of those of his partner, either by longer moves or because, as nearly invariably occurs, the latter have been 'chopped' and have re-entered behind him.

When he is in this position in the above-noted squares the partner must get two counters into the square at the beginning of the last outer row (at the end of which the obstructed counters are waiting), where they are said to have 'the foot tied,' (*aḍiya baendā*). Out of this square they must move simultaneously, that is, they can only leave it when their owner throws 2 ones, 2 threes, 2 fours, or 2 sixes. As they are not now allowed to enter the squares of the waiting counters a throw of 2 sixes sometimes cannot be utilised. After the partner has made this double throw, and taken his two counters out of the corner square, the waiting counters are released, and are now ready to move forward down the middle row of squares. Of course the delay gives the opponents an opportunity of 'chopping' some of the counters. In one game that I watched the player who had first brought his counters round and was waiting to take them into the middle row of squares, lost the game because his partner was unable to come to his assistance in time to save him. Thus the blocking of the counters in that position is clearly a device to prevent one player's running out too quickly.

When the player who requires to throw pairs of numbers fails to do so, he uses the throws to bring on his other counters, which, however, cannot pass his two in the corner square. They must occupy the next two squares behind them, and wait there until a pair of numbers has been thrown to permit the first two to make way for them. Thus there are sometimes eight counters awaiting this double throw before being able to move onward; and the enemy is almost certain to 'chop' some of them, especially the later four, if he can succeed in getting two counters into the squares at the outer end of the last row on the left, the row preceding theirs. The first batch of counters are then left hopelessly stranded on the very edge of the safe squares. The knowledge of this adds considerably to the interest of the play; and when, as is generally the case, there is a monetary pool the players become greatly excited at this point, and as they throw the dice shout in a loud voice the number they require, by way of causing it to fall. Evidently the great aim in this exciting game should be to 'chop' the counters of one of the opponents, so as to make him re-enter behind his partner, who will then be blocked at the edge of the safe squares.

Players who know Pahaḍa Keliya well are of opinion that it is the finest game in the world. It certainly contains elements of excitement in a greater degree than the other Eastern games; and it appears to me to be a decided improvement to place all the counters in the game from the commencement, and thus avoid stupid delay in beginning the play.

Āsi Keliya, 'the Shell Game'[1] or Sōnāru. The latter word is a variation of the Tamil name *Sōnālu*; the two portions *sō* and *nālu* each meaning 'four'[2], the whole word is equivalent to 'Four-four,' that is, 'Double-four.'

[1] *Āsi* is said to be equivalent to *Bellā*, shell; I believe that the game is sometimes called *Bellan Keliya*, 'the Shells Game.'

[2] Such is the meaning of *Sō* in this word, according to information given to me by players of the game. It is not found in Clough's

This game is a modification of Pahaḍa Keliya, and is played on a similar diagram, which, however, has only four sets of squares in each arm of the cross, instead of eight (Fig. 263). It is always drawn on the ground or on a plank, and two diagonals are marked in the central enclosure, separating it into four parts. In counting, the ordinary Sinhalese words for the numbers are used, with the exception that 1 is expressed by the word *Oṇḍuwa*, derived from the Tamil *oṇḍu*. In each middle outermost square the counters are not liable to be 'chopped,' as well as when inside the middle row.

There are four players, each opposite pair being partners, and each player has four counters like those used in the last game.

As the name implies, cowry shells are used as dice. Of these, five are the common yellow ones; the sixth one is white, and is termed *Sō-bellā*, 'the Four-Shell,' the others being called merely *bellā*. The scoring is the same as that of Pancha Keliya, excepting that when two shells fall with their backs upward and one of them is the Sō-bellā, this is known as *Sō-hatara*, 'Double-four,' which however counts only 4, but has special powers.

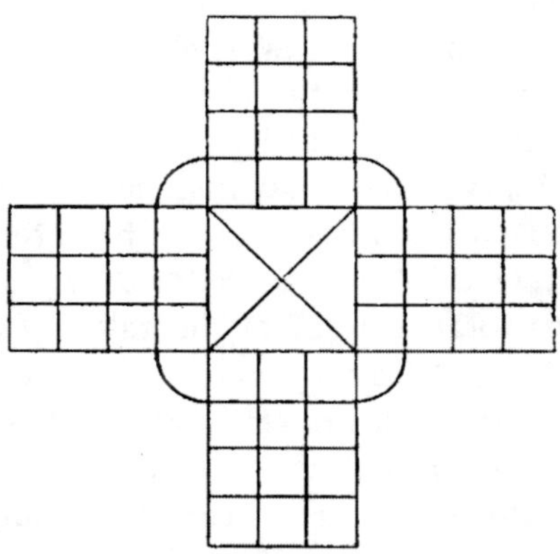

FIG. 263. Āsi-Keliya Diagram.

When the throw is 1, 5, or Sō-hatara, it is termed a 'win (*dinuma*), and the player has an additional throw, which is repeated as often as he obtains one of these 'wins.'

The entry and re-entry of the counters into the game must be paid for, and until 1, 5, or Sō-hatara has been thrown they cannot come into play. After one of these 'wins' has been obtained, and the additional throw which follows it has been made, the player must pay 1 off the score for the entry or

Dictionary, nor in Winslow's Tamil Dictionary. See my note to the next game.

re-entry of each counter. Thus a throw of 1 releases one counter, and a throw of Sō-hatara will, if desired, release all four counters, or the 5 may be given for the release of all four. Or one, two, or three counters may be released by Sō-hatara, and the rest of its score be used for moving other counters forward.

When Sō-hatara is thrown the score may be subdivided in any way whatever among the counters, or the whole of it may be used for sending one of them forward. At each subsequent throw of Sō-hatara the whole score may be used in the same way, excepting in the special case where their re-entry must be first paid for. In all other cases only the amount of each separate throw can be scored on the board; no subdivision of the amount is allowed. Counters (called, as in other similar games, *Ittō*) the entry of which has been paid for, may be left in the central triangle of each player to await a later move onward.

I give an actual instance as an example. A player who had two counters waiting to enter the board on one occasion threw a Sō-hatara, followed by 1, and then by 6. Out of this total score of 11, he gave up 2 to release his two waiting Ittō, and leaving one in the central triangle, ready to move forward at his next throw, used the remaining 9 in advancing the other and thus 'chopping' one of his opponent's Ittō. In this case, part of the total score being Sō-hatara, he might have divided the score of 9 among his four counters, or three of them, had he so desired.

A player's counters may pass over or enter the squares in which his own counters or those of his partner are placed, but except in the case mentioned below they are not permitted to jump over the opponent's counters, which can only be 'chopped' when a counter of the other side enters their square. If the amount of a throw would take a player's counter over one of them it cannot, excepting as specified below, be utilised for that counter. When one counter enters a square in which are two of the enemies' counters it 'chops' both, but in that case they have the right to re-enter the game together at the price ordinarily paid for one re-entry.

As in all similar games, the throwing of the shells and the scoring pass round by the right hand. There is no block at the end of the last row of outer squares as in Pahaḍa Keliya. When the counters enter the final central row they can only move to the extent of one square at a time, for which 1 or Sō-hatara must be thrown. They are then laid on their sides at the junction of the transverse and longitudinal lines on the player's left side of the row, and not inside the squares.

Sō-hatara has a special power of permitting the player who throws it to pass over any opposing counters, and to 'chop' them in doing so, excepting those in the middle outer squares, which are always free from all attack. The theory which explains this is that the score of Sō-hatara is composed of 1+1+1+1; each component of it may be used separately for striking the opposing piece. This quality of Sō-hatara is transmitted to the whole score of which it may form part. In all other cases the opponent's counters can only be 'chopped' when the exact amount of one throw will bring a player's counter into the square occupied by them. The winners in this and allied games are those whose counters first pass round the board and into the central enclosure.

TĀYAM SŌṆĀLU, the Tamil game, commonly pronounced *Chōṇālu.*

Either two or four persons, forming two opposing sides, play this game, each having eight or four counters respectively, termed *Kāy*, 'unripe fruit.' The board, called *Manei*, 'house,' resembles that used for Pahaḍa Keliya, and, as in that game, the score is obtained by throwing two dice, termed *Kaṭṭei.* They differ greatly in shape and marking from those previously described, being oblongs only $\frac{7}{8}$ in. long and nearly $\frac{3}{8}$ in. wide, made of ivory, bone, or wood. They are marked alike, excepting on the fourth side, as follows:—first side, one diagonal cut counts 1; second side, two diagonal cuts crossing each other count 4; third side, blank, counts 0; fourth side, on one oblong two transverse cuts count 2; on the other three tranverse cuts count 3 (see Fig. 267).

If a blank and 1 fall uppermost the score counts 1, and is

called *Tāyam*; if a blank and the second face be upward the score is 4; if both second faces be upward the score is still 4, but it is now called *Sō-ṇāl*[1] (pronounced *Chōnāl*), the 'Double-Four' of the Sinhalese game. In other cases the face values of the counters are added together and receive the ordinary Tamil names for such numbers.

No counter or Kāy of a player can enter the board until he has once thrown Tāyam; this is the indispensable and often irritating preliminary, and it introduces the first counter onto the first square. All squares are called *Kōḍu*. Afterwards, each of the throws 1, 5, or Chōnāl releases one of the other counters that are waiting to enter the board, and in each case one Kāy is placed on the first square, and no more is counted for that throw. These three numbers also permit the player to have an additional throw, which may be repeated as long as one of these three scores is thrown. The total score, or the rest of the score after the entry of a counter or counters, is used for moving forward the counters; or each part of the score may be employed separately for it, but not be subdivided.

The counters are never free from capture excepting while passing down the last middle row of squares. They may pass into or over the squares occupied by counters of their own side, but not over those occupied by the counters of the opposing players. In order to 'cut' the opponent's counters they must enter the same squares by means of the score of one undivided throw. When two opposing counters are in one square both may be cut at once, but in that case both may re-enter the board together when 1, 5, or Chōnāl is thrown by their owner.

For a counter to enter the central enclosure the exact num-

[1] In Winslow's Tamil Dictionary the meaning of *Sōṇālu* is stated to be a lucky throw of the dice, and that of *Pāṇālu*, an unlucky throw. If this be correct, the former word would appear to mean literally 'the Excellent Four,' and the original form may have been *Sūṇālu*, *sū* meaning 'good, excellent,' and also in old Sinhalese the number 4, as in *Sūvisi*, 24. *Sū* does not mean 4 in Tamil. As the actual throw called Chōṇāl consists of two fours, the Sinhalese explanation given previously may be a later invention to suit the case.

ber required must be thrown ; and the counter having passed into it is out of the game, and is now called *Paḷam,* 'ripe-fruit.' The partners all of whose counters first become Paḷam are the winners. Thus in most respects the game resembles the Sinhalese Āsi-keliya, which is evidently a variant of it.

PACHĪS, 'Twenty-five,' is the Indian form of the same game. Its Tamil name is *Sokkaṭṭāṇ* (commonly pronounced in Colombo

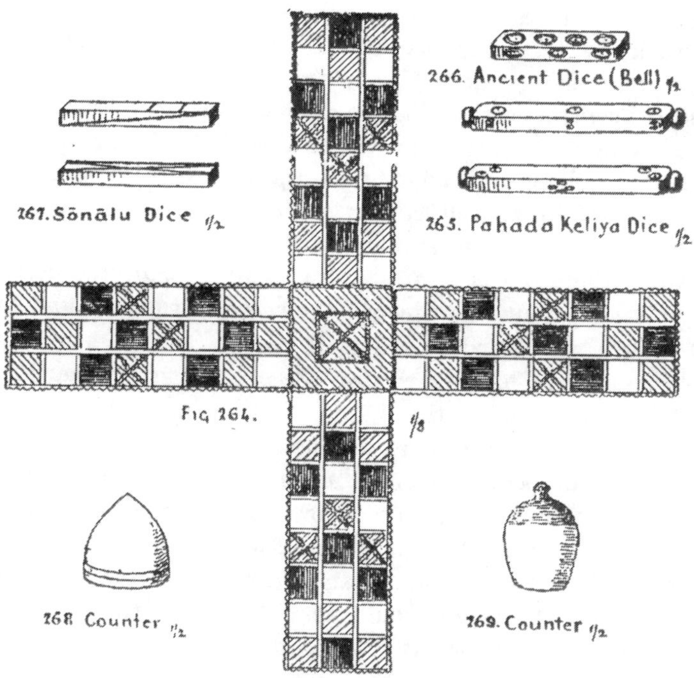

FIGS. 264–269. Pachīs Cloth.

Shok'otaṇ) ; or according to Winslow's Dictionary[1] *Soṛkēṭṭāṇ* or *Soṛkaṭṭāṇ.*

This popular Indian game may be played by two, three, or four persons, and twelve counters are used, called *Kāy* in Tamil and *Sar* in Hindustāni ; and also coloured red, yellow,

[1] Evidently the compiler of this excellent Dictionary had a confused idea of the game ; he describes it as 'Tick-tack, draughts, or Hindu Backgammon.'

black, and green, in sets of three. Blue being an unlucky colour is never used for counters in any game. If there be only two players each takes six counters. They are more or less dāgaba-shaped, like those previously described.

The board, called *Sīlei*, 'the cloth,' in Tamil, is like that used for Pahaḍa Keliya, and is always worked on cloth or velvet (Fig. 264). Crosses are marked on the fifth outer squares from the central enclosure, and on the fourth squares of the middle rows. In these squares the counters cannot be 'struck' by the opponents; they are termed *Chīra*. The ordinary squares are called 'House' (*ghara*, Hind., or *vīḍu*, Tamil), and the central enclosure is the *chār-koni* (Hind.), 'the Square.'

Six cowry shells are thrown as dice, after being shaken in the closed hands. The score is as follows:—When all the mouths are upward it counts 12, *bārah*; if five mouths be upward it is 25, *pachīs*; if two, three, or four mouths be upward the score is 2, *dō*; 3, *tīn*; and 4, *chār*, respectively. If only one mouth be upward the score is 10, *das*; and when no mouth is upward it counts 6, *choka*.

Whenever 10 or 25 is thrown the player has another throw, and if at the second throw one of the same numbers fall it counts accordingly, that is, another 10 or 25. But if either of these numbers be thrown a third time consecutively nothing is counted, and this throw cancels the two previous throws of 10 or 25, the score of the whole three throws being now 0. The right to have an additional throw would still remain, and the score would then begin afresh. There are also additional throws after 6 or 12 has fallen.

To begin the game, each player throws the shells in his turn in the right-hand order; until he obtains a 10 or 25 his counters cannot enter the board. Whenever either of these two numbers is thrown it is called a 'win,' and an addition of 1 is made to the score. If the player have counters awaiting entry or re-entry at the time, this extra allowance must always be expended in paying for one of them, 1 being charged for the entry or re-entry of each counter. If all be in the game the extra 1 is added to the rest of the score; thus a throw of 10 is counted as 11, and 25 is reckoned as 26. Excepting that this extra 1 may be used separately, the amount of each throw cannot be subdivided among different counters. In the case of the additional throw of the shells after a throw of 6, 10, 12, or 25, the amounts of the two throws may be used separately, without subdivision—either to bring a counter into an opponent's square so as to 'strike' his counters, and then move onward to the extent of the other part of the score; or the two parts may be employed in moving forward two counters.

The counters are not blocked as in Pahaḍa Keliya. As they pass down the middle row on their way into the central enclosure they are laid on their sides to distinguish them from counters that may be moving outwards. To enter the central enclosure the exact number required must be thrown. If the counter be in the last square this can only be obtained by throwing 10 or 25, the extra score of 1 which either of these receives being utilised for the purpose.

The variations in the four forms of what must have been originally one game are a proof of its antiquity. Even the two Sinhalese variants exhibit such changes that they must be many centuries old. It is possible that Āsi Keliya may represent an older type of the game than Pachīs.

Card Games.

These undoubtedly have been introduced into Ceylon by Europeans, probably the Dutch, who held the coast districts from 1655 to 1796.

The names of the cards are thus:—Diamonds are termed *Ruyita* or *Ruwita*; Hearts are *Harta*; Clubs are *Kaelāēbara*; and Spades are *Iskōp*, 'scoop' or 'shovel.' The Ace is Āsiya; the King is Rajjuruwō, a word with the same meaning; the Queen is *Dēvin-unnānsē*, 'the Queen'; and the Knave is known as *Poro*, 'Axe-(man).' The others are called after the number of pips on the face, as with us.

Only two games are usually played in the villages of the interior. One is 'Napoleon' or 'Nap,' which goes by the name of *Paswāsi*, 'Five-wins,' and is played as in England.

The name of the other game is *Bēbī-kapanawā*, 'Cutting the

Baby.' It is an extremely simple but exciting gambling game, over which considerable sums are lost and won.

A gambling party sit down at night on mats round a central cloth or mat in the middle of which is the 'pool,' and on which the cards are dealt, face upwards, to each player, after being shuffled and cut. Before each deal one person calls for any card he chooses to name, the right to do this of course passing round the players in turn. The person to whom this card is dealt becomes the winner of the pool.

On one occasion a carpenter employed by me joined a gambling party after getting his monthly pay, and when morning broke he had not only lost this money, but even the clothes on his back, which he was obliged to borrow from the winner until he could replace them. I have heard of ordinary villagers who have lost three hundred rupees in one night's play of this description, and been reduced to poverty. It is far from unusual for them to gamble away not only their money, but also their gardens, fields, and cattle, at this simple game. It is well known that the local headmen are the abettors of these gambling bouts. They always receive a substantial fee for ignoring them; this is more profitable than suppressing them.

PUZZLES.

These are included among the indoor amusements of the villagers of the interior. Among them are to be placed MAGIC SQUARES; but few understand them. The only one which I have seen was the arranging one hundred small stones in four rows, each containing four heaps. The sum of the stones in each line vertically, horizontally, and diagonally, in the four corner heaps, the central square of four heaps and the four corner squares, must amount to a quarter of the whole. The arrangement is this:—

9.	1.	6.	9.
10.	5.	5.	5.
2.	7.	8.	8.
4.	12.	6.	3.

In this square there are altogether 26 symmetrical combinations of four numbers which yield a sum of 25. This is an irregular square; in the regular Magic Square no number is repeated. Probably these are also known in Ceylon.

CROSSING THE RIVER.

A King and Queen wish to cross a river, but the only persons to row them over are a *Hēnayā-māmā*, 'a washerman,' and a *Ridī-naendā*, 'washer-woman,' who must also cross the river, but are of low caste. The single boat which is available for the purpose holds only two persons. The King and Queen must cross without one of them being left behind on the shore with one of the low-caste persons, as this would be *kilutu*, 'defilement,' for them. This will be avoided if the King can be rowed across by the man and the Queen by the woman.

The solution is very simple. The washerman first takes his wife across; he then returns and takes the King. Then he brings back his wife, who rows the Queen across, after which she returns for the washerman.

In another puzzle of the same kind three Leopards and three Goats must be taken across a river by a ferry-man whose boat only holds two besides himself. If the Goats be not left on both banks in excess of the Leopards the latter will eat them, and this must be avoided.

At first two Leopards are ferried over, and one of them is brought back. A Leopard and a Goat are then taken over. The two Leopards are then carried back, and the other two Goats are taken across. The man then returns twice for the three Leopards.

The number of simple *Conundrums* is almost countless, most of them being doubtless of Indian origin. All forms of *Acrostics* are practised also, but the commonest amusement of this kind among the villagers is found in what is termed *Perali Bāsa*, or Transposition of Letters, of which some examples have been given among the pre-Christian inscriptions.

Acrostics reached their limit in one consisting of a square of eighteen letters on each side, as given in Alwis's Introduction to the 'Siḍat Sangarāwa,' an early Sinhalese Grammar, p. 108. This acrostic was composed in 1786; it is so arranged that all the lines may be read both vertically and horizontally, backwards and forwards; they form a series of rhyming verses.

MAGUL PARAKKUWA, 'The Delay of the Feast.'

This is a very good puzzle which is sometimes brought out at marriage festivals, the guests being required to solve it before partaking of the feast. It consists of a thin wooden disk with two holes bored through it near the centre and twelve others round the margin, at equal distances apart. Twelve strings knotted at one end, on the underside of the disk, pass through all the outer holes and meet in a knot at about eight or nine inches above the disk. From their meeting-point another passes through a central hole, back through the other central hole and upwards to the same knot, where it is tied. Running on the two middle strings is a silver finger-ring. The puzzle consists in taking off the ring without untying any knots.

This is effected by drawing a loop of one of the middle strings through each marginal hole in turn, passing it round the knot of the outer string, and drawing it back. By this means all the outer strings are brought within the two inner strings and the ring, which can then be drawn off them.

ARASADI KELIYA.

This is an excellent game, which requires two confederates. After a diagram of sixty-four squares, like an ordinary chess-board, has been drawn on the ground one of the confederates absents himself. The other requests an onlooker to select any square on the diagram. He then recalls the confederate, who asks him "Which country?" the reply is either "Arasadi," or "Koḷamba" (Colombo), or "Puttalama," or "Mīgamuwa" (Negombo), the last three being towns of Ceylon. The confederate then asks "Which street?" and the reply is again one of the same four words. Lastly he asks "Which house?" and again the answer is one of the same words. Almost as soon as it is given, the confederate points out the selected square, and the effect is striking.

The explanation of the solution lies in the fact that although in the actual diagram no letters are written, those shown in the illustration are understood to be present at the four corners . they are, in fact, written there if the players are not well trained. The same letters, which are the initials of the four words of the replies, are to be understood as also belonging, in the same order, to the rows of each quarter of the diagram, as in the illustration, but they are never written in actual play. It will be seen that with their assistance any square can be picked out with ease, the vertical rows representing the 'streets,' and the horizontal rows the 'houses,' or *vice versâ*. The difficulty lies in thoroughly remembering that the progression of the letters runs from each corner only to the middle of the adjoining sides, all lines being drawn of equal thickness.

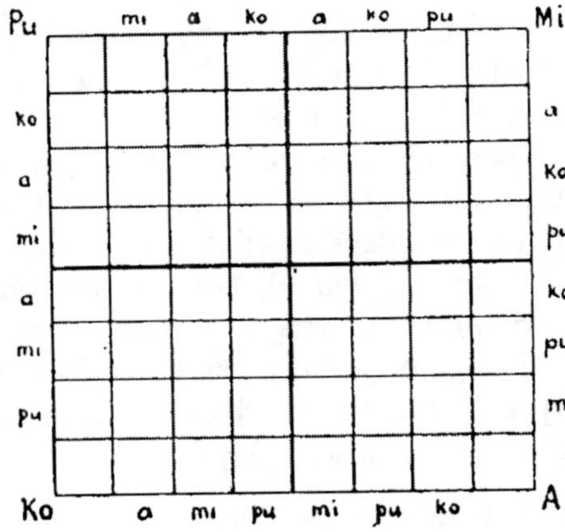

FIG. 270. Arasadi Diagram.

THE OUTDOOR GAMES

BŌLA KELIYA, 'the Ball Game' or 'Marbles.'

There is evidence that this game was played in Ceylon in the second or third century B.C. Several round small balls, some being exactly like the 'marbles' used by children in England, while others have a segment cut off so as to leave a flat base,[1] were found by me in the earliest pottery stratum at Tissa. Three of them were excellently cut or turned stone balls, while the rest were made of hard-burnt earthenware. They must have either belonged to the children of the potters

[1] Similar balls of stone were found among the 'Late Celtic' Lake Dwellings of La Tēne, at Lake Neuchatel. (Munro. *Lake Dwellings of Europe*, p. 296.)

and artizans whose rubbish heap was cut through, or have been new ones which those people made for sale.

Similar articles are still used by children in Ceylon, the phere being held between the ends of the fore-finger and thumb of the right hand and propelled by placing the end of the fore-finger of the left hand between them, behind the ball, and employing it, with the left wrist, as a spring which propels the ball. The ball is set against the last joint of the fore-finger, the back of that hand being towards the player; and not, as in England, between the knuckle of the right thumb and the tip of the fore-finger of that hand.

The game usually played is that in which the players follow up each other's 'marbles,' each in turn endeavouring to strike that of the other player.

WALA SALLI, 'Hole Money.'

This game may be looked upon as the Eastern representative of the modern game of Quoits. It was played in Ceylon by the second or third century B.C. In the Tissa excavations I found many circular thin earthenware disks in the lowest or pottery stratum, and elsewhere, some being evidently well worn at the edges with much use. The majority were a little over one inch in diameter, but some were much larger, as the game requires. I have also seen such disks, often made from pieces of broken jars, among the fragments of rough pottery which mark the sites of former villages in Northern Ceylon. They prove that the game in which they were used was a favourite amusement in ancient times throughout the island; and it has maintained its popularity down to the present day as a well-known gambling game which is now often played with money, as its modern name indicates. The present name of the disks used for playing it—*Silla*, pl. *Sillu*, a Tamil word meaning 'an earthenware disk'—suggests that before suitable money was available for this purpose the game may have been called after this word. It is known in Egypt, where it is termed *Nil'ab fil bōra*, bōra being the name of the hole made for it.

As played in Ceylon, a small cup-shaped hole is formed in

a piece of flat ground free from grass or weeds, and a line about three feet long is drawn a few inches away from it. The players, two or three, or more, in number, take their stand at a mark ten or twelve feet from the line, which is thus between them and the hole, and each in turn holds a disk made from a piece of broken earthenware, or a cent piece, between his thumb and first two fingers and carefully pitches it at the hole.

The player whose aim is best now takes up all the disks that have been thrown at the hole in this manner, and from the same mark tosses all together at the hole. Then, while he is at the same spot, with a larger and heavier disk, a five-cent piece if they are playing with money, he must hit one of the pieces which the other players select among those lying round the hole and beyond the transverse line. If he miss it his turn is finished, but if he succeed in hitting it he again tosses all the disks at the hole, and those which fall in it become his property.

The next player begins in the same manner, using the disks that have not been won by the first one, and the game continues until all are won. Accuracy of aim when tossing the first disk at the hole, and at the one selected to be struck, is quite as important in this game as in Quoits.

TATTU KELIYA, 'the Touching Game,' or SURĀ KAWADIYAN KELIYA.

In this game a rectangular diagram from 40 to 50 feet long and from 20 to 25 feet wide is described on a piece of level ground, and a line is drawn longitudinally down the middle of it. Three tranverse lines are then drawn, dividing the whole into eight equal squares (Fig. 271).

Three players are stationed at the transverse lines and a fourth at the end line, while a fifth, called *Tāchchiyā*, patrols along the lateral border. The four former players endeavour to touch any one crossing their

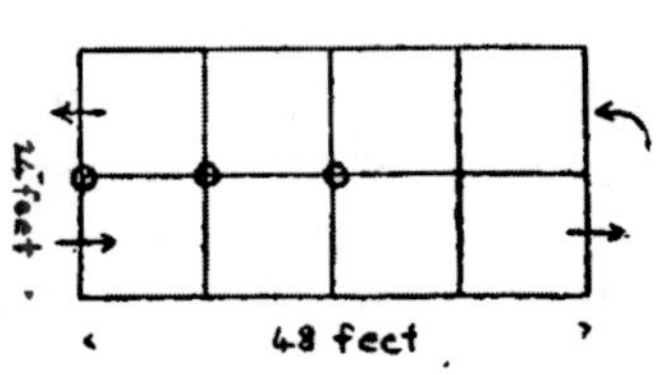

FIG. 271. Tattu Keliya.

respective lines, and the Tāchchiyā may touch any one whom he can reach while he stands anywhere on the outer side lines.

The players of the opposite side enter the first right-hand square at one end and endeavour to pass longitudinally through all the squares without being touched by the watchers. They go up the squares on the right side of the longitudinal centre line, out at the far end, and back down the squares on the left of the centre line, finally passing out across the transverse border line of the first left-hand square.

A player who passes successfully through the first four squares is termed *Pachcha Kuttiyā*; and when he has returned through the second row of squares he becomes *Uppu.* The nomenclature shows that this game was introduced into the island by Tamils.

In another and simpler form of Tattu Keliya, which is often played by both Sinhalese and Tamils, whether boys or men, a long line is drawn on the ground, and the opposing parties stand on opposite sides of it. Those on one side then endeavour to cross it without being touched by their opponents while doing so.

A third game is like one played by boys in England. Some players stand inside a series of posts or marks arranged in a wide circle round them. At these a number of others are stationed, and each one endeavours to get across to the next station without being touched by those inside while doing so. The parties in these games exchange places when all have been caught or touched.

BUHU KELIYA, 'Throwing the Ball.'

I have not seen this game played in the interior. As described by Mr. Ludovisi,[1] who terms it, 'perhaps the only purely indigenous Sinhalese game,' it appears to be an adaptation of English cricket. According to his account it is chiefly played before and after the Sinhalese New Year.

Captains are chosen who form two equal teams, and the

[1] *Journal of the Ceylon Branch of the Royal Asiatic Society*, 1873, p. 25.

first innings is settled by mutual consent, or by tossing. For a wicket, two cocoanut shells with the husks on are placed on end, three or four inches apart, with a stick laid across them. The ball is formed of an unripe Pumelo fruit, rendered soft and elastic by being placed under hot ashes, and protected by a closely plaited envelope of strips of bark.

One party or team station themselves behind the wicket as fielders, and the captain of the other side opens the game by bowling at the wicket, which is not defended by any one. If he knock it down one of the opposing team goes out of play. If the ball pass the wicket those behind endeavour to catch it while rebounding, above the height of the knee, and on their doing so the bowler is out. 'The ball, whether caught or not, having passed into the ground of the second team, one of them becomes the bowler, and the game goes on alternating between the two sides, until one team has all gone out,' leaving the others the winners.

'The victim of defeat has to sit on the bridge of cocoanut shells, his head bowed on his knees, and submit with patience and resignation to the sneers and jibes of the victors,' which apparently are sometimes of a rather coarse character. This resembles the jeering and coarse language used at the Aṇ-keliya or Horn-pulling game, described below, and in its origin it may have been intended to have a similar effect—the protection of the village from evil influences.

Kalli Keliya.

This is a form of Tip-cat played by boys, which Ludovisi stated (*op. cit.*, p. 28)—he does not say on what evidence—to have been known long before our occupation of Ceylon. The 'Cat,' a stick three or four inches long, and pointed at both ends like that used in England, is 'pitched' or tossed at a small hole, three inches long by one inch wide, which slopes downward at one end, from a distance equal to the height of the tallest player, measured to the tips of the up-stretched fingers. An opponent who stands at the side of the hole endeavours to strike the 'cat' before it reaches the ground, with a stick eighteen inches long. Should it fall in the hole, or within eighteen inches of it, or be caught when struck, the striker goes out, and the boy who pitched the 'cat' succeeds him. If, however, the striker hit it on its way to the hole, the distance at which it falls is measured in lengths of the striker's stick, and if it reach a number of lengths, ten or fifteen or more, that had been previously agreed upon, a player of the opposite party goes out of the game.

There is a penalty for the losing players which is not very clearly explained by Mr. Ludovisi. In it the stick for hitting the 'cat' is struck by the 'cat,' and followed up until the player who is doing this fails to hit it, or to send it more than the length of the loser, measured to the end of his up-stretched fingers. The loser must then run back to the hole while holding his breath, crying "Gūdo, gūdo, gūdo." I have not seen this game played in the villages of the interior, and I should expect that it is of European origin.

ETTAN KALLI.

This is a nearly similar game played in Colombo, and described by Mr. Ludovisi (*op. cit.*, p. 29) as being quite like the English Tip-cat. The 'cat' is struck as it springs forward on being 'tipped' by the striker's stick. The same penalty as above is paid by the losers. This game is also not played in the interior, but is common in Colombo.

FOOTBALL.

An Eastern kind of football is played in Colombo, especially by Malays, with a skeleton ball, called *Rāgama bōla*, 'the Rāgama ball,' which is made of interwoven strips of bamboo. The game consists in two parties kicking it backwards and forwards, apparently without any special rules, and there are no goals or 'scrimmages.'

The POPGUN, *Unaliya*, 'Bamboo-stick,' is, as its name implies, made from a short section of bamboo about seven inches long. The small globular unripe seeds of the Pāvaṭṭā (*Pavetta indica*) and Tarana (*Webera corymbosa*) are used as pellets.

STILTS, *Borupaya*, 'False-foot,' are sometimes used by youths as in England. I have seen one Sinhalese man, a professional

FIG. 272. Pattinī and her husband.

To face p. 631.

stilt-walker, perform extraordinary feats on a single high stilt, on which he progressed rapidly in kangaroo-like jumps. His feet were raised three or four feet from the ground on it.

RELIGIOUS GAMES

There are four religious games, all intimately connected with the worship of Pattinī, the Goddess of Chastity and Controller of Epidemics, in her aspect as a deity who possesses powers over certain infectious diseases such as small-pox, measles, and, as Ludovisi says, an outbreak of murrain among the cattle, the injury of crops by insects and grubs, or the occurrence of a serious drought. These games are (1) *Aṇ Keliya*, 'the Horns (pulling) Game'; (2) *Dodan Keliya*, 'the Orange (striking) Game'; (3) *Pol Keliya*, 'the Coconut (breaking) Game'; and (4) *Mal Keliya*, 'the Flower Game.'

Pattinī is a South Indian Goddess whose cult was introduced into Ceylon at an early date. In the tradition which is current regarding her in Ceylon and Southern India, she was Kannakī, the wife of a person called in India Kovilan or Kovālan, and in Ceylon Pālā Gurunnānsē, or Pālanga, who was unjustly charged by a goldsmith with the theft of the Queen's hollow jingling gem-set bracelet or anklet, termed a *Salamba* (Tamil *Silampu*) at Pāṇḍi Nuwara, that is, Madura. Without proper inquiry into the truth of the accusation, he was executed by the orders of the King of Madura. In revenge, Kannakī cursed the royal family and the city, and as the result the king and his family and all the inhabitants were destroyed by fire. The illustration (Fig. 272) shows two wooden statues which are said to be those of Pattinī and Pālanga; they are in one of the caves at the early monastery at Nikawaewa, to which reference has been made in the chapter on the dāgabas, and they may date from the eleventh century A.D. In this statue, which is probably the earliest existing representation of Pattinī in Ceylon, she has plain anklets, but ornamental jewelled bracelets.

According to the Chilappatikaran, a Tamil poem which claims to be written by Ilanko-Adikal, the younger brother of the King of Madura, called Sen Kudduva Chēra or Imaya Varman,[1] when the story of Kannakī was related to this monarch and his queen the latter remarked that the chaste widow was worthy of being worshipped as a goddess. The king agreed with her, caused a statue of Kannakī to be carved from a stone brought from the Himālayas, and inaugurated the new cult.[2]

Mr. Kanakasabhai gleans from the poem the following particulars which indicate the origin of the belief in the power of this goddess over rain and epidemics : ' From that memorable day on which Kovilan was beheaded there was no rain in the Pāndiyan kingdom, and famine, fever, and small-pox smote the people sorely. Verri-Vel-Cheliya, who held his court at Korkei, believing that these misfortunes were brought on by the curse of Kannakī, sacrificed one thousand goldsmiths at her altar, and performed festivals in her honour. Copious showers of rain then fell, and famine and pestilence disappeared from the kingdom. Kosar, King of Kongu, Gajabāhu, King of Lanka [Ceylon], and Perunkilli, the Chōla, erected temples and performed festivals in her honour, and their kingdoms were blest with never-failing rain and abundant crops.' The king consecrated the image of the Goddess ' with grand ceremony in the presence of the kings of Kongu and Malava, and of Gajabāhu, King of Lanka.'[3]

The last part of the account is not quite in agreement with the Sinhalese Rājāvaliya, which states that as a result of his successful expedition Gaja-Bāhu brought away—evidently an act of spoliation—the jewelled bracelets or anklets of the Goddess, and the insignia of the Four Guardian Gods, as well as the Sinhalese who had been carried off as prisoners by a successful Tamil invader in his father's life-time, and double that number of Tamil prisoners of war. The Sinhalese account would thus lead one to suppose that Kannakī had become a goddess before Gaja-Bāhu's war with Madura in the second century A.D.

In the Sinhalese legend, Kannakī was re-born as a demoness

[1] V. Kanakasabhai. *The Tamils Eighteen Hundred Years Ago*, p. 6.
[2] V. Kanakasabhai, *op. cit.* p. 93.
[3] *Op. cit.* p. 161.

because of the destruction she had caused—some say she became a goddess—and came to Ceylon, bringing with her the two sons of the Madura king, who had also become Yakās, and accompanied by some other demons. By means of her magical powers she succeeded in forcing an entry into the country in spite of the opposition of the Four Guardian Gods, who, according to one story, endeavoured to keep her and her undesirable companions out of the island. She created a fence or mountain of fire all round the coast which the Four Gods could not face, but which she crossed successfully. In commemoration of her victory in passing through the fire on this occasion she instituted a fire-sacrifice or fire-walking ceremony, which was to be performed annually, together with at least three other festivals, in her honour. It is still maintained throughout a great part of the Sinhalese districts of Ceylon.

Several stories are told of her, and according to one of them she is now ranked as one of the Four Guardian Deities of Ceylon, the north of the island being supposed to be in her special charge.

She is believed to have handed over the control of the thirty-two epidemic diseases to one of the Madura prince-Yakās, to cause and to cure them, while to the other prince she gave charge of all illnesses of cattle and the lower animals. As the supreme controller of the epidemics these religious games were inaugurated according to her orders, by way of pleasing and propitiating her. In some parts of the country they are played annually for the benefit of the district, and in order to ensure general prosperity and freedom from epidemics; in others apparently the Aṉ Keliya is customary only at the time when a district is threatened with an infectious disease, especially small-pox.

There can be no doubt that in another aspect Pattinī is looked upon as an incarnation of the Goddess Durgā, the wife of Śiva, and as such she is considered to have the Goddess Kālī, another form of Durgā, as her attendant. In Ceylon there are said to be seven different manifestations or incarnations of Pattinī. According to an old manuscript of the

Kurunāēgala district, in the first she was produced from or connected with Handun, or Sandal-wood ; in the second with a Mānel, or Blue-lotus flower ; in the third with ' Gem-sand ' ; in the fourth with water ; in the fifth she was the ' Fire-Pattinī,' who burnt Madura ; in the sixth she is connected in some way with the leaf of a Bō-tree ; and in the seventh she was found inside a Mango fruit at Pāṇḍi-nuwara or Madura, and was married there to a man of the Cheṭṭi caste. Other lists vary slightly.

In the Sinhalese legend, the Aŋ Keliya game commemorates an incident which is supposed to have occurred during the life of Pālanga, the husband of the Goddess. While they were both endeavouring to break a flower off the top of a Sapu tree (*Michelia champaca*) by means of two hooked sticks, the hooks became interlocked ; and although Pattinī and Pālanga exerted all their strength they were unable to unloose them. They summoned large numbers of people to help them, the men joining Pālanga and the women assisting Pattinī, and eventually the men's hook was broken, amidst the jeers of the females.

Mr. Bell, the Archaeological Commissioner, in giving a translation of part of the poem which describes this event [1] has expressed his opinion that the story may contain a reference to the cult of the reproductive powers typified in the Lingam and Yōni. In its later development this may be one meaning attached to it. But if so this was probably a mere after-thought, invented as an explanation of an ancient and pre-existing religious ceremony, which, as related in the Tamil poem, was believed to have a beneficial effect in counteracting certain wide-spread evil influences.

In the *Indian Antiquary*, Vol. v, p. 355, a ceremony in the Sāngli district is described, in which, after the cattle and ' implements of industry ' have been worshipped, the body of cultivators engage in a tug of war, pulling at a leather rope until it breaks. ' It is then divided into numerous pieces which are eagerly sought after ; for happy is the man who is able to throw one of these pieces into his granary, as his store is sure

[1] *Journal of the Ceylon Branch of the Royal Asiatic Society*, 1884, p. 393.

not to fail.' Here we see a nearly similar rope-pulling contest to ensure good luck and good crops, apparently unconnected with the cult of any special deity.

Some further light is thrown on the practice by customs of this nature among other Eastern races. The rope-pulling ceremony is found among the Kāsiyas of Āsām, and the Chukmas of the Chittagong hills, and in Burma; while in some East Indian islands the medium for the tugging which is to bring a rainy wind is a bamboo.[1] According to Dr. Fraser it is distinctly stated by the Chukmas that one party in the pulling contest represents the good spirits and the other the evil spirits.

In the Indian plains, the men of two villages join in a tug of war across the village boundary, as a ceremony by which the winners secure a plentiful season.[2] Mr. Crookes states that there are numerous instances in Northern India of mock fights as charms to secure fertility or freedom from disease. At a festival in Kumaun the fights between the two parties with stones, which were thrown across a stream, were so serious that it was considered necessary to suppress them, an act to which the increase of cholera and other epidemics was afterwards attributed by some of the people.

In some of these rites, foul and indecent language and gestures form an important part of the ceremony as scarers of demons, the authors of bad luck and misfortune; and usually the worse the words and actions are the more effective they are supposed to be.

The final torch-light procession through the village is also doubtless undertaken in Ceylon with the same object—to frighten away the malignant spirits, this being a well-known method of driving off evil influences, or the demons to whom they are due, from houses and villages.

Even so long ago as the time when the earliest part of the Rig Veda was composed, Agni, the Fire God, is repeatedly mentioned as one of the greatest foes of the demons, at whose presence they take to flight, and who preserves mankind from

[1] Dr. Fraser. *The Golden Bough*, 1890, Vol. ii, p. 114, note.

[2] Crookes. *Folk-lore of Northern India*, Vol. ii, p. 321.

their malevolent assaults. In the translation by Griffiths, the prayer to Agni in the 36th hymn of Book i, runs in fervent supplications that might be fitly chanted by the epidemic-stricken villagers of Ceylon as they march through their hamlets :—

Erect, preserve us from sore trouble ; with thy flame burn thou each ravening demon dead.
Raise thou us up that we may walk alive : so shalt thou find our worship mid the Gods.
Preserve us, Agni, from the fiend ; preserve us from malicious wrong.
Save us from him who fain would injure us or slay, Most Youthful, thou with lofty light.
The flames of Agni full of splendour and of might are fearful, not to be approached.
Consume for ever all demons and sorcerers, Consume thou each devouring fiend.'

AṈ KELIYA. The Horns Game.

As its name implies, the Aṇ Keliya, or Horn-pulling game, must have been played originally by pulling at ropes attached to deer-horns ; but now two hooked pieces of extremely tough wood, especially the Andara (*Dichrostachys cinerea*), or the heart-wood of the Tamarind tree, are generally employed instead. In some of the more secluded northern villages the horns are still used. For this purpose the lower part of the antler and the brow tine of the Sambar deer (*Rusa aristotelis*) are taken, the former being shortened to about six inches, and the latter cut down to two inches. These are about the sizes of the wooden 'horns' now made.

Each horn is fitted into a groove cut across a separate substantial bar of wood called the *Aṇ-mōla*, to which it is firmly lashed. The lower hook is upright and the upper one is laid behind it horizontally. The bars, to which they are attached with the greatest care, are utilised for steadying the horns, and preventing them from becoming unhooked during the contest, the lower bar being fixed transversely, and the upper one vertically, and they are held in these positions by several men during the ceremony. In some places the wooden horns are passed through holes bored longitudinally from the under side and through the end of two pieces of coconut log, the transverse bar for steadying the horns being fixed through the log behind the horn, and another short cross-bar through a hole behind it again, to prevent the longitudinal rope on which the strain falls from slipping off the coconut log.

Usually, on a propitious day chosen by an astrologer, a large body of people accompanied by a kapurāla, or devil-priest, repair to the foot of a selected tree surrounded by open ground, and there, at the distance of a few yards from the tree, a narrow hole about six feet long and four or five feet deep is dug, in which a substantial coconut stump called *Henakanda* (which according to Ludovisi is—or was—always taken from a tree that has been struck by lightning [1]) is loosely inserted, with the root end upwards. The toughest jungle creepers are looped round the lower part of the sheltering tree, and a loop of them is placed round the stump; to these are tied ropes that have been attached to the Aṉ-molas, which are placed between the tree and the stump. Other strong ropes of considerable length are fastened to the upper part of the Henakanda, and these are now pulled by the united force of the villagers, or in some places only by the section of them who form the party of Pālanga, until one of the horns gives way.

Although in some cases all except the men who are steadying the horns unite at the pulling, they in reality form two entirely separate parties, one of which is that of the Goddess Pattinī, while the other is supposed to be on the side of her husband Pālanga. The former party is called the *Yaṭa-pila*, or 'Lower Row,' whose horn is the lower one and is attached to the short rope which is tied to the loop fastened round the tree. The latter party forms the *Uḍa-pila*, or 'Upper Row,' and has the upper horn which is attached to the rope that is fastened to the Henakanda.

Membership of these two sides is hereditary; and so strong is the party feeling or jealousy between them that those of one side usually avoid marriage with the members of the families

[1] As *Hena (gahāpu) kandaṉ* is the term applied to a tree stump struck by lightning it would appear that originally such a stump was always used as the post.

belonging to the other side, and in fact never have much intercourse or friendly relations with them. In places where the *Uḍa-pila* men alone do the pulling, the *Yaṭa-pila* men stand as onlookers under the tree. For managing the whole ceremony each party elects a temporary leader.

At the beginning of the ceremony the two bars—the Aṉ-mōla—and the ropes to be attached to the horns are either first dedicated to the Goddess at the local dēwāla or temple, if there be one devoted to Pattinī at the village; or are separately taken in procession by their respective parties to the site of the contest, and placed on platforms or altars covered with flowers, each set in a separate small shed, which has been erected there for it. They are first purified by being deposited on the altar covered with flowers and there sprinkled with saffron water; incense is also waved round them. The kapurāla invokes the aid and favour of the Goddess, to the accompaniment of the jingling of hollow anklets or bracelets such as she wore, and of various musical instruments, such as tom-toms, small trumpets called *horanǣwa*, and cymbals.

After this necessary preliminary, the horns are sometimes carried by the leaders in procession round the Henakanda, and followed by the kapurāla and musicians. They are then attached to the bars which are to steady them, and are interlocked and bound round with cords which at first are placed loosely and then, after the accurate adjustment of the horns, are tightened by means of a tourniquet (tirinki).

After a trial pulling at the respective ropes by the two parties, the Yaṭa-pila rope is tied to the loops round the tree, and the Uḍa-pila rope to the Henakanda, which is inclined towards the tree for the purpose. Where it is the custom of the Yaṭa-pila men to join in the final pulling both parties then unite in tugging at ropes attached to the top of the Henakanda, or passed though a hole in it and fastened to the Uḍa-pila log—until one horn is broken.

The leaders then examine the horns and ascertain whether the Yaṭa-pila or Uḍa-pila one has given way. The victorious horn is removed, wrapped in white cloth, and carried under a white canopy round the Henakanda in a procession, accompanied by the music, and is again placed in the dēwāla, or the temporary shed erected for it.

A rope is then stretched from the tree to the Henakanda, and the losing party are made to stand or sit on one side of it while the winners take up a position on the opposite side and jeer at them, exhausting their vocabulary, which is a somewhat replete one, of abusive and foul language. In the expressive words of Captain Robert Knox 'Upon the breaking of the stick, that Party that hath won doth not a little rejoyce, which rejoycing is exprest by Dancing and Singing, and uttering such sordid beastly Expressions together with Postures of their Bodies, as I omit to write them, it being their shame in acting, and would be mine in rehearsing. For he is at that time most renowned that behaves himself most shameless and beastlike.'[1]

After one or two [properly seven] horns have been broken, Mr. Bell states that the final victorious horn, wrapped in white cloth, is again sprinkled with saffron-water and incensed as before. It is then brought out of the dēwāla or the shed in which it had been carefully placed, and is carried through the village by the kapurāla, or on the head of a kattādiyā (a 'devil-dancer'), over whom a white canopy is held, in a nocturnal procession, with torches and censers, and accompanied by kapurālas, or devil-priests, and the available music and dancers, some preceding and some following it. The houses of the victorious party, which have been prepared beforehand by cleaning and white-washing, are visited in turn, and blessings, to the accompaniment of the jingling of the hollow bangle or bracelet of Pattinī, are invoked on their residents, who offer refreshments in return.

The whole ceremony is considered to be a religious one to a Goddess, and is therefore termed a *pūjāwa*, that offered to a demon being denominated a *pidīma*. Where it is an annual ceremony it is usual for the opposing parties to pay in alternate years any expenses connected with it.

Although there are local variations in the form of the cere-

[1] *An Historical Relation of the Island Ceylon*, 1681, p. 97.

mony, the essential parts of it are everywhere similar; these are the purification and dedication of the articles used, the pulling at the horns until one gives way, and the employment of abusive and foul language and gestures against the losing party.

DODAṆ KELIYA, 'the Orange Game,' or DEHI KELIYA, 'the Lime Game.'

In the North-western Province this game comes after the Aṇ Keliya. The two parties take the oranges intended for the game to the dēwāla, where they are placed in heaps in front of the entrance. They are then purified by sprinkling them with saffron-water, and waving incense and lights around them; and they are afterwards consecrated to the Goddess, like the articles used in the Horn-pulling game.

In playing the game the Yaṭa-pila and Uḍa-pila parties are arranged on opposite sides of a long line, and the oranges are thrown or rolled across it from each side alternately, those on the opposing side striking them with oranges held in their hands as in the following game, until all belonging to one side have been broken. Limes are sometimes used instead of oranges, being then thrown over the line at the opponents, who must prevent them from passing over a boundary line at the back, which they also may not cross.

POL KELIYA, 'the Coconut Game.'

This follows the Orange game. The Yaṭa-pila and Uḍa-pila parties bring up large numbers of Coconuts of a special small green variety with very thick shells, called *Pora-pol*, 'Fighting Coconut.' It is allowable to purchase them for the ceremony, and Mr. Ludovisi stated that very high prices were sometimes paid for those taken from trees which were known to produce nuts with shells of extreme thickness. He mentioned an instance in which as much as thirty shillings were paid for a single nut. Other nuts are procured from trees the produce of which the owner, when sick, has vowed to devote to the yearly Pol Keliya in case of his recovery through the good offices of Pattinī. The nuts of the Pora-Pol trees may be eaten as usual during the rest of the year.

Like the Oranges, the Coconuts are heaped up by the two parties in front of the dēwāla, and are there purified by lustration and the waving of incense and lights round them, these being technically known as 'the three *Tēwāwa*.' They are then dedicated to the service of the Goddess, after which they are removed to the site of the contest.

The two leaders then proceed to divide them into equally-matched pairs, large nuts against large ones, and small nuts against those of similar size. A long line is also drawn on the ground, on the opposite sides of which the two parties take up their positions.

The game is then commenced by the Yaṭa-pila leader's throwing a nut across the line at the leader of the opposite party, who stops it by striking it as it comes with the paired nut which he holds in his hand. The result of the blow is that one nut or the other is usually broken by the shock, and this broken nut then belongs to the side of the victor. The Uḍa-pila leader in his turn throws a nut at the captain of the Yaṭa-pila side, who receives it in a similar manner; and the game is continued in this way by the members of the two parties alternately until all the consecrated nuts on one side or the other have been broken. If the number of nuts be very large other batches may be consecrated on succeeding days, and broken in the same manner; but the game often ends in one day, after fifty to eighty nuts have been broken. On special occasions the number is said to rise up to three hundred nuts, or even more; and in one game the breaking occupied six days.

As in the Horn-pulling game, the losing party who have no unbroken nuts are subjected to the abuse of the victors.

After the nuts of one side have been exhausted, oil is expressed from all the consecrated nuts for the use of the dēwāla, as well as for any lights required in connection with these ceremonies.

MAL KELIYA, 'the Flower Game.'

This game takes place at the dēwāla of the Goddess, and the flowers used are those of the Coconut palm and the Areka palm. These are placed under a tree near the dēwāla, and, I was informed, are not offered to Pattinī.

The game consists in dancing and in playing the double kettle-drum which is used at Buddhist temples. I do not possess any detailed information regarding it. In some places the ceremony of 'Cutting the Waters' is performed after the Mal Keliya; but these customs and the order of the games appear to differ in various districts.

Commonly, all these games or ceremonies are concluded by a village feast, for which both the opposing parties provide the materials, and of which both partake. At the end of it all shout "Hōyiyā," and disperse to their homes.

If the Uḍa-pila party be victorious in these games it is looked upon as a prognostic of misfortune and sickness in the district, according to my information. Ludovisi reversed the omen. They are all believed to be efficacious in driving away sickness, and even in causing rain to fall when needed.

XV

THE ORIGIN AND SIGNIFICATION OF THE CROSS AND THE SWĀSTIKA

IN the last chapter reference was made to a series of diagrams cut upon the roofing slabs of the Kūrna temple in Egypt, which was completed by Seti I (1366–1333 B.C.). I now give illustrations of the different types of these designs, including those which were partly cut away by the masons when they came to fit the slabs together on the spot (Fig. No. 273).

Among these engravings it is interesting to observe the forms of Guarded Crosses, of which several examples occur, with the lines at the ends of the arms straight in some instances and forked in others. It will be recognised that some of them resemble certain designs on the terra-cotta whorls found by Dr. Schliemann in the ruins of the early cities at Hissarlik or Troy. In addition, there are some Swāstikas and designs allied to them, and outlines of sandals [1] and hands, which are well-known guards against the Evil Eye; and especially there is to be seen the nearest approach, so far as I am aware, to the raised Swāstika symbol of early Ceylon.

Several of the designs are employed in Ceylon at the present day, as magical diagrams for protection against the unlucky influences of planets and demons, whether the evil be in the form of sickness, or misfortune, or merely evil dreams (which are always evil omens); and the star with papyrus buds at the ends of the arms occurs, with circles instead of buds, among the magical signs on an Egyptian amulet of the fourth or fifth century A.D., which is illustrated by Dr. Budge in his work on Egyptian Magic, p. 179. The guarded crosses probably can be explained in no other way than as magical diagrams; and the general connection of nearly all the designs

[1] There were many examples of the outline of the right foot, and duplicates of some of the other simpler designs.

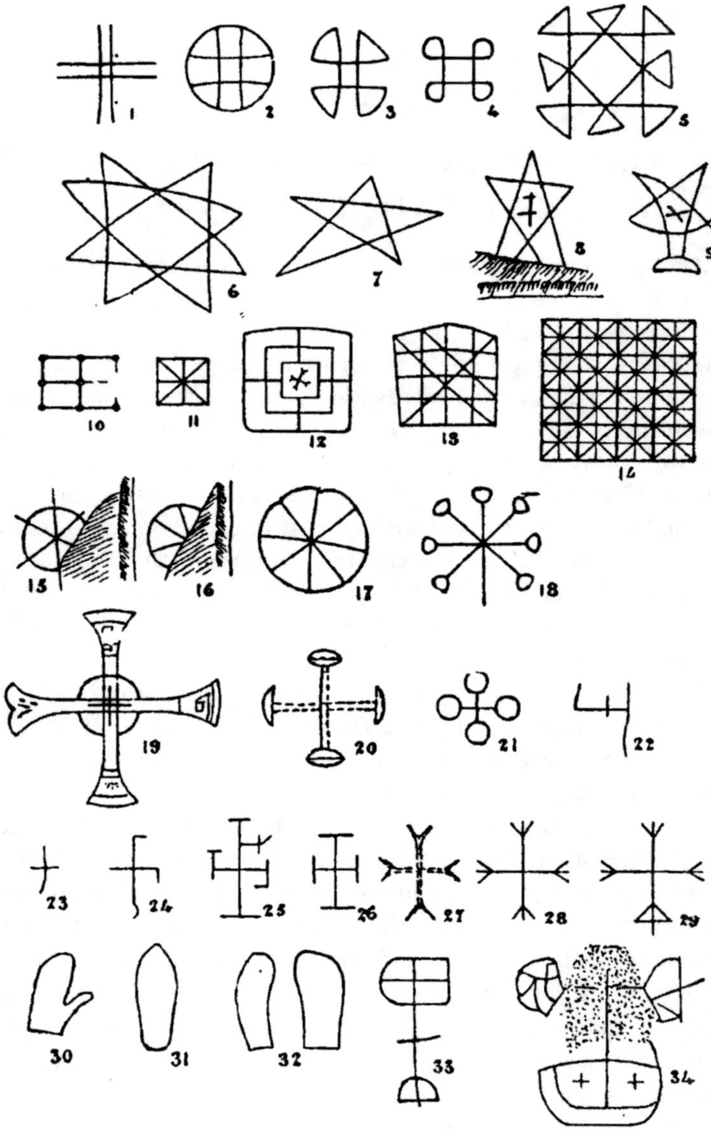

FIG. 273. Masons' Diagrams on Roof at Kūrna Temple

is so self-evident that it is safe to assert that the whole have a mystical signification which is based on their protective functions, as I have already explained in the chapter on the ancient coins of Ceylon.

We learn from Egyptian records that immediately before and immediately after the period when the Kūrna temple was being constructed, much attention was paid in Thebes to the action of magic. It is stated of Amenhetep, the minister of King Amenhetep III (1450–1430 B.C.), 'Profound knowledge of the mysteries of magic were (*sic*) attributed to him. On this subject he wrote certain works which maintained their reputation for more than a thousand years after his death.'[1] Copies of two of them are preserved in European libraries. He himself claimed in the inscription on his statue that he knew all the deep mysteries of literature, and that every secret thing was known to him.[2]

Professor Maspero says of Prince Khāmoīsīt (Khā-em-Uast), the grandson of Seti I, 'He had a great reputation for his knowledge of abstruse theological questions and of the science of magic—a later age attributing to him the composition of several books on magic giving directions for the invocation of spirits belonging to this world and the world beyond.'[3] In the story of Setna, the manuscript of which is attributed by Professor Maspero to the third century B.C., it is recorded of this prince, 'Satni Khāmoïs was well acquainted with all matters: he could read books in the sacred text and the books of the Double House of Life [explained by the learned professor as 'the magical books of the priestly library'], and the works which are engraved on steles and on the walls of the temples, and he knew the virtues of amulets and talismans, and he understood how to compose them and to draw up writings of power, for he was a magician who was unequalled in the land of Egypt.'[4]

Decorations composed of various highly developed forms

[1] Maspero. *The Struggle of the Nations*, English Translation, p. 448.
[2] Dr. Budge. *History of Egypt*, Vol. iv, p. 106.
[3] Maspero. *Loc. cit.* p. 425.
[4] Maspero. *Contes Egyptiens*, 1882, p. 47.

of Swāstika were painted on the ceilings of tombs of the eighteenth dynasty, which held the throne at this time, and the upright cross is also found on Egyptian glazed pottery of about the thirteenth century B.C.[1]

It is therefore not surprising that the intelligent stone-cutters and masons who executed the admirable works of this period should possess some knowledge of magical diagrams and, possibly in the quarries, should have chiselled many of them on the upper side of the slabs of the Kūrna temple, and perhaps at other sites where they have not been searched for. The fact that three diagrams were partly cut away in fitting the stones together is itself an absolute proof that some, at least, were incised while the construction of the temple was in progress, and before the roof stones were finally laid in position. The whole probabilities therefore lead me to believe that all were cut by the workmen at the same date, which must be about 1360 to 1370 B.C.

I have already stated that probably the earliest known Swāstika to which a definite age can be assigned occurs on pottery of the lowest remains of the first city on the site of Troy, which was in existence before 2500 B.C. As it is not a simple design, but forms part of a diagram in which it is surrounded by three rectangles, one outside the other, it must have been invented at an earlier time the date of which is unknown, but may possibly belong to the fourth millennium B.C. But some of the Kūrna figures, and other diagrams that are unmistakably closely allied to them, can be traced back to an even earlier period.

Of these designs, the upright cross enclosed in a square was much used in ancient times. It is found throughout Europe, Asia, and Central America. It is a character in Accadian and Assyrian writing, and forms the side of the throne of the deity on some Chaldean cylinders,[2] and is on a mould from Kouyunjik.[3] It is on Egyptian pottery of the

[1] Hall. *The Earliest Civilisation of Greece*, p. 185.

[2] Maspero. *The Dawn of Civilization*, p. 681. Perrot and Chipiez. *A History of Art in Chaldea and Assyria*, Vol. ii, p. 266.

[3] Layard. *Discoveries in the Ruins of Nineveh and Babylon*, p. 597.

thirteenth century B.C. It appears on a vase of the second city of Troy,[1] on the early pottery of Mycenae,[2] on a gem from Cyprus,[3] and on a vase from Cyprus.[4] It is not uncommon among the objects found at European Lake Dwellings.[5] It is figured on some of the earliest coins of India and Ceylon, it occurs among Chinese characters, and it is to be seen in the carvings of Uxmal in Yucatan. Thus it is certain that it had some other signification than a mere decorative one, and also that it was not simply a diagram used for playing a game like Nerenchi.

In Egyptian drawings a plain square represents an enclosure or a house, as in the ideograph of a hawk standing in a square—'the House of Horus.' In Dr. Sayce's Elementary Grammar, second edition, its meaning in Accadian and Assyrian characters is stated to be 'to bind, gathering, enclosing.' Col. Conder says of the 'Hittite' character which represents it, 'it clearly signifies an enclosure.[6] In Chinese characters the plain square also means 'an enclosure.' Its function in the design is therefore to house or to enclose, and thus to protect, the cross placed inside it; and apparently it is not an essential part of the figure.

The early meaning of the upright cross is less obvious. According to Professor Maspero a double cross, consisting of a vertical one and a diagonal one, enclosed in a circle, originally represented a map of the sky.[7] When the circle was omitted the interlaced crosses came to symbolise planets or stars, and as the greater Gods had astral powers,[8] eventually any god; and this emblem accordingly accompanies the names of all gods in the earliest Chaldean inscriptions, and in a simplified shape the names of all Assyrian gods.

But this is a compound design, composed of three symbols,

[1] Schliemann. *Troy*, p. 50.
[2] Schliemann. *Mycenae*, Plate 10, Fig. 47.
[3] Cesnola. *Salaminia*, Plate 15, Fig. 51.
[4] Wilson. *The Swāstika*, p. 841.
[5] Munro. *The Lake Dwellings of Europe*, pp. 72, 173, 175.
[6] *The Hittites and their Language*, p. 227.
[7] *The Dawn of Civilization*, p. 726.
[8] King. *Babylonian Magic and Sorcery*, p. 109.

each of which, when considered separately, must have had its own meaning in primitive times. It is not probable that the upright cross was obtained by a dissection of the complex sky symbol into its three components, the circle, and the vertical and oblique crosses; but rather that the symbol which represented the sky was formed by the union of these three ancient simple forms, with only one of which we are at present concerned.

To ascertain the early meaning of the upright cross we must go back, as in the case of the square, to its use in the first alphabets.

In Egyptian hieroglyphics the cross formed of two upright lines connected at the ends, with one central cross-bar, signifies 'to be in,' or 'to dwell in.'[1]

In Accadian and Assyrian, according to Dr. Sayce's Grammar, a vertical cross made with two wedges has several meanings, some of which are 'to dwell, to take; oracle, heap, family, offspring, liver, white, high.' The upright cross also forms part of an ideogram used for fire, which is interpreted 'Cross wood'; but possibly—as the remarks which follow show—may mean 'auspicious' wood. The upright cross of two upright lines and one transverse bar—representing the Egyptian form—when combined with the four wedges which compose the character for 'good, great, multitude, propitious,' means 'wind, breath, brightness, heaven, rain, Rammānu (the Air-god), sky, earth.' The whole of these are terms which in the East and in Africa, even at the present day, would be thought to be very auspicious, there being in them nothing to indicate loss or deficiency, or defect, but, on the contrary, the opposites.

The upright cross inside a square is also an auspicious expression. As the word *lu* it means 'flocks, sheep'; as *udu*, 'sheep, lamb, gazelle,' that is, animals suitable for offering to the gods. As *dib* its meaning is 'tablet, to cross, to seize, to hold.' These are also auspicious, as indicating success, gain, and a slab on which a god or king may be depicted

[1] Dr. Budge. *Easy Lessons in Egyptian Hieroglyphics.*

The sound *khi* which means 'good' in Accadian is represented in 'Hittite' inscriptions by a vertical cross.[1]

In Chinese writing the upright cross occurs as the chief part of the character for rice[2]; and the vertical cross in the square forms an important part of the characters meaning 'happiness,' and therefore must have been thought to be very auspicious. The whole design, according to Doolittle, is much used as an emblem of good luck.[3]

In dealing with magical ideas it is an invariable rule that whatever is auspicious is protective. It is an omen of good and good-luck, and as such it necessarily excludes whatever is evil and unlucky. As all unlucky acts or states are—according to primitive ideas—due to the injurious influence of evil spirits it follows that all auspicious acts and things and terms have guardian powers against such influences. It is manifest, therefore, that at the time when the earliest alphabets were being invented the Cross, having auspicious significations, was a protecting emblem.[4]

As an example we may take the Accadian ideograph for 'tomb,' which is formed of the character for 'corpse,' enclosed in an oblong—the coffin or grave—in which, at the head of the body, is placed an upright cross formed of two wedges—apparently, as the idea of 'tomb' is complete without it, depicted there with the belief that it will guard the body from demoniacal interference. This seems to be evidence that the upright cross actually had a protective signification at so early a date as, say, 5000 B.C.

In India, also, it was employed in a similar manner. General Maisey remarked in *Sānchi and its Remains* (p. 12, foot-note), 'Many of the relic-chambers opened at Sānchi, and other places, were Swāstika-shaped in plan, as also were the funeral chambers found in some of the kistvaens of Southern India;

[1] Col. Conder. *The Hittites and their Language*, p. 254.

[2] The Atharva Veda calls Rice and Barley, 'the two healing, immortal children of Heaven.'

[3] *Social Life of the Chinese*, Hood's revision. 1868, p. 569.

[4] A cross of reeds is employed by the Bushmen of South Africa, and is placed upon the body as a remedial agent in cases of extreme sickness (Stow. *The Races of South Africa*, p. 120).

and in the centre of a Sthūpa (dāgaba] lately opened in the Madras Presidency this form of cross was found, marked in masonry, at the central place of deposit for relics.' I have already mentioned that Mr. Bell examined a dāgaba at Anurādhapura in which the relic-chamber was in the form of an 'even cross.' Whatever may be thought of the Accadian ideograph, there can be no doubt that in these instances the function of the cross was to protect the relics, which were human remains, from interference by evil-disposed spirits.

The function of the upright cross in the square or circle which constantly appears among the amulets and ornaments of the Neolithic and later Lake Dwellings, and American Mound Builders, was probably similar. As an auspicious symbol it would be thought to defend its wearer from evil.

Although it may have had a very simple foundation, it is not easy in these days to comprehend the primitive reasoning according to which the upright cross came to acquire its peculiarly propitious character. An illustration of the early belief in its defensive properties occurs in the Atharva Veda, iii, 12 (Bloomfield's translation), in which on the erection of a dwelling it is the Cross Beam of the house, and not, as might be expected, the central post on which the roof rests, that is prayed to guard the building, in these words: "Do thou, O Cross Beam, according to regulation ascend the post; do thou, mightily ruling, hold off the enemies." Until the beam is in position the Cross is not present; as the member which completes the protecting emblem it is therefore more important as the defender of the house than the post which supported the roof. The 'enemies' would be chiefly or entirely spiritual foes, of course.

The upright Cross is also carved as an emblem carried by a guardian deity, probably Ayiyanār, the Guardian Forest God, on a pillar at the Jētavana dāgaba at Anurādhapura (Fig. No. 37), and it is the common emblem of the Egyptian gods.

For an elucidation of this belief in the power of the Cross it appears to be necessary to consider the diagram as a symbolical pictograph of a simple idea which would appeal to the mind of early man. The cross may be described either as four equidistant straight lines radiating from a central point, or, as in the example just given, one straight line laid at a right angle across another straight line. The latter is the simpler and therefore probably earlier notion of it, and also the one that the most obviously aids a solution of the difficulty which appears to me not to overstrain probabilities, although I expressly bring it forward as a tentative explanation.

Although the upright cross forms part of the characters which represent fire, it does not appear that the sacred fire of the Assyrians was obtained by means of the transverse friction described in the chapter on the Modern Vaeddas. The statue of the Fire-god of Assyria, Gibil, shows him holding an upright twirling-stick which he is turning with his hands, like the Vaeddas. In India, also, the sacred fire is obtained with the twirling-stick and not by cross friction.

Thus although some part of the auspicious character of the upright cross is probably due to its being a representation of the two sticks used in primitive times for causing fire by transverse friction, the various meanings to express which this symbol is employed seem to show that some other additional interpretation must be found for it.

Remembering that in Egyptian and Assyrian drawings an oblong with ripples marked on it represents a pool of water, or if open at the ends, a river ; and that in Accadian, a horizontal oblong with two wedges inside it, one behind the other, pointing to the right, signifies running water, I suggest that it is within the bounds of possibility that, as one meaning of the Cross, one bar originally symbolised a river, and afterwards any other obstruction in a person's path, while the transverse bar typified a successful crossing of it. It will be noticed that in Accadian and Assyrian 'to cross' is actually one of the meanings of the upright cross in the square. The Cross might thus eventually come to typify success in overcoming obstacles in general. s all obstacles or dangers were, and are still by many persons, believed to be due to the unfavourable actions of evil spirits, the Cross would in that case indicate a general freedom from the interference of all such opposing evil influences.

If some notion of this kind was idealised in the upright Cross it may explain the adoption of it as a suitable emblem for the Gods, and as a symbol of life—that is, of continued existence, and not of generation, or the calling of new life into being—the cessation of life being due only to evil magic or the influence of evil powers, the action of which would be prevented by it, through its being a powerful auspicious emblem.

The early Indian Āryans were acquainted with the same metaphor as illustrating a successful overcoming of obstacles, whether physical, or mental, or spiritual. In the Rig Veda, Book i, hymn 99, 1 (Translation by Griffiths), the hymn runs : 'May Agni carry us through all our troubles, through grief as in a boat across a river.' This takes the idea back to the third millennium B.C.

In Book ix, hymn 73, 1, it is stated, 'that Asura has formed, to seize, three lofty heights. The ships of truth have borne the pious man across.'

The author of one of the hymns of the Atharva Veda (Bloomfield's Translation, viii, 2, 9 ; p. 56) seems to have had the Cross in the square or circle in his mind when he composed the verse—"The missile of the Gods shall pass thee by. I pass thee across the mist (of death) ; from death I have rescued thee. Removing far the flesh-devouring Agni, a barrier do I set around thee that thou mayest live." That is, as the mystical Cross is protected by its enclosing line, so shall the patient's life be preserved by the barrier against evil influences raised by the magical virtues of the incantation. In this case one bar of the Cross might typify the 'misty road' of death (*v.* 10), and the other the safe passage across it.

Sir F. Max Müller said of Buddhist teaching that 'the very definition of virtue was that it helped man to cross over to the other shore.' [1]

[1] *Chips from a German Workshop*, Vol. i, p. 248.

If such metaphors as these were to be rendered ideographically in the simplest manner by a mystical diagram, the design would almost necessarily adopt the form of either one or two straight lines crossed by another line which would indicate the track taken by the person.

In Cheiromancy, an Eastern art, we find an actual example of a journey represented by a single line. A single line round the base of the thumb typifies the owner's journey through life, and breaks in it or lines across it indicate obstacles or dangers encountered or overcome on the way.

The theory regarding the action of magic which is adhered to by Sinhalese magicians, although far from agreeing with the opinions of many European authorities of the present day, appears to correctly preserve the primitive ideas on the subject, if we may judge by the notions current in Early Egypt,[1] Western Africa,[2] Australia,[3] and China.[4] According to it, injurious magic does not perform, and cannot possibly in any way perform the required acts of itself, but is merely the authorisation, or some say—as in Egypt[5] and China,[6]—the command, issued to malevolent spirits to intervene in the manner desired by the magician. The position is defined in terms which nearly coincide with the Sinhalese ideas, in one of Asvaghosha's sermons as translated in Beal's *Buddhist Literature in China*, p. 110:—

> 'Because of lust and anger and ignorance
> These wicked charms [spells] are used;
> And when these harmful words are woven,
> Then the evil spirits catch the words
> And with them hurt the world,
> And do deeds of mischief everywhere.'

It is evident that, conversely, beneficial magic must act

[1] Dr. Budge. *Egyptian Magic.*

[2] Dr. Nassau. *Fetishism in West Africa*; Baudin. *Fetichism and Fetich Worshippers.*

[3] Dr. Howitt. *The Native Tribes of South-east Australia.* Spencer and Gillen. *The Native Tribes of Central Australia.*

[4] Dr. de Groot. *The Religious System of China.*

[5] Dr. Budge. *Egyptian Magic*, p. 4.

[6] Dr. de Groot, *op. cit.* Vol. v, p. 917.

in a similar manner, through its influence over benevolent spirits, in addition to its own inherent protective action in some cases, owing to its power of repelling evil spirits.[1] Thus the Cross, being continually a powerful beneficial and protective symbol, becomes the permanent dwelling of a favourable spirit, exactly like the fetish amulets of Africa. Its Egyptian and Accadian meaning 'to dwell' may possibly have some connection with this belief.

Like the later magical circle, the enclosing line round the Cross would be thought to guard it from the intrusion of unfavourable spirits, who might neutralise its beneficial qualities. Both benevolent and malevolent spirits have a well-marked partiality for Crosses, and cross-roads are universally supposed to be favourite spirit-haunts. In West Africa I learnt from the Jōlas of the Gambia Valley that the treatment for some diseases is only effective when the medicine is prepared and applied in the middle of a road-crossing. In India, cross-roads are included with the temples of the Gods as auspicious objects,[2] and the Rig Veda (ii, 5, 6) states that Agni stands 'on sure ground where paths are parted.' Buddha specially pointed out that such places are suitable sites for the erection of dāgabas.[3] Of course the relics deposited in them would there receive the protection of favourable spirits. This will explain why it was usual to make four (or at any rate three) entrances to the enclosures in which the early dāgabas were erected; by their construction the edifices became situated at cross-roads. To what extent the guardian spirits are thought to defend such structures may be judged by the general belief in Ceylon that any persons who break into one unlawfully will certainly die within a year. Several instances of such deaths have been related to me.

Notwithstanding the opinions which several learned authors have expressed on the subject, I am unable to feel satisfied

[1] As when their names, or, as in the Kalevala, their origins, are mentioned. Compare also Rig Veda, i, 156, *v.* 2, 3.

[2] S.B.E., Vol. ii, *The Sacred Laws of the Āryas*, p. 223.

[3] S.B.E., Vol. xi, *Buddhist Suttas* (Davids), pp. 93 and 125. See also *The Jātaka*, No. 418, Vol. iii p. 260.

that among the earliest ideas regarding the upright cross, and especially the upright cross in the square, there was any notion that it indicated generation, or the production of the sacred fire, or more than one attribute of even the sun.

As regards the first of these, the reason of the delineation of the Cross [1] or Swāstika [2] on female figures is probably because of its inherent protective powers, the need of which is explained by Crawley in '*The Mystic Rose*.'

I am not aware of any instance in which the Cross or Swāstika is used in fire-making excepting the cross-friction or sawing method previously described, which, as I have already stated, does not appear to have been the mode adopted for obtaining the sacred fire of the Euphrates valley and is not used for that of Hinduism. That the Cross had no special primitive connection with this idea is perhaps shown by its being employed in Accadian in expressing the words 'earth, rain, white.' In the Arani which is used for producing the holy fire (Agni) of India, a single piece of wood, the Adharārani, is laid on the ground, and the drill, the Uttarārani or Pramantha is held vertically on it, and turned by a string the two ends of which are pulled alternately by another officiator. The point of the drill rests in a hole 'a small shallow round cavity' in the lower piece.[3] That such was the early form of the instrument is shown by the hymn 29 of Book iii of the Rig Veda, which says :

> Here is the gear for friction, here tinder made ready for the spark.
> Bring thou the Matron [the lower stick] ; we will rub Agni in ancient fashion forth.
> In the two fire-sticks Jātavedas [Agni] lieth. . . .
> Lay this with care on that which lies extended

With regard to its being a symbol of the sun, it has not this signification in Accadian, or Assyrian, or Egyptian writing.

[1] Schliemann. *Troy*, p. 35. Cunningham. *The Stūpa of Bharhut*, Plates of statues in relief.

[2] Wilson. *The Swāstika*, p. 829.

[3] Crookes, *The Popular Religion and Folklore of Northern India*, Vol. ii, p. 194.

Against it may also be cited the shapes of several early forms of Swāstika from Troy, such as

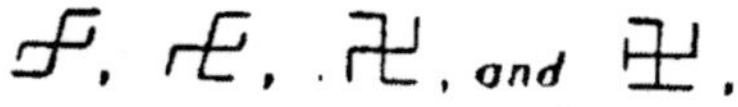

which are opposed to the identification of the Swāstika as the wheel of the sun. In Chaldea and Assyria, in most instances the sun is symbolised as a six or eight-rayed star or wheel, which equally stands for stars and several other gods; and the upright cross often forms no portion of the diagram. If it actually represented the sun it could not be omitted from such designs in the cases where the Sun-God is indicated.

The Assyrian design with only four arms appears to be an incomplete picture of the compound type that had eight rays, four of which have been omitted. In the examples of the eight-rayed symbol which typify the sun, and consist of two crosses, a diagonal and an upright one, the diagonal cross certainly represents the vivifying and brilliant light-giving rays,[1] while the upright one may indicate another attribute of the Sun-God, that is, his protective quality. If it represented the God himself there could be no need to surround it by a circle, as is usually done when there are only four arms. When this portion of the design was alone pourtrayed the intention probably was to emphasise chiefly the guarding power of this deity, referring to which Lenormant remarked, 'according to the magical hymns, the diurnal sun, shining in the highest regions of the heavens and dissipating the darkness, was one of the most active protecting gods.'[2] In numerous prayers in the magical texts supplications are addressed to him for his protection. As a matter of fact, the Accadian as well as the Egyptian emblem of the sun was not a cross but, as one would naturally expect, a circle, the sun's disk, which when depicted by means of wedges became a lozenge.

[1] Maspero. *The Dawn of Civilization*, p. 657. King and Hall. *Egypt and Western Asia*, p. 256. The light rays are shown unmistakably in these illustrations.

[2] *Chaldean Magic*, p. 178.

Both the cross in the square and the sun symbol occur in an inscription cut on the surface of a large rock at the side of an early dāgaba at a monastery at Oṭṭappuwa, in the North-central Province of Ceylon. It is a record left by a king who is variously termed in the histories Kaṇī-raja, Kaṇijānu, or Kaṇirajānu (30–33 A.D.). As the names of the two symbols are also appended in it, the inscription is of considerable interest, and I therefore give a fac-simile (Fig. No. 153), with a transliteration and translation of it.

> (1) Sirikaṇa raja (2) maha dama yaha (3) tubahi c(e)tiya (4) (n)ti bojana halā (5) pama maḷuka ca (6) hoti. Two symbols. Nā sara ru (7) go ravi.

The two symbols are an upright cross in a square, and a circle with a central dot, having a small cross dependent from its circumference.

> 'King Sirikaṇa, having established the glory of the Great Law [the Buddhist faith], built a refectory near the dāgaba, and enlarged the enclosure. (Two symbols). Figure of a Nāga pool; rayed Sun.'

The cross below the sun evidently symbolises the protecting rays; it appears to represent one of the 'arrowy rays' of the Rig Veda, which discomfited the demons. The square alone may be the figure of the pool inhabited by Nāgas, the cross which is marked on it being in that case simply a protective emblem intended to keep out evil demons such as Rākshasas, who according to the Jātaka stories were accustomed to haunt pools of water. Plain rectangles with fish inside them or at their side represent pools in the earliest Indian coins. It is obvious that in this instance the cross can have no connection with fire.

There can be no doubt that both emblems are cut at the site on account of their powers as demon frighteners. I have already stated that slabs on which are carved the figures of Cobras (Nāgas) in high relief are set up as protectors at the base of dāgabas and at the outlets of the larger sluices in Ceylon. In the present case the belief of the carver, or perhaps the king himself, appears to have been that the existence of the Nāga pool would ensure the presence of the guardian Nāgas for the protection of the relics in the dāgaba.

This example of the representation of the sun shows how necessary it is to guard against reading astrological, and I may add also Phallic, meanings in early diagrams where their designers may have never intended them to be understood.

The upright cross inside an oblong is also represented in

274. Flower Altar, near Vammiyaḍi, E. P.

275. Yantra-gala, Anurādhapura.

FIGS. 274, 275. Early Crosses in Ceylon.

relief on the surface of a stone altar slab for flower offerings at a ruined monastery in thick uninhabited forest near Vammiyaḍi tank in South-eastern Ceylon (Fig. 274). The dividing walls of the hollows in the stone receptacles termed *yantra gala* in Ceylon, for containing treasures, especially 'the nine gems,' which were often deposited in the base of dāgabas or at other monastic sites, are commonly cut in the form of a rectangular cross composed of four lines in each direction, enclosed in a square or oblong (Fig. 275). In all these instances the guarding power of the cross against evil influences, especially when enclosed in the rectangle, is doubtless the reason of the adoption of these symbolic designs. We have the same idea represented in the protecting fence round the sacred tree or other sacred symbols in the early Indian and Ceylon coins; each side of it is usually in the form of the upright cross enclosed in the rectangle.

Possibly it is to be seen also in the common 'Buddhist railing' round early dāgabas and monastic edifices in India and Ceylon, in which the horizontal bar is usually supplemented by two others. The three bars may be intended to typify the three Protections or 'Refuges' (the Buddha, the Law, and the Community of Monks) on the defensive power of which against all forms of evil every Buddhist depends. The whole forms a magical circle or boundary round the edifice.

I now suggest that it was from such a magical cross, defended by its enclosing square, that the Swāstika was developed, as a magical protective diagram. This derivation is rendered the more probable by the fact that in the most carefully drawn Swāstikas the second portion of each arm forms exactly half the side of the enclosing square. A later type of the diagram still adhered to the lines of the same enclosing square, and has a third short line, forming a quarter of the next side of the square, at the end of the usual arm. These four forms are

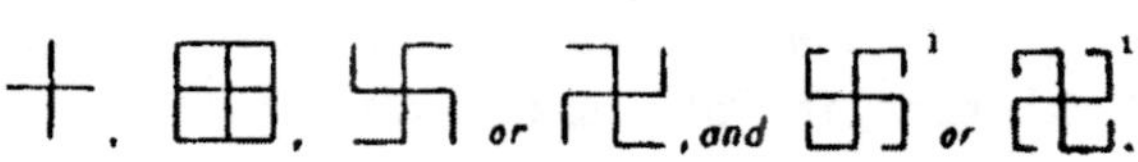

In symbolism it is unnecessary to depict a design in full; a portion of it may stand for the whole, like the single ray of the sun-emblem in the Sinhalese inscription at Oṭṭappuwa. Thus the bent arms of the Swāstika would sufficiently show

[1] Wilson. *The Swāstika*, pp. 850, 851, 852, 856, 867, 876; Du Chaillu. *The Viking Age*, Vol. i, pp. 192 and 206.

that the Cross was guarded by its enclosing square, and it would be optional to turn the second part of the arm in either direction, to the right or left. All magic being enveloped in mystery by its professors, the omission of an unessential part of the primitive diagram may have been thought to increase the mystical effect.

Another form, which some might think more protective, consisted of the Cross with the second part of the arms turned in both directions, to the right and left, leaving, in its simplest shape, only the angles of the square unrepresented, perhaps because internal corners in houses are liable to become lurking-places for evil spirits. It has been called by Mr. J. M. Campbell the 'Guarded Cross.'[1] This design occurs on early terra-cotta whorls of Troy, and on pottery from Mycenae. In the British Museum there are three specimens from Honduras, cut in flint; and it appears in the Palenque reliefs of Central America. It is also included in the Kūrna designs. That it is only a variant of the Swāstika is shown by the last form from Troy previously illustrated[2] (see p. 656).

A third type, which may be termed the Barred Cross, or Barred Swāstika, was subsequently developed. In it, one or two lines are placed across the arms of the Cross or Swāstika, at their ends or at a short distance from them. Specimens of this variety of Swāstika occur on early Indian and Ceylon coins, and the Cross is found on pottery of the first city at Troy, and on a fragment of pottery from the later Lake Settlement at Paladru in France, and of course very commonly in later Christian art.

In addition to the Swāstikas already illustrated, some of the simpler types of these early designs are as follows:—

[1] *The Indian Antiquary*, Vol. xxiii, p. 161, 'Notes on the Spirit Basis of Belief and Custom.'

[2] Schliemann. *Troy*, Plate 24, Fig. 355. Compare also Coin No. 35, *ante*.

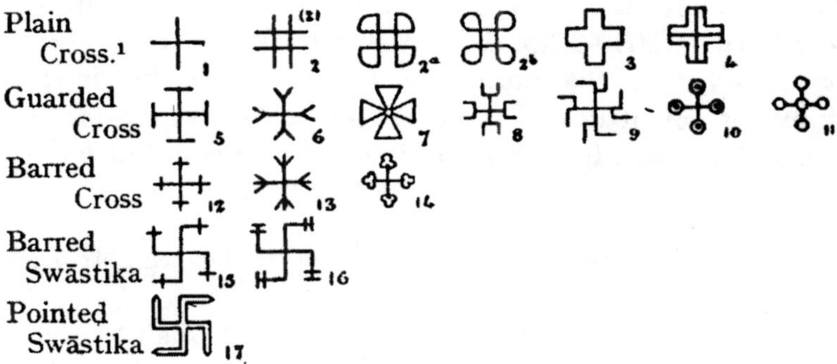

Dr. Schliemann also found a Swāstika at Troy with a square at the end of each arm. All these guards or bars on the arms are equally intended for the protection of the Cross from the intrusion of evil influences, and symbolise the enclosing square; they give increased protective powers to the cross or prevent its powers from being neutralised.

I exclude the curved Swāstikas from consideration, as they are unmistakably derived from the straight-lined figures, and because in them the ornamental character often predominates. The meaning of the dots which sometimes accompany the first five designs is obscure. It may be doubted if there are any grounds for terming them 'nails.'

It will be observed that excepting special instances in which its meaning cannot be mistaken, I have omitted all reference to the oblique cross. It is not a figure from which the Swāstika has been developed. Although in some cases it may have an import similar to that of the upright cross, in others it appears to possess a different meaning.

No hypothesis regarding the signification of the Swāstika can be satisfactory unless it furnishes a reasonable explanation of all the simpler forms which I have illustrated. This I

[1] Each of these plain types numbered 1, 2, 3 and 4 is also often enclosed in one or more squares or circles.

[2] The types numbered 1 and 2 are sometimes drawn with more lines, up to seven in number. The forms numbered 2 and 3 are used by some members of the Kurnai tribe of South-east Australia, as personal marks on opossum skin rugs (Howitt, *The Native Tribes of South-East Australia*, p. 74).

believe has not been previously attempted to be given, excepting in part by Mr. Campbell in his article in the *Indian Antiquary*. Whether the present solution be accepted in its entirety or not, it does at least provide a possible reason for them; it remains for others to decide if this is an adequate one.

Among other sites these diagrams are to be seen at the following places.

No. **1**. A prehistoric character in the earliest of all writing, the linear Sumerian or Accadian script—say 5000 B.C. (Boscawen. *The First of Empires*, p. 57).

No. **2**. On the earliest Egyptian red vases, possibly of the sixth millennium B.C. (Capart. *Primitive Art in Egypt* p. 106). Enclosed in a square this forms an Egyptian hieroglyph on a plaque of King Āḥa, about 4400 B.C. (Dr. Budge. *A History of Egypt*, Vol. i, p. 78). Troy (Schliemann. *Troy*, p. 162, Fig. 116; Plate 46, Fig. 447; Plate 51, Fig. 495). Mycenae (Schliemann. *Mycenae*, p. 105, Fig. 160). Archaic Greek Pottery (Waring. *Ceramic Art in Remote Ages*, Plate 33, Fig. 35). Egypt (Perrot and Chipiez. *Hist. of Art in Ancient Egypt*, Vol. ii, p. 359). Cyprus (P. and C. *Hist. of Ancient Art in Phoenicia*, pp. 11 and 297). In a peculiar Phrygian circular stone tumulus the body was deposited in the square made by the intersections of the stone-work built in this form (P. and C. *Hist. of Art in Phrygia*, etc., p. 50). Lake Dwellings (Munro. *The Lake Dwellings of Europe*, pp. 175 and 255). Kūrna, both separately and enclosed in a circle. Early Indian Coins (Theobald. *Journal of the Asiatic Society of Bengal*, 1890, 'Notes on some of the Symbols found on the Punch-marked Coins of Hindustan,' Nos. 78, 108, 112, 123). India (Sir A. Cunningham. *The Stūpa of Bharhut*, Plate 49, Fig. 6; Report No. xi of the Arch. Survey of India, Plate XI, Fig. 3, where the cross is formed of four Swāstikas). American Indian Burial places (Wilson. *The Swāstika*, p. 929). Ceylon (Magical diagrams).

No. **2a**. Kūrna.

No. **2*b***. Kūrna. American Grave-mounds (Second Annual Report of the Smithsonian Bureau of Ethnology, Plates 53, 58, 59).

No. **3.** Enclosed in a circle it forms an Egyptian hieroglyph. Troy (Schliemann. *Troy,* in 'hundreds,' p. 105). Mycenae (Schliemann. *Mycenae,* p. 194, Fig. 294; p. 259, Fig. 383; p. 265, Fig. 419). Cyprus (Cesnola. *Cyprus,* p. 68; *Salaminia,* pp. 254, 255; Plate 13, Fig. 30; Plate 15, Figs. 50 and 52). It is a character in a 'Hittite' inscription from Jerābīs (Dr. Wright. *The Empire of the Hittites,* inscription J. I.). Phrygia, where it is a relief on a large panel at the end of a tomb (P. and C. *Phrygia,* etc., p. 65). Lake Dwellings (Munro. *op. cit.* pp. 14, 17, 173, 255). Central America (Wilson. *The Swāstika,* p. 972). Early Indian Coins (Theobald. *loc. cit.* Nos. 162, 177, 225, 227, 269; Smith. *Catalogue of the Coins in the Indian Museum, Calcutta,* Plate 22, Fig. 16; Sir A. Cunningham. *Coins of Ancient India,* Plate II, Figs. 15, 16, 20; Plate III, Figs. 5 and 6; see *ante* Fig. No. 154 coin **b**). Ceylon (see *ante,* Inscription No. 73; Bell. Arch. Report, 1895, p. 2; a relic chamber in a dāgaba was of this form, see *ante*). American Grave-mounds (Second Ann. Rep. of Smithsonian Bureau of Ethnology, Plates 51, 53, 58, 59; Third Ann. Rep., p. 24, Aztecs, Borgian Codex, Plate 43).

No. **4**. This form enclosed in a circle appears as an Egyptian hieroglyph on a vase of King Besh, 4100–4133 B.C. (Dr. Budge. *Hist. of Egypt,* Vol. i, p. 208). Early Cylinder (Dr. Forster. *The Monuments of Assyria, Babylonia, and Persia,* pp. 158 and 166). Assyria (Waring. *Ceramic Art,* Plate 40, Figs. 3 and 4—from Lajard). Mycenae (Schliemann. *Mycenae,* p. 265, Fig. 417). Cyprus (P. and C. *Art in Primitive Greece,* Vol. ii, p. 378). As a 'Hittite character at Jerābīs (Dr. Wright. *The Empire of the Hittites,* Inscription J. II.). On a Lydian mould (P. and C. *Hist. of Art in Phrygia,* etc., p. 293). Lake Dwellings (Munro. *The Lake Dwellings of Europe,* pp. 14, 56, 62, 72, 173, 175). Central America. American Grave-mounds (Second Ann. Rep., S.B. of Ethnology, Plates 52, 53, 61).

No. **5**. Troy (Schliemann. *Troy*, p. 55). Mycenae (Schliemann. *Mycenae*, p. 203) Rhodes (Wilson. *The Swāstika*, pp. 849, 906). Egypt, Kūrna and Gnostic (British Museum). Aztecs (Plate 44, Fejervary Codex, in Third Ann. Rep. S.B. of Ethnology, Plate III ; Fig. 9, p. 60).

No. **6**. Troy (Schliemann. *Troy*, p. 130, Fig. 78 ; Plate 48, Fig. 480). Archaic Greek Pottery (Waring. *Ceramic Art*, Plate 27, Fig. 9). Cyprus (Cesnola. *Salaminia*, p. 282). Kūrna. Honduras (British Museum). Aztecs (Plates 65 and 66, Vatican Codex B, Third Ann. Rep. S.B. of Ethnology, Plate IV). Ceylon (see *ante*, 'The Earliest Coins,' No. 15, on which the Swāstika has similar forked ends. This form of cross is carved in relief on the four faces of the capital on which stands the winged lion of St. Mark, at Venice.

No. **7**. Assyria (P. and C. *Hist. of Art in Chaldea and Assyria*, Vol. ii, Fig. 116, where it is worn as an amulet by King Samas Vul. II). A symbol on a royal necklace (P. and C. *op. cit.* p. 366 ; Layard. *Monuments*, 1st Series, Plate 59 ; 2nd Series, Plate 4). It is also among the rock carvings at Bavian, where it is bounded by a circle ; and with forked ends on Persian pottery from Kouyunjik (Layard. *Discoveries*, p. 591). Troy (Schliemann. *Troy*, Plate 36, Fig. 427 ; Plate 45, Fig. 470). Mycenae (Schliemann. *Mycenae*, Plate 12, Fig. 56, closely resembling the Honduras example ; p. 203, Fig. 316 ; p. 259, Fig. 385 ; p. 264, Fig. 404 ; p. 265, Fig. 420). Cyprus (Cesnola. *Cyprus*, p. 481 ; *Salaminia*, pp. 80, 243). Lake Dwellings (Munro. *op. cit.* p. 15). Honduras (British Museum). Kūrna. Mexico (Waring. *Ceramic Art*, Plate 33, Fig. 35). Aztecs (Plate 44, Fejervary Codex in Third Ann. Rep. S.B. of Ethnology, Plate III ; Fig. 9, p. 60). Sometimes the central circle is absent, and the diagram is employed without it in Ceylon against evil planetary influences.

No. **8**. Mycenae (Schliemann. *Mycenae*, p. 74).

No. **9**. Scandinavia (Waring. *Ceramic Art*, Plate 44, Fig. 18).

No. **10**. 'The Ujjain Cross.' Troy (Schliemann *Troy*, terra cotta cover of a vase or box, p. 286, Fig. 200). Kūrna. Early Indian Coins. In many Indian examples a smaller circle is enclosed in each of those at the ends of the arms, and on one coin a third is inside the inner one. In some other cases Swāstikas or 'taurine' designs are figured in the circles.

No. **11**. Ceylon (Magical diagram). The same form appears in the plan of the Ortu Nūragh in Sardinia (P. and C. *Hist. of Art in Sardinia and Judea*, Vol. i, p. 33).

No. **12**. Kūrna. Paladru Lake Dwellings (Keller. *Lake Dwellings*, 1878, Plate 193). Central America.

No. **13**. Troy (Schliemann. *Troy*, pp. 80, 284. Kūrna. Early Indian Coins (Waring. *Ceramic Art*, Plate 41, Fig. 24). Ceylon, Early Coins (see *ante*, Nos. 53, 54, 55, where the branches of the tree are of this shape. In Coin No. 54 the tail of the elephant is also in the form of one arm of this Cross).

No. **14**. Early Indian Coins. (Theobald. *loc. cit.* No. 196).

No. **15**. Early Indian Coins (Cunningham. *Ancient Indian Coins*, Plate 10, Fig. 11).

No. **16**. Ceylon, Early Coin (see *ante*, No. 14).

No. **17**. Santorin (Wilson. *The Swāstika*, p. 843). Early Indian Coins (Smith. *Catalogue*, Plate 19, Fig. 10). Ceylon. Early Coins (see *ante*, Nos. 8, 10, 11, 13, 15, 16, 17, 43, 44).

ADDENDA

VALLIYAMMĀ (*p.* 115).

Valliyammā is addressed with Skanda in an invocation for the cure of sickness caused by the Sohon Yakā; and I find that she is also included in a Low-Country list of seven Kiri-Ammās, who are goddesses. They are as follows:—

1. Polawē Mahikāntāwā, the Goddess of the Earth.
2. Mūdē Maṇimēkhalā, the Goddess of the Sea.
3. Saraswatī, the wife of Brahmā.
4. Sītā Pramēswarī, the wife of Rāma, and an incarnation of Lakshmī.
5. Māē-anganāwā, or Ammā Dēvī, or Umayanganāwā, the wife of Siva.
6. Valliyammā, the wife of Skanda.
7. Pattinī Dēvī, an incarnation of Durgā.

AYIYANAR (*p.* 158).

Ayiyanār is said to have five Ministers, who are termed 'The Five Dēvatās.' They appear to be the deities of the Wanniyas, who may have erred in including Ayiyanār among these five deities. The list varies in different places, but all agree that three are Ilandāra, Kalu Dēvatā, and Kaḍawara Dēvatā, while another is said to be Kambili Unnaehae, and the fifth may be Gurumā Dēvatā. In that case Ayiyanār is their Wanniya Baṇḍāra.

THE SWĀSTIKA (*p.* 492).

In the case of the peculiar elevated Swāstika of Ceylon an alternative and perhaps preferable explanation of the four basal uprights is that they typify the Four Guardian Gods who protect the four quarters of the island. The base line would then represent the country itself.

The pointed ends of the lines on some coins may be intended not merely to close them against the entry of evil spirits. The pointed uprights resemble the right spear-head amulet on the crown of Duṭṭha-Gāmiṇi (p. 538), and pointed weapons are well known to be demon-scarers. The points would thus increase the protective power of the symbol.

According to the kapurālas, the Four Guardian Gods (*Hatara Waran Deviyō*) of Ceylon are, Saman 'Divya Rāja,' in the east; Skanda, in the south; Vishnu, in the west—he is said to have delegated his powers to Vibhīsana, the Rākshasa king of Ceylon, who is now treated as a god in the Western Province—and Ayiyanār (called also by Low-Country Sinhalese Boksal), in the north.

It is probably due to Rāma's being an incarnation of Vishnu, whose brother is Indra, that Saman Deviyā (or Sumana) is sometimes identified with Lakshmana, Rāma's brother, who assisted him in conquering the Rākshasas in Ceylon. According to Forbes (*Eleven Years in Ceylon*, i, p. 185), the colour of Saman is yellow (Dr. Davy says white), and his emblems are a golden bow and arrow; these are Indra's emblems, and he is the Guardian of the East in India. Buddha is stated to have placed Ceylon under the special protection of Sakka (Indra), who delegated the duty to his brother Vishnu, 'the [blue] lotus-coloured' God (Mah. i, p. 32).

Saman or Sumana was evidently a mountain deity in Ceylon, the seat of his worship being Adam's Peak, called Sumanakūṭa in the histories. It is clear that the early annalists believed him to be settled on it before the first visit of Buddha, since it is stated that on that occasion he asked Buddha for 'something worthy of worship,' and received some of 'his pure blue [black] locks,' which he enclosed in the emerald dāgaba at Mahiyangana (p. 315).

APPENDIX

TABLE OF MEASURED BRICKS

	Length in Inches.	Breadth in Inches.	Thickness in Inches.	Bt.	Contents in Cubic Inches.
PRE-CHRISTIAN BRICKS. Contents not under 366 cubic incnes.					
Central Province.					
Bambā Wihāra, Galewela . . .	(19·80)	10·30	3·30	34·0	(673)
,, ,, ...	16·28	9·04	2·66	24·0	392
Dambulla cave temple	19·45	—	2·45	—	—
Eastern Province.					
Raddila sluice	—	—	3·06	—	—
North-central Province.					
Angamuwa. Waehaera-gala monastery	17·00	8·80	2·58	22·7	386
Anurādhapura. Abhayagiri dāgaba	18·92	9·62	3·20	30·7	583
,, Abhayagiri. Large hall near Colossal Buddha . . .	—	—	3·00	—	—
,, Building with Buddhist railing (Bell)	18·00	9·00	3·00	27·0	486
,, ,, ,, wall of inner floor	17·78	8·55	2·60	22·2	395
,, Lankārāma dāgaba	17·37	8·94	2·62	23·4	407
,, Miriswaeṭi dāgaba.	—	10·41	3·00	31·2	—
,, Ruwanwaeli dāgaba, inner work . .	—	9·67	2·79	27·0	—
,, Ruwanwaeli dāgaba, outer work . .	14·06	8·99	2·90	26·1	366
,, Ruwanwaeli dāgaba, elephant wall . .	17·00	(8·80)	2·80	(24·6)	(418)
,, Thūpārāma dāgē .	19·00	9·15	3·00	27·4	521
Awukana wihāra	—	—	2·92	—	—
Ipalagama. Waehaera-gala dāgaba	17·00	9·21	2·83	26·1	443
Kaṭiyāwa. High-level sluice. . .	(18·96)	9·60	3·16	30·3	(575)
Kitikaḍawala sluice	(17·40)	9·00	2·90	26·1	(454)
Lunu-oya dam below Angamuwa tank	(16·56)	9·18	2·76	24·6	(408)
Maha Waehaera-gala, Eppāwala Kōrale	—	8·80	2·75	24·2	—
Mihintale. Building at Stone Boat.	(17·30)	8·80	2·88	25·3	(437)
,, Maha Sāēya dāgaba .	17·92	8·87	2·91	25·8	461
,, Wihāra on hill . . .	(18·00)	9·00	3·00	27·0	(486)
Nuwara-waewa. H.L. sluice . .	(18·90)	9·85	3·15	31·0	(586)
,, Malwatta-oya dam	(18·10)	9·05	3·25	30·9	(559)
Oṭṭappuwa dāgaba	18·60	9·52	3·12	29·7	552

	Length in Inches.	Breadth in Inches.	Thickness in Inches.	Bt.	Contents in Cubic Inches.
Polannaruwa. Pabulu dāgaba . .	(18·20)	9·10	3·10	28·2	(513)
, Waṭa-dāgē dāgaba .	—	—	3·00	—	—
Sangili-Kanadara sluice	18·18	9·12	3·22	29·3	534
,, ,, ...	17·75	—	2·75	—	—
Talaguru wihara (early letters) . .	—	—	3·00	—	—
Tantiri-malei dāgaba	(18·00)	9·04	3·23	29·2	(525)
Tumbulla cave at Tissa's inscription	15·70	8·80	2·77	24·4	382
Yakā-baendi Ella dam on Kalā-oya	—	—	2·92	—	—
Northern Province.					
Allēkaṭṭu dam	(18·00)	9·45	3·00	28·3	(510)
Kacca Samilan-kuḷam dāgē . . .	13·57	8·30	3·40	27·4	383
,, monastery wall .	14·60	8·68	2·95	25·7	375
Kumārapuram temple (from Kurundan-kuḷam)	(17·40)	8·50	2·90	24·6	(428)
Maha Iramba-kuḷam sluice . . .	—	—	3·00	—	—
Maḍukanda, Hall of Tooth-relic . .	(17·20)	8·60	3·00	25·8	(444)
Māmaḍu, N. sluice.	(17·80)	9·30	2·96	27·5	(489)
Matirankuli dāgaba	(18·00)	9·05	3·05	27·6	(497)
Neḍunkēṇi, Ruin on Kūllan-kuḷam road	—	10·41	3·20	33·3	—
Pāvaṭ-kuḷam. Catchwater bund sluice	(17·80)	9·52	2·97	28·2	(503)
,, N. high-level sluice .	16·70	8·29	2·94	24·4	408
,, S. sluice	17·36	8·60	2·89	24·8	433
Sēmamaḍuwa dāgaba.	(18·00)	8·93	3·08	27·5	(495)
Vavuṇik-kuḷam	—	9·10	2·70	24·6	—
Veḍikkiṇāri-malei hall	(18·00)	9·30	2·90	27·0	(486)
North-western Province.					
Batalagoḍa. S. sluice	(17·00)	9·90	2·83	28·0	(476)
,, (? wihāra)	(18·00)	9·50	3·00	28·5	(513)
,, Waste-weir . .	—	9·00	2·86	25·7	—
Dāgama dāgaba and cave . . .	16·38	8·70	2·80	24·4	399
,, poya-gē	16·42	—	2·80	—	—
Galgiriya-kanda. Galpadi dāgaba .	(17·40)	8·83	2·90	25·6	(445)
,, ,, cave. .	(17·60)	8·85	3·10	27·4	(482)
Gaṇē wihāra (early letters) . . .	—	—	3·00	—	—
Mirihampiṭiya. Maha Waehaera-gala dāgaba	(18·00)	9·34	2·98	27·8	(500)
Nikawāē-kanda small cave dāgaba .	16·41	8·16	3·39	27·6	454
Nuwara-kanda cave wihāra . . .	16·76	8·76	3·09	27·0	454
Pēddawa wihāra	(18·00)	8·93	3·12	27·9	(502)
Siriwaḍḍhana-Nuwara dāgaba . .	(17·58)	9·06	2·93	26·5	(466)
Wellangolla cave	(16·80)	9·00	2·80	25·2	(423)
Southern Province.					
Maha Debara-hela dāgaba . . .	16·20	8·50	3·15	26·8	434
Tissa. Mahānāga ,, ...	17·35	8·84	2·83	25·0	434
,, Maeṇik ,, ...	16·57	8·86	2·80	24·8	411
,, Sandagiri ,, ...	17·14	8·67	2·81	24·4	418
,, Small ,, ...	17·16	9·11	2·85	26·0	445
,, Yaṭṭhāla ,, ...	17·85	8·64	2·90	25·0	447

	Length in Inches.	Breadth in Inches	Thickness in Inches.	Bt.	Contents in Cubic Inches.
POST-CHRISTIAN BRICKS. Contents 300–375 cubic inches. 0–300 A.D.					
Eastern Province.					
Sigaraṭa-hēna monastery, Pulugannāwa	(15·00)	8·50	2·50	21·2	(319)
Vammiyaḍi tank	14·30	7·50	3·30	24·7	353
,, ,,	—	7·57	2·80	21·2	—
North-central Province.					
Angamuwa tank. Dam in inlet channel	—	7·50	2·74	20·5	—
,, ,, Kānu horowwa	—	8·50	2·36	20·0	—
Anurādhapura. Abhayagiri, large hall S. of dāgaba	15·34	8·18	2·43	19·9	305
,, Abhayagiri, large hall near colossal Buddha	—	—	2·70	—	—
,, Dakuṇu dāgaba	16·36	8·18	2·31	18·9	309
,, Daḷadā Māligāwa, inner room	14·10	8·45	2·52	21·3	300
,, Jētavana dāgaba	15·82	8·41	2·26	19·0	301
,, Ruwanwaeli dāgaba, behind E. shrine	16·78	8·26	2·36	19·5	327
,, Sēla caitya	(15·2)	9·00	2·53	22·8	(346)
,, ,, ,,	—	8·37	2·33	19·5	—
,, Thūpārāma, large hall to S. of dāgaba	15·50	8·80	2·42	21·3	330
,, Thūpārāma, wall of court	15·27	8·93	2·60	23·2	345
Ellakaṭuwa dam on Malwatta-oya	—	—	2·60	—	—
Hurulla, high-level sluice	(14·50)	8·35	2·51	21·0	(304)
,, sluice at breach	(14·50)	8·40	2·70	22·7	(329)
Ihala Siyambalan-gamuwa waste-weir	(14·50)	8·45	2·56	21·6	(313)
Kalāwaewa. Balaluwaewa sluice	—	—	2·60	—	—
,, No. 1 sluice	—	—	2·56	—	—
Mihintale. Aet dāgaba	14·50	8·46	2·44	20·6	303
,, 'Mahinda's monastery'	(15·0)	8·06	2·50	20·4	(306)
,, Sena's cave—dāgaba to W.	(14·50)	8·40	2·54	21·3	(308)
Millāēwa-gala dāgaba	15·57	8·00	2·72	21·7	339
Miṇṇīriya, low-level sluice	—	—	2·50	—	—
,, statues	—	—	2·50	—	—
Moragoḍa wihāra, N. of dāgaba	14·82	7·60	2·90	22·0	326
Nāccāduwa sluice	(14·50)	8·50	2·56	21·8	(316)
,, waste-weir	—	7·66	2·60	19·9	—
Nuwara-waewa, High-level sluice	(14·50)	8·48	2·64	22·4	(325)
Padawiya. Vaṇṇāṭṭi Pālama dam	13·61	8·48	2·70	22·9	311
Polannaruwa. Gal wihāra	16·00	8·95	2·56	22·9	366
Tantiri-malei, at large Buddha	—	9·05	2·62	23·7	—
Tumbulla cave with partly-cut figure	14·80	8·80	2·65	23·3	345
Wambutuwā-gama. Maha Waehaera gala	—	8·80	2·75	24·2	—
Yakā-baendi Ella dam on Kalā-oya	—	8·80	2·43	21·3	—

	Length in Inches.	Breadth in Inches.	Thick-ness in Inches.	Bt.	Con-tents in Cubic Inches.
Northern Province.					—
Giant's Tank. Alavakka Head-sluice	(14·50)	8·57	2·51	21·5	(312)
,, ,, Dam on Aruvi-āru .	—	8·30	2·48	20·5	—
Īraṭperiya-kuḷam sluice	14·50	—	3·10	—	—
Kacca Samilan-kuḷam dāgaba . .	14·48	8·88	2·60	23·0	332
Māpānar Periya-kuḷam sluice . .	13·70	8·09	2·90	23·4	321
Periya Kaccaṭkoḍi cave	14·80	—	2·72	—	—
Piḷima-gala, Kallukuṇḍa-maḍu . .	—	8·56	2·70	23·1	—
Putumurippu bund	—	9·00	2·60	23·4	—
Seppakāran-kallu monastery, Īrat-periya-kuḷam	(14·50)	8·31	2·59	21·6	(313)
North-western Province.					
Kahatagaswela dāgaba and wihāra .	15·22	7·84	2·65	20·8	316
Nikawāē-kanda ,, ,, .	16·22	8·66	2·51	21·7	320
,, ,, head of colossal statue	—	—	2·60	—	—
,, ,, wall at ,, ,,	14·67	8·63	2·62	22·7	333
,, ,, small cave . . .	—	7·60	2·65	20·1	—
Nīrammulla sluice	—	8·45	2·70	22·8	—
Polkumbura. Rāgala cave . . .	15·70	8·62	2·52	21·7	341

POST-CHRISTIAN BRICKS. Contents 210–300 cubic inches. 300–800 A.D.

	Length in Inches.	Breadth in Inches.	Thick-ness in Inches.	Bt.	Con-tents in Cubic Inches.
North-central Province.					
Anurādhapura, large hall near colossal Buddha . . .	—	7·75	2·48	19·2	—
,, Building with Buddhist railing . .	—	7·30	2·60	19·0	—
,, Miriswaeṭi dāgaba .	14·20	8·20	2·34	19·2	272
,, Ruwanwaeli ,, building E. of road	13·92	7·43	2·05	15·2	212
,, Thūpārāma dāgē .	14·50	8·35	2·35	19·6	285
Awukana wihāra	—	8·30	2·44	20·2	—
Hurulla tank, Bīri-horowwa . . .	12·78	7·20	2·25	16·2	207
Kaṭiyāwa tank, High-level sluice .	—	8·10	2·44	19·7	—
Mihintale. Maha Sāēya	—	7·30	2·42	17·7	—
,, Rajagiriya Cave wihāra .	13·60	7·30	2·52	18·4	250
Nuwara-waewa High-level sluice. .	—	7·50	2·30	17·2	—
Oṭṭappuwa dāgaba	12·62	8·65	2·70	23·3	294
Padawiya. High-level sluice . .	14·02	8·50	2·46	20·9	293
,, Ruin on rock . . .	12·20	8·62	2·34	19·4	246
Polannaruwa. 'Koṭuwa' . . .	14·10	8·27	2·34	19·3	272
,, Pabulu dāgaba . .	—	7·80	2·50	19·5	—
,, Tōpāwaewa channel House on rock .	—	8·10	2·40	19·4	—
,, Tōpāwaewa Low-level sluice	—	7·40	2·43	18·0	—
,, Waṭa-dāgē dāgaba .	13·20	8·35	2·30	19·2	253
Sīgiriya gallery.	13·09	7·32	2·31	16·9	220

	Length in Inches.	Breadth in Inches.	Thick-ness in Inches.	Bt.	Con-tents in Cubic Inches.
Northern Province.					
Allekaṭṭu dam	—	7·65	2·43	18·6	—
Āriyamaḍu dāgaba	—	7·60	2·60	19·7	—
Kacca Samilan-kuḷam Wihāra-gē .	12·50	8·03	2·44	19·6	245
Maḍukanda Tooth-relic hall . . .	—	7·53	2·27	17·1	—
Maha Iramba-kuḷam sluice . . .	—	7·30	2·35	17·1	—
Matirankuli dāgaba	—	8·30	2·07	17·2	—
Pāvaṭ-kuḷam dāgaba	11·23	8·47	2·46	20·8	234
,, N. Low-level sluice .	13·72	8·49	2·51	21·3	292
Putumurippu sluice	—	7·37	2·73	20·1	—
,, ,, ...	—	8·60	2·35	20·8	—
Vavuṇik-kuḷam	—	8·20	2·23	18·2	—
North-western Province.					
Arankaeḷē monastery.	—	8·30	2·38	19·7	—
Batalagoḍa S. sluice	13·20	7·60	2·42	18·2	241
Galgiriya-kanda cave	12·85	7·85	2·20	17·3	222
Mallawaewa cave temple of Galē Deviyā	—	7·50	2·52	18·9	—
Nayindanāwa dāgaba.	13·40	8·30	2·50	20·7	277
Nikawāē-kanda dāgaba and wihāra.	12·25	7·65	2·25	17·2	211
Nīrammulla sluice.	12·70	8·50	2·16	18·8	239
,, ,, ...	—	8·45	2·70	22·8	—
Pūjāgala monastery	12·25	7·77	2·43	18·9	231
Raṇagiriya Uḍa-wihāra	12·75	8·12	2·75	22·3	285
Siriwaḍḍhana-nuwara dāgaba . .	—	7·80	2·30	17·9	—
Southern Province.					
Māgama City	14·12	7·88	2·34	18·4	260
Small dāgaba near river	12·92	7·73	2·34	18·1	234

POST-CHRISTIAN BRICKS. Contents under 210 cubic inches. 800–1350 A.D.

	Length in Inches.	Breadth in Inches.	Thick-ness in Inches.	Bt.	Con-tents in Cubic Inches.
North-Central Province.					
Anurādhapura. Ruwanwaeli dāgaba, below sedent statue	13·80	7·70	1·90	14·6	202
,, Sēla caitya . . .	—	7·58	2·18	16·5	—
,, ,, ,, . . .	—	6·77	2·00	13·5	—
,, Toluwila dāgaba, outer bricks . .	9·50	7·40	1·95	14·4	137
,, Two story building	12·47	6·12	1·91	11·7	146
,, ,, ,, ,,	10·05	5·00	1·55	7·7	77
Awukana wihāra	—	7·10	1·98	14·0	—
Issambaessa-gala dāgaba. . . .	9·08	7·20	2·53	18·2	165
Kiribat dāgaba, shaft.	—	6·80	2·26	15·4	—
Mihintale. Cave dwelling near Kala-diya Pōkuna . . .	11·60	6·10	2·30	14·0	162
,, Rajagiriya Cave wihāra.	11·30	2·27	2·28	16·6	187
Moragoḍa (Padawiya) dāgaba . .	9·62	6·84	2·25	15·4	148
,, ,, . . .	8·20	5·35	2·17	11·6	95

	Length in Inches.	Breadth in Inches.	Thickness in Inches.	Bt.	Contents in Cubic Inches.
Moragoda dāgaba near breach . .	8·79	6·00	1·87	11·2	99
,, fort wall	11·25	6·93	1·98	13·7	154
,, ,, ...	8·76	5·80	2·31	13·4	117
,, Hindu temple	9·38	6·65	1·97	13·1	123
,, pilima-gē	10·40	6·73	2·41	16·2	169
,, wall at Sangbo's pillar .	9·34	6·97	1·89	13·2	123
,, well, radiated bricks . .	8·67	6·29	2·28	14·3	124
,, wihāra N. of dāgaba . .	8·60	5·90	2·00	11·8	101
Nāccāduwa sluice	12·55	7·40	2·04	15·1	189
Polannaruwa, fortification wall . .	12·63	8·20	2·00	16·4	207
,, 'Jētawanārāma' . .	13·20	7·20	1·70	12·2	161
,, 'Koṭuwa' . . .	13·33	7·57	2·00	15·1	201
,, Pabulu dāgaba tee .	11·10	6·80	2·20	15·0	167
,, Thupārāma inside. .	12·00	8·36	2·00	16·7	201
,, ,, outer side.	13·20	—	2·00	—	—
,, Tōpāwaewa, low-level sluice	over 11·80	6·95	2·12	13·7	—
,, Waṭa-dāgē wall . .	11·82	7·23	1·85	13·4	158
Tantiri-malei dāgaba	10·10	7·60	2·33	17·7	179
'Wijayārāma'.	—	7·45	1·90	14·1	—
Northern Province.					
Āriyamaḍu dāgaba	—	7·00	2·10	14·7	—
Giant's Tank. Alavakka head-sluice	11·20	6·87	2·03	17·6	156
,, ,, Mukkuwa Murippu sluice	—	7·65	1·81	13·8	—
Iratperiya-kuḷam wihāra	9·60	4·74	2·45	11·6	111
Kacca Samilan-kuḷam dāgē . . .	12·00	7·65	2·50	15·6	187
Kanakarayan-kuḷam sluice . . .	—	7·47	2·23	16·6	—
Kurinjā-kuḷam dam on Kall-āru . .	—	7·37	2·06	15·2	—
Kurundan-kuḷam, building at inscription	—	7·55	1·95	14·7	—
Maha Iramba-kuḷam sluice . . .	11·20	6·87	2·03	17·6	156
Māmaḍu N. sluice	—	7·17	2·18	15·6	—
,, S. ,, ...	—	8·40	2·02	17·0	—
Mutaliyar-kuḷam piḷima-gē . . .	10·70	6·85	2·56	17·5	187
Pāvaṭ-kuḷam N. high-level sluice .	12·75	6·52	2·07	13·6	173
Putumurippu sluice	8·50	6·10	2·17	13·2	113
Sēmamaḍuwa dāgaba.	11·02	7·80	2·25	17·5	176
Seppakāran-kallu monastery. . .	11·90	7·25	2·21	16·0	191
Taṇṇir-murippu sluice . . .	12·27	7·83	1·93	15·1	185
Tattaya-malei monastery. . . .	—	7·20	2·30	16·5	—
North-Western Province.					
Batalagoḍa S. sluice	—	7·50	1·90	14·2	—
Nikawāē-kanda small cave . . .	12·20	—	2·10	—	—
Pēddawa wihāra	—	7·40	2·26	16·7	—
Pūjā-gala ,, ...	—	7·90	1·88	14·8	—
Yāpahuwa Bō-tree	11·50	7·35	2·07	15·2	175
Southern Province.					
Rambhara wihāra	12·47	7·73	2·04	15·8	196

INDEX